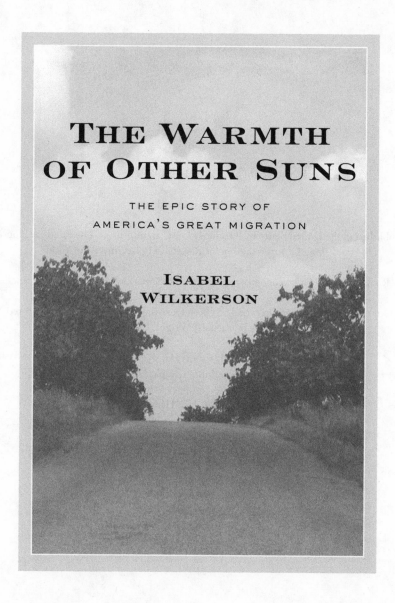

THE WARMTH OF OTHER SUNS

THE EPIC STORY OF AMERICA'S GREAT MIGRATION

ISABEL WILKERSON

RANDOM HOUSE  NEW YORK

Published in the United States by Random House, an imprint of The Random House Publishing Group, a division of Random House, Inc., New York.

RANDOM HOUSE and colophon are registered trademarks of Random House, Inc.

Our title *The Warmth of Other Suns* is taken from the final pages of the unrestored edition of *Black Boy* by Richard Wright. Used by permission.

Permissions acknowledgments for previously published material can be found beginning on page 621.

ISBN 978-0-679-44432-9
eBook ISBN 978-0-679-60407-5

Printed in the United States of America

www.atrandom.com

16 18 17

Book design by Christopher M. Zucker

THE WARMTH
OF OTHER SUNS

To my mother and
to the memory of my father,
whose migration made me possible,
and to the millions of others like them
who dared to act upon their dreams

I was leaving the South
To fling myself into the unknown. . . .
I was taking a part of the South
To transplant in alien soil,
To see if it could grow differently,
If it could drink of new and cool rains,
Bend in strange winds,
Respond to the warmth of other suns
And, perhaps, to bloom.

       —RICHARD WRIGHT

CONTENTS

PART ONE

In the Land of the Forefathers

Our mattresses were made
of corn shucks
and soft gray Spanish moss
that hung from the trees. . . .
From the swamps
we got soup turtles
and baby alligators
and from the woods
we got raccoon,
rabbit and possum.
—MAHALIA JACKSON, *Movin' On Up*

LEAVING

This land is first and foremost
his handiwork.
It was he who brought order
out of primeval wilderness . . .
Wherever one looks in this land,
whatever one sees that is the work of man,
was erected by the toiling
straining bodies of blacks.
—DAVID L. COHN, *God Shakes Creation*

They fly from the land that bore them.
—W. H. STILLWELL

I

CHICKASAW COUNTY, MISSISSIPPI, LATE OCTOBER 1937
IDA MAE BRANDON GLADNEY

———

THE NIGHT CLOUDS were closing in on the salt licks east of the oxbow lakes along the folds in the earth beyond the Yalobusha River. The cotton was at last cleared from the field. Ida Mae tried now to get the children ready and to gather the clothes and quilts and somehow keep her mind off the churning within her. She had sold off the turkeys and doled out in secret the old stools, the wash pots, the tin tub, the bed pallets. Her husband was settling with Mr. Edd over the worth of a year's labor, and she did not know what would come of it. None of them had been on a train before—not unless you counted the clattering local from Bacon Switch to Okolona, where, "by the time you sit down, you there," as Ida Mae put it. None of them had been out of Mississippi. Or Chickasaw County, for that matter.

There was no explaining to little James and Velma the stuffed bags and chaos and all that was at stake or why they had to put on their shoes and not cry and bring undue attention from anyone who might happen to see them leaving. Things had to look normal, like any other time they might ride into town, which was rare enough to begin with.

Velma was six. She sat with her ankles crossed and three braids in her hair and did what she was told. James was too little to understand. He was three. He was upset at the commotion. *Hold still now, James. Lemme put your shoes on,* Ida Mae told him. James wriggled and kicked. He did not like shoes. He ran free in the field. What were these things? He did not like them on his feet. So Ida Mae let him go barefoot.

Miss Theenie stood watching. One by one, her children had left her and gone up north. Sam and Cleve to Ohio. Josie to Syracuse. Irene to Milwaukee. Now the man Miss Theenie had tried to keep Ida Mae from marrying in the first place was taking her away, too. Miss Theenie had no choice but to accept it and let Ida Mae and the grandchildren go for good. Miss Theenie drew them close to her, as she always did whenever anyone was leaving. She had them bow their heads. She whispered a prayer that her daughter and her daughter's family be protected on the long journey ahead in the Jim Crow car.

"May the Lord be the first one in the car," she prayed, *"and the last out."*

When the time had come, Ida Mae and little James and Velma and all that they could carry were loaded into a brother-in-law's truck, and the three of them went to meet Ida Mae's husband at the train depot in Okolona for the night ride out of the bottomland.

2

WILDWOOD, FLORIDA, APRIL 14, 1945
GEORGE SWANSON STARLING

———

A MAN NAMED ROSCOE COLTON gave Lil George Starling a ride in his pickup truck to the train station in Wildwood through the fruit-bearing scrubland of central Florida. And Schoolboy, as the toothless orange pickers mockingly called him, boarded the Silver Meteor pointing north.

A railing divided the stairs onto the train, one side of the railing for white passengers, the other for colored, so the soles of their shoes would not touch the same stair. He boarded on the colored side of the railing, a final reminder from the place of his birth of the absurdity of the world he was leaving.

He was getting out alive. So he didn't let it bother him. "I got on the car where they told me to get on," he said years later.

He hadn't had time to bid farewell to everyone he wanted to. He stopped to say good-bye to Rachel Jackson, who owned a little café up on what they called the Avenue and the few others he could safely get to in the little time he had. He figured everybody in Egypt town, the colored section of Eustis, probably knew he was leaving before he had climbed onto the train, small as the town was and as much as people talked.

It was a clear afternoon in the middle of April. He folded his tall frame into the hard surface of the seat, his knees knocking against the seat back in front of him. He was packed into the Jim Crow car, where the railroad stored the luggage, when the train pulled away at last. He was on the run, and he wouldn't rest easy until he was out of range of Lake County, beyond the reach of the grove owners whose invisible laws he had broken.

The train rumbled past the forest of citrus trees that he had climbed since he was a boy and that he had tried to wrestle some dignity out of and, for a time, had. They could have their trees. He wasn't going to lose his life over them. He had come close enough as it was.

He had lived up to his family's accidental surname. Starling. Distant cousin to the mockingbird. He had spoken up about what he had seen in the world he was born into, like the starling that sang Mozart's own music back to him or the starling out of Shakespeare that tormented the king by speaking the name of Mortimer. Only, George was paying the price for tormenting the ruling class that owned the citrus groves. There was no place in the Jim Crow South for a colored starling like him.

He didn't know what he would do once he got to New York or what his life would be. He didn't know how long it would take before he could send for Inez. His wife was mad right now, but she'd get over it once he got her there. At least that's what he told himself. He turned his face to the North and sat with his back to Florida.

Leaving as he did, he figured he would never set foot in Eustis again for as long as he lived. And as he settled in for the twenty-three-hour train ride up the coast of the Atlantic, he had no desire to have anything to do with the town he grew up in, the state of Florida, or the South as a whole, for that matter.

3

MONROE, LOUISIANA, EASTER MONDAY, APRIL 6, 1953
ROBERT JOSEPH PERSHING FOSTER

IN THE DARK HOURS OF THE MORNING, Pershing Foster packed his surgery books, his medical bag, and his suit and sport coats in the trunk, along with a map, an address book, and Ivorye Covington's fried chicken left over from Saturday night.

He said good-bye to his father, who had told him to follow his dreams. His father's dreams had fallen apart, but there was still hope for the son, the father knew. He had a reluctant embrace with his older brother, Madison, who had tried in vain to get him to stay. Then Pershing pointed his 1949 Buick Roadmaster, a burgundy one with white-wall tires and a shark-tooth grille, in the direction of Five Points, the crossroads of town.

He drove down the narrow dirt roads with the ditches on either side that, when he was a boy, had left his freshly pressed Sunday suit caked with mud when it rained. He passed the shotgun houses perched on cinder blocks and hurtled over the railroad tracks away from where people who looked like him were consigned to live and into the section where the roads were not dirt ditches anymore but suddenly level and paved.

He headed in the direction of Desiard Street, the main thoroughfare, and, without a whiff of sentimentality, sped away from the small-town bank buildings and bail bondsmen, the Paramount Theater with its urine-scented steps, and away from St. Francis Hospital, which wouldn't let doctors who looked like him perform a simple tonsillectomy.

Perhaps he might have stayed had they let him practice surgery like he was trained to do or let him walk into the Palace and try on a suit like anyone else of his station. The resentments had grown heavy over the years. He knew he was as smart as anybody else—smarter, to his mind—but he wasn't allowed to do anything with it, the caste system being what it was. Now he was going about as far away as you could get from Monroe, Louisiana. The rope lines that had hemmed in his life seemed to loosen with each plodding mile on the odometer.

Like many of the men in the Great Migration and like many emigrant men in general, he was setting out alone. He would scout out the New World on his own and get situated before sending for anyone else. He drove west into the morning stillness and onto the Endom Bridge, a tight crossing with one lane acting like two that spans the Ouachita River into West Monroe. He would soon pass the mossback flatland of central Louisiana and the Red River toward Texas, where he was planning to see an old friend from medical school, a Dr. Anthony Beale, en route to California.

Pershing had no idea where he would end up in California or how he would make a go of it or when he would be able to wrest his wife and daughters from the in-laws who had tried to talk him out of going to California in the first place. He would contemplate these uncertainties in the unbroken days ahead.

From Louisiana, he followed the hyphens in the road that blurred together toward a faraway place, bridging unrelated things as hyphens do. Alone in the car, he had close to two thousand miles of curving road in front of him, farther than farmworker emigrants leaving Guatemala for Texas, not to mention Tijuana for California, where a wind from the south could blow a Mexican clothesline over the border.

In our homes, in our churches,
wherever two or three are gathered,
there is a discussion of what is best to do.
Must we remain in the South
or go elsewhere? Where can we go
to feel that security which other people feel?
Is it best to go in great numbers or only in several families?
These and many other things are discussed over and over.
                    —A COLORED WOMAN IN ALABAMA, 1902

THE GREAT MIGRATION, 1915–1970

———

THEY FLED as if under a spell or a high fever. "They left as though they were fleeing some curse," wrote the scholar Emmett J. Scott. "They were willing to make almost any sacrifice to obtain a railroad ticket, and they left with the intention of staying."

From the early years of the twentieth century to well past its middle age, nearly every black family in the American South, which meant nearly every black family in America, had a decision to make. There were sharecroppers losing at settlement. Typists wanting to work in an office. Yard boys scared that a single gesture near the planter's wife could leave them hanging from an oak tree. They were all stuck in a caste system as hard and unyielding as the red Georgia clay, and they each had a decision before them. In this, they were not unlike anyone who ever longed to cross the Atlantic or the Rio Grande.

It was during the First World War that a silent pilgrimage took its first steps within the borders of this country. The fever rose without warning or notice or much in the way of understanding by those outside its reach. It would not end until the 1970s and would set into motion changes in the North and South that no one, not even the people doing the leaving, could have imagined at the start of it or dreamed would take nearly a lifetime to play out.

Historians would come to call it the Great Migration. It would become perhaps the biggest underreported story of the twentieth century. It was vast. It was leaderless. It crept along so many thousands of currents over so long a stretch of time as to be difficult for the press truly to capture while it was under way.

Over the course of six decades, some six million black southerners left the land of their forefathers and fanned out across the country for an uncertain existence in nearly every other corner of America. The Great Migration would become a turning point in history. It would transform urban America and recast the social and political order of every city it touched. It would force the South to search its soul and finally to lay aside a feudal caste system. It grew out of the unmet promises made after the Civil War and, through the sheer weight of it, helped push the country toward the civil rights revolutions of the 1960s.

During this time, a good portion of all black Americans alive picked up and left the tobacco farms of Virginia, the rice plantations of South Carolina, cotton fields in east Texas and Mississippi, and the villages and backwoods of the remaining southern states—Alabama, Arkansas, Florida, Georgia, Kentucky, Louisiana, North Carolina, Tennessee, and, by some measures, Oklahoma. They set out for cities they had whispered of among themselves or had seen in a mail-order catalogue. Some came straight from the field with their King James Bibles and old twelve-string guitars. Still more were townspeople looking to be their fuller selves, tradesmen following their customers, pastors trailing their flocks.

They would cross into alien lands with fast, new ways of speaking and carrying oneself and with hard-to-figure rules and laws. The New World held out higher wages but staggering rents that the people had to calculate like a foreign currency. The places they went were big, frightening, and already crowded—New York, Detroit, Chicago, Los Angeles, Philadelphia, and smaller, equally foreign cities—Syracuse, Oakland, Milwaukee, Newark, Gary. Each turned into a "receiving station and port of refuge," wrote the poet Carl Sandburg, then a Chicago newspaper reporter documenting the unfolding migration there.

The people did not cross the turnstiles of customs at Ellis Island. They were already citizens. But where they came from, they were not treated as such. Their every step was controlled by the meticulous laws of Jim Crow, a nineteenth-century minstrel figure that would become shorthand for the violently enforced codes of the southern caste system. The Jim Crow regime persisted from the 1880s to the 1960s, some eighty years, the average life span of a fairly healthy man. It afflicted the lives of at least four generations and would not die without bloodshed, as the people who left the South foresaw.

Over time, this mass relocation would come to dwarf the California Gold Rush of the 1850s with its one hundred thousand participants and the Dust Bowl migration of some three hundred thousand people from Oklahoma and Arkansas to California in the 1930s. But more remarkably, it was the first mass act of independence by a people who were in bondage in this country for far longer than they have been free.

"The story of the Great Migration is among the most dramatic and compelling in all chapters of American history," the Mississippi historian Neil McMillen wrote toward the end of the twentieth century. "So far reaching are its effects even now that we scarcely understand its meaning."

Its imprint is everywhere in urban life. The configuration of the cities as we know them, the social geography of black and white neighborhoods, the spread of the housing projects as well as the rise of a well-scrubbed black middle class, along with the alternating waves of white flight and suburbanization—all of these grew, directly or indirectly, from the response of everyone touched by the Great Migration.

So, too, rose the language and music of urban America that sprang from the blues that came with the migrants and dominates our airwaves to this day. So, too, came the people who might not have existed, or become who they did, had there been no Great Migration. People as diverse as James Baldwin and Michelle Obama, Miles Davis and Toni Morrison, Spike Lee and Denzel Washington, and anonymous teachers, store clerks, steelworkers, and physicians, were all products of the Great Migration. They were all children whose life chances were altered because a parent or grandparent had made the hard decision to leave.

The Great Migration would not end until the 1970s, when the South began finally to change—the whites-only signs came down, the all-white schools opened up, and everyone could vote. By then nearly half of all black Americans—some forty-seven percent—would be living outside the South, compared to ten percent when the Migration began.

"Oftentimes, just to go away," wrote John Dollard, a Yale scholar studying the South in the 1930s, "is one of the most aggressive things that another person can do, and if the means of expressing discontent are limited, as in this case, it is one of the few ways in which pressure can be put."

By the time it was over, no northern or western city would be the same. In Chicago alone, the black population rocketed from 44,103 (just under three percent of the population) at the start of the Migration to more than one million at the end of it. By the turn of the twenty-first century, blacks made up a third of the city's residents, with more blacks living in Chicago than in the entire state of Mississippi.

It was a "folk movement of incalculable moment," McMillen said.

And more than that, it was the first big step the nation's servant class ever took without asking.

———

The passenger train came wheezing through the north Georgia mountains after the colored school let out, and when it passed through the hill town of Rome, Georgia, back during the Depression, a little girl would run down the embankment and wait for it to rush past the locust trees. She would wave to the people in the metal boxes on wheels, the important people, their faces looking away, and dream of going wherever it was they were rushing to.

Years later, she got on a train herself, heading north. The railcar was filled with the expectant faces of people hoping for all the rights and privileges of citizenship. She stepped off at Union Station in the border city of Washington, D.C. It was the start of the North, filled as it was with grand squares and circles named after northern heroes of the Civil War—Ulysses S. Grant, William Tecumseh Sherman, George Henry Thomas, David G. Farragut—names, to this day, reviled in the South. She made her way to the address she had been given and settled onto the fold-out sofa in the front room of a second cousin she barely knew. Soon afterward, she performed a ritual of arrival that just about every migrant did almost without thinking: she got her picture taken in the New World. It would prove that she had arrived. It was the migrant's version of a passport.

The picture is sepia, two by three inches, from the forties. Two young women sit on the front steps of a row house on R Street in Washington, looking very Bette Davis. Stacked heels and padded shoulders, wool coats brushing their knees. They are new in town. Childhood friends from Georgia meeting up now in the big city. Their faces give no hint of whatever indignities the South had visited upon them. That was over now. Their faces are all smiles and optimism. The one in the pearls used to greet the train when she was little and dream of going with it. She would become a teacher and, years later, my mother.

As a girl, I found the picture in a drawer in the living room, where many of those artifacts of migration likely ended up. I stared into the faces, searched the light in their eyes, the width of their smiles for clues as to how they got there.

Why did they go? What were they looking for? How did they get the courage to leave all they ever knew for a place they had never seen, the will to be more than the South said they had a right to be? Was it a braver thing to stay, or was it a braver thing to go? What would have happened if she had not gone north and met and married the Tuskegee Airman from Virginia, a migrant himself, who would become my father? Would I (and millions of other people born in the North and West) have even existed? What would have happened had all those people raised under Jim Crow not spilled out of the South looking for something better? If they had not gone north, what would New York look like? What would Philadelphia, Detroit, Pittsburgh, Chicago, Los Angeles, Washington, and Oakland look like? What, for that matter, would the South look like? Would it have changed on its own? Or did the black exodus force the South to face itself in ways no one could ever have thought possible?

"What would have happened if I'd stayed?" my mother asked out loud, repeating a question put to her one day. "I don't even want to think about that."

She never used the term "Great Migration" or any grand label for what she did nor did she see her decision as having any meaning beyond herself. Yet she and millions of others like her were right in the middle of it. At one point, ten thousand were arriving every month in Chicago alone. It made for a spectacle at the railroad platforms, both north and south.

"I went to the station to see a friend who was leaving," Emmett J. Scott, an official at Tuskegee Institute in Alabama, wrote shortly after the Migration began. "I could not get in the station. There were so many people turning like bees in a hive."

———

Those millions of people, and what they did, would seep into nearly every realm of American culture, into the words of Ralph Ellison and Toni Morrison, the plays of Lorraine Hansberry and August Wilson, the poetry and music of Langston Hughes and B. B. King, and the latter-day generation of Arrested Development and Tupac Shakur. It all but consumed the work of Richard Wright, the bard of the Great Migration. He gave voice to the fears and yearnings of his fellow migrants through his novel *Native Son* and his autobiography, *Black Boy*. He had been a sharecropper's son in Natchez, Mississippi. He defected to the receiving station of Chicago, via Memphis, in December 1927, to feel, as he put it, "the warmth of other suns."

Yet for all of its influence, the Migration was so vast that, throughout history, it has most often been consigned to the landscape, rarely the foreground. Scholars have devoted their attention to the earliest phase of the Migration, the World War I era. "Less has been written about the more massive sequence of migration that began during World War II," the historian James N. Gregory wrote in 2005, "and a comprehensive treatment of the century-long story of black migration does not exist."

This book addresses that omission. The stories in this book are based on the accounts of people who gave hundreds of hours of their days to share with me what was perhaps the singular turning point in their lives. They were among more than twelve hundred people I interviewed for this book in New York, Chicago, Los Angeles, Milwaukee, and Oakland. All of them journeyed from the South during the Great Migration, and it is their collective stories that inform every aspect of this book.

For the three main characters—Ida Mae Brandon Gladney, George Swanson Starling, and Robert Joseph Pershing Foster—and for others like them, the circumstances of their migrations shaped who they were and defined the course of their fortunes or misfortunes and the lives of their descendants. The events were thus easily recounted when the participants were called upon to do so. Official records corroborated those details that were indeed verifiable. But it is the larger emotional truths, the patient retelling of people's interior lives and motivations, that are the singular gift of the accounts in this book. With the passing of the earliest and succeeding generations of migrants, it is these stories that have become the least replaceable sources of any understanding of this great movement of people out of the South to the American North and West.

This book covers a span of some one hundred years. As the narrative moves through time, the language changes to retain the authenticity of each era. The word "colored" is used during the portion of the book in which that term was a primary identifier for black people, that is, during the first two-thirds of the twentieth century, as evidenced by the colored high schools the people attended and the signage that directed them to segregated facilities. As the narrative moves into the 1960s, it shifts to the use of the term "black," after it gained popularity during the civil rights era, and then to both "black" and "African American" in the current era.

Over time, the story of the Great Migration has suffered distortions that have miscast an entire population. From the moment the emigrants set foot in the North and West, they were blamed for the troubles of the cities they fled to. They were said to have brought family dysfunction with them, to more likely be out-of-work, unwed parents, and on welfare, than the people already there.

In the past twenty years, however, an altogether different picture has emerged from ongoing research by scholars of the Great Migration. Closer analysis of newly available census records has found that, contrary to conventional thought, black migrants were actually more likely to be married and to raise their children in two-parent households, and less likely to bear children out of wedlock. "Compared with northern-born blacks," writes the sociologist Stewart E. Tolnay, a leading expert on the Migration, "southern migrants had higher rates of participation in the labor force, lower levels of unemployment, higher incomes, lower levels of poverty and welfare dependency." The lives of the people in this book bear out this more complex understanding of the Great Migration and, based on the new data, represent the more common migrant experience than many previous accounts.

Despite the overlapping of time and place in the text, the three main people in this narrative never met or knew one another. Their paths never crossed except through their experiences with me and metaphorically through the interlocking chapters of this book. The narrative portrays the phenomenon through people unknown to one another, in the way that migrants moving along different currents would not have intersected, their anonymity a metaphor for the vast and isolating nature of the Migration itself.

The actions of the people in this book were both universal and distinctly American. Their migration was a response to an economic and social structure not of their making. They did what humans have done for centuries when life became untenable—what the pilgrims did under the tyranny of British rule, what the Scotch-Irish did in Oklahoma when the land turned to dust, what the Irish did when there was nothing to eat, what the European Jews did during the spread of Nazism, what the landless in Russia, Italy, China, and elsewhere did when something better across the ocean called to them. What binds these stories together was the back-against-the-wall, reluctant yet hopeful search for something better, any place but where they were. They did what human beings looking for freedom, throughout history, have often done.

They left.

PART TWO

BEGINNINGS

This was the culture
from which I sprang.
This was the terror
from which I fled.
—RICHARD WRIGHT,
Black Boy

Ida Mae Brandon Gladney

CHICAGO, 1996

———

FROM THE OPEN DOOR IN THE VESTIBULE, I see her. She is sitting in a cotton housedress on a baby blue, plastic-covered easy chair by the window. She is looking through a parting of the curtains at the street circus below. There they are, all scuffling beneath her: urban drug dealers, falling-down sweatpants pooling at their feet, now bent over the driver's-side window of a late-model sedan from the suburbs; fourth-graders doing lookout for men who could be their fathers; young girls with their stomachs swelling already; middle-aged men living out of their Pontiacs; gangsters who might not make it to the weekend.

She lives on the second floor of a three-flat on the South Side of Chicago. She taps her foot and moves closer to the sill. This is not what she had come to Chicago for, nor was it what she expected it to be. But here she is, and this is what it has become, a place so dangerously absurd that it is living entertainment in her old age. She knows the street names and the code words for all the hustlers and pushers playing out their lives beneath her window, and even though they may have just shot a rival or just got out on parole, they look out for her and greet her kindly—*you watch yourself now, Grandma*—because there is something sweet and kind about her, and she is from the Old Country and has survived a life of fear and privation they will never know.

She has an endearing gap in her teeth, which go just about any which way they please, and her hair is now as soft and white as the cotton she used to pick not particularly well back in Mississippi. She is the color of sand on a beach, which she had heard of growing up but had never seen for herself until she arrived in Chicago half a lifetime ago. She has big searching eyes that see the good in people despite the evil she has seen, and she has a comforting kind of eternal beauty, her skin like the folds of a velvet shawl.

Her name is Ida Mae, and she is a long way from where she started back in the hard soil of the eastern foothills of Mississippi during the century's adolescence. She leans forward and adjusts herself for a long conversation. Her hazel eyes grow big as she begins to tell her story.

VAN VLEET, MISSISSIPPI, 1928
IDA MAE BRANDON GLADNEY

IT BEGAN, LIKE MANY STORIES DO, with a man.

Actually, two men. They both came calling in the quiet hours of the hot season, when the cotton lay gestating in the field. Ida Mae had just sprouted into a woman of fifteen, and the suitors were out front clutching their hats to their chests.

They descended from opposite corners of old Chickasaw County, down the dirt roads that became mud rivers in the wet season and dust clouds in the dry but were the only route to the bottomland by the Natchez Trace and an audience with Ida Mae, who was amused by it all.

David McIntosh came after church on a tall red horse, the sun slanting heat through the hackberry trees, and he was always the first one there. He sat stiff in his Sunday clothes and sugar-talked the daughter in an old chair in the front room while her mother, Miss Theenie, stood peeping by the door. When he had said all he had to say, which was never soon enough for Miss Theenie, he climbed back on his horse and, as the daughter suspected, rode off to another girl he was weighing, named Sallie.

George Gladney walked three or four miles past the salt licks of Long Creek and over the railroad tracks to see Ida Mae. It took him longer than it took David McIntosh, and by the time he got there, his shirt was wet with perspiration and brown from the dust clouds stirred up on the road. Sometimes David's horse was still tied out front. George was a quiet, austere man and felt a certain proprietorship toward Ida Mae. He waited for David to finish before going in himself. He stood outside and watched David mount his horse and gallop away before walking up the plank steps of the porch. Coming in second would give him more time to win the girl over and assess her fitness as a wife.

Miss Theenie was not particular about either one of them. To begin with, they were too old for Ida Mae, trotting up the porch in their twenties when Ida Mae hadn't long turned fifteen. David was barely as tall as Ida Mae, and both of them were too dark by Miss Theenie's reckoning. She had little assurance of her daughters' upward mobility in a world where most colored women were sharecroppers' wives, but she could hope for the more favorable economic prospects of a lighter man, based on his acceptability to white people and even kinship to them, maybe, which would be all the better.

Ida Mae didn't go for that kind of talk and didn't pay it much attention. One color of wildflower was no better than another to her, so she made no distinctions whatsoever. She had a way of looking past the outer layer of people and seemed to regard everyone she met with a kind of searching intensity, as if this were the first person she had ever seen.

In any case, Miss Theenie's protests were likely just an excuse. Whatever his attributes, Miss Theenie was not inclined to like any man that came courting her second girl. Miss Theenie gave birth to her in a little wood house on Cousin Irie's land and named her Mae Ida after her husband's mother, Ida.

It was March 5, 1913, some three years after the start of the Great Migration that Ida Mae would unwittingly become a part of. There was a spark inside of her, and, when she got big enough, she told people to call her Ida Mae instead of Mae Ida. She would later say it sounded less old-timey to her, but it was an early indication that she could think for herself when she chose to.

She was a small-framed girl with a chiseled face the color of nut butter and her dark brown hair in plaits most of the time. It turned out she was fearless and spirited and liked doing the kinds of things men are known for doing. She was no good in the field, but she could chop wood and kill snakes and didn't mind doing it, and that was a good thing for Miss Theenie.

By the time men started showing up on the porch for Ida Mae, Miss Theenie was a widow, left to tend the land they lived on all by herself. She stood eye to eye with most men and suffered no fools, but she had little help now. Her oldest daughter, Irene, had gone off and gotten married. Her two grown sons, Sam and Cleve, had fled north to Ohio like more and more colored boys chafing in the South seemed to be doing. Her husband, Joseph, had just about run them off before he died. Joseph would beat them for any little thing, since they weren't his blood like the girls were. And that didn't make them want to stay either. So they went up north. That left Miss Theenie with her youngest daughters—Josephine, who was able to work but wouldn't, and Talma, who was too young to work—and her second, the tomboy, Ida Mae.

On her way home from school, Ida Mae climbed up the hickory and walnut trees on the side of the road and shook them down. She picked the skittle bumps off the ground and cracked them on her teeth. She saw how her brothers relieved themselves in the woods at the side of a tree and tried it herself. Being a girl, it didn't work as well when she tried it standing up.

Sam and Cleve, before they left, had to shoo her away when they went out hunting rabbit. She crouched behind the trees, and they heard her rustling near them and threw tap sticks at her, the sticks they took to kill the rabbits with. Sometimes she spotted a rabbit sleeping and popped it with a tap stick, and, along with whatever her brothers took in, they would eat well that night.

Sometimes her brothers didn't want to be bothered. So they gave her a quarter and let her plow in their place so they could go to a pickup baseball game. She'd get behind the mule and go up and down the field cutting lines in the earth as if it were the most important job in the world. The kids started calling her Tom because she acted more like a boy.

———

They lived on the curving land in the hill country of northeast Mississippi. It was a voluptuous place, more beautiful than the Delta land along the Great River, and like anything beautiful, had a tendency to break grown people's hearts. It was not meant to work as hard as it was made to when it came to sowing cotton, and, of the two regions, it had the more difficult birthing pains.

Joseph Brandon had come into ownership of a piece of bottomland, where he planted cotton and grew hogs. The land that colored men managed to get was usually scratch land nobody wanted. Still, he courted the land every spring. He cut lines in the earth with an old till, a swayback mule, and a horse named Jim. He planted cottonseed in the topsoil and tried to conjure rain. When the land turned green, he chopped the unwanted leaves that got in the way of the buds trying to grow.

By late summer, if the rains had come but not rotted the seed, if the sun had burned long enough by day and the dew had descended by night, dry snow sprang from the earth at the tips of low scrub that came to bud with his prayers and sweat. The land would be salted with white confetti that spread out to the tree line. Then he had to bend down in the beating sun to pick the bolls and crouch and crawl to reach the lowest buds.

Before she was big enough to see over the cotton, Ida Mae followed her father out to the field. He gave her a flour sack to keep her occupied, and she tagged behind him and gathered cotton bolls even though what little she brought in was not of much use. It turned out she had no talent whatsoever for the field and didn't like the chore of picking. But her father was always out there, and picking gave her time with him.

"That's how come I know about the field," she would say half a life later. "Wherever he went, I went."

When he wasn't nursing the cotton, he was tending the hogs. Sometimes the hogs ran off and got stuck in the creek water swollen up after the gully washers that poured from the sky in the spring. Ida Mae followed her father down to the creek and watched him slosh in the water to save his drowning hogs. The rains brought moccasin snakes to the surface and left them alive on the creek bank when the water fell back. Ida Mae took sticks to pick them up with and played with them like toys.

The rains beat down on Mississippi in May of 1923. The hogs went down to the creek and got stuck like they always did, but when her father slogged in after them, he had trouble bringing them in for all the floodwater that had risen up. He got sick from exposure and never recovered. He was forty-three years old.

He was diabetic, and the grown people said he was dead. But Ida Mae sat at the side of his bed and touched him, and he was warm. No doctor ever tended to him. There were no colored doctors around. The white ones were all in town, and the family would have had to meet them halfway, if they were going to see them at all, because the doctors in town didn't know the backwoods. Even if they had been inclined to come, the roads were too muddy from the rains to get through.

Ida Mae thought the grown people should give him more time; maybe he would come out of the spell he was in. Years later, she learned that educated people had a name for what her father appeared to be in. They called it a coma. But in that world and in that time, nobody could know for sure and nobody would pay a little girl any attention, and so they set the date for the burial.

She and her sisters Irene and Josie and Talma didn't have any shoes and went trailing behind their mother in their bare feet to the funeral. Nobody felt sorry for them because most other people didn't have shoes either.

When they closed the casket, Ida Mae thought for sure that her father was alive in there. "I still say today he wasn't dead," she would say three-quarters of a century later. "At that time, they didn't have a way to know."

Not long after the funeral, Ida Mae was sitting on the bin where they stored the hay and corn, in an enclosure they called a crib. She looked up and saw what looked to be her father walk in. It was both startling and natural. He reached his hand out to her and took her hand in his and held it. When she realized what was happening, she ran out screaming and went to get Miss Theenie.

"Daddy's in the crib!" she cried. "I saw him!"

"Girl, get away from me with that lying," Miss Theenie said. "Joseph wouldn't scare you."

"I held his hand, just as plain as day," Ida Mae said.

She never saw him again. As the summer wore on, it sank in that he wasn't coming back, and she started resenting the world and the people who had fathers. She started fighting and picking fights with people for no reason.

School was out because colored children only went to school when they were not needed in the field. Ida Mae and other colored children in rural Mississippi didn't start school until the cotton was picked, which meant October or November, and they stopped going to school when it was time to plant in April. Six months of school was a good year.

She was still grieving when it was time to go back the next fall. She walked a mile of dirt road past the drying cotton and the hackberry trees to get to the one-room schoolhouse that, one way or the other, had to suffice for every colored child from first to eighth grade, the highest you could go back then if you were colored in Chickasaw County.

The children formed a walking train to get there. It started with the child farthest away and picked up more children as it moved in the direction of the schoolhouse until just about the whole school was in a cluster at the front door.

Ida Mae was easily distracted by the nut trees along the way and had a hard time keeping up. "I be lagging behind hollering and crying, 'cause they run off and leave me," she said.

When the rains came and the water got too high for the children to pass through the hog wallows in places like where Ida Mae lived, the old people cut down a tree and trimmed the limbs so the children could cross over the log to get to school.

The school was a narrow frame cabin with wood benches and long windows, run by a teacher who was missing a leg. Amos Kirks was a source of unending curiosity and whispers among the children. He was of an age where he might have lost his leg in World War I, but none of the children knew for sure. He walked into the schoolroom, hobbling on crutches, in a suit and with a stern face. He rotated the grades as if the room were a railroad switch yard, calling the second- and third-graders to the front when it was their turn, while the other children moved to the back to do their lessons.

He towered above them and always wore a tie. But all the children could see was the left pant leg pinned up at the knee and air where a calf and foot should have been.

One day Mr. Kirks came in, and his pant leg wasn't pinned at the knee. He had a new leg. But he couldn't walk on it like a real one. "He throwed the leg, like it was tiresome to him," Ida Mae said. "And it would swing. He kind of swing it around."

It was the talk of the schoolyard.

"He finally got him a leg!" the children whispered to each other.

When Mr. Kirks wasn't looking, Ida Mae tried to tug at his pant cuff. "I sat side of him," Ida Mae said years later. "I try to do all I know how to get up under there and see how that leg look. I'd sat by him, and I just rub and do. He couldn't feel it no way. And I could see the clear foot in the shoe."

Ida Mae had to make sure Mr. Kirks didn't catch on. For the slightest infraction, Mr. Kirks would send some boys out to the woods to get branches off a tree. Then the child who was talking out of turn or drawing when he should be listening was called up front for lashings with the switch.

Ida Mae knew how that felt. In the fall after her father died, they were in the middle of a spelling lesson. One of the words was a city in the North called Philadelphia. Mr. Kirks called on Ida Mae to spell it. Some words, the children turned into jingles to help them remember. For geography, it was *George Eat O Gray Rat At Poor House Yesterday.* For Mississippi, it was *M eye crooked-letter crooked-letter eye crooked-letter crooked-letter eye humpback humpback eye.*

Ida Mae had heard about the North but didn't know Philadelphia or any ditties for it. She stumbled over the word. Mr. Kirks thought she was acting up. He told some boys to go out to the woods and get him a switch. He held the branches over the fire and told Ida Mae to come up front. He told her to bend over. He drew his arm back, and, in front of all the other children, he whipped her. And each time the switch snapped her back, he shouted a letter: P-H-I-L-A-D-E-L-P-H-I-A.

She was hurt to be singled out that day. She wasn't saying she hadn't done a devilish thing in her life. She was just thinking to herself all she had done was miss the word, and the whipping wasn't called for. After school, she went up to Mr. Kirks and told him so.

"If I had a daddy, you wouldn'ta whoop me," Ida Mae told him. "You whoop me 'cause I don't have a daddy."

He never whipped her again.

She seemed to be more aware of how life was harder now. Things she wouldn't have paid attention to before, she seemed to be noticing.

On her way to and from school, she passed the farm of a man named Mr. Bafford. His wife had left him to raise their son by himself, and he seemed to take out his grief on those around him. He had a yard full of trees that bore more fruit than he could ever consume or pick fast enough to sell. The peaches and apples and pears were some of the biggest and sweetest in the bottoms. They ripened and fell to the ground, and still he dared anyone to come onto his land to get any.

Ida Mae figured out a way to get some. She stopped by and talked with Mr. Bafford and made sure to keep him talking. And if he ever looked away, she reached down and slipped a pear or an apple into her dress. "You know they fall off, he coulda give us some of 'em," she said. "Every time I got a chance, I got me some."

It was approaching Christmas, the first Christmas since her father had died. One day when Ida Mae stopped to see Mr. Bafford, she started wondering aloud whether Santa Claus was going to come this year, what with her daddy gone and all.

"That's the first thing they teach y'all, a lie," Mr. Bafford said. "Ain't no such thing as Santa Claus."

It crushed Ida Mae to hear him say that. She was ten, and, even in the gaunt world she lived in, she still believed in Santa Claus. She started crying when Mr. Bafford said it.

"That taken all the joy out of life then," she said.

———

There would be no Christmas that year. "I'm not able to pay Santa Claus to come to us," Miss Theenie told the girls. Ida Mae began to resent everybody now. She was getting into more scrapes coming and going to school and getting ornery without cause.

A boy named Henry Lee Babbitt used to ride his horse to school every day and brought corn to feed him with. Ida Mae lived farther than Henry Lee did and had to walk. Something got into Ida Mae one day, and she told Henry Lee she was going to set his horse loose. She went up to the horse and reached for the bridle bit that tied the horse to the hitching post.

"Tom, you bet not turn my horse aloose," Henry Lee said.

"What if I do?" Ida Mae shot back.

"You do, I beat your brains out."

The two of them stood there next to the horse, Ida Mae holding the bridle bit and threatening to pull it off and Henry Lee trying to keep her from doing it.

"I dee-double-dog-dare you to pull that bridle," Henry Lee said. "You take that there, and you take a nickel off a dead man's eye."

She yanked the bridle off the horse and dropped it to the ground. "And down the road we went, me and the boy there, fighting," she said years later.

Henry Lee reached down and grabbed the bridle bit from where she left it and raised it up against her. "He took it and nearly beat me to death," she said. "I got a knot in back of my head now where he hit me with that bridle bit."

Without her half brothers and her father around, she was on her own. "You had to fight," she would later say. "Them boys would mess with you. You couldn't whoop 'em. But you did what you could."

Within a few years, the boys would not want to fight with her anymore. They wanted to sit and hold her hand and talk. The spark that made her fight them drew the quiet ones to her when it came time for courting. She was fifteen when two in particular started showing up at the front porch with those intentions.

———

On a Sunday after service in the summer of 1928, the church mothers at New Hope Baptist set out the hot platters of corn bread and collards and salted hams. Whoever made the collards worried if they were tender enough. Whoever baked the pound cake prayed that people would favor her cake over somebody else's potato pie.

It was the time of the year they called the lay-by, when the people left the cotton alone and waited for it to sprout. The people had turned the benches up and spread the food on the tables outside the little frame church. They called the event Children's Day, in the spirit of Men's Day and Women's Day other times of the year. An event like this was all there was on colored people's off day in the backwoods of Chickasaw County. People came in from Buena Vista, or Bewnie as they called it, and from over near Houston, the county seat, and even Okolona, arriving in their wagons and surreys.

These were the times when sharecroppers and servants could recede into a world of their own making, where Jim Crow didn't bother to enter. They could forget that there was such a thing as colored or white and just be. Sundays like this turned the churchyard into courting grounds for marriageable girls and young men looking for wives or diversions.

George Gladney showed up with a bunch of other young men from across the creek in somebody's old Model T Ford. He was twenty-two, stern-faced, and serious even then. "He wasn't no smiling man," Ida Mae said.

He was from around Bewnie, which was seven or eight miles south of Van Vleet. He was among the last of twelve to fifteen children. (No one alive knows for sure how many there were; his father had children by several wives, who died young or at least before he did.) George's mother died before he acquired much to remember her by. He was raised by an older brother, Willie, and the weight of his circumstances seemed to show in his face.

It was getting to the time when he should settle down. So he walked up to Ida Mae that afternoon. She was eating on the grass in her Sunday dress. He introduced himself, but she didn't pay him much attention. Her mind was on someone else, and she was mad at the moment. A boy by the name of Alfonso Banks had shown up at church that day with another girl.

Alfonso was the love of her short life. He was friends with her brothers, older and sure of himself in a way that drew the girls to him. No one had really taken her anywhere her whole life, and she felt grown up and free when he did. Excitement seemed to follow him even when he had nothing to do with it. One time he took her to a church revival, which was the country equivalent of a night on the town. It was Alfonso and Ida Mae and Ida Mae's big sister, Irene, and another young man who was escorting Irene that night. They drove up to the church and got out of the car, all of them young and giddy. They attracted the attention of a man named Bay-Bay, who had designs on Ida Mae's sister. He saw them and got enraged.

"Who is this out here laughing?" he said to them.

They ignored him. They started up the steps, and as they walked toward the church door, Bay-Bay pulled out a gun and shot at them six times, aiming at Irene or her escort or both. He was a bad shot and didn't hit anybody. But it was exciting and the talk of the woods and further proof to Ida Mae that Alfonso Banks sure knew how to show a girl a good time, even though he had nothing to do with it.

She had been out with Alfonso enough to feel a kind of ownership that was implied if not outright said. When she saw Alfonso come to Children's Day with another girl, she went up and spoke her mind.

"What'd you bring her here for?" Ida Mae said.

"I brought her for Children's Day."

"Unh-huh."

Something rose up in her. She took the umbrella in her hand and knocked it across his head. "Boy, I loved that boy," she said years later. "And he come bringing that girl over there. And I hit him all cross the head. My mother hit me with a poker when I got home. Everybody was talking about it. You know how folks talk. Said I was wrong. Had no business hitting him cross the head on church grounds."

When George showed up that day, she was distracted and didn't give this new face much thought. But he seemed to have made up his mind about her and started coming by her house on Sunday afternoons, giving her time to see the light.

He endured the stone face of Miss Theenie's disapproval and the teasing curiosity of Josie and Talma to spend time with Ida Mae. When he felt he was on firm enough ground to do so, he began making noises about the other young men: David McIntosh, Alfonso Banks, and another one, Freddie McClendon. He didn't like them coming around, and it showed on his face.

The other men must have noticed an intensity of purpose in George that they could not have fully understood, and they avoided running into him. It got to the point where, during his final visits, David McIntosh, sensing the hour growing late, would say, "Well, I guess I better go 'fore Gladney get here."

George's steadfastness won her over, and she finally agreed to marry him and be free of life under her mother. But she and George had to keep it to themselves. Miss Theenie wouldn't allow it if she knew. She never liked any of the boys courting Ida Mae, and she didn't like George.

"He's old enough for your daddy," Miss Theenie used to say of George, who was by now twenty-three to Ida Mae's sixteen.

In the middle of October 1929, George made arrangements for them to run off and get married. He found a preacher and a place near Bewnie outside her mother's circle. He went into Houston and bought a yellow dress with a blouson waist low on the hip, as was the style back in the twenties, for Ida Mae to wear.

The morning of October 14, 1929, Ida Mae fed the chickens and did her chores like any other day and kept a lookout for George to come and take her to a new life. But before he could get there, a neighbor man pulled up to their cabin and went in to see her mother.

"I heard your daughter gettin' married in Bewnie tonight," the man said.

Miss Theenie started cursing and went looking for Ida Mae. Ida Mae knew she would pay for plotting under her mother's nose. She ran and hid under the bed and wondered how she would get out when George came for her. Now that Miss Theenie knew George was on his way, Miss Theenie would be ready for him.

Josie and Talma and Miss Theenie looked out in the crib and out by the cows and called out to her in the little wood house and couldn't find her. The search for Ida Mae must have touched something in Miss Theenie. Something must have told her it was time for Ida Mae to leave her. She got through cursing, and Ida Mae felt safe to come out.

Miss Theenie went up to her second daughter and told Ida Mae her decision about the wedding.

"Well, I give you tomorrow," Miss Theenie said, "providing all us can go with you."

The next day, October 15, 1929, they all went to the minister's house.

Ida Mae put on the yellow dress with the blouson waist that George had chosen for her. The yard was filled with people as they stood on the porch steps and George Gladney and Ida Mae Brandon were declared man and wife.

"We wish you much joy," the people in the yard said.

George took her to the Edd Pearson plantation, a few miles away, where he would sharecrop cotton and she would learn to be a wife. Two weeks later, something called the stock market crashed, and things would get harder than they ever knew they could. Because, if the planters suffered, so much more would the sharecroppers under them.

An invisible hand ruled their lives and the lives of all the colored people in Chickasaw County and the rest of Mississippi and the entire South for that matter. It wasn't one thing; it was everything. The hand had determined that white people were in charge and colored people were under them and had to obey them like a child in those days had to obey a parent, except there was no love between the two parties as there is between a parent and child. Instead there was mostly fear and dependence—and hatred of that dependence—on both sides.

The particulars of all this eluded Ida Mae. White people were everywhere around her, but they were separate from her, in a separate schoolhouse, on separate land on the other side of a firewall that kept white and colored from occupying the same sidewalk. Colored people had to step off the curb when they passed a white person in town, and if the minutest privilege could be imagined, the ruling class claimed it. Ida Mae lived only a few towns away from Calhoun City, Mississippi, where there were white parking spaces (the ones closest to the bank in the town square) and colored parking spaces (on the other side of the street) well into the 1950s. There were no signs for them; it was just the work of the invisible hand.

Neither Miss Theenie nor George ever took Ida Mae into Houston or Okolona, where white people transacted their business affairs, and, growing up, Ida Mae had few direct dealings with white people. When she did, it was in the service of them and their whims whether she wished it or not, and, in the short time she was in their presence, it seems they made sure to remind her what her place was in their eyes even when she was too young to understand it.

She was about six or seven years old when one day her father told her to take a small section of plow to get sharpened at the blacksmith. That way, he wouldn't have to quit working to go himself. She rode the horse down the dirt path through the hackberry trees to the blacksmith's house.

The blacksmith was a kind and middle-aged white man with two grown sons. The blacksmith pulled the plow sweeps off the horse and went into the back to sharpen them. As Ida Mae stood waiting, the blacksmith's two sons came up to her. They were in their twenties and, with their father occupied, were looking to have some fun.

"We gon' put her in the well," they said to each other and laughed.

Each man took an arm, and as she screamed for them to let her go, they dragged her to a well with a wall around it and dangled her over the mouth of it. Ida Mae could see down the black hole of the well, her legs hanging over the rim. She fought and kicked and screamed at the men to let her go. She looked around and saw nobody there to help her. The men's father was still working on the plow bits.

The men watched her squirm and laughed at the sight of her squirming. They held her over the well until the fun wore off. Then they put her down, and she ran to where the blacksmith was and waited for him to come out with the freshly sharpened sweeps.

Her father used to send her there all the time. After that, he never sent her anymore. When it came down to it, there was nothing he could do to keep it from happening again. Decades later, she would think about how they could have dropped her, even by accident, and how she would have died and nobody would have known where she was or how she'd gotten there.

"They wouldn't have never told," she said.

Ida Mae soon discovered that, when it came to white people, there were good ones and bad ones like anything else and that she had to watch them close to figure out the difference. She was too good-natured to waste energy disliking them no matter what they did but looked upon them as a curiosity she might never comprehend. She learned to give them the benefit of the doubt but not be surprised at anything involving them. This alone probably added decades to her life.

A white lady named Miss Julie McClenna lived across the pasture, and she was nice to Ida Mae. After Ida Mae's father died, Miss McClenna paid Ida Mae to gather up eggs in the henhouse. Sometimes she took her into town to help her carry eggs to sell. She gave Ida Mae live chickens and leftover food, knowing that Ida Mae's mother had just been left a widow.

After school, Ida Mae walked a mile to the big house across the pasture to gather eggs for Miss McClenna in the evenings. She always hoped for a lot of eggs. If there were too many for Miss McClenna to carry herself, she would take Ida Mae into Okolona with her. It was the only chance Ida Mae got to go into town.

Ida Mae gathered more than usual one time, and Miss McClenna took her into Okolona to help her sell them to the white people in town. They delivered the eggs to customers' houses, straight to their doors, and Miss McClenna had Ida Mae carry the basket of eggs for her.

The day had gone well until they knocked on one woman's door to make a delivery. Ida Mae stood with the basket behind Miss McClenna as Miss McClenna prepared to step inside.

"You can't bring that nigger in," the woman said from her front door as soon as she saw Ida Mae.

Miss McClenna knew what that meant. She motioned for Ida Mae to go to the back door to deliver the eggs while Miss McClenna stepped inside to complete the transaction.

On the way back home, Miss McClenna seemed unsettled by it.

"Did you hear what she called you?" Miss McClenna asked Ida Mae.

"Yeah, but I ain't pay it no attention," Ida Mae said. "They call you so many names. I never pay it no attention."

The incident jarred Miss McClenna. The "hardware of reality rattled her," as the artist Carrie Mae Weems would say decades later of such interactions.

What few people seemed to realize or perhaps dared admit was that the thick walls of the caste system kept everyone in prison. The rules that defined a group's supremacy were so tightly wound as to put pressure on everyone trying to stay within the narrow confines of acceptability. It meant being a certain kind of Protestant, holding a particular occupation, having a respectable level of wealth or the appearance of it, and drawing the patronizingly appropriate lines between oneself and those of lower rank of either race in that world.

An attorney's wife in Alabama, for instance, was put on notice one day at a gathering at her home for the upper-class women in her circle. Between the hors d'oeuvres and conversation, one of the clubwomen noticed, for the first time apparently, a statuette of the Virgin Mary on a cabinet in the hostess's living room. The guest cattily remarked upon it. *Why, she never knew that the hostess and her family were Catholics!*

The attorney's wife was shaken by the accusation, and quickly replied that *of course not, they were Methodists and she thought everyone knew that. She only had the statuette because she happened to like it.*

But after the party was over and the guests were gone, the accusation haunted her, and she fretted over the implication that she might be seen as a member of a lesser tribe. That day, the attorney's wife took down the statuette of Mary that she liked so much and put it away for good. She could not afford even the appearance of having stepped outside the bounds of her caste.

Neither could Miss Julie McClenna. As far as Ida Mae knew, Miss McClenna never sold eggs to that lady again. But that was also the end of her brief employment with Miss Julie McClenna and the end of the trips into Okolona. "She never did take me no more after that," Ida Mae said.

———

In the bottoms where Ida Mae grew up, it was a crazy enough world that they could almost time the weekends by a white farmer who lived down the road.

He was fine when he was sober and actually liked colored people. But he got drunk on Fridays and came staggering on his old horse to the colored people's cabins. They could hear the hoof steps and hollering as he rode in waving his gun.

"I'm coming through!" he shouted.

Grown people dropped their buckets and went running. Children hid under the cabins on the dirt floor between the stilts, while he huffed and cussed and tried to smoke them out.

"I'm a shoot y'all!" he hollered. "I'm a kill y'all!"

There was always a commotion and a panic whenever he came through. It could happen day or night. There was never much warning, and they had to scramble to escape his ragged gunshots. Then they had to lie perfectly still. "We'd run under the house, and, wherever he hear a bump, he would shoot," Ida Mae said.

One day when he came through, Ida Mae was outside and couldn't get under the house in time. Josie and Talma had scattered already, and she didn't see where they had gone. The man had wobbled off his horse and was coming through, firing his gun.

A barrel of cornmeal was right next to her, and she saw it and jumped inside. She sank into the grit cushion of meal with her chin digging into her knees. All the while, the man hollered and grunted around her, and the bullets made the pinging noises of metal against tin. She pulled the top over her head and tried not to breathe. She stayed in the barrel until the shooting and the cussing stopped.

He was drunk and a bad aim and never actually hit anybody as far as Ida Mae knew. No sheriff or police were ever called in. There would have been no point in calling. And so the drunk farmer could go on shooting and scaring the Brandons and other colored people in the bottoms whenever he felt like it.

"He call hisself having fun," Ida Mae said.

As she grew older, she learned that there was more to the southern caste system than verbal slights and the antics of a crazy white farmer. In the summer of 1926, when she was thirteen, a cloud passed over the grown people, and it showed in their faces. She could overhear them whispering about something that had happened in town, some terrible thing they didn't want the children to know about. It had to do with two colored boys—the Carter brothers, as she heard it—and a white woman.

"They said something to the white lady," she said.

And, as best as Ida Mae could make out, the white people had taken the boys and hanged them in Okolona that morning. Ida Mae would always remember it because that was the day her cousin was born and they named the baby Thenia after Ida Mae's mother. The grown people wept in their cabins.

After the funeral, the surviving Carters packed up and left Mississippi. They went to a place called Milwaukee and never came back.

In three years' time, Ida Mae and George would move to the Pearson plantation, and things would unfold in such a way that Ida Mae would eventually follow the Carters up north. Although she didn't see how it might apply to herself at the time, the Carter migration was a signal to Ida Mae that there was, in fact, a window out of the asylum.

THE STIRRINGS OF DISCONTENT

Everybody seems to be asleep
about what is going on right under our noses.
That is, everybody but those farmers
who have wakened up on mornings recently
to find every Negro over 21 on his place gone—
to Cleveland, to Pittsburgh,
to Chicago, to Indianapolis. . . .
And while our very solvency
is being sucked out beneath us,
we go about our affairs as usual.

—EDITORIAL, *The Macon Telegraph,*
SEPTEMBER 1916

SELMA, ALABAMA, EARLY WINTER 1916

———

NO ONE KNOWS WHO was the first to leave. It was sometime in the middle of World War I. The North faced a labor shortage and, after centuries of indifference, cast its gaze at last on the servant class of the South. The North needed workers, and the workers needed an escape. No one knows exactly when or how it commenced or who took the first actual step of what would become the Great Migration.

One of the earliest references came on February 5, 1916, and was seen as an isolated, random event. It merited only a paragraph in the *Chicago Defender,* the agitator and unwitting chronicler of the movement, and was likely preceded by unremarked-upon departures months before. Railroads in Pennsylvania had begun undercover scouting of cheap black labor as early as 1915. But few people noticed when, in the deep of winter, with a war raging in Europe and talk of America joining in, several hundred black families began quietly departing Selma, Alabama, in February 1916, declaring, according to the *Chicago Defender*'s brief citation, that the "treatment doesn't warrant staying."

Ida Mae Brandon was not yet three years old. George Starling, Pershing Foster, and millions of others who would follow in the footsteps of those first wartime families from Selma had not yet been born. But those early departures would set the stage for their eventual migration.

The families from Selma left in the midst of one of the most divisive eras in American history—the long and violent hangover after the Civil War, when the South, left to its own devices as the North looked away, dismantled the freedoms granted former slaves after the war.

The plantation owners had trouble imagining the innate desires of the people they once had owned. "I find a worse state of things with the Negroes than I expected," wrote General Howell Cobb, a Georgia planter, shortly after the slaves were freed. "Let any man offer them some little thing of no real value, but which looks a little more like freedom, and they catch at it with avidity, and would sacrifice their best friends without hesitation and without regret."

"They will almost starve and go naked," wrote a planter in Warren County, Georgia, "before they will work for a white man, if they can get a patch of ground to live on and get from under his control."

For all its upheaval, the Civil War had left most blacks in the South no better off economically than they had been before. Sharecropping, slavery's replacement, kept them in debt and still bound to whatever plantation they worked. But one thing had changed. The federal government had taken over the affairs of the South, during a period known as Reconstruction, and the newly freed men were able to exercise rights previously denied them. They could vote, marry, or go to school if there were one nearby, and the more ambitious among them could enroll in black colleges set up by northern philanthropists, open businesses, and run for office under the protection of northern troops. In short order, some managed to become physicians, legislators, undertakers, insurance men. They assumed that the question of black citizens' rights had been settled for good and that all that confronted them was merely building on these new opportunities.

But, by the mid-1870s, when the North withdrew its oversight in the face of southern hostility, whites in the South began to resurrect the caste system founded under slavery. Nursing the wounds of defeat and seeking a scapegoat, much like Germany in the years leading up to Nazism, they began to undo the opportunities accorded freed slaves during Reconstruction and to refine the language of white supremacy. They would create a caste system based not on pedigree and title, as in Europe, but solely on race, and which, by law, disallowed any movement of the lowest caste into the mainstream.

The fight over this new caste system made it to the U.S. Supreme Court. Homer A. Plessy, a colored Louisianan, protested a new state law forbidding any railroad passenger from entering "a compartment to which by race he does not belong." On June 7, 1894, Plessy bought a first-class ticket on the East Louisiana Railroad, took an empty seat in the white-only car, and was arrested when he refused to move. In 1896, in the seminal case of *Plessy v. Ferguson,* the Supreme Court sided with the South and ruled, in an eight-to-one vote, that "equal but separate" accommodations were constitutional. That ruling would stand for the next sixty years.

Now, with a new century approaching, blacks in the South, accustomed to the liberties established after the war, were hurled back in time, as if the preceding three decades, limited though they may have been, had never happened. One by one, each license or freedom accorded them was stripped away. The world got smaller, narrower, more confined with each new court ruling and ordinance.

Not unlike European Jews who watched the world close in on them slowly, perhaps barely perceptibly, at the start of Nazism, colored people in the South would first react in denial and disbelief to the rising hysteria, then, helpless to stop it, attempt a belated resistance, not knowing and not able to imagine how far the supremacists would go. The outcomes for both groups were widely divergent, one suffering unspeakable loss and genocide, the other enduring nearly a century of apartheid, pogroms, and mob executions. But the hatreds and fears that fed both assaults were not dissimilar and relied on arousing the passions of the indifferent to mount so complete an attack.

The South began acting in outright defiance of the Fourteenth Amendment of 1868, which granted the right to due process and equal protection to anyone born in the United States, and it ignored the Fifteenth Amendment of 1880, which guaranteed all men the right to vote.

Politicians began riding these anti-black sentiments all the way to governors' mansions throughout the South and to seats in the U.S. Senate.

"If it is necessary, every Negro in the state will be lynched," James K. Vardaman, the white supremacy candidate in the 1903 Mississippi governor's race, declared. He saw no reason for blacks to go to school. "The only effect of Negro education," he said, "is to spoil a good field hand and make an insolent cook."

Mississippi voted Vardaman into the governor's office and later sent him to the U.S. Senate.

All the while, newspapers were giving black violence top billing, the most breathless outrage reserved for any rumor of black male indiscretion toward a white woman, all but guaranteeing a lynching. Sheriff's deputies mysteriously found themselves unable to prevent the abduction of a black suspect from a jailhouse cell. Newspapers alerted readers to the time and place of an upcoming lynching. In spectacles that often went on for hours, black men and women were routinely tortured and mutilated, then hanged or burned alive, all before festive crowds of as many as several thousand white citizens, children in tow, hoisted on their fathers' shoulders to get a better view.

Fifteen thousand men, women, and children gathered to watch eighteen-year-old Jesse Washington as he was burned alive in Waco, Texas, in May 1916. The crowd chanted, "Burn, burn, burn!" as Washington was lowered into the flames. One father holding his son on his shoulders wanted to make sure his toddler saw it.

"My son can't learn too young," the father said.

Across the South, someone was hanged or burned alive every four days from 1889 to 1929, according to the 1933 book *The Tragedy of Lynching,* for such alleged crimes as "stealing hogs, horse-stealing, poisoning mules, jumping labor contract, suspected of killing cattle, boastful remarks" or "trying to act like a white person." Sixty-six were killed after being accused of "insult to a white person." One was killed for stealing seventy-five cents.

Like the cotton growing in the field, violence had become so much a part of the landscape that "perhaps most of the southern black population had witnessed a lynching in their own communities or knew people who had," wrote the historian Herbert Shapiro. "All blacks lived with the reality that no black individual was completely safe from lynching."

In this atmosphere, *The Clansman,* a 1905 novel that was the basis of the 1915 film *Birth of a Nation,* became a national bestseller. It fed whites' panic over freed blacks in their midst and inspired people in Georgia to revive the Ku Klux Klan the year the film was released. Soon Klansmen in full regalia were holding public parades before cheering white crowds across the South like celebrations of the Fourth of July, the Klan then seen not as a rogue outlier but as the protector of southern tradition. Thus the fragile interdependence between the races turned to apprehension and suspicion, one race vowing to accept no less than the total subjugation of the other.

The planter class, which had entrusted its wives and daughters to male slaves when the masters went off to fight the Civil War, was now in near hysterics over the slightest interaction between white women and black men. It did not seem to matter that the danger to white women of rape by a black man, according to the white South Carolina–born author Wilbur Cash, "was much less, for instance, than the chance that she would be struck by lightning."

White citizens, caught up in the delirium in the decades following Reconstruction, rioted in Georgia, North and South Carolina, Tennessee, Florida, Texas, Arkansas, and central Illinois. They killed colored residents and set fire to their homes on rumors of black impropriety, as authorities stood by or participated.

In the darkest hours of this era, the abolitionist Frederick Douglass saw his health fade just as everything he spent his life fighting for was falling apart. He said, in his last great public lecture, delivered in Baltimore in January 1894, a year before his death, "I hope and trust all will come out right in the end, but the immediate future looks dark and troubled. I cannot shut my eyes to the ugly facts before me."

It was during that time, around the turn of the twentieth century, that southern state legislatures began devising with inventiveness and precision laws that would regulate every aspect of black people's lives, solidify the southern caste system, and prohibit even the most casual and incidental contact between the races.

They would come to be called Jim Crow laws. It is unknown precisely who Jim Crow was or if someone by that name actually existed. There are several stories as to the term's origins. It came into public use in the 1830s after Thomas Dartmouth Rice, a New York–born itinerant white actor, popularized a song-and-dance routine called "the Jim Crow" in minstrel shows across the country. He wore blackface and ragged clothes and performed a jouncy, palsied imitation of a handi-

capped black stable hand he had likely seen in his travels singing a song
about "Jumping Jim Crow." Jim Crow was said to be the name of either
the stable hand or his owner living in Kentucky or Ohio. Rice became a
national sensation impersonating a crippled black man, but died penni-
less in 1860 of a paralytic condition that limited his speech and movement by the end of his life.

The term caught the fancy of whites across the country and came to
be used as a pejorative for colored people and things related to colored
people, and, by 1841, was applied to the laws to segregate them. The first
such laws were passed not in the South, but in Massachusetts, as a means
of designating a railcar set apart for black passengers. Florida, Mississippi, and Texas enacted the first Jim Crow laws in the South right after
the Confederates lost the Civil War—Florida and Mississippi in 1865
and Texas in 1866. The northerners who took over the South during Reconstruction repealed those hastily passed laws. The Federal Civil
Rights Act of 1875 explicitly outlawed segregation. But the northerners
who were there to enforce the law retreated by the late 1870s and left the
South to its own devices. As the twentieth century approached, the
South resurrected Jim Crow.

Streetcars, widely in use from the 1880s, had open seating in the
South, until Georgia demanded separate seating by race in 1891. By
1905, every southern state, from Florida to Texas, outlawed blacks from
sitting next to whites on public conveyances. The following year, Montgomery, Alabama, went a step further and required streetcars for whites
and streetcars for blacks. By 1909, a new curfew required blacks to be off
the streets by 10 P.M. in Mobile, Alabama. By 1915, black and white textile workers in South Carolina could not use the same "water bucket,
pails, cups, dippers or glasses," work in the same room, or even go up or
down a stairway at the same time.

This new reality forced colored parents to search for ways to explain
the insanity of the caste system to their uncomprehending children.
When two little girls in 1930s Florida wanted to know why they
couldn't play on a swing like the white children or had to sit in a dirty
waiting room instead of the clean one, their father, the theologian
Howard Thurman, had to think about how best to make them understand. "The measure of a man's estimate of your strength," he finally
told them, "is the kind of weapons he feels that he must use in order to
hold you fast in a prescribed place."

All told, these statutes only served to worsen race relations, alienating
one group from the other and removing the few informal interactions

that might have helped both sides see the potential good and humanity in the other.

Now the masses of black workers cast about on their own in a buyer's labor market with little in the way of material assets or education or a personal connection to even the coldest slave master, who would have shown a basic watchfulness if only to protect his financial investment. Their lives were left to the devices of planters with no vested interest in them and, now, no intimate ties to ease the harshness of their circumstances or to protect them, if only out of paternalism, from the whims of night riders, a hell-bent jury, or poor whites taking out their resentment at their unwitting competitors for work.

David L. Cohn, in the 1935 book *God Shakes Creation,* wrote that, for a colored man without a white sponsor, "his fate is in the lap of the gods."

Each year, people who had been able to vote or ride the train where they chose found that something they could do freely yesterday, they were prohibited from doing today. They were losing ground and sinking lower in status with each passing day, and, well into the new century, the color codes would only grow to encompass more activities of daily life as quickly as legislators could devise them.

Thus, those silent parties leaving Selma in the winter of 1916 saw no option but to go. Theirs would become the first volley of a leaderless revolution. There was no Moses or Joshua or Harriet Tubman, or, for that matter, Malcolm X or Martin Luther King, Jr., to organize the Migration. The best-known leader at the start of it, Booker T. Washington, was vehemently against abandonment of the South and strongly discouraged it. Frederick Douglass, who saw it coming but died before it began, was against the very thought of it and considered an exodus from the South "a premature, disheartening surrender."

Those entreaties had little effect.

"The Negroes just quietly move away without taking their recognized leaders into their confidence any more than they do the white people about them," a Labor Department study reported. A colored minister might meet with his deacons on a Wednesday, thinking all was well, and by Sunday find all the church elders gone north. "They write the minister that they forgot to tell him they were going away."

Ordinary people listened to their hearts instead of their leaders. At a clandestine meeting after a near lynching in Mississippi, a colored leader stood before the people and urged them to stay where they were.

A man in the audience rose up to speak.

"You tell us that the South is the best place for us," the man said. *"What guaranties can you give us that our life and liberty will be safe if we stay?"*

The leader was speechless.

"When he asked me that, there was nothing I could answer," the leader said afterward. "So I have not again urged my race to remain."

Any leader who dared argue against leaving might arouse suspicion that he was a tool of the white people running things. Any such leader was, therefore, likely to be ignored, or worse. One Sunday, a colored minister in Tampa, Florida, advised from the pulpit that his flock stay in the South. He was "stabbed the next day for doing so."

———

In the years leading up to and immediately following the turn of the twentieth century, a generation came into the world unlike any other in the South. It was made up of young people with no personal recollection of slavery—they were two generations removed from it. The colored members of this generation were free but not free, chafing under Jim Crow and resisting the studied subservience of their slave parents and grandparents. They had grown up without the contrived intimacy that once bound the two races. And it appeared that young whites, weaned on a formal kind of supremacy, had grown more hostile to blacks than even their slaveholding ancestors had been.

"The sentiment is altogether different now," William C. Oates, the old-guard former governor of Alabama, said in 1901 of the newer generation of white southerners. "When the Negro is doing no harm, why, the people want to kill him and wipe him from the face of the earth."

The colored people of this generation began looking for a way out. "It is too much to expect that Negroes will indefinitely endure their severe limitations in the South when they can escape most of them in a ride of 36 hours," the Labor Department warned. "Fifty years after the Civil War, they should not be expected to be content with the same conditions which existed at the close of the war."

Younger blacks could see the contradictions in their world—that, sixty, seventy, eighty years after Abraham Lincoln signed the Emancipation Proclamation, they still had to step off the sidewalk when a white person approached, were banished to jobs nobody else wanted no matter their skill or ambition, couldn't vote, but could be hanged on suspicion of the pettiest infraction.

These were the facts of their lives:

There were days when whites could go to the amusement park and a day when blacks could go, if they were permitted at all. There were white elevators and colored elevators (meaning the freight elevators in back); white train platforms and colored train platforms. There were white ambulances and colored ambulances to ferry the sick, and white hearses and colored hearses for those who didn't survive whatever was wrong with them.

There were white waiting rooms and colored waiting rooms in any conceivable place where a person might have to wait for something, from the bus depot to the doctor's office. A total of four restrooms had to be constructed and maintained at significant expense in any public establishment that bothered to provide any for colored people: one for white men, one for white women, one for colored men, and one for colored women. In 1958, a new bus station went up in Jacksonville, Florida, with two of everything, including two segregated cocktail lounges, "lest the races brush elbows over a martini," *The Wall Street Journal* reported. The president of Southeastern Greyhound told the *Journal,* "It frequently costs fifty percent more to build a terminal with segregated facilities." But most southern businessmen didn't dare complain about the extra cost. "That question is dynamite," the president of a southern theater chain told the *Journal.* "Don't even say what state I'm in."

There was a colored window at the post office in Pensacola, Florida, and there were white and colored telephone booths in Oklahoma. White and colored went to separate windows to get their license plates in Indianola, Mississippi, and to separate tellers to make their deposits at the First National Bank of Atlanta. There were taxicabs for colored people and taxicabs for white people in Jacksonville, Birmingham, Atlanta, and the entire state of Mississippi. Colored people had to be off the streets and out of the city limits by 8 P.M. in Palm Beach and Miami Beach.

Throughout the South, the conventional rules of the road did not apply when a colored motorist was behind the wheel. If he reached an intersection first, he had to let the white motorist go ahead of him. He could not pass a white motorist on the road no matter how slowly the white motorist was going and had to take extreme caution to avoid an accident because he would likely be blamed no matter who was at fault. In everyday interactions, a black person could not contradict a white person or speak unless spoken to first. A black person could not be the first to offer to shake a white person's hand. A handshake could occur only if a white person so gestured, leaving many people having never shaken hands with a person of the other race. The consequences for the slightest misstep were swift and brutal. Two whites beat a black tenant farmer in Louise, Mississippi, in 1948, wrote the historian James C. Cobb, because the man "asked for a receipt after paying his water bill."

It was against the law for a colored person and a white person to play checkers together in Birmingham. White and colored gamblers had to place their bets at separate windows and sit in separate aisles at race-tracks in Arkansas. At saloons in Atlanta, the bars were segregated: Whites drank on stools at one end of the bar and blacks on stools at the other end, until the city outlawed even that, resulting in white-only and colored-only saloons. There were white parking spaces and colored parking spaces in the town square in Calhoun City, Mississippi. In one North Carolina courthouse, there was a white Bible and a black Bible to swear to tell the truth on.

These were the facts of their lives—of Ida Mae's, George's, and Per-shing's existence before they left—carried out with soul-killing efficiency until Jim Crow expired under the weight of the South's own sectarian violence: bombings, hosing of children, and the killing of dissidents seeking basic human rights. Jim Crow would not get a proper burial until the enactment of federal legislation, the Civil Rights Act of 1964, which was nonetheless resisted years after its passage as vigorously as Reconstruction had been and would not fully take hold in many parts of the South until well into the 1970s.

And so what started as a little-noticed march of the impatient would become a flood of the discontented during World War II, and by the tail end of the Migration, a virtual rite of passage for young southerners—brothers joining brothers, nieces joining aunts, as soon as they got big enough to go.

Many of the people who left the South never exactly sat their children down to tell them these things, tell them what happened and why they left and how they and all this blood kin came to be in this northern city or western suburb or why they speak like melted butter and their children speak like footsteps on pavement, prim and proper or clipped and fast, like the New World itself. Some spoke of specific and certain evils. Some lived in tight-lipped and cheerful denial. Others simply had no desire to relive what they had already left.

The facts of their lives unfurled over the generations like an over-wrapped present, a secret told in syllables. Sometimes the migrants dropped puzzle pieces from the past while folding the laundry or stirring the corn bread, and the children would listen between cereal commercials and not truly understand until they grew up and had children and troubles of their own. And the ones who had half-listened would scold and kick themselves that they had not paid better attention when they had the chance.

And in this way, the ways of the South passed from one generation to the next in faraway cities by the Pacific Ocean and on the shores of the Great Lakes and along the Hudson and Potomac and Allegheny rivers. These are the stories of the forgotten, aggrieved, wishful generations between the Harlem Renaissance and the civil rights movement, whose private ambition for something better made a way for those who followed. Of the three whose lives unfold in these pages, Ida Mae Brandon Gladney left first, in the 1930s, George Swanson Starling in the 1940s, and Robert Joseph Pershing Foster in the 1950s, in a current that swept up millions of others like them.

George Swanson Starling

HIS WORLD IS THE BASEMENT of a brownstone on 132nd Street west
of Lenox Avenue, a shaft of light streaking through the burglar bars on
a single window. Outside, there is Harlem—Tupac on boom boxes,
street preachers on soap crates. Crack addicts scrounging for change.
There are middle-aged volunteers planting beds of impatiens in a footprint of earth in the concrete, German tourists pressed against bus windows to see the Apollo Theater and the Abyssinian Baptist Church.

He has lived here so long that not much of this fazes him anymore.
He is a widower now. He walks lean and upright, and he towers over
you as he leads you to the one room he keeps for himself out of the whole
brownstone he owns. It is the product of all the hustling and saving he
had to do when he arrived here a country boy from the South. His apartment is a cluttered storeroom, really, with a single bed, a couple of
chairs, a dresser with a picture of his grandmother, Annie the root doctor, on it, and half-open boxes of his accumulated highs and regrets.

The knees that used to climb suckling tree limbs to pick grapefruit
back in Florida and worked the train aisles up and down the East Coast

all those years are giving way to arthritis now. He takes a seat by the bed and talks in a monotone without taking a breath, there is so very much to say. He has catalogued in his mind every character who ever passed his way, can mimic their toothless drawl with wicked precision, recall every good and bad thing he has ever done or that has ever been done to him, every laughable contrivance of Jim Crow, every grievance and kind turn, all the people who made a way out of no way in that world growing up.

George Swanson Starling came from the featureless way station of citrus groves and one-star motels between the Georgia border and Orlando, Florida, a place of cocksure southern sheriffs, overworked pickers, root doctors, pool hustlers, bootleggers, jackleg preachers, barely a soul you could trust, and a color line as hard as Mississippi's. It comes back to him, one image after another, how Jim Crow had a way of turning everyone against one another, not just white against black or landed against lowly, but poor against poorer and black against black for an extra scrap of privilege. George Starling left all he knew because he would have died if he had stayed.

His face is long and creaseless. He was handsome in his day, a basketball player in high school, good with numbers, a ladies' man. He holds out a crate of Florida oranges like the ones he used to pick and offers you one, says, even after all that picking and all that it cost him, they're better than the ones from California. A smile lifts his face at the absurdities of the world he left, and which, in some ridiculous way, he still loves. Then his eyes well up over all that they have seen.

EUSTIS, FLORIDA, 1931

———

BEHIND THE ST. JAMES A.M.E. Church over at Prescott and MacDonald was an old orange tree that turned out oranges with dimpled skin as green as saw grass on the outside but inside sweet as sugarcane by September. To look at it, no one would know the fruit was ripe unless they climbed up and tried one, which George Starling and some other boys did once they made the discovery.

The tree was taller than a telephone pole, and it was hard for the boys to pass it by knowing what they did about those oranges. They waited for nightfall, when church would start and the deacons would light the kerosene lamps by the pews.

The boys climbed the twenty-foot tree and picked the oranges by the sanctuary light as the church people sang about Jesus. They steadied themselves in the crook of a limb and stuffed their shirts and trouser pockets until the buttons gaped. Then they turned back home, peeling and slurping, a trail of orange hulls following them all the way down MacDonald Avenue.

The church people tried to wait for the fruit to turn orange. But George and the other boys picked the tree clean before the church people could get to it. And so it went, George Starling and others in his impatient generation outwitting the old folks they saw as too content in their spirituals and their place in that world.

Here they were in Eustis, Florida, in the interior Citrus Belt of the state, hemmed into the colored part of town called Egypt. It was the haphazard cluster of dirt yards and clapboard bungalows, juke joints and corner churches where the colored people lived and conducted their affairs. It was unofficially policed by a man named Henry McClendon, a steward at another church in town. He lived across the street from St. James and saw George and his friends Sam Gaskin and Ernest Sallet sneak around the side of the church as he sat on his front porch one night.

When the boys got up into the tree, he started probing the limbs with a flashlight.

"Come down outta that tree in the name of the law!" he said.

The boys froze and hoped he would go away.

"I'm gonna come and tell your daddies. Y'all 'round here stealing these oranges, and y'all 'bout the same ones been stealing the wood from on the back porch."

"Man, we don't eat no wood. We been getting these oranges from around here for years. Ain't nobody want no wood."

"Oh yeah, y'all 'bout stole the wood. I'm coming out there, and I'm a tell your daddy."

The boys scrambled out of the tree and got on their knees because the worst thing that could happen to a colored child in the South was for a parent to hear that a child was acting up. There would be no appeals, the punishment swift and physical. The arbitrary nature of grown people's wrath gave colored children practice for life in the caste system, which is why parents, forced to train their children in the ways of subservience, treated their children as the white people running things treated them. It was preparation for the lower-caste role children were expected to have mastered by puberty.

For a young colored boy in the South, "the caste barrier is an ever-present, solid fact," John Dollard, an anthropologist studying the region's caste system, wrote at the time. "His education is incomplete until he has learned to make some adjustment to it. . . . The Negro must haul down his social expectations and resign himself to a relative immobility."

Indeed, breaking from protocol could get people like George killed. Under Jim Crow, only white people could sit in judgment of a colored person on trial. White hearsay had more weight than a colored eyewitness. Colored people had to put on a show of cheerful subservience and unquestioning obedience in the presence of white people or face the consequences of being out of line. If children didn't learn their place, they could get on the wrong side of a white person, and the parents could do nothing to save them.

"The question of the child's future is a serious dilemma for Negro parents," wrote J. W. Johnson around the time George and his friends got caught picking those oranges. "Awaiting each colored boy and girl are cramping limitations . . . ; and this dilemma approaches suffering in proportion to the parents' knowledge of and the child's innocence of those conditions."

There was no time for childish ideals of fair play and equality. *Oh, you calling them grown folks a lie?* George remembered parents saying. *Them grown folks wouldn't a said it if they didn't see you doing it.*

So the boys pleaded with Mr. McClendon that night. "We make a promise. You don't tell our daddies. We won't come back here to get no more fruit. We won't bother the oranges no more."

George didn't actually believe this as he said it. He knew they were wrong, but he didn't like how the grown people wouldn't believe him no matter what he said, and he didn't see the punishment as fitting the crime. He was getting to be a teenager now. He was learning that you didn't have a right to stand up for yourself if you were in his position, and he wasn't liking it.

———

George Starling was a fairly new boy in town. He had spent most of his short life circling north-central Florida as his parents hunted for work.

He was born on a tobacco farm out by the scrub oaks and wire grass near Alachua, Florida, halfway between Jacksonville and the Gulf of Mexico, on June 1, 1918. Lil George and his father—called Big George to distinguish him from the son—his mother, Napolean, and his half brother, William, all lived with a cast of uncles, aunts, and cousins headed by a hard-bitten curmudgeon of a grandfather, a man named John Starling.

John Starling was a sharecropper who smoked a corncob pipe and had few good words for anybody. Once he kicked the cat into the fire when it tried to rub his leg. He was from the Carolinas, where the plantation owner he worked for used to come down to the field and flog the workers with a horsewhip if they weren't going fast enough, as a rider might snap a whip at his mule. One day, the owner came down with the horsewhip, and the sharecroppers killed him. They swam across the river and never went back. That's all the grandfather would say.

It was before the turn of the twentieth century, and instead of going north, where there would have been no place for a colored farmer like him, John Starling went south to the warm, rich land of the Florida interior. There, Big George and the rest of that generation were born, and the family acquired its surname. Originally, they were Stallings. But nobody could pronounce it right. When they first joined their little country church, the preacher welcomed the newcomers every Sunday with a different mispronunciation.

"And we're glad to have the Stallions here with us today," the preacher announced during service.

"Stallings! Stallings!" John protested.

He eventually settled on Starling, which was a close enough compromise to suit him and the people around them.

By the time little George was born, John was working for a planter by the name of Reshard. He was living a hard enough life as it was and had other grandchildren in his care for whom he had little patience. He liked to put cotton between their toes and light it to wake them up in the morning. But the grandfather and his second wife, Lena, took a liking to little George. He was the only child of John's firstborn (George's half brother, William, had a different father), and Lena used to grab him close.

"Come up here, boy, give your grandma some sugar."

He could see a bulge in her cheeks from the snuff in her mouth and snuff juice dripping down her chin. George tightened his face and twisted his head, but that didn't stop her from planting a snuff-scented wet one right on the lips.

They were farming tobacco and cotton, among other things, and the grandfather liked to take little George out to the field with him and out to the boiler when he went to fire up the tobacco. He would let George sleep on top of the boiler shed when he got tired. He'd have George right by him and seemed to make a show of it, which only made life tougher for little George, propped up as he was distinct from his cousins.

"My cousins would be out there with their fists shaking at me," he remembered.

There were aunts and uncles all around. One of the younger aunts, called Sing, was married to a short-tempered man named Sambo. Sing attracted the attention of men without trying, and Sambo could never get used to it. As it was, colored men had little say over their wives since the days when slave masters could take their women whenever they pleased and colored men could do nothing about it. Planters were known to take the same liberties the slave masters had, and the contradictions were not lost on colored men: white men could do to colored women what colored men could be burned alive for doing to white women. In this sexual testing of wills, Sambo was overcautious toward his wife. He told her if she kept it up with what he saw as flirting, he was going to kill her one day. She just laughed. He was always talking like that. Big George told his sister not to make light of her husband. But she didn't pay it any mind.

One day, Sambo went to John's house and told Big George he was going rabbit hunting and needed some shells. Big George went and got the shells for Sambo. A few minutes later, he heard a shot from the woods.

"I guess Sambo done got him a rabbit," Big George said.

Sambo had just killed Big George's little sister.

————

These became some of Lil George's earliest memories. Each year, he saw his grandfather return from the planter's house after another dispiriting settlement and recount to the family what had transpired.

At the end of every harvest, the planter would call John Starling up to the big house. John would knock on the back door, the only door colored people were permitted to enter, according to southern protocol. He and the planter met in the planter's kitchen.

"Come on in, John," the planter said. "Come here, boy. Come here. Have a seat. Sit down here."

The planter pulled out his books. "Well, John," the planter began. "Boy, we had a good year, John."

"Yes, sir, Mr. Reshard. I'm sure glad to hear that."

"We broke even. You don't owe me nothing. And I don't owe you nothing."

The grandfather had nothing to show for a year's hard toiling in the field.

"This is all he ends up, 'We broke even,' " George would say years later. "He has no money, no nothing for his family. And now he's ready to start a new year in the master's debt. He'll start all over again. Next year, they went through the same thing—'We broke even.' "

The following year, the grandfather went to the big house and got the same news from Reshard.

"Well, by God, John, we did it again. We had another good year. We broke even. I don't owe you nothin, and you don't owe me nothin."

George's grandfather got up from the table. "Mr. Reshard, I'm sho' glad to hear that. 'Cause now I can go and take that bale of cotton I hid behind the barn and take it into town and get some money to buy my kids some clothes and some shoes."

The planter jumped up. "Ah, hell, John. Now you see what, now I got to go all over these books again."

"And when he go over these books again," George said long afterward, "he'll find out where he owed that bale. He gonna take that bale of cotton away from him, too."

John had no choice but to tell Reshard about that extra bale of cotton. In the sharecropping system, it was the planter who took the crops to market or the cotton to the gin. The sharecropper had to take the planter's word that the planter was crediting the sharecropper with what he was due. By the time the planter subtracted the "furnish"—that is, the seed, the fertilizer, the clothes and food—from what the sharecropper had earned from his share of the harvest, there was usually nothing coming to the sharecropper at settlement. There would have been no way for George's grandfather to sell that one extra bale without the planter knowing it in that constricted world of theirs. In some parts of the South, a black tenant farmer could be whipped or killed for trying to sell crops on his own without the planter's permission.

Even though John wouldn't be able to keep the extra bale, Reshard was considered "a good share, a good boss, a good master," in George's words, " 'cause he let us break even."

Most other sharecroppers ended deeper in debt than before. "They could never leave as long as they owed the master," George said. "That made the planter as much master as any master during slavery, because the sharecropper was bound to him, belonged to him, almost like a slave."

The anthropologist Hortense Powdermaker, studying the sharecropping system back in the 1930s, estimated that only a quarter to a third of sharecroppers got an honest settlement, which did not in itself mean they got any money. "The Negro farm hand," a colored minister wrote in a letter to the *Montgomery Advertiser* in Alabama, "gets for his compensation hardly more than the mule he plows, that is, his board and shelter. Some mules fare better than Negroes."

There was nothing to keep a planter from cheating his sharecropper. "One reason for preferring Negro to white labor on plantations," Powdermaker, a white northerner, observed, "is the inability of the Negro to make or enforce demands for a just statement or any statement at all. He may hope for protection, justice, honesty from his landlord, but he cannot demand them. There is no force to back up a demand, neither the law, the vote nor public opinion. . . . Even the most fair and most just of the Whites are prone to accept the dishonest landlord as part of the system."

That did not keep some sharecroppers from trying to get what they were due after a hard year's labor. During the lull before harvest time, one of George's uncles, Budross, went to the little schoolhouse down in the field and learned to read and count. When it came time to settle up over the tobacco George's grandmother Lena had raised, the uncle stood by while the planter went over the books with her. When they got through, George's uncle spoke up.

"Ma, Mr. Reshard cheatin' you. He ain't addin' them figures right."

The planter jumped up. "Now you see there, Lena, I told you not to send that boy to school! Now he done learn how to count and now done jumped up and called my wife a lie, 'cause my wife figured up these books."

The planter's men came and pistol-whipped the uncle right then and there.

The family had to get him out that night. "To call a white woman a lie," George said, "they came looking for him that night. They came, fifteen or twenty of them on horseback, wagon."

George's grandparents knew to expect it. "We got to get you away from here 'cause you done call Mr. Reshard a lie. And you know they ain't gon' like that."

George was too young to understand what was happening but heard the grown people talk about it in whispers. It was the middle of the 1920s, and George never knew exactly where the uncle went. The particulars were never spoken.

"They hid him out" was all George would say. "He left from out of there."

———————

Lil George and his parents didn't stay in Alachua much longer after that. They fled to St. Petersburg on the Gulf of Mexico, where they would no longer be under a field boss or overseer. They could work in the big high-rise hotels going up, and with all the tourists from up north and the building boom in the beach towns on the coast, they could be free of the farm and find plenty of work.

They were living in a row house off Fifth Avenue in the colored district. The father found work in construction, and things were good. But by the late 1920s, when the Great Depression descended on the country, things weren't so good. Big George took to drinking and would lie in wait on the porch for Lil George's mother to get back from church on Sunday. Once, instead of coming straight back, she stopped a few doors down to chat with a neighbor. Big George saw her dawdling, and that set him off.

"You making plans to meet some other man," Big George said.

He jumped on her and started hitting her. Lil George and his half brother, William, were sitting on the porch and could see it.

It wasn't the first time. Lil George cried over it. He was torn between the two of them. Sometimes William, who had a different father and was two years older than Lil George, would throw rocks at Big George to make him stop. Lil George hated it when William did that. He adored his parents. This time, Lil George got mad. The two boys went and got a brick from under a wash pot in the kitchen and hit Big George with it. Then they ran down the street to get away. Big George was hurt more by the pain he had caused his son than by the brick itself and went calling after his namesake. *Son, come back here. I'm not gonna bother you.*

The marriage gave out after that, and the family split up. The mother kept William on the Gulf Coast with her. And Big George headed east to the town of Eustis, where he said he would send for Lil George after he got established. For the time being, Lil George was sent to live with his mother's mother in Ocala, a town in the scrublands midway between Alachua and Eustis.

The grandmother was a root doctor named Annie Taylor who was a big-boned woman as tall as a man. She lived on a corner lot and grew pole beans alongside the fence. She was already raising one daughter's two boys, and here came another one from another daughter, Napolean, now that she had quit her husband.

Annie set George to work right away. She took him and his cousins out to the woods and showed them which twigs and roots to dig up: sassafras, sulfur, and goldenrod. They would tramp behind her through the scrub and wire grass back to the house—George and his cousins James and Joseph, whom they called Brother. She would stir the roots into foul-smelling potions that people bought to thin their blood, cut a fever, shush a hacking cough. She knew all the roots and could identify them, and she knew what they were good for.

The boys were her nearest patients, and every season brought a new torture. Sulfur and cream of tartar at the first sign of spring to thin the blood for the summer. Castor oil to clean your system out in the winter. Balls of asafetida hung around the neck to ward off flu and tuberculosis, the asafetida resin rolled up like flour dough and smelling only slightly worse than cow dung. She put the asafetida paste into little sacks and made necklaces for the boys to wear (which they took off and put in their pockets as soon as they got from around her). In between, she plied them with goldenrod for fever, asafetida with whiskey for a bad cold, and any number of bitter-tasting concoctions that made the boys hate to get sick.

If she detected a cold in the chest, she unscrewed the top of the kerosene lamp, tipped it over a spoonful of sugar, and let four or five drops of kerosene saturate the sugar. Then she stuck the spoon into their tight faces for them to swallow. There was no point in trying to run and hide. "You better not be talking about no run-and-hide," George said years later. "She didn't play that. 'Now you gonna get a whippin' on top of it.' "

The three little boys were left in Annie Taylor's care because there was a great churning among the young people of working age like her daughters. Her oldest girl, George's mother, was off on the Gulf Coast. And her two youngest girls, Annie (whom they called Baby) and Lavata (who actually was the baby but whom they called Date), were up in New York. Baby couldn't keep little James and Brother in New York with her, so she left them with her mother to raise, like a lot of migrants did when they went up north.

Young people like them weren't tied to a place like their slave grandparents had been forced to, and they weren't content to move from plantation to plantation like their parents. Ever since World War I had broken out and all those jobs had opened up in the North, there had been an agitation for something better, some fast, new kind of life where they could almost imagine themselves equal to the white people. And so they had gone off to wherever the money seemed to be raining down—to the Gulf Coast rising up in a construction boom or the orange groves at picking season or the turpentine camps if they couldn't manage anything else; or, if they had nerve in the early days of the Migration, they'd hop a train to the edge of the world, straight up the coast, past Georgia and both Carolinas and straight through Virginia and up to New York, where people said you could get rich just mopping floors.

To the old folks who stayed, the young people looked to be going in circles, chasing a wish. Some went crossways to someplace in Alabama or Georgia, where they heard things were better, only to find the South to be the South wherever they went. Some went north, high and mighty, and came back south, low and broke. Some people's pride wouldn't let them come back at all. So they shoehorned themselves into tenements and made like they were rich or just plain made do and dazzled the folks back home with all the money they wired back.

Some people back home came to depend on that money, to half expect it, and they got agitated when it didn't come. They figured the people who left were making all that money up north and just about owed it to them, especially if they left children behind. Baby and Date kept up fairly regular payments to their mother to cover Baby's two little boys. George's father sent money for George, too. At first. But after a while, it got to the place where he wouldn't send any money, and the grandmother had to stretch what her daughters sent for two into enough to take care of all three of them.

Sometimes George heard his grandmother fretting about how she was running out of money and hadn't heard from Big George. It was the Depression, and sometimes even the daughters got slow sending money for the two which had stretched to three, and the grandmother had a problem on her hands. The daughters had gotten themselves out in that big world way up north—who knew what kind of fix they were in?—and here she was left with the little ones.

When the money got low, Annie Taylor got in her rocking chair on the porch and rocked back and forth. She hummed and sang as she rocked. *Guide me o'er, thou Great Jehovah, pilgrim to this barren land. I am weak, but thou art mighty. Guide me with thy loving hand.*

George and James and Brother heard her humming.

"Grandma humming that song again," George told James. "Somethin' gonna happen soon."

The palm of her hand started to itch, or so she said. And before long, a Western Union man came rolling up the street, announcing a telegram for Miss Annie Taylor.

"Somebody would be done wired us some money," George would say years later. "Yes, sirree."

The waiting and hoping went on for two years, and then it was decided that it was best for George to be with his father, and he joined his father in Eustis.

———

Big George worked at the loading dock of a packinghouse and ran a one-room convenience store over on Bates Avenue. He sold baked goods and castor oil to the fruit pickers and day workers and the children on their lunch break from the colored high school across the street in a citrus farming town in the underdeveloped midsection of a still-isolated state.

Lake County and the rest of central Florida were far from the lights of Miami and the palm-tree version of paradise that tourists came for. This was the Florida that had entered the Union as a slave state, where a Florida slaveholder could report without apology, in 1839, that he worked his slaves "in a hurrying time till 11 or 12 o'clock at night, and have them up by four in the morning." Florida went farther than some other slave states in the creativity of its repression: Slaves could not gather together to pray. They couldn't leave their plantations, even for a walk, without written permission from their owner. If they were accused of wrongdoing, "their hands were burned with a heated iron, their ears nailed to posts," or their backs stripped raw with seventy-five lashes from a buckskin whip. The few free blacks in the state had to register with the nearest probate court or could be automatically enslaved by any white person who stepped forward to claim possession.

As the country neared the point of collapse over the issue of a state's right to slavery, Florida, in the early winter of 1861, became one of the first to secede from the Union in the months leading up to the Civil War. Florida broke away on January 10, 1861, three weeks after the first rebel state of South Carolina, and a day after Mississippi. Florida heartily joined a new country whose cornerstone, according to the Confederacy's vice president, Alexander Hamilton Stephens, was "the great truth that the negro is not equal to the white man; that slavery—subordination to the superior race—is his natural and normal condition." This new government, Stephens declared, "is the first, in the history of the world, based upon this great physical, philosophical, and moral truth."

Thus began the bloodiest war on American soil, after four years of which the Confederates fell in the spring of 1865. Immediately, Florida, Mississippi, and Texas took steps to begin imposing a formal caste system, becoming the first in the South to do so. They hastened to pass laws restricting the newly freed people barely before the cannons had cooled. Florida's 1865 law set forth, among other things, that "if any negro, mulatto or other person of color shall intrude himself into any railroad car or other public vehicle set apart for the exclusive accommodation of white people," he would be sentenced to "stand in pillory for one hour, or be whipped, not exceeding thirty-nine stripes, or both, at the discretion of the jury."

Florida was shut off from the rest of the world by its cypress woods and turpentine camps. It was another country, with its own laws and constitution. And all through the 1920s, when George was a toddler and then in grade school, the grown people hung their heads over the violence that descended over them and passed the stories among themselves and to the children when they got old enough to understand.

They talked about the white mob that burned down the colored section of Ocoee, over by Orlando, when a colored man tried to vote back in 1920, how the man was hanged from a tree and other colored people were burned to death and the remaining colored people packed up and never returned. They whispered about the time the white people burned and leveled Rosewood, a colored settlement by the Gulf of Mexico, halfway between St. Petersburg and Tallahassee, because a white woman said a colored man had attacked her. It was where, a survivor said, "anything that was black or looked black was killed." That was in 1923.

And then, in the fall of 1934, when George was a teenager and old enough to take note of such things, perhaps the single worst act of torture and execution in twentieth-century America occurred in the panhandle town of Marianna, Florida, a farm settlement halfway between Pensacola and Tallahassee.

That October, a twenty-three-year-old colored farmhand named Claude Neal was accused of the rape and murder of a twenty-year-old white woman named Lola Cannidy. Neal had grown up across the road from Lola Cannidy's family. He was arrested and signed a written confession that historians have since called into question. But at the time, passions ran so high that a band of more than three hundred men armed with guns, knives, torches, and dynamite went searching for Neal in every jail within a seventy-five-mile radius of Marianna.

The manhunt forced the authorities to move Neal across the panhandle, from Marianna to Panama City by car, to Camp Walton by boat, to Pensacola by car again, with the mob on their trail at every turn. Finally, the Escambia County sheriff, fearing that his jail in Pensacola was too dilapidated to withstand attack, decided to take Neal out of state altogether, to the tiny town of Brewton, Alabama, fifty-five miles north of Pensacola. Someone leaked Neal's whereabouts, and a lynching party of some one hundred men drove several hours on Highway 231 in a thirty-car caravan from Florida to Alabama. There the men managed to divert the local sheriff and overtake the deputy. They stormed the jail and took Neal, his limbs bound with a plow rope, back to Marianna.

It was the early morning hours of October 26, a Friday. Neal's chief abductors, a self-described "committee of six," an oddly officious term commonly used by the leaders of southern lynch mobs, set the lynching for 8 P.M., when most everyone would be off work. The advance notice allowed word to spread by radio, teletype, and afternoon papers to the western time zones.

Well before the appointed hour, several thousand people had gathered at the lynching site. The crowd grew so large and unruly—people having been given sufficient forewarning to come in from other states— that the committee of six, fearing a riot, took Neal to the woods by the Chipola River to wait out the crowds and torture him before the execution.

There his captors took knives and castrated him in the woods. Then they made him eat the severed body parts "and say he liked it," a witness said.

"One man threw up at the sight," wrote the historian James R. McGovern.

Around Neal's neck, they tied a rope and pulled it over a limb to the point of his choking before lowering him to take up the torture again.

"Every now and then somebody would cut off a finger or toe," the witness said. Then the men used hot irons to burn him all over his body in a ritual that went on for several hours.

"It is almost impossible to believe that a human being could stand such unspeakable torture for such a long period," wrote the white undercover investigator retained by the NAACP.

The crowd waiting in town never got to see Neal die. The committee of six decided finally to just kill him in the woods. His nude body was then tied to the back of a car and dragged to the Cannidy house, where men, women, and children stabbed the corpse with sticks and knives. The dead girl's father was angry that Neal was killed before he could get to him. "They done me wrong about the killing," the father said. "They promised me they would bring him up to my house before they killed him and let me have the first shot. That's what I wanted."

The committee hanged the body "from an oak tree on the courthouse lawn." People reportedly displayed Neal's fingers and toes as souvenirs. Postcards of his dismembered body went for fifty cents each. When the sheriff cut down the body the next morning, a mob of as many as two thousand people demanded that it be rehanged. When the sheriff refused to return it to the tree, the mob attacked the courthouse and rampaged through Marianna, attacking any colored person they ran into. Well-to-do whites hid their maids or sent cars to bring their workers to safety. "We needed these people," said a white man who sat on his porch protecting his interests with a loaded Winchester. Florida Governor David Sholtz had to call in the National Guard to quell the mob.

Across the country, thousands of outraged Americans wrote to President Franklin D. Roosevelt demanding a federal investigation. The NAACP compiled a sixteen-page report and more files on the Neal case than any other lynching in American history. But Neal had the additional misfortune of having been lynched just before the 1934 national midterm elections, which were being seen as a referendum on the New Deal itself. Roosevelt chose not to risk alienating the South with a Democratic majority in Congress at stake. He did not intervene in the case. No one was ever charged in Neal's death or spent a day in jail for it. The Jackson County grand jury, in the common language of such inquests, reported that the execution had occurred "at the hands of persons unknown to us."

Soon afterward, it was learned that Neal and the dead girl, who had known each other all their lives, had been lovers and that people in her family who discovered the liaison may have been involved in her death for the shame it had brought to the family. Indeed, the summer after Neal was lynched, the girl's father was convicted of assault with intent to kill his niece because he suspected that that side of the family had had a hand in his daughter's death.

In sentencing the father to five years in prison for attacking the relative, the judge said, "I hate to pass this sentence on an old man such as you, but I must do it. To be perfectly fair with you, I don't believe you have any too many brains."

The father replied, "Yes, judge. I am plumb crazy."

Thereafter, Florida continued to live up to its position as the southernmost state with among the most heinous acts of terrorism committed anywhere in the South. Violence had become such an accepted fact of life that, in 1950, the Florida governor's special investigator, Jefferson Elliott, observed that there had been so many mob executions in one county that it "never had a negro live long enough to go to trial."

———

The grown people's whispers of unspeakable things seeped into George's subconscious like a nursery rhyme, even though he was too young to know the particulars or understand the meaning of it all. Surrounded as he was by the arbitrary violence of the ruling caste, it would be nearly impossible for George or any other colored boy in that era to grow up without the fear of being lynched, the dread that, in the words of the historian James R. McGovern, "he might be accused of something and suddenly find himself in a circle of tormentors with no one to help him."

By the time Lil George was old enough to notice, it seemed as if the whole world was crazy, not because of any single event but because of the slow discovery of just how circumscribed his life was turning out to be. All this stepping off the sidewalk, not looking even in the direction of a white woman, the sirring and ma'aming and waiting until all the white people had been served before buying your ice cream cone, with violence and even death awaiting any misstep. Each generation had to learn the rules without understanding why, because there was no understanding why, and each one either accepted or rebelled in that moment of realization and paid a price whichever they chose.

No one sat George down and told him the rules. His father was quiet and kept his wounds to himself. George's teachers were fear and instinct. The caste system trained him to see absurdity as normal.

Like the time George went for an ice cream cone at the pharmacy in downtown Eustis. He wouldn't be able to sit at the counter, he knew that going in. Anytime a white customer walked up, he had to step back and wait for him or her to be served first. George had learned this, too, by now. The pharmacist had a dog, a little terrier. And when George walked up to the counter, three or four white men who were standing around looked at one another and then at the pharmacist. The owner called out to the dog. And the dog jumped up onto the counter.

When the pharmacist had everyone's attention, he turned to the dog.

"What would you rather do?" the pharmacist asked the dog. "Be a nigger or die?"

The dog rolled over on cue. It flipped onto its back, folded its legs, shut its eyes, and froze. The grown people at the counter and up front near George shook with laughter.

George was a teenager and outnumbered. He was the only one of his kind in this place. All he could do was stand there and take it. Any other response would require an explanation. *What's the matter with you, boy? You don't like it?* he could hear them saying.

All kinds of thoughts went through his mind. "A whole lot of things," he said. "How you'd like to kill all of 'em, for one thing."

On its face, it looked to be a black-and-white world, but George learned soon enough that the caste system was a complicated thing that had a way of bringing out the worst in just about all concerned. Sometimes it seemed that loyalty didn't stand a chance against suspicion and self-preservation. Even on the lowest rung, some people would squeeze what little they could even when nobody had anything.

Reverend J. W. Brinson was a jackleg preacher who ran the colored grocery store on MacDonald in Egypt town. The store had a slot machine that took customers' nickels and dimes but gave hardly any back. People went in and played the dime machine for an hour or two, and everybody could see that the machine was ready to deliver. That's when Reverend Brinson would step in and close up shop. "He figure that machine is getting hot and is gonna start paying off," George recalled. "And he run everybody out the store."

George and his friends walked out as told. Then they watched old man Brinson take the slot machine to his house next door. "We would tip up on the porch," George said, "and we could hear him in there in the bedroom and hear that slot machine just ringing. And he just be burning it up trying to get that jackpot for himself."

On top of that, the merchandise in the grocery store was unjustly high, to hear George tell it, and he and his friends resented it. They found a way to get back what they figured they had overpaid.

They noticed that Reverend Brinson went into town the same time every day, leaving the store in the care of his wife, Mary, who was a sweet woman but couldn't count. One day the boys sat under a big old oak tree and waited for Reverend Brinson to pull away. Then they went in and played nice to Miss Brinson.

"Hi, Miss Brinson."

"Hello, boys. How y'all?"

"We wanna get something, Miss Brinson."

"Yeah, alright. What y'all want?"

"We want ten cent worth of bologna."

The Brinsons had a scale in the back of the store where the icebox was, which required Miss Brinson to go back in the icebox, get the roll of bologna, and bring it to the butcher block near the counter. She carved enough slices until it looked about right, cutting less than she needed so as not to waste slices the customer didn't want. Then she went back to the scales to weigh the bologna as the boys watched.

"Oh, Miss Brinson, you ain't quite got ten cent worth up there yet. You got to get some more."

"Yeah, that's right," she said, admitting the discrepancy.

She hauled the loaf of bologna back to slice some more, leaving the slices she had already cut on the counter, two or three of which the boys slipped into their mouths. She came huffing back with the extra slices, only to learn it still wasn't enough.

"Oh, you ain't got it yet, Miss Brinson."

Back and forth she went, the loaf shrinking and the scale not budging, until the boys were full from the extra slices they'd eaten.

"Aw, that's alright, Miss Brinson. That's close enough. Just wrap it up."

Come summer, the Brinsons set watermelons out on the bare floor in front of the counter. George and the other boys saw them there and decided to go in one day. They lined up along the counter and started looking around. One pointed to a jar of pickles on the very top shelf.

"Miss Brinson, how much is that jar of pickles up there?"

"Well. Let me see now. Which one?"

Miss Brinson went to get the ladder and climbed up to check. And as she stretched herself to reach the last jar, one of the boys took his foot and started a watermelon rolling. He kicked it to the next boy, who kicked it to the next boy, until the melon had rolled and creaked down the wood plank floor toward the front screen. The last boy was positioned to kick it outside, none of them for a second taking his eyes off Miss Brinson, still reaching for the jar of pickles. They would get two or three watermelons that way.

Poor Reverend Brinson must have suspected that they stole from him, and he kept his prices high, which only encouraged more pilfering. It was George's and the other boys' way of getting justice in an unjust world. And so it went in Egypt town, the poor at odds with the broke.

———

George was a boy interested in the things boys are interested in and not particularly wanting to live the life the preachers set out at Gethsemane Baptist Church. Not then, anyway. There wasn't much to do around Eustis when school was out. Sure, they could fish and swim awhile in one of the lakes. But there weren't any jobs, and so they got into the things that boys get into, like picking green oranges while the church people sang about Jesus.

He was friends with a bootlegger's brother who lived behind the poolroom. Grown men roosted on the benches out front like crows on a fence, and there were big trees all around. The boys shot pool when the grown men let them and then made off with a pint of the bootlegger's moonshine. They poured water in place of the liquor and put the bottle back where they found it. They figured they weren't hurting anybody. The bootlegger was breaking the law anyway. They figured it was like taking something that wasn't supposed to exist in the first place.

George was growing taller and bigger and was in high school now. He grew to over six feet and started playing basketball at Curtright. He was walking taller and straighter. One day he went up to Ocala to see his grandmother the root doctor. He liked to surprise her, so he didn't let her know that he was coming. But she knew anyway. "You think you slipped up on me," she said once. "I knew you was coming 'cause my nose was itching. I just told somebody, 'Somebody's coming to see me.'"

She saw the change in him, how he was wearing grown folks' clothes, walking taller, straighter, suddenly aware of how he looked in a mirror. It always happened that the young people got to a certain age and thought they were the best thing that ever walked the earth. "I see George got you in long pants now," she said. "You must be smelling yourself."

———

It's true that George got into his share of devilment, but, fortunately for him, it turned out that he had a thing for numbers and words. He could remember just about anything that was set in front of him, and school came easy to him. He devoured books even though they were the white schools' leftovers and had pages missing. He started to think about how he could escape this place, maybe even go to college.

The kids noticed and looked to George to help them with their lesson. But they seemed to wish they didn't have to ask. They would turn around and tease him for doing what they should have been doing.

"So what you doing tonight, George?"

"Getting my lesson."

"Yeah, you go on and get your lesson, and we'll get the girls."

George couldn't abide the teasing and didn't believe they were doing all they said they were anyway. He would finish his homework and tip over to the house of whatever girl they said they were having their fun with. He would sweet-talk the girl, and since he was tall and not, as they say, hard on the eyes, he managed to do quite well, in his estimation.

The next day in school, the boasting would commence.

"They brag about how they were with this girl last night," George said years later. "I say to myself, 'I know you lying.' But I couldn't tell them. I used to walk the back roads. Nobody would see me."

George was always observing the developments around him, and here was a lesson in the underhanded nature of some human relations. "I know they would be telling lies on the girls," he said years later, " 'cause I be setting up there with that same girl in her house. That's how I found out how the boys lie on girls."

He didn't want them knowing his business. He indulged them instead.

"What'd you do last night, Lil George?"

"Man, I had so much work. I was getting my lesson."

By the time they got old enough to work, most of the kids had dropped out of school altogether. By graduation day, there were only six seniors in the Class of 1936 at Curtright Vocational Training School, and George Swanson Starling was valedictorian. He got accepted to Florida Agricultural and Mechanical State College in Tallahassee. His father did not really understand why he would want to go when he could be making a little money picking in the groves. But he sent him anyway.

George came home with better than decent grades. But a year passed and then another whole six months with other people working and George just reading books. His father didn't see the point of it. In the middle of George's sophomore year, his father told him he had gotten enough schooling and it was time for him to work. Maybe he could pick it up later.

Big George didn't see where it made much difference anyway, hardly anybody they knew went to college. The father had only gone to fifth grade, and he was doing alright, running the store and packing fruit at the Eichelberger Packing Company.

"With two years of college, you should be able to be president of the United States," his father figured.

"But I'm taking a four-year course number, and you dropping me in the middle of the stream. I'm not prepared to do anything because I'm only halfway there."

George had made valedictorian at Curtwright and, just as significant to him, was the only one from his high school to finish the first year of college without failing any subject. He thought he deserved better.

But his father had made up his mind. Lil George was his namesake, but he wasn't his only concern. Big George had remarried since coming to Eustis. He had a wife now and two stepsons to think about. He had that little store to keep up and dreams of a little orange grove of his own for his old age. He wasn't willing to spend what money he had to send George back to school to study Socrates and polynomials. It was an outrageous indulgence when everybody else was working the groves every day.

A few days later, George was looking for some papers. Rummaging through a dresser drawer, he found some postal receipts for deposits his father had made in a savings account at the post office.

"He had a drawer full of them where he was saving in the post office," George said years later. "But he was telling me he didn't have any money. And that made me angry, and I couldn't sense it into him that I needed to go on and get the other two years. So I just got angry and evil, and I decided I would do something to hurt him."

———

George had gotten around with the girls, but he always seemed to come back to one in particular. Inez Cunningham was a girl from the backwoods with full cheeks and a narrow waist who had endured an even more unsettled childhood than he had. Her parents had died young and left her in the care of a Pentecostal aunt who trotted her to late-night church meetings with holy rollers talking in tongues. She spent so much of her girlhood in the quaking pews of the Pentecostal church that she swore she would never join a church again if she got free. She kept her word and never did.

She wore plaits and plain dresses and didn't have the pomaded hair some other girls had or the stockings and jewelry that made certain girls look more refined. But she had a way of smiling and tilting her head to the side and some kind of simpatico, outsider way of looking at the world that appealed to a young man like George who felt life had never cut him a fair deal.

She had graduated from high school and was doing the common and necessary job of cleaning white people's homes. But with George up in Tallahassee around those well-turned-out coeds training to be teachers, she fixated on her deficiencies. She imagined her competition in high heels and straight hair, their dignified talk turning George's head. She convinced herself he would choose one of them over her and told him as much.

Big George didn't want Inez around his son either. She was from the backwoods and, in the pecking order that emerged even on the lowest rung—people with house notes versus people who paid rent, factory workers versus servants—Big George saw Inez as lower than the Starlings.

During spring break of his sophomore year, the subject of school came up again. George asked his father if he would send him back, and again the answer was no. George was incensed and decided to do something about it. It was April 19, 1939. He took his father's car and drove up to the house where Inez lived.

"Come on, let's take a ride," he said.

"What you doing?"

"Come on, let's ride."

"Well, where you going?"

"Oh, just a ride."

She hopped in, and he drove south for five miles to Tavares, the county seat. He drove around to the back of the courthouse, where the jail was, and slowed to a stop.

"Where you going?" Inez asked, alarmed now.

He grabbed her hand. "Come on. I want to show you something."

He led her upstairs and into the magistrate's office.

"Well, what can I do for ya, boy?" the magistrate said.

"We come to get married," George said.

Inez nearly fainted. She looked to George to explain himself.

"Well, you been pressuring me about gettin' married. You're telling me that I'm gonna end up marrying one of those college girls that's getting a schoolteacher's education. And you're not gonna be good enough for me. And I keep telling you that that wouldn't make any difference. But you can't seem to believe that, and you don't want to wait. I wanted to show you that you the only one that I wanted. So we just gonna get married now."

Inez stood there with her mouth open. "I—I didn't know" was all she could manage.

She was wearing whatever dress she happened to put on that morning, and he had on whatever he'd thrown on, too.

"Now, you know that'll cost you a dollar fifty, boy," the county judge, A. S. Herlong, said. "A dollar for the license. Fifty cent for a witness."

"Yes, sir."

The judge went through the vows and declared them man and wife. She was twenty-one. He was twenty and not legally old enough to marry.

"I told the man I was twenty-one," George later said. "They didn't care. If you black, they don't care nothin' about Negroes. They didn't check it out. I would be twenty-one in a couple of months. But anyway, we got married."

As they drove back to Eustis, George told Inez his plan.

"You gon' have to continue to stay with your people. We got to keep this secret until I find out whether I'm going back to school or not."

George left out a crucial bit of information in what he told Inez, although it wouldn't take her long to figure it out. "I didn't tell her my ulterior motive," he said years later. Now, in all fairness, he said, "I was in love with her. But I didn't have no intention of getting married, not at that stage, until I got mad with my daddy. He didn't even want me to be courting this girl, much less talking about marrying her.

"So I figured that would fix him up good 'cause he won't send me back to school," he said. "I got in all that trouble for a dollar fifty cents."

George hadn't really thought his revenge scheme through to completion. He held out hope that his father would change his mind. George would spring the news about Inez on him only if his father didn't come around. The two of them kept their secret through the spring and into the summer, when George went to New York like a lot of college students from the South to make spending money for school.

He worked at a dry cleaner's in Flatbush and lived with the aunts who had sent money to his grandmother, the root doctor in Ocala. Toward the end of the summer, he wrote his father: *I have my money for my books and everything. I bought what clothing I'll need. Are you going to be able to pay my tuition?*

Lil George didn't know it, but the people back home had been grumbling in Big George's ear. The father had already done more than he had to. Nobody else was spending all that money for school. None of them had gone off to college, and they had made out alright. Their kids were working in the groves and bringing in good money. What was Lil George doing? His father wrote him back: *No, I just won't be able to do it. You'll have to work this year, and we'll see how things are next year.*

The summer was almost over. The semester would be starting soon. George had run out of time. He realized his dream was over. He wrote his father again. He wanted to get back at him now: *Well, that's alright, don't worry about it 'cause I'm married anyhow. I'm married to Inez.*

George waited for the fireworks. But they never came. He caught the bus back home, and the old people who hadn't seen him in months recognized him as he walked from the bus station. They called out to him from their front porches.

"Hey, ain't that Lil George Starling?"

"Yes, ma'am, this is me."

"Come here, boy. Lord have mercy, what is wrong with you? You done gone plumb fool. They tell me you done jumped up and married that Cunningham girl. And your daddy said, he was here gettin' ready to send you back to school."

George couldn't speak. The old people went on.

" 'Cause your daddy said he was gettin' ready to send you back to school, and, before he know anything, you come writing him about you done got married."

The word had spread all across Egypt town, and everybody knew about the ingrate son who had ruined his chance at college, marrying some girl from the wrong side of town.

Dog, the ole man done tricked me, George thought to himself. He knew how they talked. And in the old people's sweet scolding, he could hear how the story got repackaged in the telling, people in town with nothing better to do, who never had the chance at college themselves, maybe never tried or even wanted to go, delighting in the confusion and goading Big George over it.

"George, where is that boy? Is he going to school?"

"No, you know what that devilish boy done? I'm here gettin' ready to send him back to school, and here he come writing me the other day tellin' me about he married."

"Well, I declare! You mean to tell! Now, I know that boy ain't done nothin' like that! And hard as you workin' trying to send him to school!"

And so it went. If the father had ever intended on sending him back, he now had a publicly acceptable excuse for not doing so, and he had come out the hero in the deal.

As for Lil George, no colleges near Eustis nor any state universities in Florida, for that matter, admitted colored students. The closest colored colleges were hours away. He had a wife to support now. So he would have to do precisely what his father had intended all along. It looked as if he might never make it back to school.

And he would have to live with vows made in anger for the rest of his life. It would not be happy because he knew and she knew how it had come to be. But they would both try to make the best of it now that the deed was done.

ROBERT JOSEPH PERSHING FOSTER

LOS ANGELES, 1996

———

THE PANELED DOOR RISES a story high and would befit a museum or government office but is actually the front door of a Spanish Revival south of Wilshire. The door opens, and there stands a onetime bourbon-swilling army captain and deft-handed surgeon who, now in his later years, is a regular at the blackjack tables and the trifectas at Santa Anita. But he is, at the heart of it all and perhaps most important, a long-standing, still bitter, and somewhat obsessive expatriate from the twentieth-century South, the heartbreak Jim Crow land he chose to reject before it could reject him again.

He is a Californian now, this Robert Joseph Pershing Foster. He is the color of strong coffee and has waves in his hair, which he lets grow as untamed as Einstein's but then brushes back like the boys in the band. He's wearing a white cotton island shirt, loose slacks, and sandals, the uniform of the well-to-do L.A. pensioner. He has the build and bearing of a Sammy Davis, Jr., and not a little of the showmanship and delightful superficiality that seem to grow on people in certain circles of L.A.

He walks straight-backed and slew-footed into the foyer, past the curved, faux–*Gone With the Wind* staircase and the East Asian pottery. He gestures toward the living room, an imposing museum of a space that dwarfs him in its volume, fairly frozen in the sea foam carpet and hot pink tulip chairs out of a sherbety Doris Day movie from the fifties. The whole effect is as starched and formal as the tuxedos he used to wear to the parties he threw for himself back when his wife, Alice, was alive and the money was raining down like confetti. He seems accustomed to people fawning over the place and, with the prim air of leading men of his favorite movies from back in the forties, insists on serving his guests a slice of lemon pound cake and vanilla ice cream on Rosenthal china, whether they would like to have it or not.

His heavy-lidded eyes look straight into those of his listener and have a distractingly thick fringe of lashes like those seen on babies and starlets.

He is a physician—or was for most of his adult life and, by most accounts, a very good one—and is prone to pontificate like a man of his years and accomplishments. But he is just as likely to interrupt himself and check the time to see if he can still make the one o'clock at the Hollywood Park racetrack.

His photo albums are filled with an unlikely assortment of bookies and blues singers and dentists and fraternity men and surgeons and society people whose approval he craved even though he knew they were too pretentious to matter, really. He doesn't say it because it would be gauche and hardly worth mentioning from his point of view, but there happen to be a lot of little Roberts around town, due to the fact that, over the years, he delivered a number of baby boys whose mothers were so grateful for his firm hand and calming reassurances at the precise moment of truth that they named their sons not after their husbands, but after the doctor who delivered their babies.

Before he begins his story, he tells you it's a long one and you can't get it all. He's lived too many lives, done too much, known too many people, ridden so high and so low that there's no point in fooling yourself into thinking you can capture the whole of it.

You could try, of course, and he agrees to give as much as he can.

"I love to talk," he says, a smile forming on his still-chiseled face as he sits upright in his tulip chair. "And I am my favorite subject."

MONROE, LOUISIANA, 1933

IT WAS SATURDAY. Pershing Foster, the teenage son of ambitious but barely paid schoolteachers, began to stir in the thin light of morning. He lived across the railroad tracks from the rest of Monroe, in the worn colored section mockingly known as New Town despite its dirt roads and old shotgun houses on stilts. He pulled out his good pants with the three-inch waistband and the buttons on the side. A few hours from now, the Paramount Theater would go dark, and Jean Harlow or Errol Flynn or some other airbrushed and porcelain movie star would appear out of nowhere, big as a building.

Pershing wanted to be there when the curtain went up and escape his segregated cell of a life, if only for ninety-four minutes. But his father reminded him he couldn't leave just yet. The cows had to be brought in from the grazing pasture and milked before he could go.

Morning after morning, his father had tried to teach him how to milk. Each time, Pershing bent down and pulled hard on the teats, but he could never get the hang of it, nor, truth be told, really wanted to. One time, the cow kicked over the bucket, and the milk spilled everywhere, which only proved to Pershing, who didn't want to be there in the first place, that he wasn't cut out for this line of work.

"I told you that cow didn't like me," Pershing said.

His father couldn't afford to lose a whole bucket of milk. Madison Foster was the principal of the colored high school—a misnomer because it included every grade from the first through the eleventh, but, in any case, paid him a fraction of what the state openly and unapologetically paid his white counterparts and left him and his family only slightly better off than the colored servants in town. He needed that milk to supplement his wages, and he didn't have milk to waste.

"Let him go," his father finally conceded to his wife, Ottie. "Unloose him. Unloose him."

Pershing got his way. He was the last child Ottie would ever bear, and, to the degree that a colored child could be spoiled when so much of the world was cut off to him, he was.

There were three children above him. Madison was the oldest and away most of the time, off in medical school. He was going to be the first doctor in the family, as Ottie, who set her sights higher than the teacher that she was, liked to say of her firstborn. Leland, the second son, was a star pitcher at Morehouse College in Atlanta. His parents had big plans for Leland, naming him as they did after their alma mater, Leland College in New Orleans. People were saying Leland had a shot at the Negro Leagues. He had to fight the girls off him as it was. He had a sculpted mahogany face and waves in his hair. He had the best mind of all the four children but, to his mother's great sorrow, was a regular at the pool hall and the juke joints, despite her best efforts. The women called him Woo, which is what they whispered when they saw him.

There was a sister named Emlyn. They called her Gold owing to the sunset cast to her skin and her place as the only surviving girl. Her twin, Evelyn, had died as an infant. Everybody fussed over Gold and told her how beautiful she was, which she was.

The table seemed set before Pershing was even born, and he couldn't see how to stand out on his own or figure out how he fit in as the youngest. A few years before, when he was about ten, he hit upon something that he thought he could do. He was in fifth grade, and when the school bell rang, he ran to meet his mother in her seventh-grade classroom. He told her his discovery as they walked home together.

"Mama, I believe I can play the piano."

"You think you can?"

"Yes, Mama, I know I can."

"What makes you know?"

"Mama, all you got to do is do like this," he said, banging his fingers on an invisible keyboard as he walked, "and hum the song, and it'll come out."

"You think so, baby?"

"Yes, Mama."

"Well, tomorrow after school, you go down, and you try it on the piano, and you let me know how you come out."

The next day, he did as she said. Noise came out of the piano instead of the music in his head, and that was the end of his short career as a pianist. He never spoke of it again. And, seeing that he didn't bring it up, neither did his mother.

The day the cow kicked over the bucket, they let Pershing have his way. He was a teenager now and off to the Paramount. It sat gaudy and beautiful on the other side of the Missouri Pacific Railway tracks from the colored section of town. He stepped out of the white frame bungalow with his pants creased to a knife edge, the crinkled waves in his hair pomaded and patted down, and proceeded down the dirt roads leading downtown. He went past the little plank houses that stood on cinder blocks due to the rains and floods and jumped over the dirt ditches that made grass islands of every yard around.

He picked up paper-shell pecans that fell in people's yards like litter. Soon he came to the places where the white people lived. The streets were paved and smooth now. In New Town, the roads were earthen humps with a ditch on either side to catch the bayou when it ran out of places to go. Whenever it rained, the streets turned to mud, and Pershing and the other children jumped in the ditches and splashed around as if the ditches were a swimming pool. They didn't know what a real pool was like because the only one in town didn't allow children who looked like them.

Trucks rumbled down the road and flung dust on the porches and through the screens and into the front rooms of the houses on Pershing's side of town. The mud and dust were an affront to Pershing, and he defied it the best he could. He made a game out of proving he could outwit his lower-caste world.

"It was my personal pride to wait till a rainy day and polish my black-and-white shoes," he said, "and wear them when the rain had stopped and jump over puddles and not get a spot of anything on them."

Those dirt roads were the reason he never learned to skate, and he could never forget that.

"We could buy skates," Pershing would remember even as an old man. "But we couldn't buy sidewalks."

Downtown was called Five Points, the intersection of Eighteenth and Desiard, and when Pershing got there, he walked further down Desiard Street past Piccadilly's restaurant, where the white people ate, and on to the Paramount straight ahead. He could see the double glass doors in front and a crowd forming outside. He knew to ignore the front entrance. It was off-limits to people like him.

He went to get his ticket. It was a more complicated affair than it had to be, owing to the whims and peculiarities of how Jim Crow played out in a particular town or establishment. For a time, there was a single ticket agent working both booths—the window for the colored and the one for the white. The agent swiveled between the two openings to sell the movie tickets, a roll to the white line and then a pivot to the colored. It created unnecessary confusion and waiting time for one line or the other, the waiting borne more likely by the colored moviegoers than the white, as waiting to be served after colored people would have been unacceptable to the white clientele. By the time Pershing was nearly grown, the swiveling ticket agent was dispensed with in favor of altogether separate windows and ticket sellers, which would cost a little more but would move the white and colored lines along more quickly and was more in keeping with the usual protocols of Jim Crow.

The Paramount fancied itself like one of the great opera houses of Europe with its crimson velvet curtains and pipe organ rising from the orchestra pit. A double-wide staircase ushered theatergoers to its box seats. But Pershing would not be permitted near them. He followed the colored crowd to the little door at the side entrance, while the white people passed through the heavy glass doors on Desiard. He saw Jimmy and Clarence and Nimrod and just about every other kid from New Town on his way in.

The side door opened onto a dark stairway. Pershing mounted the steps, anxious to get a seat before the lights went dim. He went up one flight, two flights, three, four, five flights of stairs. The scent of urine told him he was getting closer to the colored seats.

At the top of the stairs, there was Bennie Anderson, the colored ticket taker, ready to take his stub. The urine aroma was thick and heavy now. The toilet was stopped up most of the time, and the people did what they had to. Some relieved themselves on the way up. Pershing thought they did it on purpose—a protest maybe for the condition of the place, not registering that it was other colored people who had to suffer for it. He could understand it, but he didn't much approve.

Pershing sat hard in the wooden seat and tried not to notice the stuffed upholstery on the main floor below. Sometimes the kids would rain popcorn and soda pop on the white people. At last, the place went dark, and Pershing left Monroe. He was on a bright veranda with Myrna Loy and Tyrone Power out in California. It was a perfect world, and he could see himself in it.

———

The only way that someone as proud and particular as Pershing could survive in the time and place he was in was to put his mind somewhere else. He grew up watching his parents exercise exquisite control over the few things they were permitted to preside over in life. Their domain was the Monroe Colored High School, where Madison was principal and Ottie taught seventh grade. It was a small brick building with 1,139 pupils and a teacher for each grade, from kindergarten to eleventh, and run with the precision of a military institution.

Madison James Foster was a short man partial to vested suits and Bible scripture. He had had a hard, orphan-like childhood which he kept to himself other than to say that he had been raised not by his parents but by white people in New Iberia, down by the Gulf. As a boy in the 1880s, he showed a gift for reciting verse, and his white guardians had him perform for their guests as parlor entertainment. There he stood in the middle of a Victorian front room, white guests gathered around him, and was told to recite scripture for their amusement. They saw that he had a facile mind and, when the time came, offered him some assistance to get a degree. He landed at an old colored school called Leland College in New Orleans, where he met a preacher's daughter named Ottie. They graduated from Leland in 1905 and married the same year. They had big plans for themselves just as Jim Crow was closing doors on them.

They set out to teach far from New Orleans, in a moated land of cotton gins and oak trees dripping plant feathers between the Ouachita River and the bayou. An opportunity had arisen in Monroe, an old mill town near the upper brim of the Louisiana boot, not far from where the shoelaces would be. Monroe was three counties west of Mississippi, seventy-five miles from Vicksburg. It was closer to the cotton fields of the Delta than the bons-temps-rolling high life of New Orleans, where the two of them had met. To the north was the tenant-farming Ozark land of warm springs and hard living in Arkansas, where an attempt by sharecroppers to unionize in the town of Elaine would be crushed with bloody efficiency in 1919. To the west was Texas, the wide-open grazing and cotton land of vigilante justice and lynching spectacles that drew people by the thousands and made the newspapers all over the country.

In the midst of this violence, Monroe was a quietly hierarchal town with its two castes remaining in their places and separated by two sets of railroad tracks. The town had been founded by French traders in the nineteenth century and became a mill town serving the nearby cotton plantations and lumber concerns by the time the Fosters got there.

The town came into its own in the 1920s with the arrival of a crop-dusting outfit out of Macon, Georgia, the company having decided to move to the more strategically located town of Monroe, closer to the Mississippi Delta. In 1928, a businessman named C. E. Woolman purchased what was then known as Huff Daland Dusters. He switched from crop dusting and began running the first passenger flights between Mississippi and Texas, via Monroe and Shreveport, in 1929. The company would later come to be known as Delta Air Lines, named after the region it originally served. Delta's presence in Monroe was little more than a distant point of pride to the colored people there, as they could not have become pilots, stewardesses, or gate agents for the airline and might glean only the ancillary benefits of cleaning the airport and serving the now wealthier and well-positioned white people working there. Delta would remain headquartered in Monroe until 1941, when it relocated to Atlanta with the United States's entry into World War II.

———

It was in Monroe that Madison and Ottie Foster spent their honeymoon hoping to prosper despite the limits of their era, a time when Jim Crow was closing in on them and mutating all over the South. Madison took a position as principal and she as a teacher of the colored children who spilled out of the shotgun houses on the colored side of the Kansas City Southern and Union Pacific railroad tracks. They eventually bought a white frame bungalow on Louise Anne Avenue surrounded by icemen, barbers, sawmill workers, and domestics. The colored people took to calling the husband "Professor Foster" out of an overinflated respect for his bachelor's degree and the position he held over them. It came out " 'Fessor Foster," though, by the time people got through saying it.

He cut a tight-buttoned bearing in his Kuppenheimer suits and Arrow shirts with detachable white collars and cuff links, always gold cuff links. By the late twenties, he was in a position of some prestige among colored people in town, the president of the Louisiana Colored Teachers Association, and was regularly mentioned in the Louisiana News section of the *Chicago Defender* for attending or speaking at some important colored meeting or convention.

He rose early to open his school and greeted the people on their porches as he passed. He had authority of some sort over practically every child in New Town. Some Sundays, he preached at Zion Traveler Baptist Church. It was a world unto itself. The striving colored people in town, stooped and trodden the rest of the week, invested their very beings into the church and quarreled over how things should be run and who should be in charge of the one thing they had total control over.

In the summer of 1932, the church actually split into two rival factions as to who should be the pastor. One side was backing the Reverend W. W. Hill, an old-school preacher who had just been ousted; the other was supporting Professor Foster, a starched man with a standoffish wife and brilliant children whom some people saw as having enough influence as it was, seeing as how he already ran the school. The church grew so divided that people were no longer speaking. Enemy lines were drawn. The church had to shut down for two whole months. The authorities in Monroe took away the keys.

The church reopened the first Sunday in September 1932, along with the wounds and hostilities that were no closer to healing than the day the church was shuttered. That morning, Sunday school had barely begun when "there arose a contention between the two factions as to who was in charge of the church," the *Chicago Defender* reported.

There was a question as to whether the apparent victor, Professor Foster, should speak, the Hill people saying it was perhaps best that he not, the anti-Hill faction urging him to go forward.

Professor Foster was accustomed to running things. He arose and stood stiff and pious and was reading Bible scripture, when four women walked up to the pulpit and demanded he stop preaching, as if to suggest he had no right to be taking over as he had.

It was an outrageous, unheard-of disruption, practically blasphemous, and the church broke into an uproar. Several men rushed the pulpit and began fighting. A deacon backed out of the door, hitting back at those who pursued him and falling down in the street. A parishioner named James Dugans, who was either a supporter of Professor Foster or merely enraged at the show of disrespect, picked up a chair, drew a pistol, and started shooting. A bullet struck a woman named Patsy Daniels in the stomach. Incensed, her father ran to a house next door and got a pistol of his own. The father came back to a fight that had now spilled out to the front of the church.

When the first gunman, Dugans, saw the woman's now-armed father, he shot him in the chest. The bleeding father continued firing as he fell, killing Dugans and wounding three other parishioners. Patsy Daniels died from her wounds. In all, as many as seven people were left wounded, including the dead woman's father. Professor Foster and his family managed to escape unharmed—physically, in any case. The Monroe police again had to take the keys of the church. Until the congregation could settle its dispute, "the doors of the church were securely nailed up," the *Atlanta Daily World* reported.

Pershing was thirteen. He would now end up seeing the world as a beleaguered and underappreciated Foster, a member of a resented clan in a small, clannish subculture inside a segregated pressure cooker of a life. The incident was so unseemly and beneath him that he never spoke of it. But he carried the sense of betrayal and insecurity with him and in some ways would spend the rest of his life both running from those who rejected his family and craving their acceptance.

After the melee, neither Reverend Hill nor Professor Foster would ever muster the full support of the congregation or get to run Zion Traveler Baptist Church. In time, life somehow returned to some version of normalcy, and Professor Foster instead took comfort in his place as the leading black educator in town. On school mornings, he stood at the front steps of the school with a pocket watch in one hand and a paddle in the other. Sometimes the students came running across the school yard late and out of breath.

"The trains cut us off, 'Fessor Foster," the children would tell him.

"I'm gon' cut *you* off," he'd say, raising his paddle. "Get up early. Get up early."

He held chapel before class started, quoting the Old Testament in the auditorium for an hour every morning, and he believed in sparing neither the rod, paddle, or switch. He half waited for some child to get out of line so he could make an example out of him. But as anybody who grew up in that world could tell you, he was no better or no worse than any colored schoolmaster in the South when it came to such things.

His wife, Ottie Alberta Wright Foster, was a prim and ambitious woman, who made the society pages of the colored papers as president of the Golden Seal Embroidery Club and for hosting such things as a wedding breakfast for a bridal party in what the *Defender* called a "lovely home . . . prettily decorated for the occasion." Ottie was raised in New Orleans, a magic circus of a place compared to Monroe, braided with openly mixed-race Creole people and their patois and jambalaya. She brought the food and ways with her and spent hours on the roux for her gumbo when things were good. To be reputed to be Creole was enough to make her exotic to some colored people, whether she was actually Creole or not—which no one ever established for sure but most assumed was true.

She was a small woman with skin the color of chestnuts and wavy black hair. It was said she would have been considered quite a beauty if it weren't for the tight bun she wore low on her head with the severe center part at her forehead and the fact that she seemed rarely to smile at anyone other than her children.

All of the children were bright. But in the family hierarchy, there was not much Pershing could do to distinguish himself with one big brother off in medical school and another a star athlete. He played softball with the neighborhood kids, where they used broomsticks for bats and made their own rules because nobody had seen an official baseball game. But he wasn't especially good at it.

Pershing looked for a way to prove himself. There were three fig trees in their yard, and he picked the figs and sold them to the neighbors, thirty-five cents for a gallon bucket. He gave them a broad smile and charmed them into believing they needed the figs for breakfast or for preserves or to can for the coming winter.

He practiced smiling in the mirror and writing with his left hand even though he didn't need to. He lived for the pat on the head from his father but especially his mother for washing out the washtub or any little thing that he did. He took to cleaning the house to make them happy and to keep the compliments coming, but it only felt good as long as he did it before they could ask.

He was crushed whenever he fell short. His parents punished him by making him go to the back steps and sit there. He sat hugging his dog and cried. Sometimes his mother got tired of him sitting on the steps and called him in. Otherwise, he couldn't leave until his father said so.

"Alright," Professor Foster would say. "Come back in."

It was true he couldn't milk a cow, but he didn't mind churning. He churned the milk as it soured and clabbered. Ottie skimmed the butter off, and he proceeded to go door to door, selling the butter and the buttermilk in a lard bucket with a cultivated earnestness and the crisp airs he was beginning to master.

Mrs. Poe, don't you wanna buy some milk from me? Can I start bringing you milk on Thursdays?

He found that he could get people to like him and that if people liked him he could get what he wanted.

———

For each grade there was one teacher. And when Pershing got to the seventh grade, Mama taught him. She stood at the front of the room and drilled math and verse into him and the rest of the class without humor or partiality. Sometimes Pershing got restless and leaned over to talk to Moses Potter or Nimrod Sherman or maybe Jimmy Peters. When he did, Ottie stopped in the middle of the lesson and glared down hard at him.

"Pershing, be quiet."

She stood by the blackboard and waited.

"Pershing, be quiet."

He didn't hear her, engrossed as he was. She marched over to his desk. He felt her shadow looming over him and continued to talk. She raised her left hand and smacked him in front of the class.

The other children laughed and laughed. Pershing put his head down and knew not to test Mama anymore. He could get away with less with his mother than with any other teacher in the school.

It seemed to him that for every good thing about being the teacher and principal's son there was a bad thing to it. If he was caught running down the street, somebody would stick her head out the window and remind him who he was.

"Boy, get on out the street. I'm a tell Miss Foster on you."

To further complicate his life, the Fosters were bookish, small-boned people and the children of the sawmill hands towered over Pershing. The days when he didn't walk home with Mama, when he was alone on the streets of New Town, some of the boys lay in wait for him. They surrounded him and taunted him for the way he carried himself and the half inch of extra privilege he had over them.

"You think you somebody 'cause you 'Fessor Foster's boy. You think you better than anybody else 'cause you a Foster."

They made a circle around him and felt bigger because of it. If Professor Foster had whipped the boys with his strap that day, Pershing paid for it that afternoon. They beat him and had a good time doing it. He took it because he had to and fighting wasn't in him. Telling his father would have made things worse. Professor Foster knew no other way to keep errant children in line and would have beat the boys again if he knew what they'd done to his youngest boy, which would have only made life harder for Pershing. So he kept it to himself.

As Pershing got to be a teenager, he started venturing out into the neighborhood, poking his head into the juke joints and the pool hall where the hip cats drank late into the night. It was where the men slapped Woo on the back as they poured him another shot of whiskey. But whenever Pershing poked his head inside, he got the same wave of the hand from the proprietor and the men lining the wall.

"Boy, get outta here. You ain't got no business in here. 'Fessor Foster wouldn't want you in here."

Woo wouldn't have minded and never told him not to come in, but the word had spread somehow that Professor Foster and his wife had a different life in mind for Pershing.

There were pressures coming at him from every direction—his high-minded parents trying to make up in a single generation all that they had been denied through generations of slavery; bullying kids who taunted him and resented his station, tentative though it was; neighbor-hood people watching his every move. Then there were the reminders that no matter what he did or how smart he might be, he would always be seen as inferior to the lowliest person in the ruling caste, which only meant he had to work even harder to prove the system wrong because it had been drilled into him that he had to be better than the system con-strued him to be.

He lived under the accumulated weight of all these expectations.

"People in the town demanded more of us," he said years later, "and we had to give it. I respected what they told me. And anything I didn't want them to see, I kept it out of their sight."

————

Every few years, a teacher from Monroe Colored High loaded a band of students onto the flat bed of a pickup truck and rattled across the Mis-souri Pacific Railway tracks. They passed the rich people's porticos and pulled up to the back entrance of the white high school in town. The boys jumped out and began stacking the truck bed with the books the white school was throwing away. That is how Monroe Colored High School got its books. The boys loaded the truck with old geography and English texts, some without covers and with pages torn out and love notes scrawled in the margins, and headed back to their side of town.

By the time he was old enough to understand where the books came from, Pershing was fast putting together the pieces of the world he lived in. He knew there was a dividing line, but it was hitting him in the face now. He was showing a talent for science and was getting to the point that he needed reference books to do his lesson. But it was against the law for colored people to go to the public library. "And the library at the Colored High School did not live up to its name," he said years later.

He was in the eighth grade when word filtered to his side of the tracks that Monroe was getting a new high school. It wouldn't replace the old building that Monroe Colored High was in. It was for the white students, who already had a big school. It would be called Neville High. The colored people could see it going up when they ventured to the other side of the tracks. It rose up like a castle, four stories of brick and concrete with separate wings and a central tower, looking as if it be-longed at Princeton or Yale. It opened in 1931 on twenty-two acres of land. The city fathers made a fuss over the state-of-the-art laboratories for physics and chemistry, the 2,200-seat balconied auditorium, the ex-panded library, and the fact it was costing $664,000 to build.

As the new high school took shape across town, Pershing watched his
father rise in the black of morning to milk the cows and walk the mile
and a half to open his building the size of a grade school. His father, his
mother, and the other teachers at Monroe Colored High School were
working long hours with hand-me-down supplies for a fraction of the
pay their white counterparts were getting. In Louisiana in the 1930s,
white teachers and principals were making an average salary of $1,165 a
year. Colored teachers and principals were making $499 a year, forty-
three percent of what the white ones were.

Pershing's parents could console themselves that they were faring
better than colored teachers in other southern states, a reflection not necessarily of their superior performance but that there were states even
worse than Louisiana when it came to teachers' pay. In neighboring
Mississippi, white teachers and principals were making $630 a year,
while the colored ones were paid a third of that—$215 a year, hardly
more than field hands. But knowing that didn't ease the burden of the
Fosters' lives, get their children through college, or allow them to build
assets to match their status and education.

The disparity in pay, reported without apology in the local papers for
all to see, would have far-reaching effects. It would mean that even the
most promising of colored people, having received next to nothing in
material assets from their slave foreparents, had to labor with the
knowledge that they were now being underpaid by more than half, that
they were so behind it would be all but impossible to accumulate the assets their white counterparts could, and that they would, by definition,
have less to leave succeeding generations than similar white families.
Multiplied over the generations, it would mean a wealth deficit between
the races that would require a miracle windfall or near asceticism on the
part of colored families if they were to have any chance of catching up or
amassing anything of value. Otherwise, the chasm would continue, as it
did for blacks as a group even into the succeeding century. The layers of
accumulated assets built up by the better-paid dominant caste, generation after generation, would factor into a wealth disparity of white
Americans having an average net worth ten times that of black Americans by the turn of the twenty-first century, dampening the economic
prospects of the children and grandchildren of both Jim Crow and the
Great Migration before they were even born.

For now, each day, Pershing's parents and the families whose children they taught had to live with the reality that they had to do more
with less. Southern states made no pretense as to the lopsided division of

resources to white and colored schools, devoting as much as ten dollars per white student for every dollar spent on a colored student and showing little interest beyond that meager investment.

"The money allocated to the colored children is spent on the education of the white children," a local school superintendent in Louisiana said bluntly. "We have twice as many colored children of school age as we have white, and we use their money. Colored children are mighty profitable to us."

When a fire broke out in the basement of Monroe Colored High School, destroying classroom furniture and equipment, the city refused to so much as replace the desks and teaching supplies that had burned to ashes, as the *Monroe News Star* reported. The tax dollars were earmarked for Neville. The colored parents, already strapped, would have to raise the money themselves. That would be just one more thing weighing on Professor Foster. As it was, he wasn't making half of what the Neville High School principal made. Nobody in New Town would be allowed in the new building when it opened, other than to clean it, and the idea of Pershing attending it, no matter how smart he was, was unthinkable.

It was not something the Fosters would have wanted to dwell on, as it would have done them no good, but their very existence, their personal aspirations, and the purpose of their days were in direct opposition to the white ruling-class policy on colored education—that is, that colored people needed no education to fulfill their God-given role in the South.

"If these Negroes become doctors and merchants or buy their own farms," a southern woman told the celebrated journalist Ray Stannard Baker, "what shall we do for servants?"

The unfairness started to eat at Pershing. It was a curse to be able to see it. Better not to know. But the older he got, the more he was starting to want. And the more he wanted, the harder it was to accept that he might never get it—all because of a chemical in his skin that some people resented and felt superior to and that no one on this earth could change. To make matters worse, he had the misfortune of having developed exquisite taste and what little he was exposed to only fed his ambitions.

"Everything you wanted was white and the best," he said.

Pershing had started to notice the girls, and they started to notice him. They were getting to an age where they would walk home from school together, meet at the Paramount for the picture show, and eventually end up in a park or a field somewhere. Somebody would get a car from an uncle or someone or other, and they would drive up to where the new Neville High was, shiny new and perched high on a hill. It was lush and secluded, and when they had finished with the girls, they whirred past the grounds and flung their spent condoms on the green.

"That's how we showed our resentment," he said years later. "Don't think we were blind."

———

Just before dark, when the sky is neither blue nor black but purple, Pershing stepped out of the tin tub to get ready for a Saturday night. He put on long pants and cheap cologne and walked in the direction of the Miller and Roy Building on the colored side of Five Points, about a mile from the center of town.

It was in the shadow of downtown in a world of its own. The axis was Eighteenth and Desiard. Across from the office building was the drugstore. Behind the drugstore was a café. Behind the café was a liquor store. Across from the liquor store was the pool hall.

He had his shirt buttoned low and open as he strutted down Desiard. He was two blocks from the Miller and Roy Building when a car pulled up to the curb. The exhaust spit and coughed. A white man leaned out of the window.

"Hey, boy."

Pershing kept walking. He hated being called boy even though he was one. They barked it at the sawmill hands and at bent-over, old colored men and even upstanding men like his father. He was fourteen, and it was already beginning to grate on him.

"Hey, boy!"

Pershing stopped and consoled himself: *You can answer him because you are a boy. You're not twenty-one yet. Technically you're still a boy. That makes it okay for him to address you as boy.*

He turned toward the car and kept it to "Yes," instead of "Yes, sir."

"Boy, I'll pay you if you get me a nice, clean colored girl."

Pershing breathed deep. Ever since his sister, Gold, had hit puberty, he could hardly walk down the street with her without white men with snuff in their mouth yelling out what they would do to her. It made him want to vomit. She kept her head up and held his hand tight and walked through it. He could never defend her, never stand up to a gang of them on a street corner. "That was death," he would say years later.

Pershing knew it from the sheer insanity all around him. When he was eleven years old, a white mob burned down the courthouse across the border in Sherman, Texas.

It started with a colored man accused of raping a white woman, a confession extracted, a trial hastily set. But just as the trial opened, a mob stormed the courtroom and torched the building to get to the defendant, George Hughes. Court officials fled through a second-story window and left Hughes in a steel vault with a bucket of water.

Firefighters tried to save the courthouse, but the mob slashed the water hoses to keep the blaze going. The mob then dynamited the vault where Hughes had been left. The mob found him dead, crushed by the explosion, the water bucket almost empty. The courthouse then burned to the ground.

Disappointed that they had not gotten to Hughes before he died, the people in the mob hanged his body from a cottonwood tree and set it on fire with furniture they looted from a nearby colored hotel. Then they torched the colored district, as the colored people of Sherman fled to the homes of white friends or left town. A half-dozen colored homes escaped the torching only because a white man told the mob the houses belonged to him.

This was the world Pershing was growing up in. He had learned the rules early in life. Now he was standing at a vacant curb, just him and a white man out prowling. He had never seen the man before, imagined he must have come in from the country and made a beeline for the colored section with one thing in mind, as was his prerogative. Not just any colored girl. *A nice, clean colored girl.*

The man waited, and Pershing assessed the situation. He was on the colored side of town, a block from the rooming house. He knew every turn and alley. He was in the majority around here.

He looked at the man. "A nice, clean colored girl," he said, calculating the risks of what he might say next. "Let me see. I tell you what. You get your mama for me, and I'll get you one."

He didn't wait for the man's reaction. Pershing vanished into the colored alleys of Five Points. He couldn't believe what had come out of his mouth. His face was flushed, and his hands shook. He could get hanged for that. Nothing more needed to happen to remind him who had the power over him and what they could do if they wanted.

"You lived with it," Pershing said years later. "But it wasn't that you liked the taste of it."

And I'd whisper to myself that someday
the sun was going to shine down on me
way up North in Chicago or Kansas City
or one of those other faraway places that
my cousin . . . always talked about. . . .
I felt the same restlessness in me.
— MAHALIA JACKSON, *Movin' On Up*

THE SOUTH, 1915 TO THE 1970S

———

AT EASTER AND AROUND THE FOURTH OF JULY, the people from the North came. They looked like extras out of a movie at the Saturday matinee. They wore peplums and bergamot waves. Even the wind moved aside as they walked.

They flashed thick rolls of cash from their pockets—the biggest bills on the outside covering the ones and fives. They said they were making all kinds of money. But they didn't have to say it because the cars and the clothes did the talking. They had been wiring more money to their families back home than they truly could spare and had been saving up all year for those gloves and matching purse. But they weren't telling the people in the South that.

They made sure to show up at their mother-churches, where everyone would see them: at Gethsemane Baptist Church in Eustis, Florida, where Lil George went; at Thankful Baptist Church in Rome, Georgia, where my mother saw the people visiting from the North; at New Hope Baptist Church in Chickasaw County, Mississippi, where Ida Mae lived.

Even at Zion Traveler Baptist Church in Monroe, Louisiana, where Pershing grew up, the partisans set aside their rivalries and sat upright in the pews when the people from the North came. The pastor would ask the visitors to rise, and it was then that the people from up north or out west stood up in their butterfly hats and angel dresses and in suits upholstered to the tall men's frames. People who hadn't seen them in ages now craned their necks to see how Willie and Thelma looked and if they had changed any. And the pastor went on about how this one was building cars in Detroit and that one was doing us proud in Oakland.

They were received like visiting dignitaries. They had once been just like the people who stayed. Now they were doing important-sounding work for the government in Washington, in the hotels on Michigan Avenue in Chicago, in the garment district in New York or in the apartments of the rich people on Riverside Drive. They wore the protective coating of the North. They lived in big cities too distracted to care what the colored people did as long as they did it to themselves, and that was the greatest blessing of all.

———

At night when the junebugs came out, the children sat at the knees of the people from the North and heard stories of doing unimaginable things like sitting in the front of a trolley car and saying "Yes" instead of "Yes, sir" to a white person and living to tell it.

In Grenada, Mississippi, two little boys couldn't wait for their big sister Francie to come visit from Ohio. Gilbert and Percy Elie would crouch at her feet and listen to her.

"We would sit on the porch in the moonlight," Gilbert remembered, "and she would tell us about the North."

Then she went back to Ohio. And life returned to the way it was for Gilbert and Percy, living as they were in the altogether different country of the Mississippi Delta.

They and Ida Mae and George and Pershing and children all over the South were growing up, trying to comprehend the caste they were born into, adjusting or resisting, lying in bed at night and imagining a world that was different and free, and knowing it was out there because they had seen it in the casual airs, the haughtiness even, and the clothes and the stories of the people from the North. Now nothing around them made sense, and everything that happened to them imprinted itself into their psyches and loomed larger because they had glimpsed what was possible outside the bars of their own existence.

Yet they were too young to escape. So they had to endure their peculiar station in the feudal world they were consigned to and the madness that could intrude at any given moment.

Like the night back in the 1940s, "a moon-shining night, bright, like it's almost day," when little Gibert and Percy were sitting on the front porch steps of their family's cabin.

The boys could hear voices coming from the woods. The voices echoed through the trees in the night. The boys got quiet and still and tried to make out what was happening. They could hear the crackle of a whip and a hollow wailing coming from the woods. A colored man was being lashed in the pine scrub beyond their cabin.

The boys heard the man cry out with each blow.

"Alright, we gonna take a break," some voices finally said.

There was silence. Then the men took up the task again.

"We gonna kill you," the voices said from the woods.

"Please, *please,* don't," the colored voice said. "Before y'all do, will you let me pray?"

The man began to pray. "The man prayed a prayer like a Baptist preacher," Gilbert remembered decades later. "I ain't never heard a man pray like that man."

"Father, forgive them, for they know not what they doing," Gilbert remembered the man praying. *"I lived a good life for you, if you never done nothing for me, Lord, please . . ."*

"Alright, that's enough," the other voices said.

The man continued to pray. The beating and wailing commenced again. Then the wailing stopped.

"The sonabitch dead," came a voice from the woods.

Gilbert could never get the man's cries out of his head. "We don't know who he was," Gilbert said some fifty years later, "or what he was supposed to have done."

The seeds of Gilbert's departure from Mississippi were sown that night. More seeds were planted another day, when he and his father and brother were walking home from the movie theater in town.

The street was little more than an alley, barely wide enough for two people to walk astride. Gilbert was about twelve. He was reading a comic book and not paying attention. Three white boys not much older than Gilbert came in their direction. Gilbert's father and brother instinctively jumped out of the way. Gilbert was looking at his comic book and bumped into one of the boys.

The boy grabbed Gilbert by the collar.

"Who do you think you are?" Gilbert remembered the boy asking him.

The boy spat at him, and Gilbert hit the boy back. Gilbert's father was shaking with fear. He begged forgiveness from the boy who spat on his son. Then he turned to his son and upbraided him.

"Boy, what's the matter with you?" his father said. "Are you crazy?"

The father fumed at him. "All the way home, he didn't talk to me," Gilbert remembered decades later.. "I got home, he didn't say a word."

That night, Gilbert could hear his father confiding to his mother through the cardboard-thin walls of their cabin. "Sugar, that one son we got, Gilbert, I'm afraid for him," the father whispered. "That boy'll never live if he stays in Grenada."

Gilbert knew that. He shared his dreams with Percy when they worked in the field hoeing and plowing and weighing up the cotton.

"We would plow side to side," Gilbert remembered. "He'd have a row, and I'd have a row. We would talk. We would talk about school or what I'm gonna do when I get to be grown, when I leave here."

His big sister's stories of life up north had seeped into him, and one day when he got big enough, he told himself, he was going to follow her to Ohio. And he did.

———

Hundreds of miles away, out in the country near Jackson, North Carolina, a family named DeBreaux was in a tizzy whenever cousin Beulah was expected in from New York. The mother cooked all day. The daughters, Virginia and Lee, cleaned and swept and tried to imagine how she would look. It was as if the queen of England were coming.

Beulah blew into town in the latest silk dresses, her high heels click-clacking on the pavement. Her hair was pressed and shiny and swung when she turned her head. The girls touched it to see how it felt.

"If we could just look like that," Virginia told her sister.

Virginia started dreaming then and there. *Someday, I'm going to New York.*

She sat and planned the whole thing out with her little brother. She wouldn't have to pick cotton anymore or feel the spike of frost on the wet grass going barefoot to the outhouse in the morning.

In the early 1940s, she did, in fact, join the multitudes. The day she left, her mother made fried chicken and broke down crying. Her father was too hurt to speak. He stayed in the house as they left. "He did not bid us good-bye," she said. She ended up in Brooklyn, where the elevated train shook the apartment and looked as if it were coming straight into the window, and where she would get her hair pressed and wear high heels click-clacking on the pavement like Beulah.

Sometimes, the young people had little choice but to leave, sooner than they had imagined. Such was the case with my mother's older brother. He was a teenager in Rome, Georgia, working as a driver and office boy for an upstanding white man in town during the Depression. He would drive the man from Georgia to Miami for the man's business trips, alone with him in the car for hours at a time. He liked the man because he let him keep the big new shiny car after dropping the man off at the white hotel. It was one of the few company jobs accorded colored teenagers in the South at that time and was thought to be a good one.

One day, he was straightening the man's office when he opened a drawer and saw something white folded inside. He pulled it out and unfurled the fabric.

It was a white robe and hood.

Trembling, he put it back in the drawer, and had to reconsider everything he thought he knew about the man he had trusted and the world in which he lived. That night, he went home and told his parents and little sisters that he was leaving Georgia for Detroit, one of the receiving stations for people from that part of the South. He had made his decision, was shocked into it, really. He would get a job at Chrysler like a cousin of theirs. He was joining the Great Migration for the most personal and profound of reasons, and, without knowing it, planting a seed in my mother's imagination, knowing as she did why her big brother had fled.

Several seeds were planted, too, in Ida Mae, Lil George, and Pershing. Ida Mae heard about this one or that one going north to freedom after a lynching or a raw deal at settlement. Her big brothers, Sam and Cleve, had fled to Toledo, her big sister Irene was talking about going to Milwaukee, and, as Ida Mae came of age, she saw the cloche hats and unobtainable finery of city living in the pages of the Sears, Roebuck catalogue out of Chicago.

Lil George watched the Blye brothers, Babe and Reuben, older boys who'd gone north to New York, come back to Eustis in their zoot suits and fedoras. They talked about all the money they were making building the 9W highway up in Jersey, about the skyscrapers and streetlights, the dance halls in Harlem, the parties in Corona, and the boulevards paved where the colored people lived.

"We used to sit up all night," George remembered, "and listen to Babe and M.B. and Reuben and Freeman and all them talkin' about New York. And I said, 'Boy, that sounds just like heaven. I wanna see some of that. *New York*. I'm sure going to New York soon as I get big enough.'"

And in Monroe, Louisiana, if Mantan Moreland passed through town, there was a stir in the pews and talk in the pool hall. Everyone wanted to sit down with the native son who had made it to Hollywood, even if it was only as a shuffling sidekick in the movies.

Pershing saw the parade of people from the North and the movie scenes at the Paramount of life beyond Louisiana and began dreaming of escape, too. When he was still small enough to fit in the crawl spaces of the houses on cinder-block stilts, he played pretend with a girl down the street named Clara Poe. They peeked out from under the floor joists and waited for a car to rumble down Louise-Anne Avenue and fought over whose it was. *It's my car. No, it's my car.* Then they pretended they were in the car leaving.

Clara always said she was going to Chicago, where her uncles were. But no matter how many times Clara said Chicago, Pershing said he was going to California. He didn't have any family there. All he knew was that, one day, somehow, whenever he got big and whatever it took, he was going.

A Burdensome Labor

> This land is first and foremost
> his handiwork. . . .
> Wherever one looks
> in this land,
> whatever one sees
> that is the work of man,
> was erected by the
> toiling straining bodies of blacks.
> —DAVID L. COHN, *God Shakes Creation*

> But the Egyptians
> mistreated
> and oppressed us,
> assigning us a
> burdensome labor.
> —DEUTERONOMY 26:6

CHICKASAW COUNTY, MISSISSIPPI, 1929
IDA MAE BRANDON GLADNEY

IDA MAE'S NEW HUSBAND took her to live in a little wood cabin on
Edd Pearson's plantation on a clearing past the Natchez Trace. Ida Mae
was sixteen. In the morning, the sun poked at them through the gaps in
the roof. At night, they could see the stars through the ceiling cracks
over their bed. It just about rained inside as much as out.

They set about working cotton for Mr. Edd. All around them, the land was in a state of being cotton or becoming cotton, brown and rutted for planting, green shoots willed into rows of coddled bushes until the land was white out to the tree line. Every so often, a wood cabin broke the clearing, raw and thrown-together, built uneasily on a footprint of land that was a fraction of what was devoted to the field.

The people who lived in the cabins gave the best hours of their days to cotton, working until the sun went behind the trees and they couldn't see their hands anymore.

Early morning, the mist rose over the fields and made a halo on the surface of the earth. Ida Mae's new husband and the sharecroppers working other sections of Pearson's land tried to pick as much as they could before the sun got high.

Edd Monroe Pearson was a decent boss man, as decent as could be expected from a planter in Mississippi in the 1920s. He presided over the lives of some dozen families who grew his crops, as Ida Mae would recall, and he took half of whatever they produced, whether it was cotton or turkeys or hogs. At the end of the season, he deducted the debts he said they owed—cottonseed, fertilizer, implements, ginning fees, cornmeal, salt pork—the "furnish," as it was called, of their half of the harvest. Money rarely changed hands between planter and sharecropper, as the entire system was built on credit. The sharecroppers owed the planters, the planters owed the merchants, the merchants owed the banks, and the banks were often beholden to some business concern in the North, where most of the real money was in the first place.

Unlike some planters, Mr. Edd actually gave George and Ida Mae a few dollars when settling time came at the end of the harvest, although they never knew whether they would get anything or how much it might be or if it was actually what they were due, nor could they complain if it wasn't. Edd Pearson was about the best boss man a colored sharecropper could hope for.

But he was a ranking member of the dominant caste and felt it within his right to involve himself in the private affairs of his serfs.

He came through the field on his horse one day and saw George bent over picking through the rows. George and Ida Mae had been out for hours and the sun had cooked their backs. Ida Mae had no gift for picking like her new husband did and had fallen farther and farther behind, stooping from the weight of the sack.

George had called out to her, but she was too far back and too beat from the sun to catch up. After a few dozen pounds, her knees gave way.

She saw a clear path up ahead and dropped onto her sack, collapsed in the dirt aisle between the cotton rows.

Mr. Edd rode up to George and questioned him about it.

"Your wife don't do nothing, do she, but sit down," Mr. Edd said to George.

George would have liked to have said it was his business and not Mr. Edd's, but colored men could not say such things to a white man in Mississippi and get away with it in 1929.

When Mr. Edd was gone, George went back to Ida Mae.

"See can't you try and do a little bit better," George said, caught between the two of them.

She said she would try, but there was no use pretending. She was not going to be of much help in the field. She had never been able to pick a hundred pounds. One hundred was the magic number. It was the benchmark for payment when day pickers took to the field, fifty cents for a hundred pounds of cotton in the 1920s, the gold standard of cotton picking.

It was like picking a hundred pounds of feathers, a hundred pounds of lint dust. It was "one of the most backbreaking forms of stoop labor ever known," wrote the historian Donald Holley. It took some seventy bolls to make a single pound of cotton, which meant Ida Mae would have to pick seven thousand bolls to reach a hundred pounds. It meant reaching past the branches into the cotton flower and pulling a soft lock of cotton the size of a walnut out of its pod, doing this seven thousand times and turning around and doing the same thing the next day and the day after that.

The hands got cramped from the repetitive motion of picking, the fingers fairly locked in place and callused from the pricks of the barbed, five-pointed cockleburs that cupped each precious boll. The work was not so much hazardous as it was mind-numbing and endless, requiring them to pick from the moment the sun peeked over the tree line to the moment it fell behind the horizon and they could no longer see. After ten or twelve hours, the pickers could barely stand up straight for all the stooping.

Ida Mae had watched people do it all her life and knew how it was done. But when it came time to actually go out and pick it, she would look up and see everybody else far down the row. At weighing time, she would empty her sack on the scale and never get three digits.

Above her was an entire economy she could not see but which ruled her days and determined the contours of her life. There were bankers, planters, merchants, warehouse clerks, fertilizer wholesalers, seed sell-

ers, plow makers, mule dealers, gin owners. A good crop and a high
price made not much improvement to the material discomforts of Ida
Mae's existence but meant a planter's wife could "begin to dream of a
new parlor carpet and a piano" and a salesman of farm implements
could be "lavish with more expensive cigars than he smoked last year."
On Wall Street, there were futures and commodities traders wagering
on what the cotton she had yet to pick might go for next October. There
were businessmen in Chicago needing oxford shirts, socialites in New
York and Philadelphia wanting lace curtains and organdy evening
gowns. Closer to home, closer than one dared to contemplate, there
were Klansmen needing their white cotton robes and hoods.

———

In the half light of morning, when the mist hung low and the dew was
thick on the bolls, the pickers set out to the field as their slave foreparents had done year in and year out for two centuries. *"The first horn was
blown an hour before daylight as a summons for work hands to rise."* Each
one looked out across the field to infinity. The quarry was spread over
acres and rows far from the starting plant, and they could not see the
end of what they were expected to pick.

On large fields during the height of the season—which began in August in south Texas and moved eastward, reaching the Carolinas by
early fall—the star pickers sped like fan blades through the cotton, a
blur of fingers and bolls, arms and torsos switching from the left row to
the right, picking on both sides of them and tossing the cotton like feathers into their sack. The sacks were strapped over their shoulders and
dragged in the dirt behind them like an extra limb, the sacks weighing
as much as a human adult by the end of the day and making them stoop
all the more.

They picked until they were hypnotized by the picking. By midday,
the fast ones and the slow ones were far from the center, the stars way up
ahead and not looking back, the slow ones trailing behind, the most
watchful of everyone's placement. The field was flat and unbroken by
trees, and there was no escape from the hundred-degree heat. The sun
bore down on them through the head rags and the Panama hats and
made the cotton field shimmer like the ocean. Pickers thought they saw
things, like people who had died and come back, and waved a handkerchief in the air to call the water boy from under a shade tree. He was
usually a picker's child, the one designated to fetch the bucket of well

water when they needed it, half the water splashing out of the bucket and onto the ground as the water boy trudged down the rows.

Throughout the cotton kingdom, the act of picking cotton was the same. But in the hills, the cotton was sparser and shorter, not thick and shoulder high like cotton in the Delta. It was harder to get a hundred, much less more. You had to pick a wider field and stoop to pick the lowest bolls to reach the same benchmark.

There were ways to make life easier or harder for yourself when it came to picking cotton. Experienced pickers knew to pick in a rapid, flowing motion, trancelike and efficient. The strongest of the men, men like George, could pick two or three times their weight in cotton—four hundred pounds gave a man bragging rights in anybody's field. A woman could hold her head up if she picked a hundred.

It was a mean enough world that people got desperate. For one thing, for day pickers, there was the money. For another, there was their pride. And then there was the fact that they did not want to be there in the first place. Some people collected rocks, hid them in their pockets, and threw them into their sack at weighing time to make a heavier load. Some people picked the stalk and all to add extra weight. Some were the first out in the morning, picking early while the dew was on the bud, which meant much of the weight was water. It was a trick they could get away with unless the planter set the cotton out in the sun to dry it out, which some did. When those who were so inclined didn't outright lard their sacks, they helped themselves to the peaches and berries on the edges of the boss's cotton and gave themselves a raise for breaking their backs in the field.

Many years later, the people would stand up to water hoses and sheriffs' dogs to be treated as equal. But for now the people resisted in silent, everyday rebellions that would build up to a storm at midcentury. Rocks stuffed into cotton sacks in Mississippi at weighing time. The COLORED ONLY signs pulled from the seat backs of public buses and converted into dartboards in dorm rooms in Georgia. Teenagers sneaking into coffee shops and swiveling on the soda fountain stools forbidden to colored people in Florida and then running out as fast as they'd come in before anybody could catch them. Each one fought in isolation and unbeknownst to the others, long before the marches and boycotts that were decades away.

Sometime in the 1930s, a crew of pickers had been assembled to harvest a wide field of cotton near Brookhaven, Mississippi, some two hundred miles south of Chickasaw County, where Ida Mae lived. On the crew was a big man who had just gotten out of Parchman Prison. Word spread through the field that the man had killed somebody, but no one knew for sure. It was clear from the start that the man could pick. He was used to picking with a gun to his back. He could pick like a machine when he got paid for it.

People could hardly pick for watching the man. One of the slower pickers was a teenager who figured if he could just stick behind the prisoner, he could make more money for himself. So he got behind him and did what he did, or tried to anyway. The prisoner did not speak. He just picked until he was a faint figure in the distance. The slow picker fell behind, and when dusk approached, he knew from his sack that he was underweight. The other pickers headed to the scales. But the slow picker dragged his sack behind a tree. He looked to his left and to his right and in front of him to see that no one was watching. Then he pulled down his coveralls. He opened the sack that represented a day's worth of work and his bent back and the pennies he would get for this bent back because he knew it did not amount to a hundred pounds. That was when he positioned the sack just so and relieved himself in the boss man's cotton for spite and the extra dime because he didn't like having to pick cotton anyway.

Ida Mae grew up isolated in the hills and never heard about these things until it was too late to do her any good. So she and her husband worked the piece of Pearson land apportioned to them with duty and resignation.

She herself could not afford a dress made out of the cotton that ruled their days. What she wore was pieced together from flour sacks that she boiled for hours until the flour company's name finally faded away. Burlap scratching her skin and the sun hunting her down, she dragged a sack behind her and plucked and picked, not figuring she was clothing a small piece of the world and never giving much thought to where the contents would land.

———

All around her in raw cabins leaning in different corners of the plantation were offshoots of her husband's family: half brothers, whole sisters, uncles, cousins, and their wives and husbands and children. A nephew, Robert Pulliam, whom they called Saint, helped them pick cotton sometimes. A cousin named Joe Lee was willing to help, but nobody much wanted him around because he was known for taking things that weren't his. A neighbor named Addie B. raised turkeys on the half for Mr. Edd and fretted over them when they went roosting in the woods. George's brother Willie was the patriarch because he was the oldest of them all.

Ida Mae tried to learn who all these people were and set about trying to become a wife. Willie's daughter, Callie Mae, showed her how to roll dough and make blackberry cobbler and tomato pie. They went picking blackberries on the running vine up and down the ditch bank to bake their cobblers with. George liked his greens with fatback or hog maws, and she learned how to cook them like he liked. She got up early and chopped wood as well as a man for the cooking fire. She put the meat on, and before the meat was brown and near ready to fall off the bone, she stuffed the greens in the pot and they cooked down and swam in pot liquor so good it made you want to swallow your tongue, as they used to say in their highest compliment to a cook. George would never just come out and say he liked it; he just ate, and that's how she knew he did.

Saturday was for washing and ironing. She hauled water in from the well and washed their clothes in the iron kettle. Sunday was for church. The rest of the time, she was out in the field beside George, hoeing or chopping or picking cotton around the army worms that nested in the leaves. It took fourteen hundred pounds to make a bale, and George needed to make a bale every two or three days in the picking season. Mr. Edd took half. "You know he comes first," Ida Mae would say years later.

They saved a little piece of land behind the house to plant corn and collards and peanuts and sweet potatoes. George hauled Ida Mae out to plant and till their little garden in the off hours, but Ida Mae didn't much want to be out there. They had been working all day and were planting the last of the corn. George dug a trough in the earth and told her to come behind him and scatter the kernels in the trench he made, which she did until she got tired of it. She had a pail full of seeds left. She threw the whole pail of kernels into the hole he dug and told him she was just fresh out of seeds.

In the fall, the corn came up. It was full and dense in one spot of land, the corn stalks elbowing one another in the row. George and Ida Mae ate well that season. George didn't have much to fuss about.

There were things she was good at and things she was not so good at, and she saved herself a lot of aggravation by knowing the difference between the two. She was good at raising chickens, and she kept one in a coop to press into service whenever she needed it. "If I wanted it for breakfast, I'd kill it in the morning," she said. "I go out there wring the neck off, have my hot water scalding, cut him up, and fry him for breakfast."

Nothing scared her. Like that morning at picking time when George had already left for the field. She lay in bed and heard a rattling in the kitchen. *"I know ain't nobody in that kitchen,"* she told herself, rising to see what it was. A speckler—a snake as long as a broom handle—had slithered over the edge of a bucket and was helping itself to the drinking water she had hauled in from the well. She backed out of the door and got the pitchfork and stuck it through him. She held up the pitchfork with the snake dangling from it and dropped it into the dirt yard. Then she took a stick and beat it until it stopped making *S*'s with its body. The snake was full of guinea eggs it had swallowed from the guinea nest, and it hadn't had a chance to wrap itself around a tree to break the eggs in it yet. The eggs broke when she killed it.

She told George about it when he dragged in from the field. He didn't praise her for her bravery or say much of anything. "I been seeing 'em all day" was all he said.

It was getting to be the 1930s. It was a hurting time, and the farm people almost couldn't give the cotton away. The value of what they harvested, the worth of their hard labor and the measure of their days, plummeted after the crash of 1929. A bale of cotton had gone for nearly thirty cents in the mid-1920s and for nearly seventeen cents in the late 1920s. By 1931, the planters couldn't get six cents for the same bale of cotton. The people in New York and Boston were not ordering up new seersucker suits and cotton pillowcases like they did just a few years before. The cotton ripened in the bud, but there was nobody to buy it. So the boss men went without new Model T Fords. The sharecroppers went without shoes.

Ida Mae fed the chickens and worked the field barefoot. She watched George haul in cotton with no assurance of what, if anything, the planter might give him for it and tried not to worry her mind over what she could not fix. Before long, she started feeling full around her belly. She didn't think much of it. She went about her chores and rode horseback when she went to visit her kin people. No horse was fast enough for Ida Mae, and she raced now like she always did. It wasn't good for the life that was growing inside her, and she miscarried riding those horses before she knew she was expecting.

Her belly got full again, and she didn't ride horses this time. She hated waddling into church with her flour sack dress pulling tight across the front and her belly sticking out. She was in the field when the thunder came. It started as a light knocking deep inside her. She ran into the house, and the thunder got violent. It shot to the top of the ceiling and hurled itself back into her. She got up and started walking, walking in a circle around the bed. The midwife came and watched her rock from foot to foot.

"I could see the pain comin' down on the top of the house and keep comin'," she said.

The men don't know what the women go through, was what she was thinking, don't feel the stab of lightning inside.

"Oughta be so they could," Ida Mae said.

She stopped her pacing and squatted beside the bed. She was on her knees. The life force reached out of her and into the light.

It was a girl. Ida Mae never wanted a girl. She was still thinking like a tomboy wanting to climb a tree. The baby had big eyes and a brown, narrow face like her husband's. They named her Velma. In time, Ida Mae took to her and held her close.

Within a year or so, she started feeling full again. It was another girl. They named her Elma but called her Baby Sis. Ida Mae took them to the field with her when it was time to plant. She set them both down in the shade of a plum tree. It got too hot for them out in the field. They were toddlers now. Ida Mae told them to sit still and then took her place behind her husband at the turnrow.

The sun bore down on Ida Mae and George, and soon they heard crying near the plum tree. It was Velma wailing and Baby Sis lying sick with half-eaten plums beside her. Velma had reached up and gotten her some, and Baby Sis ate them and got the flux, as the country people called whatever stomach ailment, poison, or virus had got into the baby. It was a perilous world in the early 1930s, even without Jim Crow. Dysentery, typhus, malaria all thrived in the backwoods of the Deep South before penicillin or common vaccines were invented. There were no doctors nearby, and, by the time they got Baby Sis to one, it was too late. They buried her in a little box at the church cemetery near Bewnie.

Ida Mae told herself that day that she would never leave a child of hers alone again.

In September of 1935, she finally got the boy she wanted. He had the brown, narrow face of her husband. When it came time to name him, a neighbor girl stepped forward. The girl looked after Velma when Ida Mae was in the field and took care of a little white boy in town when she was summoned to do so. His name was James Walter. George and Ida Mae had never laid eyes on the boy, but they named their son after him and hoped maybe good fortune would rain down on their son like it seemed to fall on the white people.

Not long after he had begun walking, something took over little James. He began rearing back and shaking all of a sudden. It could happen anytime, and it so worried Ida Mae that she went looking for advice.

"Next time he has a seizure," a neighbor lady told her, "whatever he got on, pull it off."

George had managed to scrape together a pair of shoes and socks and pants for his only son and was still paying on them. On a Sunday after church, when George was out in the field somewhere, little James had a shaking fit. Ida Mae pulled off his shoes and tore off his socks as the neighbor lady told her to do. Off came his little shirt and pants. She made a wood fire and held little James tight as she threw his clothes into the flames.

George got home, and she gave him the good news that she had cured little James. But that's not what stood out in George's mind.

"Whatchu doing burning up his shoes?" George asked her. George didn't have a decent pair himself.

Reason can't explain it, except that maybe little James outgrew whatever afflicted him or maybe it wasn't really seizures in the scientific sense of the word or maybe her belief that she had exorcised the thing actually killed it. In any case, whatever James had, it never came back after she burned his clothes to cinders.

———

A new year rang in. It was 1937. It looked to be no better than the year before. They were calling it the Depression now. People took to begging and scraping to eat. A man down the road started stealing hogs to sell and eat as his own. He was white and a friend, so to speak, to George. He rounded up somebody's hogs one day and came by George and Ida Mae's to get George to help skin them.

George didn't want to get blamed for somebody else's misdeeds. He could get killed for stealing a white man's hogs. He told the man to do it himself. The man didn't like hearing no. George and the man argued, and the man stormed off.

"I'll be back," he said. "I'm a fix you."

Chickasaw County had a sheriff, but calling him would have never crossed George's mind. No sheriff would take a colored man's side against a white man, no matter who was right. George called out to Ida Mae.

"Ida Mae, you take the kids and go on in the house," he said. "I'm a sit right here till they come back."

He sat on the porch waiting with his shotgun on his knee. He looked out for an open-bed truck trailing dust in the road or a car packed with men looking for trouble. Ida Mae crouched down and tried to still little James and Velma. George waited and waited. But they never came. "The next day or two," Ida Mae said, "him and George back friends again, I reckon, getting the hogs."

People learned to want less and live with whatever they had. The boss men said there was little to nothing to give at settlement time. They told the day pickers they wouldn't be needing them. The cast-off croppers and field hands moved from place to place. They walked to the next farm up the road to see if they could use an extra hand and to the relatives who might make a place for them in their cabin. Mr. Edd kept George and Ida Mae on. They were good workers, Ida Mae's picking notwithstanding, and he was an optimist. But now there were five people in their little sharecropper cabin. Besides them and Velma and James, they had taken in a boarder, so to speak. It was George's sister Indiana. She helped with the picking of crops and the raising of turkeys, and she slept by the door in the front room.

———

In the spring, when George and Ida Mae planted cotton and prayed for rain, the turkey hen laid her eggs. "She'd set there and set there," Ida Mae said. "Just sit there about three or four weeks. She'd get up, shake herself off, and go get her some water, dust water all over her and do round and all, take a bath, I reckon, what it was. She'd be setting while we planted cotton."

By the time the cotton was in the ground, the chicks poked out of their shells and required Ida Mae's attention. Ida Mae and Addie B. and other women on the Pearson plantation scooped up the chicks and tended them for Mr. Edd. He would be coming back just before Thanksgiving to take half of however many turkeys each woman managed to raise.

Ida Mae pulled off the beak crust that they came into the world with and crushed corn for them to eat because they were too little to eat feed corn. The hawks circled overhead, waiting for her to leave, ready to swoop down and pick off a baby chick and fly back into the air before you knew it.

Ida Mae didn't worry about the hawks. She knew the hens moved in a flock and didn't leave their babies like humans do.

"You know a hen will take up for her chickens more so than people will take up for one another," Ida Mae said. "Whenever a old hawk would come along—you heard talk how a hawk will hover and all the chicks run under her wing—she hugs them and she sticks up for 'em and keep a funny noise, and you knew that hawk was somewhere around."

She trusted God and nature more than any man and learned to be a better person watching the lower creatures of the earth. "The ant see a crumb, he can't carry it himself," Ida Mae said. "Don't you know another ant will come and help him? They better than people."

Addie B. and the other women fretted over their turkeys, worried when they went off and when they took forever coming back because Mr. Edd was going to want his turkeys soon. Ida Mae let her turkeys run free and pick after bugs and ants and twigs in the dirt. They went exploring out in the woods and roosted wherever they pleased. And when they came back, she threw corn at their feet.

The turkeys grew big and plump as September approached, and the land was turning white with cotton.

EUSTIS, FLORIDA, 1939
GEORGE SWANSON STARLING

A FLATBED TRUCK creaked down a highway through rattlesnake scrub and okra growing wild in the field. George Starling should not have been on that truck. He should have been in a college classroom up in Tallahassee. But his father said he'd had enough schooling, and schools nearby did not allow colored students. So Lil George went and got himself a wife out of spite and love, too, and had to feed her now, and so was sitting on a flatbed truck en route to the groves instead of in the library stacks at a college in the state capital.

The truck was on its way between the groves on a chill morning at picking season. It was hauling men to pick fruit for fresh juice and frozen concentrate, for gift boxes of temple oranges and ruby grapefruit, and the perfect balls of citrus stacked high on grocery shelves for people in New York to pick through.

The owners of the groves rode their dogs in the covered front seats safe from the wind. The pickers rode on the flatbed truck with the frost cutting their faces. Twenty or thirty men hunched on the open barge, their legs dangling over the sides of it and a stack of ladders tied loose along the rim.

George sat pinned between the regular pickers, who were missing teeth and taking liberties with the language and knew more about picking than he ever cared to know. They got a kick out of bouncing over potholes, grove to grove, next to the college boy. They looked to be the smart ones now, hadn't had to squint over any textbooks or waste time in somebody's high school. And here they were carrying a bushel sack in the same flatbed truck as Lil George. Back when he was still in school and picking only during semester break, they started calling him "Schoolboy."

"Schoolboy," one of them said, "I don't know whatchu goin' to school fuh. You right out'chere with us. I ain't went so far as the sixth grade, and I can pick more fruit in one hour than you pick all day. You ain't had to go no twelfth grade to learn how to do this."

"Yeah, you right," George said. "But the difference between you and me, is I can leave from out here, and you can't. When the opportunity presents itself, I can leave."

That was easy to say when he was back and forth to Tallahassee, calling himself a freshman and then a sophomore and looking like he could do anything in the world. Now he was picking because he had to, no different from them.

He told himself that this picking situation was a temporary setback and kept himself busy doing whatever came up. Some days, the high school had him substitute for a sick teacher. He had more education than most colored people in town anyway. He sold insurance on the side to the colored people out in the woods. But the groves were all there was most days, and he climbed the flatbed like every other colored citizen who could use the money, which was just about all of them at one time or another.

Fruit was the currency of central Florida. The land was given over to citrus trees, groves of them spanning the low hills from Eustis up to

Ocala and down to Orlando. Tourism hadn't yet bloomed the way it would decades later in central Florida, and Eustis, Ocala, and even Orlando were just places to pass through on the way to Miami. Each year in the late thirties and early forties, some two million tons of oranges and grapefruit were coming out of the state, most of it from the region where George lived.

The people who picked the fruit and the big owners of the groves were often at odds with each other, one side poor, one side landed, one needing more money than the other was willing to give. But they agreed on one thing: they wanted the trees heavy with oranges and the people of the North flush and hungry because then there would be work enough for everyone.

So they pampered the trees like infants. When a hard freeze afflicted the groves, the people burned logs and rubber tires and lit the oil heaters to keep the orange trees warm. They prayed for a miracle like the one at a grove they called Ole Natural. A big freeze had settled in back in 1895, and most of the other groves looked as if they had been set on fire after it left. But Ole Natural survived the big freeze, and its orange trees came back on their own.

Lake County held a high place in the Citrus Belt and once was the orange capital of the world. But Lil George never took it that seriously and never got but so good at picking. He could never claim to have picked the most bushels in the least amount of time. It was piecework, and the winners of the race were not necessarily the quickest minds but the fastest hands. George had a quick mind.

———

In the late fall, a crowd gathered before the sun came up, when the fog hung close to the earth. The people stood watching at the corner of Bates and Palmetto and in front of the pool hall over in East town, near Egypt. They waited in the wet dark for the flatbed truck to roll up. The foreman climbed down and picked out the best pickers for his crew. The foremen were the middlemen between the packinghouses and the pickers, and both sides might have cause to distrust them now and then. They chose the pickers and oversaw the picking and each had their own way of supervising. It might be Oscar Lipscomb or Uncle John Fashaw or a man they called Mr. Pat choosing his pickers for the season.

George hoped to get on the Blye brothers' crew. They were ten years older than he was. They knew their way around the juke joints and the raccoon woods around Eustis. One of them was named Arnette, but they called him Whisper because he had got his throat cut and could speak no louder than that.

The other brother, Reuben, towered over the tallest of men. He had a stone face, a long series of wives, and had seen just about everything. When he was a little boy, an uncle told him to come help him with an errand. The two of them rode out into the woods and came to a stop at a tree. A colored man was hanging dead from a limb. The uncle needed Reuben's help cutting the rope and getting the limp, lynched body down. Reuben was ten years old. He would never forget that.

When Reuben got big, he fled to New York, worked at a tombstone factory in Brooklyn, on the 9W highway through Kingston up into Albany. He worked crushing tomatoes at a ketchup factory and had seen so many of the unmentionable things that got mangled into the ketchup that he never ate ketchup again. Now he was back in Eustis working as a foreman in the groves. He looked straight at you and through you and had a way of making women forget their husbands when they saw him.

It was a buyer's market in the picking world. There were always plenty more people who wanted to pick than there was room or need for in the groves. The lucky ones loaded onto the truck, their legs dangling from the rim of the flatbed.

At the grove, they each picked a number out of a hat and went to the row with that number. They got paid by how many boxes of fruit they picked by sunset and had to keep up with little tickets to prove what they had picked. If the row was thick with fruit, it would be a good day. They could stand at the underskirt and fill a two-bushel box. If it was sparse, they had to climb into two or three trees to get that much.

It tempted good people to try to outtrick one another. You looked for a way out. You learned to watch everybody and the rows coming up. The rule was that when you finished yours, you moved in order to the next row available. If it was a dud row like the one you were working, you did your best to avoid it.

"If that next row is a bad row," George said, "and you on a bad row, and here's somebody else by you on a bad row, you lag back, you keep watching them. You let them get through first, ahead of you, so they can get that bad row. Then you hurry up and get through."

If the next one up was thick with fruit and "you on a bad row, you run through it," George said. "But you be sure they done moved over before you leave your row. You get cagey. It's little tricks in all this."

Some men could pick a hundred boxes a day. They called them high rollers. George never managed more than sixty-five or seventy. He never cared enough about it to get proficient.

They set the ladders in the tree, ladders sixteen and twenty feet high, sometimes spliced like extension cords and leaning forty feet up, a full four stories, along the spine of the tree. They had to set them so the ladder wouldn't kick when they reached the top and wouldn't split the tree in two, which was liable to happen with a ladder set in the fork of a young bud. They learned to plant their ladders deep in the soil.

The trees were wet from the rain, and George and the pickers had to balance themselves on the slick limbs of the old seedlings. They disappeared into the branches with a bushel sack on their shoulders and a clipper in their hand and only came down when the sack was full and their shoulders ached and they were sick from the sight of fruit. Tangerines, tangelos, temple oranges, navel oranges, Valencia oranges, seeded grapefruit, seedless grapefruit, red navels, ruby reds, lemons, and kumquats. If he had to pick, which he did, George would rather pick grapefruit because they filled a box quicker. But the packinghouses knew that, too. So they paid less for grapefruit than just about anything else.

Up and down the ladders they went, working top to bottom, snipping fruit and filling boxes. Sometimes they heard a voice cry out way down the grove; a picker had come across a wasp nest and pulled at it instead of an orange. Every now and then, they heard a thud and then a cry. A limb had snapped. Somebody fell out of a tree, broke an arm or leg or neck.

George climbed the high limbs of four or five grown seedlings one morning and was climbing deep into the next. The foreman that day was an old colored man named Deacon John Fashaw. They called him Uncle John. George knew him from Gethsemane Baptist Church. The deacon oversaw the harvest of some of the groves at the Eichelberger Packing Company. He called George out of the tree in the middle of the grove.

"Number fourteen!" he yelled.

Deacon Fashaw presided over his pickers with a suckle from an orange tree. It looked like a switch a mother whipped her children with. He called George over to him with the suckle in his hand.

"Now, number fourteen," the deacon said, looking up into the limbs at George.

"Yes, sir."

"Come down here. Bring ya ladder."

"Dog, what Uncle John want?" George said under his breath and then, out loud, "I'll be there, Uncle John."

If he didn't move fast, next thing he'd know, Deacon Fashaw would be there shaking his ladder from under the tree.

"Come down, young man. Come down."

George climbed down, and Deacon Fashaw swooshed the switch at him. Anybody else, and George would have had him on the ground. But it was Deacon Fashaw, and the men respected his position too much to fight him.

"Now, you bring your ladder back here. I told you to bring your ladder back here."

George ran back to get the ladder and followed Deacon Fashaw back to the first tree he had picked.

"Now, you see that orange up there in the top of the tree?"

"Yeah, Uncle John."

"Well, you know they want that orange in New York, and you done left it up there in that tree. And I don't like it. And Mr. Eichelberger don't like it. Mr. Eichelberger don't like it, and I ain't gon' have it. Now, you put that ladder back in that tree, and you go right on up there and pick that orange right now."

Deacon Fashaw stood and watched George position his ladder and climb into the tree for that one orange as the other pickers peered through the branches. It was all part of Uncle John's plan. "He let you get four or five trees away so you have to drag that back," George said. "You probably done lost five or six boxes while you doing that. You do that two or three times, you soon get the message that 'I'm gonna be sure I clean my tree before I leave it.' I mean clean it."

They moved from grove to grove in a single day. The flatbed truck rumbled down a highway past the bean fields and the turpentine stills. Midday, they finished one grove and were moving to the next. The truck reached an intersection and swung a hard left. The ladders broke from their lashes and shifted under the men. The loose ladders pushed the men off the open bed of the truck and onto the rough surface of the highway as if they had been shot from a gun.

George felt himself thrown to the gravel. His heels nearly hit his back, and he tried to break the fall with his elbow and knee. Half the workers were on the ground. Some had fallen onto their heads and were lying unconscious. A man named Nathan Bailey was never able to work again. He got two hundred dollars for his injuries after the men petitioned the packing company for help. George got twelve dollars and forty-eight cents for his swollen knee and elbow, which he would re-member for as long as he lived; they sent him two payments of six dol-lars and twenty-four cents each.

Most of the men took it and were grateful. George wasn't. The work was hard, and now it was dangerous. "You not getting anything to begin with, you know, at the best," he said.

George had some schooling, and the old men who teased him for it put their pride in their sack when they thought the packinghouse was cheating them.

"Schoolboy, look a here," a man said. "Tell me how much I got for my work. Here my envelope."

George took it and looked at it and turned to the man. "How many boxes of oranges did you pick?" George asked. "How many boxes of tangerines did you pick? How many boxes of grapefruit?"

The man told him what he thought he had picked, and George did the math.

"No, you three dollars short. They done cheated you out of three dol-lars somewhere 'cause if you picked the number of boxes you say you picked, you didn't get paid for all of it."

Two or three days' pay had disappeared. It was hard to keep up. Each kind of fruit paid a different rate—four cents a box for grapefruit one day, ten cents a box for tangerines the next, six cents a box for oranges. If they didn't know how much they picked of each kind of fruit or lost the little ticket that said what they had picked or if the foreman added the numbers on the ticket wrong, whether on purpose or by acci-dent, the pickers didn't get what little they were due.

"Sometimes they would tell you that they paying one thing and when you get your pay, you got less," George said. "And if you couldn't figure, you didn't know the difference. They were very good at that. They promise you four cents for a box of grapefruit, and you get two cents."

The pickers took whatever they got. Some asked about the difference but didn't dare press it. Some wrote it off, blamed themselves, said they must have been the ones who'd lost their ticket. There was no point in protesting. There wasn't enough work as it was. It was the Depression. And for every man waiting at the corner of Bates and Palmetto in the black wet morning at picking time, hoping to board a truck to the groves, there were ten more out there hoping he would miss it.

MONROE, LOUISIANA, 1935
ROBERT JOSEPH PERSHING FOSTER

————

PERSHING WAS SIXTEEN and making his first trip out of Monroe on his own on a bus ticket his brother Madison had given him for graduation. Pershing had just finished the eleventh grade, which was as far as you could go if you were colored in Louisiana, and he was beside himself with anticipation.

The sign on the front of the bus said ST. LOUIS and Pershing climbed on board with his suitcase in his hand and his back propped straight as if he were stepping onto the *Queen Mary* and going to France. He dusted the folds of his tweed suit and headed down the central aisle of the bus in search of a seat. The bus was not going to take him to the Big North of southern dreams but to a modest city in a border state where his brother was serving out his medical residency, and well enough out of the South.

He scanned the aisle to find a place for himself. His eye caught the wooden shingle with the metal prongs on the bottom, the shingle that said COLORED on one side and WHITE on the other. It was set into holes at the top of a seat back toward the latter half of the bus. He didn't like seeing it, but he knew to expect it. He took a seat behind the wooden shingle and looked out the window at the view.

Those white and colored shingles were as much a part of the southern landscape as cotton growing in the field. Each state and city had a different requirement or custom to signal how the races were to be separated and to what extent the races were to be divided. In North Carolina, white and colored passengers could not occupy "contiguous seats on the same bench." Virginia prohibited the two races from sitting side by side on the same bench unless all other seats were filled. Several states required that the placard saying WHITE or COLORED be "in plain letters, not less than two inches high." In Houston, the race to which the seat belonged was posted on the back of the seat. In Georgia, the penalty for willfully riding in the wrong seat was a fine of a thousand dollars or six months in prison. Colored passengers were assigned to the front of the railcar on the train but to the rear of other conveyances to, in the words of the mayor of Birmingham, do "away with the disagreeable odors that would necessarily follow the breezes."

The bus headed north along the Mississippi River into Arkansas, picking up more people at stops along the way. The seats began to fill. More white passengers than colored seemed to be boarding. They had taken up some of the seats in the very front and were spreading further back. Now, each time new white people got on, they picked up the wooden shingle and inserted it in the seat back where Pershing was sitting. It seemed only the white people could touch the shingle and set the musical chairs in motion.

"Go 'head, boy. Move on back," the driver told him.

Pershing rustled himself up from the seat he was in. Gathered his things. Looked for an empty space behind him. Moved back a row. Sometimes the new passenger took up a whole row by himself, forcing Pershing back just so the newcomer wouldn't have to sit next to anyone else.

At every stop, they had to move again until the colored passengers were now crowded into a few seats in the back and Pershing found himself in the very last row.

It was early summer, and road dust flew into the windows and rushed to the back seat, where Pershing in his brand-new tweed suit was pressed among the other colored passengers.

The dust coated the tweed and his skin and his hair, and Pershing found it unbearable, packed as he was like livestock.

"I was dressed as good as I could be," Pershing said years later. "And I felt very down that I had to submit to this."

He looked around him at the other colored passengers to his left and to his right, grown people, beaten down, hunched in their seats. They dropped their eyes, and he dropped his.

"Some have endured, and that's all they've known," Pershing said. "They don't expect anything better, and nobody's demanding anything better. You wouldn't have survived if you had done too much demanding anyway."

It was a long ride, there was no toilet on the bus, and the back seats took every bump on the road. Before Pershing could make it to St. Louis, he passed his urine and sat in his soaked tweed pants and felt lower than he had in his entire short life.

———

St. Louis was a blur. Madison carted Pershing all over St. Louis, took him into Homer G. Phillips Hospital, where Madison was a resident and where the nurses fawned over the cute little brother with the thick eyelashes and waves in his hair. Madison reminded him it was time to get ready for college. For a while, when he was thirteen or fourteen, Pershing actually thought he didn't have to go. He told his mother that one day.

"Mama, I'm gonna stop school."

He didn't realize how impossible that was, his father being principal and all.

Ottie indulged him.

"Baby, why are you gonna stop school?"

"I want some of the things the other boys got."

"Like what?"

"Like clothes."

"Well, what do you want?"

Pershing couldn't think of much in particular that he didn't already have.

"I want a suit. I want a pair of shoes."

"Now, I tell you what you do," his mother said. "You save your little money you get from the milk. Now, get you a little job after school or in the summer, and you work and save your money. And when you got half of whatever it cost, I'll give you the other half."

Pershing listened.

"And you don't pay down on anything," she told him. "You can keep your money as well as that white man can."

––––––––

The nearest college was right in Monroe, across the railroad tracks from where they lived. Northeast Louisiana College had a brand-new campus with reasonable fees, built with taxpayer money, to which his parents' meager salaries contributed. Students who looked like Pershing weren't permitted there. So the family debated where Pershing would go.

His mother wanted him at Morehouse, the most prestigious college in the country for colored men. It was in Atlanta, which might as well have been Paris, and she wanted the biggest she could get for her baby. All these years she had saved up her teaching money, kept it in a chifforobe with a key, which the children knew not to touch. It would be their future. The last time she opened the chifforobe, it was to send Leland to Morehouse. It was expensive, and he had not fared well. Professor Foster blamed the school, but anyone who knew Leland knew the trouble was with Leland, whom the women called Woo and who was brilliant, beloved, and weak to life's temptations. They had wasted their precious,

second-class, colored teacher's wages on Leland at Morehouse. Now
Ottie was trying to send Pershing there, and Pershing wanted to go.

"No, you don't go to Morehouse," Professor Foster said.

"You'll go to Morehouse," his mother said.

So it was settled. He would go to Morehouse. But the family had to
save up the extra money it would take. Pershing would have to spend
two years at the lesser-known alma mater of his parents, Leland College, before living out his mother's dream.

The summer after his freshman year at Leland, he needed a job. He
heard the furniture store downtown needed janitors. He dressed and
went down and got in line with all the other colored boys wanting to
work.

The white foreman called him to the front when it was his turn for an
interview.

"Boy, do you go to school?" the foreman asked.

"Yes, sir, I do," he said. "I just completed my first year at Leland College."

"Boy, if you go to college, you don't need a job as a janitor."

Few people, white or black, in Ouachita County had the chance to go
to college. Resentments ran deep, especially when it came to a colored
boy getting to go when some southerners were still debating whether
colored people were worth educating at all. Too many educated colored
people, and it would upset the whole balance of power in the caste system and give other colored people ideas.

The man turned to some other boys in line, who weren't in school
and didn't need tuition, and hired them. Pershing had a long memory,
and he would nurse that wound for years. Here he was trying to make
something of himself, and the invisible hand was punishing the ambitious, and rewarding the servile to keep colored people in their place.

Later in the summer, he went looking for work at the sawmill.

He saw a classmate there from high school and was told the work
wasn't too hard. It was stacking wood staves to make barrels. Pershing
asked the foreman for a job. There was nothing available, he was told.
He was getting desperate. He spotted his friend stacking staves.

"Show me how to do this."

The friend showed him what to do, and Pershing worked beside
him. He looked up and saw the foreman watching him. Pershing pretended not to see him, worked even harder. The foreman left, and,
when he came back, Pershing was still at work. At the end of the day,

the foreman hired him. Pershing finished out the summer stacking staves, not minding the hard work and not finding it demeaning.

"Sometimes," he said, "you have to stoop to conquer."

————

Morehouse was a heavenly place. Colored boys racing straight-backed and self-important in their sweater vests, hair brushed back with a hint of a center part. Arriving at chapel to sit with their respective fraternities and daring not take the wrong row. There was a sister school, Spelman, the women sealed off in their cloistered dormitories and emerging in fitted dresses and gloves to be paired with Morehouse men, who were the only men worthy of them. There was the graduate school, Atlanta University, where the brightest of both schools were expected to go to take their master's and doctorates. It was all too perfect for words.

Whatever future there was for colored America, they believed themselves to be it, and they carried themselves accordingly. Then there was Atlanta. Too many colored doctors and lawyers and businessmen to count, living in brick houses set back from the road and with staircases inside, driving fancy cars and not apologizing for it.

"I saw blacks living like people ought to live," Pershing would say years later.

Atlanta was big enough to get lost in. Enough colored people to be anonymous. The colored people drew a fence around themselves and manufactured a world so grand they told themselves they didn't want whatever Jim Crow was keeping from them.

Pershing was at peace. It was the fall of 1937.

After the first homecoming game, Pershing and a science classmate by the name of Morris Williams took two girls out dancing. They both chipped in the money they needed and bought sloe gin for the four of them and whiled away the night.

They took the girls home and were walking back to the dormitory. As they crossed the intersection of Fair and Ashby, Pershing slowed down to a stop in the middle of the street. He was wobbling from the gin. He stood and looked around. He was in Atlanta in the middle of the night, far from the stooping and yessums of Monroe. He was surrounded by a whole campus of somebodies like him and doing whatever he pleased.

He stood in the street, half drunk and half dreaming. Cars slowed and honked, and he paid them no mind.

"Boy, come on," his friend said. "Get out the street. That car's gon' hit you, you drunk fool."

"Yes, I'm drunk," Pershing said. "I ain't in Monroe, don't nobody know me, and I don't give a damn.

"I'm free," he said.

Pershing did not know precisely where he would end up or how. But he knew at that moment that he would never live in another country Jim Crow town again. He would do whatever it took to get as far away as he could.

"That bug got in me," Pershing would later say. "I wanted, I wanted to get out."

————

Shadows still hung over him. His big brother Leland was rarely in class but was a four-letter man at Morehouse and a star pitcher on the baseball team. The Spelman women called out his name on the yard. And then there was Madison, his oldest brother. Madison still hung over him from afar. Madison was a doctor. Madison sang. Madison dressed. The women loved Madison.

"So you hit school," Pershing would remember years later, "and 'That's Foster's brother. That's Foster's brother.' It's hard to be the little one. You fightin' for identity. And everybody discussing everything you did. And when it was bad, they blew it up."

Pershing threw himself into the one thing that brought him the most attention. He had a voice as rich as an organ, so he joined the school choir. He started singing solo at the Christmas concert at Sisters Chapel at Spelman and made a name for himself. In time, people didn't ask about Leland and baseball as much anymore or about his brother the doctor.

In his senior year, sometime in 1939, Pershing arrived for choir practice one day when the head of the music department, a man by the name of Harold Stotford, called him over. They stood in the rehearsal room as students gathered to practice.

"Foster, wait here a minute," Professor Stotford said. "I want you to meet this young lady."

A young woman of modest dress and perfect manners stepped forward. She was a gifted pianist and a newer member of the choir. She was the color of the buttermilk he used to make with his mother and had brown hair brushing her shoulder. She looked out from wire-rimmed glasses that were an accurate barometer of how studious she was.

Pershing recognized her instantly. She could have been a celebrity on campus had she not had the breeding and sweet nature not to make a fuss of her position. She was the beloved only daughter of the president of Atlanta University, the campus's graduate school, and was well known to anyone with the least awareness of social standing.

Her name was Alice Clement.

She was a sophomore at Spelman. Her family lived in a mansion high on a hill on university grounds. It was redbrick with black shutters. The estate was called Hickory Hill and looked like Mount Vernon. Her father, President Rufus Clement, had a car and driver. Her cotillions and bridge parties were chronicled in the society pages of the *Atlanta Daily World*, the colored newspaper in town. She was bookish and would not likely have been made Miss Spelman had she even cared to run, but she would know how to throw a dinner party for twelve. She was the embodiment of most everything an ambitious colored man of the day was trained to want.

"This is the daughter of President Clement," Professor Stotford said, "who happens to be that gentleman there. President of Atlanta University. I want you to meet Alice Clement."

"How do you do?" Pershing said. He made a mental note to himself to make the most of his good fortune.

At the next choir rehearsal, he made it his business to start a conversation with her in the hope that something might come of it. She finally asked him to take her to a party. He was all too happy to oblige.

He put on his wittiest, most charming self, and soon the boy from Monroe, Louisiana, was courting the quiet and self-contained daughter of a university president. Pershing escorted her to parties, took her to dances with a foursome. He was spending more time up at Hickory Hill and gaining automatic admission to the world of the most influential colored people in all of Atlanta.

Pershing Foster was not what Rufus Early Clement would have had in mind for his only daughter. Clement had risen from a bellhop and delivery boy in Kentucky to become the head of one of the most elite colored universities in the country and its longest-serving president. He was a square-jawed, politically astute academic who rarely smiled and wore a look of professorial detachment at both the lectern and the many social engagements that demanded his attendance. He met regularly with the likes of Eleanor Roosevelt and Paul Robeson in his capacity not only as a university president but as a leading figure among the colored bourgeoisie in the South.

Clement gained a reputation as a cautious and incurious steward whom history will record as the man who ousted W. E. B. Du Bois, the leading black intellectual of his time, from a professorship at Atlanta University after years of clashing egos and temperaments.

W. E. B. Du Bois arrived at Atlanta University, already in his seventies and with plans for an ambitious study on race relations, at around the same time that Clement was confronted with this new boy interested in his only daughter. Clement would be at odds with Du Bois almost from the start, perhaps threatened by the long shadow of his celebrity or put off by the elder man's impertinent disregard for Clement, who was thirty years younger than Du Bois. But it was just as likely a contest between the accommodating pragmatism of the southern-born Clement and the impatient radicalism of the northern-bred Du Bois. The two men were the very embodiment of the North-South divide among black intellectuals.

In any case, Clement blocked Du Bois's every move, even standing in the way of a thousand-dollar grant Du Bois was pursuing, according to Du Bois's biographer David Levering Lewis. Du Bois suspected Clement of sabotaging him and said he "regretted the necessity of having to work with a president who seemed incapable of appreciating the great opportunity facing the university." For his part, Clement complained that Du Bois "had become extremely difficult" and that he believed Du Bois's age was impairing him. In 1943, Clement found a way to get rid of Du Bois altogether by invoking, with the support of the board of trustees he had lobbied, an arbitrary loophole requiring compulsory retirement at sixty-five. He informed Du Bois that he would be retired when his contract ended at the close of the school year.

"The result of this action was disastrous," Du Bois wrote in his autobiography. "Not only was a great plan of scientific work killed at birth, but my own life was thrown into confusion." Du Bois "fought back in despair" against his termination, Lewis wrote. Students from Morehouse, Spelman, Clark, and Atlanta University rose up in support of Du Bois in a scornful letter to President Clement: "Our regret," they wrote, "is that we did not have more courses under him, and the students who follow us will not have the opportunity which we have had in absorbing his rich experience and inspiration."

Du Bois was beside himself. "There was no earthly reason why this wish of mine should not have been granted and applauded," he said.

His northern friends thought they knew what the trouble was. "He's buried himself in the South too long," Arthur Spingarn, the NAACP president, concluded, "protecting ideas nobody but he understands, and raising hope for change which may be comprehended in a hundred years."

Du Bois returned north, to New York, where he took a position as director of special research at the NAACP, the organization he had co-founded thirty-four years before, and moved into an apartment on Sugar Hill in Harlem.

For his part, Rufus Clement had proven that, even if out of his own insecurities and desire for control, he could be a cunning and formidable adversary. He had prevailed in the short run, regardless of the consequences or of which side of history he would ultimately fall on.

————

As for this new young man at his doorstep wanting to court his only daughter, Clement was still sizing him up. Pershing was respectful and well mannered, as Dr. Clement would have expected of any Morehouse man. He was a math major—smart, clearly. But on the face of it, Pershing was just another student who had worked waiting tables at the cafeteria and who was just now making a name for himself as a soloist in the choir. He had come from some country town out in Louisiana. Someone said his parents taught school or something. Dr. Clement had never heard of the Fosters, nor had he any reason to recognize Monroe.

No young man with the courage to come courting his daughter would have had an easy time of it. Worse still, this was not looking like a move up in Dr. Clement's estimation, so he looked judgingly through his spectacles.

But Pershing told of the great plans he had for himself. He talked about pursuing his doctorate in biology at Atlanta University. Or maybe going to a graduate school up north, like the University of Michigan or the University of Chicago. Pershing figured that southern elites always loved those northern status symbols even if they didn't care to live there themselves. Maybe he would get a scholarship to go. Then he would apply for a fellowship in New York, maybe. His brother was a doctor, internal medicine, and he was considering that, too, by the way.

Pershing was talking the president's language, the vocabulary of upward mobility. He had potential. He was ambitious, if nothing else. And Alice—quiet, demure Alice—had taken to him. He had a street wit about him that made her laugh. He was the life of the party she never was, and she seemed content to bask in his light.

Pershing graduated Morehouse with a major in math and a minor in biology in the spring of 1939 and sang solo at commencement. He took up graduate studies at Atlanta University while Alice completed her time at Spelman. He was moving into a world where great things were expected of him. Dr. Clement looked for him to make good on his promise to become someone worthy of his daughter. Madison wanted his baby brother to follow in his footsteps. His mother, too, wanted a second doctor in the family and knew her youngest had it in him. So he applied to Meharry Medical College in Nashville and was accepted. His mother sent him the registration fee.

"I sat awake all night," he said. "Do I want to go? Or don't I want to go?"

If he could have done anything in the world at that moment, he would have dropped it all and gone up north to New York or out west to California. He'd always had a thing for California. He would go into show business, maybe, and sing and perform onstage. The audiences would love him, and he would be who and where he was meant to be. But he kept his dreams to himself and did what was expected of him. He sent in the registration fee and would start medical school in the South, in the state of Tennessee, a place far from his dreams, in the fall.

A Thin Light Far Away

In the winter of 1919, when Ida Mae was trailing her father out to the field, George and Pershing were learning to crawl, and the first wave of migrants was stirring to life, an astronomer made a startling discovery. The astronomer, named Edwin Hubble, working out of the University of Chicago, looked through one of the most powerful telescopes of his time.

What he saw would eventually become the most significant astronomical find of the century and would come to parallel the awakening of an isolated people in his own country. It would confirm what for generations had been whispered of but dismissed as impossible. It occurred near the start of a long pilgrimage of Americans seeking to escape their own harsh, known world.

Hubble identified a star that was far, far away and was not the same sun that fed life on Earth.

It was another sun.

And it would prove for the first time in human history that there were galaxies other than our own, that the universe was much bigger than humans had ever imagined, that there were, in fact, other suns.

THE AWAKENING

You sleep over a volcano,
which may erupt at any moment.
—LAURA ARNOLD, DESCRIBING
THE SOUTH IN A DEBATE
ON THE MERITS OF MIGRATION,
TWO WEEKS BEFORE SHE HERSELF
LEFT NORTH CAROLINA
FOR WASHINGTON, D.C.

I am in the darkness
of the south
and I am trying
my best to get out.
O please help me
to get out of
this low down county
I am counted no more thin a dog
help me please help me.
—AN UNIDENTIFIED
LETTER WRITER FROM
BIRMINGHAM, ALABAMA

CHICKASAW COUNTY, MISSISSIPPI,
LATE SEPTEMBER–EARLY OCTOBER 1937

———

ADDIE B., who lived down the road on the same plantation as Ida Mae, rose early to feed the turkeys at her cabin across the field. Addie B. always fretted about her turkeys. She looked all over and called out to them. But there was no clucking or nipping or kicking of dust. The yard was barren. The turkeys were gone. Mr. Edd, the boss man over all of them, would be coming for his turkeys soon, to sell in time for Thanksgiving. There would be no explaining the disappearance to Mr. Edd. The economics were simple. The turkeys were money when money was the one thing nobody had. The punishment—she did not want to think about the punishment. Besides, she had an idea of what happened to her inventory. She decided to tell Mr. Edd her suspicions before he could ask. Mr. Edd rounded up some men.

Later that night, around nine or ten o'clock, the pounding started on Ida Mae's door. It was like the sound of wild dogs trailing raw meat. It seemed far away at first, and then it drew closer, mad fists beating the bare face of the cabin. The cabin was dark, and Ida Mae was asleep. She was alone in the house with little Velma and James and her sister-in-law Indiana, who was meek and of little help. Her husband was not yet back from his errands in town. She threw back the coverlet and fingered the sides of the walls to get to the front door. She stumbled past the two little ones, who were, by some miracle, still asleep, stepped around the hearth and between the two beds on each side of the door. Indiana, in the bed closest to the ruckus, got up to follow her and stood behind her and watched.

Ida Mae cracked open the door and saw the men, four or five of them with chains and shotguns. She recognized the boss man, Mr. Edd. And she recognized his friend Mr. Willie Jim, another planter, but could not make out the faces of the others standing before her in the middle of the night.

She tried to dispense with them, told them her husband wasn't in and she didn't know when he would be back. That wasn't why they were there. Willie Jim stepped forward to speak for them all. They wanted to know if Joe Lee was in her house.

Joe Lee was her husband's cousin, who lived further down the road and would have had no business there that time of night, which is what she told them. He worked the land like the rest of them and, though well into his twenties, still lived on his father's farm. He had a reputation for taking things that weren't his. She said she hadn't seen him.

"*Joe Lee is in there. And we want him outta there.*"

"*What'd he do?*"

"*That's alright, we want him outta there.*"

They had searched the other sharecropper cabins. Somebody said they saw Joe Lee escape to her house. Willie Jim was getting agitated, thought she was ornery, disputing them like she was, and raised up his chain and drew it back to hurl at her. Mr. Edd stepped forward and told him not to. He liked George and Ida Mae, and he needed that cotton out of the field.

"*Don't you hit her,*" Mr. Edd said.

"*That's alright. Let 'em hit me,*" Ida said, stiffening herself.

"*No, he ain't gon' hit you now,*" he told her.

Willie Jim stepped back, reminded of what they had come for. The men fanned out, their heavy boots clomping the old wood boards on the porch. They surrounded the house and ran toward the back door of the kitchen, the cabin's only other way out, and caught Joe Lee trying to get away. He had fled into the house as Ida Mae slept. He had darted past Indiana as she lay in bed in the front room. But Indiana was too afraid to tell anybody.

"Why ain't you tell me you saw Joe Lee come through here?" Ida Mae asked her afterward. Then she thought about it and realized that if they had caught her in a lie, it would have been worse. And so the two of them concluded it was best that Indiana knew but didn't tell and that Ida Mae didn't know and didn't lie.

Ida Mae couldn't go back to sleep, and she couldn't wait for her husband to get back home. Finally, she heard a motor rumbling outside. She ran out to get him.

"Get out. I got something to tell you."

"What is it?"

"They come and got Joe Lee out the house."

"Who?"

"Your boss."

"I know Mr. Edd ain't did that."

"They caught him trying to step out the back door."

They stood absorbing what it meant and not knowing why it happened.

"What way they went with him?" George asked.

A part of him wanted to go and set things straight, try to talk some sense into his boss man. Ida Mae didn't want him to go. No good could come of it. She didn't see which way they went anyway, black as it was. And they had been gone a good while.

EUSTIS, FLORIDA, DECEMBER 1941

GEORGE SWANSON STARLING

———

ON THE OTHER SIDE OF THE EARTH, at a harbor in Hawaii, a bomb exploded. It was at a naval base. Pearl Harbor. People heard it on the radio, not knowing what it meant.

The United States was joining the war over in Europe. George Starling got notice to report for an army physical. But the doctor looked him over and disqualified him on account of what the doctor said was a weak heart. George was scared he would die at any minute. But the minutes turned into weeks and then months, and he figured either the doctor didn't know what he was talking about or his heart had recovered.

In the spring, there would be no work after the fruit was picked from the trees. George was hearing talk of war jobs up in a place called Detroit. The factories that made cars were rolling out planes and weapons twenty-four hours a day. He did not particularly want to go to Detroit. He didn't have people there, nor did he know much about it. But they were paying a ridiculous sum of money—dollars an hour instead of pennies a box. He could make enough in a couple of months to last him a year. He heard they were so desperate you could get a job right off the bus. He floated the idea to his wife.

Inez didn't want him to go. For most of their marriage, they had been living with Big George at his house on Bates Avenue. She spent her days sweeping up after the white family she had inherited from her mother and aunt and from her grandmother before them. She was scrubbing toilets when what she really wanted to do, she told George, was to go to beauty school in Tampa, the Angelo Beauty College, it was called, and learn how to fix hair.

She hardly ever saw George as it was. When he wasn't out picking fruit, he was out in the backwoods selling insurance. Lately, he had taken to ferrying people around in his old car as if he were a cab driver. There were no taxis for colored people, so he took people to town for groceries or picked them up after the show to make a little extra money. Friday nights, all day Saturday, and into Sunday evening, George was gone, carrying other people to the things he and Inez could be doing together.

He called himself saving for the future. He had it all planned out. He would save enough money to put her through beauty school. Then she would start working and help him finish college in Tallahassee. That would be their freedom.

So he gave his weekends to his passengers. Sometimes they just showed up at his house for him to take them somewhere. Inez was stirring the grits for breakfast when Lil George came into the kitchen one morning.

"Well, I'm a run this guy downtown to do his shopping," George said. "I'll be back by the time you get breakfast ready."

He took the man downtown and dropped him off with his groceries. On his way home, somebody else flagged him down.

"Hey, Lil George, whatchu doin'?"

"I'm not doing anything."

"How 'bout running me downtown?"

He would start his morning with the best of intentions and not get back until dark. "But all the while I'm away from home, I'm working," George said.

He knew he would be in for a fight as soon as he stepped in the door. "My wife would be swole up big as this room by then 'cause I'm gone all day."

George figured as much and tried to soften her up.

"I know you thought I wasn't never coming back," he said.

She grunted, fuming still.

He told her what had happened and how people had flagged him down in the street and had no way to get their groceries and how one thing had led to another and you know there was no way to reach you because there weren't any phones to call from and, anyway, look at what I got.

Fifty cents on this trip, a dollar on that one, and at the end of the day, George pulled in five, ten, twenty, sometimes thirty dollars in change.

"See how much money I made while I was out. I made all of this."

He dumped it all on the bed, quarters, halves, and paper money. Inez was too mad to look at it.

"Well, all of this goes toward your going to school. That's what I'm scuffling for. So you can go to school."

She kept quiet. So he went on.

"I'm a let you save it now," he said. " 'Cause you know I was sincere. You put it in the trunk so you know where it is. So when you get enough to go you can go."

But she wouldn't get over all those lost weekends so easily. If he took her wants for granted, she would do the same for his. She stood there as if she hadn't heard him. So George went and put the money away himself. Soon he had Mason jars full of quarters and halves, fruit jars filled with nickels and change rattling in tin cans, the start of a future in bottles all over the house.

It was the start of 1943. When the picking season was over and it was nearing spring, everybody's money went dry. The people needing rides trailed off. George saw it coming and started talking again about going to Detroit for the summer to make enough for them to go to school. He made a note to himself: 1943 was the year for Inez to go to beauty school.

"When it gets a little bit warmer, when the fruit season is over," he told her, "I'm going to Detroit to work. Then I could send you to school. It's nothing to do around here during the summer. Ain't no working. I can't even make no money hustling. So I'm going out to Detroit and work and send you to school."

George had it all worked out. Inez just listened. The neighbors had been telling her to watch after her husband. He wasn't going to Detroit to work, they said, he was going to be with some woman, probably one of those schoolteachers he went to school with up in Tallahassee. *Heard one of them was up in D.C. Bet he's going up there to be with her. He's not going to Detroit.*

Inez was quiet. So he repeated himself.

"This year, you going to Tampa. I want you to go to school."

"I don't want to go to no school. I changed my mind. I want to go to Detroit with you."

"What you talking 'bout? You been preaching about Angelo Beauty School, now you want to go to Detroit? You go on to beauty school, where you wanted to go. You can always see the world. You can't always go to school. You're not going to Detroit with me. That's it."

The neighbors would surely talk now. Some came up to George himself. "Why you not letting your wife go with you? They say you not going to Detroit. You going to D.C."

He paid them no mind and caught a bus up to Detroit with his friends Sam Gaskin and Charlie Bollar, whom they called Mud.

The day he left, Inez was too mad and too hurt to say good-bye.

She headed to work. "I hope you all take care of yourselves" was all she could manage.

———

They made B-29 cargo planes at a plant in Hamtramck. George arrived in the late spring of 1943, and they put him to work on a jig making frame covers for the hatch doors and rudders of the cargo planes. They applied chemicals to the covers to make them strong but light. The chemicals were so flammable that anyone caught with a cigarette in his pocket was fired on the spot.

George set about learning the job and adjusting to a gray concrete city he wasn't particular about when a cousin of his wife's showed up unannounced. That was the point. Inez had sent him to see if George was really there and not with some other woman. The cousin reported back that George was doing what he said he was, and only then could Inez feel halfway good about going on to Tampa to take a short course in beauty culture.

George worked nights drilling holes around hatch door frames to attach the covers with screws. He had to bend or lie flat or get on his knees and twist himself to drill the holes straight.

The place was swimming with Communist sympathizers and alleged saboteurs, or so people said, in the hothouse of wartime. Because spies were believed to be inside the plants themselves, any missing or wrongly placed screws were enough to draw suspicion and reprisals in an already cheerless endeavor.

"This made it a nervous, nerve-racking situation," George would say years later. "You know, you drilling all kind of ways and you trying at your very best, and every now and then, you gonna get a hole angle, it's not gonna be right. But if you got too many of them, then you were in trouble."

And every minute, George was scared the whole place would blow up from all the chemicals and paranoia.

Then on the humid night of Sunday, June 20, 1943, a fight broke out between several hundred white and colored men on Belle Isle, a park extending into the Detroit River on the east side of town. The fighting spread north, south, and west as rumors circulated among blacks that white men had killed a colored woman and thrown her baby into the Detroit River and, among whites, that colored men had raped and killed a white woman in the park.

Neither rumor turned out to be true, but it was all that was needed to set off one of the worst riots ever seen in the United States, an outbreak that would mark a turning point in American race relations. Until the 1943 uprising in Detroit, most riots in the United States, from the 1863 Draft Riots in New York to the riots in Tulsa in 1921, to Atlanta in 1906 to Washington, D.C., to Chicago, Springfield, and East St. Louis, Illinois, and Wilmington, North Carolina, among others, had been white attacks on colored people, often resulting in the burning of entire colored sections or towns.

This was the first major riot in which blacks fought back as earnestly as the whites and in which black residents, having become established in the city but still relegated to run-down ghettos, began attacking and looting perceived symbols of exploitation, the stores and laundries run by whites and other outsiders that blacks felt were cheating them. It was only after Detroit that riots became known as primarily urban phenomena, ultimately centered on inner-city blacks venting their frustrations on the ghettos that confined them.

The Detroit riots went on for close to a week, ending in thirty-four deaths and more than one thousand wounded. The Sunday night the riots began, as many as five thousand people joined in the stoning, stabbing, beating, and shooting, so many people injured that the municipal hospital was admitting riot victims at a rate of one a minute.

George was living at 208 Josephine near Hastings and Woodward and heard the mayhem in the streets and on the radio all through the night. He was living in the middle of the crowded colored quarter mockingly called Paradise Valley, where blacks were stoning the cars of passing whites, whites were beating up blacks as they emerged from the all-night theaters on Woodward, and an inspector on the scene reported to the police commissioner that the situation was out of control.

The rioting continued into the next morning. It was now Monday, the start of the work week. A co-worker of George's called him up.

"Hey, Starling, what you gonna do?"

"Do 'bout what?"

" 'Bout going to work."

"I'm going."

"Man, you must be crazy."

"What you talking about?"

"Don't you know? Where you been? You didn't know it was a riot going on?"

"Yeah, but I ain't got nothin' to do with it. I ain't in no gang."

"This ain't no gang fight. This is a riot."

"Well, they ain't gonna bother me. I ain't done nothing to nobody. I'm going on to work."

"You gonna get yourself killed."

George had to take two trolleys to get to Hamtramck. He boarded the first in a colored neighborhood and instantly knew something was wrong. The colored people were sitting up straight; the white people were crouched in their seats so they couldn't be seen out the window.

Wonder why these people down on the floor like they are? he asked himself.

The trolley made its way to a white neighborhood, and now the colored people crouched down and the white people sat up.

Well, what in the devil is going on? he said to himself.

The trolley pulled into the intersection. A mob two blocks long stood cursing outside the trolley.

What's wrong with all them people? he thought.

The mob became a single organism descending on the trolley. The trolley operator moved fast. "He went back the other way," George said. "That's the only thing that saved us. And that's when I began to realize the seriousness of this thing."

He managed to make it to work that day. But the trouble wasn't over. The rioting continued all day Monday and into a second night. When he got back home to Hastings Street that evening, a mob was approaching from Woodward, howling and turning over cars.

"I ran so fast till my heels were hittin' my back," he said.

And as he rounded the corner onto Josephine, he could see a colored mob forming. "They were turning over white cars," he said, "dumping the people out like you dump ashes out an ashtray and setting the cars on fire."

Some colored men in his block stood on the sidewalk, trying to figure out what to do. They had gathered the empty bottles in their flats to throw at people if it came to that. "We were wondering how it was gonna end up," George said.

A white undertaker in the block joined the colored men contemplating the situation. He did not leave when the other white people fled. He fixed his feet on the ground with the neighbors who happened to be colored and let it be known where he stood. He might need their protection if it came to that.

"You know, them white folks raising hell over there on Woodward Avenue," the white undertaker started to say.

"Yeah, they sure are," George said.

The white undertaker drew closer and into their circle. "But us colored folks is giving 'em hell over on Hastings," he said.

The colored men welcomed a new brother, and they all laughed at the meaning of that.

———

George stood on the porch and watched the National Guard tanks with machine guns on top parade through the streets. He sat up all night looking out the window as they passed.

He heard windows smashing and then saw a man with a sofa on his back. Another one had a shoulder of meat. A third had about five or six loaves of bread in his arm.

One morning, as the riots wore on, he passed a Florsheim shoe store while heading to work. People were grabbing shoes through the broken glass and running in the morning sun.

A co-worker was with him and ran over to the store.

"Come on, let's get some," he said.

"Man, I don't want no shoes," George said. "I don't need no shoes like that."

The friend went in without him, grabbed two shoes, and went tearing down the street. He was giddy until he looked at what he had. He had made off with two left shoes.

"Now he gonna go back and try to find the mates," George said. George told him he was crazy.

"No, man, these *good* shoes," his friend said. "If I find the mate to these shoes, I don't have to buy no more shoes for a good while."

He went back in the store, and in that instant the police showed up and caught him in the act. They fired shots, and one hit him in the stomach. He later landed in jail.

The looters took over after the mob cleared out. Within days, the freight trucks rolled up to Hastings and Josephine and all over Detroit and came to a stop in front of suspect stoops. Out came men in overalls pushing dollies, coming for the stolen merchandise. Minutes later,

George saw a sofa come out of a two-flat. Somebody had seen the tenants looting and told.

When the time came to go back to work, George rounded the corner to get to the entrance and felt sick. "I got the feeling like I was walking into Alcatraz or Sing Sing," he said, "to begin a lifetime sentence."

At the plant he learned that several men he worked with had gotten shot in the rioting. One or two had been killed. Between the riot and the anti-Communist paranoia and the plant itself, it was time to go.

"Look, I can't take it," George told his foreman. "I can't come in here another day."

"Well, you know you are frozen on this job."

"But I'm defrosting. I cannot, I cannot come in here no more. Now, you can take it any way you want. I'm just not coming back."

"You know, if you walk out of here, you subject to be in the army in the next twenty-four hours."

"I can't help that," George said, knowing he'd already been rejected for army duty. "I'm gone."

"You have to wait till the pay period to get your money."

"I want my money now. I'm a sit right here. I ain't goin' nowhere until y'all give me all of my money. Now, y'all can do what you want. I'm leaving."

Finally they cut him a check. "And I left the next day."

It was late summer now and going into autumn. There were only two places he knew of to go and live. One was New York, where he had aunts and uncles and no job. The other was Florida, where he had a wife, a father, the dim hope of going back to school, and a patched-together work life of whatever came up.

He caught a bus home to Florida with a sense of dread and defeat. He had gone to college and gone up north and now was returning to exactly the same place he had left. He went back to picking fruit. But instead of hundreds of men in their prime standing at the corner of Bates and Palmetto hoping to board the truck, a small cluster gathered there—old men and women, errand boys and domestics, children, too, who would never have made the cut before the war, along with the few young men like Charlie "Mud" Bollar, and Sam Gaskin and George, who hadn't been chosen to go off to fight.

With the high rollers gone, the three of them reveled in their good fortune. Here they were the only strong pickers left. The trees heavy with fruit. The fruit rationed and prized like never before. The packinghouses helpless to get the fruit out of the trees and, not knowing how long the situation, meaning the war, would drag on, forced to pay an extra nickel a box to entice anybody who could crawl to get on the truck to come pick.

George, Mud, and Sam boarded the truck with the newcomers and rode out thirty, forty miles into the grove. Only it was different this time. George was seeing the world in a new light after being in Detroit. The three of them had gotten used to fair wages for their hard work up north and walked with their backs straight now. George, in particular, never had the constitution to act subservient, and his time up north, where colored people didn't have to step off the sidewalk, only made him more impatient with the role the southern caste system assigned him.

He had gotten used to carrying himself in a different way, talking to white people as equals in Detroit. Now that he was back in Eustis, he made a point to do whatever he could to keep from addressing white people as "sir" or "ma'am." "They'd say, 'So and so and so, boy,'" he said. "I would never say, 'Yes, sir' or 'No, sir.' I'd say, 'That's right.' 'Sure.' 'Certainly.'"

"What you mean by *certainly*?" would come the indignant reply. "You don't know how to say, 'Yes, sir'?"

A colored teacher who had finished the University of Michigan ran into the same trouble in Mississippi at around the same time. He needed to send a wire to a colleague and went into a drugstore to do so. The drugstore owner asked where the wire was going.

"Do they have a phone there?" the druggist asked.

"Yes, they do," the colored teacher replied.

"Do they have a phone there?" the druggist asked again.

"Yes, they have a phone," the colored teacher said, wondering why the druggist hadn't understood him the first time.

"Goddamn it, when you talk to a white man, you say, 'sir'!"

The teacher, to avoid further escalation, addressed him as "sir" and walked out the door. There he saw a group of white men waiting. The teacher jumped into his car. "I didn't run," the teacher said, "but I made haste to my car and left that town just as fast as I could."

George knew that the minutest breach of protocol could be risky but had a hard time submitting to it. The North had changed him, and Mud and Sam, too, and they couldn't go back to the way they were before. The three of them had a plan. They were tired of having to take whatever pennies the packinghouses decided to pay them, and with the war on and not enough pickers, this was one of the few times the workers had any leverage.

George, Mud, and Sam decided to make the most of the situation and stand up for themselves like men. They took to strolling the grove and assessing it themselves before setting their ladders in a tree. Sam and Mud walked the grove as if they were the foremen and looked over the density of the fruit to see what they were in for.

George stayed with the crew of old men and women warming themselves by a fire in the fog. The workers wanted to know when they could start picking. George stood with them and told them the plan.

"Now, look," he said. "Everybody sit down till we get the price straight. Nobody go to work."

"What about the foreman?"

"I don't care what the foreman say. Nobody go to work until we give the word."

The old men and women were used to cleaning white yards and cooking in white kitchens ten or twelve hours a day for seventy-five cents, maybe a dollar. George told them if they could get a good price, they could make that much in an hour or two. Sounded like voodoo talk to them.

"We got to take what the white folks tells us," they told him. "You can't do no different."

George looked back down the row for Mud and Sam to show up and back at his skeptical army.

"I don't want to hear that stuff," George said. "I been listening to that all my life."

The old men and women worried what would happen if they didn't get their price and worried all the more if they got it. With the war on, it was a new day, George told them.

"We got a chance to kind of get back at them," he said, trying to inspire them to stand up for themselves. "I ain't thinking about no future. I'm thinking about right now."

Besides, Sam and Mud had already tried to scare the pickers into submission.

"Anybody put a ladder up under them trees," Mud told them, "we gonna snatch it from under you and stomp you when you hit the ground!"

The pickers waited. Mud and Sam emerged from deep in the grove.

"Well, what it looks like?" George asked.

"It's pretty good over here in one spot," they said.

"Well, what do you think?"

"We'll do it for twenty-two cents."

George spoke for the group since he was the one who had been to school. He went to the foreman to start the unthinkable act of negotiating with a white man.

"What you paying for this?" George asked the foreman.

"Well, you know, this is good fruit, boy," the foreman said. "Now, you can get well in here. These oranges big as grapefruit."

"How much you paying?"

"We paying good. That's fifteen cents a box."

"That ain't good enough. Nope. We can't pick it for that. We want twenty-two cents a box."

"Naw, we can't give you that."

George thought it over.

"Okay, we'll do it for twenty-two cents. Straight through, good and the bad."

"Naw, we can't."

"Well, we can't pick it, then."

"We forty miles from town."

"I know. We still not gonna pick it."

"Well, y'all pick a load. I don't want to send the truck driver back empty. So y'all pick enough so he can take a load into the packing-house. Then I'll send word to the boss and tell him what y'all wantin' to do."

"No, we not gonna pick one. You can send the truck back to town, and we'll wait. Got nothing to do."

"Y'all just doing us this way because y'all got the advantage over us. This war ain't gon' last forever, and, by God, y'all gon' pay for this."

"We already paid," George said. "All these years we couldn't even ask how much you were paying for a box of fruit or we'd get fired. You gave us what you wanted to give us. You promised us one thing and give us another. You put the payday off whenever you get ready. Sometime you didn't pay us, period. So now, far as I'm concerned, this is reckoning day. And I ain't worried about after the war. You can pay us what we want, or else your fruit gonna hang out there. And they want it in New York. They want it all over the world, and you ain't got nobody to pick it."

The foreman needed the fruit out of the trees. He left with the truck

driver and before long was back from the packinghouse. He told them
to go to work. He would pay them twenty-two cents. This time.

The old men and women set their ladders in the trees and commenced picking, and by nightfall, they and these cocksure boys had
made more in a day than they would have otherwise made in a week.

———

People could buy stew meat now and put Sunday suits on will-call at
Ferran's. The Mason jars of quarters Lil George was saving up multiplied. He knew the wages they were making out in the groves couldn't
last forever. Everything depended on the supply and demand created by
the war, and who knew how much more time they had? He decided to
make the most of it while he could. The way things were going, he
could earn enough money for college and then some. Until then, while
the money was flowing, he thought it was time to rent a place of their
own and get out from under his father. Maybe that was what he and
Inez needed, now that she was back from her short course in beauty culture.

"Go downtown and look in Thompson's," he told her. "Pick out some
things you think you would like to have for the house, so we know what
we're doing when we move."

"I don't want to go down there and ain't got no money," she said.
George always had these grand ideas, planning their future in his head.
"How you gon' buy any furniture?" she asked. "You ain't got no money
to buy no furniture with."

"Don't worry about it. Just go and look. You never can tell what
might take place."

One day he just took her by the hand. "Come on," he said. "I'm a take
you down to Thompson's, and you gonna pick out some furniture."

"Pick it out? What you gon' pay for it with?"

"Get your coat and come on, let's go." George scooped up seven or
eight jars of quarters and halves, and they went to Thompson's.

"What you see in here that you like?" he asked her.

She saw a bed, a sofa, a dining room set.

"How much is that?" George asked the clerk, a white man.

"You could pay two dollars down and seventy-five cents a week on
it," the clerk said.

"I don't want to know all of that. I want to know how much does it
cost, and if I pay cash for it, how much can I get off?"

"Cash?" the clerk asked. "You gon' pay cash for all this, boy?"

"I just might."

"Let me see now."

The clerk gave him a figure. George did some adding himself and figured the quarters and halves would cover it.

"Okay, I'll take it."

"Well, you know this is for cash, you know."

"Yeah, I'll take it."

George went out to the car and came back with a box of Mason jars and set the jars on the counter.

"You got a can opener?" George asked. He had glued the tops on to keep the money from falling out or a thief from getting in. They cut the tops off, and George dumped the quarters and halves out on the counter. The coins clinked and rolled, and George started counting.

Inez stood looking first at the money and then at George. The clerk ran out into the street.

"By God, y'all come in here. You ain't gon' believe this. This damn boy in here got over three hundred dollars in jars."

They counted out quarters and halves until George paid him for every bit.

"And when I left out of there," George said, "he was still shaking his head." Inez too.

The pickers had more money in their pockets than they were raised to think they had a right to, and times were the best they had ever been, which said more about how meager the past had been than how great the present was. There was a war going on, after all. They hated that there was a war, but they knew that it made them indispensable for once, and deep inside they wished it would never end.

ATLANTA, 1941

ROBERT JOSEPH PERSHING FOSTER

———

THINGS WERE SPINNING FAST AROUND PERSHING, and, before he knew it, he had allowed himself to be pulled completely into the bourgeois world that he had become besotted with and that would be his ticket out of the world he had come from. He had been squiring around the daughter of the president of Atlanta University for two years now. The daughter, Alice Clement, finished Spelman on June 4, 1941, and it was decided that it was time the two be married. Shortly after commencement, a breathless announcement ran in the *Chicago Defender*:

> *Enlisting widespread interest is the engagement of Miss Alice Clarissa Clement, charming and attractive daughter of President and Mrs. Rufus E. Clement of Atlanta University, to Robert Joseph Pershing Foster, son of Mr. and Mrs. Madison James Foster of Monroe, La.*
>
> *The announcement was made on Thursday evening at a party honoring Miss Clement.*

That December, on the evening of the twenty-third, a Tuesday, and not by coincidence the anniversary of Dr. and Mrs. Clement's own wedding twenty-two years before, Robert Joseph Pershing Foster married Alice Clarissa Clement and entered the insular and parallel universe that was colored society. Dr. Benjamin Mays, the president of Morehouse College and a celebrated figure of the day, married them. The groom was two days shy of his twenty-third birthday. The bride was twenty-one.

The Japanese had attacked Pearl Harbor just a few weeks before. But the troubles of the outside world were put aside that night. It was the social event of the season, played up in the *Atlanta Daily World,* the *Chicago Defender,* and the *New York Amsterdam News;* and here was Pershing right in the middle of it.

"The wedding—" Pershing began many years later. "Can I brag a little? It was a monster. If you can visualize a Gothic chapel. Stained-glass windows. Long mahogany benches. Then a balcony. Pipe organs up the wall. A master organist."

There were eight bridesmaids and a maid of honor in floor-length white taffeta and with tiaras on their heads. They carried long-stemmed red roses, heavy in their arms. There were eight groomsmen, including Pershing's brothers Madison and Leland, in white tie and tails.

"White kid gloves," Pershing continued. "Patent-leather shoes. We were clean as chitlins."

As he recounted that day half a century later, he would not for some reason speak of the bride as much as the details of the spectacle itself. The *Atlanta Daily World* reported that she wore a gown of ivory satin, its neckline embroidered with seed pearls, and a floor-length veil that "fell from a crown of orange blossoms." The altar was "banked with palms and ferns," "numerous sixteen branch candelabra and three huge urns of gladioli and lilies," in what the paper called "a setting of splendor and beauty."

One of the groomsmen, Jimmy Washington, would always remember the night they got married. Because it was beautiful, he said years later, and it rained in sheets that night.

———

There would not be much of a honeymoon. School took them in opposite directions. Alice went off to New York to study music at Juilliard, an extraordinary thing for a young colored woman of the day. Pershing prepared to go to Nashville to attend Meharry Medical College, and the two saw each other when they could. It was wartime, and it seemed everybody was separated from their sweethearts.

Alice completed a year at Juilliard, and then it was decided that it was better for her to stay with her parents and teach in Atlanta than to live in Nashville with Pershing, who was caught up in his medical studies. She would be in familiar surroundings in Atlanta. Her father could secure an ideal position at a public school there for her, and neither she nor Pershing would have to trouble themselves with the messy details of keeping house at this stage in their lives.

By the time Pershing found out, it had all been decided. Pershing had no choice but to go along with it. What money he and Alice had was coming from Dr. Clement, and he was calling the shots. So Alice taught in Atlanta and visited Nashville when she could.

After a visit in the early spring of 1943, Alice discovered she was pregnant. She gave birth to a girl that December. They named her Alberta Ann, after Pershing's beloved mother, Ottie Alberta. She had a brown velvet Gerber baby face. They wrapped her in baby bunting and began to call her Bunny, a name that would stick for as long as she lived.

Pershing finished Meharry in 1945 and moved to St. Louis to serve out his residency at Homer G. Phillips Hospital, the colored facility where Madison had served his. Alice was expecting their second child now, and her parents argued against her trying to raise two babies in St. Louis with Pershing working three and four nights straight as a resident.

"Why do that when you can live here?" they asked.

"See, they can show you a million reasons to keep that daughter and granddaughter at home," Pershing said years later. "They were logical reasons. And you couldn't beat 'em."

That October, the second girl was born. Pershing named her Alice Emlyn, after his wife and the beloved sister he could never protect from the white men who called out to her in Monroe. Little Alice inherited her father's big eyes and sharp nose and looked like a lighter incarnation of him. Everyone came to call her Robin, similar to Pershing's actual first name, Robert.

She was born in Atlanta surrounded by the Clements while Pershing was working the ward twenty-four hours straight, until he was cross-eyed and crazy from it.

"In the evening when you got through work," Pershing said, "you said, *Whew, thank God.*' And you run upstairs, taking your clothes off on the elevator. Run to the shower. Get you a gulp, throw your whiskey, and get you two, three shots. Towel around you and hit the shower. And get out and get a cab and hit the streets. Anywhere. It didn't matter where you went. *Let me get away from this.* And then you had to come home sober. And you had to sleep fast 'cause you had to get up the next morning looking bright-eyed and bushy-tailed in a crisp, clean uniform and white shoes. And you had to *'Good morning, Mr. So-and-So.'* "

A resident ahead of him noticed his work and suggested he go up for a surgery residency when the time came.

"You think I can do it?" Pershing asked.

"Yes," the resident said. "Try."

Pershing did as he said and started a new round of training that would last several more years and take him to hospitals in North Carolina and New York City to train in surgery.

Soon he began getting disturbing reports from home. His mother had taken ill.

It was cancer. Her kidney. He left to be with her. She had prayed to God every night to let her see her baby become a doctor. There he sat, a doctor in training now, reading aloud the *Reader's Digest* to her. She tried to stand up to go over to him. But she couldn't.

"What's the matter?" he asked her.

He got up to kiss her on the cheek. She tried to speak. She was worried what would become of her son in this bourgeois world he was entering.

"Baby," she said, "always be independent. You don't want to be dependent all your life and have to depend on someone else for a drink of water."

Pershing kept those words inside of him. In a few years, he completed his training, and, though she would not live to see it, he would become a surgeon at last.

————

For a time, Madison was the only colored physician in all of Ouachita County, Louisiana, after a doctor by the name of Chandler died. Years before, two colored doctors had been forced out of Monroe, the author Ray Stannard Baker reported, "because they were taking the practice of white physicians."

So Madison learned to step judiciously in his practice. He tended to the students at a colored college out from town and the poor people out in the country where the white doctors would not go. The country people paid him with the side of a freshly killed hog until they could get the money, which some never did. When Madison's patients needed to go to the hospital, Madison could not admit them. He was not allowed in the hospital to practice. So he carried a hospital in his medical bag and made the front room of every shotgun cabin an operating room.

Madison had his hands full, and he enlisted Pershing's help with his patients out in the countryside when Pershing was on break from his residency. Pershing was glad to help. But he did not want to be a country doctor. And he was thinking even then that he would have to get out of Monroe to be the doctor and the man he knew he could be. He wanted the shiny fixtures of a modern hospital and a staff of nurses at his side that he could direct like an orchestra.

Pershing was visiting once when someone sent for him to deliver a baby out in the country. He arrived with his satchel. Someone met him at the door.

"Doc, I think she's ready."

The fireplace was spitting ashes. The woman's kinfolk stood drinking strong coffee and waiting for the woman to pass the baby.

Pershing saw her splayed flat on a cot, looking ready to burst. He set down his satchel and went over to her. He reviewed in his head the principles of the obstetrics course he had only recently completed. There was no point in pining for the trappings of a modern hospital or the equipment he was used to in medical school. He would have to make do with whatever was in the cabin and his medical bag. They would get through it somehow.

He reached toward her and felt for the hard surface of a human head at the beginning of life. The woman bore down and grunted. He in turn made note of the contractions and the baby's position. He tried to help her bear down. But the baby didn't come.

The woman had been through more births than Pershing had and could sense the tentative touch of a book-learned delivery. All this analysis, and still no baby.

"That's alright, Doc," she finally said. "Get on out the way."

She rolled her round body off the edge of the cot. She grunted and squatted on the bare surface of the floor and pushed hard. Pershing watched and did as she said.

"Come on, now," she said. "Catch it."

He moved into position. A few grunts more, and the baby plopped into his hands. *Shoop, bingo.*

The woman paid what she could, which in the usual currency was not much more than food and a promise but was beyond calculating when it came to wisdom. He learned that all the book knowledge and equipment in the world didn't make you a good doctor if you didn't know what you were doing or listen to your patients. He learned a lesson that night that would stay with him for the rest of his life and would pay off in ways he couldn't imagine.

————

Things appeared to be looking up for Pershing. He had traveled across the South for his degrees, been to St. Louis, spent summers picking tobacco in Connecticut with other Morehouse students, visited New York, seen the differences between North and South, and now, having deferred his military duty during medical school, was reporting to Fort Sam Houston, Texas, for a training course for army medical officers about to begin their tours. He would be called Captain Foster, and it was from his short time in the army that he would plot the rest of his life.

He was bright and earnest, and, while that didn't always get him what he wanted or deserved in the Jim Crow South, he was getting a break now, it seemed. The colonel, impressed with him, pulled him aside and suggested that Pershing could well make chief of surgery at his new posting.

"Foster, you're the only colored officer with surgical training here," the colonel said. "You don't get this often, but I'm going to give you first choice."

Pershing threw his shoulders back.

"Thank you, Colonel," Pershing said. "Alright. Now what are my choices?"

World War II was over, and another, smaller one was brewing in Korea. He could go on to Korea, stay in the South at Fort Sam Houston, or go to Austria, a base of the European theater. The colonel encouraged him to go to Austria, and that's what Pershing chose.

Thousands of colored soldiers had preceded him overseas during the two great wars—more than a million in World War II alone—and that service had been a defining experience for many of them. They were forced into segregated units and often given the most menial tasks or the most dangerous infantry tours. But they also experienced relief from Jim Crow in those European villages, were recognized as liberating Americans rather than lower-caste colored men, and felt pride in what their uniform represented.

They returned home to a Jim Crow South that expected them to go back to the servile position they left. Most resented it and wanted to be honored for risking their lives for their country rather than attacked for being uppity. Some survived the war only to lose their lives to Jim Crow.

In the spring of 1919, a colored soldier named Wilbur Little returned home to Blakely, Georgia, after a tour of duty in World War I. A band of white men saw him at the train station in his uniform. They ordered him to take it off and walk home in his underwear. He refused. Soon anonymous notes were warning him to leave town if he wanted to wear his uniform. Days later, a mob attacked him as he greeted friends congratulating him on his achievements. He was found beaten to death on the outskirts of town. He was wearing his uniform. He had survived the war only to be killed at home. Cases like that were cause enough for some men to go north.

Pershing put those things aside and chose to revel in the idea that he could actually be chief of surgery. Alice was elated. They had been married for eight years now and had never lived together more than a few weeks at a time. The two girls, Bunny and Robin, were just about school age now. Alice had been rearing them in Atlanta with her parents while Pershing did his medical training in different parts of the South. Now the four of them could be a family.

They arrived just outside Salzburg, and Pershing went straight to his new commanding officer. He wanted to make a good impression.

"Captain Foster has reported for duty, sir," he said.

The new colonel was from Mississippi, and, in an instant, Pershing found himself hurled back to the South. The colonel had not expected his new surgeon to be colored, nor had he been told that this colored surgeon was supposed to be in charge—or, if he did know, he chose to ignore it. He told Pershing he had nothing for him to do.

"Why don't you go out?" the colonel said. "Can't you go somewhere? Come back in a week."

"Well, I don't have any money," Pershing said. "I've come all the way from Fort Houston, and the next payday hasn't come, Colonel."

The southern colonel had no assignment for him, so Pershing had no choice but to wait until the following week. When he returned, he learned there would be no leadership position for him. A white officer would be chief of surgery, as it had always been. Pershing would have no title other than staff doctor. Jim Crow had followed him across the Atlantic, and it was hitting him that he would never get ahead as long as these apostles of Jim Crow were over him.

Still, he dutifully made his rounds when it was his turn, tending to the basic needs of the soldiers, itching to do something more in keeping with his credentials. It turned out that many of the patients were soldiers' wives with gynecological and obstetrical complications that called for interventions that by now he was well equipped to handle. But for one reason or another, a superior officer always seemed to intervene and never let him treat the white ones.

One day a patient was in labor on his watch. The nurse thought it might be time. Pershing said it was still too soon.

"She's not quite ready yet," he told the nurse. "Watch her close, now."

Other doctors tended to deliver when it was most convenient, pump general anesthesia into the patient and get it over with, he recalled years later. Cesarean sections were all the rage. But Pershing had learned from the woman in the cabin back in Louisiana that everything had its own time. He liked to let a baby come when it was ready. Others said he let the labor go on too long. But he thought it was a more welcoming way for one to enter the world if one were not rushed into it. So, while other doctors relied on general anesthesia, he preferred local for the sake of the mother and the baby.

A white doctor of his same rank caught wind of the delay. He stepped in over Pershing's head and delivered the baby as Pershing watched, too hurt to speak and not daring to.

Never was there a rule written down somewhere, but that was how it played out. "You make the rounds," Pershing said years later, "and you're standing behind other doctors, and they're talking about your patient."

He was noticing it more and more, like how, whenever a white woman needed surgery, they never let him in the operating room. They sent him over to operate on the men. It was Jim Crow all over again, and he thought again about his short- and long-term prospects. It was reminding him that he had a decision to make. When he got out of the army, he would get as far away from Jim Crow's disciples as he could.

For now he had no choice. He was under these people and had to make the best of it. He pushed the hurt and anger inside himself and decided that if all they would let him do was take somebody's pulse, he would take it better than any doctor there. And so he doted on the few patients he got.

"I treated every white boy like he was the king of Siam," he said, "and didn't lose dignity. It's a fine art."

It all changed one day when a woman in labor suddenly stopped contracting. It was another doctor's patient, the one who had intervened when he thought Pershing had let a labor go on too long. The doctor was getting second opinions and let Pershing come in this time. Pershing saw the woman on the operating table in preparation for a C-section.

He looked the patient over and gave his diagnosis.

"She's in uterine inertia," Pershing said. "The uterus is tired. It's stopped pushing. You need to start a glucose drip of Pitocin to make the uterus start contracting."

The doctor decided to try it. The nurses later went to Pershing and gave him the news.

"The baby's crawling," they said. "The baby came."

One evening soon afterward, he and Alice were at dinner in the officers' club. The waiter asked what they were drinking and soon reappeared with another round.

"Compliments of the lieutenant over there," the waiter said.

Pershing reached for Alice's hand. They danced their way over to the table where the lieutenant, a white man from Kentucky, was sitting with his wife.

"You wouldn't remember me," the wife said. "But I'm the patient whose baby you just delivered. I must give you a kiss for saving me from a C-section."

She gave him a kiss in front of everyone.

"You were the talk of the commissary," she said.

People were taking notice. He was young, charming, and brilliant. People saw him in line and tittered about him.

"I hear we got a new doctor, and he's colored," people were saying.

"Would you have a colored doctor deliver your baby?" somebody else would throw in.

CHICKASAW COUNTY, MISSISSIPPI, FALL 1937

IDA MAE BRANDON GLADNEY

———

THE MEN WHO pounded on Ida Mae's door that black night, who raised a chain up to her, frightening her and the children and her sister-in-law Indiana, who slept by the door, went and hunted down her husband's cousin Joe Lee over the turkeys that had disappeared.

They tied Joe Lee's hands behind him with hog wire and took him to the woods out by Houston, a few miles away.

They tied him up for stealing Addie B.'s turkeys, which belonged to Mr. Edd.

Joe Lee did not work for Mr. Edd—his father had a piece of land he farmed on his own. But it didn't matter because any boss man in the ruling class could claim jurisdiction when he pleased. A colored man, a few miles west of here, was whipped when he asked a storekeeper for a receipt. If what Addie B. said was true, Joe Lee had committed a serious crime against Mr. Edd, and it didn't matter who he worked for.

So they took him out to the woods.

They laid him across a log by the schoolhouse. They beat him with the chains that Willie Jim had raised up to Ida Mae. And when he said he didn't know anything about any turkeys, they paid it no mind. They beat him until his coveralls turned red with blood and stuck to the surface of his skin as if with adhesive. Then they took him to the Chickasaw County jail and left him bleeding alone in the cell.

———

The next morning, Addie B.'s turkeys wandered back on their own to her cabin across the field. They had been roosting in the countryside and came cawing and clucking before George and Ida Mae knew why Joe Lee was captured in the first place or what had become of him. There were no apologies. Sometimes they just got the wrong man. Joe Lee was known for taking what wasn't his, but this was one time when he hadn't.

George went to Mr. Edd first thing in the morning to find out what happened and where his cousin was and to register his discontent. Ida Mae didn't want him going in the state of mind he was in and told him to mind his words. He had to walk a thin line between being a man and acting a slave. Step too far on one side, and he couldn't live with himself. Step too far on the other, and he might not live at all.

He got there and asked Mr. Edd what happened.

"Where is Joe Lee?" George asked.

"We tried to wait till you got there," Mr. Edd said.

George thought it best not to press the matter of what happened to Joe Lee. All these years he had been loyal to Mr. Edd, and Mr. Edd had been fair with him. So he spoke only as a husband and father, which he felt was within his right.

"Very idea you upsettin' my family," he said, looking down as he prepared to leave and not quite knowing what else to do.

Joe Lee survived the night. The boss man told George to go get him at the jail. George, Willie, Saint, and the other colored men on the plantation took grease to peel the overalls off him, just as their slave forefathers had done after whippings generations before. They carried Joe Lee back to his father's farm in the fresh clothes they put on him, and the people went back to picking cotton. The lash wounds on Joe Lee's back healed in time. But Joe Lee was never right again, people said. And, in a way, neither was George.

On the drive back home, George searched himself, hard and deep. This wasn't the first beating, and it wouldn't be the last. Joe Lee had lived, but he just as easily could have died. And there was not a thing anybody could do about it. As it was, Ida Mae felt George was in danger for asking Mr. Edd about it at all. Next time, it could be him. George had a brother in Chicago. Ida Mae's big sister, Irene, was in Milwaukee and had been agitating for them to come north.

He made up his mind on the way back. He drove into the yard and went into the cabin to break the news to Ida Mae.

"This the last crop we making," he said.

EUSTIS, FLORIDA, 1944
GEORGE SWANSON STARLING

———

WORD SPREAD THROUGH THE CITRUS GROVES that a cell of pickers had taken to demanding twenty-two cents a box and refusing to pick if they didn't get it. It was a miracle wage, and soon other pickers were trying to join Lil George's roving union. But some got scared at the way George talked to the white people like he was equal and never went picking with him again.

The foremen who assembled the crews and oversaw the citrus harvest knew they were in for a long day when they saw George, Mud, and Sam awaiting pickup with other hungry workers at the corner of Bates and Palmetto. Most foremen had little sympathy for the pickers. Their job was to get the fruit out of the trees as fast as they could, and this back-and-forth over pay was wasting time. Even worse, these boys had no business telling white men what to do. Most foremen told the pickers to take whatever the packinghouses were offering.

The Blye brothers were different. They were among the few colored foremen around and had grown up with most of the pickers. Reuben, who towered over most men and had a way of making women forget their husbands; Babe, who liked to gamble and hunt possum; and Whisper, who could speak no louder than that because he had got his throat cut, had been pickers themselves and knew the packinghouses could pay more if they wanted to. Florida growers were grossing fifty million dollars a year from that fruit back in the forties, and the brothers felt the pickers deserved better.

After assessing a grove, George and the Blye brothers conferred on the price the pickers should ask for. Then the brothers went and told the packinghouse it looked like the pickers flat-out wouldn't work if they didn't get their price, and they didn't know what had got into them. The Blye brothers hoped to convince the packinghouses that, with the war on, there weren't enough good pickers to choose from and they were stuck with whoever was left, crazy though these pickers may be, that the packinghouses needed to think about paying more if they wanted the fruit out of the trees, at least for now. Of course, the Blye brothers, being colored and walking a fine line themselves, didn't put it like that. They just said the pickers were refusing and they didn't know what in the world had got into them.

Back in the groves, the brothers confided to George, Mud, and Sam that they were within their rights to ask and that there was room to maneuver. The packinghouses were wringing the most they could out of all of them, including the Blye brothers, who had reason to believe they themselves weren't getting paid what the white foremen were, this being the South in the 1940s.

The grove owners and their packinghouses had a near monopoly on the growing and selling of citrus. They were among the richest men in central Florida; their European vacations and their daughters' cotillions and the visits of their children from the best boarding schools in the South were all chronicled in the local papers that everyone, including workers like the Blye brothers and George, could read. It was a multimillion-dollar industry fed by the demands of wealthy and middle-class families from Chicago to Long Island who expected orange juice with their toast and coffee every morning.

The brothers urged the three men and their frightened, thrown-together crew of pickers to stand their ground.

"Man, sock it to 'em, sock it to 'em," Reuben told George, knowing how much the grove owners were making off the fruit and that they were likely cheating them all.

"Don't pick it no less," Whisper said. "Don't pick it no less than twenty-two cents. Goddammit, I'm a tell the man y'all ain't gon' do it."

Most times George, Mud, and Sam got their price right there on the spot. But sometimes they didn't. They couldn't depend on getting the Blye brothers as their foremen every time. And when they didn't, some foremen just said no without telling the packinghouse at all. Some went to the packinghouse but accepted whatever the packinghouse told them. Others went ahead and sent the truck back to the packinghouse empty of fruit and waited to see what the owners said. Sometimes the packinghouses relented. But sometimes the driver would come back from the packinghouse saying, "Well, they say they not gon' pay that."

The pickers dragged back to the truck when that happened for the empty-handed ride back to town. George started to climb up with them. But most foremen weren't like the Blye brothers and wouldn't let him on the truck if he told the crew not to pick.

"You big with your big-mouth self," one foreman said. "You get back to town best way you can."

And so George had to thumb a ride for thirty or forty miles after facing down a foreman while his followers rumbled past him on the flatbed of the truck.

He was developing a reputation for stirring up trouble in the groves. These walkouts were beginning to look something like a union. The grove owners didn't like unions, didn't allow unions, and weren't going to stand for it, especially from a band of colored pickers trying to take advantage of the war. Inez was scared for her husband but too disgusted to let it show. Didn't he realize that he was colored in the South? Why couldn't he be satisfied like everybody else?

Big George had been working with them when Lil George stood up to a foreman in Orlando.

The next day, Big George begged off. "I ain't going with you," he said. "Y'all too crazy."

He knew, and everyone else knew, that every time George went out to the groves standing up to packinghouses, he was pushing the limits of what a colored man in Florida in the 1940s was allowed to get away with.

In the months that George had been rousing up the pickers, their world had grown even more dangerous due to the state's desperate wartime need for labor. From the panhandle to the Everglades, Florida authorities were now arresting colored men off the street and in their homes if they were caught not working. Charged with vagrancy, the men were assessed fines of several weeks' pay and made to pick fruit or cut sugarcane to work off the debt if they did not have the money, which few of them did and as the authorities fully anticipated. Those captured were hauled to remote plantations or turpentine camps, held by force, and beaten or shot if they tried to escape.

It was an illegal form of contemporary slavery called debt peonage, which persisted in Florida, Georgia, Alabama, and other parts of the Deep South well into the 1940s. Federal investigations into neoslavery in Florida uncovered numerous abuses of kidnapping and enslavement and led to a 1942 indictment and trial of a sugar plantation company in the Everglades.

Lake County, too, needed as many workers as could be rounded up and in 1944 elected a new sheriff to see to it. He was Willis Virgil McCall, the six-foot-tall son of a dirt farmer who policed the county with a ten-gallon hat, size thirteen boots, and a Winchester rifle he did not hesitate to cock. He was openly linked to white supremacists and would be implicated in the deaths and abuse of dozens of blacks in what would become a twenty-eight-year reign. As soon as he took office, he set to work. He arrested forty pickers for vagrancy, including a man from Deacon Fashaw's crew, in late January and early February 1945.

They were arrested for not working on a Saturday, at a time when George, Sam, and Mud were leading actual strikes in the groves.

Each day, the danger was drawing closer, and there was now even more pressure on George's pickers to work no matter how much George managed to win for them. McCall stepped up his arrests. In February, he showed up at the home of a picker from a crew in Leesburg, fifteen miles west of Eustis. The picker, Mack Fryar, had already worked that week, but, to the sheriff's way of thinking, the picker had no business being at home on a Saturday instead of out in the groves. McCall ordered Fryar to come with him. When he asked why, McCall replied, "None of your damn jaw, just come on with me." McCall struck the picker in the head with a blackjack for such impudence, knocking him unconscious in front of the picker's wife and fourteen-year-old son. He then hauled the picker to the Lake County jail.

The FBI began an investigation, and an agent was seen visiting the picker's wife, Annie. Local whites got wind of it and began plotting mob action because they saw her as "stirring up trouble for the sheriff and the county" by talking to the FBI. Neighbors warned the wife, and upon the picker's release, the Fryars fled to Harlem, "leaving all their possessions, except some money from the sale of her chickens."

George, now an unintended union organizer, somehow managed to stay under the radar screen for months, or so it appeared, in the eleven hundred square miles of citrus land being policed by Sheriff McCall. But that could not go on forever. The orange groves had become a battlefield over more than just fruit but over the rights of the people lowest down in the citrus world and the caste system itself, and the only thing that couldn't be known was how far George, Mud, and Sam could push it.

———

For several days late in the picking season, no rain fell from the sky. The limbs of the tangerine trees shrank in response. The stems became a tough rubber, harder to cut.

Lil George and his crew landed in a tangerine grove out in Sanford in the middle of this unpleasant development. They hated picking tangerines. The fruit was small, and it took more of them to fill a box. The very properties that made them easy to peel made them harder to pick. The rind broke and bruised almost at the touch, meaning it was harder to get a box of perfect tangerines. They had to be clipped flush without scraping the fruit, all while the picker was reaching between the branches and trying to steady himself on a limb. Then they had to be packed just so in the crate so the stem of each tangerine wouldn't injure the rest.

However difficult they were to pick, tangerines were big sellers at market. Growers in Lake County were known for holding down their production costs, and thus netting "returns to the grower considerably above the state average," according to a newspaper report.

To do that, the grove owners were holding the pickers to nickels on a box. But, with the war on, tangerines were selling an average of four dollars and forty cents a box at auction in 1944, nearly twice the going rate before the United States entered World War II. Across the state, tens of thousands of tangerines were being shipped out every week, a good portion of them coming out of Lake County. There were 2.6 million citrus trees in Lake County, the third most in the state next to Polk and Orange counties.

George's crew arrived at the tangerine grove out in Sanford that morning. The foreman said the packinghouse would pay ten cents a box. George said that wasn't enough what with all they had to do and how hard it was to pick fragile tangerines in the best of conditions, which, after the lack of rain, these weren't.

The price was always in flux depending on the circumstances anyway. This was one time where the pickers saw more work for themselves and thought the price should reflect that. So, no, they needed twenty cents. The foreman held his ground. Lil George started to round up the pickers to head back home, to see if twenty cents sounded better to the foreman than no tangerines at all. George told his crew to get back on the truck, *we're going back to town.*

"Well, we done come all this far now," they said. "We may as well work today, and then we won't come back tomorrow."

This was always the hard part. The pickers liked the miracle money on the days when the foreman gave in. But when the foreman turned them down, they were scared to leave with ill will in the air. *What was the point of antagonizing the boss man? Let's go on and work while we're out here.*

But George knew that walking out was the only leverage they had.

"No, we not gonna work today," George told the pickers. "We are *not* going to work today. Now, you made enough money yesterday. You already made more in one day than you make in a week doing day's work. You ain't never made over six dollars a week. Yesterday, you made seven, eight, nine dollars. So you not losing anything. You gaining. So you can afford to go home and sit down today. Now, we *not* picking."

The pickers didn't move.

"What are you worried about?" George asked them. "Just take it easy."

"Well, we done warmed our pail."

"So now you don't have to cook. Just take that on back home and eat."

Word got back to the owner of the grove that there was trouble in the tangerine stands, and he came out to the field himself. He demanded to know why they were standing there not picking.

"We not gonna pick tangerines for less than twenty cents a box," George told him.

The man cursed and called them names. He had a gun on him like many a man, colored and white, in those parts at that time and told them he would use it if he had to. George, Mud, and Sam knew from hunting squirrel and possum how to handle a gun, too, and told him as much. The pickers, too frightened to speak, watched the standoff between George and the grove owner, not knowing how far either of them would take this thing or how all of them would manage to get out of this.

The men came to no agreement. The owner stormed back to his truck and sped away in a cloud of dust down an alley of his unpicked tangerine trees. George tried to step onto the flatbed truck to head back to town with his pickers. The foreman pushed him off.

"No, boy," he said. "Y'all can't work, you ain't gon' ride. These others can go back on here, but you ain't going back on there."

The pickers were scared to get on the truck and scared not to.

"Y'all go 'head," George said. "Don't worry about me. Go on and get in the truck. You ride. I'll get back to town. Don't worry about me. Just get on the truck."

He hitched a ride back to town and wondered how long his little union would hold.

———

Fear spread among Lil George's band of pickers after that losing day in the tangerine groves. The owner had come out and seen them not picking. All these walkouts, and there might come a time when the packinghouse wouldn't let them work at all. The boss men might blame them for the fruit hanging unpicked in the trees. A picker would end up hanging from a tree himself before long, if this kept up.

They talked among themselves when George, Mud, and Sam weren't around. They didn't like how George, in particular, had a way of being what they considered impudent with white people in a way that made everyone nervous.

Things had gone too far, as the other pickers saw it. These boys had been up north and were going to get all of them killed. That night, after the defeat over the tangerines, they went in secret to the owners of the grove.

"Us come by to tell y'all how come us didn't work today," they said. "Them boys, Sam and Mud and Lil George. You know them is bad. Them boys is bad. We know y'all is always done a good part by us colored folks, and we wanted to work. But them boys told us if we put a ladder in that tree, they gonna snatch the ladder up and stomp us when we hit the ground. So we scared. We know y'all is good white folks and has always done a good part by us. And it wasn't none a us."

———

Sometime later, a young man was tending the grove owner's yard. He was clearing debris around the garage when he heard voices inside. They were the voices of grove owners talking among themselves about people on the colored side of town, something about the trouble some men were causing in the groves.

The yard man recognized the name of Lil George Starling. School-boy had helped him fill out ration papers for sugar and gasoline. It was wartime, and he wouldn't have gotten any if he didn't have papers, and he wouldn't have had papers if George hadn't filled them out for him.

That night after work, the yard man went to Lil George.

"Lil George, I come to tell you what I heard them saying about you boys today in the garage up there," he said.

George looked at him and listened.

"I heard them plottin' that they gon' take you boys out," he said. "Say if they get rid a you three, that the rest of them they could handle. Say 'cause y'all got a big influence over them others. And so they scared a y'all. So they planning to get rid a y'all."

The yard man said he heard mention of a cypress swamp eighteen miles out from town.

"They talking 'bout taking y'all out to Blackwater Creek," he said. "They talking 'bout giving y'all a necktie party. They gon' take y'all out there and hang y'all in one of them cypress trees."

Something in George half expected as much. The man went on.

"I thought I would tell you 'cause you always were nice to me," he said. "When I had papers to fill out, I would bring my papers to you.

You would always do it for me. You never charged me anything. And I wanted you to know. I came out here to tell you y'all better watch yourself."

"I appreciate that," George told him, not wanting to betray the churning in his stomach. "Man, I ain't studyin' 'bout them people."

Inside was a different story. "I couldn't rest comfortable," he said.

———

Leaving was his only option. He went to tell his father. Big George was trying to set out a little grove of his own at a place called Grand Island five or six miles out from town. He had just put his orange trees in the ground and had to haul water out to them to soak them so they could catch root.

Lil George helped him haul lake water in barrels. Together, they poured the pails of water at the roots of the trees every evening.

Out in the grove that night, Lil George told him his plans.

"After today, I'm not gonna be able to help you haul no water," he said. "I'll help you water these trees. Then I'm gonna get my clothes together, and I'm gonna take on off. Because I'm not gonna change."

He told his father what his father already knew. Men had been hanged for far less than what George was orchestrating. And there would be no protecting him if he stayed. In Florida and in the rest of the Deep South, "the killing of a Negro by a white man ceased in practice even to call for legal inquiry," a white southerner observed in the early 1940s.

George and his father lived with that reality every day of their lives, and now it was right before them.

"So the best thing for me to do," George told his father, "is to get on out from around here."

FORT POLK, LOUISIANA, EARLY 1953
ROBERT JOSEPH PERSHING FOSTER

———

BY THE TIME his tour of duty in Austria was over, Pershing had worked his way to a position of esteem if not authority and won awards for his medical skills. He had worked long hours, odd hours, building up his reputation, but it had left him no further ahead. Most southern hospitals wouldn't allow him inside an operating room no matter how gifted he was or what he'd done in the army. There was simply no place for a high-minded colored surgeon who thought he was as good as, or, to hear him tell it, better than most anybody else. He was now discharged to Fort Polk, Louisiana, and, with no job prospects and a family to support, was plotting his escape from the world he had known. But where? And to what?

He stayed awake at night weighing the options. All this education and no place to practice and live out his life as he imagined it to be. The only assurance of a job was back home in Monroe. Madison would be overjoyed to have his little brother join his small-town practice. But Louisiana was out of the question. In the time Pershing had been away, the Fosters had lost their place as the leading and often resented colored family in Monroe. His mother, Ottie, had passed away. His father, Professor Foster, had been edged out of his position as principal of Monroe Colored High School, to which he had devoted most of his adult life and identity. He had been forced into retirement and had to watch as a younger rival from his own faculty, Henry Carroll, not only ascended to the principal's desk but also, through carefully tended connections to a former governor of Louisiana, James A. Noe, managed to get a new colored high school built and named after himself.

Robert watched the school go up and grieved for his heartbroken father. Just being a Foster in Monroe was like being in exile now. Besides, Alice had no interest in that small town. She wouldn't stand for it, and Pershing couldn't bear it.

He could return to Alice's home in Atlanta. The Clements would be beside themselves. And that was the problem. Dr. Clement could surely set him up in practice, and Alice and Pershing could join colored society as the daughter and son-in-law of a distinguished university president. They would have a place card calligraphied for them whenever dignitaries came to visit—Eleanor Roosevelt, the Rockefellers, and so forth. They would have everything they aspired to. But at what price? He imagined he couldn't so much as choose the seasoning on the roast with Dr. Clement down the street.

As it was, Dr. Clement was growing in prominence in Atlanta, looming larger than ever before, running for the Board of Education, seeking to become the first colored holder of a major office since Reconstruction.

Back in medical school, Pershing had begun suspecting he had lost his place as the man in his family. While he was away learning to be a doctor, the family grew accustomed to Pershing's absence, had settled into routines and ways of being that could not be turned off overnight.

Alice and the girls were living in President Clement's brick Georgian mansion with its circular driveway and Doric-columned veranda, its groundskeepers and servants, its chintz draperies and damask uphol-stery in grand parlors and receiving rooms. There, dignitaries gathered for tea and, in the evenings, Dr. Clement read to his beloved grand-daughters in a club chair by the fireplace, pictures of the girls on the mantel next to the porcelain figurines. The Clements and Alice would gather the girls around the baby grand to sing along as Alice played.

Bunny and Robin had become adorable little girls in pigtails and rib-bons and patent-leather shoes, but Pershing didn't truly know them. He had missed the milestones in their lives, their first steps, their first words, their first day of school. It was the Clements who dried their tears when they fell and went over their homework with them.

Pershing could not blame anyone for what had become of his role in the family. He had agreed to the arrangement. Now he decided he needed to get as far from the Clements as he could to take possession of the family that was slipping from his influence. Atlanta was in the South, anyway. Atlanta was off the list.

He sat down and tried to figure out—*where else did he know anybody?* There must be someplace outside the South he could go. In the years since World War I, a large colony of colored people from Monroe had established themselves in Detroit. Faroker Johnson was one hometown man he knew. He was a dentist who had preceded him at Meharry and was practicing up in River Rouge. Then there was his boyhood friend Nimrod Sherman. He was a psychiatrist up in Detroit and doing alright for himself. But Detroit didn't have the sophistication Pershing was looking for, and he didn't consider it for very long. Same for St. Louis, where he had done his residency, and even Chicago, which was cold be-sides.

What he wanted was New York, where they never turned the lights out and had the best of anything you could think of. But he didn't know anybody there. That wasn't the natural route people from Louisiana took to get out of the South. They went where the railroad took them, straight north to Chicago and Detroit. Or west to California, where the climate was more to their liking.

So Pershing would have to think West, which was not a difficult thing to do. He had been hearing about California all his life, played pretend with Clara Poe and always said he was going to California before he even knew what it was. Seemed like everybody who left Monroe was talking California. There was a contingent up in Oakland, a branch down in Los Angeles, spreading out to Fresno and over to San Bernardino. He had names, lots of names. More than enough to make a practice out of. Not only was it out of the South, it was about as far as you could get from the South and the Clements, too.

He began to get excited at the very thought. No more stepping to the side door to get your meal like a hog at a trough. No more operations in somebody's kitchen and lynchings in the next county. He could dress like he wanted, act like he wanted, be who he wanted and how he wanted to be it. He would not have to try to protect his daughters from some planter with snuff in his mouth and know he couldn't. In California, he could stand up straight and not apologize for it. He would know what white people's water tasted like and drink it whenever he wanted. It wasn't one thing. It was everything. He was going to be a citizen of the United States, like the passport said.

He told Alice his decision. They could start out fresh in California, the four of them. He would go first and see it for himself. She and the girls would stay in Atlanta for now, and she could start packing their belongings. He would send for them after he got settled. All he had to do now was save a little money. And figure how best to get out.

AMERICA, 1915–1970

A SERIES OF UNPREDICTABLE EVENTS and frustrations led to the decisions of Ida Mae Gladney, George Swanson Starling, and Robert Pershing Foster to leave the South for good. Their decisions were separate and distinct from anything in the outside world except that they were joining a road already plied decades before by people as discontented as themselves. A thousand hurts and killed wishes led to a final determination by each fed-up individual on the verge of departure, which, added to millions of others, made up what could be called a migration.

If there was a single precipitating event that set off the Great Migra-

tion, it was World War I. After all, blacks had tried to escape the South
with limited degrees of success from the time the first slaves arrived in
Virginia in 1619. The Underground Railroad spirited hundreds of
slaves out of the South and as far north as Canada before the Civil War.
Later, in 1879, Benjamin "Pap" Singleton, a former slave who made
coffins for colored lynching victims and was disheartened by the steadi-
ness of his work, led a pilgrimage of six thousand ex-slaves, known as
Exodusters, from the banks of the Mississippi River onto the free soil of
Kansas.

In the ensuing decades, a continuous trickle of brave souls chanced an
unguaranteed existence in the unknown cities of the North. The trickle
became a stream after Jim Crow laws closed in on blacks in the South in
the 1890s. During the first decade of the twentieth century, some 194,000
blacks left the coastal and border states of the South and settled in relative anonymity in the colored quarters of primarily northeastern cities,
such as Harlem in New York and in North Philadelphia. Some were
domestics for wealthy northerners; others were musicians, intellectuals,
and exiled politicians of the Reconstruction era who would inspire colored people in the South by their very existence.

But the masses did not pour out of the South until they had something to go to. They got their chance when the North began courting
them, hard and in secret, in the face of southern hostility, during the
labor crisis of World War I. Word had spread like wildfire that the
North was finally "opening up."

The war had cut the supply of European workers the North had relied on to kill its hogs and stoke its foundries. Immigration plunged
by more than ninety percent, from 1,218,480 in 1914 to 110,618 in 1918,
when the country needed all the labor it could get for war production.
So the North turned its gaze to the poorest-paid labor in the emerging
market of the American South. Steel mills, railroads, and packinghouses
sent labor scouts disguised as insurance men and salesmen to recruit
blacks north, if only temporarily.

The recruiters would stride through groupings of colored people and
whisper without stopping, *"Anybody want to go to Chicago, see me."* It
was an invitation that tapped into pent-up yearnings and was just what
the masses had been waiting for. The trickle that became a stream had
now become a river, uncontrolled and uncontrollable, and about to
climb out of its banks. Some 555,000 colored people left the South
during the decade of the First World War—more than all the colored
people who had left in the five decades after the Emancipation Procla-

mation, which promised the freedoms they were now forced to pursue on their own.

At first the South was proud and ambivalent, pretended that it did not care. "As the North grows blacker, the South grows whiter," the *New Orleans Times-Picayune* happily noted.

Then, as planters awoke to empty fields, the South began to panic. "Where shall we get labor to take their places?" asked the *Montgomery Advertiser,* as southerners began to confront the reality observed by the *Columbia State* of South Carolina: "Black labor is the best labor the South can get. No other would work long under the same conditions."

"It is the life of the South," a Georgia plantation owner once said. "It is the foundation of its prosperity. . . . God pity the day when the negro leaves the South."

"With all our crimes of omission and commission, we still retain a marked affection for the Negro," wrote David L. Cohn in the 1935 book *God Shakes Creation.* "It is inconceivable to us that we should be without him."

The Macon Telegraph put it more bluntly: "We must have the negro in the South," it said. "It is the most pressing thing before this State today. Matters of governorships and judgeships are only bagatelle compared to the real importance of this negro exodus."

Yet as reality sank in, nobody could agree on what to do about it, debating to the point of exasperation. "Why hunt for the cause when it's plain as the noonday sun?" wrote a white reader in the *Montgomery Advertiser.* "He doesn't want to leave but he knows if he stays here he will starve. They have nothing to eat, no clothes, no shoes, and they can't get any work to do and they are leaving just as fast as they can get away. . . . If the Negro race could get work at 50 cents a day he would stay here."

And a newspaper in Columbia, South Carolina, put this question to the ruling caste: "If you thought you might be lynched by mistake," the paper asked, "would you remain in South Carolina?"

When the South woke up to the loss of its once guaranteed workforce, it tried to find ways to intercept it. Southern authorities resurrected the anti-enticement laws originally enacted after the Civil War to keep newly freed slaves from being lured away, this time, however, aimed at northern companies coveting the South's cheapest and most desperate workers.

"Conditions recently became so alarming—that is, so many Negroes were leaving," wrote an Alabama official, that the state began making anyone caught enticing blacks away—labor agents, they were called—

pay an annual license fee of $750 "in every county in which he operates or solicits emigrants" or be "fined as much as $500 and sentenced to a year's hard labor."

Macon, Georgia, required labor agents to pay a $25,000 fee and to secure the unlikely recommendations of twenty-five local businessmen, ten ministers, and ten manufacturers in order to solicit colored workers to go north. But by the middle of World War I, those laws were useless. Northern industries didn't need to recruit anymore. Word had spread, and the exodus took on a life of its own. "Every Negro that makes good in the North and writes back to his friends, starts off a new group," a Labor Department study observed.

So the South tried to choke off the flow of information about the North. The chief of police in Meridian, Mississippi, ordered copies of the *Chicago Defender* confiscated before they could be sold, fearing it was putting ideas into colored people's heads.

When the people kept leaving, the South resorted to coercion and interception worthy of the Soviet Union, which was forming at the same time across the Atlantic. Those trying to leave were rendered fugitives by definition and could not be certain they would be able to make it out. In Brookhaven, Mississippi, authorities stopped a train with fifty colored migrants on it and sidetracked it for three days. In Albany, Georgia, the police tore up the tickets of colored passengers as they stood waiting to board, dashing their hopes of escape. A minister in South Carolina, having seen his parishioners off, was arrested at the station on the charge of helping colored people get out. In Savannah, Georgia, the police arrested every colored person at the station regardless of where he or she was going. In Summit, Mississippi, authorities simply closed the ticket office and did not let northbound trains stop for the colored people waiting to get on.

Instead of stemming the tide, the blockades and arrests "served to intensify the desire to leave," wrote the sociologists Willis T. Weatherford and Charles S. Johnson, "and to provide further reasons for going."

To circumvent the heavy surveillance, some migrants simply bought tickets to cities two or three stations away where they would not be recognized or where there was less of a police presence. There, under less scrutiny, they bought tickets to their true destination. Those who had somehow gotten on the wrong side of somebody in the ruling class had to go to unusual lengths to get out, one man disguising himself as a woman to flee Crystal Springs, Mississippi, for Chicago in the 1940s.

Chastened by their losses, some businessmen tried conciliation, one delegation going so far as to travel to Chicago to persuade former share-croppers that things had changed and it was time they came back. (The sharecroppers showed no interest and instead took the opportunity to complain about being cheated and whipped while in their employ.) In the 1920s, the Tennessee Association of Commerce, the Department of Immigration of Louisiana, the Mississippi Welfare League, and the Southern Alluvial Land Association all sent representatives north to try to bring colored workers back. They offered free train tickets and promised better wages and living conditions. They returned empty-handed.

When these efforts didn't work, some planters increased wages, if only temporarily, and tried easing up on their workers to induce them to stay. "Owing to the scarcity of labor," the Labor Department reported, "a Georgia farmer near Albany this year laid aside his whip and gun, with which it is reported he has been accustomed to drive his hands, and begged for laborers."

Oblivious to the hand-wringing, trainloads of colored people took their chances and crowded railroad platforms. Men hopped freight trains and hoboed out of the South in grain bins. Women walked off cotton fields in Texas, hiding their Sunday dresses under their field rags, bound for California. A granite quarry in Lithonia, Georgia, had to shut down because its workers had vanished. "One section gang left their tools on the spot, not stopping to get their pay," Arna Bontemps wrote of one work site.

All the while, in the places they left, the weeds grew up over the cotton, the rice and tobacco lay fallow and unpicked, and the mules wandered the pastures because, as the historian James R. Grossman noted, there was no one to hitch them to a plow.

BREAKING AWAY

I was leaving without a qualm,
without a single backward glance.
The face of the South that I had known
was hostile and forbidding,
and yet out of all the conflicts
and the curses . . . ,
the tension and the terror,
I had somehow gotten the idea
that life could be different. . . .
I was now running more away
from something than toward something. . . .
My mood was:
I've got to get away;
I can't stay here.
— RICHARD WRIGHT, *Black Boy*

CHICKASAW COUNTY, MISSISSIPPI, OCTOBER 1937
IDA MAE BRANDON GLADNEY

IN A DAY, the world had changed. Everything was in a commotion, but George and Ida Mae could not let it show. Joe Lee had been beaten half dead over a false accusation about some turkeys that had run off. He had been left in a jail cell, barely conscious, his clothes sticking to his bloodied skin, and nothing was done about it. Ida Mae and George bent their heads and prayed for light. Then they went out in the field the next day. They picked long and hard and more urgently than before. They decided they would leave as soon as they got the cotton out of the ground.

They would give Mr. Edd no cause to suspect their intentions or to withhold their pay. They needed whatever was due at settlement to get out
of Mississippi.

They could not risk telling anyone but Saint and Miss Theenie and
the one or two other relatives they needed to help them get out. And so
they continued to gather the cotton. The land went from white to brown
as they made their way across it. They began selling off their possessions, one by one, so as not to attract attention. The cows. The hogs. The
chickens. The feather beds and quilts. The tin tub. The wash pots. The
rusted old Model T Ford. The double-blade axes Ida Mae used to chop
wood and kill snakes with. They went into town and sold what livestock was theirs and not Mr. Edd's. What they didn't sell they gave away
or left with Saint to dispense with.

And if anybody asked what was going on, they knew to say, "We just
running out of room."

For some reason, Ida Mae was dragging more than usual. But there
was so much to do and so little time, there was no point in mentioning
it. They needed to get out before people started speculating about what
it was they were doing. The way people talked, it wouldn't take long to
get back to Mr. Edd. Someone would love to curry favor, alert him to a
sharecropper trying to leave. There were spies and Toms all over the
place, setting up fellow colored men and sending them to their deaths
for an extra privilege or two. Planters did not like to lose good help.
They had ways of keeping sharecroppers under them, claimed they
owed money when they didn't, that they had to work off the debt,
which meant they were working for free and made fugitives of them if
they left. The planters kept the books, and, even if a sharecropper had
the nerve to keep his own, a colored man's numbers didn't count.

If George and Ida Mae didn't get out, life could be harder than it already was. The quicker they got the cotton out of the ground, the better
off they would be.

It was already late in the season, and before long they had picked
their last bale. George had to figure out how best to leave. He decided
first to get off Mr. Edd's land. They quietly gathered up what little they
were taking and carried it over to Miss Theenie's after the cotton was
picked. They would leave from the house where George had courted
Ida Mae.

George wanted to settle with Mr. Edd as soon as possible and prepared to go see him. After what happened to Joe Lee, Ida Mae worried
whenever George went out.

"George, be careful," she said.

"I ain't gon' be careful. I ain't done nothing to him."

George went up to Mr. Edd like it was any other end-of-the-season settlement. He gave no indication that it was his fervent hope never to see him again in life or ever again to set foot in the state of Mississippi.

He looked over the list of credits and debits Mr. Edd had tallied—the bales of cotton he and Ida Mae had gathered, the seed and cornmeal they had consumed. It didn't matter what he thought of it. He couldn't dispute it no matter what it said. At the bottom of the page was a figure that showed he had a few dollars coming to him for a year's worth of labor.

It was not much, but it was more than many sharecroppers got. Fewer than one out of five sharecroppers ever saw a profit at the end of the year. Of the few who got anything, their pay came to between $30 and $150 in the 1930s for a year of hard toil in the field, according to a leading Yale anthropologist of the era, or between nine and forty-eight cents a day. The remaining eighty percent either broke even, meaning they got nothing, or stayed in debt, which meant they were as bound to the planter as a slave was to his master.

There was no place to appeal. "How a man treats his tenants is not felt to be a matter of public concern," the anthropologist Hortense Powdermaker wrote, "but is as much his private affair as what brand of toothpaste he uses."

George did the math in his head and saw that, along with what he had managed to save up to this day, it was enough for four tickets north on the Illinois Central Railroad.

Mr. Edd handed him the bills, and George completed the transaction without so much as a smile, which was his way. He tucked the money in his pocket and thought about what next to say. There before him stood his boss man and overseer of close to ten years. Mr. Edd was a man a full head taller than George and partial to ten-gallon hats. Whatever he may have done to other colored people in the name of the white man's law, Mr. Edd had been honorable in his dealings with him. He had never raised a hand to him or Ida Mae, and George gave him no cause to do so.

George could have left after settlement without saying a word. It was a risk to say too much. The planter could rescind the settlement, say he misfigured, turn a credit into a debit, take back the money, evict the family or whip the sharecropper on the spot, or worse. Some sharecroppers, knowing they might not get paid anyway, fled from the field, right in midhoe, on the first thing going north.

The planters could not conceive of why their sharecroppers would want to leave. The dance of the compliant sharecropper conceding to the big planter year in and year out made it seem as if the ritual actually made sense, that the sharecropper, having been given no choice, actually saw the tilted scales as fair. The sharecropper's forced silence was part of the collusion that fed the mythology.

And so it came as a shock to many planters when their trusted sharecroppers expressed a desire to leave. Like one planter in Florence, Alabama. Year after year, he would go down the list of staples he said his sharecropper, Jack Fowler, owed:

I LB FLOUR

I LB RICE

I LB CORN MEAL

I LB COFFEE

The planter scanned the page and decided to add a few more pounds of coffee, increasing Fowler's debt to him. One year, the sharecropper finally spoke up, careful not to suggest the planter was a liar or an outright cheat.

"Mr. Perry, you know I don't drink coffee."

With that, the planter added another pound of coffee to the list. The sharecropper could do nothing but watch.

One year, the planter's son happened to come in during settlement and spoke up himself.

"Pa, you know Jack don't drink coffee."

And, for once, the sharecropper didn't have to pay for something he had never consumed in the first place.

Sometime after settlement, he went to tell his boss man he was leaving for a place called Lake Forest, Illinois. The planter had already settled with Jack Fowler and had no rational excuse to keep the sharecropper on his plantation, which didn't mean he couldn't have if he wanted to. Instead, the planter tried to scare the sharecropper out of leaving.

"Jack, you gonna go up there and freeze your brains," the planter told his sharecropper. "And who is going to handle my horses when you leave?"

———

Knowing the dangerous and arbitrary rules of the world he was in, George stood before Mr. Edd and weighed what he should say. Mr. Edd had already paid him, so George thought he was safe. They had agreed that George did not owe him and was not in the planter's debt. Mr. Edd had always been a man of his word, and George trusted him to keep it now. George made the calculation that the truth would serve him better than if he were later caught in a knowing omission. He prayed and breathed deep before speaking.

"Well, this'll be my last crop with you, Mr. Edd," George said. He told him he and Ida Mae were moving to Milwaukee.

Mr. Edd did not see it coming.

"Oh, you ain't gon' leave, George," Mr. Edd said.

George was a quiet man who could pick a whole field by himself without complaint. He took whatever was given him and knew not to question. Yet he had a way of walling off his family that even a segregationist could respect. George was the kind of sharecropper a planter could depend on, and Mr. Edd showed his appreciation by letting him clear a few dollars most years. Mr. Edd didn't want to lose George. He wanted to know what he was leaving for. George told him he didn't like what happened to Joe Lee.

"Oh, you ain't gon' leave for that," Mr. Edd said. "It wasn't none a you."

"I know," George said. "It wouldn't been me."

———

Ida Mae was gathering their belongings while George settled with Mr. Edd. She lumbered as she went about her packing. Miss Theenie looked at her hard. She saw something that nobody else would notice, how Ida Mae loped now, the way the burlap tugged across the front of her.

"Look to me like you pregnant," she said.

"Oh, no, I ain't."

"What you goin' up there for pregnant?"

"*I ain't pregnant.*"

She was a couple of months along now and had kept it to herself. George might tell her to stay in Mississippi, leave her and the children with Miss Theenie, say he would send for her like the other men who say they're going to send for their wives and don't, get up to the big city and forget all about what they left. If Miss Theenie knew, she would kick up a fuss and scare George into leaving Ida Mae there. So she lied to Miss Theenie, denied up and down that she was expecting, and Miss Theenie couldn't prove it but knew that time would tell and prove her right.

There was no way for Ida Mae to know what was transpiring between her husband and Mr. Edd at settlement. George had prayed over it and had hoped Mr. Edd would remain a man of his word. If all went well, George told Ida Mae, he would go to the train station in Okolona ahead of them. He wanted to get the tickets right away. He had arranged in advance for one of his brothers to take Ida Mae and the children to the station to meet him. The plan was for them to leave that night.

EUSTIS, FLORIDA, APRIL 1945

GEORGE SWANSON STARLING

———

LIL GEORGE BROKE THE NEWS to Inez that he was getting out of Eustis on the next train out of Wildwood. The grove owners had it in for him because he had roused up the pickers. The pickers had turned on him out of fear for themselves. He had no choice but to get out. He told Inez he was going up to Harlem, where his aunts were.

He started gathering his things right away. There was no time to waste. The yard boy who warned him about the grove owners' meeting didn't seem to know any more than what he'd happened to overhear—that the grove owners were plotting to take George and Mud and Sam out to the cypress swamps over at Blackwater Creek and hang them at "a necktie party," that the owners were bent on teaching them a lesson for stepping out of their place, demanding an extra dime for the fruit they picked, and turning the heads of the faithful other pickers who had been content with whatever the owners gave them.

There was no telling whom the grove owners might have enlisted, when or how they might round the boys up, whether it would be the new big-hat sheriff, some crew foremen, or Klansmen currying favor, whether it might be somebody George would recognize right away after all these years or not know at all. He went about his last-minute arrangements, watchful of everybody and careful to mind his steps.

He could not be seen anywhere near the groves again. It was dangerous enough just being in Eustis during the hours it took to get out. There were so many things he wanted or needed to do—he was leaving forever, after all—but he was running out of time.

He dashed off a letter to his aunts, Annie and Lavata, to alert them to his situation. They would need to know to expect him.

He tried to reassure Inez that everything would work out, but she was still seething over the fact that he had turned their lives upside down and put all of them in danger. She hadn't approved of what he had been doing anyway and didn't know why he couldn't make himself satisfied like everybody else.

"What did you expect from a bunch of handkerchief heads?" she asked him. "What do you expect?"

"I guess I expect the unexpectable," he said, "because they don't look at things like the way I do."

Here he was running for his life, and the two of them were arguing over what couldn't be undone. George didn't ask Inez what he should do. He didn't consult her as to where he should go or whether she would join him. He just told her he was going up to where his aunts were.

"I'm going to New York and get situated," he said. "And when I get situated, I'll send for you."

Their anniversary, April 19, was coming up in a few days, but if everything worked according to plan, he would be gone by then. He felt there was no time for debating and thought he should be the judge of what would happen to him. "After all," he would say years later, "it was my neck on the block."

Inez heard the magic words—"I'll send for you"—and did not put up much more of a fuss. He had not taken her to Detroit, but he would bring her to New York, and that was good enough for now. She warmed to the idea and felt better and better about it. She thought less now of the danger of the circumstances than of their new life up north. A chance to start over in a new place together.

———

He told Mud and Sam he was leaving. They were leaving, too. Sam was talking Washington, D.C., where he had a brother. Mud was talking about a place he had heard of called Rochester, New York. Then Lil

George said good-bye to Inez and good-bye to his father, who, if he was worried, kept it to himself.

"Yeah, well," Big George said, "I think this will be the best. I guess if you gonna still act that way, it's best for you to go."

MONROE, LOUISIANA, MARCH 1953
ROBERT JOSEPH PERSHING FOSTER

———

PERSHING WAS WORKING AT FORT POLK, an hour's drive from Monroe, for the singular purpose of saving up the money to go to California. His heart was already gone. His mother had died. His widowed father, Professor Foster, had been forced out as principal of the school to which he had devoted his life, by one of his own teachers. The coup left Professor Foster a leader in exile. He watched the new colored high school he had always dreamed of rise up under the name of his rival. Pershing grieved for his father and all that had happened in a caste system that seemed to rely on pitting the lowliest people against one another.

He drove between Monroe and Fort Polk at the edge of spring, blind to the wild grasses that blushed on either side of the Bayou Desiard. The bayou cut through town and bent toward the west, and the land was thick with crimson clover crawling up the folds in the land.

It was beautiful, but it didn't matter. Pershing was thirty-four years old. His life was in front of him, and he was not going to live it out in a one-stoplight town in the South.

On that, he and Alice had agreed, and she would wait for him to send for her and the girls once he got situated. Still, his brother Madison tried to get him to stay, reclaim the family's former glory. Madison had a small practice there and was ready to etch Pershing's name beside his on the door. The two of them could work out of Madison's second-floor office on Desiard. They could travel the parish in their portable hospital and tend to the colored schoolteachers and the women who took in washing, the athletes out at Grambling and the sharecroppers who might pay with buttermilk or the side of a freshly killed hog.

But Pershing did not want to be paid with buttermilk or the side of a freshly killed hog and did not want to deliver babies in somebody's kitchen.

There was a respectable hospital in town. St. Francis. It was a brick building that stood with the color and trim efficiency of a manila folder. It had white beds in one wing and colored beds in another and was closed to colored doctors. Pershing put St. Francis out of his mind and figured he would work at Fort Polk until he had the money to leave.

One day he went into town and walked into the old clothing shop of a white storekeeper. He had known the man since he was a little boy picking up clothes for his father.

"I'm M. J. Foster's boy. I think you have a suit for him," he used to go in and say.

Pershing was grown up now. He was in uniform with his captain's bars and medical caduceus. The storekeeper noticed and asked what he was going to do when he got out of the army.

"Well, I'm going to go into practice, private practice," Pershing said.

"Are you gonna come here with your brother?"

"No, I'm going to California and start my practice there when I get out of Fort Polk. And this is what I plan to do."

"What's wrong with St. Francis?"

Pershing shook his head. The man had lived there since before Pershing was born, and a central fact of colored people's existence hadn't registered after all these years.

"You know that colored surgeons can't operate at St. Francis, Mr. Massur."

The man looked startled and caught himself. White-only and colored-only signs were all over town, but the storekeeper had not thought about how segregation applied to the hospital. The storekeeper had watched Pershing grow into an upstanding young man and had known the Fosters for years. For a split second, the storekeeper seemed to see Pershing as no different than any other bright young physician. But Pershing's words brought him back to reality: the rest of the white world did not see Pershing the way the storekeeper did, and that gave the storekeeper an uncomfortable glimpse of the burdens on one of his best customers.

There was a moment of awkwardness between the two men. And as the realization hit the storekeeper, the truth hit Pershing, too. He stepped outside himself and considered the absurdity that he was doing surgery for the United States Army and couldn't operate in his own hometown.

The man tried to recover, offer advice and encouragement. "Well, why don't you all build a hospital, you and your brother?"

"Mr. Massur, do you realize that we are doctors and not businessmen? The cost of building a hospital and operating one would be astronomical."

There was very little to say after that. Even the storekeeper could see the impossibility of the situation. He wished Pershing well in whatever he did, and Pershing went on his way.

Mr. Massur had meant well. Still it made no sense to Pershing that one set of people could be in a cage, and the people outside couldn't see the bars. But he told himself it didn't matter anyway because he was through with Monroe, through with small towns and small minds and particularly small-minded small towns in the South.

He didn't like how you couldn't get your teeth cleaned without everybody knowing it. He didn't like how the white people couldn't quite manage to call him "Dr. Foster" but spat out "Doc" as if they were addressing the cook. He didn't like how his brother Madison denied himself certain twentieth-century conveniences to avoid submitting to the indignities of Jim Crow.

Madison never went to the side window of a white restaurant, never sat in the back of the Paramount Theater like other colored people. Because he never went. He drove his son, little Madison James, to the theater and watched the colored people climb the back stairs and pack the balcony to see whatever was playing. But he never went inside himself.

In the 1940s, Madison had petitioned St. Francis Hospital for a position on staff. The hospital rejected him. But he refused to leave town, and he didn't let it stop him from working. If he couldn't practice at a hospital, he would carry a hospital in his trunk. He had a portable operating table built especially for his patients and lugged it into their shotgun houses when it was time to do surgery or deliver their babies.

He didn't suffer the humiliation of seeing a suit he wanted to try on in a store but couldn't because colored people weren't allowed that courtesy. He just never went. He sent his wife, Harriet, instead. The two of them would drive up and down Desiard Street from Hanes to the Palace, the finest men's stores in town. Madison sat in the car and waited while Harriet went from store to store and came out with an armload of clothes. She held up each suit on its hanger. He inspected the weave and the cut from the car window and told her which ones to buy. And that is how Madison got his wardrobe.

Pershing wouldn't stand for that. Pershing wanted to walk right into the Palace and try on a suit if he pleased and sit in a corner booth at The Lounge if he wanted. He was restless for a basic kind of freedom that was crazy at best and arrogant at worst for a colored man in that place at that time, and the two brothers knew it.

One last time, each made his pitch to the other. Pershing tried to get Madison to go with him to California, set up practice there. After all, they practically had a clientele waiting for them. Half of colored Monroe was already out there. Madison tried to get Pershing to stay. Louisiana was home, and things would never change if everyone gave up and left. What did Pershing know about starting a practice in California? He had never set foot in California. Running away meant Jim Crow had won, and Madison wasn't going to give the rascals that. And besides, there was no guarantee Jim Crow wasn't out in California.

It was getting to be early April. The brothers made a necessary peace. Pershing decided to leave the day after Easter with Madison's blessing, if not approval, and readied for the round of formal good-byes.

———

The Covingtons, who lived down the street from Madison, heard Pershing was leaving and planned the going-away party for the Saturday night before Easter. The Hills, the Browns, January the Tailor, and all the better-off colored people in New Town gathered at the Covingtons' white frame bungalow with the azaleas out front at the corner of Eleventh and Louise Anne Avenue.

Ivorye Covington cooked all day for the Fosters—fried chicken and waffles and collard greens and corn bread. The place was prim with white tablecloths and upholstery and smoky from the Camels and Chesterfields.

Pershing, the bon vivant in sport coat and ruler-creased trousers, made the rounds through the dining room and living room and Ivorye's yellow kitchen with a shot of bourbon in his hand. He was leaving first thing Monday morning, he told everyone, heading southwest to Houston on his way west to first stop by and see a Dr. Anthony Beale—*you remember Anthony Beale, who used to go out with my sister, Gold; he's practicing in Houston now, and he said he could help me get started there, but I said thank you very much, but I'm set on California.*

Late into the evening, Ivorye's husband, N.E., turned down the record player in the front room, clearing the haze of chatter and bebop. The dancing by the credenza came to a stop. And Napoleon Brown and

Pless Hill, Big Madison and Harriet and the rest raised their glasses to Pershing, who was joining the Migration without them.

Pershing looked out into the faces and could not for the life of him figure out why these people were frittering away their lives in a place like this.

"How in the world can you stay in Monroe," he finally said, "and live in this Jim Crow situation?"

It was pompous, as he was at times known to be, and perhaps out of place at so well meaning a send-off. But he had convinced himself it was crazy to stay and wrong if he left without coming right out and saying it.

"How can you stay here and take the crumbs?" he said. "Come go to Heaven with me. To California."

He knew no more about California than they did, and he won no immediate converts that night. But he had planted the seed and would follow up once he had seen the state for himself.

I pick up my life
And take it with me
And I put it down in
Chicago, Detroit,
Buffalo, Scranton . . .
I pick up my life
And take it on the train
To Los Angeles, Bakersfield,
Seattle, Oakland, Salt Lake,
Any place that is
North and West—
And not South.
    —LANGSTON HUGHES,
    "ONE-WAY TICKET"

AMERICA, 1915–1975

AS THEY SUMMONED THE WILL TO LEAVE, it would never have occurred to Ida Mae, George, and Pershing, or the millions of others who continued to flee the South over the decades of the Great Migration, that it was supposed to have ended in World War I, when they were just coming into the world. They joined a flight already in progress when the narrow straits of their lives compelled them to do so. Theirs is a kind of living testimony that migrations fed by the human heart do not begin and end as neatly as statisticians might like.

The Great Migration in particular was not a seasonal, contained, or singular event. It was a statistically measurable demographic phenomenon marked by unabated outflows of black émigrés that lasted roughly from 1915 to 1975. It peaked during the war years, swept a good portion of all the black people alive in the United States at the time into a river that carried them to all points north and west.

Like other mass migrations, it was not a haphazard unfurling of lost souls but a calculable and fairly ordered resettlement of people along the most direct route to what they perceived as freedom, based on railroad and bus lines. The migration streams were so predictable that by the end of the Migration, and, to a lesser degree, even now, one can tell where a black northerner's family was from just by the city the person grew up in—a good portion of blacks in Detroit, for instance, having roots in Tennessee, Alabama, western Georgia, or the Florida panhandle because the historic rail lines connected those places during the Migration years.

"Migratory currents flow along certain well-defined geographical channels," wrote E. G. Ravenstein, a British historian, in his landmark 1885 study of human migration. "They are like mighty rivers, which flow along slowly at the outset and after depositing most of the human beings whom they hold in suspension, sweep along more impetuously, until they enter one of the great . . . reservoirs."

The Great Migration ran along three main tributaries and emptied into reservoirs all over the North and West. One stream, the one George Starling was about to embark upon, carried people from the coastal states of Florida, Georgia, the Carolinas, and Virginia up the eastern seaboard to Washington, Philadelphia, New York, Boston, and their satellites. A second current, Ida Mae's, traced the central spine of the continent, paralleling the Father of Waters, from Mississippi, Alabama, Tennessee, and Arkansas to the industrial cities of Cleveland, Detroit, Chicago, Milwaukee, Pittsburgh. A third and later stream carried people like Pershing from Louisiana and Texas to the entire West Coast, with some black southerners traveling farther than many modern-day immigrants.

The chronology of this Great Migration, as is the case in many immigrant experiences, was sometimes a more circuitous affair than might be expected and has at times been reported. Some participants of the Great Migration made trips outside the South before their actual and final leaving, which suggests that a great deal of ambivalent churning preceded a fair number of departures. Many served overseas during wartime, in the First and Second World Wars and in the conflict in Korea. Some managed to visit relatives up north; some tried to make a go of it in one city before trying out another. These trips often exposed them to the freedoms they were denied back home, served as way stations where they could earn enough money for the next leg of their journey, or otherwise emboldened them and fed their desire to migrate. Thus, leaving the South was not always a direct path but one of testing and checking of facts with those who had left ahead of them, before making the great leap themselves.

Yet the hardened and peculiar institution of Jim Crow made the Great Migration different from ordinary human migrations. In their desperation to escape what might be considered a man-made pestilence, southern blacks challenged some scholarly assumptions about human migration. One theory has it that, due to human pragmatism and inertia, migrating people tend to "go no further from their homes in search of work than is absolutely necessary," Ravenstein observed.

"The bulk of migrants prefers a short journey to a long one," he wrote. "The more enterprising long-journey migrants are the exceptions and not the rule." Southern blacks were the exception. They traveled deep into far-flung regions of their own country and in some cases clear across the continent. Thus the Great Migration had more in common with the vast movements of refugees from famine, war, and genocide in other parts of the world, where oppressed people, whether fleeing twenty-first-century Darfur or nineteenth-century Ireland, go great distances, journey across rivers, deserts, and oceans or as far as it takes to reach safety with the hope that life will be better wherever they land.

PART THREE

EXODUS

There is no mistaking
what is going on;
it is a regular exodus.
It is without head, tail, or leadership.
Its greatest factor is momentum,
and this is increasing,
despite amazing efforts on the part
of white Southerners to stop it.
People are leaving their homes
and everything about them,
under cover of night,
as though they were going
on a day's journey—
leaving forever.
    —The Cleveland Advocate,
        APRIL 28, 1917

We look up at
the high southern sky. . . .
We scan the kind black faces
we have looked upon
since we first saw the light of day,
and, though pain is in our hearts,
we are leaving.
    —RICHARD WRIGHT,
    12 Million Black Voices

THE APPOINTED TIME
OF THEIR COMING

Even the stork
in the sky knows
her appointed seasons,
and the dove,
the swift and the thrush
observe the time
of their migration.
—JEREMIAH 8:7

NEAR OKOLONA, MISSISSIPPI, LATE AUTUMN 1937
IDA MAE BRANDON GLADNEY

IDA MAE AND THE CHILDREN rumbled over curled ribbons of dirt road in a brother-in-law's truck from Miss Theenie's house to the train depot in Okolona. Piled high around them were all the worldly possessions they could manage to carry—the overalls and Sunday clothes, the cook pots and kerosene lamps, a Bible and the quilts that Ida Mae and Miss Theenie had sewn out of used-up remnants of the clothes they had worn out tilling the Mississippi soil. Miss Theenie had not wanted them to go and had prayed over them and with them and then watched as her second-born daughter left the rutted land of the ancestors. *"May the Lord be the first one in the car,"* Miss Theenie had whispered about the train they were hoping to catch, *"and the last out."*

Heading to the depot through the dust hollows and the cotton fields and away from the only place she had ever lived, Ida Mae did not know what would become of them or if her husband could actually pull this thing off. She did not know if Mr. Edd would let them go or stand in their way, if her husband would get anything from Mr. Edd at settlement, if they would be better off up north or, if they failed, worse off for having the nerve to try to leave—and if, in the end, they would truly make it out of Mississippi at all.

But there at the depot was her husband, the taciturn man who kept his emotions to himself, who had courted her and won her over despite Miss Theenie's objections, and who had decided that he did not want his family under the mercurial thumb of Mississippi for one more hour. He had not asked Ida Mae what she thought about leaving or whether she wanted to go. He had merely announced his decision as the head of the family, as was his way, and Ida Mae had gone along with it, as was hers.

She had not wanted to leave Miss Theenie and her sister Talma and all the people she had ever known, but her lot was with her husband, and she would go where he thought it best. Both she and Miss Theenie could take comfort in knowing that Ida Mae's sister Irene would be there to receive them in Milwaukee and that half her husband's siblings were up north in Beloit, Wisconsin, and in Chicago, and so Ida Mae would not be alone in that new land.

Mr. Edd had been a man of his word. He did not try to keep George and Ida Mae from leaving. George had gotten a few dollars from Mr. Edd and managed to secure four train tickets to Milwaukee via Chicago, having likely secured them not in Houston, where he might have been recognized, but in Okolona, where he was less likely to be noticed and where they would be leaving from.

And so the family—Ida Mae, George, Velma, James, and the little one still forming in Ida Mae's belly—boarded a train in Okolona. They were packed in with the baggage in the Jim Crow car with the other colored passengers with their babies and boxes of fried chicken and boiled eggs and their belongings overflowing from paper bags in the overhead compartment. The train pulled out of the station at last, and Ida Mae was on her way out of Chickasaw County and out of the state of Mississippi for the first time in her life.

EUSTIS, FLORIDA, APRIL 14, 1945
GEORGE SWANSON STARLING

———

GEORGE HAD NO TIME for formalities or the seeking of advice or reas-surance. He had to go. There was no point in discussing it, and no one he told tried to argue him out of leaving, except for Inez, who wasn't so concerned that he was going but that he wasn't taking her with him. He hadn't had time to figure out what to do with Inez. All he knew was he had to get himself out of Lake County, Florida, before the grove owners got to him first.

All three of the men who had stirred up the commotion in the groves were heading out quick: George to New York, Charlie to Rochester, Sam to Washington, D.C. They each had to figure out where they knew somebody up north and the most direct route to wherever the people they knew were located. They did not so much choose the place as the place presented itself as the most viable option in the time they had to think about it. They did not dare travel to the train station together or allow themselves to be seen together once it was clear they had to get out.

George would be traveling fast and light—a few books, some papers, a change of clothes. He got a man most people wouldn't associate him with but whom he felt he could trust, old Roscoe Colton, to drive him to the train station at Wildwood, a good forty-five minutes' drive on the two-lane gravel roads from Eustis. They rode through the groves that George had picked and that he knew the names of and were the reason he was forced to leave. But he wasn't feeling sentimental about it. He had to get out of the county first. The two of them had to make sure they didn't attract attention to themselves, didn't get stopped along the way, and weren't being followed.

They went west with the sun, rambling along the southern edge of Lake Eustis, passing the county seat of Tavares, where George and Inez had gotten married at the courthouse almost exactly six years before, and crossing into Sumter County between Lake Deaton and Lake Okahumpka. Roscoe Colton's truck pulled up to the depot at Wild-wood, and George, tight and sober-faced, walking slow and deliberate so as not to look like the fugitive he had unwittingly become, climbed the colored steps onto the Silver Meteor, headed for New York.

MONROE, LOUISIANA, THE MONDAY AFTER EASTER 1953
ROBERT JOSEPH PERSHING FOSTER

IN THE DARK HOURS OF THE MORNING, Pershing Foster pulled
away from his father and brother, the house on Louise Anne Avenue,
and his caged existence in the caste-bound, isolated South. The night
clouds crawled eastward, the sky itself floating in the opposite direction from him in the damp, cool air. He pointed his Buick Roadmaster
to the west, away from Monroe, and settled into the tufted bench seat
for the nearly two thousand miles of road ahead of him, the distance
that now stood between him and California, between Jim Crow and
freedom.

He was setting out on a course that was well trodden by 1953. In the
years before Pershing's migration, many hundreds of people from Monroe and thousands more from the rest of Louisiana had joined the river
to California. Mantan Moreland, a minor Hollywood figure who made
a name for himself as the fumbling manservant and loyal incompetent
of black-and-white comedies and Charlie Chan capers, left Monroe for
Los Angeles during the Depression. It spread around New Town that
he had been on his way to shining shoes in West Monroe and passed a
tree with a colored man hanging from it. He left that day and headed to
California.

A toddler named Huey Newton was spirited from Monroe to Oakland with his sharecropper parents in 1943. His father had barely escaped a lynching in Louisiana for talking back to his white overseers.
Huey Newton would become perhaps the most militant of the disillu-
sioned offspring of the Great Migration. He founded the Black Panther
Party in 1966 and reveled in discomfiting the white establishment with
his black beret, rifle, and black power rhetoric.

Another boy from Monroe who migrated with his parents to Oakland took an entirely different path. He would go on to become one of
the greatest basketball players of all time. Bill Russell was born in Monroe in 1934 and watched his parents suffer one indignity after another.
His father once went to a gas station only to be told he would have to
wait for the white people to get their gas first. He waited and waited,
and, when his turn seemed never to come, he started to pull off. The
owner came up, put a shotgun to his head, and told him he was not to
leave until all the white people had been served.

"Boy, don't you ever do what you just started to do," the station owner said.

As for Russell's mother, a policeman once grabbed her on the street and ordered her to go and take off the suit she was wearing. He said that she had no business dressing like a white woman and that he'd arrest her if he ever saw her like that again. Bill Russell watched his mother sit at the kitchen table in tears over the straits they were in.

Soon afterward, his parents packed up the family and moved to Oakland, where a colony of people from Monroe had fled. Russell was nine years old. He would get to go to better schools, win a scholarship to the University of San Francisco, and lead his team, the Dons, to two NCAA championships, a first for an integrated basketball team, collegiate or professional. He would join the Celtics in 1956 and lead Boston to eleven championships in his thirteen seasons. He would become perhaps the greatest defensive player in NBA history and the first black coach in the NBA. There is no way to know what might have happened to Bill Russell had his parents not migrated. What is known is that his family had few resources and that he would not have been allowed into any white college in Louisiana in the early 1950s, and thus would not have been in a position to be recruited to the NBA. The consequences of his absence from the game would now be unimaginable to followers of the sport.

In Pershing's own circle, a funeral director named John Dunlap went to Oakland. Pershing's boyhood friend Jimmy Marshall had been out in Los Angeles since the war. A friend named Limuary Jordan moved out to L.A. in 1950. By the time Pershing turned the corner of Desiard Street for good, more than 462,000 colored people, many of them from Louisiana and Texas, were already out in California, most of them people he never knew but who had joined the march before him.

World War II had set off a virtual stampede. In all of California, there had been only 124,306 colored people in 1940, before the United States entered the war. But during the rest of that decade, the population almost quadrupled—337,866 more hopeful souls flooded into California for the shipyard jobs and the defense industry jobs and the ancillary jobs that came with the wartime and postwar economy. More colored people migrated to California in the 1940s than had come in all the previous decades put together. And so, heading out as he was in 1953, Pershing left with the feeling that the Great Migration had passed him by, that he was playing catch-up with a tide that had already rolled away. He drove with a sense of urgency, not knowing that he was, in fact, right in the middle of a wave that was more than fifteen years from ebbing. Another 340,000 colored people would go to California in the fifties, the decade he left Louisiana. Another quarter million would follow in the sixties.

For now, he imagined there was a whole world just waiting for him to get there, people living the high life in Los Angeles and building businesses in Oakland. He had no idea which city he would end up in. He was partial to Los Angeles, based on what he knew of it from the movies he had seen at the Paramount, but there were more people from Monroe in Oakland. He decided not to worry about that now. He would visit them both and decide once he got there. The thing he knew for sure was he was going to California.

———

He drove west and slightly south in the direction of Houston, where he would visit a Dr. Anthony Beale and knew he could be assured of a place to rest for the night. The sun rose behind him in his rearview mirror. He drove alone with only the radio to keep him company, stations moving in and out like guests at a party. As soon as he got used to one, another would break in and take its place, often the new one not nearly so engaging as the last.

He had nothing but time, time to think, and, as he drove, he knew this was the time to shed his southern self for good, starting with the name. *Pershing*. It was stiff and archaic and not him at all. It was for another man and time. His mother had meant well when she named him after John J. Pershing, the World War I general. It was the fall of 1918. She was growing full with her last son forming inside her, and General Pershing was pushing the Germans past the Argonne Forest when an armistice ended the Great War. The general was a household name at the time, an American hero, and she decided to add the name to the list she had in mind for her unborn child.

The baby was delivered by a midwife on Christmas Day 1918. His full name would be Robert Joseph Pershing Foster. His mother called him Pershing after the general and insisted that everyone else do the same.

A name was a serious undertaking. It was the first and maybe only thing colored parents could give a child, and they were often sentimental about it. They had a habit of recycling the names of beloved kinpeople, thus ending up with three or four Lou Dellas in one or two generations. Out of the confusion it created, children got nicknames like Boo or Pip or Sweet, which after repeated use meant nobody knew anybody's given name until they got married or died. It left mourners at southern funerals not knowing for sure who was in the casket unless the preacher called out "Junebug" in the eulogy. *Oh, that's Junebug that died!*

Sometimes parents tried to superimpose glory on their offspring with the grandest title they could think of, or, if they were feeling especially militant, the name of a senator or president from the North. It was a way of affixing acceptability if not greatness. It forced everyone, colored and white, to call their janitor sons Admiral or General or John Quincy Adams, whether anybody, including the recipient, liked it or not. White southerners who would not call colored people Mr. or Mrs. were made to sputter out Colonel or Queen instead.

And so, growing up, he was called not by his first name, Robert, but by the more imperial-sounding Pershing. The problem was that by the time he got to grade school nobody in Monroe knew or cared much about the feats of an ancient general way off in Europe somewhere. It had no meaning to the people around him, and he was the only Pershing they knew. The colored children in New Town had a hard time pronouncing it. They called him *Percy, Purly, Persian, Putty,* which made an ill-fitting name even less bearable and a mockery of his mother's intentions.

He was starting over now. His mother was gone. What he would be called would be up to him. In California, he would be Robert or, better yet, Bob. Bob with a martini and stingy-brim hat. It was modern and hip, and it suited the new version of himself as the leading man in his own motion picture. He had tested it out in Atlanta, and it had caught on. The people in California who knew him back home would get used to it in time. *Bob.* Simple and direct and easy to remember. He rolled the word around in his mind, and he liked it.

ON THE ILLINOIS CENTRAL RAILROAD, OCTOBER 1937
IDA MAE BRANDON GLADNEY

———

IDA MAE SAT UP and watched Mississippi blur past her through the film of soot on the train window. By some miracle, she and her husband had managed to keep their secret from most of the plantation through-out the picking season and left whole branches of the family and people they had known since childhood in the dark as to what they were up to. They couldn't chance it and had no choice. "You didn't go around telling neighbors and everybody else in the farm. A lot of 'em didn't know we was gone," she said, "till we was gone."

The two of them, along with little James and Velma, boarded a screeching metal horse on wheels, heading north and slightly west on the Mobile and Ohio Railroad, a feeder line to the main rail. They rode in the darkness on an old train called The Rebel, a mule-headed relic of the Confederate South, rattling toward something they had never seen and did not know. Over the course of the next twenty-four hours, they would have to collect their belongings and change trains in Jackson, Tennessee, to board the Illinois Central Railroad, the legendary rail system that, for a great portion of the twentieth century, carried upward of a million colored people from the Deep South up the country's central artery, across the Mason-Dixon Line, and into a new world called the Midwest. It carried so many southern blacks north that Chicago would go from 1.8 percent black at the start of the twentieth century to one-third black by the time the flow of people finally began to slow in 1970. Detroit's black population would skyrocket from 1.4 percent to 44 per-cent during the era of the Migration.

It would not have occurred to them that they were riding history. They were leaving as a family, not as a movement, on the one thing going north. But as it happened, the Illinois Central, along with the At-lantic Coast Line and Seaboard Air Line railroads, running between Florida and New York, and the Union Pacific, connecting Texas and California, had become the historic means of escape, the Overground Railroad for slavery's grandchildren. It hurtled its passengers along the same route and under the same night sky as the Underground Railroad, the secret network of safe houses leading north that had spirited slaves to freedom the previous century.

Even before the first anxious sharecroppers boarded the Illinois Cen-tral, sometime in the early stages of World War I, the railroad had a pedigree that made it inadvertently synonymous with freedom to black southerners who could manage to secure a ticket. The Illinois Central Railroad was founded in 1850 as a connector between Chicago and Cairo, a river town at the southern tip of the state, adding steamboats down the Mississippi and ultimately rail lines to New Orleans and the Gulf of Mexico. For a time, Mark Twain piloted the railroad's steamboats up and down the Mississippi, and Abraham Lincoln was a rising attorney on retainer to the railroad before his election to the White House.

The Civil War brought an end to regular passenger use, and the railroad was pressed into the service of the Union Army, funneling troops and supplies from the North to the South for the war effort. At war's end, the railroad laid or acquired tracks into the more isolated precincts of Mississippi, Arkansas, Tennessee, and Louisiana and unwittingly made the North a more accessible prospect for black southerners desperate to escape. Each train route of the Illinois Central had a name of its own. The trains were called The Planter, The Creole, The Diamond, The Panama Limited, and, most famous of all, the one that Ida Mae rode, The Louisiane, later renamed The City of New Orleans, which went straight up the country's spine from the Mississippi Delta to the flat wheat prairie land and Chicago itself.

The Illinois Central brought more than merely the chance to leave. It brought parcels from the North that became accidental marketing brochures—the catalogues from Sears, Roebuck, the lovingly wrapped boxes of hand-me-downs from relatives who had made it north, and the discreetly bound copies of the *Chicago Defender,* the colored newspaper that was virulently anti-South and for that reason virtually banned in the region. Pullman porters smuggled the paper into the luggage holds during their regular runs between Chicago and the Deep South, hurling them out by the bundle at strategic points along their routes and thus spreading the word about the possibilities of the North. This makeshift distribution system helped make the *Chicago Defender* one of the most widely circulated black newspapers in the country by the end of World War I and its founder, a migrant from Georgia named Robert Sengstacke Abbott, one of the richest colored men in the country.

The Illinois Central sped past the pine woods and the cotton fields, and in time the railroad's cars were packed with the peasant caste of the South, "the huddled masses yearning to breathe free" in their own country and, save for their race and citizenry, not unlike the passengers crossing the Atlantic in steerage with the intention of never returning to the old country.

Ida Mae and her family boarded the Illinois Central in the middle of the Great Migration, during the statistical lull between the peak outflows of colored southerners during the world wars, unaware of the enormity of the thing and what it might mean beyond themselves.

ON THE SILVER METEOR, APRIL 14, 1945
GEORGE SWANSON STARLING

———

GEORGE WAS STUFFED into a hardback seat in the baggage car on the Silver Meteor up the East Coast. He was packed in with other colored passengers breaking open their cold chicken and hard-boiled eggs and shushing their children. He didn't pay them much mind. He was still too mad thinking about why he was on that train in the first place.

"I was angry," he said later, conjuring up emotions of fifty years before. "I was angry with my people. We caused them to earn more money in one day than they ever earned in a whole week. And they would complain, 'us not lettin' them work' one or two times. It was only about two or three occasions where we didn't work because we didn't get the price we asked for. And they go to the man's house at night and complain. They made it even worse for us. They couldn't see that we were helping them till after we all scattered."

For once he was riding in the front of something, as opposed to the customary back of everything else. On the railroad, the Jim Crow car was usually the first car behind the coal-fired locomotive that belched soot, fumes, and engine noise. It was the car that would take the brunt of any collision in the event of a train wreck. It was where the luggage and colored passengers were placed, even though their train fare was no different from what white passengers in the quieter rear of the train paid for the same class of service. He and the other colored passengers just had to live with it. George gave it little thought because he was on his way out.

EAST TEXAS, APRIL 1953
ROBERT JOSEPH PERSHING FOSTER

THE LAND WAS CHANGING now as Robert passed over into Texas, the
two-lane road fringed yellow with buttercups, the pine stands giving
way to cattle ranches and barbecue joints in Panola County. He passed
Fish Lake Slough and Flat Fork Creek north of Timpson. The air was
moist and heavy now. As he drew near to Splendora County and on to
Houston, there was a drizzle in the air and fog on the ground that hid
the trees behind a gray veil.

He would eventually follow the country's southern hemline along the
Rio Grande. He could have taken the worn Mother Road of the Dust
Bowl itinerants and young easterners in their convertibles with the
wind whipping their Elvis pompadours. He could have joined Route 66
early on in Oklahoma City, due northwest of Monroe, or in Elk City,
Oklahoma, or in Amarillo, Texas.

But that was not considered the most direct route to Los Angeles, and
all along he had planned to stop in Houston, where he could stay with
Dr. Beale, his friend from back in medical school. And as he never did
anything ordinary and as he wanted to cross into another country if only
by a few yards to say that he had tasted the tequila, he took a circuitous
route to Nuevo Laredo on the Mexican border, which would satisfy his
craving for adventure and for doing whatever he did with style and
grandiosity.

He pulled into Houston and up to Dr. Beale's house feeling good
about his decision and the world. The trip so far had been smooth, as of
course it would be in that Buick Roadmaster. He didn't know when he
had ever been so happy as the day he bought that car. It made a good impression wherever it went, which is exactly what he wanted.

"If you had seen it, you would have wanted it, too," he would say
years later. "They just took chrome and splashed it on that car when
they made it, the Roadmaster Buick. And it rode like a chariot. I bought
it in St. Louis and drove through a housing project, and I can hear the
little kids screaming now, *'Good Lord, look at that car.'* "

Dr. Beale knew he was coming and took it upon himself to show
Robert around Houston. They relived their medical school days, and
Dr. Beale repeated his offer to help Robert set up practice there if Robert
was willing to consider it. But Robert's heart was set on California. He

was trying to get away from the South. Texas, with its segregation and cotton fields, never stood a chance. And so Robert declined the offer and, after thanking his friend for the hospitality, set off in the direction of the nearest border town, Laredo.

There he crossed the bridge over the Rio Grande into Nuevo Laredo in Mexico. He drove past the clay storefronts where they sold garlic cloves and pictures of Jesus. The music cried out from second-floor windows, and the streets felt like alleys. He slowed near the places that peddled *vinos y licores* and came to a stop near the cantinas with their gringo girlie posters and red vinyl-top bar stools off Guerrero Street.

He got there in time to sample the margaritas before nightfall and, though he enjoyed the tequila, thought it best to head back before too long. He crossed the Rio Grande again and awaited clearance at U.S. customs. He waited longer than he thought he should, which might have been trivial under normal circumstances but was an eternity to him at the time.

He had a long drive ahead of him. There were 766 miles between Laredo and a town called Lordsburg, New Mexico, where friends had assured him he'd find safe lodging. That meant he had fifteen hours of driving without sleep, and that was only if he managed to keep an ambitious pace of fifty miles an hour on those two-lane highways winding through every whistle stop en route.

Robert was anxious to get back on the road. His turn in line had finally come, and here were the border patrolmen smoking and chatting it up with each other.

"I shouldn't have to wait this long for you to check me clear," he finally said.

"If you want to cross the border, you better shut up," a patrolman said.

Night was forming and Robert needed to get on his way. He didn't have the luxury of checking into a hotel that night as long as he was in the state of Texas. He didn't need any further delay. So he did as they said. They waved him through.

He was more tired now than before. He had more than half of Texas in front of him and a couple of hours of margaritas in his veins. There were roadside motels on both sides of the highway, but he drove past them and gave them no thought. There was no point in asking for a room. They didn't take colored people, and it did no good to think about it. They might as well not have existed.

He reassured himself with the advice he'd gotten that there was a motel in Lordsburg, New Mexico, that took in colored people. He drove over dry riverbeds and through the Stockton Plateau and came parallel to the Texas Pecos Trail near Del Rio.

He was leaving the wet green land for the dry dust land, and there were times he couldn't go any further. The eyelids grew heavy, and the road seemed to blur. He would look for a safe place, the next town maybe, a mile or ten miles or twenty miles down the road, a place not so isolated and alone but quiet enough to be still. He would have to keep himself awake until he found such a place. He would pull over into an empty filling station or a wedge in the road and shut his eyes to rest.

He wouldn't sleep in another bed until he got out of the state of Texas.

The long and thinly populated stretches were the hard gasp of the journey. Every fifty or sixty miles, you saw a crippled Hudson or Pontiac, overheated, engine trouble, out of gas. It reminded you of the treachery of it all and how lucky you were still to be moving. In west Texas, there were fewer and fewer towns, and what towns there were, were smaller and farther apart. If you got stranded, you could only sit and hope that help arrived before the next meal. There was no assurance of a telephone and no way to reach anyone in the event of an emergency. If a tire went flat or a fan belt broke or the car let out a strange crackle or groan, your fate was in the hands of the gods. You could go an hour without seeing another car on the road.

At night, when you couldn't see, you were grateful for the occasional truck wheezing up the hill ahead of you and lighting your path. You might piggyback him even though he was going slower than you would like.

There developed a code of the road among colored people making the crossing. When you got sleepy, there were places you stopped and places you didn't. You stopped at a filling station and asked if the owner minded if you parked there. If you saw a car or two stopped on the side of the road, you might pull up. Somebody else might pull up behind you and do the same.

You tried to stay awake until you found such a place. It might take fifteen minutes. It might take an hour. Before stopping, you ran your eyes over the resting car's bumper and rear windshield, checked for a Confederate flag. You would be crazy to pull up behind one of those. If you saw a pack of cars, you were wary. If you had to stop, you wanted to stop behind one car resting, someone tired and alone like yourself.

The next morning, not having been able to check into a motel, you might stop at a gas station and slap water on your face in the restroom or gargle with ginger ale or fountain water under a colored-only sign.

It called for exquisite planning and a certain surrender to whatever lay ahead. In making the crossing two years before, Limuary Jordan, whom Robert knew back in Monroe, loaded up on bread and lunch meat at the grocery store for himself and his family. They stopped only once, at a colored motel in El Paso. They would drive their DeSoto for three full days and three full nights.

They carried with them twenty-five pounds of ice in a lard bucket as a makeshift air conditioner—or for the radiator if it overheated, an affliction so many of those wheezing old jalopies were prone to suffer—along with a copy of the 121st Psalm:

> *I raise my eyes toward the mountains.*
> *From where will my help come?*
> *My help comes from the Lord,*
> *the maker of heaven and earth.*
> *God will not allow your foot to slip;*
> *your guardian does not sleep. . . .*
> *By day the sun cannot harm you,*
> *nor the moon by night.*
> *The Lord will guard you from all evil,*
> *will always guard your life.*
> *The Lord will guard your coming and going*
> *both now and forevermore.*

Robert was not a particularly religious man, but he was a determined one. He might not have known the blessing for pilgrims making a dangerous trek, the Old Testament prayer some other migrants carried with them, but the spirit of it would follow him nonetheless, and, whether he knew it or not, he would come to need its reassurance and protection for the long, lonely journey into the desert.

ON THE ILLINOIS CENTRAL RAILROAD, OCTOBER 1937
IDA MAE BRANDON GLADNEY

THE RAILCARS CLATTERED ALONG THE TRACKS, and Ida Mae and her family swayed with every rocking motion as the train wound north in the pitch black of night. The countryside gave way, and they passed out of Mississippi into Tennessee and away from the Pearson Plantation and the arbitrary rules they had lived under. They did not know precisely what they would do for work in the North, but they would never again drag another sack of cotton on their backs through a hot, bearing-down field.

From the overcrowded seats in the Jim Crow car, Ida Mae could not have imagined what finery filled the buffet lounges and Pullman cars where the white people sat and would not have let her mind dwell on it even if she had. While the Illinois Central and its counterparts on the East Coast and along the Rio Grande were effectively freedom trains for colored people, deliverance out of the South did not come without its own humiliations, which could eat away at the spirit if one let it. There was no guarantee, for instance, that they could get food on the long ride in either direction because the great bulk of the dining car was reserved for whites and partitioned off by an insistent green curtain.

There was rarely enough room for the many people in steerage. My father would remember trying to get from Washington to Tuskegee, Alabama, where he was a pilot during World War II, and having trouble just getting food. "I rode the train from Washington to North Carolina standing up," he said decades later, "waiting to get into the dining car." The line was several cars long, and there were only four seats in a back corner of the dining car where colored people could sit. For that reason, colored people learned to pack their own food to avoid needing what they couldn't get—cold fried chicken, hard-boiled eggs, and biscuits in a shoe box—which Ida Mae and thousands of others carried on board and which led people to call the migration trains "the Chicken Bone Special."

Still, just being on the train set them apart from the people they left behind. These great creatures on tracks were as big as buildings and longer than roads. They had grand, triumphant-sounding names—Silver Meteor, Broadway Limited—and took people to grand, triumphant-sounding places, and just a little bit of that prestige could rub off on them, and they could walk a little taller in their overalls knowing they were going to freedom.

The train rumbled toward the western tip of Kentucky, wending north toward Illinois. There, on the stiff seats of the colored car, they sat bundled together, George, stoic and straight-backed, keeping whatever apprehensions he had to himself, Ida Mae, wide-eyed and homesick at the same time, Velma's head pressing against her arm, James wriggling in her lap, and another one restless in her belly.

ON THE SILVER METEOR,
SOMEWHERE IN THE CAROLINAS, APRIL 15, 1945
GEORGE SWANSON STARLING

———

GEORGE HAD BEEN RIDING for close to half a day, only it was the dark hours of the morning of the day after he left Eustis, Florida. The hard, upright seats made it tough to get any sleep. He looked out the window at the blur of countryside and the train depots where they stopped to collect and deposit passengers. The train passed from South Carolina into North Carolina, and with each mile that moved him closer to New York, he began to get exhilarated.

The further north the train got, the more he started thinking about this new life ahead of him and what he had been through. "I was hoping that the conditions would be better," he said. "But I know one thing, I was sick of them gossiping, lying Negroes in Eustis, and I wasn't never coming back there no more. I was never gonna put my foot back there no more in life because they had spoiled my experience. And I was finished."

SOMEWHERE EAST OF EL PASO, APRIL 1953
ROBERT JOSEPH PERSHING FOSTER

ROBERT CROSSED WEST TEXAS through the dry sandpaper fields, past the blur of oil drills and ranches set back from the road and the yucca plants with flower stems like fishing poles. There would appear on either side of the road a drive-in theater with pink cursive lettering or a pit stop that sold liquor and ammo.

The land was red now. Bulls grazed on the scratch land to the south. The red suede hills began a slow roll at Uvalde, and he found himself driving through cuts in the rise of the hills. Now and again, he passed over another dry river waiting for the rain to come home.

He drove parallel to the Rio Grande. The hills became washboard steppes in Hudspeth County. He was almost at El Paso, the last southern town heading west, a border town. Under the circumstances, borders could be deceptive. They are a blend of the two lands they straddle, not fully one or the other, ripe for ambiguity and premature assumptions. El Paso, the unspoken border between the Jim Crow South and the free Southwest, was no different.

Heading to California, Jim Crow was no longer the law after El Paso. The signs that said COLORED above the railcar doors went blank, a metaphor for crossing into a land without segregation. Colored rail passengers heading west were free to move to the seats in the white cars for the remainder of the ride to California. Apparently few ever did, too afraid to push convention, and with good reason. In border towns, freedom was arbitrary and unpredictable. Not every restaurant was open to colored people, hotel access still dependent on local convention and the owner's whim. A colored traveler could never be sure where rejection might greet him. Thus the real border stretched farther than by law it had a right to.

Heading back from California, the South officially began in El Paso. There, Jim Crow laws took over again for any colored person crossing into the state of Texas. There began the spectacle of colored passengers moving to their places from the integrated cars to the Jim Crow cars. The colored and white signs went back up. The colored people knew to gather their things a few stops ahead and move before being told to, to spare themselves the indignity.

It was a spectacle played out in one way or the other on every train coming into or out of the South until Jim Crow died a violent death in the 1960s. At particular stops, which had less to do with the old Mason-Dixon Line than with the psychological border claims of the South, the train cars would undergo a similar transformation.

Up and down the East Coast, the border crossing for Jim Crow was Washington, D.C., which was technically south of the Mason-Dixon Line but was effectively the honorary North, as it was the capital of the Union during the Civil War. Later, it was the first stop on the migration route up the East Coast, the place where colored southerners could escape the field or kitchen and work indoors for the government and sit where they liked on the buses and streetcars. But to blacks in the Deep South, Washington had a significance beyond perhaps any other city in the North. A colored tailor in Georgia told the author Ray Stannard Baker that he was leaving the South for Washington because he wanted "to be as near the flag as I can."

Between Alabama and Detroit, the dividing line was the Ohio River, as it had been during slavery, where, once across it, blacks were free if they only could manage to get there. Between Mississippi and Chicago, Jim Crow went out of effect in Cairo, Illinois, at the southern tip of the state. For a time in the 1920s, the ride to Chicago was interrupted after the train crossed the Ohio River into Cairo, as if the train were passing from Poland into the old Soviet Union during the Cold War. Once over the river and officially in the North, the colored cars had to be removed in a noisy and cumbersome uncoupling and the integrated cars attached in their place to adhere to the laws of Illinois. Colored passengers had to move, wait, reshuffle themselves, and haul their bags to the newly attached integrated cars. Going south, the ritual was reversed. The railroad men now had to reattach the colored-only cars and remove the integrated cars in a clamorous ordeal to meet the laws of Kentucky. Colored passengers had to gather up their things and take their second-class seats, reminded, in that instance, that they were now reentering the South. Such was the protocol of a border crossing.

Colored travelers needed to be aware of these borders whether they were riding the rails or not. The border sentiments spilled over into a general protocol that colored people had to live by. It determined whether or how easily they might find a room or food. They could look silly asking for a colored restroom in a border town that felt more northern than southern and presumptuous in a town that felt the opposite.

"How a colored man, or a white man either, for the matter, can be expected to know all the intricacies of segregation as he travels in different parts of the country is beyond explanation," wrote Robert Russa Moton, the black scholar who succeeded Booker T. Washington as president of Tuskegee Institute in Alabama. "The truth of the matter is, he is expected to find out as best he can."

Usually, colored travelers wanted to avoid insult at all cost and protected themselves by assuming that segregation was the rule whenever they needed a place to eat or sleep. But heat and fatigue could make people do anything to get out of the fix of driving for days without sleep.

Around the same time that Robert was making his way across the country, a family from Beaumont, Texas, near the Louisiana border, was making the same drive. The patriarch of the family was doing the driving. With him were his wife, his grown daughter, and her three children—two boys, between eight and ten, and a girl, about five or six. They had piled into a '49 Chevrolet and were rumbling across Texas en route to California.

They had driven all day and had come into night, and they reached the border city of El Paso. The man could not drive any farther and, as this was the border and he was almost out of Texas, decided to stop and ask if the motel took colored people.

As could be expected, the answer was no. But he was tired. He had the three grandkids, the wife, and the grown daughter with him. And he was colored but was different from the majority of colored people. He had straight hair and pale skin. He looked white, and so did his wife and daughter and two of her three children.

He decided to try another motel. He had been honest, and it hadn't gotten him anywhere.

"Well, I know what to do here," the grandfather said.

This time he would not ask about a room for colored people. He would just ask for a room, like a white person would.

But the family had a problem. One of the grandchildren, a boy, about ten at the time, did not look white. His skin was brown. His hair had a tight curl. He would blow their cover. There would be no way to explain it.

For the plan to work, the motel must not know about the boy, and for that to happen, the grandfather needed the children's cooperation. They were playing in the back seat, counting the stars and pointing out the window at the Big Dipper in the sky. The grandfather needed them to be quiet and to keep their heads down. He told them to pretend to be asleep.

"Now, don't get up, don't get up," he said as he and his wife prepared to go to the front desk. "Don't y'all raise your head up. Somebody come over here, don't raise your head up. Stay down."

The instructions were primarily meant for Jules, the ten-year-old who looked like what he was. But the grandfather told all the children in the hope that what one did, they all would do.

The children could sense his fear and were afraid to move. "You scared, somebody talking to you like that," Pat Botshekan, then the little granddaughter in the back seat, said almost half a century later.

The grandfather and his wife walked up to the front desk, and he asked for a room as a white person would. The clerk checked him in and gave him the key and pointed him in the direction of the room.

Now he had a place for the night, but he also had a problem. They had to get Jules into the room without the front desk discovering what Jules was.

They went back to the car to gather their things. The grandfather got his wife and daughter and the two children who looked white out of the car. It was late at night now, and the grandfather, tired from the drive and the stress of the moment, scrambled to sneak Jules out of the car without detection.

For the plan to work, Jules would have to do what was not natural for a ten-year-old boy. He would have to keep still and be perfectly quiet and not let his arms and legs stick out or rear up his head out of the blanket or let anybody see him. There was no time to explain why they had to hide him and not the other children, or why he was the only one who couldn't under any circumstances be seen while the others would walk in like normal. Somehow he had to understand how imperative it was that he not let a patch of his brown skin show.

Everywhere the family went, little Jules stood out from the rest of the family, and that was hard enough. Now he was being sneaked into a strange place in the middle of the night as if he were contraband.

The grandfather put the blanket over Jules, sitting in the back seat. He tucked the little boy's brown arms and legs under the blanket to make sure they didn't show. He lifted the little boy in his arms like a bag of groceries and carried him into the room. That is how they managed to get a bed for the night. But it was said that the memory stayed with Jules and that he was not quite ever the same after that.

———

Like most colored people making the journey, Robert could not pass for white and was not in a position to try to fool his way into a room, which is not to suggest that all who could did. In fact, he found it sad and equally humiliating to have to deny who you were to get what you deserved in the first place.

No, for him and for most people in his predicament, you were not free till you had cleared the gate. But even a border's borders are not always clear. Where is it safe to assume you are out of one country and well into another? When can you sigh a sigh of relief that you have passed from the rituals of one place into those of the other side?

Robert took nothing for granted. He assumed he was not out of the South until he was a safe distance from El Paso. He gave himself breathing room and was more cautious than most. He did not want to subject himself to the indignities of being colored any more than he had to and so would make no attempt to stop and inquire until he was all but certain he had a shot at a room.

He crossed into New Mexico and drove some more until he reached Lordsburg, some four hours past the border on those old two-lane roads.

Lordsburg was a dusty old frontier town with saloons famous for fistfights and a Southern Pacific Railroad track paralleling Main. He would have had no reason to stop there if it didn't happen to be the only place in New Mexico he had been told that he could be assured of a place to sleep.

The rooming house in Lordsburg was part of a haphazard network of twentieth-century safe houses that sprang up all over the country, and particularly in the South, during the decades of segregation. Some were seedy motels in the red-light district of whatever city they were in. There were a handful of swanky ones, like the Hotel Theresa in Harlem. But many of them were unkempt rooming houses or merely an extra bedroom in some colored family's row house in the colored district of a given town. They sprang up out of necessity as the Great Migration created a need for places where colored people could stop and rest in a world where no hotels in the South accepted colored people and those in the North and West were mercurial in their policies, many of them disallowing blacks as readily as hotels in the South.

Thus, there developed a kind of underground railroad for colored travelers, spread by word of mouth among friends and in fold-up maps and green paperback guidebooks that listed colored lodgings by state or city.

Colored travelers, hoping to plan their journeys in advance and get assurance of a room, carried the guidebooks in their glove compart-

ments like insurance cards. But the books were often out of date by the
time they were printed, the accuracy of their entries based on the fortunes of "hoteliers" who may have only been renters themselves. A colored traveler had to prepare for the possibility that he might arrive at a
place in the guidebook only to find that the proprietor had been gone for
years and then have to take up the search for a room all over again. Still,
the mere presence of the guidebooks and of word-of-mouth advice
about places to stay gave a sense of order and dignity to the dispiriting
prospect of driving cross-country not knowing for sure where one
might lay one's head.

The rooming house in Lordsburg was forgettable and left no impression on him other than it was like all the other rooming houses that took
in colored people. A bedroom with no assurance of a key, an old toilet
down the hall, sheets the previous guest may have slept on. The rooming houses that catered to a colored trade usually had no competition,
and their clientele had no choice.

And so neither would Robert. The only bed he knew between Houston and Lordsburg was the bench seat of the Buick. Lordsburg was the
first chance in a thousand miles of road to sleep and was the only certain
sleep and shower before Los Angeles. He made the most of it. He was
fussy about such things as the proper shave and a well-pressed shirt, so
he took his time the next day. He got a later start than he should have.

He had known that there were no guarantees for the first half of the
journey, meaning the South, except for his Buick and Dr. Beale back in
Houston. Now he was crossing over into the land of the free. He had
known the rules in the South. He hadn't liked them, but he had expected them. "There were no hotels taking blacks then," Robert remembered years later. "No. None. So if you had a friend who would
take you in, you went there, period, and you were through. And then
you worried about the next stop."

He was putting that all behind him now. He drove toward Arizona,
confident that this was one thing he didn't have to worry about anymore.

Crossing Over

Do you remember any good stopping places
in Arizona or western Texas?
Anything in Phoenix or El Paso?
And what is the best route from here to the coast?
I have never driven it, you know.

— THE POET ARNA BONTEMPS IN A LETTER
TO THE POET LANGSTON HUGHES BEFORE
A CROSS-COUNTRY TRIP FROM ALABAMA
TO CALIFORNIA

WESTERN NEW MEXICO, APRIL 1953
ROBERT JOSEPH PERSHING FOSTER

LATE AFTERNOON. The desert was different from anything he had seen before. Great bowl of sky. Fringe of mountain in the distance. He was soon in Arizona. The desert began playing tricks on the eyes. It seemed he was driving and standing still at the same time. Road signs began warning of dust storms. Gas stations sold bags of water for people to placate their overheated radiators. He couldn't wait to get to California.

He drove through the dry earth and yucca as heat vapor stirred at the surface. He soon entered the flat plains of the Salt River Valley. The dry land sprouted fields of sorghum and soybeans. Crop dusters flew low in the distance.

Night moved in from behind. The mountains were now crisp against the light of the falling sun.

The next big city was Phoenix, and he drove in anticipation of it. As he drew nearer, a curtain of night cloud fell behind him to the east. He could see it coming in his rearview mirror. The sky turned navy, then black. He soon saw the outline of Phoenix off to his right, north of the highway.

But the road would not take him where he wanted to go. It veered away from the lights and continued south and west along the outskirts of town. The fifteen hundred miles of driving caught up with him now. His eyelids grew heavy, and his head filled with the fog of the onset of sleep.

It occurred to him that he had squandered his energy on the easiest leg of the journey, on the closely set hamlets with their billboards and ranch signs, the distractions and margaritas at the Mexico border, even gassing up and eating in Lordsburg. He did not regret it, but he was paying for it now. Ahead was the long stretch of aloneness in the desert.

He thought he'd better stop now. If he looped back to Phoenix, he could poke around for a colored boardinghouse and be in a bed of uncertain hygiene in a couple of hours. But the highway continued away from the lights and into a vast darkness. He could lose an hour just trying to find his way back to town.

He considered the options. He was a safe distance from the South, long past Texas and well beyond New Mexico. This far west, he wouldn't have to wander the city and hunt down the first colored person he saw for directions to where the colored people board. He was free now, like a regular American.

Up ahead, a bank of neon signs popped up in the distance and fought one another over guests for the night. The motels sat low to the ground at angles from the road, little more than stretch trailers with rhinestone facades. He pulled up to the parking lot of the first one he came to.

The car kicked up gravel dust as it crawled up to the vacancy sign that blinked the promise of a decent night's sleep. He noticed a white Cadillac convertible pulling into the parking lot, its mirror-slick chrome and the headlights shining onto the building. A man who could have been in a Brylcreem commercial was at the wheel and next to him a blond lady friend. The man was laughing. The woman had her head on his shoulder. They were in their own world as they stepped out of the car and floated into the motel in front of him. It was a scene right out of the movies and Robert's kind of place. He felt even better about this new citizenship he was acquiring.

He had been driving since noon and was wrinkled from the ride. He was a formal man in a formal age, and so he couldn't go in like this. He brushed his fingers along the sleeves of his shirt and ironed the front with his palm. He got his sport coat, shook the dust out of it, and afterward straightened his tie. He didn't have a comb within reach; he hadn't thought that far ahead. So he smoothed the top and sides of his head with his hand.

He caught sight of his face in the mirror and the dark wood finish of his skin. The skin was moist and glistened in the blinking neon of the vacancy sign. *Good lord.* He had been sweating in the heat all day. They might think he was a common laborer. He felt his pockets for a handkerchief. He took it and wiped the shine off his nose, off his cheeks and chin, and mopped the sweat from his forehead. It was not his best presentation, but it would have to do.

When he got out of the car, he dusted his coat sleeves and checked for wrinkles again. He stood up as if there were a brace strapped to his back. Then he walked up to the front desk for a room. At reception, he took a deep breath and put on the most charming rendition of himself.

"I'd like to get a room for the night, please," he said.

The man looked flustered. "Oh, my goodness," the man at the front desk said. "We forgot to turn off the vacancy sign."

Robert tried to hide his disappointment.

"Oh, thank you," Robert said.

He climbed back into the car and drove away from the motel and the vacancy sign that continued to blink. He had been in the South long enough to know when he had been lied to. But there were plenty of motels on the road, and it didn't matter what one man thought of him.

He wasn't thinking rights and equality. "I thought a bed and a shower and something to eat," he would say years later.

He drove to the next motel in the row, a hundred or so yards away.

"I'd like to get a motel room," he said, stiffer than before. He was cautious now, and the man must have seen his caution.

"I'm sorry," the man said, polite and businesslike. "We just rented our last room."

Robert looked into the face, tried to read it. He noticed that "the face was awkward, trying to be loose and matter of fact. All calm and uncomfortable."

He thanked the man anyway, tried to prove himself even in rejection. "Usually when we try to fit in, we're above them," Robert thought to himself, sad and indignant at the same time. "If we're going to be nice, we're nicer than they would be to each other."

Knowing that wasn't helping him now. He was getting anxious. The pulse was racing. He was agitated, sweating on a cool desert night.

He went to a third motel and was sweetly rejected a third time. It was fully night now, the sky black and dense. He should have been in bed hours ago. His was the only car on the road now. The motel lots were quiet and still. The lamp lights on bedside tables were clicking off, that young couple in the Cadillac all situated now. The road was getting darker, lonelier, as the world settled in for the night.

Anybody looking for a room had one by now. Any leftover rooms would go empty. And still they were turning him away.

He replayed the rejections in his mind as he drove the few yards to the next motel. Maybe he hadn't explained himself well enough. Maybe it wasn't clear how far he had driven. Maybe he should let them know he saw through them, after all those years in the South. He always prepared a script when he spoke to a white person. Now he debated with himself as to what he should say.

He didn't want to make a case of it. He never intended to march over Jim Crow or try to integrate anybody's motel. He didn't like being where he wasn't wanted. And yet here he was, needing something he couldn't have. He debated whether he should speak his mind, protect himself from rejection, say it before they could say it. He approached the next exchange as if it were a job interview. Years later he would practically refer to it as such. He rehearsed his delivery and tightened his lines. "It would have been opening-night jitters if it was theater," he would later say.

He pulled into the lot. There was nobody out there but him, and he was the only one driving up to get a room. He walked inside. His voice was about to break as he made his case.

"I'm looking for a room," he began. "Now, if it's your policy not to rent to colored people, let me know now so I don't keep getting insulted."

A white woman in her fifties stood on the other side of the front desk. She had a kind face, and he found it reassuring. And so he continued.

"It's a shame that they would do a person like this," he said. "I'm no robber. I've got no weapons. I'm not a thief. I'm a medical doctor. I'm a captain that just left Austria, which was Salzburg. And the German Army was just outside of Vienna. If there had been a conflict, I would have been protecting you. I would not do people the way I've been treated here."

It was the most he'd gotten to say all night, and so he went on with his delivery more determinedly than before. "I have money to pay for my services," he said. "Now, if you don't rent to colored people, let me know so I can go on to California. This is inhuman. I'm a menace to anybody driving. I'm a menace to myself and to the public, driving as tired as I am."

She listened, and she let him make his case. She didn't talk about mistaken vacancy signs or just-rented rooms. She didn't cut him off. She listened, and that gave him hope.

"One minute, Doctor," she said, turning and heading toward a back office.

His heart raced as he watched her walk to the back. He could see her consulting with a man through the glass window facing the front desk, deciding in that instant his fate and his worth. They discussed it for some time and came out together. The husband did the talking.

He had a kind, sad face. Robert held his breath. "We're from Illinois," the husband said. "We don't share the opinion of the people in this area. But if we take you in, the rest of the motel owners will ostracize us. We just can't do it. I'm sorry."

By now, if they had agreed to it, Robert would have been willing to check out before dawn, before anybody could see him, if that's what it took. It was a long shot, but some white proprietors had been known to sneak a colored traveler in on occasion, harbor them like a fugitive or a runaway slave, so long as he was out before the neighbors got wind of it. Robert would have accepted that even if he didn't like it.

In his delirium, he imagined the exchange between husband and wife in the back office minutes before, the woman arguing his case, the husband skeptical, wary.

"Nobody'll see him anyway," the wife's whispering.

"Yes, they will," the husband's responding.

"How will they know?"

"Somebody might see him when he drives out of here. Or somebody might see his car. Where he's been before, the people that turned him down. They'd know we let him stay here."

And so the answer was no. Robert thanked them anyway, especially the woman. If it had been up to her, he would have had the room. "I believe that with everything that's in me," Robert said when he was older and grayer. "This thing I've analyzed three thousand times."

Somehow Robert made it back to the car. He was in the middle of the desert and too tired to go on and too far along not to keep going. His mind took him back to Monroe, to the going-away party they gave him just a few nights ago. His own words rose up and laughed at him. *How in the world can you stay here in this Jim Crow situation? Come go to Heaven with me, to California.*

————

He drove, erratic, in the direction of the road and, thus, California, although he was nowhere near California, and saw the lights of a filling station. He needed gas and could use some coffee if he was to make it through the desert and the night. He drove into the station and stopped at a pump.

The owner, a middle-aged white man, came right out.

"May I help you?"

Robert couldn't answer. The man repeated himself.

"Hey, fella, what's wrong? What's the matter? Are you sick?"

"No," Robert said, unable to manage much more.

The man sensed something. He put his hand on Robert's shoulder, and Robert tried to tell him what had happened. The man shook his head as if he understood.

Something in the voice, in the way the man looked into his eyes and touched his shoulder and tried in the middle of a cool desert night to console him, made Robert feel all the sadder. It confirmed he wasn't crazy, and that made him feel utterly alone. Yes, there was an evil in the air and this man knew it and the woman at the motel knew it, but here he was without a room and nobody of a mind to do anything had done a single thing to change that fact. And that made the pain harder, not easier, to bear.

Robert broke down. The exhaustion, the rejection, the unwinding of his dreams in a matter of minutes, it all caught up with him at once. He had driven more than fifteen hundred miles, and things were no different. In fact, it felt worse because this wasn't the South. It wasn't even close to the South. He sat unable to speak for longer than is comfortable in front of a total stranger. His voice cracked as the story tumbled out of him.

"I came all this way running from Jim Crow, and it slaps me straight in the face," Robert said. "And just think, I told my friends, why did they stay in the South and take the crumbs? *'Come to California.'* "

The man listened with the helplessness of the well-intentioned and tried to cheer him up.

"Come on, let me get you a cup of coffee. Where are you going anyway?"

"Los Angeles."

"Well, I went to USC, and I hate to disappoint you, but Los Angeles ain't the oasis you think it is."

Robert was feeling sick now. It was too late to turn back, and who knew what he was heading into? The man told him to gear himself up. The man didn't use the term, and nobody had bothered to tell Robert ahead of time, but some colored people who had made the journey called it *James* Crow in California.

"You will see it, and it'll hit where it hurts," the man said. "What are you in?"

"I'm a doctor."

"Well, you're going to find it in the hospitals going to work."

Robert was thinking fast, reconsidering, weighing, and waking up. The dream looked to be over before he could even get to California. The man brought him a cup of coffee and filled his tank. Robert got back on the highway and drove into the black hole of night. Soon he came to a fork in the road and saw a sign that made his heart sink:

LOS ANGELES 380 MILES

SAN DIEGO 345 MILES

He knew he couldn't drive a mile farther than necessary in this condition, and so San Diego it would be. "I could just see numbers in my mind now," he said many years later. "Los Angeles this way and San Diego that way. And the number was far less distance, and I chose that."

———

In the absolute darkness he found himself in, he could not see the will of the road. He went on faith that he was not driving off into a ravine.

Every cell wanted sleep. He bit his tongue to keep his eyelids from sneaking shut. He sang, sang anything, to keep his mind from turning in for the night. Now when he needed the radio, there was no radio, just a crackle of white noise from someplace far away.

Suddenly, somewhere around Gila Bend, the road got mean, turned without warning, a sharp left, then a sharper, uglier right, back and forth, and all over again. The car tilted upward, gaining elevation and resisting the climb as any car would. It forced him into an alertness his body wasn't prepared for and that he hadn't anticipated.

212   THE WARMTH OF OTHER SUNS

The road shot more curves at him, one right after the other, so that he was going north and south as much as west, and he had to slow down to absorb the blind hooks and horseshoes coming at him. He knew he wasn't the best driver in the world, hadn't done that much of it really. And so he would have to brake to a crawl if he was going to make it.

Before it hadn't mattered much that this was a two-lane road with no reflector lights and no guardrails to catch him. Now it did. Interstate highways didn't exist yet. Dwight D. Eisenhower, the president who would go on to build them, had only recently taken office. Of course, Robert didn't know that, and knowing it wouldn't have helped him.

The mountains closed in on him. He couldn't make out the earth from the sky. The sky was black, the road was black. He could see the black shape of saguaro cactus standing helpless as he passed. He drove into the cave of night, more alone now than ever.

It got to the point where he could go no further, and he pulled over to the side of the road. He unfolded himself from behind the wheel and caught an hour of half sleep. He would have to stop again two or three times that night. Each time, it left him not much more refreshed than before. He had no choice but to start the engine and take up the task again.

He wound through rock canyons and crossed Fortune Wash near the Gila River. A film stuck to his skin and to his wrinkled shirt and trousers. He had not had a chance to wash yesterday off. He opened the windows and vents to get air.

Another hour passed, and ahead was a valley, a black velvet plain with diamonds on it. It was the city of Yuma. He saw motel signs with amusing desert names. He gave them no thought. He knew better now.

Soon he came upon the Colorado River. A road sign said he had reached the California line. But he was too beat down now to pay it much attention.

His back pinched from days and nights of driving. His fingers were sore from clutching the steering wheel. His wrists ached, and still there was more road. The road would not end.

Just past Felicity came the warnings of the desert: CHECK YOUR RADIA-TOR. LAST CHANCE FOR WATER. LAST CHANCE FOR GAS STATIONS. STRONG WINDS POSSIBLE.

What was this place he was going to? What was he doing behind the wheel in the middle of the pitch-black desert by himself? Could it be worth all this? It had seemed so clear back in Monroe. Now he fought with himself over the fear and the doubt. He couldn't bear to hear the I-told-so-so's. If he turned

*back now, if he changed his mind or lost his nerve, the I-knew-its would ring
in his ear. Dr. Clement would be the first to say it.*

He was dreading the place already. "But there was no turning back," he would say years later. "I had to get here. I had to try."

He blinked at oncoming headlights, willing himself awake. Orion stretched over the highway and made an arc across the sky. It filled the windshield and stayed with him until the sun came back.

Near the Tecate Divide, the pink light of morning came in from behind. He was in San Diego County. Another fifty miles to the coast. The sun was on his back as he pulled away for good from the South and the center of gravity.

ON THE ILLINOIS CENTRAL AT THE ILLINOIS BORDER,
OCTOBER 1937
IDA MAE BRANDON GLADNEY

IN THE DARK HOURS OF THE MORNING, Ida Mae and her family crossed the Mason-Dixon Line, at the Ohio River, the border between Kentucky and Illinois, between the provincial South and the modern North, between servitude and freedom, without comment.

The black night pressed against the windows and looked no different in the New World than in the Old. It was as thick and black in Illinois as it was in Kentucky or Tennessee. From the railcar window, the land looked to be indistinguishable, one state from another, just one big flat plain, and there was nothing in nature that one could see that said colored people should be treated one way on one side of the river and a different way on the other.

Crossing the line was a thing of spiritual and political significance to the guardians of southern law and to colored people escaping it who knew they were crossing over. But going north, most migrants would have been asleep or unable to see whatever the line looked like if they even knew where it was.

On the red-eye going north, the railroad would not likely have disrupted the entire train just so colored people could sit with white people now that they legally could. Ida Mae had no memory of such a commotion in any case, only that they'd made it out of Mississippi. They crossed into Illinois at *Cairo* and passed through *Carbondale* and *Centralia.* Then *Champaign. Kankakee. Peotone. Matteson. Grand Crossing. Woodlawn. Hyde Park. Oakland. Twenty-second Street. Twelfth Street Station. Chicago.*

They would have to change trains yet again to continue on to Milwaukee, where Ida Mae's sister Irene lived and where they could set about finding work to sustain them in the New World.

ON THE SILVER METEOR, NORTHERN NEW JERSEY, APRIL 15, 1945
GEORGE SWANSON STARLING

AT DAYBREAK, the Silver Meteor wound its way into Pennsylvania Station at Newark, New Jersey. The conductor called out the name of the station and the city, and after so long a ride through the night and now into day, some passengers from the South gathered their things and stepped off the train, weary and anxious to start their new lives and relieved to have made it to their destination at last.

"Newark." It sounded so tantalizingly close to "New York," and maybe, some assumed, was the way northerners, clipping their words as they did, pronounced New York. It was confusing to have their intended destination preceded directly by a city with such a similar name and with an identically named station. And as they had been riding for as many as twenty-four hours and were nervous about missing their stop, some got off prematurely, and, it is said, that is how Newark gained a good portion of its black population, those arriving in Newark by accident and deciding to stay.

George Starling knew better. He had been to New York before, just not on the train. He remained in his seat until he arrived at the real New York, where the aunts who had sent money to his grandmother, the root doctor, to help raise him and his cousins were waiting for him at their Harlem doorsteps.

SAN DIEGO COUNTY, APRIL 1953
ROBERT JOSEPH PERSHING FOSTER

———

IT WAS EARLY IN SAN DIEGO. Robert Foster could see the concrete skyline and the headlights of a city waking up. He drew closer to the heart of town. Trolley cars clanked past the palm trees on C Street. The Pacific Ocean was up ahead. He was finally on the other side of the desert. He was hours from Los Angeles but well into California, the end of the line when it came to the Migration. It was more a relief now than a wonder.

His eyes scanned the pedestrians for pigment. He stopped at the curb and flagged down the first colored person he saw. He had not talked to a soul during his night in the desert. This would be the first encounter in this new adopted land. His heart sank as he uttered the words that seemed an admission of failure.

"Pardon me," he said, edgily, to the man. "Where can you find a colored hotel?"

"What do you mean, a *colored* hotel?" the man said with the casual annoyance of an urbanite interrupted by a tourist. "I can tell you where a hotel is. There's a hotel right there."

"No, I don't want that," Robert said. "Just tell me where most of the colored folks stay."

Robert was too tired to argue. Three states without sleep. He had a stubble of beard on his face that he would otherwise never be seen in public with. He could not bear rejection again.

"I could not," he began, still searching for the right words decades later, "the thought—it was overwhelming—of me being turned down again. I couldn't do that."

Robert repeated himself to the man. The man assured him he didn't have to stay in a place like that in San Diego but gave him the name of a small, featureless hotel anyway, a place for colored people, since he was so insistent on that.

Robert found the place. He slept and showered and shaved for the first time since New Mexico. When he opened his eyes hours later, there he was in a segregated hotel. A week on the road, and he was in the exact same place, it seemed, that he left.

Later in the day, he headed north past the Joshua trees. Los Angeles was another 121 miles from San Diego. He didn't know which city would be the right one for him—Los Angeles or Oakland—or where he would work or how he would set up a practice wherever he ended up. He had just come out of the desert, in every sense of the word, and the details of his future were too much to think about right now.

He drove north toward whatever awaited him. Billboards popped up on both sides of the highway. They whizzed past him as he drove. They had women in rouge and lipstick and men with stingy-brim hats with the cord above the brim selling lager beer and cigarettes. The people in the billboards were smiling and happy. They looked out onto the highway and straight into the cars.

They kept him company, and, although they weren't talking to him, he told himself they were. "I played a game that it was for me," he later said.

Soon one billboard stood out from the others. IT'S LUCKY WHEN YOU'RE IN CALIFORNIA, it said cheerfully. It was hawking Lucky lager beer to every car that passed. Robert repeated those words in his mind.

"It's gonna be lucky for me in California. It's gonna be good."

It had to be. He said it over and over to himself until he actually started to believe it.

THE SOUTH, 1915–1975

FROM THE MOMENT the first migrants stepped off the earliest trains, the observers of the Great Migration debated what made millions of rural and small-town people turn their backs on all they knew, leave the land where their fathers were buried, and jump off a cliff into the unknown.

Planters blamed northern recruiters, who were getting paid a dollar a head to deliver colored labor to the foundries and slaughterhouses of the North. But that only held for the earliest recruits, usually young men, field hands, with nothing to lose. Others said the *Chicago Defender* seduced them. But they could only be seduced if there was some passion already deep within them.

Economists said it was the boll weevil that tore through the cotton fields and left them without work and in even greater misery, which likely gave hard-bitten sharecroppers just one more reason to go. Still, many of them picked cotton not by choice but because it was the only work allowed them in the cotton-growing states. In South Carolina, colored people had to apply for a permit to do any work other than agriculture after Reconstruction. It would not likely have been their choice had there been an alternative. And besides, many of the migrants, people like George Starling and Robert Foster and many thousands more came from southern towns where they did not pick cotton or from states less dependent on it and thus would have made their decisions with no thought of the boll weevil or the pressure on cotton prices.

The Chicago Commission on Race Relations, an investigative body created after the World War I wave of migration, decided to ask migrants why they had left. A few of their responses were these:

- SOME OF MY PEOPLE WERE HERE.

- PERSUADED BY FRIENDS.

- FOR BETTER WAGES.

- TO BETTER MY CONDITIONS.

- BETTER CONDITIONS.

- BETTER LIVING.

- MORE WORK; CAME ON VISIT AND STAYED.

- WIFE PERSUADED ME.

- TIRED OF THE SOUTH.

- TO GET AWAY FROM THE SOUTH.

The earliest departures were merely the first step in a divorce that would take more than half a century to complete. At the time it was misunderstood as a temporary consequence of war and declared over when the war ended. But the people who before had been cut off from the North now had the names of neighbors and relatives actually living there. Instead of the weakening stream that observers predicted, the Great Migration actually gathered steam after World War I.

It continued into the twenties with the departure of some 903,000 black southerners, nearly double the World War I wave. It did not stop in the thirties, when, despite the Depression, 480,000 managed to leave. Among them was Ida Mae Gladney. World War II brought the fastest flow of black people out of the South in history—nearly 1.6 million left during the 1940s, more than in any decade before. George Starling was one of them. Another 1.4 million followed in the 1950s, when Robert Pershing Foster drove out of Louisiana for good. And another million in the 1960s, when, because of the more barefaced violence during the South's desperate last stand against civil rights, it was actually more treacherous to leave certain isolated precincts of the rural South than perhaps at any time since slavery.

The numbers put forward by the census are believed by some historians to be an underestimate. Unknown numbers of migrants who could pass for white melted into the white population once they left and would not have been counted in the Migration. Colored men fearful of being extradited back to the South over purported debts or disputes would have been wary of census takers. And overcrowded tenements with four or five families packed into kitchenettes or day workers rotating their use of a bed would have been hard to accurately account for in the best of circumstances. "A large error in enumerating southern blacks who went North," wrote the historian Florette Henri, "was not only probable but inescapable."

———

The journey north was a defining moment for the people embarking upon it. Many years later, most everyone would remember how they chose where they went, the name of the train they took, and whom they went to stay with. Some would remember the exact day they departed and the places the train stopped on the way to wherever they were going. A man named Robert Fields, who as a teenager hid in the freight cars to flee Yazoo City, Mississippi, remembered arriving in Chicago on the day Rudolph Valentino died, which would make it August 23, 1926, because the news of Valentino's death was on the front page of every newspaper and was all anyone was talking about that day.

Robert Pershing Foster would remember leaving right after Easter, which, unbeknownst to him, was a popular time to leave. Given a choice, southerners preferred not to go north facing winter, and leaving at Easter gave them plenty of time to adjust to the North before the cold set in. George Starling would remember that he left Florida on April 14, 1945, as if it were his birthday, which in a way it was.

Decades after she left, Ida Mae Gladney would remember that they got the cotton clean out of the field before they left, which would make it mid- to late October, and that she was pregnant with her youngest child but not yet showing, which would make it 1937.

Well after Ida Mae, George, and Robert made their way out of the South, a man by the name of Eddie Earvin would always remember how he left because he went to such great lengths to escape the Mississippi Delta. It was the spring of 1963.

Many of the observers and participants of the first wave of the Migration had passed away, having concluded that the phenomenon was long over. They would not have imagined that someone like Earvin might have a harder time leaving than many before him.

But in the early 1960s, secluded regions of the rural South— Alabama and Mississippi in particular—had become war zones in the final confrontation between segregationists and the civil rights movement. Spies and traitors were everywhere, the violence raw and without apology, the segregationists standing more boldfaced, clamping down harder as outsiders tried to force integration on them. No one was exempt—not well-to-do white northerners like Andrew Goodman and Michael Schwerner, not upstanding family men like Medgar Evers, or even four little middle-class girls in church on a Sunday morning in Birmingham in 1963.

Earvin's story is evidence of just how long the Great Migration stretched across a hard century, how universal were the impulses of those who left, and how treacherous it could be to try to leave certain remote and Victorian pockets of the American South throughout the sixty-odd years the Great Migration lasted.

Eddie Earvin was twenty in the spring of 1963. He was a day picker at a plantation in Scotts, Mississippi, walking with pieces of cardboard tied to his one pair of shoes to cover the bottoms of his feet. "We were still in slavery, like," he would say years later.

He started picking when he was five and chopping weeds off the cotton at six. And when he was seven or eight, a boy named Charles Parker was skinned alive for opening a door for a white woman and speaking to her in a way she didn't like, as the grown folks told it. Eddie would never forget that.

He picked because he had to and crawled on his knees to cut spinach because spinach is low to the ground. He got ten cents for a fifty-pound basket of spinach. He could pick only two or three baskets a day because spinach is light.

One day when he was out cutting spinach, he sliced into his finger but was afraid to leave the field. It was six miles to the doctor in town. He worked two more days and on the third day decided to walk to town to see the doctor. The boss man passed him on his way back to the field and jumped out of his truck.

"Don't you know you don't go nowhere unlessen I tell you to?" the boss man said.

He pulled a Winchester rifle out of the truck. "Maybe I ought to kill you right now," he said.

The man put the rifle to Eddie's head.

"You don't go nowhere unlessen I tell you to go," he told him.

Eddie was seventeen. He decided that, somehow or other, he would find a way out. When he was twenty, he made his plans. A bus ticket to Chicago was twenty-one dollars, as he remembered it. It took him six or seven months to save up for it. But that was the easy part. Now he had to find out how to use it without calling attention to himself in that little town where everybody knew everybody and it seemed everyone was watching.

There was a bus that stopped near him, but he couldn't catch that bus or inquire about it. "Everybody knew what you'd be trying to do if you caught that bus," he said. And you had to walk six miles to get to it.

There was another little bus stop in a town nearby. It did not post the bus schedule, and he was not in a position to ask. "They didn't tell you the schedule," he would say years later. "A lot of things you'd want to know, you couldn't ask."

So he went to the station at different times of the day. Each time, he sat and waited for the bus to leave, and when it belched out of the depot, he looked at the station clock and made a note of it. Sometimes the bus left early, he found. Sometimes it left late. He tried to get an average time so he would not miss it on the day he wanted to go. That was how he learned the bus schedule.

"We had been checking for months," he said.

He decided to leave in May 1963 and take his sister and her two children with him. He didn't tell anyone what he was doing. "You didn't talk about it or tell nobody," he said. "You had to sneak away."

That day, he acted as if it were any other day. He went up to a man named Eason and casually asked him if he could give them a ride.

"We going to Greenville today," he told Eason. "Could you take us?"

He didn't tell Eason he was leaving Mississippi for good or that he needed to catch a bus pulling out at a certain time or that this was the moment of truth after planning this in his mind for most of his short adult life. The man might not have taken them if he knew. So Eddie kept it to himself.

The four of them got in the car with nothing but a few clothes in a paper bag. When they got to Greenville, they paid the man three or four dollars. Eason figured out what they were up to when he saw where they wanted to be dropped off.

"What do you call yourself doing?" he asked them.

"We getting out of town," Eddie said. The man got scared himself after that.

Eddie and his sister and her two kids got on the bus, and before anybody knew it, they were out of the county with everything they had in a shopping bag wrapped in a rope of sea grass.

They sat in the back and kept their mouths shut. "The white folks could talk," he would say years later. "You sit and be quiet. Where we came from, we didn't move from the back. We just sat there. We weren't the type to move around. We wasn't sure we could move. So we didn't move. That fear."

He had learned that fear when he was little and once passed the white people's church. The kids came out of the church when they saw him. They threw rocks and bricks and called him the vilest names that could spring from a southern tongue. And he asked his grandparents, "What kind of god they got up inside that church?"

He was getting away from all that now. He looked out at the lights and the billboards. The driver announced that they were passing out of Mississippi and into Tennessee. He was out for sure now and on his way to Illinois, and at that moment he could feel the sacks of cotton dropping from his back. Years later, he would still tremble at the memory and put into words the sentiments of generations who went in search of a kinder mistress.

"It was like getting unstuck from a magnet," he said.

PART FOUR

THE KINDER MISTRESS

The lazy, laughing South
With blood on its mouth. . . .
Passionate, cruel,
Honey-lipped, syphilitic—
That is the South.
And I, who am black, would love her
But she spits in my face. . . .
So now I seek the North—
The cold-faced North,
For she, they say,
is a kinder mistress.
—LANGSTON HUGHES, "THE SOUTH"

CHICAGO

Timidly, we get off the train.
We hug our suitcases,
fearful of pickpockets. . . .
We are very reserved,
for we have been warned not to act green. . . .
We board our first Yankee street car
to go to a cousin's home. . . .
We have been told
that we can sit where we please,
but we are still scared.
We cannot shake off three hundred years of fear
in three hours.
  —RICHARD WRIGHT, *12 Million Black Voices*

CHICAGO, TWELFTH STREET STATION, OCTOBER 1937
IDA MAE BRANDON GLADNEY

———

THE LEAVES WERE THE COLOR of sweet potatoes and of the summer sun when it sets. They had begun to fall from the branches and settle in piles at the roots of the elm trees. The leaves had begun to fall when Ida Mae and George walked into the cold light of morning for the very first time in the North.

Ida Mae and her family had ridden all through the night on the Illinois Central and had arrived, stiff and disheveled, in a cold, hurrying place of concrete and steel. People clipped past them in their wool finery and distracted urgency, not pausing to speak—people everywhere, more people than they had maybe seen in one single place in their entire lives, coming as they were from the spread-out, isolated back country of plantations and lean-tos. They would somehow have to make it across town to yet another station to catch the train to Milwaukee and cart their worldly belongings to yet another platform for the last leg of their journey out of the South.

Above them hung black billboards as tall as a barn with the names of connecting cities and towns and their respective platforms and departure times—Sioux Falls, Cedar Rapids, Minneapolis, Omaha, Madison, Dubuque—footfalls, redcaps, four-faced clocks, and neon arrows pointing to arrivals and track numbers. The trains were not trains but Zephyrs and Hiawathas, the station itself feeling bigger and busier than all of Okolona or Egypt or any little town back home or anything they could possibly have ever seen before.

They would have to ride the La Crosse and Milwaukee Railroad for three more hours to get to their final stop in their adopted land. They could not rest easy until they had made it safely to Ida Mae's sister's apartment in Milwaukee. In the end, it would take multiple trains, three separate railroads, hours of fitful upright sleep, whatever food they managed to carry, the better part of two days, absolute will, near-blind determination, and some necessary measure of faith and just plain grit for people unaccustomed to the rigors of travel to make it out of the land of their birth to the foreign region of essentially another world.

The great belching city she passed through that day was the first city Ida Mae had ever laid eyes on. That first glimpse of Chicago would stay with her for as long as she lived.

"What did it look like at that time, Chicago?" I asked her, half a life later.

"It looked like Heaven to me then," she said.

NEW YORK

A blue haze descended at night
and, with it, strings of fairy lights
on the broad avenues....
What a city! What a world!...
The first danger I recognized...
was that Harlem would be
too wonderful for words.
Unless I was careful,
I would be thrilled into silence.
— THE POET ARNA BONTEMPS UPON
FIRST ARRIVING IN HARLEM, 1924

NEW YORK CITY, PENNSYLVANIA STATION, APRIL 15, 1945
GEORGE SWANSON STARLING

———

IN THE SPACE OF TWENTY-FOUR HOURS, George Starling had put
behind him the slash pines and cypress swamps of his former world and
was finally now stepping out of Pennsylvania Station. He walked beneath the Corinthian columns and the iron fretwork of its barrel-
vaulted ceiling and into the muted light of a spring morning in
Manhattan. He could see a blur of pedestrians brushing past him and
yellow taxicabs swerving up Eighth Avenue. Concrete mountains were
obscuring the sky, steam rising from sewer grates, the Empire State
Building piercing the clouds above granite-faced office buildings, and,
all around him, coffee shops and florists and shoe stores and street ven-
dors and not a single colored- or white-only sign anywhere.

This was New York.

He had made it out of Florida and was now reaching into his pocket for the address and telephone number of his aunt Annie Swanson, the one they called Baby, who lived up in Harlem. But he couldn't find the slip of paper with her number on it, and, in his fatigue and confusion and the upset of all he had been through, couldn't remember precisely where she lived even though he had been there before, and so he made his way to the apartment of the only friend whose Harlem address he could remember and who just happened to be home.

"He took me in, and I sat there, and I tried to think," George said. "The more I tried to think, the more confused I got."

All the streets were numbered. What number street was she on? All the tenements looked the same. Which tenement was she in? She had moved so much. Where was she the last time he was here?

"Don't worry about it," the friend said. "It'll come to you eventually. I'm a let you take you a good, hot bath, lay down, and relax a while."

George got in the tub, and it came to him. "Oh shoot, I know where my aunt lives," he said, and he hurried out of the tub. "Now I remember it. Now it has come to me. Maybe I needed to relax."

He had crossed into another world and was feeling the weight of it all. "I think I was overtired," he would say years later, "from getting ready to leave and getting out of there."

The friend directed him to Aunt Baby's three-room apartment on 112th Street between Fifth and Lenox, where he would sleep on the sofa in the front room until he could find work and a place of his own.

He set his things down just inside her front door, and, at that moment, he became a New Yorker, because, unlike on his other visits to the North, this time, he planned to stay. He would have to get accustomed to a concrete world with the horizon cut off by a stand of brownstones, to a land with no trees and where you couldn't see the sun. Somehow, he would have to get used to the press of people who never seemed to sleep, the tight, dark cells they called tenements. He would quicken his steps, learn to walk faster, hold his head up and his back stiff and straight, not waving to everyone whose eyes he met but instead acting like he, too, had already seen and heard it all, because in a way, in a life-and-death sort of way, he had.

Curiously enough, one thing was for sure. He didn't see himself as part of any great tidal wave. "No," he said years later. "I just knew that

I was getting away from Florida. I didn't consider it like it was a general movement on and I was a part of it. No, I never considered that."

He could only see what was in front of him, and that was, he hoped, a freer new life for himself. "I was hoping," he said years later. "I was hoping I would be able to live as a man and express myself in a manly way without the fear of getting lynched at night."

LOS ANGELES

Maybe we can start again,
in the new rich land
—in California,
where the fruit grows.
We'll start over.
— JOHN STEINBECK, *The Grapes of Wrath*

LOS ANGELES, APRIL 1953
ROBERT JOSEPH PERSHING FOSTER

———

ROBERT DROVE UNDER A GRAY GAUZE SKY through the thicket of shark-fin taillights, up Crenshaw and Slauson and Century, the stickpin palms arched high above him. He went screeching and lurching with the distracted urgency of a man meeting a blind date, picturing the first glance and dreading the faint chance of disappointment.

He drove into the white sun. Everything was wide open and new. The city unfurled itself, low and broad, the boulevards singing Spanish descriptions, *La Cienega, La Brea, La Tijera*. There were orange trapezoid signs staked high above the diners and auto dealerships and neon lights at the coin-op laundries.

The farther he went, the better it got. The trees were not trees anymore but Popsicles and corncobs. The lawns spread out like pool tables, and you could cut yourself on the hedgerows. Everything was looking like a villa or a compound now, statues and gumdrop trees marching down overdone driveways and Grecian urns set out on the porticoes.

The whole effect was like a diva with too much lipstick, and he loved it. The too-muchness of it all.

He was drawing near the Wilshire district and was looking for St. Andrews Place, where a Dr. William Beck, an old professor from medical school, now lived.

Dr. Beck started practicing medicine when Robert was just learning to crawl. However hard Robert thought he had it, Dr. Beck had had it rougher. It began with why Dr. Beck had become a doctor in the first place. Decades before, his father had tuberculosis. There were no colored doctors around, and no white doctors would come out to the farm. The father died, and so the son decided he would be the doctor that didn't exist when they needed one. He specialized in tuberculosis and diseases of the lung and would spend the rest of his life fighting what took his father away.

No colored man out on a farm was going to die abandoned if he could help it. He took a job teaching at Meharry and on the weekends went out into the country making house calls on colored families who couldn't make it into Nashville. Every Sunday he drove the back roads to the sharecropper shacks and the shotgun houses in his crisp suits and late-model car. Some of the white people accused him of being uppity and not knowing his place. Threats and shots were fired. One afternoon, some roughnecks pulled him from his car and beat him. From then on, his wife, Reatha, and their two young children, William, Jr., and Vivian, rode with him whenever he went.

"They would drive out as a family, figuring that they wouldn't kill him in front of them," his granddaughter, Reatha Gray Simon, said years later.

Mrs. Beck was prominent in her own right in the South's distorted world of colored privilege. Her father, a dentist, was said to have been an outside child of an Alabama governor, a condition that afforded the family land and means when the son decided to set up house outside Monroe, Louisiana. The son had thirteen children, and all of them went to college in the days when most colored people did not make it to high school.

Dr. and Mrs. Beck were in their fifties now, Robert's parents' generation. They themselves had arrived in Los Angeles only six years before. They were part of the postwar flood of colored Louisianans that was turning Los Angeles into New Orleans west. Dr. Beck arrived as an elder statesman who had taught many of the colored doctors practicing

there, and Mrs. Beck arrived the very picture of a doctor's wife. She was
a beauty of the Lena Horne variety, who had never spent a day at work
and was accustomed to maids and cooks and would thus not know what
to do with either a typewriter or a mop. When they first arrived, they
noticed to their dismay that most colored people were living on the
more congested east side of town, east of Main Street and far from the
circular driveways of Beverly Hills.

They looked further west and found a house more in keeping with
their vision of themselves. It was a four-bedroom peach stucco mansion
set back from the road on St. Andrews between Pico and Country
Club. The address was 1215 St. Andrews. It had a wide portico with
balustrades like the bridges of Paris. It was surrounded by houses that
were equally grand. And they wanted it.

But the neighborhood was all white, and there was a covenant on the
house that forbade the owners from selling to colored people. Still a real
estate agent managed to secure the house for them in spite of the restric-
tion. During the early testing of limits that presaged the white flight
from northern and western cities in the 1960s, realtors found ways
around the covenants by buying properties themselves and selling them
at a higher price to colored people, by arranging third-party transfers
that hid the identity of the true purchasers, or by matching defiant or
desperate white sellers with equally anxious colored buyers, which together were just about the only way colored people could get into certain
neighborhoods. In any case, Dr. and Mrs. Beck, bourgeois though they
were, waited until after dark to move into 1215 St. Andrews Place. But
someone must have seen them. That night, as they began unpacking, an
orange light danced in front of the picture window. The palm tree on
their manicured lawn was on fire. It was not unlike the crosses that
burned in the South, except this was California.

They were not new to this kind of hostility, and they decided not to
run from it. They had survived the South during far uglier days. And
they considered themselves upstanding people that anyone should be
proud to live next to. They went to court to challenge the covenant and
defend the means by which they had acquired the house; and, when it
was over, they had won the right to stay. The white people emptied out
of the block within months.

On a spring afternoon six years later, Robert Pershing Foster drew
near the vicinity of the peach stucco house that his mentor had to sue to
live in, to begin his own life in California.

Robert had arrived in one of the last receiving stations of the twentieth-century migration out of the South. For most of the state's history, the distance between California and the old Confederacy had discouraged all but the most determined of black pioneers. The people were of so little means that they could scarcely take a chance on someplace so far away in the decades before the Great Migration. There was already an abundance of unskilled labor from China, Japan, and Mexico, which gave California industries little need to recruit cheap black labor from the South, had they been so inclined.

Still, a small contingent of blacks had lived in California since the eighteenth century. There were two blacks among the forty-four settlers who founded Los Angeles on September 4, 1781. Some arrived over the ensuing decades, when slaveholders who moved west brought their slaves with them. Others worked as fur traders, scouts, cowboys, and miners. But even before the end of the Civil War, California, like other states outside the South, strongly discouraged the migration of freed slaves across its border. The state constitutional convention seriously considered prohibiting colored people from living in California. The measure did not pass but was a reflection of the fear and intolerance directed toward them.

By 1900, there were only 2,131 black people in the city of Los Angeles out of a total population of 102,479, and only 11,045 in the entire state of California. The numbers rose slowly but steadily over the years but did not take off during the labor shortage of World War I as in the North. California had not been as dependent on European labor as had other parts of the country, and Los Angeles, the state's largest city, did not then have an industrial base as did the cities of the North.

But even in the low-status laborer and domestic positions that were the caste-ordered preserve of colored people in the South, colored migrants to California faced stiff competition from the many immigrants already there, the Mexicans and Filipinos working the loading docks, the Europeans in personal service to the glamorous and the wealthy.

"Even the seeming inapproachable shoe-shining field was competed for by the Greeks," observed a report by the Works Progress Administration in the 1930s on the challenges facing black workers in Los Angeles. "Trained English servants succeeded them as valets and butlers."

The polyglot nature of Los Angeles made it harder for colored migrants to figure out this new terrain, where competition was coming from every direction and each minority was pitted against the others. "In certain plants, Mexicans and whites worked together," the Works Progress Administration reported. "In some others, white workers accepted Negroes and objected to Mexicans. In others, white workers accepted Mexicans and objected to Japanese. White women worked with Mexican and Italian women, but refused to work with Negroes. . . . In the General Hospital, Negro nurses attended white patients, but were segregated from white nurses in dining halls: in a manufacturing plant white workers refused to work with Negroes, but worked under a Negro foreman."

Into this world arrived the migrants from the South, looking for a place for themselves far from home, not knowing what to expect in a city with a whimsical caste system and no rules that anyone could see.

———

The Becks were expecting him. Word had reached them that he was heading to California, although Robert did not alert them himself or assume he could stay with them. Driving in the middle of a foreign city, it hit him that he had arrived in Los Angeles without any assurance of anything. It was not clear who would take him in or for how long. The nearest relative was two thousand miles away. And he suddenly started to feel alone and uncertain again. "I knew I could find a place to sleep in any hotel I knew would take me in," he would say years later, "but I didn't know what my future was."

He decided to look up Dr. Beck's office and go by there first. He didn't want to give the impression that he expected to live off the Becks. "These were not relatives I was going to see," Robert said. "I didn't know the Becks would take me in."

He found the address in the phone book. It was an office building on South Figueroa, number 4240. It turned out Dr. Beck was delighted to see him.

"Come here, boy," Dr. Beck said greeting him. "Of course you'll be staying with us. We've got a big house, plenty of room."

Robert regaled the Becks with the story of his journey. And he told them that it was not yet over, that he was going up to Oakland to see about the prospects there.

"Now, when you get through looking it over," Dr. Beck said, "come on back here, and I'll give you all the surgery out of my practice."

Robert was relieved and knew that Dr. Beck had the best of intentions. But he also knew he couldn't make a living on one man's referrals alone. So he made plans to drive up to Oakland and to see if it better suited him. In the meantime, he would take in L.A.

Johnny Warmsley, an old schoolmate from Morehouse, took him around, brought in another guy they knew from Atlanta, Wilbur Pew Beulow, who owned a gas station now, and showed him Hollywood and Vine, which actually meant something in those days, and Beverly Hills, the hills in general, the colored nightclubs on Central Avenue, the department stores on Wilshire, the palm trees, the billboards, the people dressed like Dean Martin and Doris Day, the broad silver sidewalks, and the mansions the color of cotton candy.

They rode and rode, and Robert drank it in. He saw what he had driven all this way for and had had in his mind for as long as he could remember, and there it was laid out before him better than a dream.

"I loved it," Robert said. *"I loved it, loved it, loved it, loved it."*

You could drive for hours and still not see the end of it. He could get lost in a town like this, be whoever he wanted to be. It was a blank canvas waiting for him to start painting on it. "Big, open, hustle and bustle," he said. "It was big, big, big. It was the cleanest city I'd ever seen. It was clean enough to eat breakfast off the sidewalk. *Beautiful.* I loved it."

Johnny Warmsley gave him the verbal map of the city.

"Now, Los Angeles is divided into East and West by Main Street," Johnny told him. "All the boulevards go this way, and the streets go that way. The colored neighborhoods are mostly east. There are very few of us west of Crenshaw." That meant most of the places you heard about in the movies: Bel-Air, Brentwood, Beverly Hills, Malibu. They were off-limits to colored people, Johnny Warmsley told him.

Robert would have expected as much after his ordeal in Arizona and was too excited to muster much disappointment. After all, the Becks were living west of Crenshaw, the lawsuit notwithstanding, and that gave him hope that Los Angeles was making as much progress as most any city he might choose.

Johnny and Wilbur were happy to take him to where the movie stars lived and maybe make a sighting. But Robert said he didn't care about that. He had already seen Barbara Stanwyck once. It was when he was based in Austria for the army and the colonel from Mississippi, rather than giving Robert an assignment, ordered him to make himself scarce. The Clements gave him and Alice the money for a trip. They went all over Europe and when they were in Venice, they were standing in St. Mark's Square when they saw Barbara Stanwyck and whoever her husband was at the time.

"And she whispered to him, 'Look at the blacks over there,'" Robert remembered. "I read her lips. She didn't say it in a demeaning manner, but I saw him look over to where we were. And they were giving false grins for all the populants of the city. If you see a celebrity, sure, I want to see the celebrity. But I'd seen enough not to go gaga over it."

He woke up from the city's spell. The glamour was all well and good, but he had other things on his mind.

"I was thinking of more urgent things," he said. "What will I do? *What will I do?* I had to think about surviving."

And so something compelled him several hundred more miles through the mountains, a fear that he was on his own now, far from home, that failure was a distinct but unbearable possibility and that everyone was watching and ready to comment on how things turned out. There was a dread deep within him that he might not make it in L.A., however besotted he was. And so he prepared to drive to Oakland in order to settle on a city for good.

He was weighing every nuance and eventuality, and the stars seemed to have preordained Oakland. It had more people from Monroe than any other place on the coast. He would have a ready-made clientele. He would be looking up his old friend John Dunlap, who had been in the mortuary business in Monroe, knew everybody from back home, and had assured him of plenty of patients. It was as if Oakland were sitting there waiting for him. He could not rest until he had seen it.

He rode at God's knee between the two great cities of California and saw the clouds search out folds in the mountains. He made his way across the San Francisco Bay and into Oakland, which by the early 1950s had become a satellite of colored Louisiana. The shipyards and the loading docks and the railroad jobs had called out to the southerners running from Jim Crow and had given them haven and jobs paying more than a dollar an hour. They settled in the foothills of west Oakland and Richmond, far from the wealthy white cliff-side mansions and nearer to the shipyards. They planted their collards and turnip greens, and let chickens forage out back.

Robert drove into west Oakland, past the fussy Victorian row houses and the worker cottages, turreted and marching in lockstep, barely a foot between them, roosters and pole beans growing in some of the postage stamp yards. It was looking familiar. It was looking like Monroe, which was perhaps one reason why people from Monroe had gravitated there in the first place and made a colony for themselves. It was precisely what Robert was looking to get away from. It was not living up to his glamour vision of California. It felt as if he had driven all this way for the same place he had left.

He was searching for Forty-second and Lusk, where John Dunlap lived. Dunlap, as Robert called him, had moved to Oakland at the height of the war, in 1943, not knowing a soul. The climate agreed with him. He got a room and sent for his wife. From then on, he saw southerners like Robert show up in Oakland looking for something they couldn't name. "They started coming every week," Dunlap said decades later. "They were coming in carloads."

Dunlap had married into a family of morticians and so had taken up the trade himself. Robert was counting on Dunlap to show him around and help him build a clientele. Morticians were always good people to know. Having seen the villas in Los Angeles, Robert was expecting a spread befitting someone with the guaranteed customer base a mortician enjoys. But he pulled up to Lusk and found the little white worker cottage belonging to Dunlap.

Dunlap was glad to see him and showed Robert where he would be sleeping—on a makeshift bed in the front room. He apologized for not being able to take Robert around. But he was working hard to make ends meet in this new world and was too beat at the end of the day to be of much help. It turned out Dunlap hadn't found work as a mortician in Oakland. He and other middle-class migrants from the South, it turns out, were not unlike the immigrant taxi drivers you hear about who had been doctors or engineers back in Pakistan. Dunlap had been somebody back home, but it didn't translate at his destination. And so he had taken a job as a laborer at the shipyard.

Dunlap pointed Robert in the direction of the hospitals he knew of and the people Robert might like to see from back home in Monroe. Robert set out in the morning for the hospitals and clinics he'd heard about. He went to Kaiser, the big industrialist-shipping conglomerate, to see what possibilities there might be for a medical position. He came back empty.

"I'm not finding what I want," he told Dunlap.

Dunlap knew what that meant. Not only was Robert having no luck finding a place to practice, he wasn't liking Oakland. As Dunlap saw it, Dr. Beck had gotten to Robert first. Los Angeles had seduced him. And Oakland did not stand a chance. Robert made up his mind and phoned Alice and the Clements about his decision. And as soon as he did, he drove back to Los Angeles to start living for the first time in his life.

THE THINGS THEY
LEFT BEHIND

There were no Chinaberry trees. No pecan trees. . . .
Never again would I pick dew berries
or hear the familiar laughter from the field truck.
This was my world now, this strange new family
and their cramped quarters over the tiny grocery store
they grandly called the "confectionery."
—CLIFTON TAULBERT, *The Last Train North*

IN THE NORTH AND WEST, 1915–2000

WHEN THEY FLED, there were things they left behind. There were people they might not see again. They would now find out through letters and telegrams that a baby had been born or that a parent had taken ill or passed away. There were things they might not ever taste or touch or share in again because they were hundreds of miles from all that they had known. From this moment forward, it would take great effort and resources merely to sit and chat over salt pork and grits with a beloved mother or sister who had chosen not to go. Perhaps the greatest single act of family disruption and heartbreak among black Americans in the twentieth century was the result of the hard choices made by those on either side of the Great Migration.

The South was still deep within those who left, and the sight of some insignificant thing would take them back and remind them of what they once were. For my mother, a vase of Casablanca lilies far from home took her back to the memory of this:

Once a year on a midsummer night that could not be foretold, a curious plant called the night-blooming cereus would decide to undrape its petals. It was said, among the colored people in the small-town South who followed such things and made a ritual of its arrival, that if you looked hard enough, you could see the face of the baby Jesus in the folds of the bloom.

My mother's mother, who sang to her camellias and made showpieces of the most recalcitrant and unlovable of plants—the African violets and Boston ferns that died when other people just looked at them—did not want to leave the land of her ancestors, the drawl of small-town convention, the hard soil she had willed into a cutting garden. There was chaos in the Jim Crow world outside her picket fence. But inside, there was peace and beauty, and she insulated herself in her perennial beds.

She grew a night-blooming cereus on the front porch of her yellow bungalow. Its gangly branches coiled out of its pot and snaked along the porch planks. It was an unpleasant-looking orphan of a plant that was only worth growing for the one night in the year when its white, lily-like petals managed to open for a few hours when nobody would be up to see it.

My mother's mother tended its homely stalks all through the year. She watched it close and made note when the buds were plump and ready to unfurl. As soon as she was certain, she alerted the neighbors as they passed her front yard with its roses the size of saucers, which she sold after some cajoling for a dollar apiece, and its crape myrtles the color of cotton candy.

"My night-blooming cereus is going to open tonight," she told them.

Amanda Poindexter, Miss Lilybell Nelson, who lived up the hill and sang like a bird, Mrs. Jacobs next door, and a few other neighbor ladies on Gibbon Street would arrive at my grandmother's front porch at around midnight. They drank sweet tea and ate freshly churned vanilla ice cream. They rocked in the porch swing, which creaked as they rocked, and they waited. As a young girl, my mother sat watching on the porch steps, mystified by the grown people's patience and devotion.

The opening took hours. Sometime around three in the morning, the white petals spread open, and the women set down their sweet tea to crane their necks over the blossom. They inhaled its sugary scent and tried to find the baby Jesus in the cradle in the folds. Most exclaimed that they saw it; my mother said she never did. But she would remember the wait for the night-blooming cereus, the Georgia heat stifling and heavy, and take the memory with her when she left, though she would never share in the mystery of that Gibbon Street ritual again.

———————

As best they could, the people brought the Old Country with them— a taste for hominy grits and pole beans cooking in salt pork, the "sure enoughs" and "I reckons" and the superstitions of new moons and itchy palms that had seeped into their very being.

In the New World, they surrounded themselves with the people they knew from the next farm over or their Daily Vacation Bible School, from their clapboard Holiness churches, from the colored high schools or the corner store back home, and they would keep those ties for as long as they lived. The ones from the country fired their shotguns into the night air on New Year's Eve like they did back home in Georgia and Mississippi and ate black-eyed peas and rice for good luck on New Year's Day. The people from Texas took Juneteenth Day to Los Angeles, Oakland, Seattle, and other places they went. Even now, with barbecues and red soda pop, they celebrate June 19, 1865, the day Union soldiers rode into Galveston, announced that the Civil War was over, and released the quarter-million slaves in Texas who, not knowing they had been freed, had toiled for two and a half years after the Emancipation Proclamation.

Whole churches and social rituals in the North and West would be built around certain southern towns or entire states. Well into the 1990s, at the Bridge Street Church in Brooklyn, for instance, when people from South Carolina were asked to stand and make themselves known, half the flock would rise to its feet. To this day, people still wear sequins and bow ties to the annual Charleston Ball in Washington, where a good portion of the Carolinas went.

It turned out they were not so different from Sicilians settling in Little Italy or Swedes in Minnesota.

In the New World, colonies organized themselves into Mississippi and Arkansas Clubs in Chicago; Florida Clubs in Harlem; Carolina Clubs in Brooklyn and Philadelphia; and numerous Texas Clubs, general Louisiana Clubs, several New Orleans Clubs, and, among others, a Monroe, Louisiana, Club and a Lake Charles, Louisiana, Club in Los Angeles.

They met over oxtails and collard greens well into the turn of the new century or for as long as the original migrants lived to recall among their dwindling membership the things they'd left behind: the ailing parents and scuffling siblings and sometimes even their own children; the courtly tipping of one's hat to a stranger; the screech owls and whip-poorwills wailing outside their windows foretelling an imminent death; paper-shell pecans falling to the ground; mimosa trees, locust trees, dog-wood trees, and chinaberries; the one-room churches where the people fanned themselves through parching revivals and knelt by the ancestors buried beside the sanctuary light. These things stayed with them even though they left, because a crying part of them had not wanted to leave.

"If I were half as well treated home as here," a migrant in Pittsburgh told the economist Abraham Epstein early in the Migration, "I would rather stay there."

They wired money back home, as expected, and sent a larger share of their straining paychecks than they could truly afford to the people they left behind. In his study of the Migration, Epstein found that eighty per-cent of the married migrants and nearly half of the single ones were sending money home, most sending five dollars per week and some sending ten or more dollars per week out of weekly wages of fifteen dol-lars back then for unskilled laborers, as many of them would have been.

There was something earnest and true-hearted about them. They greeted people on northern sidewalks a little too quickly and too excit-edly for the local people's liking and to the stricken embarrassment of their more seasoned cousins and northern-born children. They talked of a lush, hot-blooded land to children growing up fast and indifferent in a cold place too busy to stop and visit.

Transplanted in
Alien Soil

Should I have come here?
But going back was
impossible. . . .
Wherever my eyes turned,
they saw stricken,
frightened black faces
trying vainly to cope
with a civilization
that they did not understand.
I felt lonely.
I had fled one insecurity
and embraced another.
— RICHARD WRIGHT,
Black Boy

MILWAUKEE, WISCONSIN, NOVEMBER 1937
IDA MAE BRANDON GLADNEY

———

IDA MAE REUNITED WITH HER BIG SISTER, Irene, at the train station
in Milwaukee, and it was clear to both sisters that Ida Mae and George
had a long way to go before they could survive on their own in the
North. Ida Mae had made it out of Mississippi, but her task had just
begun. Irene took them to her walk-up apartment in a two-flat off
Reservoir on the North Side of the city. The sister had been in Milwaukee only a couple of years herself, having followed her husband, the

third one, Richard, there in 1935. Ida Mae and her family camped out in Irene's front room with all their worldly belongings while Ida Mae's husband went out hunting for work.

Ida Mae had landed in Milwaukee because her sister had migrated there along a not altogether random route established at the start of the movement, back when the two of them were just little girls. It was one of the by-products of the Great Migration that particular southern counties became feeder lines to specific destinations in the North, based on where the earliest migrants went and established themselves, which in turn was often based on something as random as where the northern companies recruiting southerners in World War I just happened to be based. Irene had followed one of those tributaries.

A map of the crosscurrents of migration would link otherwise completely unrelated southern counties and towns with seemingly random northern cities that, other than the train lines and sometimes in spite of them, made little practical sense but nonetheless made sister cities of the unlikeliest of pairings: Palestine, Texas, and Syracuse, New York; Norfolk, Virginia, and Roxbury in Boston; Brookhaven, Mississippi, and Bloomington, Illinois. Small colonies of migrants from Chickasaw County, Mississippi, ended up in Toledo, Ohio, where Ida Mae's older brothers fled, and in Kalamazoo, Michigan, when the call came for workers.

But for most sharecroppers in Chickasaw County, the Promised Land was, oddly enough, a place called Beloit, Wisconsin, on the Rock River seventy-five miles southeast of Milwaukee, which, along with Chicago, because of the *Chicago Defender* and the mail-order catalogues, would have figured prominently in their minds.

The foundries and metalworking factories in Beloit and the steel mills and manufacturers of farm implements in Milwaukee went to northeast Mississippi to hire workers used to hard labor for little money back during World War I. With so many northerners nosing around the South for cheap black labor, the recruiters had to work undercover and spread themselves out among the targeted states to escape detection, arrest, or fines that could run into the thousands of dollars.

Ultimately, southern protectionism had limited effect, and neighbors and cousins of Ida Mae's husband made their way from Okolona to Beloit, some later fanning out to Milwaukee and Chicago. And so, arriving as she did deep into the Depression, Ida Mae's sister, Irene, followed a quiet but well-trod rivulet from Chickasaw County to Milwaukee.

The city's colored population had not skyrocketed as it had in De-

troit, which rose sevenfold from 5,741 to 41,000, or Gary, which shot up
from 383 to 5,300, during World War I. But the number of colored people in Milwaukee had risen from a mere 980 in 1910 to 2,229 by 1920, an
increase of 127 percent, and continued to rise in the 1920s and 1930s.

Once Irene got to Milwaukee, it didn't take her long to start sending
gift boxes of clothes from the North and talking up Wisconsin—not
pressuring Ida Mae, who was too easygoing to take anything too seriously anyway, but just telling her flat out, "If I was you, I just wouldn't
stay down there."

———

Milwaukee was a frank and clattering workhorse of a town, a concrete
smokestack of a place with trolley cars clanking against a web of power
lines and telephone cables filling the sky. Curls of steam rose from the
rooftops and factory silos and from the gray hulk of the Schlitz brewery
over by the Cherry Street Bridge.

It was the other side of the world from the wide-open, quiet land of
the cotton fields. Ida Mae saw things she never imagined, bridges that
lifted into the air to let ships pass through, traffic lights and streetlamps
and flocks of white-robed women—nuns, she was told they were—
their habits fluttering in the wind and their crisp headdresses making a
stiff halo around their faces. Ida Mae had never seen anyone like them
before. She felt drawn to them, and she liked to watch them float by,
regal and otherworldly.

There were unknown tongues and aromas drifting out of the beer
gardens and delicatessens. There were Germans, Poles, Slavs, Hungarians, Irish, Italians, Greeks, and Russians who had come here, as Ida
Mae and her husband had, willing to work their way up from the bottom and make a life for themselves in a freer place than the one they had
left. Before World War I, Milwaukee had not extended itself to the la-
boring caste of the South, nor had it needed to, with the continuing supply of European immigrants to work its factories.

But, as in the rest of the industrial North, the number of Europeans
immigrating to Milwaukee plummeted from 22,508 in the first decade
of the twentieth century to a mere 451 during all of the 1920s because
of the war. Factories that had never before considered colored labor
came to see the advantages of colored workers from the South, even if
some of the so-called advantages were themselves steeped in stereotype.
"They are superior to foreign labor because they readily understand
what you try to tell them," one employer reported. "Loyalty, willing-

ness, cheerfulness. Quicker, huskier, and can stand more heat than other workmen."

Most colored migrants were funneled into the lowest-paying, least wanted jobs in the harshest industries—iron and steel foundries and slaughtering and meatpacking. They "only did the dirty work," a colored steelworker said of his early days in Milwaukee, "jobs that even Poles didn't want."

But it was now the fall of 1937, and even those jobs were disappearing. George and Ida Mae arrived in Milwaukee as the city was falling deeper into the Depression. The automotive, farm, and heavy machinery sectors suffered crushing layoffs in August 1937, two months before they arrived, layoffs that would continue well into the following year. The kinds of jobs George was looking for and that most colored men performed—unskilled labor that was often hot, tedious, backbreaking, or dangerous—plunged by seventy percent, from 1,557 such jobs in 1930 to only 459 at the end of the decade, around the time George and Ida Mae arrived.

With jobs scarce, the old tendency toward intolerance and exclusion reasserted itself. Hiring managers at A. O. Smith Company, a tank and auto frame factory, said there was no use in colored people applying for jobs there because the company "never did and didn't intend to employ Negroes." Company guards knew to stop colored job seekers at the gates.

———

Still, the urge to get out of the South was so strong that by the mid-1930s, Milwaukee's North Side, a neighborhood of tenements and two-flats just above the city's central business district, was already becoming the colored side of town. Since World War I, it had been filling each day with more and more colored people from the South, so much so that in some grade-school classrooms, nearly every child was from Mississippi, Tennessee, or Arkansas, and those born in the North were in the minority. The way things looked, Ida Mae's children would add three more to that demographic equation.

By now Ida Mae couldn't hide the fact that she was pregnant and was already making plans to head back to Mississippi to give birth. She didn't quite trust whatever it was they did to people in hospitals. She had never been inside one but had heard that they strapped women down during delivery, and so she decided to surrender herself to a Mississippi midwife as she and everybody she knew had always done.

It was calculated that the baby was due sometime in the late spring, so she would be heading back to Mississippi in three or four months. George hadn't found steady work yet, and Ida Mae would have to leave him with her sister and brother-in-law while he continued to hunt for work. Ida Mae's return to Mississippi delayed her adjustment to the New World, planning as she was to leave nearly as soon as she arrived. But her decision had assured her that she wouldn't end up like so many other wives, left down south waiting for a husband who might never get around to sending for them.

HARLEM, SPRING 1945
GEORGE SWANSON STARLING

———

GEORGE HAD THE GOOD FORTUNE to have made it out of Florida and to have arrived in New York well into World War II, and was thus able to find a job right away. It was a job doing the one thing, whether he sought it or not, that would keep him tied to the South. It was a job on the railroad, the Seaboard Air Line, it was called, which would keep him on the rails up and down the East Coast for days and weeks at a time, expose him to the temptations of women and drink, and do little to help his already colicky marriage to Inez.

He was overqualified and overeducated for the job as a coach attendant, hauling luggage into the baggage car and helping people stow their carry-ons in the overhead bins for a dime or a nickel tip. But it was a step up from what they had wanted him to do when they first got a look at him.

"We need some big, tall, husky boys like you to carry the trays in the dining room," the manager told him.

"Well, you need some big husky boys to carry the bags on the coaches too," George said.

"We need waiters."

"But I don't want to wait no tables."

The war was on and labor was short, so George got the job as coach attendant. He wouldn't get paid what his white counterparts were getting even in the enlightened North. He would be getting more than he ever had as a fruit picker down south, which was not particularly a great triumph but was a fact known to anyone, including and perhaps especially railroad management, as it was a convenient way to explain away the lower pay scale for black employees. *At least you're making more than you did down south,* they could say.

The job meant working twenty-four- and forty-eight-hour runs up and down the East Coast on trains called the Silver Comet, the Silver Star, and the Silver Meteor, the very train he rode when he migrated north. He would work the Jim Crow car and the white car behind it, stacking trunks and suitcases up to the ceiling, getting ice, and polishing shoes. He would make close to a hundred dollars every two weeks for it.

In attending to the needs of his white clientele, he would be addressed as "boy," as was the custom when he was working the white cars, even though by now he was twenty-seven years old and towered over most everyone who addressed him as such.

———

They could call him what they wanted on the train. He didn't like it, but it didn't define him. He lived in Harlem now and was free.

He had avoided the racial turf wars that characterized other cities during the Great Migration. In Manhattan, those fights had been settled long before World War II, when George got there.

The first blacks in Harlem were actually a small group of seventeenth-century slaves of the Dutch West India Company. They built the original road between lower Manhattan and Harlem and worked the farms and estates of what was then undeveloped marshland and countryside.

As more Africans were shipped in to build the colony, the majority were concentrated in lower Manhattan, where the first eleven African captives had landed on the island in 1625. They and those that followed were imported by the Dutch to clear timber and construct the city's roads and buildings. They worked in captivity for two hundred years, until New York abolished slavery in 1827. Emancipation set free ten thousand slaves in Manhattan. But they found their economic conditions little changed, confined as they were to the lowliest positions and facing steep competition from newly arrived immigrants.

Their tenuous condition and the state of race relations in general reached a nadir in the city during the Civil War Draft Riots of 1863, when Irish immigrants launched a five-day assault on freed slaves in lower Manhattan.

The trouble began when the federal government announced it would start drafting men to serve in the Union Army. Wealthy men could avoid the draft by paying three hundred dollars or hiring a substitute. Anger rose among Irish working-class men, in particular, who couldn't afford to buy their way out of a war they felt they had no stake in. They saw it as risking their lives to defend southern slaves, who would, in their minds, come north and only become competition for them. As it was, the Irish were already competing with former slaves in New York, whose very presence undercut the wages of working-class whites because blacks had little choice but to accept lower pay for whatever work they did.

The draft began July 11, 1863. Two days later, on the morning of July 13, mobs began assaulting blacks on the streets. They attacked a fruit vendor and a nine-year-old boy in lower Manhattan and set fire to a colored orphanage in Midtown. They attacked white women married to colored men and burned boardinghouses and tenements where colored people lived, stripping the clothes off the white property owners. They dragged a black coachman out of his home, hanged him from a lamppost, and then dragged the body through the streets by the genitals.

In five days of rioting, anti-war mobs lynched eleven black men and drove the colony of former slaves in lower Manhattan into a continual search for housing. Black residents moved steadily north from one unestablished and unsavory neighborhood to the next, from lower Manhattan to Greenwich Village to the coldwater flats of the Tenderloin District and finally to pockets of upper Manhattan, in the emerging district north of Central Park known as Harlem.

By the late nineteenth century, Harlem was no longer isolated farmland but, due to the rise in immigration from eastern and southern Europe and the completion of new subway routes, was now a fashionable district of middle-class Germans, Russians, Jews, and Irish living in recently built brownstones on broad boulevards and of newly arrived Italians living in the more working-class outskirts of East Harlem. It was where Oscar Hammerstein bought and sold property during the boom years at the turn of the twentieth century and it was the district represented by Fiorello La Guardia in the U.S. House of Representatives during the Depression.

As a stream of colored people trudged north from other parts of Manhattan and from the countryside of the American South, the Italians and Jews ceded much of Harlem to the new arrivals in the early decades of the twentieth century for the greener hamlets of Westchester, Queens, and the Bronx or the stylish apartments on Riverside Drive.

By 1930, some 165,000 colored people were living in Harlem, packed so densely that some tenants had to sleep in shifts—"as soon as one person awoke and left, his bed was taken over by another," the historian Gilbert Osofsky wrote. Harlem had become majority black, its residents having built institutions like the Abyssinian Baptist Church, regaling white audiences at the Cotton Club, reciting poetry at private salons, running numbers rackets, and baptizing themselves in the Harlem and East Rivers.

Even during the Depression, people continued to pour in by the tens of thousands, such that the Reverend Adam Clayton Powell, Sr., wrote, "There was hardly a member of Abyssinian Church who could not count on one or more relatives among the new arrivals."

———

The changeover in Harlem was not a smooth one and went to the very heart of the basic difference between the North and South, between the authoritarian control over colored lives under Jim Crow and the laissez-faire passivity in the big, anonymous cities of the North and West.

The receiving stations of the Great Migration were no more welcoming of the colored migrants than the South was—in fact, the arrival of colored migrants set off remarkable displays of hostility, ranging from organized threats against white property owners who might sell or rent to blacks to firebombing of houses before the new colored owners could even move in.

White Harlemites banded together into committees to fight what they openly called "a growing menace," an "invasion" of "black hordes," and a "common enemy," using what Gilbert Osofsky called "the language of war." They formed organizations like the Save-Harlem Committee and the Harlem Property Owners Improvement Corporation to protect against "the greatest problem Harlem has had to face."

Panicked property owners drafted restrictive covenants in which they swore not to let colored people into their properties for fifteen years or "till when it was thought this situation . . . will have run its course." Some covenants covered entire blocks and went so far as to limit the number of colored janitors, bellboys, butlers, maids, and cooks to be employed in a Harlem home or business. White leaders tried to segregate churches, restaurants, and theaters, the Lafayette Theater on Seventh Avenue permitting colored people to sit only in the balcony, no different from Mississippi.

White leaders warned colored real estate agents not to seek housing on certain streets and tried to negotiate a boundary line that colored people would agree not to cross. On the other side of the color line, they took recalcitrant white neighbors to court if they broke down and rented to colored people against the rules of the covenants.

In the end, none of these things worked, not because anti-black forces gave up or grew more tolerant but because of the more fluid culture and economics of the North—the desire of whites to sell or rent to whomever they chose whether for profit or out of fear, necessity, or self-interest, or the temptation of higher rents that could be extracted from colored tenants with few other places to go.

Just as significantly, these things didn't work because of what might be called the dispassion of the indifferent. The silent majority of whites could be frightened into lockstep solidarity in the authoritarian South but could not be controlled or willed into submission in the cacophonous big cities of the North.

The Great Migration forced Harlem property owners to make a choice. They could try to maintain a whites-only policy in a market being deserted by whites and lose everything, or they could take advantage of the rising black demand and "rent to colored people at higher prices and survive," Osofsky wrote. Most were pragmatic and did the latter.

The flood of colored migrants soon broke down the last of the racial levees in Harlem, and signs went up all over the place, alerting people to the opening up of the market. The following notice, one among many, was posted in front of a Harlem tenement in 1916, at the start of the Great Migration:

NOTICE

We have endeavored for some time to avoid turning over this house to colored tenants, but as a result of . . . rapid changes in conditions . . . this issue has been forced upon us.

The posted concessions, addressed to white neighbors with a sense of defeat and resignation, offered a glimpse into the differences between the North and South. The South, totalitarian and unyielding, was at that very moment succeeding at what white Harlem leaders were so desperately trying to do, that is, controlling the movements of blacks by controlling the minds of whites.

"The basic collapse of all organized efforts to exclude Negroes from Harlem was the inability of any group to gain total and unified support of all white property owners in the neighborhood," Osofsky wrote. "Landlords forming associations by blocks had a difficult time keeping people on individual streets united."

The free-spirited individualism of immigrants and newcomers seeking their fortune in the biggest city in the country thus worked to the benefit of colored people needing housing in Harlem. It opened up a place that surely would have remained closed in the straitjacketed culture of the South.

By the 1940s, when George Starling arrived, Harlem was a mature and well-established capital of black cultural life, having peaked with the Harlem Renaissance, plunged into Depression after the 1929 stock market crash, climbed back to life during World War II, and, unbeknownst to the thousands still arriving from Florida, the Carolinas, Georgia, and Virginia, not to mention Jamaica and the rest of the Caribbean when George got there, was at that precise moment as rollickingly magical as it was ever likely to be.

Seventh Avenue was the Champs-Élysées, a boulevard wide and ready for any excuse for a parade, whether the marches of the minister Father Divine or several thousand Elks in their capes and batons, and, on Sunday afternoons, the singular spectacle called The Stroll. It was where the people who had been laundresses, bellmen, and mill hands in the South dressed up as they saw themselves to be—the men in frock coats and monocles, the women in fox stoles and bonnets with ostrich feathers, the "servants of the rich Park and Fifth Avenue families" wearing "hand-me-downs from their employers," all meant to evoke startled whispers from the crowd on the sidewalk: *My Gawd, did you see that hat?*"

Virtually every black luminary was living within blocks of the others in the elevator buildings and lace-curtained brownstones up on Sugar Hill, from Langston Hughes to Thurgood Marshall to Paul Robeson, Duke Ellington, and W. E. B. Du Bois, on and off, to Richard Wright, who had now outgrown even Chicago, and his friend and protégé Ralph Ellison, who actually lived in Washington Heights but said it was close enough to be Harlem and pretty much considered it so.

Of course, George, having just arrived from Florida, was nowhere near the Sugar Hill set. He was, however, good with money and managed to save up enough fairly quickly to find a more than decent place to live. He located a brownstone on 132nd Street off Lenox in what the people on Sugar Hill called the Valley, which accounted for most of what would be considered Harlem and was thought of as perfectly respectable, even admirable, for someone like George. Now that he had a place and had put a down payment on it, he was in a position to send for Inez. In the meantime, he made the most of his free, new self.

———

When he wasn't on the rails, he was at the Savoy Ballroom, the rum-boogie emporium that took up a whole city block at Lenox and 140th Street. It had a marble staircase and a cut-glass chandelier in the lobby, settees for guests to rest on between dances, two bands alternating so the music never stopped. Anyone might be there, from a shoeshine boy to Greta Garbo or the Prince of Wales. For a time, Ella Fitzgerald was the house vocalist, Benny Goodman or Jimmy Lunceford might be there on any given night, and if you stayed there long enough—which, having come all this way, George, of course, did—you were bound to run into someone from back home in the South—someone from Durham, Charleston, Richmond, Augusta, or, to George's delight, Eustis, Florida.

Gussie Robinson, Louis and Cleo Grant, "Babe" Blye—old Reuben's brother—John Burns, Mary McClendon, and a whole bunch of the Youngs. All of them might show up at the Savoy or at a place called Big George's or the Monte Carlo out in Corona, where a colony of Eustis people were living, which meant that pretty much every weekend, there was a Great Migration convention, a reunion of onetime fruit and cotton pickers, yard boys and house girls and country schoolteachers who had left all the sirring and ma'aming behind. They were jitterbugging on a floating wood floor in the sequins and Florsheims they now could afford, toasting themselves in another world altogether, a world of their own making in the North—if only for a Saturday night.

LOS ANGELES, 1953
ROBERT JOSEPH PERSHING FOSTER

———

ROBERT WAS HEADING BACK to Los Angeles sometime in the late spring of 1953 with the relief and uncertainty of a discriminating man having finally made the decision of his life. He would no longer be a visitor here. For better or for worse, it was home now, and yet he knew little of it. It was as if he had married a perfect stranger and was now confronting the enormity of getting to know her after the deed was done. He had to convince himself that he had made the right choice, that, after all, there really had been no choice for an educated and ambitious colored man like him at the time.

He had driven clear across the country and more than halfway up the California coast and back, with an unsatisfying flirtation with Oakland in between. But his task had just begun.

What little he had when he set out from Louisiana had now dwindled to almost nothing. He pulled into Los Angeles with all of a dollar and a half in his pocket. Now it somehow had to be converted into enough money to buy equality, meaning, to him, enough to go anywhere, do anything, buy the best of whatever he might want. He could not erase half a lifetime of sirring and stepping off the sidewalk, but he would have a good time trying.

He did not have enough to put a security deposit on an apartment, so he had to return to Dr. Beck, who put him up in the guest room of his house and made good on his promise to throw some surgery his way.

Dr. Beck called Robert into his office early on.

"I want you to examine this lady," Dr. Beck told him, starting to describe the patient. "This is Mrs. Brown. I think she has a tumor. Check her out. Tell me what she needs."

Dr. Beck had already examined the patient and knew precisely what she needed, but it was his way of easing Robert into this part of his practice. "That would feed you," Robert said years later. "It wouldn't give me quail, but it would feed me."

He needed to find a place so he could send for Alice and the girls. He was itching to be on his own and make a name for himself. He couldn't do that sitting in somebody else's office waiting for a patient to need surgery.

He heard that the Golden State Mutual Life Insurance Company, the largest colored insurance company in the West (founded by William Nickerson, Jr., a migrant from Texas; George Allen Beavers, a migrant from Georgia; and Norman Oliver Houston, a native Californian, in 1925), was hiring doctors to go house to house to collect urine samples and do routine examinations of customers seeking coverage. Years later, this kind of work would be performed by people with a fraction of his education, and it would be unthinkable for a doctor to show up at a patient's house for any reason, much less to collect urine samples.

It was beneath him, and it was exactly the kind of thing he was running from in Louisiana. He never wanted to be a country doctor going out to people's shotgun houses with a satchel in his hand. Now he would be a city doctor going out to people's bungalows with a satchel in his hand, and not to deliver babies or patch wounds but to take people's blood pressure, of all things. There was no way he could let the people back in Monroe, and, Heaven forbid, his in-laws, the Clements, know how humble his existence was and how desperate he had become.

But he needed the money and had no choice. He was better off than most other new arrivals from the South, who didn't have his credentials. So he made himself grateful for the $7.50 he got for each exam and for the extra $2.50 for the cup of urine.

It was as if he were a young boy again, going door-to-door as he had in Monroe, asking people if they wanted some figs to can for the coming winter. As he had before, he tried to make the best of the situation. He learned to ingratiate himself to the customers while making sure not to miss anything lest he not get paid. But he never knew what he was in for, because here, unlike in Monroe, he was a small person in a big place, a colored man who had memorized the rules of the South and was now in a place with no rules, none that he could see anyway, and where the Foster name could not help him.

One day he showed up at the modest home of a colored couple in their fifties somewhere in South Central. The wife met him at the door and called her husband to the front room.

"John, the doctor's here," the wife said before disappearing into the kitchen.

Robert checked off the answers the husband gave about preexisting conditions, fractures, and surgeries. He gave the man a cup to collect the urine in and later began the physical.

He put a blood pressure cuff on the man's arm and began listening for the systolic pressure. Just then the wife walked in and turned the television on so loud that Robert couldn't hear the beat.

"Could you ask your wife to please cut the television off?" Robert asked. "I can't do my examination."

The woman complied, and soon Robert was finished with the husband.

"Now," Robert said, "I also have a form to examine your wife."

"Alright," the husband said. "Baby, come on. The doctor's ready to do your physical."

The wife came out. She was a large woman in a housedress and apron. She had her hands on her hips. And Robert was unprepared for what she had to say.

"I told you I wasn't going to let no nigger doctor examine me."

Robert was beside himself. There were many things one could say about the South, but he had never experienced rejection by patients of his own kind and hadn't anticipated such a thing in this new place. Colored doctors in the South were revered because there were so few of them and because they were the only ones who could be counted on to go into the country to tend to colored people. They were greeted like Union soldiers come to free the slaves. Because of the great chasm between blacks and whites, colored doctors also had a virtual monopoly on colored patients.

He realized he had entered a more complicated universe than he had imagined. Colored people in California didn't have to go to colored doctors if they didn't want to. They had choices colored people in the South couldn't dream of. To make matters worse for a colored doctor new in town, the very system that instilled privilege and superiority in southern whites also instilled a sense of inferiority in their colored workers, and when the latter got the chance to get all that had been denied them, some sought out whatever they were convinced was superior—and thus white.

In that one exchange, Robert experienced a by-product of integration that would affect nearly every black business and institution when the doors of segregation flung open—rejection by a black customer base for the wide-open new world. It didn't take Robert long to realize that he would have to work doubly hard to win over his own people and get any patients at all. But at the moment, he was so hurt and rattled by the woman's rejection that he couldn't think straight.

"It frightened me so," Robert said years later, "I threw all my things in my bag and dashed out of the house to leave."

"I'm sorry, Doctor," the husband was saying.

"That's alright, that's alright," Robert said, the door closing behind him.

Robert got into his car and only then realized that, in his haste, he had forgotten something.

"Oh, my gosh, I've undergone this embarrassment," he thought to himself, "and I don't have the urine specimen. I'll only get $7.50."

He needed every nickel, so he had no choice. "I cut the motor off," he said, "swallowed my pride, and went back and got the urine specimen."

The woman never let him examine her, and it was just as well. The experience had begun to shape his vision of this new world. "To think that I had come all the way from the Deep South," he would say many years later, "out here to this Land of Milk and Honey and Opportunity and Intelligence, to find that one of my own color was disrespecting me."

He endured such slights for years, and drove all over South Central Los Angeles doing perfunctory examinations and collecting urine as if he were a traveling salesman and not a surgeon with military awards, and he did it because he had to. "That's the cut that you took to get your foot in the door," he would say years later.

The ready-made clientele of old Louisianans he had imagined in his more cocksure moments in Monroe did not materialize. The people were there, alright. He saw them spilling onto Jefferson after Mass on Sunday mornings and packing into the clubs and cafés on Central Avenue and shopping on Crenshaw. But he had no easy way to get to them. Some were going to white doctors over in Leimert Park. Some were going to colored doctors they already knew. Specialists like him often built a practice through referrals, but few doctors knew him well enough to refer patients to him, and they seemed content with the surgeons already on their roster. Los Angeles was turning out to be bigger than he thought, and it was harder to make inroads.

Even the people he knew from back in Monroe were slow to seek him out for treatment. Some people acted different when they got out to the New World. Some changed their names, no longer wanted to be called Boo but by their given name, Henry or William, as Robert himself had done. Some were anxious to leave the South and the past behind and preferred doctors from California, because people from California were seen as better educated, more sophisticated, untainted by the South, and just "better." Some people disappeared completely—the palest Creoles passed into white society, never to be seen again in the colored world. But mostly, the same cliques and assumptions people had had back home had migrated with them to the New World. Some people had resented Robert and the Fosters back in Monroe and brought the feelings with them. And some just couldn't bear the idea of little Pershing from back home examining them.

"All that crowd over there, and then some," Robert said. "They didn't come. My father taught half of 'em. There's enough people in this town to give me the biggest practice in the world that I went to grade school with."

He learned he would have to make do without them. He was feeling anxious and slightly desperate and could not bear the thought of failure. Big Madison was back in Monroe, looking to hear how his little brother was handling all those patients he bragged about. Alice and the girls were awaiting word as to when they would join him in what everyone expected would be a fabulous new home. And his father-in-law was surely expecting a progress report on how his practice was faring in Los Angeles, a city the father-in-law had argued against in the first place.

As it was, the Clements were beside themselves with excitement over developments back in Atlanta. President Clement had decided to make a historic bid to become the first colored member of the Atlanta Board of Education. Colored people could not vote in most of the South and could lose their lives for even trying to register, and here was Clement running for public office in the biggest city in the South. It was such a long shot that Robert was too weary to pay it much attention.

———

Somehow Robert had to find a way out of this new desert he was in. So he wasted no time seeking out prospects wherever he could. Rather than bemoan his lowered position as a traveling hack for an insurance company, he started viewing every insurance customer needing a physical as a potential patient. He dug deep into himself and resurrected the earnest little boy selling figs and buttermilk back in Monroe. He put on his most charming self and tried to win over whoever was placed before him, no matter how surly or resistant or lowly the patient was.

"If people saw you and liked you," he began, "it's your job to charm 'em, show how efficient you were."

He spent many lonely hours crisscrossing neighborhoods in South Central Los Angeles, far from the Becks' and the manicured places he wanted to be, conducting those insurance examinations.

Then, in May, a month after he had arrived in Los Angeles, he got word from Atlanta: President Clement had beaten the longest of odds and been elected to the Board of Education. He had defeated an incumbent, 22,259 votes to 13,936 votes, in an election in which Red-baiting

detractors tried to get him disqualified in the eleventh hour and his opponent, who had been on the board since 1927, had been so confident
that he didn't even campaign.

"I didn't think the people were ready for this," his opponent, J. H.
Landers, told *The Atlanta Constitution.*

The win made Clement the first colored man to win a major office in
Georgia since Reconstruction and was significant enough to merit a
story in *The New York Times* and articles in *Time* and *Newsweek.* "For
the first time since Reconstruction days," the *Times* wrote, "a Negro won
nomination to Atlanta's Board of Education."

The news filtered back as Robert was knocking on doors collecting
urine samples and still boarding with the Becks. He was feeling even
more isolated and alone and could not let on to anyone back home the
truth of his situation. Just as he was needing to muster more faith than
ever, the South chose a rare instance to let slip a colored victory—and to
President Clement, no less, the man who had never thought Robert
measured up, who had taken over his role as the head of his own family,
and who second-guessed his every decision, even his choice to leave the
South. Robert was struggling with that choice at that very moment and
now could not escape his father-in-law's triumph because it was national
news.

Robert was now feeling the accumulated weight of all the pressure he
was under. With the Clements unwittingly gaining a greater hold on
Alice and the girls as President Clement rose in stature, Robert fretted
over his options. He had to get himself established, and soon. He devised
a new plan to gain a foothold in Los Angeles: he now decided to canvass
physicians door-to-door to try to build up referrals. He would market
himself at the big middle-class churches in town. He would court potential patients wherever he could and dress in such a way that they
wouldn't forget him.

So, in between insurance exams, he went from building to building,
office to office, up and down Jefferson Avenue and off Vermont and
Figueroa, tracking down physicians like a homeless man looking for
change. He knocked on glass doors with a doctor's name etched on them
as he dreamed his, too, would be one day. He sucked in his pride and
took in a deep breath and tried introducing himself to physicians who
knew or thought little of him to get into their good graces. He showed
them his surgery credentials and asked if they wouldn't mind referring
cases to him if they didn't do surgery themselves.

"That was met with poor success," Robert said. Here he was, a perfect stranger from someplace down south—Louisiana, was it?—asking for a favor. The big-city doctors who happened to beat him to California or had grown up there didn't take to it kindly. "So you took a lump in the jaw and kept on to the next office."

He made his pitch again and again and got the same response. "All the cordiality in the world," Robert said. "They would say, 'I've been using Dr. XYZ for all these years. Show me one good reason I should change to you.'"

He didn't have an answer then, but he was determined that one day he would. So he set about trying to make a name for himself the best he knew how. He started going to churches even though he was rarely seen in them otherwise. He decided to put on his loudest, most ostentatious suit and tie so the people would remember him. He made a show of dropping more than he really could afford when the collection plate came his way, enough for the church people to be sure to notice. He asked the ministers if they would introduce him to their congregations from the pulpit as they did politicians and visitors from back South.

"I didn't have any responses," he said.

But Golden State Insurance kept sending him out, and those after-hours insurance examinations were adding up. So he decided to turn his attention to the people themselves. He was doing more and more of those exams, and the anonymous working-class colored people of South Central L.A., many newly arrived from Texas or Arkansas or parts of Louisiana that Robert did not know, began to notice this smooth-talking physician, who looked more like a high roller than a doctor in his loud, tailored suits and stingy-brim hats and who made you feel as though you were the most important person in the world.

He conducted enough of those examinations and collected enough of those critical vials of urine to move into an apartment west of Crenshaw, near the Becks. He had been in Los Angeles a couple of months, getting himself set up, and could send for Alice and the girls now. His name was now forming on the lips of cleaning ladies and laborers, gamblers and seamstresses, postal workers and stevedores scattered all over South Central who wanted a doctor they could relate to, the humble and exuberant people who would eventually become the foundation of everything he would ever do in Los Angeles and among the most loyal people ever to enter his life.

DIVISIONS

I walked to the elevator and rode down with Shorty.
"You lucky bastard," he said bitterly.
"Why do you say that?"
"You saved your goddamn money and now you're gone."
"My problems are just starting."
— RICHARD WRIGHT, *Black Boy/American Hunger*

THE NORTH AND WEST, 1915 TO THE 1970S

UNKNOWINGLY, the migrants were walking into a headwind of resentment and suspicion. They could not hide the rough-cast clothes ill suited for northern winters or the slow syrup accents some northerners could not decipher. They carried with them the scents of the South, of lye soap and earthen field. They had emerged from a cave of restrictions into wide-open, anonymous hives that viewed them with bemusement and contempt. They had been trained to walk humbly, look down when spoken to. It would take time to learn the ways of the North.

What they could not have realized was the calcifying untruths they would have to overcome on top of everything else. As soon as the North took note of the flood of colored people from the South, sociologists and economists began studying the consequences of their arrival and drawing conclusions about who these people were and why they were coming.

"With few exceptions," wrote the economist Sadie Mossell of the migration to Philadelphia, "the migrants were untrained, often illiterate, and generally void of culture."

"The inarticulate and resigned masses came to the city," wrote the preeminent sociologist E. Franklin Frazier of the 1930s migration to Chicago, adding that "the disorganization of Negro life in the city seems at times to be a disease."

In 1965, Daniel Patrick Moynihan, then an official in the U.S. Department of Labor, called the inner cities after the arrival of the southern migrants "a tangle of pathology." He argued that what had attracted southerners like Ida Mae, George, and Robert was welfare: "the differential in payments between jurisdictions *has* to encourage *some* migration toward urban centers in the North," he wrote, adding his own italics.

Their reputation had preceded them. It had not been good. Neither was it accurate. The general laws of migration hold that the greater the obstacles and the farther the distance traveled, the more ambitious the migrants. "It is the higher status segments of a population which are most residentially mobile," the sociologists Karl and Alma Taeuber wrote in a 1965 analysis of census data on the migrants, published the same year as the Moynihan Report. "As the distance of migration increases," wrote the migration scholar Everett Lee, "the migrants become an increasingly superior group."

Any migration takes some measure of energy, planning, and forethought. It requires not only the desire for something better but the willingness to act on that desire to achieve it. Thus the people who undertake such a journey are more likely to be either among the better educated of their homes of origin or those most motivated to make it in the New World, researchers have found. "Migrants who overcome a considerable set of intervening obstacles do so for compelling reasons, and such migrations are not taken lightly," Lee wrote. "Intervening obstacles serve to weed out some of the weak or the incapable."

The South had erected some of the highest barriers to migration of any people seeking to leave one place for another in this country. By the time the migrants made it out, they were likely willing to do whatever it took to make it, so as not to have to return south and admit defeat. It would be decades before census data could be further analyzed and bear out these observations.

One myth they had to overcome was that they were bedraggled hayseeds just off the plantation. Census figures paint a different picture. By the 1930s, nearly two out of every three colored migrants to the big cities of the North and West were coming from towns or cities in the South, as did George Starling and Robert Foster, rather than straight from the field. "The move to northern cities was dominated by urban southerners," wrote the scholar J. Trent Alexander. Thus the latter wave of migrants brought a higher level of sophistication than was assumed at the time. "Most Negro migrants to northern metropolitan areas have had considerable previous experience with urban living," the Taeuber study observed.

Overall, southern migrants represented the most educated segment of the southern black population they left, the sociologist Stewart Tolnay wrote in 1998. In 1940 and 1950, colored people who left the South "averaged nearly two more years of completed schooling than those who remained in the South." That middle wave of migrants found themselves, on average, more than two years behind the blacks they encountered in the North.

But by the 1950s, those numbers would change. As the Migration matured, the migrants would arrive with higher levels of education than earlier waves of migrants and thus greater employment potential than both the blacks they left behind and the blacks they joined. A 1965 study of ninety-four migrants to Chicago, most of them from Mississippi and Arkansas, found that thirteen percent were illiterate (defined as having five or fewer years of schooling), compared to forty-five percent of the people in the southern counties they came from. The migrants and the blacks they encountered in the poor west side neighborhood of North Lawndale had roughly the same amount of schooling—an average of about eight years, the study found. "There is no support," the sociologist Frank T. Cherry wrote, for the notion of "a less-well-educated" pool of migrants entering Chicago "than it already has."

A seminal study that would be published that same year went even further. Across the North as a whole, the post–World War II migrants "were *not* [italics in original] of lower average socioeconomic status than the resident Negro population," the Taeubers wrote in their 1965 census analysis of migrants arriving north from 1955 to 1960. "Indeed, in educational attainment, Negro in-migrants to northern cities were equal to or slightly higher than the resident *white* population."

Against nearly every assumption about the Migration, the 1965 census study found that the migrants of the 1950s—particularly those who came from towns and cities, as had George Starling and Robert Foster—had more education than even the northern white population they joined. The percentage of postwar black migrants who had graduated from high school was as high as or higher than that of native whites in New York, Cleveland, Philadelphia, and St. Louis and close to the percentage of whites in Chicago.

As for blacks who had the advantage of having come from the urban South, the percentage who had graduated from high school was higher than that of the whites they joined, by significant margins in some cases, in each of the seven northern cities the study examined.

In Philadelphia, for instance, some thirty-nine percent of the blacks who had migrated from towns or cities had graduated from high school, compared with thirty-three percent of the native whites. In Cleveland, forty percent of migrants from the urban South were high school graduates compared to thirty-one percent of the native whites. This was the case for George Starling, Robert Foster, and hundreds of thousands of other colored migrants from the small-town South, who, it turns out, often had as much as or more education than those they met, colored or white, in the cities to which they fled, though they were often looked down upon.

Indeed, when it came to their black counterparts, the Taeuber study found that, in every major city the migrants fled to, a higher percentage of migrants had completed at least one year of high school than the black population they joined—sixty-one percent of migrants compared to fifty-three percent of native blacks in New York, fifty-six percent of migrants compared to fifty-two percent of native blacks in Chicago, sixty-three percent of migrants compared to fifty-four percent of native blacks in Cleveland, sixty-six percent of migrants compared to fifty-four percent of black natives in Washington, D.C., sixty percent of migrants compared to forty-eight percent of native blacks in Philadelphia, and so on.

The migrants, the Taeubers found, "resemble in educational levels the whites among whom they live," and they tended to be "of substantially higher socioeconomic status, on the average, than the resident Negro population." The researchers added that "these findings are at variance with most previous discussions of Negro migration."

The misconceptions about the migrants carried over to their presumed behavior upon arrival. Contrary to popular convention, the migrants were more likely to be married and remain married, less likely to bear children out of wedlock, and less likely to head single-parent households than the black northerners they encountered at their destinations. They were more likely to be employed, and, due to their willingness to work longer hours or more than one job, they actually earned more as a group than their northern black counterparts, despite being relegated to the lowliest positions.

"Black men who have been out of the South for five years or more are, in every instance, more likely to be in the labor force than other black men in the North," wrote Larry H. Long and Lynne R. Heltman of the Census Bureau in 1975. They found that, among young black men in the North, fifteen percent of those born in the North were jobless as against nine percent of the southern migrants they studied. "The same pattern applies to all other age groups and to the West," the census found.

Whatever their educational level, the migrants "more successfully avoided poverty," wrote Long and his colleague Kristin A. Hansen of the Census Bureau, "because of higher rates of labor force participation and other (unmeasured) characteristics."

There developed several theories as to why. One was that, because of the migrants' hard-laboring lives in the South, they had "a stronger attachment to the labor force as a result of their work-oriented values," Long and Hansen wrote. Another explanation pointed to disadvantages facing the northern-born blacks in the migrants' destinations— "exposure to drugs, crime and other conditions in big cities that may be handicaps in obtaining and holding jobs."

There is yet another possible reason—that the migrants who would make it out of the South and outlast others who gave up and returned home were a particularly resilient group of survivors. "The migration of blacks out of the South has clearly been selective of the best educated," Long and Hansen wrote. "It is possible that the least capable returned, leaving in the North a very able and determined group of migrants."

Those who would tough it out in the North and West were "not willing to risk relocation in the South because of possible greater advantages in their current location," wrote the sociologists Wen Lang Li and Sheron L. Randolph in a 1982 study of the migrants.

This would suggest that the people of the Great Migration who ultimately made lives for themselves in the North and West were among the most determined of those in the South, among the most resilient of those who left, and among the most resourceful of blacks in the North, not unlike immigrant groups from other parts of the world who made a way for themselves in the big cities of the North and West.

There appeared to be an overarching phenomenon that sociologists call a "migrant advantage." It is some internal resolve that perhaps exists in any immigrant compelled to leave one place for another. It made them "especially goal oriented, leading them to persist in their work and not be easily discouraged," Long and Heltman of the Census Bureau wrote in a 1975 report. In San Francisco, for instance, the migrants doubled up like their Chinese counterparts and, as in other cities, tended to "immigrate as groups and to remain together in the new environment for purposes of mutual aid," wrote the sociologist Charles S. Johnson.

The willingness to do whatever it took to survive appeared to offer some protection from the ills surrounding them, North and South. The San Francisco study found that the migrants were half as likely to be separated, divorced, or widowed as the blacks they encountered upon arrival. Overall, wherever they went, they tended to be "more family-stable compared both to those they left behind at their origin and those they encountered at their destination," the sociologist Thomas Wilson wrote in 2001. "They are less likely to bear children outside of marriage and less likely to be divorced or separated from their spouses."

The findings, he wrote, "are once again clearly at odds with earlier claims that family dysfunction was carried north by southern migrants."

———

Still, the stereotypes persisted despite the evidence and extended to even the youngest migrants. The children, having emerged from one-room schoolhouses with their southern English, were often labeled retarded by northern school officials, regardless of their native abilities. Segregation was not the law, but northerners would find creative ways to segregate the migrant children from the white children when so inclined.

"Colored pupils sometimes occupy only the front seats or the back seats," wrote the researcher W. A. Daniel in 1928. "They are grouped on one side, or occupy alternate rows; sometimes they are seated without regard to race; or they share seats with white pupils, a method used regularly by one teacher for punishing white pupils."

The absurdities of the South seemed to follow the migrants north despite their efforts to escape. One migrant child faced altogether different seating and circumstances in each classroom he entered. In this case, the student, Daniel wrote, "is literally forced to take the back seat" in one classroom. "In another room, he is the president of his class, and in another the editor of the paper, in another in charge of the tool room, while in another he is expected to do more than his share of menial tasks."

It was in the early 1920s that a little boy named James Cleveland Owens migrated with his sharecropper parents from Oakville, Al-

abama, to Cleveland, Ohio, when he was nine years old. The city of
Cleveland was the Promised Land to colored people in his part of Alabama, as reflected by his middle name. The parents had debated for
months over whether to leave, the mother anxious to do so, the father,
having been beaten down by sharecropping, worried and fearful. As
they prepared to leave, the little boy happened to bump into his father
while they were packing for the train. The father put both hands on his
son's shoulders to steady himself but quickly removed them out of embarrassment. Only then did the boy realize that his father's hands were
"shaking with fright."

The boy's first day of school in the North, he was assigned to a grade
lower than the one he'd been in where he had come from, and the
teacher couldn't understand his southern accent. When she asked him
his name, he said he was called J.C. The teacher misheard him and,
from that day forward, called him Jesse instead. So did everyone else in
this new world he was in. He would forever be known as Jesse Owens,
not by his given name. He would go on to win four gold medals at the
1936 Olympics in Berlin, becoming the first American in the history of
track and field to do so in a single Olympics and disproving the Aryan
notions of his Nazi hosts.

It made headlines throughout the United States that Adolf Hitler,
who had watched the races, had refused to shake hands with Owens, as
he had with white medalists. But Owens found that in Nazi Germany,
he had been able to stay in the same quarters and eat with his white
teammates, something he could not do in his home country. Upon his
return, there was a ticker-tape parade in New York. Afterward, he was
forced to ride the freight elevator to his own reception at the Waldorf-
Astoria.

"I wasn't invited to shake hands with Hitler," he wrote in his autobiography. "But I wasn't invited to the White House to shake hands with
the President either. I came back to my native country, and I could not
ride in the front of the bus. I had to go to the back door. I couldn't live
where I wanted. Now, what's the difference?"

It would take the arrival of millions of more migrants and many
more decades of perseverance on their part and on the part of protesters
for human rights before they would truly become accepted.

But his father, a man of few words who had come north with the
greatest reluctance and worry, was overcome with the enormity of the
moment and how it had come to be. His son had had the chance to go to

good schools, run on real tracks, and be coached at Ohio State University, rather than spend his life picking cotton. "My son's victories in Germany," Henry Owens said, "force me to realize that I made the best move of my life by moving out of the South."

CHICAGO, AUGUST 1938

IDA MAE BRANDON GLADNEY

MISS THEENIE HAD BEEN RIGHT about her daughter. Ida Mae was expecting when she left Mississippi with her husband and two little ones in the fall of 1937. That spring, she returned south for the express purpose of having the baby in the familiar hands of a midwife. She had heard that up north, doctors strapped women down when they went into labor, and she wasn't going to submit to that kind of barbarity. So she gave birth to her last child in Miss Theenie's house, on May 28, 1938. It was a baby girl, and Ida Mae named her Eleanor, like the first lady of the land, Eleanor Roosevelt.

She kept the baby in Mississippi until she was plump and strong and then carried her and little James and Velma north on the Illinois Central sometime in August to rejoin her husband. Only this time, Ida Mae didn't return to Milwaukee. She got off in Chicago, the city of skyscrapers and Montgomery Ward that she had thought was Heaven when she first set foot in the North.

While she was away giving birth, George had left Milwaukee, having found little work and given up on the prospects of making a living there. One of his brothers had settled in Chicago. So George turned to the bigger city with its steel mills, blast furnaces, slaughterhouses, and tanneries. He would have been willing to take just about anything to feed his family, having stooped to pick cotton all his life, but what he found first was a job on another man's ice wagon.

Up and down the rutted streets they went, steering the horse and wagon in the early-morning hours, delivering ice to the colored people in their cold-water flats on the South Side.

"Iceman! Iceman!" they shouted as they steered.

"Bring me fifty pounds!" someone would yell from the window of a three-flat.

"Bring me a hundred!" came an order from another.

George slung a rug across his shoulders and hoisted a block of ice on his back to carry it up the tenement steps. He was used to hauling a hundred pounds of cotton in a day for fifty cents. Now he could make that with each fifty-pound block of ice. And he was delivering a lot of it. Ice melted fast in the summer heat. Some people needed to replenish their iceboxes every day. He was already making more money than in Mississippi, and not under the shotgun scrutiny of a planter. It was stoop labor, and he couldn't do it forever. But it would have to do for now.

By the time Ida Mae got back with the baby and little James and Velma, he had secured for his family a one-room basement apartment among the frail tenements and dilapidated lean-tos in the roped-off colored section of town.

It was a kitchenette in a two-flat in the low Forties off St. Lawrence. Preceding waves of European immigrants had lived there before them in creaking buildings from the nineteenth century, the streets now pockmarked and piled so high with rubbish that ice wagons couldn't get through some of them. It was only a few miles south but a world away from the boulevards and skyscrapers Ida Mae had seen when she first arrived, gray and weed-strewn as this new place of hers was.

———

They were confined to a little isthmus on the South Side of Chicago that came to be called "Bronzeville," the "black belt," "North Mississippi." It was "a narrow tongue of land, seven miles in length and one and one half miles in width," as the midcentury historians St. Clair Drake and Horace Cayton described it, where a quarter-million colored people were packed on top of one another by the time Ida Mae and her family arrived.

Up and down Indiana and Wabash and Prairie and South Parkway, across Twenty-second Street and down to Thirty-first and Thirty-ninth and into the low Forties, a colored world, a city within a city, rolled out from the sidewalk, the streets aflutter with grocers and undertakers, dressmakers and barbershops, tailors and pressers, dealers of coal and sellers of firewood, insurance agents and real estate men, pharmacists and newspapers, a YMCA and the Urban League, high-steepled churches—Baptist, Holiness, African Methodist Episcopal churches practically transported from Mississippi and Arkansas—and stacked-heeled harlots stumbling out of call houses and buffet flats.

There were temptations a southern sharecropper couldn't have known existed and that could only catch root when so many people were packed into one place, the police could be bought, and the city looked away: reefer pads, card sharks, gangsters and crapshooters. The so-called mulatto queen of the underworld running poker games. Policy kings running the numbers racket, ready to take a migrant's newly earned dollar fresh from the slaughterhouse. The migrants could see Ma Rainey at the Regal or just melt into the neon anonymity of city life without a watchful uncle or jackleg preacher knowing about it.

This was the landing place in Chicago for most colored people just in from the South. They had left the wide-open spaces and gravel roads of the cotton fields and had to watch their every step. Ida Mae and George, in particular, pious and churchly as he was, wanted nothing to do with the devilment crowding in on them but had to make the best of it and just be thankful for having made it out of Mississippi alive.

———

By the time Ida Mae and her family arrived, Chicago was a major terminus of the Great Migration of colored people out of the South and of latter-day immigrants from central and eastern Europe. It had first been settled in 1779 by a black man named Jean Baptiste Point DuSable in what was then wilderness. He was a fur trader who built a "rude cabin on the sandpoint at the mouth of the river."

Ida Mae found the living conditions not much better than those back home and, in some cases, worse. "A few goats and an occasional pig" roamed alleyways that reeked of rotting vermin. Front doors hung on single hinges. The sun peeked through cracks in the outer walls. Many rooms sat airless and windowless, packed with so many people that some roomers had to sleep in shifts, all of which made a mockery of city codes devised to protect against these very things.

"Families lived without light, without heat, and sometimes without water," observed Edith Abbott, a University of Chicago researcher who studied tenement life in Chicago in the 1930s, the time when Ida Mae arrived. "The misery of housing conditions at this time can scarcely be exaggerated."

They were living in virtual slave cabins stacked on top of one another, wives, like Ida Mae, cooking on hot plates and hanging their laundry out the window, if they had a window at all, unable to protect themselves or their children from the screams and conversation and sugar talk and fighting all around them. It was as if all of them were living in one room without space for their own thoughts or for their dreams of how best to get out.

Ida Mae soon discovered that there really was no getting out, not right off anyway. "Negro migrants confronted a solid wall of prejudice and labored under great disadvantages in these attempts to find new homes," Abbott wrote. The color line in Chicago confined them to a sliver of the least desirable blocks between the Jewish lakefront neighborhoods to the east and the Irish strongholds to the west, while the Poles, Russians, Italians, Lithuanians, Czechs, and Serbs, who had only recently arrived themselves, were planting themselves to the southwest of the colored district.

With several thousand black southerners arriving each month in the receiving cities of the North and no extra room being made for them, "attics and cellars, store-rooms and basements, churches, sheds and warehouses," according to Abraham Epstein in his study of the early migration, were converted to contain all the new arrivals. There was "rarely a place in these rooms for even suitcases or trunks."

People like Ida Mae had few options, and the landlords knew it. New arrivals often paid twice the rent charged the whites they had just replaced for worn-out and ill-kept housing. "The rents in the South Side Negro district were conspicuously the highest of all districts visited," Abbott wrote. Dwellings that went for eight to twenty dollars a month to white families were bringing twelve to forty-five dollars a month from black families, those earning the least income and thus least able to afford a flat at any rent, in the early stages of the Migration. Thus began a pattern of overcharging and underinvestment in black neighborhoods that would lay the foundation for decades of economic disparities in the urban North.

Ida Mae tried never to worry about things she couldn't change and so made do with what they could get. She wasn't the only one. "Lodgers were not disposed to complain about the living conditions or the prices charged," Epstein wrote. "They were only too glad to secure a place where they could share a half or at least a part of an unclaimed bed."

The story played out in virtually every northern city—migrants sealed off in overcrowded colonies that would become the foundation for ghettos that would persist into the next century. These were the original colored quarters—the abandoned and identifiable no-man's-lands that came into being when the least-paid people were forced to pay the

highest rents for the most dilapidated housing owned by absentee landlords trying to wring the most money out of a place nobody cared about.

It would soon come to be that anyone living in any American city
would know exactly where these forgotten islands were, if only to make
sure to avoid them: under the viaduct along a polluted stream in Akron,
Ohio; in the Hill District in Pittsburgh; Roxbury in Boston; the east side
of Cincinnati; the near east side of Detroit; nearly all of East St. Louis;
whole swaths of the South Side of Chicago and South Central in Los
Angeles; and much of Harlem and Bedford-Stuyvesant in New York.

Like other migrants with limited options, Ida Mae and her family
moved from place to place, from one unacceptable flat to a slightly
larger and less odious option a few blocks away, not unlike sharecroppers moving from farm to farm looking for a less exploitive arrangement with, they hoped, a fairer planter. Soon they were living on the top
floor of a three-flat at Thirty-sixth and Wabash. It was well into the
Great Depression, and a man took to sleeping at odd hours of the day on
the little landing outside their kitchen door.

"I open the door and put garbage out there, and he still be sleep," Ida
Mae remembered. "I don't know who he was. He stayed there winter
and summer. He didn't bother nobody. He was sleeping like he was in a
bed. He had his little cover out there."

Did he ever wake up when you went out there? I asked her once.
"No," she said. "Because I reckon he done did his devilment all night."

———

Ida Mae didn't know it, but, with the Great Depression deepening, she
and her family had arrived in a city unprepared for and utterly resistant
to the continuing influx of migrants. City fathers and labor experts had
expected the Great Migration to end with World War I. Jobs and housing were scarcer now. White unions were refusing colored workers
membership, keeping colored wages low, restricting the work that migrants could do, and leaving them unprotected during cutbacks.

The colored old-timers who were already there were not especially
happy to see them. Even as the Migration was a bonanza for colored
storekeepers and businessmen, it meant more competition for the already
limited kinds of jobs blacks were allotted and made the black presence in
the city more conspicuous and threatening to the city's racial alchemy.

As it was, the city was still recovering from the tensions of one of the
worst race riots in American history. The riots had set the city on edge
and hardened race lines that would persist for generations.

The trouble began after an incident only blocks from the three-flat at Thirty-sixth and Wabash where Ida Mae's family would live exactly two decades later. It was the summer of 1919. World War I, the stimulus of the first wave of the Great Migration, was over. Munitions plants had shut down, the factories that lured black southerners were now letting workers go, the country was on the verge of recession, not able even to imagine the actual Depression that was brewing. The migrants, hemmed in and living on top of one another, even as more of them arrived, pressed against the white neighborhoods on their borders and were met with death threats and bombings when they ventured to the other side.

The demilitarized zone was a moving target that no one could see but that everyone knew in his bones. Blacks were finding more things off-limits than it would otherwise appear, defined by custom and whites' discomfort rather than by law. Even the beaches of Lake Michigan were segregated. Everyone was feeling the strain of a declining economy. Whites saw the migrants as competition for a scarcer pool of jobs and took to attacking them along the western boundary of the black belt.

Then on Sunday, July 27, 1919, a seventeen-year-old black boy named Eugene Williams, swimming along the shore of Lake Michigan, drifted past an invisible line in the lake into the white side of the Twenty-ninth Street beach.

As was common in the North, there were no white or colored signs. It was merely understood that whites entered and used the beach at Twenty-ninth Street and blacks were to stay near the Twenty-seventh Street entrance two blocks north. The imaginary color line stretched out into the water. Swimming as he was, the boy couldn't see the line where the white water began because the water looked the same.

Carl Sandburg, the future poet who was then a reporter for the *Chicago Daily News,* recounted it this way: "A colored boy swam across an imaginary segregation line. White boys threw rocks at him and knocked him off a raft. He was drowned."

Blacks demanded that the white police officer on the scene arrest the whites they said had hurled rocks at Williams. The officer refused, arresting, instead, a black man in the crowd "on a white man's complaint."

Within hours, tensions reached a boil on both sides, and a riot was in full cry. Whites dragged black passengers from streetcars and beat them. Blacks stabbed a white peddler and a white laundryman to death. Two white men were killed walking through a black neighborhood, and two black men were killed walking through a white neighborhood.

White gangs stormed the black belt, setting houses on fire, hunting down black residents, firing shotguns, and hurling bricks.

All told, the riots coursed through the south and southwest sides of the city for thirteen days, killing 38 people (23 blacks and 15 whites) and injuring 537 others (342 blacks, 178 whites, the rest unrecorded) and not ending until a state militia subdued them.

———

Contrary to modern-day assumptions, for much of the history of the United States—from the Draft Riots of the 1860s to the violence over desegregation a century later—riots were often carried out by disaffected whites against groups perceived as threats to their survival. Thus riots would become to the North what lynchings were to the South, each a display of uncontained rage by put-upon people directed toward the scapegoats of their condition. Nearly every big northern city experienced one or more during the twentieth century.

Each outbreak pitted two groups that had more in common with each other than either of them realized. Both sides were made up of rural and small-town people who had traveled far in search of the American Dream, both relegated to the worst jobs by industrialists who pitted one group against the other. Each side was struggling to raise its families in a cold, fast, alien place far from their homelands and looked down upon by the earlier, more sophisticated arrivals. They were essentially the same people except for the color of their skin, and many of them arrived into these anonymous receiving stations at around the same time, one set against the other and unable to see the commonality of their mutual plight.

Thus these violent clashes bore the futility of Greek tragedy. Yet the situation was even more complicated than the black migrants could have imagined. As they made their way north, so did some of the poorer whites from the South, looking not for freedom from persecution but for greater economic rewards for their hard work. Slavery and sharecropping, along with the ravages of the boll weevil and floods, had depressed the wages of every worker in the South. The call of the North drew some of the southern whites the migrants had sought to escape.

Initially, they came to the North in greater numbers, but they were much more likely to return south than colored southerners were— fewer than half of all white southerners who left actually stayed in the North for good, thus behaving more like classic migrant workers than immigrants. Still, many brought their prejudices with them and melted into the white working-class world of ethnic immigrants to make a potent advance guard against black inroads in the North.

As a window into their sentiments, a witness to the Detroit riots in 1943 gave this description of a white mob that had attacked colored people in that outbreak. "By the conversation of the men gathered there, I was able to detect that they were Southerners and that they resented Negroes working beside them and receiving the same amount of money," the informant said, adding that these southern whites believed that the black migrants "ought to be 'taken down a peg or two.' "

———

Perhaps the earliest indication of what the migrants were unknowingly up against came from an outbreak directly related to the Great Migration, or rather to how the North reacted to the newcomers from the South. These were the riots that erupted in East St. Louis, Illinois, in the summer of 1917 after companies being struck by white workers hired colored migrants to replace them. The migrants were flocking to the city at a rate of a thousand a month, some eighteen thousand having arrived that spring, and they instantly became the perfect pawns, an industrialist's dream: they were desperate to leave the South, anxious for work, untutored in union politics or workers' rights—as most could not have imagined unionizing themselves as field hands, thus uncomprehending of the idea of a worker making demands and unlikely to complain about whatever conditions they might face.

Once the strike was over, the colored migrants, resented by the unions and unprotected by the plants that had hired them, paid the price. One union wrote its members that "the immigration of the southern Negro into our city for the past eight months has reached a point where drastic action must be taken" and demanded that the city "retard this growing menace, and devise a way to get rid of a certain portion of those who are already here."

On the night of July 1, a carload of whites fired shots into colored homes. The colored residents fired back when a second car filled with whites passed through, killing two policemen. The next day, full-scale rioting began. Colored men were "stabbed, clubbed and hanged from telephone poles." A colored two-year-old "was shot and thrown into the doorway of a burning building."

"A black skin was a death warrant on the streets of this Illinois city," wrote an observer shortly afterward.

The police, charged with quelling the riot, in some cases joined in, as did some in the state militia sent in to restore order, actions that resulted in seven courts-martial. All told, thirty-nine blacks and eight whites were killed, more than a hundred blacks were shot or maimed, and five thousand blacks were driven from their homes.

After the two riots, city leaders in Chicago could see no end to the racial divisions without intervention and a public appeal for tolerance. A white-led, biracial commission set up to investigate the climate and circumstances leading to the riots produced a 672-page report, *The Negro in Chicago.* It stands to this day as one of the most comprehensive examinations of both the early stages of the Great Migration and race relations in a northern American city.

With a sense of urgency, it set out fifty-nine recommendations for improving race relations. It urged that the police rid the city's colored section of the vice and prostitution that plagued the black belt; that the schools hire principals with an "interest in promoting good race relations"; that white citizens seek accurate information about blacks "as a basis of their judgments"; that restaurants, stores, and theaters stop segregating when they weren't supposed to; that companies "deal with Negroes as workmen on the same plane as white workers" and stop using them as strikebreakers and denying them apprenticeships; that labor unions admit colored workers when they qualified; that employers "permit Negroes an equal chance with whites to enter all positions for which they are qualified by efficiency and merit"; that the press avoid using epithets in referring to blacks and treat black stories and white stories with the same standards and "sense of proportion."

With the commission having no authority to enforce its recommendations and a good portion of the citizenry not likely even to have seen them, much of its counsel went unheeded. So Ida Mae arrived in a world that was perhaps even tenser than before the riots. In the ensuing decades, the color line would only stiffen. The South Side would become almost totally black and the North Side almost totally white. Ida Mae's adopted home would become one of the most racially divided of all American cities and remain so for the rest of the twentieth century.

NEW YORK, SUMMER 1945
GEORGE SWANSON STARLING

———

GEORGE FINALLY BROUGHT INEZ to New York in June of 1945 to begin life on their own for the first time in their marriage. Now that he had a decent job on the railroad, he was hoping she could now get a job as a beautician like she had trained for and they could make a go of it in New York.

But Inez was still nursing a grudge over how little time they had spent together since they'd been married, how he'd gone off to Detroit without her, how he had taken so long to send for her, and now, here he was, likely to be gone half the time working the rails.

He was always the one with big dreams, and he had them now. He wanted to make up for all they didn't have and couldn't have back in Florida. He located a little beauty shop around the corner from the brownstone where they lived that had six available booths for her to use.

"Inez, this is your chance," he told her. "We can rent this place, and you can do hair in one booth and rent out the other five booths. You can build you up a business here, and then after a while you don't have to do no hair at all, just supervise."

But Inez wasn't of a mind to do much of what he said, given all they had been through, so she decided to forgo hairdressing after all. She would never work at it a day in her life. Instead she took a short nursing course and got a job at a hospital to show her independence, to spite him, or both.

———

George had escaped Florida but could not run away from the frustrations of an impulsive, ill-advised marriage. Inez had arrived in Harlem, but nothing had changed. They were getting along no better than before. So when he wasn't on the rails, he began to fall under Harlem's spell like many of the new arrivals suddenly free of the South. Between the people he knew from back in Florida and the co-workers he met riding the rails, he had a ready-made set of diversions every night of the week in a place that never shut down and was spilling over with people.

It was said that Harlem was one of the most crowded places in all of the country. Some half a million colored people were crammed into a sliver of upper Manhattan that was about fifty blocks long and only seven or eight blocks wide. A 1924 study by the National Urban League confirmed what colored tenants already knew: that colored renters paid from forty to sixty percent higher rents than white tenants for the same class of apartment. So colored people in Harlem took in boarders and worked second and third jobs.

Beginning in World War I, as many as seven thousand people were estimated to be living in a single block in Harlem. The crush of people begging for space forced rents even higher in what became a landlord's paradise. Cash-strapped renters looked for new ways to make their rent. They began throwing end-of-the-month parties, "where they drank bathtub gin, ate pig knuckles and danced with the lights off," as Arna Bontemps wrote. They called them rent parties. They charged twenty-five cents admission for a few hours of smoke-hazed, gin-juiced, tom-tom caterwauling, and poker playing with people from back home and with worldly-wise northerners they did not know just to help make that month's rent.

Up and down the side streets off Lenox and Seventh Avenues, people flung open their apartment doors the Saturday night before the rent was due. They served pork chops and pigs' feet and potato salad just like down south, except that the food and spirits were for sale, and they put Count Basie on the record player to give people something to dance to. Total strangers looking for a good time could stroll down the block looking for a red, pink, or blue light in a window and listening for the rabble of a rent party in progress. Signs went up inviting anybody willing to pay. One read:

> There'll be brown skin mammas
> High Yallers too
> And if you ain't got nothing to do
> Come on up to Roy and Sadie's
> West 126 St. Sat. Night May 12th.
> There'll be plenty of pig feet
> An lots of gin
> Jus ring the bell
> An come on in.

Tenants stood to make the most money if they got the partygoers playing poker, and George was all for it. There were some people from

Eustis, Florida, living up on Seventh Avenue, between 146th and 147th Streets. They lived right next door to each other and started running their parties simultaneously.

"We just go from one house to the other," George said. "We get tired of playing over to Freeman's, or we get mad with him about something, and we go over to M.B.'s. We go from one house to the other. We would be gambling the whole weekend."

When they got tired of the people on Seventh Avenue, they went over to the Bronx, where the Blye brothers had a sister named Henry living over at Third Avenue and Seventeenth Street, and played some more.

The wives and girlfriends served the gin and bourbon and the grits and eggs and biscuits and smoked pork from the pork store down the street, the big poker players never getting up from the table, shoveling forkfuls of grits into their mouths between hands.

They were playing five-card stud, and sometimes there were so many people there'd be two or three games running, people just in or visiting from Eustis and Ocala, people who had been in Harlem for years, hustlers who made a life out of circulating at the gambling tables of the rent parties to beat the tenants out of their own rent money. It was an open invitation, after all.

George saw the money they were making—some of them were pulling in hundreds of dollars a weekend—and decided to throw some parties himself.

He went in with his friend Babe Blye, one of the Blye brothers from back home in Florida (there were nine brothers in all, plus three girls that the parents had given boys' names to, but that's another story). Babe was working as an auto painter for General Motors in New York and was living upstairs from George and Inez in the brownstone George was buying. Sometimes Inez served food, sometimes she wouldn't. Sometimes she would stay down in their apartment. Working the rails mostly for tips, George could use the extra money for the house note and went in with Babe to run some poker parties.

George figured out the system. "If you stay outta the game, and if you run a game for four or five hours or more, you gonna have most of the money," George said. "You're gonna have most of the money and the cut. Because most of the players are going to lose."

Trouble was, Babe couldn't just sit back and watch. "See, that was our weakness," George said. "Babe couldn't stay outta the game. He just had to get in the game, and he'd lose pretty near everything that we take in."

Like most migrants from the South, George had surrounded himself with the people he knew from back in the Old Country, but the Old Country was still in the people no matter where they went, and George found that, as much as he loved the people from back home, he could never truly move up with the country people still acting country. He never put it in so many words, but he didn't keep his resentment to himself.

"We done sat up here all night, and you done gambled all the money out of the cut box," he told Babe. "We just set this whole thing up for nothing. And now we got to clean up and see how many cigarette spots somebody done burned in the furniture. And we don't have a thing to show for it."

Then one night, George had had enough. They were gambling upstairs in Babe's apartment. They had a big game going, and Babe and George were both in the game. George looked to be winning the pot when Babe called him. Two men they didn't know and who looked to have been in Harlem much longer than George and Babe were in the game, as often happened when the migrants threw open their doors to make extra money to make ends meet. George caught Babe dealing off of the bottom of the deck. He hit himself from the bottom with an ace, giving himself a better hand than everyone else.

Babe had cheated to win the pot, but it did not appear that the two other men had caught on. "I couldn't say anything because of the other guys in the game," George said. "If they caught you cheating, some of them guys would kill you right on the spot. So I had to sit there and let Babe go with that. I lost thirty dollars down the deal."

George made a show of borrowing thirty dollars from the pot.

"Well, I'm borrowing thirty dollars," he said to no one in particular, figuring Babe would get the message that George was onto his cheating and wanted him to stop.

"That was for the benefit of the other guys around the table, not to become suspicious," George said.

When the game was over, George headed downstairs. Babe called out to him.

"Hey, son. You know you owe me thirty dollars."

"I do?" George asked. "Let me tell you one thing. I will never in life play with you again. Because you dealt yourself off the bottom with an ace that beat my hand, and the only reason I let you go, I didn't want you to get me and you both killed because there were other people in the game. And you know the rule is, if you caught cheating, you in trouble.

Now, I don't want no killing in the house. It might have been me. So I had to let you go with that."

George wasn't finished.

"Didn't you hear me saying, 'I'm borrowing thirty dollars out the pot?' I took my money out that I lost. I don't owe you nothing. You owe me your life 'cause if I had squawked about you dealing off the bottom, you and I both might have got killed."

He told Babe, who was, after all, his tenant, that he was through with him when it came to gambling. "I ain't gon' never pay you," George said. "And, furthermore, I ain't gon' never gamble with you no more. If you can't gamble with your friends without being cheated, who can you gamble with?"

That was the end of George's short, unhappy career running a gambling den. He wasn't making money, and now it was dangerous.

The city had a way of bringing out the best and now the worst in everyone. People got up to the big city and either forgot where they came from and took on the meanest aspects of a hard life or kept a kind of sweet country blindness and fell victim to what looked to be city charms but could be traps if you weren't wise to them. Or they somehow managed to keep the best of both worlds, keep the essential goodness of the old culture and the street wit of the new. George had to learn to recognize that admixture in the people who surrounded him, even as he tried, sometimes successfully, sometimes not, to do the same himself.

LOS ANGELES, JUNE 1953
ROBERT JOSEPH PERSHING FOSTER

ROBERT HAD BEEN IN CALIFORNIA for a couple of months now, taking whatever work Dr. Beck threw his way and doing physicals for Golden State Insurance. He had set aside some of what he had been making and was starting to feel he could pull a practice together, what with all the people he was meeting through Golden State.

He decided it was time he got an office of his own. He could never get ahead on those ten-dollar physicals, and he wouldn't be able to make the most of Dr. Beck's referrals or treat any patients without an office they could come to. Besides, Alice and the girls were wanting to know when they could come out to California, and the Clements, just waiting for him to fall short, wanted to know what was taking him so long since he had raved so much about the place before he had seen it.

Robert didn't want an office in the predictable places where colored businesses went. He didn't want to be in Compton or Watts or South Central. He wanted to be as far north as he could afford, which wouldn't be but so far north given his resources and wouldn't be practical anyway, given where his current roster of potential patients was living. He wanted a location with some prestige so he could live out the California dream he had in his head and justify the fees he thought he deserved, not knowing that a shot of penicillin generally went for five dollars no matter where you were.

He went driving around the west side looking for the right kind of place for himself. He found an office to let at 959 West Jefferson, well west of Central Avenue, right across the street from the University of Southern California campus. He could always say he was near Southern Cal, and he liked the sound of that.

It was a ground-floor suite at the front of an office building with a dentist upstairs and a doctor and an Asian import-export company on the ground floor with him. The office directly behind his was occupied by an internist from Los Angeles who was neither willing to nor interested in extending himself to this newcomer just in from the South, as seemed to be the distancing and disdainful attitude of many of the people who happened to have gotten to the North or West first or had the advantages of having grown up outside the walls of Jim Crow.

The internist had come from a completely different world, an integrated world that Robert both distrusted and envied, a world he could only hope his young daughters could grow to master and benefit from but not completely lose themselves in one day.

The building was just a few blocks south of the apartment on Ellendale he had secured for himself and his family until they could afford the house everyone expected of him. Everything finally seemed to be coming together.

That office was where he would start his new life. "And it was a beautiful building," Robert said. "It had a nice marquee in front of it. My office was at the front of the building, and my name was on the window, beautifully etched."

He put a deposit on an X-ray machine and the draperies for the office, a desk in the waiting room, chairs for the patients he hoped to attract. Now that he was nearly established, the people from Monroe turned out. Limuary Jordan and his wife, Adeline, came and helped him set up the office.

"We built his operating table in a room over there," Limuary would remember.

Howard Beckwith, a friend from back home, built furniture and opened his line of credit for Robert to use to get on his feet. Limuary loaned him money, too. They all made sure he ate.

"Come on, Doc, you can't practice on your empty stomach," they said. "You gotta eat."

Mrs. Beck and her daughter, Vivian, planned an open house for that July. They supplied the linens, the lace tablecloths, the crystal punch bowls. They made the punch and refreshments and served as hostesses in their cinched-waist dresses and pumps.

"I spent my last dime buying whiskey at Mick's for the open house," Robert said. "We had two fifths of whiskey."

He invited twenty people. The friends from Morehouse and Spelman and Atlanta University all came out, and Robert was in business.

———

He called Alice to say it was time. He was ready for them to join him in Los Angeles. They had been waiting in Atlanta for him to give them the word. The girls were growing up fast, and he had missed most of it. Bunny was nine already, and Robin was seven. He was all packed and ready to receive them. He would move out of the Becks' and into an apartment a few blocks north of his new office.

But when it came time to actually move in, the manager told him she was sorry but it was already rented to somebody else.

"That was my introduction to the deception of California," he said.

Alice and the girls had come all this distance, and he didn't have a place for them. He had to scramble to find something else before word got back to the Clements. He heard about a Dr. Anderson he knew from back in Louisiana, who happened to be moving out of his apartment. It was on St. Andrews Place, near the Becks'. It had two bedrooms. It was a far cry from Hickory Hill, the president's mansion back at Atlanta University, where Alice and the girls had been living. But the family would be together for the first time since Austria.

"And he rented it to me for my family," Robert said.

Alice set about making the apartment a home, while Robert began building a practice. He discovered he was having trouble attracting his most obvious patient base. For some reason, even with the new office on the fashionable side of town, the people from back home—from Monroe and from his days at Morehouse and Alice's days at Spelman—weren't coming. They had shown up for the hors d'oeuvres and whiskey at the open house, but they weren't coming in for appointments.

"Some were going to white doctors," he would say years later. "But not all of them went to white doctors. I really don't know who they were going to. I wasn't really interested in who they were going to. I wanted them to come to me."

He figured he was a hometown patient's dream. He was board-certified in surgery but was doing family practice, knew their family histories, could talk their language, and, as he had done all his life, would do just about anything to please them.

But among the gumbo recipes and family Bibles they brought to California were the petty rivalries from back in Louisiana. People had long memories, and if Professor Foster had taken a switch to them without cause or Robert's mother had been too hard on them in the seventh grade or if one of the Fosters had happened not to speak to them at Zion Baptist Church one Sunday back in 1932, they remembered it and carried it with them across the desert to California.

And that wasn't all. Some of the middle-class people from back in Monroe—the insurance agents and teachers and salesclerks—seemed to resent even the early signs of success and the fact that he was wanting people to call him Robert instead of Pershing after all these years.

They seemed to be second-guessing him more than his other patients did. They questioned the motives of his every instruction and stood up to him like they did when they were back in the third grade, especially when it came to surgery.

"See, they got lots of time before they get on the table," Robert remembered. "They can think a whole lot. They can get another consultation. They'd be quick to say, 'I'll get another consultation.' Or somebody would say, 'What you tryin' to do? Buy a mink coat for Alice?' Now, that slaps you. People can be little."

The rejection hurt him and gnawed at him. It stayed with him for decades. He set out to prove he could make it without them. He would be the very best doctor he knew how. He would focus not on the grudging people from Monroe but on the people who wanted him as their doctor. He would put on a show so they wouldn't forget him. He would pull in more of the cooks and laborers from Texas and the Mardi Gras–celebrating people from New Orleans and Baton Rouge, who would appreciate his loud suits and stingy-brim hats and folksy, one-of-the-people bedside manner.

The people from Monroe would learn how wrong they had been.

TO BEND IN
STRANGE WINDS

I was a Southerner,
and I had the map of Dixie on my tongue.
—ZORA NEALE HURSTON, *Dust Tracks on a Road*

CHICAGO, LATE 1938
IDA MAE BRANDON GLADNEY

———

THERE WAS A KNOCK on the door at Ida Mae's tiny flat one afternoon when she was at home alone taking care of the children. It was a neighbor lady who had taken notice of the new family just up from Mississippi, seen that the young mother was by herself with the little ones much of the time, the husband likely off to work somewhere, and the neighbor lady was saying she had come to introduce herself.

Ida Mae thought it was awfully nice of the lady to drop by. She hadn't been in Chicago long, as the woman likely knew. George had secured the apartment while Ida Mae was in Mississippi giving birth to Eleanor.

On days when there was no work to be had, Ida Mae was cooped up in the kitchenette apartment, far from home, in a big, loud city she didn't yet know. She was used to wide-open spaces, trees everywhere, being able to see the sun set and rise and the sky stretched out over the field. She was used to killing a chicken if she needed one, not lining up at a butcher and paying for it in pieces with money she didn't have. As much as she hated picking cotton, she missed her sisters-in-law and the other families on the plantation and her mother and younger sister. She didn't know too many people in Chicago yet and was isolated with only little James and Eleanor with her during the day, as Velma was off in grade school.

So Ida Mae welcomed the neighbor lady and invited her in to sit a while. The lady had brought something with her. It was a bottle of homemade wine. Ida Mae had never had wine before. George didn't believe in it, and Ida Mae never had occasion to try it.

The woman opened the bottle and poured some for the two of them to drink while they talked. Ida Mae took a few sips and started feeling woozy as the woman asked her how she'd gotten there. The woman learned all about how Ida Mae's family first tried Milwaukee and how Ida Mae went back to Mississippi to have the baby when George told her he was going to try Chicago. The woman poured more wine, and Ida Mae got giddy and light-headed. She had never felt this way before.

The woman was from Mississippi but had been in Chicago for some time, had gotten to know the city's virtues and vices and how a city resident, which Ida Mae now was, should comport oneself. She told Ida Mae that now that she was in the North, she shouldn't wear her head scarf out in public—that was for back when she was in the field; that she shouldn't hang her wet laundry out the front window, even though there was no place else to let the linens dry out in the open sun like back home; that she should make sure the kids had shoes on when they went out, even though the kids hated shoes and shoes cost money they didn't have.

Ida Mae told the lady she appreciated that advice, but soon she wasn't comprehending much of anything the neighbor lady was saying. When the bottle of wine was finished, the lady said she'd better be heading back home.

George came home soon after the neighbor lady left. He found Ida Mae giggling and slurring her words, talking gibberish, and the children needing to eat and get their diapers changed. She told him that a nice neighbor lady had stopped by and that she had tried some of the wine the lady brought.

George was furious. The devilment of the city had come right into his home, as hard as he tried to protect his family from it. Ida Mae was too sweet-natured to recognize when someone might be taking advantage and wasn't wise to the machinations of the people who had preceded them to Chicago. She wouldn't have noticed if they made fun of them, looked down on them, or took pleasure in seeing the simple country people fall under the city's spell. He had to make it clear to Ida Mae that she was not to just let anybody in—this was Chicago, after all. He told her he didn't want that lady coming around anymore and that Ida Mae wasn't to drink any more wine, which was a sin in his estimation anyway.

When Ida Mae came to her senses, she was shamefaced about what had happened. She was waking up to the ways and the people of the North. She soon learned that the colored people who had gotten there before her and had assimilated to the city didn't look too kindly upon her innocent country ways.

————

In the receiving cities of the North and West, the newcomers like Ida Mae had to worry about acceptance or rejection not only from whites they encountered but from the colored people who arrived ahead of them, who could at times be the most sneeringly judgmental of all.

The northern-born colored people and the long-standing migrants, who were still trying to keep their footing in the New World, often resented the arrival of the unwashed masses pouring in from the very places some of the old-timers had left. As often happens with immigrant groups, some of the old-timers would have preferred to shut the door after they got there to protect their own uncertain standing.

The small colony of colored people already in the New World had made a place for themselves as an almost invisible minority by the time the Migration began. Many were the descendants of slaves the North had kept before Abolition or of slaves who fled the South on the Underground Railroad or were among the trickle of pioneers who had migrated from the South in the decades after the Civil War.

A good portion were in the servant class—waiters, janitors, elevator operators, maids, and butlers to the wealthiest white families in the city. But some had managed to create a solid though tenuous middle class of Pullman porters, postal workers, ministers, and businessmen who were anxious to keep the status and gains they had won. The color line restricted them to the oldest housing in the least desirable section of town no matter what their class, but they had tried to make the best of it and had created a world within a world for themselves.

From this group came the letters and newspaper stories about the freedoms of the North that helped inspire blacks to leave the South in the first place. The Great Migration brought in many a northerner's sweetheart, aunts, uncles, siblings, nieces, nephews, parents, and children. It also delivered hundreds of thousands of new customers, voters, readers, patients, and parishioners to the black institutions that stood to profit and be forever changed by the influx.

"They have been our best patrons," a colored physician in Chicago told researchers studying the Migration in the 1930s. "We have increased from five to two hundred and fifty doctors. We are living in better homes, and have more teachers in the schools; and nearly every colored church has benefitted."

Businessmen jumped at the opportunity. They opened restaurants serving hog maws and turnip greens. A man named Robert Horton opened Hattiesburg Shaving Parlor in a five-block stretch along Rhodes Avenue where some 150 families from that Gulf Coast town were huddled together. A few blocks away, there sat the Mississippi Coal and Wood Company, the Florida East Coast Shine Parlor to pull in the Floridians, and the Carolina Sea Island Candy Store for those who'd made it from there.

The Migration made giddy landlords of some of the old-timers. It gave them the chance to get extra money and bragging rights, too, by renting their spare rooms and garages to the new people. In Los Angeles and Oakland, it became a status symbol to have the wherewithal to take in roomers.

"I got a sharecropper," a woman in Los Angeles was heard boasting.

"Honey, I got me three sharecroppers!" another one said.

The churches stood to gain the most, and did. They ran notices in the *Defender* proclaiming, "Strangers welcome." Walters African Methodist Episcopal Church in Chicago tripled in membership. The city's Olivet Baptist Church got five thousand new members in the first three years of the Migration, making it one of the largest Baptist churches and one of the first megachurches in the country. A migrant from Alabama said she couldn't get in the first time she went. "We'd have to stand up," she said. "I don't care how early we'd go, you wouldn't get in."

But soon the cultural and class divisions between the newcomers and the old-timers began to surface. Many of the migrants, seeking the status and security they could not get back home, filled the stained-glass sanctuaries of the mainline churches. Others were overwhelmed by the size of the congregations and the austerity of their services. One migrant said she "couldn't understand the pastor and the words he used" at Olivet and couldn't get used to the singing. "The songs was proud-like," she said.

A migrant from Louisiana felt out of place at Pilgrim Baptist, an-

other big, old-line church. "Nobody said nothing," the mi~
"But there were whispers all over the place."

The migrants did as much moving around from church to chu~
they did from flat to flat. They tended to favor smaller storefront
churches opened up by ministers fresh from the South, where they
could sing the spirituals, catch the spirit, and fan themselves like they
were used to. The reason one woman left a mainline church was because
it was "too large—it don't see the small people."

The migrants brought new life to the old receiving stations. But by their
sheer numbers, they pressed down upon the colored people already
there. Slumlords made the most of it by subdividing what housing there
was into smaller and smaller units and investing as little as possible in
the way of upkeep to cash in on the bonanza. It left well-suited lawyers
and teachers living next to sharecroppers in head scarves just off the Illinois Central. The middle-class and professional people searched for a
way out.

"They tried to insulate themselves by moving further south along the
narrow strip that defined the gradually expanding South Side Black
Belt," wrote the historian James Grossman. "But the migrants inevitably
followed."

Unlike their white counterparts, the old settlers had few places to go
and were met with hostility and violence if they ventured into white
neighborhoods. The color line hemmed them in—newcomers and old-
timers alike—as they all struggled to move up. "The same class of Negroes who ran us away from Thirty-seventh Street are moving out
there," a colored professional man said after moving further south to
Fifty-first Street ahead of the migrants. "They creep along slowly like a
disease."

The fate of the city people was linked to that of the migrants, whether
they liked it or not, and the city people feared that the migrants could
jeopardize the status of them all. A colored newspaper called *Searchlight*
chastised them for boarding the streetcars in soiled work clothes after a
day at the stockyards and accused them of threatening the freedoms colored people had in the North. "Don't you know that you are forcing on
us here in Chicago a condition similar to the one down South?"

A survey of new migrants during World War II found that an overwhelming majority of them looked up to the people who were there be-

fore them, admired them, and wanted to be as assured and sophisticated as they were. But a majority of the colored people already in the New World viewed the newcomers in a negative light and saw them as hindering opportunities for all of them.

The anxious old settlers were "like German Jews who in the late nineteenth century feared that the influx of their coreligionists from eastern Europe would endanger their marginal but substantial foothold in gentile Chicago," wrote the historian James R. Grossman.

"Those who have long been established in the North have a problem," the *Chicago Defender* acknowledged. "That problem is the caring for the stranger within their gates."

It turned out that the old-timers were harder on the new people than most anyone else. "Well, their English was pretty bad," a colored businessman said of the migrants who flooded Oakland and San Francisco in the forties, as if from a foreign country. To his way of looking at it, they needed eight or nine years "before they seemed to get Americanized."

As the migrants arrived in the receiving stations of the North and West, the old-timers wrestled with what the influx meant for them, how it would affect the way others saw colored people, and how the flood of black southerners was a reminder of the Jim Crow world they all sought to escape. In the days before Emancipation, as long as slavery existed, no freed black was truly free. Now, as long as Jim Crow and the supremacy behind it existed, no blacks could ever be sure they were beyond its reach.

One day a white friend went up to a longtime Oakland resident named Eleanor Watkins to ask her what she thought about all the newcomers.

"Eleanor," the woman said, "you colored people must be very disgusted with some of the people who have come here from the South and the way they act."

"Well, Mrs. S.," Eleanor Watkins replied. "Yes, some colored people are very disgusted, but as far as I'm concerned, the first thing I give them credit for is getting out of the situation they were in. . . . Maybe they don't know how to dress or comb their hair or anything, but their children will and *their* children will."

In the early years of the Migration, the *Chicago Defender* took it upon itself to help correct the country people it had helped lure to the North to better fit the city people's standard of refinement. "It is our duty," the *Defender* wrote, "to guide the hand of a less experienced one, especially when one misstep weakens our chance for climbing."

The *Defender* ran periodic lists of "do's and don'ts" that recirculated over time and were repeated to newcomers like Ida Mae:

> DON'T HANG OUT THE WINDOWS.
>
> DON'T SIT AROUND IN THE YARD AND ON THE PORCH
> BAREFOOT AND UNKEMPT.
>
> DON'T WEAR HANDKERCHIEFS ON YOUR HEAD.
>
> DON'T USE VILE LANGUAGE IN PUBLIC PLACES.
>
> DON'T ALLOW CHILDREN TO BEG ON THE STREETS.
>
> DON'T APPEAR ON THE STREET WITH OLD DUST CAPS, DIRTY
> APRONS AND RAGGED CLOTHES.
>
> DON'T THROW GARBAGE IN THE BACKYARD OR ALLEY OR
> KEEP DIRTY FRONT YARDS.

The Chicago Urban League, which helped direct migrants to temporary shelter, rental options, and jobs, was the closest the migrants got to Customs in the North. It held what it called "Strangers Meetings" to help acclimate the newcomers, and its members went door-to-door, passing out leaflets advising the migrants as to their behavior and comportment. To the *Defender*'s do's and don'ts, the Urban League distributed cards adding the following admonishments:

1. DO NOT LOAF. GET A JOB AT ONCE.

2. DO NOT LIVE IN CROWDED ROOMS. OTHERS CAN BE OBTAINED.

3. DO NOT CARRY ON LOUD CONVERSATIONS IN STREET CARS AND
   PUBLIC PLACES.

4. DO NOT KEEP YOUR CHILDREN OUT OF SCHOOL.

5. DO NOT SEND FOR YOUR FAMILY UNTIL YOU GET A JOB.

————

Ida Mae didn't take it personally when people pointed these things out to her, like the neighbor lady who had brought the wine. Ida Mae wouldn't likely have seen her again because the family moved so much in those early months in Chicago. But she thanked people like her and a lady who mentioned her head scarf on the bus one day. She was grateful for the advice and, in fact, took most of it.

But there were some things she was not ever going to do. She was never going to change her name to something citified and highfalutin. She was never going to take on northern airs and name-drop about the pastor she knew from this or that church or the alderman who stopped to greet her at the polls, even though she would come to know famous people who made good up in the North because she had known their kin people back in Mississippi. She was never going to forget the folks back home and how she loved them so. She was never going to change her Mississippi drawl, not in the least, not even after she had spent more of her life in the North than in the South, not even when some northerners still had trouble understanding her decades after she'd been there; though she wasn't trying to be difficult and was just being herself, she simply didn't care what anybody thought. It didn't matter, because people seemed to love her for it.

She decided to keep the things that made her feel like home deep within herself, where nobody could judge her, and inside the walls of their kitchenette apartment where she made turnip greens and peach cobbler and sweet potato pie flecked with nutmeg and sang spirituals like in Mississippi as often as she liked.

NEW YORK, JANUARY 1947
GEORGE SWANSON STARLING

IT TOOK EIGHT YEARS OF MARRIAGE, broken by fearsome silences and fitful separations due to George's work on the railroad and the circumstances under which he had to migrate north. But finally George and Inez had a baby. It was a boy. He was born in January 1947, and they named him Gerard. There were already enough Georges in the family, and Gerard was close enough.

"I was the happiest man in the world when this boy came," George said. "I thought we weren't gonna never have no children."

George couldn't stop taking pictures of the baby. And the arrival of their son gave Inez a new purpose. She threw herself into motherhood. That was a good thing, because, soon after the baby was born, George had to take to the road again to care for his growing family.

In no time George was back on the rails, working the legendary trains that followed the East Coast route of the Great Migration. His job put him in the middle of one of the biggest population shifts in the country's history. He saw firsthand the continuing stream of people pouring out in front of him. He helped them carry their cardboard boxes tied with string, the hand-me-down suitcases, the hatboxes and steamer trunks. Some came north with only a cotton sack or a paper bag with all they owned or were able to get out with.

"Time they get their seat and their bags up, here come the shoe boxes," he said. Fried chicken, boiled eggs, crackers, and cakes.

He was working the Silver Comet from New York to Birmingham, the Silver Spur from New York to Tampa, and the other Great Migration trains. His job was to help people load their bags, direct them to their seats, warm their babies' milk, and generally attend to their needs and clean up after them. The ride could last as long as twenty-eight hours from the southernmost stop to Pennsylvania Station in Manhattan.

George walked up and down the train aisles, helping people board or disembark at every stop along the way. He rarely got a chance to sit down, much less sleep. The pay was lower than it might otherwise have been because he was expected to get tips to compensate for it. But when he was working the Jim Crow car, he was mostly servicing the lowliest, poorest-paid workers in the South—or in the country, for that matter. Many of them had never been on the train before and knew nothing about the protocol of gratuities.

They gave him food instead. "Want some fried chicken?" the colored passengers would ask him. "I give you some fried chicken. You already gettin' paid."

He had come from the place they were leaving and knew not to expect a tip or hold it against them. He knew the fear and uncertainty in their hearts because he had felt it himself. He had ridden the night train north just as they had and spoke their language and could read the worried optimism in the faces.

When the train approached Washington, D.C., the dividing line between the Jim Crow South and the free North, and rode deeper into the Promised Land, his role took on an unexpected significance.

As they neared the final stops, it became necessary for George to become more than a baggage handler, but tutor and chaperone to nervous charges arriving in the New World. At the moment of the migrants' greatest fear and anxiety, it fell to him to ease them into the Promised Land, tell them whatever he knew about this new place, which bus or subway to take, how far the station was from their cousin's apartment, to watch out for panhandlers and hustlers who might take what little change they had left, and usher them and their luggage off to whatever the future held for them.

It was his tap on the shoulder that awakened them as the train neared their stop and alerted them to their new receiving city. He and other colored porters were men in red caps and white uniforms, but they functioned as the midwives of the Great Migration, helping the migrants gather themselves and disembark at the station and thus delivering to the world a new wave of newcomers with each arriving train.

———

It seemed to George that the moment they stepped on the train going north, they became different people, started acting like what they imagined the people up north to be. Some started talking their version of a northern accent, sitting up straighter, eating their chicken wings with their pinkie out, becoming more like the place they were heading to. "A lot of them pretending to be always northerners," George said, knowing full well the difference.

Heading south, it was a quiet and sober train, filled with the people of the North returning home, in their finest suits and hats, and southern visitors having just seen the big city for themselves.

Heading north, the trains were more festive and anxious, filled with people migrating out with all their worldly goods and the people from the North returning to their adopted cities with all they could manage to take with them that they missed from back home in the South.

George could tell the people from the North. The bags that were empty heading south were now heavy with ham and hog head cheese and turnip roots and sweet potatoes and any little thing they cherished from back home and had a hard time getting in the North or that, if they could get it in the North, just didn't taste the same.

One day at a little station somewhere in South Carolina, George helped his passengers get their bags up onto the luggage rack above the seats on the Silver Comet as he always did. The train then left the station, and George was in the back of the colored railcar. He always liked to stand in the back so he could observe the passengers and see who might need his help.

"They wanted to assign us seats in the front," George said of the bulkhead crew seats, "but I never liked sitting in front of my people. I couldn't see how I could be helpful in the car, sitting in front of everybody. I like to sit behind them so I can see what's happening."

That day after the train left the station in South Carolina, he began to notice the sound of a slow drip hitting the floor of the railcar and the seats below. He looked up and saw that it was coming from a bag up on the luggage rack. Whatever the liquid was, it was red and looked to be blood, and as he got closer he discovered that it was in fact blood dripping out of the bag.

"They must have just killed a hog or something, cut him up and put him in the bag," George said. "I keep hearing something dripping, and I look up, and here's this bag with blood just drippin' all out of this bag. They done butchered up somebody's chicken or hog and had him in the bag. They must have done it on the way to the train, and they didn't get rid of all the blood, they were still draining in the bag rack."

George was used to people bringing all kinds of things, live chickens and rabbits, a whole side of a pig. But this was the first time someone brought something they hadn't even finished butchering. George took the bag and sat it on the floor. He wiped it down and mopped up the blood that had dripped from it. He never did see whose bag it was or what kind of animal was inside it, given all that he had to do tending to the train and the other customers. And no passenger claimed the bloody bag for the duration of the trip. In the commotion of arrival at one of the stations up north, the bag just disappeared into the disembarking crowd, its owner having claimed it in anonymity.

After a while, nothing surprised George, but he dreaded the work he was in for on the rides north. The bags were so heavy he could barely lift them from the ground. His knees were bad from all the basketball he used to play in high school, and the people, having morphed into northerners just by stepping onto the Silver Comet, were expecting the full rights of citizenship, to begin with George picking up their overloaded bags.

They carried jars of fig preserves, pole beans, snap peas, and peaches, whole hams, whatever the folks back home were growing on the farm and other treasured pieces of the South they could carry back with them.

One passenger came on with a big hatbox that looked innocent enough, but when George tried to pick it up, the front end flew up and he could feel something moving inside. When he tried to steady the hatbox, the other side flew up.

"I could feel it going to the front," he said. "She had a big old watermelon in there rolling down in the bag. That's why it was flopping back and forth."

———

A man with a trunk boarded at a tiny station somewhere near Abbeville, South Carolina, bound for New York. George saw him and jumped down from the train.

"I need some help with my bag," the man said.

George reached down to grab the trunk and fell trying to lift it.

"Hey, man," George said. "What do you *have* in this bag?"

"Clothes, daddy, clothes," the man said. "You know I been down here for two weeks. I had to have something to change in."

"Yeah," George said. "Okay, then, if you want your clothes up on this train, you better give me a hand with this bag. 'Cause I can't lift it off the ground."

Together they pushed it up the steps and shoved it onto the train. The train rocked from side to side as George struggled to drag the trunk down the aisle.

It was dark by now, and George managed to push the trunk to the back. He held up one end by the handle to position it in a corner away from the other passengers. Then he dropped it.

"And when it hit the floor, the latches flew off," George said.

And out came the contents.

"The potatoes rolled out that bag, and the engineer is hitting these curves," George said, "and you could hear 'em rolling all over the floor."

The man whose trunk it was got alarmed.

"Hey, daddy, you gotta flashlight?" he asked.

"I don't have no flashlight that's gonna last long enough for you to find all your clothes," George said. " 'Cause they rolling all over the train. And I need my flashlight. I'm sorry, man."

The train lurched from side to side and from one curve into the next and with each curve came the rumbling sound of mud-caked Carolina sweet potatoes. The colored car was in an uproar, the man's trunk flung open, its latch broken, the man running down the aisle in the dark after the contents, and the fifty-one other passengers rolling with laughter and very likely helping themselves to sweet potatoes they hadn't managed to bring aboard themselves but that would make a nice sweet potato pie once they got back to Harlem.

LOS ANGELES, 1954
ROBERT JOSEPH PERSHING FOSTER

ALICE BEGAN SETTING UP HOUSE in the walk-up apartment Robert had scrambled to secure for his family after the apartment he wanted mysteriously fell through. It was nowhere near the space Alice was accustomed to and had few of the amenities and not a whiff of the grandeur of her parents' brick Georgian estate back in Atlanta.

As she began to arrange what furniture they had, shop for groceries, dust, and clean, which she had never in her life really had to do before, and direct their two little girls, it soon hit Alice and Robert: they had been married for twelve years but had never lived together as husband and wife, other than their short tour of duty in Austria, where they had not so much kept house as camped out. Such was the life of ambitious black southerners trying to find a place for themselves in a not altogether welcoming world. Robert had been in medical training for much of those twelve years of marriage, and the Clements had thought it best that Alice stay with them while Robert pursued his internships and residencies and tried to figure out and save up for where he wanted to migrate.

Over the years, they had seen each other when they could. But they had both settled into their own ways of doing things, essentially living out their lives on their own. Now that they were finally all together in Los Angeles, it hit them that they didn't really know each other.

Alice didn't know how Robert liked his food cooked or that he was prone to work late hours. Robert had to learn how to be a father to two daughters who had been raised by socialite grandparents and who were missing the only world they had ever known.

He came to that realization when he was out with his older daughter, Bunny, one day. She saw a toy she wanted and was insisting that her father buy it for her. Robert had just opened his practice and was watching every nickel. Bunny had been raised like a princess back in Atlanta, and Robert thought she had more than enough toys and dolls as it was.

"Why, you don't need that," Robert told her.

"Well, if you don't give it to me, Granddaddy will."

Robert discovered that his whole family was really the Clements' and not his, and he had to figure out how to reclaim his status in the household. He and Alice began fighting over her cooking, which had become a symbol of their class differences and the variation in southern culture, depending upon which state you happened to be from.

Robert wanted oxtails and turnip greens and red-peppered gumbo like he grew up with in Louisiana. Alice had never really cooked for him before. And what she cooked was what any well-born 1950s homemaker would prepare for her family—the soufflés and casseroles of the upper classes of the day. She went to a great deal of trouble to make these Betty Crocker–era meals. But Robert didn't like them, and he took her style of cooking as a repudiation of his tastes.

"It needs some more seasoning in it," he said.

"The children don't like it that way," Alice told him.

"Children eat what their mama give 'em," Robert said. "And you give 'em the food the way I like it to be cooked."

But it was already too late. The children had become set in their expectations, the family system already established. Robert and Alice fought and fought over it. They were paying a price for the sacrifices they had made to get established outside the South. Every day, they were confronted with a difference they hadn't noticed before, something so basic as a meal suddenly becoming a metaphor of the different worlds they came from. The dinner table became a testing of wills over which culture would prevail, the high-toned world of black elites in Atlanta or the hardscrabble but no less proud black middle class of small-town Louisiana, and, more important, who was going to run the family—the Clements from afar or Robert, who was working long hours to take care of them now.

It exposed a chasm between the two of them that would never be fully resolved but that both would have to live with. "That was a big hurdle," Robert said.

As it was, they were living in a cramped apartment with temporary furniture and tacked-down rugs and trying to make the best of it.

"We were not defined by where we lived," Robert said. "We felt we'd make it in time. And we lived that way."

So long as they were in a walk-up apartment, Alice put off her socialite yearnings. She wanted to wait to make her presence known to the colored elite in Los Angeles. She wanted to wait until they could secure a house more befitting her station. She took a position teaching third grade in the Los Angeles public school system to help them save up for the house they would need before she could announce herself to L.A. society.

Robert didn't see the point of waiting. She was the same person now as she would be when they got a house. But Alice knew the value of a proper entrance when one was coming in as an outsider, as any southerner new to California would be. Robert kept asking anyway. It would be good for business to start making connections, and she was all but assured of acceptance to those patrician circles by birth alone.

"Well, when you gonna join?" he'd ask her.

"It's too expensive for us out here now," she'd say. "The time's not right."

From Atlanta, her mother had signed her up with the Links, perhaps the most elite of the invitation-only, class- and color-conscious colored women's societies of the era.

But Alice wouldn't activate her membership until they got a house. "We're not ready, Robert," she said. "No, we're not ready."

It was a reminder to Robert that he had not yet lived up to her and her family's expectations. The shadow of Rufus Clement loomed over him from across the continent. The family he was just now getting to know was used to living on an estate with formal gardens and servants, and here they were, cramped together with him in a walk-up apartment like waitstaff.

Robert was not in a position to duplicate what they had back in Atlanta. So he set out to prove himself in other ways. If Alice wasn't ready to go Hollywood, Robert was. His practice was just beginning to take off, and he had an idea of what he needed to cap off the image he was trying to create. He went to Dr. Beck for advice.

"Doctor, I wanna buy a Cadillac," Robert said, announcing his desire for the most coveted car on the market in those days. "Do you think I'd hurt myself if I bought a Cadillac?"

"Can you meet the notes, boy?"

"Yes, I can."

"Go buy it, then."

Alice was against it and said so. "How'd you like a Cadillac parked in front of an upstairs apartment? Don't you think you're a little premature?"

"Yes, but I want one."

"You don't wanna buy a Cadillac, and you live in a walk-up apartment," Alice said. "You don't have a garage to put it in."

But Robert had made up his mind. He thought he could attract more patients with it. Patients half expected their doctor to be driving a Cadillac. It would make them respect him more, give them something to brag about. And if they were bragging about him, more patients might come his way. Besides, there was something deep inside him that had to prove to the world and to himself that he had made it.

So he went downtown to Thomas Cadillac to buy himself one. But the salesclerk took him past the showroom of new Cadillacs to the dealership's used car lot.

"I told him I wanted a new car, and he kept showing me used cars," Robert said, exasperated but by now picking up on the subtleties of his interactions in the New World.

"I thanked him and went home," Robert said.

Then he wrote a letter to General Motors, Cadillac division, in Detroit: *"I'm a young black physician, just getting started,"* he wrote. *"All my life I dreamed Cadillac, and when I had enough money to go down and get one, the man insults me by showing me used cars."*

Soon after he wrote the letter, he got a call from the dealership. "We have instructions," Robert remembered the man saying, "to deliver to you a Cadillac to your liking. What day would you like to come down and select it?"

It was 1955, so he headed right over to pick out a 1955 model. "A white Cadillac," he said years later, a smile forming on his face, "with blue interior and whitewall tires. Yes, indeedy. See what you can get when you step on the right feet?"

Some of the people from Monroe thought the car pretentious and over the top. They were still having a hard time even picturing him a doctor. But just putting the key in the ignition made him feel like he had moved up in the world.

"And I learned that lesson from Dr. Beck's advice," Robert said years later. "To hell with what people think of me. Go on and do what you wanna do. They gonna do what they wanna do anyhow, say what they wanna say anyway."

He mulled over his words. "That's right," he said. "And you get more if they feel you ain't suffering."

He was already plotting new ways to prove himself to the naysayers, black and white, in Louisiana and in L.A. "My lifestyle'll blow 'em outta the water," Robert would say. "Just blow 'em outta the water, 'cause I'll go on and do what I wanna do."

THE OTHER SIDE
OF JORDAN

We cannot escape our origins,
however hard we might try,
those origins contain the key
—could we but find it—
to all that we later become.
—JAMES BALDWIN,
Notes of a Native Son

CHICAGO, NOVEMBER 1940
IDA MAE BRANDON GLADNEY

———

THE CROWDS GATHERED early at the fire station at Thirty-sixth and State on the morning of November 5, 1940. It was election day. President Franklin D. Roosevelt was in a tighter-than-expected race against a maverick businessman, Wendell Willkie. Europe was at war, the United States was in Depression despite the gains of the New Deal, and Roosevelt was now the first president in history to seek a third term, which his Republican opponent was using against him.

For weeks, precinct captains and ward volunteers had canvassed the tenements and three-flats on the South Side of Chicago. They had passed out palm cards and campaign flyers to the domestics and factory workers and to untutored potential voters like Ida Mae.

Illinois was considered crucial to Roosevelt this election, so much so that the Democrats held their national convention in Chicago that year. He had been elected twice before by landslides against Herbert Hoover and Alf Landon, and he now needed the Midwest and Chicago, in particular, to turn out for him if he were to stay in the White House.

Ida Mae didn't know what was at stake, but suddenly everyone around her was talking about something she'd never heard of back in Mississippi. The precinct captain for her area, a Mr. Tibbs, had been out in the neighborhood rousing the people to register for the upcoming election. She had seen him and gotten the slip his workers handed out and was curious about all the commotion.

Back home, no one dared talk about such things. She couldn't vote in Mississippi. She never knew where the polls were in Chickasaw County. And even if she had had the nerve to go, she would have been turned away for failing to pay a poll tax or not being able to answer a question on a literacy test for which there was no answer, such as how many grains of sand there were on the beach or how to interpret an obscure article of the Mississippi constitution to the election registrar's satisfaction. She and most every other colored person in the South knew better than even to try.

So she never thought about her senator or congressman or state representative or about Theodore Bilbo, an admitted Klansman and a famous Mississippi governor. Bilbo had been one of the most incendiary segregationists of the era, yet she didn't pay him much mind because she had nothing to do with his getting into office and couldn't have voted against him even if she knew when and how to do it.

Bilbo made it to the governor's mansion without citizens like Ida Mae or Miss Theenie having any say as to his getting into or remaining in office. He later ascended without them to the U.S. Senate, where, in 1938, the year Ida Mae finally migrated to Chicago, he helped lead one of the longest filibusters in the history of the Senate, the one to thwart a bill that would have made lynching a federal crime.

At one point in the filibuster, he rose to speak on behalf of his constituents—not the entire state of Mississippi but the white voters there—and in opposition to the interests of half the state. He spoke in defense of the right to kill black citizens as white southerners saw fit.

"If you succeed in the passage of this bill," Bilbo told his Senate colleagues, *"you will open the floodgates of hell in the South. Raping, mobbing, lynching, race riots, and crime will be increased a thousand fold; and upon your garments and the garments of those who are responsible for the passage of the measure will be the blood of the raped and outraged daughters of Dixie, as well as the blood of the perpetrators of these crimes that the red-blooded Anglo-Saxon white Southern men will not tolerate."*

Ida Mae hadn't bothered to know what politicians like Bilbo were doing because it wouldn't have done her any good. Nobody she knew had even tried to vote. Nobody made note of election day whenever it came. It was as if there were an invisible world of voting and elections going on about its business without her.

Now it was 1940, and she was in Chicago. All around her were new arrivals like herself who had never voted before and were just getting the hang of elections after a lifetime of being excluded. Suddenly, the very party and the very apparatus that was ready to kill them if they tried to vote in the South was searching them out and all but carrying them to the polls. To the Democrats in the North, each new arrival from the South was a potential new vote in their column. It was in the Democrats' best interest to mobilize these people, who, now given the chance to vote, might go Republican. The Republicans, after all, had been the party of Lincoln and of Reconstruction. The Republicans had opposed the segregationists who had held the migrants down in the South. But now the migration trains were delivering brand-new voters to the hands of whoever got to them first.

Chicago was a Democratic town, and the Democrats had the means to make the most of this gift to the party. They were counting on the goodwill Roosevelt had engendered among colored people with his New Deal initiatives. Still, the precinct captains took no chances. They went door-to-door to talk up the New Deal and to register the people. They asked them about their kids and jobs and convinced them that the Democrats in the North were different from those in the South. They printed up party slates and passed out palm cards—political crib notes that would fit in the palm of the hand—so the people would know whom to vote for when they got inside the booth.

On election day, Ida Mae walked up to the fire station around the corner from her flat at Thirty-sixth and Wabash to vote for the first time in her life. The sidewalks were teeming with volunteers to usher neophytes into the station and to the correct sign-in tables. Inside, election judges, clerks, a policeman or two monitored the proceedings.

Ida Mae was not certain what to do. She had never touched an election ballot. She walked in, and a lady came over and directed her to where she should go. Ida Mae stepped inside a polling booth for the first time in her life and drew the curtain behind her. She unfolded the palm card she had been given and tried to remember what the lady had told her about how to punch in her choices for president of the United States and other political offices. It was the first time she would ever have a say in such things.

"She showed me how to do it," Ida Mae said.

What was unthinkable in Mississippi would eventually become so much a part of life in Chicago that Mr. Tibbs would ask Ida Mae to volunteer at the polls the next time. She had a pleasant disposition, and Mr. Tibbs put her to work helping other people learn how to vote. She would stand outside the firehouse, directing newcomers who were clutching their palm cards and looking as puzzled as she had been her first time at the polls.

She did not see herself as taking any kind of political stand. But in that simple gesture, she was defying the very heart of the southern caste system, and doing something she could not have dreamed of doing—in fact, had not allowed herself even to contemplate—all those years in Mississippi.

But she had seen for herself the difference it could make the first time she had stepped inside a voting booth. Ida Mae's first vote and George's first vote and those of tens of thousands of other colored migrants new to the North were among the 2,149,934 votes cast for President Roosevelt in Illinois that day in 1940. Ida Mae's new home was a deeply divided swing state that year, and this was among the tightest of races. It turned out for Roosevelt that it was a good thing the migrants had come. The ballots cast by Ida Mae and other colored migrants up from the South were enough to help give Roosevelt the two percent margin of victory he needed to carry the state of Illinois and, by extension, the United States—to return him to the White House.

ON THE SILVER COMET, MID- TO LATE 1940S
GEORGE SWANSON STARLING

THE TRAIN HAD ROLLED OUT OF BIRMINGHAM and was wending its way toward New York. It would stop in Wattsville, Ragland, Ohatchee in Alabama, in Cedartown, Rockmart, Atlanta, Athens, Elberton in

Georgia, on its way to the Carolinas and up the East Coast. George was working the train as a railcar attendant and was settling into a twenty-three-hour workday of hauling bags, sweeping and dusting, tending and picking up after the fifty-two passengers in his car.

Somewhere along the route, he looked out of the vestibule door by the draft gears between the railcars. The train leaned into a sharp bend in the track. The railcars spread apart to take the full curve. And suddenly, George could see the figure of a man standing between the railcars, clinging to the edge by the door. The man stood as still as a piece of furniture. With the railcars spread open as they were, the man could no longer hide. He looked into George's face and did not speak. His eyes begged George not to turn him in.

It is not known how many migrants made it out of the South by hopping a freight or passenger train as this man did. They called what this man was doing "hoboing." It was one of the ways some men and boys, often the most desperate, the poorest, the most adventurous, or those who got on the wrong side of a planter or a sheriff, got out.

Years before, in 1931, a boy by the name of Johnson plotted his way out of Lake Charles, Louisiana, with three of his friends. They were hoping to make it to Los Angeles. All over the South, there were colored boys like him dreaming of hopping a train. They practiced how to jump on and off the freight cars when the trains passed through Yazoo City, Mississippi, or Bessemer, Alabama, or any number of small towns. They would ride a couple hundred feet and jump off until they got the hang of it.

Johnson and his friends talked about escaping Lake Charles, Louisiana, for months. They planned the day of departure, only to put it off because one boy's mother got sick or another lost his nerve. Finally they set a date and met at the rail yard one night in 1931. They had nothing but the clothes they were wearing and a couple dollars in their pockets. The four of them grabbed the side of a car and hopped aboard as the train wound along the tracks.

The passenger trains would have been a surer way to get out. The freights were not marked and did not announce their destinations like the passenger trains did. Anyone riding them couldn't be certain where he was headed. But scheduled trains were riskier because the passengers, the conductors, the porters, and attendants like George might see them and turn them in. So most stowaways hopped a freight train, lonely with its grain and cotton bins. If they found a car open, they hid inside. Sometimes they had no choice but to ride on top of the car, holding tight against the wind kicked up by a train going seventy miles an hour.

Johnson and his friends made it onto the freight train and were headed out of Louisiana and into Texas. But what they hadn't realized was that the freight trains had police, men who patrolled the freight cars and were on the lookout for stowaways like them. The patrolmen were called railroad bulls, and they were hired to do whatever it took to get stowaways off the train. They were known to beat or shoot anyone they caught or to send stowaways to a chain gang, where they might never be seen again. The bulls had names like "Denver Bob" and "Texas Slim."

Johnson and his friends were positioning themselves on a freight car and dreaming of California when a bull caught sight of them. It was harder to go undetected when there were four people rather than one. The bulls started hurling rocks and the boys had no choice. They jumped sixteen or seventeen feet from a moving freight train, not knowing where they were or when the next freight was coming or if whatever came through was going to California.

Now they were lost somewhere in Texas. They had to wait for hours before another train rumbled through. They hopped on it, not knowing where it was headed. Suddenly it stopped on a trestle bridge suspended two stories above a ravine. The bulls liked to stop on high bridges to force stowaways off the train. It left the boys with nowhere to hide. They could stay and face a beating from the bulls or risk injuring themselves in yet another jump.

They jumped. They tumbled downhill in the darkness. They were still in Texas, crawling through weeds, the bulls' flashlights searching the scrub brush.

In all the commotion, Johnson got separated from the other three as they rolled down the ravine. He was alone in the brush as he heard the train rattle away from him. He crawled in the brambles, hungry, lost, and jarred by the escape. He crawled toward the light of a settlement in search of food.

He came to a fire where real hoboes, men who rode trains for the thrill of it, were gathered near the tracks of the freight train. The hoboes were sitting around a pot over a fire, one man with a potato, another with a skinned rabbit over the flame. The men were covered in soot. This was what they called the hobo jungle, where they slept and cooked their food, which was whatever the group of them had managed to rustle up, before taking to the trains again.

"What'd you bring to put in the pot?" they asked the boy.

THE WARMTH OF OTHER SUNS

He didn't have anything. He was not of their world.

"You better go and look for something," they told him.

The boy walked further toward the light of the settlement in search of food to bring back to the strangers by the fire.

He approached a house. A white woman answered. She didn't seem surprised. The people in the settlement had seen a lot of boys and men hopping trains like him.

"Madame," he said, "I'm hoboing." He asked if she had food she could spare. "Anything you have."

She gave him bread and chicken. With that, he returned to the hobo jungle, handed over what he had gotten, and was finally able to eat. At daybreak, he hopped the first train that came through. He rode not knowing where he was headed and not, of course, able to ask.

The train was not going west to California. It was going north toward Chicago. There, the next morning, he hopped a train going west with the sun. The boy would make it to California and become an extra in the movies, an officeholder in the Lake Charles, Louisiana, Club, and a respectable accountant in South Central Los Angeles.

George had heard about these boys and men hoboing out of the South but had never seen one for himself until that day on the northbound train. He was as startled as the disheveled, soot-covered man in front of him.

"I can't believe what I'm looking at," George thought to himself. "I can't believe I'm seeing what I see."

The man must have sneaked onto the train as it sat boarding passengers or run alongside it and jumped up as the train either slowed to a stop or pulled out of a station.

And now he was clinging to the sides of the railcar as it rocked at top speed, the wind rushing between the cars as they rumbled and turned.

George never knew what became of the man or the others he saw hoboing on the trains. They never spoke. He himself had stared death in the face in Florida and felt sadness and awe at whatever drove them to steal onto a train this way.

"They were standing there like statues," George said. "Like they were part of the equipment. I couldn't tell whether they were living or dead there for a while."

Sometimes he would see the same few coming back and forth, as if that were the only way they could manage to go north or south. It was nerve-jangling to George to see them because he was supposed to turn them in. But he just couldn't bring himself to do it.

"I would never give them up," he said. "I'd pretend I didn't see them. One or two occasions, I'd sneak a sandwich or something out of the diner."

And after he did that, they would always disappear.

LOS ANGELES, SUMMER 1955
ROBERT JOSEPH PERSHING FOSTER

AFTER TWO YEARS OF HARD WORK, Robert managed to attract enough patients needing some sort of surgery that he was finally able to secure admitting privileges at a hospital in Los Angeles. It was nowhere near Cedars Sinai or UCLA Medical Center but was a little place called Metropolitan Hospital over at Twenty-first and Hoover Street, near his office. It had a mostly colored patient load and a mostly white staff of doctors. There were only a few colored doctors, and Robert was one of them.

They did most of their surgeries in the morning, and around noon they broke for lunch. They sat in the lounge to eat or read the newspapers and waited for their next cases to come up.

But Mondays were different. Monday was the day when the white doctors came back from the weekend, regaling one another with their exploits at the casinos and their triumphs on the golf courses in Palm Springs or Las Vegas. Robert dreaded Mondays.

One Monday, they turned and looked at him.

"Bob, have you been to Caesars?"

"No, I haven't seen it," Robert said, looking down. "I've never been there."

Robert hated to admit that. He wanted more than anything to be able to go to Vegas. He was born for Vegas. By now he had the money to go. That was what he came out here for—to be a full citizen, do whatever people of his station did, regardless of what color they were.

He began avoiding the other doctors on Mondays. He made himself

busy, buried himself in his newspaper, and avoided eye contact so they
wouldn't engage him in conversation during their animated recaps. But
he couldn't escape hearing their tales from the casinos.

He sat there having to listen to them talk about Vegas for months,
seething and saying nothing. They seemed to have caught on that he
didn't want to join in and left him alone as they compared notes among
themselves.

"Then, every now and then," Robert remembered, "somebody would
make a mistake and ask to confirm or give your feeling about a club or
gambling in Las Vegas."

One day, he spoke up.

"Listen, I'm tired of you guys asking me about Las Vegas," he said.
"You know colored people can't go to the hotels there or the casinos. It's
a thorn in my side, so don't ask me about that."

The doctors fell silent. "That embarrassed all those who heard it,"
Robert remembered years later. "They had a guilt feeling that they were
a part of that. This is the way I perceived it anyway. Maybe they didn't
give a nickel. I don't know."

The doctors stopped asking him about Vegas, but that didn't mean he
stopped thinking about it, wishing for it.

Over time, Robert began hearing rumors about blacks protesting
their exclusion from Las Vegas and that the city might be opening up.
He went to two doctor friends of his, one a brother of his classmate Dr.
Beale back in Houston, and another, Dr. Jackson, who had both gotten
into hospital management and seemed always to know the latest.

He asked them what they'd heard about Vegas.

"Is it true that blacks can go there now?"

"I ain't heard that, Bob," Dr. Jackson said.

They had, however, heard that there was a colored man in Vegas who
people said was helping get colored people into a few of the hotels and
casinos.

"I tell you what you do," Dr. Jackson said. "Why don't you call Jimmy
Gay?"

"Who's Jimmy Gay?"

James Arthur Gay was perhaps the most influential colored man in
the still-segregated world of Las Vegas. He had migrated there from
Fordyce, Arkansas, after World War II and found himself locked out of
both the mortuary trade, for which he had been trained, and the resort
industry, to which he aspired. College degree in hand, he worked his
way up from a cook at a drive-in to become one of the first colored exec-

utives at a casino, the Sands, at a time when stars like Nat King Cole and
Sammy Davis, Jr., were not permitted to stay in hotels on the Strip.
Knowing how hard it had been for him to cross the color line in Vegas,
he took it upon himself to help spirit other colored people in wherever
he could, risking his own tenuous standing to do so.

Over time, he became the contact person, a secret agent of sorts, the
one connection in an almost underground network in Las Vegas, where
a colored visitor could not otherwise be assured of getting a room at a
mainline hotel. Jimmy knew who to talk to in order to secure rooms for
colored people at the Vegas hotels and knew how to do it discreetly, and
he was in a position to screen, through word of mouth in that insular circle of colored people for whom he would perform such a service.

So Robert called him.

"This is Bob Foster, Jimmy," Robert said. "Jackson and Beale told me
to call you and find out if this was true. Have they opened Las Vegas
up?"

"You planning to come up?"

"If we can go. Can we go? Could we come?"

"Well, how many in your party? When are you planning to come?
Get your party together and call me, and I'll see what I can do."

Robert couldn't wait to tell his friends about it. It took them some
time to get it together. A total of thirteen people signed up to go in what
would be an early foray past the color line in Vegas: doctors, doctors'
wives, a school principal. They started planning right away. They made
their plane and train reservations. They read up on the casinos and the
shows they wanted to see. The women shopped for what seemed like
weeks.

"They had three different outfits for every day," Robert said. *"Three
completely different outfits."*

Jimmy had arranged for them to stay at the Riviera Hotel. Robert
couldn't wait. It was the first high-rise in Vegas. It had cost ten million
dollars to build and had just opened that spring to worries that it was
so big that the desert sand might sink under its weight. It was right
on the Strip, its name in big letters on a V-shaped marquee above the
sign for the Starlight Lounge. Dean Martin was part owner. Liberace
played there. It would become the set for *Ocean's Eleven.* It was so very
Rat Pack, and Robert could just picture himself at a dinner show in
the Clover Room. All summer, a jingle was running on the radio stations in Los Angeles about "The Riv," as it came to be called, like it was
the hottest thing going in Vegas. *There's a new high in the Las Vegas sky,*

the Riviera Hotel. Robert used to sing along with the jingle and only got more excited.

"You heard it a million times a day," Robert said. "And, oh, I'd just be thinking about the trip we were going to have."

The people who flew in piled into several taxicabs at the Vegas airport and pulled up to the canopied driveway of the Riviera with enough luggage for a celebrity road tour. They walked into the marble lobby, chatting and giddy.

"Now, we all dressed to the fingertips," Robert said, "sharp as sharp could be. Everybody."

Robert saw bellmen all around but noticed that no one stepped forward to get the luggage. Someone in the group asked for help. At last a bellman came and brought their luggage in, loads of it, to the front desk.

In the lobby, Robert's group met up with the couple who had caught the train and had arrived ahead of them. The wife was named Thurma Adams. She jumped up and ran toward Robert and the others and began acting out of sorts. She was humming under her breath as if to warn them of something, but it was in a childlike code that Robert had trouble deciphering.

She was skipping as she sang, *"La de, da, de, da, la de da, de da!"*

"Thurma, Thurma, Thurma," Robert said. "Have you lost your mind?"

"Just go on over to that desk," she told him. "You'll see."

Robert understood instantly. "And chills went through me," he remembered. "A wave of nausea."

Phoenix again.

"Oh hell, we ain't gonna get this room," he thought to himself. "The same story, 'There's no room in here.' "

Here they were, thirteen travelers just arrived in a place they thought had opened up to people like them. They couldn't have been sure of it but wanted so much to believe that they had taken the chance anyway, and now they were being told there were no accommodations for them, and they're standing there in the gilded lobby like refugees, homeless in their tailored suits and sequins and with enough luggage for a European holiday.

Robert tried to calm himself and salvage the situation. He went over to the front desk just as he had in Phoenix, but more assured this time because he had been through this before and besides, he was a Californian now.

"This is Dr. Robert Foster," he began. "We have a party of thirteen people from Los Angeles. We are supposed to have room reservations."

"Who made them?" the clerk asked.

"Mr. Jimmy Gay made them," Robert answered.

"Who's Jimmy Gay?"

"Jimmy Gay knows somebody here. I didn't get the name of the person who made them for me."

The front-desk clerk called the reservations supervisor, and he came out.

"And they looked, and they looked and they looked and they looked," Robert remembered.

"They looked for what they knew wasn't there. And I know that one, too."

The front desk said it could find no reservation for any of them, made no offer to accommodate them, and made no suggestions nor showed any interest in where else they might possibly go.

"So I'm standing there fuming," Robert said many years later. "*How do I get out of this? How we gonna get out this hotel with all this luggage?* Humiliation galore. I felt everybody in the place looking at us. I felt as if the shower door had fallen, and I looked up and saw I had an audience of fifty people. I just felt that they could see clear through me that we had been rejected. And that was what I felt at that desk."

He decided to call Jimmy Gay from a phone booth in the hotel. Maybe that would clear things up. Fortunately, Jimmy was home.

Jimmy told him that he would check on it and that Robert should stay by the phone booth.

"Don't let anybody use the phone you on," Jimmy said. "Block it. Leave the line open. I want to make a phone call, and I'll call you right back. Stay by the phone."

Jimmy couldn't locate the reservations clerk he had talked to at the Riviera, late as it was. So he came up with an alternative.

"Go to the Sands Hotel," he instructed. He told them who to ask for when they got there. "He'll take care of you and the party."

So Robert and the twelve others once again loaded into several cabs and went to the Sands Hotel. Because Jimmy had made reservations at the Riviera and not the Sands, the Sands didn't have enough rooms for the entire party that night. The Sands made arrangements for them to stay at yet another hotel, the Flamingo Capri, further down on the Strip.

"We'll come and get you tomorrow," the front-desk clerk said. The

Sands kept its word, and the next morning they were, at last, all unpacking their things at the Sands.

"I got a warm spot with Sands for what they did for us," Robert would say years later.

Jimmy Gay and his wife, Hazel, puddle-hopped them from nightclub to nightclub where Jimmy knew they would be accepted. They heard Pearl Bailey in the lounge. They made three shows a night. And Robert got to go inside the casinos he had heard his fellow physicians brag and goad him about for months and that he dreaded hearing mention of. But now he didn't have to dread it anymore.

"We lived the part," Robert said.

He remembered one night in particular. He was wearing a black mohair suit he ordered specifically for the occasion from the tailor who dressed Sammy Davis, Jr., and Frank Sinatra. He wore a black tie with a burgundy stripe, a white tab-collar shirt, gold cuff links, black shoes, black silk socks, and a white handkerchief with his initials, *RPF,* embroidered in silver.

All the humiliation melted away, the white doctors' idle chatter, the rejection at the Riviera.

He was finally in the world he belonged in, living out a dream like an honorary member of the Rat Pack. Jim Crow, the South, Louisiana, Monroe, Phoenix, the downside of L.A.—all gone for now. He was in a casino out of a movie. Dean Martin could have walked in any minute, or so it seemed, and here was Robert, right in the middle of it, acting as if he'd been to it.

"And I am playing the roulette. And I'm enjoying myself, and I'm having a good time, and I'm standing up betting over some other people there, and I hit my number, and I eased the buttons loose on the coat, and I hit number eleven, and I reached over like this to pick up my chips and open my coat and show my blood red silk lining.

"People said, 'Oh, look at that!' A white woman said that. She had never seen a red lining in a suit. That was very avant-garde. All this conservative stuff outside. And this red satin lining inside."

For once he would not be dreading lunchtime at the hospital that Monday.

CHICAGO, EARLY 1939
IDA MAE BRANDON GLADNEY

———

GEORGE AND IDA MAE had been in the North for close to two years. They had three little ones to feed and were still having trouble finding work. They had arrived in the depths of the Great Depression with the fewest skills any migrant could have but with the most modest of expectations and the strongest of backs. They had taken their chances and found even the most menial jobs hard to come by.

Anything with the least amount of status or job security seemed reserved for people who did not look like them and often spoke with an accent from a small eastern European country they had never heard of. They were running into the same sentiment, albeit on a humbler level, that a colored man in Philadelphia faced when he answered an ad for a position as a store clerk. "What do you suppose we'd want of a Negro?" the storekeeper asked the applicant.

George had been struggling since he arrived. He had worked on a coal truck, dug ditches for the Works Progress Administration, delivered ice to the tenements on the South Side, and been turned away from places that said they weren't hiring or just had nothing for him. He would just keep looking until he found something.

Finally, he landed a job that suited his temperament on the soup-making line at the Campbell Soup plant, a place so big there was bound to be some work for him if the people were open to hiring him, which, fortunately for him, they were. The plant was on twenty-two acres at Thirty-fifth and Western by the panhandle tracks, where they mixed several thousand tomatoes and oxtails at a time to make soup for customers west of the Mississippi. He had been working all his life, but this was the first indoor job he had ever had.

His days would now turn on the directions of foremen and the spinning of machinery, the orderly and finite ticking of the company punch clock instead of the rhythms of the field, where he and Ida Mae used to work according to what an anthropologist once called "the great clocks of the sky."

The plant turned out six thousand cans of soup a minute along three miles of tracks and switches. He was entering the world of assembly-line factory culture, the final destination of many unskilled black southerners once they got established in the North. Whatever reception he got, good or bad, he kept it to himself, as was his way, and he carried out whatever duties he was to perform without complaint, whatever kind of soup was coming down the vats in his direction.

Like so many others, he had gone from the mind-numbing sameness of picking cotton to the mind-numbing sameness of turning a lever or twisting a widget or stoking a flame for one tiny piece of a much larger thing he had no control over. He had moved to a different part of the country but was on the same rung of the ladder. It was, in some ways, not all that different from picking cotton. The raw bolls went off to some mill in Atlanta or Massachusetts to be made into something refined and unrecognizable from what he saw of it, from the poorly remunerated kernel of the thing that represented George's and other sharecroppers' contribution to the final product intended for someone far better off than he. Except now, in Chicago, he would get paid.

Just by being able to keep his job, which he would for many years, George would be spared the contentious relations at so many plants in the North, where the migrants were scorned if they were hired at all, or outright turned away. Most migrants like George were hired into either menial labor—janitors or window cleaners or assembly-line workers—or hard labor—longshoremen, coal miners, stokers of foundries and diggers of ditches, which is what he had done before landing the assembly-line job at Campbell Soup.

Many companies simply didn't hire colored workers at all but for altogether different reasons from the South. It wasn't because of an explicit Berlin Wall of exclusion, written into law and so engrained as to not need to be spelled out for people on either side, as in the South. Instead, in the North, companies and unions said that, however much they might want to hire colored people, their white workers just wouldn't stand for it. And, for the sake of morale, the companies and unions weren't going to force the issue.

A glass plant in Pittsburgh tried to hire colored workers, but the white workers ran them out, the researcher Abraham Epstein reported, by cursing them and "making conditions so unpleasant they were forced to quit." At a steel mill there, the white bargemen threatened to walk out "because black workers were introduced among them." The white workers at the mill were appeased only "by the provision of separate quarters" for the colored workers.

A factory in Chicago reported that after it hired colored workers, there was "friction in the washrooms" and that "for every colored girl employed, we lost five white girls."

"I find a great resentment among all our white people," the manager of a wholesale millinery in Chicago reported. "I couldn't overcome the prejudice enough to bring the people in the same building, and had to engage outside quarters for the blacks. . . . We thought it would be nice if we would start a school for machine operators. . . . I received a delegation from our sewing hall who said they resented the idea. They wouldn't listen to it at all, and I had to abandon the project. Their argument was: 'If you let them in it won't be long until we are out entirely.' The attitude against the colored is only the same as it was against the Slavs or the foreign races when they first intruded the field."

Somehow the migrants persisted, partly because they had little choice and could only hope that open-minded whites might see past the preconceptions. A Chicago laundry, for instance, reported that when it hired its first colored girl, "the white girls threatened to quit. The manager asked them to wait a week and, if they still objected, he would let her go." As it turned out, the white girls grew to like the colored girl, and she was permitted to stay.

Overall, however, what was becoming clear was that, north or south, wherever colored labor was introduced, a rivalrous sense of unease and insecurity washed over the working-class people who were already there, an unease that was economically not without merit but rose to near hysteria when race and xenophobia were added to preexisting fears. The reality was that Jim Crow filtered through the economy, north and south, and pressed down on poor and working-class people of all races. The southern caste system that held down the wages of colored people also undercut the earning power of the whites around them, who could not command higher pay as long as colored people were forced to accept subsistence wages.

The dynamic was not lost on northern industrialists, who hired colored workers as strikebreakers and resorted to them to keep their labor costs down just as companies at the end of the twentieth century would turn to the cheap labor of developing nations like Malaysia and Vietnam. The introduction of colored workers, who had long been poorly paid and ill treated, served as a restraint on what anyone around them could demand.

"Their presence and availability for some of the work being performed by whites, whether they are actually employed or not," wrote the sociologist Charles S. Johnson, "acts as a control on wages."

By the time George managed to find steady work, he was joining the forty percent of black men doing unskilled or semiskilled work in

Chicago in the 1940s. Another thirty-four percent of black men were working as servants, meaning that, for three out of four black men, the only work they could get was work that nobody else wanted—lowly and menial or hard, dangerous, and dirty. Nearly the inverse was true for white men, the majority of whom—some sixty percent—were doing skilled, clerical, business, or professional work, clean indoor jobs.

The ceiling was even lower and the options fewer for colored women, a situation that was making it even harder for Ida Mae to find work. By 1940, two out of every three colored women in Chicago were servants, as against seventeen percent of white women (most of those newly arrived immigrants). Only a fraction of colored women—a mere seven percent—were hired to do clerical work—common and upstanding positions for women of the day—compared to forty-three percent of white women.

Under these conditions, Ida Mae and George found themselves at the bottom looking up at the layers of immigrants, native-born white people, and even northern-born black people who were stacked above them in the economic hierarchy of the North. It was all well and good that George now had a job at Campbell Soup. But they would never be able to get settled in Chicago until Ida Mae found reliable work. So Ida set out to look whenever George wasn't at work and, the rest of the time, took care of the children.

———

By now it was winter in Chicago, and the cold was beginning to get to her. She had never felt anything like it before. It was a supernatural kind of cold that burned the tips of her fingers and hunted her down through the layers of sweaters to the half inch of skin that happened to have been left unprotected.

On the streets, there were perils at every turn. The sidewalks were glazed with ice, and she had to climb over hills of unmelted snow. She looked up and saw spears of icicles hanging from the gutters and soffits of the buildings. The icicles were as big as a human leg and pointed toward the sidewalk like swords. She heard that sometimes the icicles broke from the buildings and killed people. It was like being on a different planet.

"You spit, and it would be froze," she said.

She didn't complain about it. She just did what she had to do. She trudged through the snow to take baby Eleanor to the clinic at Forty-third and State for the immunizations the city said the baby had to have.

She wrapped Eleanor in so much swaddling you couldn't tell there was a baby inside.

At the clinic, the nurse gave her instructions.

"Mother," the nurse said, "take the baby's clothes off."

Ida Mae thought that was the craziest thing in the world, cold as it was outside. She didn't want Eleanor exposed like that.

"All that snow out there," Ida Mae said. "I ain't takin' my baby's clothes off."

"The doctor has to see her," the nurse told her.

Ida Mae balked but soon learned there was no point in protesting. This was the way they did things here on this new planet she was on.

NEW YORK, DECEMBER 1951
GEORGE SWANSON STARLING

———

NO MATTER HOW SETTLED the migrants got or how far away they ran, the South had a way of insinuating itself, reaching out across rivers and highways to pull them back when it chose. The South was a telegram away, the other end of a telephone call, a newspaper headline that others might skim over but that hurtled them back to a world they could never fully leave.

George had been in New York for six years when the South came back to haunt him. Sometime in late December 1951, he got word that something terrible had happened to an old acquaintance back in Florida.

It was someone he knew from his days as a substitute teacher at the colored school in Eustis during the lulls in the picking season. George had only a couple years of college, but it was more education than most colored people in town, which was why they called him Schoolboy with his proper-sounding talk. So George was a welcome and natural fill-in for the regular teachers when they took sick or went away.

He loved imparting whatever wisdom he had acquired in his twenty-odd years. But he soon came to realize that colored teachers were making only a fraction of what the white teachers were making in Florida.

He was always alert to any hint of injustice, and here was yet another example of the double-sided world he was living in. He would later lead a series of strikes in the groves, which would force him out of Florida for good, but before that time, while he was substitute teaching, he got pulled into a different crusade.

Harry T. Moore, a churchly schoolteacher from an old place called Mims over on the Atlantic Coast, was the NAACP's chief organizer for all of Florida back in the 1930s and 1940s. He wore out three cars crisscrossing the state in his stiff suit and tie, teaching colored people how to vote before Florida granted them the right to, investigating lynchings, and protesting segregated schools and unequal pay for colored teachers. He did much of this work as a volunteer, driving alone in the backwoods and small towns of Florida, "where no restaurant would serve him, no motel would house him, and some gas stations wouldn't let him fill his tank, empty his bladder or even use the phone," his biographer Ben Green wrote.

These were the dark early days of the civil rights movement, before it even had a name: Martin Luther King, Jr., was still in grade school, Rosa Parks was a young bride, and the NAACP was an underground organization in the South. It was still building a base there among its fearful constituents, and segregationists were viewing it as an uppity troublemaker meddling in the private affairs of the southern order of things. It took courage even to be associated with it in those days, let alone be its field secretary in one of the most violent states in the South. Between 1882 and 1930, vigilantes in Florida lynched 266 black people, more than any other state, so many, in fact, that, after white men killed a black man with a hatchet one day, a newspaper could smugly and correctly report, "It is safe to predict that nothing would be done about it." The same could be said for the hundreds of blacks driven out of town in that same era, their homes shot up and set afire in the all-black settlements of Rosewood and Ocoee. "We are in the hands of the devil," a black Floridian said.

It was here that Harry T. Moore began his quiet crusade. He wore out typewriter ribbons and worked a hand-cranked ditto machine to produce his measured entreaties to governors and legislators in cases of brutality or injustice in the courts, often facing ridicule or outright rejection. One case in particular spurred him to action. A young colored boy sent a Christmas card to a white girl, who showed the card to her father. A posse of white men captured the boy, hogtied him, and forced the boy's father to watch as they tortured the boy and drowned him in the river. The posse would later say the boy jumped into the water on his own.

Moore then stepped up his letters, circulars, and broadsides and threw himself into more dangerous terrain, the fight against lynching and police brutality. He began conducting his own one-man investigations into every lynching in Florida, interviewing the victims' families and writing to the government on their behalf.

When he wasn't working to hold officials to their oaths of duty, he was going door-to-door, town to town, trying to recruit people to join his cause. It was in this way that George Starling met Harry T. Moore.

The men were not friends. They only met once. But both he and George shared an outrage over the treatment of colored people when it came to the schools. Florida school boards, each its own little fiefdom, had a habit of shutting down the colored schools weeks or months before the school year was supposed to end, blaming the closures on budget shortfalls that for some reason did not affect class time at the white schools. It was a way for county school boards to save on both the cost of running colored schools and having to pay colored teachers for the already foreshortened school year colored schools had.

Even when the teachers got to work a full year under the colored school schedule, they were paid a salary of $542 a year, compared to $1,146 per year for white teachers in the late 1930s, forty-seven percent of what the white teachers were making. There was nothing the colored teachers or parents could do about it until Harry T. Moore, himself the principal at a grade school in Brevard County, started a petition to protest it.

George Starling met Moore sometime in the early 1940s when the civil rights worker arrived in Eustis to enlist colored teachers in the effort. Moore had been making his way around an unwelcoming state and was now seeking to make inroads in Lake County in the state's central interior. Moore wanted to start a local chapter in Eustis to build up state membership and widen support for the cause. He needed people on the ground to help him discreetly canvass the colored district of Eustis, allay people's fears, and take on the forbidding task of convincing them to join the NAACP.

Moore gathered the colored people of Eustis together at Gethsemane Baptist Church one Sunday after service. Moore, along with his wife, Harriette, laid out his plan to petition the state to raise colored teachers' pay and said he needed someone to lead the NAACP registration drive in Eustis. The principal of the colored school, a Mr. J. S. Pinckney, expressed support for the cause; after all, he was being cheated by the pay gap too. Everyone in town knew how vocal George could be, and the principal nominated him to lead the registration effort.

"I didn't want to do it," George said years later. But the principal assured him that he wouldn't be going it alone.

"I'll help you," the principal said. "We need somebody that knows how to organize people, how to approach people."

"So I let him talk me into doing it," George said years later. "And I started first working with the teachers."

Sunday evenings after church, George went door-to-door to try to persuade them in private to join the NAACP. Membership dues were a dollar. Sometimes the principal went with him. But George was having little success.

"I couldn't get one single teacher to join," he said years later. "And I was tight with most all the teachers out there."

The teachers were making all kinds of excuses and were flat-out saying they just couldn't do it. George thought something wasn't adding up. These were intelligent, reasonable people, people he had known all his life and worked with at school when he was a substitute. They were the ones who would benefit most from the changes the NAACP was seeking.

So one day, he cornered one of the teachers he was closest to and asked her what was going on.

"Look, now," he said. "Something is not right. Why is it that I can't get any teacher to join the NAACP? We all tight together, but I can't get none of y'all to sign up."

The teacher didn't want to talk about it. But George persisted.

"I'm not gonna take 'no' for no answer today," he said. "I wanna know what's happening."

So she told him.

"Well, the principal held a faculty meeting," she began, "and he told all the teachers that any teacher that joins the NAACP, he would personally see that they don't ever teach in this county no more."

The principal had given the impression to the colored people in town and to Harry Moore himself that he was all for progress and the NAACP. But he was undercutting the effort in private, knowing George's every move and every person George was talking to and in the perfect position to manipulate the results.

When George approached the principal, he discovered the nature of the contradictions and the compromising position the principal was in, not that George thought it was right. First, to George's surprise, the principal joined the NAACP for himself and his wife.

But he gave George a warning.

"Now, don't put my name on there," the principal said. "We'll pay our membership fee, but you don't have to put our names on the list."

Then George discovered the real problem. Word had gotten back to the county school board that Harry T. Moore, who was by then known and despised by white officials all over the state, was stirring up trouble among the colored teachers in Lake County. If the principal didn't get the situation under control and the NAACP out of the schools, he could lose his job or worse. The principal assured the board that he would take care of it, and he did.

"I told my teachers if they join that fight, I'll fire 'em all," the colored principal reported to white school board officials. "I said, not near one a y'all better not join the NAACP."

"Yeah, Pinckney, you a good man," a white school board official said, as the story was told among the colored people in Eustis. "You a good man."

Any teacher caught working with the NAACP could face retaliation in Florida. Firing teachers was a common tool of the authorities to undercut efforts to equalize their pay. In due course, the authorities fired NAACP leader Harry T. Moore from his principal's position and banned him from ever teaching in Florida again. Without work and with two young daughters to support, Moore struck a deal to work full-time for the NAACP, but he had to raise some of the money for his salary himself.

He did not let that stop him, and his biggest fight was only beginning. It involved the sheriff in the county where George grew up and would make national headlines.

It started on the morning of Saturday, July 16, 1949, when a seventeen-year-old white woman accused four black men of raping her and attacking her husband on an isolated road in Lake County, near the town of Groveland. A manhunt led to the arrests of three young black men, one of whom had been in police custody at the time the girl said the rape occurred, but was still considered a suspect. The authorities shot and killed a fourth suspect before he could be taken to jail.

Tensions ran so high that the 350 colored residents of Groveland had to be evacuated to Orlando, where the Red Cross, the Salvation Army, and colored and white churches put them up.

The three young men were reportedly beaten with rubber hoses while in police custody, with Lake County Sheriff Willis McCall, an imposing figure in a Stetson hat, announcing that a confession had been extracted from them. By then the case had become so emotionally charged that the court had a hard time finding a lawyer to represent the defendants. The one who finally agreed, Alex Akerman, said he "had no desire to handle the case," and said to himself, as he drove toward Lake County for the trial, that he knew this would be "the end" of his career.

The three suspects were luckier than many other black men accused of raping a white woman. They actually lived long enough to hear the jury's conviction. Two were sentenced to death. The one who had been in police custody at the time of the rape was shown mercy and sentenced to life in prison.

The trial had been so tense that the judge took it upon himself to show the defense team—Akerman and the NAACP lawyers, along with two northern reporters covering the case—the safest door from which to exit after the verdict was read. They would all have to get out of town quick. They hoped the verdict would be handed down before nightfall. It wasn't. They followed the judge's warning and headed out the side door into the Florida night after the verdict, convicting the men, was read. As they drove out of town, they could see the headlights of two unidentified cars tailing them. The NAACP lawyer floored the accelerator, barely able to keep ahead of the menacing headlights bearing down on them through hairpin country roads. The two cars hunted them into the darkness. The defense team finally made it to the county line and crossed over into another jurisdiction. Only then did the cars tailing them back away.

———

This was the world Harry T. Moore operated in and that George knew all too well.

The Groveland case, as it came to be known, roused Moore to action. He fired off letters of protest to the governor, to the FBI, to the U.S. attorney general. The pressure he and the NAACP headquarters put on the courts won the men a second trial. (The one who had been shown mercy because he had been in police custody at the time of the rape was advised to be grateful for his life sentence and not seek further redress through a second trial.)

The night before the trial was to begin, for reasons that remain unclear and known only to him, Sheriff McCall decided to move the prisoners to another jail. He handcuffed them together and drove them himself in his patrol car. At one point, he moved the two men to the front seat with him. Minutes later, he was calling for backup. He said the handcuffed men had attacked him and tried to escape. He said he had defended himself by shooting them, emptying his .38 Smith and Wesson in the process.

The shootings and the photographs of the two black men, their bodies splayed on the ground still handcuffed together, attracted national headlines and criticism of the sheriff, the governor, and the Florida legal system from all over the country. The heat ratcheted up further when it turned out that one of the two men had actually survived the shooting by pretending to be dead so the sheriff would stop shooting him.

Harry Moore began calling for an investigation of the shootings and for Sheriff McCall's ouster. Either the sheriff had shot two shackled men without cause or he had shown recklessness and lack of forethought in transporting the men alone, as Moore saw it. Moore was doing what no colored men dared to do in those days of southern apartheid: he was standing up to the most powerful man in all of Lake County. He was attracting more attention from white supremacists, who had resented him in the past but were incensed at him now. He began getting death threats and for the first time started carrying a gun with him on those lonely drives into the country.

At the same time, unbeknownst to the local whites who deplored him, Moore was losing the support of NAACP headquarters in New York, an organization Moore had worked hard for but which had its own national ambitions and was at that very moment seeking changes in the Florida operation Moore had built. Now that Florida was on the map, in civil rights terms, headquarters wanted to capitalize on the publicity of the Groveland case for its broader goals. It pushed for greater membership and for centralized county chapters rather than the small colonies Moore had nurtured in places like Eustis. Headquarters could not have known the tensions on the ground in those isolated hamlets or the fear in the people George tried to sign up in Eustis all those years ago, or recognize that country people couldn't risk being seen outside their homes at a countywide NAACP meeting that would attract life-threatening attention. Not then anyway.

Moore and the NAACP remained at odds through the fall and into Thanksgiving of 1951. At a statewide meeting in early December, national officers finally managed enough votes to oust Moore, who had virtually given his life to the cause. His very strength was his undoing that night. The chapters in the small hamlets that were so loyal to him, because they knew more than anyone the dangers he faced just getting there to see them, did not have the resources to send delegates to that meeting. Thus the meeting was dominated by the delegates from Miami, Tallahassee, Jacksonville, big-city groups that had their own politics and looked down upon the country teacher from a small town on the Mosquito Coast none of them had been to.

Now, despite his hard work, Moore was no longer the head of the Florida NAACP. But the white supremacists he had challenged all those years wouldn't have known that. To them he was still the NAACP's man on the ground and a target of their anger. Soon white men from outside his county started asking people in town where that colored NAACP fellow lived. There was a mysterious break-in at the Moores' house, which sat isolated on a country road surrounded by orange groves.

And then on Christmas night 1951, the Moores' twenty-fifth wedding anniversary, a bomb exploded under the floorboards beneath their bed as they slept. It hurled furniture into the air and crushed the bed into a crater in the earth. The force of the blast could be heard the next town over. Harry and Harriette Moore suffered grave internal injuries. Relatives rushed them to the nearest hospital, some thirty-five miles away. But, as was the common dilemma for colored patients in the South, they had to wait for the only colored doctor in town to get there to attend them. Harry T. Moore was dead by the time the colored doctor arrived. Harriette, saying she did not want to live without her husband, survived for eight days before succumbing herself.

The county, the state, and the FBI conducted a months-long investigation. It was determined that the Klan, specifically the Orlando Klavern, was behind the bombing. But as the investigation narrowed its focus, the Klansmen closed rank. At their meetings, they now began requiring everyone to recite the Klan oath of secrecy as the investigation closed in on them. The chief suspects all said they had been at a barbecue with twenty or thirty other members at the time of the attack, a convenient alibi for most anyone who would come under suspicion. Ultimately, no one was ever charged or spent a day in jail for the murder of Harry and Harriette Moore, considered by some the first casualties of the modern civil rights movement.

News of the bombing reached George up in Harlem, and he found it both shocking and half expected, knowing what he did about that land of raccoon woods and cypress swamps thick with fear and secrets.

When he spoke of Harry T. Moore, he spoke matter-of-factly, without emotion, flat and to the point. It was as if nothing in the world could surprise him. He had just about heard and seen it all.

Years later, when George was an old man, he would find God, become a deacon, and join the choir at a Baptist church in Harlem. People always said he had a beautiful voice. He was a tenor baritone. He knew all the words to just about any Baptist hymn. Whenever he stood up and sang, there he was, towering over all the sopranos and tenors, his voice rising up above the others but his eyes welling up and tears falling in droplets down the sides of his cheeks. It happened whenever he sang.

LOS ANGELES, MID- TO LATE 1950S
ROBERT JOSEPH PERSHING FOSTER

ROBERT WAS MAKING a bigger name for himself now. He was getting a reputation not just for making a show of his every arrival but for being the kind of doctor who could just look at somebody and tell that the problem was with the spleen.

The people from Monroe began taking notice. They started coming around, tentative and curious at first. Robert never knew what to expect when they showed up. Jimmy Marshall's mother had tried to make herself go and see Robert, but for the longest time she just couldn't get used to his being a doctor. She still hadn't adjusted to the idea of calling him Robert. She kept slipping and couldn't bring herself to say it.

"I can't believe little Pershing Foster is a doctor!" she once exclaimed.

He was becoming so popular that she finally went to see him. But she was appalled at what he asked of her at her first appointment. "How dare you tell me to take my clothes off!" she told Robert as he prepared for the examination.

"Bob got so tickled," Jimmy remembered. "Then, after he treated her, she had to admit, 'He's a good little doctor.'"

Robert's office was well situated on West Jefferson, a fashionable black business district closer to Beverly Hills than South Central, and he now had admitting privileges at several hospitals. He was getting to know other doctors but, oddly enough and just as important, was popular with the orderlies and charge nurses and even the people in the cafeteria, the kind of people other doctors ignored. And they started showing up at his office, too.

"My patients loved me," he said matter-of-factly years later. "They could tell me anything. They'd tell you in a minute, 'I can talk to you.'"

They waited for hours to see him. Many were people who back in Texas or Louisiana or Arkansas might have only rarely seen a physician, who were used to midwives and root doctors and home remedies they handed down and concocted for themselves. Here was a doctor who was as science-minded and proficient as any other but who didn't make fun of their down-home superstitions and knew how to comfort them and translate modern medicine into a language they could understand.

"It was twenty people deep on Saturdays," Malissa Briley, a patient of his, remembered. "They would come early, sign up, then leave, go shopping and run errands, come back three or four hours later and still have to wait."

Any number of times he'd ask, "How long you been waiting?"

"Don't even ask me," she'd say. "You know how long I been waiting."

People would complain among themselves. "They would sit up in the office and fuss and carry on about how he's never on time," Briley said. "And the very next time you go, you see the same people waiting."

And after hours of sitting and passing the time, when they finally made it into his office, he would light a cigarette and throw his feet up on his desk and ask them what was going on in their lives.

"Tell me about it," he would say.

Husbands shared suspicions about their wives. Mothers brought their children in.

"Doctor, I believe she's pregnant," a mother told Robert. "Make her tell you whose baby it is."

He loved it so much, he practically gave his life over to the worries and fixes his patients got themselves into.

"If you got sick and had a complication," he said, "I didn't leave your bed until you showed signs of improvement, if it took all night long. If you had tubes down your nose and through your stomach and intravenous going, I'd stay there and be sure that they worked. Then I'd get up and go home, shave, dress, get as sharp as I could get, and come back at visiting hours. And walk over to the bed, feel the pulse."

"Miss Brown, you feel any better?" he'd say.

"Baby, this is my doctor," the patient would tell her husband.

Sometimes the discussion was with the relative in the room.

"Hey, Doc. He's sick as he can be," a patient's relative might say.

It got to the point that it seemed people could tell when he stepped out of the elevator and onto the floor, and it reassured people and they almost started feeling better at the sight of him. This spread to the friends and relatives visiting the patient and to the people who weren't his patients, seeing him dote on someone else.

"You know some other doctor's patient," he said, "and they call me in to do the surgery or whatever it was. And then I wouldn't go back until the man is better. When I *know* he looks better. And I'm sharp, got on the latest fashions. I put the show on so you wouldn't forget. They called me 'the Jitterbug Doctor.' Think I'm kidding, don't you? Straight, straight just like it is. But the point was that they would not forget me. And others would see you in the room with them. And they would remember you outside the room. They'd get your card and call you."

Sometimes he'd hear from patients' relatives, people coming in from out of town or just new to California who were feeling under the weather and worried what it might be. Someone would hand them Robert's number with no more explanation than this: "If you just call this number, and tell him 'I'm sick,' he'll tell you what to do."

———

One of the people who called him one day was a cook from east Texas working the cafeteria line at the old hospital on Hoover Street. She had seen the jitterbug doctor, liked him, and told him she had a cousin she thought could use his help. The cook sent her cousin to see Robert for a physical and an assessment of her medical problems.

The cook's cousin was a woman named Della Beatrice Robinson. People called her Della Bea. She was a singer who had not long since migrated from Texas. Della Bea took her cousin's suggestion and made an appointment.

Della Bea was so pleased with the treatment and with the southern, down-home way about this doctor, something comforting and familiar about him, that she kept coming back. She also had another idea.

"My husband needs to come in to see you," she said after a few visits.

She said her husband would need the last appointment of the day and that his name was Ray Charles Robinson—Ray Charles to most of the world.

"So there I got Ray Charles," Robert would say years later. "The rest was up to me and Ray, and it flew."

Both men were from the South and had come to Los Angeles chasing a dream, Ray having migrated in 1950, three years before Robert. Both were more ambitious, controlling, and meticulous than the gaudy, juke-joint side of them might suggest. Both moved in highfalutin circles but were most at ease with plainspoken common folk, which is what they really were deep inside. They were both on the verge of making it big in their respective worlds. And neither could truly put behind them the hurts each had endured in the South or overcome the excesses of those fixations. The two would be friends from that day on.

With all these new patients, Robert's practice was taking off. He was now ready to move his family into a house more befitting their station. From his in-laws' perspective, it was about time. The Clements were living in the president's mansion, pretty much an estate, back at Atlanta University, and they felt their daughter and granddaughters had been holed up long enough in that walk-up apartment off Jefferson. It was enough that Robert had taken the three of them away from Atlanta and the Clements as it was. When was he ever going to make good on his potential, all his talk, and give Alice and the girls the luxuries to which the Clements had made them accustomed? It had been eighteen months already.

Robert found a way out. He located a house on an exclusive block of Georgians and avant-garde contemporaries with putting-green lawns and bougainvillea draping the sides of vanilla stucco walls. The block was in a neighborhood known as West Adams, just south of Pico, a few minutes' drive from Wilshire, and on the western side of Crenshaw. It already had a few colored people living there—the fights over restrictive covenants had occurred a decade before, so he wouldn't have to make a political statement just to move into a house, which, apolitical as he was, would not have interested him. He chose not to try to integrate a new neighborhood, although, by then, he could have afforded most any he wanted. Two court rulings—*Shelley v.* and *Barrows v.*—had struck down restrictive covenants by the time he arrived, but whites were still resisting black incursions into the strongholds of Glendale, Canoga Park, Hawthorne, South Gate, and through most of the San Fernando Valley. There was a bombing near Culver City and cross burning in Leimert Park.

Some neighborhood groups went so far as to buy up properties themselves, "even at a financial loss, to prevent blacks from moving in," wrote the historian Josh Sides.

But the San Fernando Valley suburb of Pacoima got especially creative when a black government worker named Emory Holmes moved in with his family in 1959. The neighbors put their heads together and decided to make calls to every business in town posing as Holmes or his wife. The first week in the neighborhood, the Holmeses were flooded at odd times of the day with visits from "a life insurance sales representative, a milk delivery service, a drinking water company, three repair services, several taxis, an undertaker, a *Los Angeles Times* newspaper carrier, a veterinarian, a sink repair service, a termite exterminator, a pool installer," Sides wrote. Finally, the neighbors threw rocks through their windows and spray-painted their garage: BLACK CANCER IS HERE. DON'T LET IT SPREAD!

Robert wasn't going to put himself through that. He found a safe place that suited him. Not only were black people there already, but they were among the finest and most socially connected in all of old Los Angeles. The house was a white Spanish Revival at 1680 Victoria Avenue, right next door to the most prominent colored architect in Los Angeles and maybe the country, Paul Williams. The street had physicians and dentists and socialites on it, people who regularly made the society pages of *The Los Angeles Sentinel*.

The family moved in on Palm Sunday 1956, three years after Robert's lonely drive through the desert. The girls each chose a room. The sofas and cocktail tables and dining room suite arrived. Now Alice could finally join the Links and host her bridge parties and socials, and they could all take up their rightful place, wherever it might lead them, in this bright new city of theirs. In the meantime, shortly before moving into their new home, Robert and Alice got a welcome surprise: a third daughter arrived in December 1955. They named her Joy.

COMPLICATIONS

What on earth was it, I mused,
bending my head to the wind,
that made us leave
the warm, mild weather of home
for all this cold,
and never to return,
if not for something worth hoping for?
— RALPH ELLISON, *Invisible Man*

CHICAGO, 1939–1940
IDA MAE BRANDON GLADNEY

———

THINGS HAD GROWN DESPERATE, and, although she had three little ones at home, Ida Mae had to find some kind of work if they were to survive another year. The options for colored women fresh from the field were limited up north—mainly, to cleaning white people's homes, doing laundry, or working a factory line, if the factory was short of men or of white women. For Ida Mae, domestic work was the likeliest option for now.

It was still the Depression, and it seemed as if the North just didn't know what to do with colored women who were still learning the ways of the cities. Even in the best of times, many industries, while accepting black men for their strong backs, and then only in limited numbers, refused to hire black women, seeing no need to have them around. Throughout the North and West, black women migrants were having the hardest time finding work of all the people pouring into the big cities, harder than Polish and Serbian immigrants to Chicago, harder than Italian and Jewish immigrants to New York, harder than Mexican and Chinese immigrants of either gender in California. They were literally at the bottom of the economic hierarchy of the urban North, the least connected by race and gender to the power brokers in their adopted lands and having to stand in line to hire out scrubbing floors when times got hard during the Depression years.

Some employers started requiring them to have college degrees, which neither they nor the vast majority of other unskilled laborers could have been expected to have. Some demanded that black women take voice tests to weed out those from the South, tests that Mississippians just up from the plantation would have been all but assured of failing. Even those lucky enough to land in a training course for assembly-line work found that they were often shunted to "positions in either the cafeteria or bathrooms."

Entire companies and classes of work were closed off to them without apology. A few years after Ida Mae arrived, a plant in Ohio, for instance, sent out a call for five hundred women, specifying that they be white. The plant had to alter its age limits, lower its requirements, and go to neighboring states like Illinois to get enough white women, who were more likely than colored women to be able to stay at home with their children. Even when it was unable to fill its quota, the plant still refused to hire colored women.

Thus colored women were left to fight for even the most menial of jobs, facing intense competition from the Irish, German, and Scandinavian servant girls preferred by some of the wealthier white families.

There emerged several classes of domestics. Those on the lowest rung resorted to "slave markets" where colored women gathered on street corners from as early as six in the morning and waited for white housewives from the Bronx and Brooklyn in New York or from Hyde Park or Pill Hill in Chicago to bid on them for as little as fifteen cents an hour.

Twenty-five such markets were active in New York City alone by 1940. One was by a five-and-dime at 167th and Gerard near the Grand Concourse in the Bronx, where the lowliest women from Harlem sat on crates waiting to be picked. Another was a few blocks north at 170th and Walton, the waiting women a little better clothed and slightly less desperate, knowing that the Bronx housewives had to pass them first before getting to the market at Gerard. In Chicago, there was a crowded market at Twelfth and Halsted, where colored women jockeyed over the white housewives who were looking them over, the whole enterprise having the effect of bidding down the colored domestics' wages. One woman at the Chicago slave market reported making fifty cents a day, what she would have made picking cotton in the field.

If she were desperate enough, a colored woman needing work would just show up in a white neighborhood, the wealthier the better, and simply walk down the street. "Someone would invariably call out the window," wrote the sociologist Barbara Clegg Gray, and hire the woman on the spot to clean the toilets or scrub the floors or whatever the white housewife discovered she needed for maybe a dollar or two.

In Los Angeles, due to the "great horde of jobless domestics, white families in one of the wealthiest cities in the country could hire colored domestics for as little as five dollars a week" in the 1930s. For that sum, families got someone who would work ten or twelve hours a day doing anything from washing dishes and clothes to cooking and scrubbing floors for not much more than she could have made picking cotton back in Texas.

One colored woman in Los Angeles said she thought getting her high school diploma would make a difference. She kept trying to find different work. Jobs on assembly lines, running elevators, clerking in stores, filing in offices, were typical jobs open to unskilled women in those days. "But everywhere I went," she said, "they wanted to keep me working as a domestic."

The randomness of this kind of work, hiring oneself out to total strangers with no standards in duties or wages, opened domestics to all kinds of exploitation for very little pay. They could never know for sure what they would be asked to do, how long they would be expected to do it, or if they would be paid what was promised.

It seemed everyone was trying to wring the most out of whatever they had, some white housewives even turning back the hands of the clock to keep from paying a domestic for all the hours she actually worked. Older domestics took to forewarning the new ones to take their own clock to work with them and to prepare for any indignity. One housewife ordered a domestic to eat her lunch out of the pet's bowl, not wanting the help to eat from the same dishes as the family.

In many cases, the housewives were neither accustomed to hired help nor familiar with colored people, harboring assumptions and prejudices of the day due to lack of exposure. The housewives and their domestics brought differing expectations, and frequently each side felt somehow aggrieved. While an employer could go out and hire someone else, some employees, having no legal recourse, took their frustrations out on their madames' homes when not paid or otherwise exploited, slashing the draperies they had just ironed or defacing the floors they had scrubbed.

Aside from these sources of friction, colored domestics could not know what perils they might face from opportunistic sons or husbands assuming that younger domestics would do more than just clean. As it was, the very act of walking the streets for work came awfully close in appearance to how prostitutes plied their trade—except that the domestics were working at the whim of Janes instead of Johns.

The expectation that any colored woman walking in the white section of town was available to scrub floors and wash windows would continue into the 1960s, such that a colored professional woman appearing in a white neighborhood in the North had to be prepared to be called out to just because she was black. "Say, girl," a woman called out to my mother in the late 1950s when she was on her way, in her tailored suit and heels, to decorate and fit slip covers in Cleveland Park, a wealthy neighborhood in Washington, D.C. "Could you come up here and clean my bathroom?"

"I'm looking for someone to clean mine," my mother yelled back to the woman.

Ida Mae's husband would not have stood for his wife to walk the streets for work, and in any case, Chicago had grown so segregated that the wealthy white neighborhoods were far from where they lived. But one day Ida Mae got word of a job from someone she knew from back home in Mississippi, and that felt a little safer.

A girl who was doing day's work for a well-to-do couple on the North Side needed someone to fill in for her. It would be temporary, Ida Mae's friend told her, but would have to do for now.

"Miss Gladney will work in your place," Ida Mae's friend told the girl.

The job was more than an hour away on the streetcar, farther north of the Loop than she lived south, almost up near Evanston. The regular girl who mopped floors and folded laundry for the family would be away for a week. The job was paying something like four or five dollars a day. Ida Mae didn't hesitate.

"I was glad to take her place," she would say years later.

She dressed for the job and took a change of clothes with her. It turned out to be a man and his wife living in a grand apartment above a shoe store the wife ran.

Ida Mae took the elevator up and went into a glorious apartment, where she found the husband alone in the couple's bedroom. He was still asleep, which seemed odd to Ida Mae, so she began looking for things to do. The husband roused himself and told Ida Mae what he expected of her.

"Get in the bed with me," he said.

He told her the regular girl stayed in bed with him all day long. He reassured Ida Mae not to worry, he'd do the cleaning later. He figured that was a fair exchange and good deal for her, a cleaning girl not having to clean at all and still getting paid for it.

Ida Mae was in her midtwenties, a mother of three by then, married to a pious man who wouldn't stand for another man touching his wife. She knew white men in the South took whatever liberties they wanted with colored women, and there was nothing the women or their husbands could do about it. All her life in Mississippi, she had managed to avoid unwanted advances because she had rarely worked in white people's homes. Now here she was in Chicago, a white man expecting her to sleep with him as if that were what any colored woman would just naturally want to do. And no matter what happened, she would have no legal recourse. There would be no witnesses. It just would be a privileged man's word against hers.

She was thinking fast. She was as mad at the girl who sent her without warning her of what the job really entailed as she was at the man expecting her to climb into bed with him with his wife just a floor below. She started to leave. But she had come all this way, had spent the train fare, and she needed the money.

Her body stiffened, and she backed away from the man.

"Just show me what you want cleaned," Ida Mae said.

Somehow, something in the way she stood or looked straight at him as she said it let the man know she meant business. He didn't press the matter. He left her alone.

"He didn't say no more 'cause he seen I wasn't that type of person," Ida Mae said years later.

And perhaps in that moment Ida Mae discovered one difference between the North and South. She would not likely have gotten out of it in Mississippi. Her refusal would have been seen as impudence, all but assuring an assault. And there would have been nothing done about it. Here, the northern man seemed to view such a conquest as a hoped-for fringe benefit rather than a right. That, along with Ida Mae's indignation over the whole thing, appeared to keep her safe.

That day, she cleaned the bathroom, the kitchen, the bedroom, and changed the linens as she had gone there to do. The man stayed in his room. She never went back.

She missed out on the rest of the week's pay, which she desperately needed. Later, she confronted the regular girl who worked for the couple.

"So you don't do nothin' but stay in the bed all day, huh?" Ida Mae said. "Don't ask me to go back up there again."

The girl paid Ida Mae out of the money she was making off the couple. The whole sordid affair stayed with Ida Mae for years. She couldn't see how the girl could live with herself.

"I just don't know," Ida Mae would say years later. "Supposing the wife came back home? I just couldn't see how she did it."

———

With five mouths to feed, the family couldn't go much longer unless Ida Mae found a job. In the fall of 1939, something finally opened up at Inland Steel, over at Sixty-third and Melvina, on the city's southwest side. George had a brother working there. At this point, Ida Mae didn't much care what it was as long as it wasn't day's work cleaning toilets and fighting off the madame's husband.

It was her first real job in Chicago. They called her a press operator. She was in the canning department, where her job was to work the presser that attached the curved tops that cover cans as they came down the assembly line. She had to fit the tops on, her arms going up and down and up and down, over and over and over again.

She was excited at first but then found it to be a nerve-jangling endeavor. The factory was loud, the noise a little like being inside a car engine. The mechanical arms that she operated were sharp and heavy and were known to slice off people's fingers and hands.

She was on the line one day when another worker, a colored woman, got some of her fingers cut off. Ida Mae was a couple of machines down from her.

There wasn't much of a commotion, as Ida Mae remembered it.

"They stopped everybody for a while," she said. "Then they went out with her so fast. And she never did come back."

Ida Mae quit soon after that. A line job turned up at Campbell Soup, where George was working. It wouldn't last long either, after a woman stole her coat that winter. She got a job at a printing press, and it looked to be a good one. But in time she would get a job at a hospital, Walther

Memorial on the West Side of Chicago, working as a hospital aide. She sterilized instruments, cheered up patients, which was her specialty, and organized the gauzes, bandages, and intravenous lines in central supply.

It took her a while to learn how everything worked and how to get the little scissors and scalpels cleaned just so.

"I wash tray by tray and put the instruments back in there till I learned it," Ida Mae said. "And I learned all them instruments. Some of them I couldn't call the name, but you better believe I know where they went."

Sometimes she would poke her head in during surgery when she dropped off a tray of instruments she had sterilized. She liked to see the babies come into the world, and the doctors let her stay sometimes.

She had been through it four times herself and still marveled at the sight and sound of a new life making its entrance. "They always come out hollering," she said. Just like her babies had.

"You know, that's amazing, ain't it?" she said.

With Ida Mae working, the family could move out of the one-room apartment at Twenty-first and State and into a flat big enough for everyone. In the coming years, they would live all over the black belt.

———

Now that they were getting situated, people from back home in Mississippi started to make their way north to stay or to visit and see what it was like.

Saint, who had helped them move their things from Edd Pearson's plantation and get out of Mississippi, came up with his wife, Catherine, and their children, and stayed for good. Ida Mae's brother-in-law Aubrey, her younger sister Talma's husband, came up for a while to see if he would like it, but he didn't and moved back to Mississippi, where the people tipped their hat to you as they passed and looked up to him because of his family's long years in the South, where he had made peace and found a way to get along with the white people and benefit from it. Joe Lee, whose flogging was the reason George and Ida Mae had left, even came up and lived there for a while. But he was never quite right after all he had been through. He never married and did not make out very well or live too long, and nobody cared to talk about him very much.

One time, George's brother Winston, whom everyone called Win, came up from the plantation just for a visit and wasn't ashamed to look up at the tall buildings reaching for the sky.

George took him around the first day, and at the end of it they settled in for the night. Win got ready for bed and then started calling for his brother.

"Come help me," Win said. "I can't blow this light out."

George found him standing by the bulb. Win had been blowing on the bulb until he was almost out of breath.

"Win, you can't blow it out, you got to turn it off," George told him, reaching for the light switch and shaking his head. It hadn't been that long ago that he, too, had been callow to the New World.

"George showed him how to cut it off," Ida Mae said, "and we never had no more trouble with him."

They were becoming Chicagoans now. They would talk about Win and that lightbulb for years.

———

It was only a matter of time before just about every colored family in the North, unsettled though they might have been, got visitors as George and Ida Mae did. There was a back-and-forth of people, anxious, giddy, wanting to come north and see what all the fuss was about. And whenever a colored guest paid a visit while the Migration was on, and even decades later, he or she could be assured of finding the same southern peasant food, the same turnip greens, ham hocks, corn bread in Chicago as in Mississippi.

But the visitors were a curiosity to the children of the North. The uncles and cousins from the South often had a slow-talking, sweetly alien, wide-openness about them that could both enchant and startle some of the more reserved nieces and nephews who barely knew them, as was the case with a character from Mississippi visiting relatives in Pittsburgh in August Wilson's *The Piano Lesson* in the following exchange:

BOY WILLIE: *How you doing, sugar?*
MARETHA: *Fine.*
BOY WILLIE: *You was just a little old thing last time I seen you. You remember me, don't you? This your Uncle Boy Willie from down South. That there's Lymon. He my friend. We come up here to sell watermelons. You like watermelons?*
(MARETHA *nods.*)
We got a whole truckload out front. You can have as many as you want. What you been doing?
MARETHA: *Nothing.*

BOY WILLIE: *Don't be shy now. Look at you getting all big. How old is you?*

MARETHA: *Eleven. I'm gonna be twelve soon.*

BOY WILLIE: *You like it up here? You like the North?*

MARETHA: *It's alright.*

BOY WILLIE: *That there's Lymon. Did you say hi to Lymon?*

MARETHA: *Hi.*

LYMON: *How you doing? You look just like your mama. I remember you when you was wearing diapers.*

BOY WILLIE: *You gonna come down South and see me? Uncle boy Willie gonna get him a farm. Gonna get a great big old farm. Come down there and I'll teach you how to ride a mule. Teach you how to kill a chicken, too.*

NEW YORK, 1950S
GEORGE SWANSON STARLING

———

GEORGE WAS JUST BACK ONE EVENING from a forty-eight-hour turnaround from New York to Florida and to New York again and had gotten his check and cashed it. Rather than head straight home to Inez, he thought he'd stop and get a drink at a bar near Penn Station.

He was with another colored railroad attendant, chugging his beer as the bar filled up. He and his co-worker barely noticed that everyone else at the bar happened to be white as they regaled each other with stories from riding the rails. When it was time to go, they paid their tab and put their glasses down.

The bartender had said very little to them the whole time they were there. Now the bartender calmly picked up their glasses, and instead of loading them into a tray to be washed, he took them and smashed them under the counter. The sound of glass breaking on concrete startled George and his co-worker, even though this wasn't the first time this had happened to them, just not at this bar, and it attracted the attention of other patrons.

"They do it right in front of us," George said. "That's the way they let us know they didn't want us in there. As fast as you drink out of a glass and set it down, they break it."

There were no colored or white signs in New York. That was the unnerving and tricky part of making your way through a place that looked free. You never knew when perfect strangers would remind you that, as far as they were concerned, you weren't equal and might never be. It was just the prerogative of whoever happened to be in a position to keep you from getting what the law said you had a right to, because nobody was going to enforce it anyway.

And so the glass he drank from went crashing under a counter in Manhattan.

———

It was hitting George in all directions. At sudden and unexpected times like these in New York, in crude and predictable ways when he went back south for his job, and now on the train itself. He was a stickler for rules and regulations and businesslike comportment even if it was only for lifting and loading bags. He was in uniform and was representing not just the railroad but himself and colored people, and he took the job of attending to his passengers seriously.

His formal bearing did not sit well with some of the southern conductors he worked for, who considered him acting above his station, which to his mind he was. He still saw himself as the college boy, someone who read the newspapers, kept up with world affairs, and knew as much as most anyone he was serving. The white southerners he worked with didn't like it any more than the grove foremen did.

"They kept me at a hardship," George said.

Somehow, without trying, he managed to get on the bad side of a southern conductor out of Tampa.

The conductor liked to tease and joke with the colored attendants, one in particular. The conductor would nudge and kick the colored attendant, and the colored attendant, knowing his place, would jump and laugh and, to George's mind, put on a show for the conductor.

"Hah, hah, don't do that, Cap!" the colored attendant would josh the conductor in mock protest.

George stood stone-faced and made no attempt to hide his disdain.

Now the conductor began making extra demands on them all. He liked to make the rail attendants wipe the railcar steps while the train was moving. He got a kick out of that.

He wanted the attendants to drop the traps of the bottom step and wipe the steps down so he wouldn't get dirt on him when he got off to direct passengers at the station. Usually, it was something the attendants did once the train had stopped. The conductor didn't want that. He liked to see them bending over, dangling along the side, and struggling to wipe the bottom step while the train was running twenty-five, thirty miles an hour.

George resisted wiping the steps until he thought it was safe. The other car attendant did as the conductor ordered. George stood to the side, his face pinched and frowning, as his co-worker tried to hold on and clean the step with the train rocking toward the station and the conductor chortling at the sight of it.

One day the conductor confronted George.

"What's the matter with you, boy? You can't laugh?"

"Yes, sir, I have a good sense of humor," George said. "But I don't see anything funny about what y'all are doing."

The conductor began singling out George from that day on, blocking him in the aisles, jabbing him as he passed. There was little George could do about it and still keep his job. George had been through worse things in the South and figured it was just one more thing he would have to watch out for.

But it got to the point that, when George saw him coming down the aisle to check tickets, he had to step between the seats to avoid a confrontation.

"He got to the place when he get along about where I was," George said, "and he would step out of the aisle in between the seats and step on my foot, like that. And then he'll walk back and look at me."

George thought to himself, *I don't know how I'm a deal with this 'cause he gonna do this one day and I'm a try to kill him.*

"I was praying that I never had to reach that point," he said.

One afternoon, they were pulling out of Clearwater on the Silver Star, a sleek, steel-encased all-reserve train that was the pride of the Seaboard Air Line Railroad. It went up the west coast of Florida along the Gulf of Mexico en route to New York. It had only the finest and highest-class people on it, as George remembered, and he had worked his way up to that route.

As the train gained speed as it headed out of the station, George was helping an elderly white lady with her two bags. He had gotten one bag into the rack overhead and was heaving the second bag over the edge of the compartment.

"And just as I went up with the next bag and set it up in the rack," George said, "something hit me from behind like a truck. *Boom!*"

The conductor, a sturdy and heavyset man, had knocked into George as George tried to steady himself on the moving train while holding the bag overhead. George's knees were bad from all the basketball he had played in high school, and, standing on the train rocking as it was, he was off balance and had nothing to hold on to.

"He come up from behind me like a football player blocking the line," George said.

The conductor shoved George into the seat where the passenger was. George managed to drop the bag onto the rack and not onto the elderly white passenger. But the force of the conductor's weight knocked George over onto the lady, a precarious situation for a colored man in the South.

The train rumbled from side to side as George stood and tried to straighten himself. He suspected he knew what had happened but looked around anyway and saw the conductor in the aisle grinning. This feud was escalating to a point that was getting dangerous for George. If the passenger were hurt or frightened by a colored man sprawled over her as he was, George would be the one to take the fall for it, and the conductor knew it. If the passenger grew hysterical and accused George of attacking her, there would be nothing George could do, and far worse could happen to him.

But it was a fortunate thing for George that the white woman saw that he had been pushed and did not let it rattle her.

"Well, what's wrong with him?" she asked George.

"Miss, you know what he was trying to do?"

She shook her head no.

"He was trying to make me drop that bag on your head. He's just that mean, and he just don't like nobody. He did that to try to make me drop that bag on your head."

"What is wrong with him?"

George started telling his story about how the conductor had been harassing him all this time, and now the conductor had pushed him and didn't even seem to care about the passengers' safety, and she listened because she had seen it for herself.

"Well, something needs to be done about that."

"Yes, ma'am. But they just don't pay me no attention if I try to do anything about it."

He paused. "But you could do something about it."

"Well, who do I write?"

"You just write it, and I'll send it," he said, not wanting to risk her forgetting about it or just not getting around to it. "You write it, and give it to me."

And so the woman wrote up her complaint and gave the letter to George. He, in turn, attached a letter of his own and sent it to the superintendent in Jacksonville, Florida, who was over that route at that time.

George never heard from the superintendent's office about the harassment he had endured.

"But when they saw her letter, they immediately went into action," he said.

The office called the conductor in to question him about the white woman's complaint and suspended him for sixty days. It wasn't long before the conductor found out that it was George who had had a hand in the suspension, and, of course, that did not sit well with him.

George only heard the outcome from other attendants and never got a response himself. Still, it could be said that he had emerged victorious. And that only created more trouble for him. He had expected as much and had prepared for it. When he dropped off the woman's letter, he decided to do it on the way north, so that by the time it got into the superintendent's hands, George would be well out of Florida and out of the conductor's orbit.

Back in New York, he went straight to the railroad office to get a route change.

"Look, I'm not going back to the west coast anymore," George told the dispatcher. "I had an incident down there with a conductor. I know it's gonna be rough. And I'm not going back down there."

George proposed switching with another attendant who had always wanted the coveted all-reserve train to Tampa–St. Petersburg but didn't have George's seniority. George was willing to take a less desirable route to avoid any more trouble.

"No, you can't do that," the dispatcher told him.

"Look, I just told you I had an incident down there. I'm not going back down there 'cause I know what they're contemplating. I'm not going back."

"Well, I don't know what to tell you. You can't change."

George decided to call the other attendant himself.

"Look, you been raving you wanna run to St. Petersburg. I tell you what, when we come out Saturday, you set up in my car in the west coast and I'll set up in your car going to Miami. We'll just switch. You can go to St. Pete, and I'll take your run to Miami."

The attendant took George's old route, was happy to take it, and, when George's stand-in got to Tampa, a group of white men met him at the train.

"Yeah, which one of you boys is that nigger boy called Starling? You George Starling?"

"No, sir, I ain't no George Starling."

"Why, by God, where is he?"

"Well, he's not on here."

"Well, by God, we gonna find him. He done got Captain Wills put in the street for sixty days, and we gonna teach him a lesson."

When the car attendant who traded routes with George got back from that first run to Tampa, he went to George and told him what had happened.

"Boy," he said, "I don't know what you did down there, but they mad with you down there. Don't you go back down there."

"Why you think I switched with you?" George asked. "You tell them, don't worry, I'm not coming back down there no time soon."

George didn't go back to Tampa for five years. New conductors and managers came in, and it was only then that George felt it safe to go back.

LOS ANGELES, 1961
ROBERT JOSEPH PERSHING FOSTER

IT WAS WELL INTO THE NIGHT of March 20, 1961, when the telephone rang at the Foster house on Victoria, and Robert took the call. A nearly hysterical voice was coming at him, and Robert tried to make out the facts tumbling out from the other end of the line. It was the wife of a man who had somehow stumbled and sliced his left hand on the edge of a glass table, severing an artery. The man was hemorrhaging and losing consciousness. The man would need to be seen right away.

Robert would drop everything for any of his patients and had done so countless times, to the detriment of his own family. But this injury got his attention more than most. It was a disoriented Ray Charles, who was facing the loss of the use of his left hand, a disaster for the piano-playing singer, or, with all the bleeding he sustained, the loss of more than that.

The circumstances of the fall were unclear and only made the situation more delicate. For several days, Ray had been under pressure to write a playbook of songs for a big tour coming up. He had put in long hours, dictating the music in his head to a collaborator writing the songs down on paper. He had been up most of the previous night, had worked all day and into a second night. He was finding it hard to stay alert, and he was running out of time. He had turned to drugs before and so now summoned his heroin dealer to help him get through the night, according to his biographer Michael Lydon.

After the dealer's last visit to Ray's house near Baldwin Hills, Ray went thrashing about alone in his den, knocking into walls and furniture, out of his mind. Ray would later say the episode had less to do with drugs than fatigue, although he was candid about his drug use. "I didn't see how the dope was hurting," he said in his 1978 autobiography, *Brother Ray.* "I don't mean I wasn't sick now and then in those years, 'cause I was. I'd hit a dry period and go through the same convulsions as any other junkie."

As for the events leading up to that night, he said, "I'm sure that sometime during that day—like all days—I had my little fix and maybe it was stronger than usual."

That night, as he remembered it, he collapsed from exhaustion and "somehow, in my state of unconsciousness, I slammed my hand against a glass table top and sliced it to ribbons." His hand went numb. He was so high, exhausted, or just out of it, the injury didn't register with him. And he just lay there, "bleeding like a hog."

It was around that time that his son, Ray, Jr., ventured into the den. Little Ray was six years old and wanted to say good night to his father. The boy opened the door to his father's den and found him with his shirt covered in blood and blood on the walls.

Ray's writing partner and his drummer rushed in to help him. They wrapped his hand in beach towels, soaking up two quarts' worth of blood, and tried to get him walking to keep him from losing consciousness.

They chose not to call an ambulance under the circumstances. His wife, Della Bea, then eight months pregnant, instead called Robert, who told them to meet him at his clinic at once. Ray arrived at Robert's office on West Jefferson Avenue bleeding so heavily that he went into convulsions. Robert quickly sewed the wound and admitted Ray into the hospital, where Ray required a transfusion of four pints of blood.

There Robert examined Ray more closely and discovered that Ray had not only sliced an artery but severed a tendon as well. Robert would have to perform emergency surgery to reconnect the tendon if Ray was to regain use of his hand. After the surgery, Robert told Ray he was not to use the hand for six weeks.

"Naturally, I refused," Ray said years later. His big tour was starting the next week, so he told Robert he would just play with one hand. A publicist had already devised an explanation for the public. They would say he had slipped in the bathtub.

Robert could not have been pleased with Ray's insistence but knew him well enough not to be surprised. With Ray determined to go on tour against doctor's orders, Robert insisted on going along with him to attend to the wound should anything happen to it, which, naturally, it did.

Robert put a cast on the hand to protect it, but that only seemed to attract attention and endanger it more. "Everyone I met couldn't resist touching it or shaking it," Ray recalled. "The hand did get infected, but Bob was there to keep me straight."

The tour was a dream of Ray's from back when he had gotten his start in those Jim Crow towns in Florida, where he could just see himself leading a big band like Duke Ellington's—with trombones, trumpets, saxophones, guitars, him on piano, of course, and the Raelettes, his doo-wopping backup singers in their form-fitting sequins and stilettos.

Robert traveled with them to St. Louis, checking on his most famous patient's most precious instrument and loving his front-row seat to smoke-filled celebrity. The tour continued on to Detroit, where Ray struck up his orchestra and somebody decided to bring a blind teenager onto the stage. It was said that the teenager had been signed up by a new outfit called Motown and could sing and play the harmonica. It was Stevie Wonder, "Little Stevie," as he was known back then, who, not surprisingly, idolized Ray Charles and got the chance to play a few songs with him that spring night in Detroit.

———

Ray's hard-driving life of drugs and women was beginning to catch up with him—he would end up arrested for drug possession in Boston and would end up fathering a total of twelve children, only three of them by his wife, Della Bea, who divorced him in 1977.

But it occurred to him as he was writing his biography that he did not want to leave the wrong impression about his physician, a man he described as "one of the dearest people I've ever known."

He said: "I must say something about Bob, though, before anyone gets the wrong idea. Although he was my personal friend, and although he traveled with me for about ten days during the time my hand was in the cast, I never let him do anything illegal for me. I liked him too well for that. If you really love a person, you won't get him involved in something which might hurt him."

The hand began to heal, and after a week and a half on the road, Robert felt it safe to return to Los Angeles and to his practice. "He sewed up my hand so smoothly that you can barely detect the cuts today," Ray said years later. "He's the man who got me through the crisis with my hand, and for a piano player, that's some serious business."

It was time for Robert to leave the tour for another reason. Not only did he have a life and practice back in Los Angeles, he had another patient to attend to. Ray's wife, Della Bea, was expecting her third child and wanted Robert to deliver her baby. She had had a difficult delivery with her first son before she had heard of Robert Foster and had now come to rely on him.

The baby was born in May of 1961. It was a boy. After all that had happened in the preceding month and the time spent tending them before that, the couple decided to name the new baby Robert.

THE NORTH, 1915–1975

FROM THE VERY BEGINNING, scholars would debate the effects of the Migration, whether it was a success or a failure, whether the people who left had done better by leaving or would have been better off staying, whether the poorest among them merely imported the disorganized family systems inherited from slavery and carried into sharecropping or whether the anonymous, overpacked cities merely brought out the worst in the weaker souls. Usually these were macroeconomic, sociological questions as to the effect of the North or South on the people who left or stayed.

But back when the Migration first began, the venerable Chicago

Commission on Race Relations, convened after World War I, chose to ask the migrants themselves about their perceptions of how they were faring in the North. These were a few of their responses:

Do you feel greater freedom and independence in Chicago? In what ways?

- *Yes. Feel free to do anything I please. Not dictated to by white people.*
- *Yes. Can vote; no lynching; no fear of mobs; can express my opinion and defend myself.*
- *Yes. Feel more like a man. Same as slavery, in a way, at home. I don't have to give up the sidewalk here for white people.*
- *Sure. Feel more freedom. Was not counted in the South; colored people allowed no freedom at all in the South.*

What were your first impressions of Chicago?

- *When I got here and got on the street car and saw colored people sitting by white people all over the car I just held my breath, for I thought any minute they would start something. Then I saw nobody noticed it, and I just thought this was a real place for colored people.*
- *Was completely lost, friend was to meet me but didn't and I was afraid to ask anyone where to go; finally my friend came; was afraid to sleep first night—so much noise; thought the cars would finally stop running so I could rest.*
- *Always liked Chicago, even the name before I came.*
- *Didn't like it; lonesome, until I went out.*
- *Liked Chicago from the first visit made two years ago; was not satisfied until I was able to get back.*

In what respects is life harder or easier here than in the South?

- *Easier, you can make more money and it means more to you.*
- *Find it easier to live because I have more to live on.*
- *Earn more money; the strain is not so great wondering from day to day how to make a little money do.*
- *Harder because of increased cost of living.*

WHAT DO YOU LIKE ABOUT THE NORTH?
- *Freedom and opportunity to acquire something.*
- *Freedom allowed in every way.*
- *Freedom of speech, right to live and work as others. Higher pay for labor.*
- *Freedom; privileges; treatment of whites; ability to live in peace; not held down.*
- *Freedom of speech and action. Can live without fear, no Jim Crow.*
- *The schools for the children, the better wages, and the privileges for colored people.*
- *The people, the freedom and liberty colored people enjoy here that they never before experienced.*

WHAT DIFFICULTIES DO YOU THINK A PERSON FROM THE SOUTH MEETS IN COMING TO CHICAGO?
- *Getting accustomed to cold weather and flats.*
- *Rooming and "closeness" of the houses.*
- *Growing accustomed to being treated like people.*
- *Getting used to the ways of the people; not speaking or being friendly; colder weather, hard on people from the South.*
- *I know of no difficulties.*

ARE YOU ADVISING FRIENDS TO COME TO CHICAGO?
- *Yes. People down there don't really believe the things we write back; I didn't believe myself until I got here.*
- *No. I am not going to encourage them to come, for they might not make it, then I would be blamed.*
- *Wish all the colored folks would come up here where you ain't afraid to breathe.*

THE RIVER KEEPS RUNNING

*"Why do they come?" I asked a Negro minister in Philadelphia.
"Well, they're treated more like men up here in the North," he said,
"that's the secret of it. There's prejudice here, too, but the colour line
isn't drawn in their faces at every turn as it is in the South.
It all gets back to a question of manhood."*
— RAY STANNARD BAKER, *Following the Color Line*

"Every train, every bus, they were coming."
— MANLEY THOMAS, *a migrant from Tennessee to Milwaukee*

WHITFIELD, MISSISSIPPI, FEBRUARY 7, 1958
IDA MAE BRANDON GLADNEY

IT WOULD BECOME LEGEND in Chicago among the migrants and their
children, the lengths to which some colored people would go to get out
of the South. The Great Migration was now into its fourth decade. People who were children when it began were well into middle age. And
back in Mississippi, people were still trying to escape. Ida Mae would
hear about these people and pray for them.

One of the most desperate souls was a perfectly well man named Arrington High, who had been consigned to the Mississippi State Hospital
for the Insane for protesting the southern order of things. The hospital
and its hundred or so outbuildings, originally called the Mississippi Lu-
natic Asylum, took up some three thousand isolated acres in the pine
woods southeast of Jackson, near Terrapin Skin Creek, in a place called

Whitfield, some 170 miles from where Ida Mae was born. From the time it opened in 1935, anyone saying, "They took him to Whitfield," meant nobody ever expected to see the person again.

What got Arrington High in trouble was a weekly newsletter he published that argued for integration. He had been editor of a two-page mimeographed broadside, the *Eagle Eye,* for some fourteen years and had made a name for himself protesting the treatment of colored people in central Mississippi. What got him declared insane, however, was exposing the segregationists who were consorting with prostitutes at a colored brothel that catered only to white politicians. It was a death wish of a crusade that actually may have fit the legal definition of insanity for a colored man in Mississippi at the time.

High was taken into custody and committed to the insane asylum in October 1957. It was a sentence that would shut him off, at age forty-seven, from the rest of the world and his wife and four children for the remainder of his life. He was held in confinement deep in the woods, surrounded by guards and hospital personnel, a good fifteen miles from the nearest city. It amounted to a total silencing of a revered dissident of the Mississippi order of things and a slow death in a crazy place where he would be subjected to whatever indignities his keepers devised.

———

The world of Mississippi and the world of Chicago were intertwined and interdependent, and what happened in one did not easily escape the notice of the other from afar. Word of his capture made it to Chicago. Ida Mae, a faithful reader of the *Chicago Defender* even in the days when it was well past its prime, would take note of people like Arrington High back in her home state and wish them safety.

A colored physician that Ida Mae and most everyone from Mississippi knew through word of mouth, a man named T. R. M. Howard, also made note of what happened to Arrington High. Dr. Howard had founded the Mississippi Regional Council of Negro Leadership, a local precursor to the civil rights groups that would become household names in the 1960s. He organized protests from his base in the all-black town of Mound Bayou in the Delta. But his activities forced him to escape Mississippi a few years before Arrington High was committed to the asylum. From Chicago, Dr. Howard tried to figure out a way to help his friend.

———

The asylum put patients to work in the dairy and truck farms and the orchards run by the state. Some of the patients had to be up at dawn to work the farms. Arrington High got up at 5 A.M. on February 7, 1958, a Friday, to milk the cows, which was one of his chores.

It was still dark outside, and instead of heading to pasture, he scurried down a deserted path on the hospital grounds and came upon a row of five cars that were parked at the side of a quiet stretch of road.

A door in the second car opened, and he got inside the only car with a colored driver. That car and the four other cars, driven by white men, inched their way to the exit so as not to kick up any more dust or engine noise. There, the white man driving the lead car in the caravan motioned to the hospital guard at the front gate. The guard waved the processional through with a tilt of his flashlight.

Arrington High was out of the asylum but not out of danger. The motorcade took the highway, careful not to drive too fast or too slow as to attract attention. They drove 105 miles through Pelahatchie, Hickory, Meridian, and Toomsuba, Mississippi, to the Alabama line. It would take them more than two hours to get there, and they had to watch for cars tailing them and sheriffs hunting them, as surely by now the asylum officials knew that High had gone missing.

At the Alabama line, the drivers took no chances. They did not cross the state border themselves with their Mississippi license plates. Instead they took Arrington High to the state line and instructed him to get out of the car and walk over into Alabama. There a caravan of five other cars, all with Alabama license plates, were waiting for him. As before, there were four white drivers and one colored driver. The caravan would attract less attention if two colored men were driving together than it would if Arrington High were riding with a white man.

He was in Alabama but still not safe. He was still in the South and within siren call of any Mississippi sheriff. The cars took him to a predetermined location. There waiting for him was a pine coffin. He was told to get inside. The coffin had breathing holes in it for him to get air. The men sealed him in the coffin and loaded it onto a hearse. On top of the coffin, the men placed a load of flowers so that it would appear that the coffin had just been driven from a funeral.

The hearse drove to a railroad station, where the coffin was loaded on a train bound for Chicago. He lay still and quiet, unable to turn over or adjust himself for the fifteen-hour ride to the North.

The moment the train pulled out of the station in Alabama bearing

Arrington High's coffin, Dr. Howard, awaiting word in Chicago, got a
long-distance telephone call.

"The Eagle has flown the coop," the voice on the line said.

High made his escape in a ritual of last resort that, in some way or another, had been used to deliver black people out of the South from the
time of the Underground Railroad, the slaves using whatever means
they had at their disposal. Men disguised themselves as women, women
dressed as men to elude detection.

A century before High was nailed into his coffin, a man named
Henry Brown, a slave on a tobacco plantation near Richmond, Virginia,
began plotting his escape the moment he saw his wife and three young
children carted away in chains to some unknown part of North Carolina. His master had sold them off. Brown did not know they were
being sold, did not get to hold them one last time, did not know where
they were being taken, and would have been flogged or worse if he tried
to search for them in North Carolina. He chose to leave the South and
the "whips and thumbscrews" altogether. He prayed over it, and it came
to him that he should pack himself into a box and get himself "conveyed
as dry goods to a free state."

He had a carpenter build a crate of a size commonly sent on the railcars. The box was three feet, one inch wide by two feet, six inches high
and had three little gimlet holes for air. Brown then went to a white man
he thought he could trust. The man asked if the box was for Brown's
clothes. Brown said, no, he was going to get into it himself. The five-
foot, six-inch Brown would have to fold himself into the fetal position
and remain that way for the twenty-odd hours it would take to reach the
North. His white friend did not think it safe and did not want to seal
Brown inside the box.

"I insisted upon his placing me in it, nailing me up," Brown wrote in
his autobiography, "and he finally consented."

The friend had promised to accompany the box to protect it on the
journey, but at the last minute decided against it. Brown would have to
go it alone. The friend sent a telegram to an acquaintance in Philadelphia "that such a box was on its way to his care."

The morning of March 29, 1849, the friend carried the box, with
Brown folded inside with a few small biscuits, to the express office.
There, it was later placed upside down, which left Brown sitting on his
head, even though the box explicitly said, THIS SIDE UP WITH CARE. From

the express office, the box went to the train depot and "tumbled roughly into the baggage car" where it happened to fall right side up, only to be put on a steamboat upside down again and left that way for close to two hours.

Brown was in agony but dared not moan. He waited for death and prayed. Then he heard the men say, "We have been here two hours and have traveled twenty miles. Let us sit down and rest ourselves." In so doing, the men happened to turn the box over.

The box then arrived at the depot in Washington. There he heard a voice say, "There is no room for this box. It will have to remain behind."

Brown, stiff and contorted and now fearful, had to keep silent. He felt a man's hands reach for the box and squeeze it onto the railcar, his head pointing down again, until someone righted it at the next stop. He arrived in Philadelphia at three in the morning. He had been doubled up in the box for twenty-six hours.

Before daylight, a wagon drove up and a white man got out and inquired about the box. He carried the box to an office on North Fifth Street. Several abolitionists had gathered to witness the opening of the parcel.

They locked the door behind them. But once the box was placed before them, the men seemed afraid to open it. Finally one of them said, "Let us rap upon the box and see if he is alive."

Someone then tapped on the sides of it.

"Is all right within?" the voice asked, trembling.

"All right," Brown replied.

The people were joyful. And Brown was free. He would go on to Boston, which was judged to be safer, and for the rest of his life he would go by the name of Henry *Box* Brown, in light of how he had gained his freedom.

———

Some one hundred years after Henry Brown shipped himself north, the train bearing Arrington High's coffin arrived at the Twelfth Street station in Chicago. Dr. Howard, the friend who had helped organize the escape, met the train at the station that had come to symbolize the Great Migration itself. The coffin would now have to be transported by hearse to a funeral home. There, a group of men opened the lid and welcomed Arrington High to the receiving city of Chicago. The people were joyful.

How many people fled the South this way during the Great Migration is impossible to know, due to the very nature of the mission. For the operation to work, it required the highest level of secrecy, coordination and planning worthy of the Secret Service, the active and willing participation of sympathetic white southerners, the cooperation of funeral homes in both the departure and receiving states, the complete trust of the person being ferried out by friends and loved ones willing to put themselves in danger to save a single soul, and a good measure of courage and faith on everyone's part.

It would appear from the precision of the Arrington High escape that this was not the first time the people involved in its execution had carried out an operation such as this. To this day, many funeral directors refuse to discuss the matter, admit their involvement, or bring unwanted attention to it—in case, it would seem, it might need to be used again.

"That underground is as effective today in the South," Arrington High told the *Chicago Defender* after his arrival, "as it was during the days of slavery."

It was Dr. Howard who, with the help of more than a dozen others, arranged for his colleague's escape and greeted him upon arrival. He knew what it meant to flee for your life. He did not have to imagine what Arrington High had been through during that dark, cramped ride to Chicago. He himself had to be spirited from Mississippi only a few years before.

NEW YORK, 1957
GEORGE SWANSON STARLING

———

GEORGE STARLING WAS RUNNING the rails up and down the East Coast, and, as he did, he was in a way running from Inez. George loved Inez. But Inez was not an easy woman to love. There was a storm inside her that nobody seemed able to calm.

It had started long before, when she and her toddler sister were left orphaned right after Inez was born. They were raised by poor, put-upon, Bible-thumping Pentecostal aunts, who couldn't afford two more mouths to feed, and by a Victorian grandmother, who thought the only way to break a girl as stubborn as Inez was to beat her the way the overseers beat their foreparents. They hauled Inez and her older sister to their Holiness church, where the aunts and the grandmother caught the spirit and talked in tongues. Inez's sister did not let it get to her. Inez rebelled from the start.

George had taken a liking to Inez back in Eustis, maybe because she was as headstrong as he was and knew what it was like to feel tossed about as a child by the people charged with caring for her. He hadn't given much thought to the consequences of marrying her, hadn't given much thought to marriage at all. But now he found himself bound to her, with a young son she adored, and as principled and stubborn as he was, he wasn't going to admit defeat no matter how blue and ornery she could be.

There were happy times, when the folks from back home paraded up from Florida. George could regale them with stories from the railroad, and Inez could show off how well they had made out in New York, how much better things were there than down south, how the little country orphan girl was living in a brownstone in the biggest, brightest city in maybe the whole world.

In the summer, it seemed as if there was someone from Eustis coming up every weekend. If George wasn't on the rails, he would throw some ribs on the grill. Babe Blye, who lived upstairs from George and Inez in the second-floor apartment, would drive out to the woods, out to Westchester or Connecticut, and bring back some possum or run to the corner store and get the whiskey and chitlins. Inez and Babe's wife, Hallie Q., would cook up the possum and the chitlins and stir up some collard greens, make the potato salad, and there would be a Florida reunion in the middle of Harlem. Everybody who came up to New York from Eustis knew to stop by George and Inez's place.

Soon, after so many years with just the three of them, their household expanded further. They had a little girl in 1954. She looked just like George and had his temperament. They named her Sonya. Now they had two little ones to raise.

Then, one day in 1957, word arrived about a death in the family that would bring more changes to the household. Inez's sister had taken ill and died back in Florida. She left behind a teenage daughter named Pat, who was bright but distraught and who everyone feared was headed for trouble.

Like many people who had come up from the South, George and Inez sent for the girl to come live with them. Inez wasn't especially happy about her niece coming. Life was hard enough in New York. Inez had put Eustis behind her and was working hard to take care of her own children. She and George had to leave the children alone more than they wanted to as it was in order to meet the house note and the property taxes, the utilities, and everything else that seemed to be high just because this was New York.

But George saw something in the girl, a quick mind and a good heart, and thought they could help her. Besides, he knew that most migrant families that moved up north took in a relative or two at some point or other. It was how a lot of newcomers got situated in the New World, and was the right and southern thing to do.

There were people in Eustis who never left and never wanted to leave and couldn't see why anybody would go up north with all the crime and drugs and devilment. They felt sorry for the sheltered teenager whose mother had taken ill and died in her arms and who now was being shipped up north to live with an aunt and uncle she barely knew in a city she had never seen.

"All the people in my little town saw doom for me," Pat said years later. "Uncle George took me in."

George knew firsthand how the folks in Eustis could be. He told Pat she needed to make the most of the mind God had given her and warned her that there would be people pitying her and expecting her to fail.

"You must not fail," George told Pat, "because they're expecting you to."

But when Pat arrived, George was hardly ever around, working the rails as he was. Inez couldn't hide her resentment, and it was just the two of them, aunt and niece, in the first floor of their brownstone sometimes. Inez told her she would give her a week, and then Pat would have to start paying rent.

Pat protested that her mother had just died, that she didn't have a job yet, she didn't know the city well enough. Inez didn't need to be told how rough life could be. She had never had the chance even to know her mother. She had little sympathy and didn't want her around.

Inez got worried about the money it was costing to have Pat there and would lock the kitchen to control who could get in. Pat would have to sneak in there when the kitchen was open.

"I would go in there and snatch everything I could outta there," Pat said.

One day, soon after she arrived, George and Inez left for work, and Gerard, now twelve, and little Sonya, who was about six, were left alone in the house with Pat, who was still getting used to all the lights and the noise and the perils of the big city.

About ten boys showed up at the front door. Gerard let them in, and they all headed straight for the kitchen.

"They had this white stuff, and they were doing something with it," Pat remembered. She had never seen this in Eustis before. The boys were doing drugs, she later learned.

It was summer, and, each day, after George and Inez left, the boys would show up and head for the kitchen.

"They would come there to roll that stuff and then hit the door," Pat remembered.

The temptations of the city had seeped into George and Inez's house when they weren't looking, when they were out trying to make a living to stay in the city that was swallowing up their son. Pat eventually got the nerve to confront Gerard.

"I'm gonna tell Inez," she warned him.

Gerard knew how much his mother adored him and dared Pat to say anything.

Pat got up the courage to tell Inez. She told her that when she went off to work, Gerard was letting in a bunch of boys, and they were doing dope in the kitchen.

Inez grew enraged.

"How dare you say that about Gerard!" she told Pat.

George wasn't around. He was on the train. And Inez told Pat she wanted her out of the house.

"I don't appreciate you talking about my son taking drugs," she said.

Pat was between jobs, was just a teenager, and had no money. But she was too proud to argue with her aunt.

"Well, if that's what you want me to do," she said.

She gathered what few things she had and started walking, not knowing where she was going. She got to a shoe-shine stand and asked the man if he knew of anyone with rooms for rent.

He took her to the apartment of a sweet old couple. The wife sang with a gospel group, and Pat stayed there until she got on her feet.

George got back from the rails, not knowing what had happened to Pat or where she was. He didn't intercede because Pat was Inez's blood relative, not his. It was only some time later that she saw George and told him what had happened.

"Pat, I had no idea," George said. "I didn't know where you were. She told me you had just left. I had no idea that she had done that."

Inez was her aunt, but it was George she would always be closer to, like a second daughter to him.

"The man cared more about me than she did," Pat said. "Had he been there that day, I would have waited and told him. My pride wouldn't let me."

———

Pat's warnings turned out to be prophetic. Gerard would only sink deeper into drugs and watch his friends die from overdoses of heroin. One of them they found dead in an elevator. Gerard would go on to steal televisions and radios and cash from his parents, anything of value that they hadn't locked up or hidden away or could be easily carried out the door. He would bring sadness and heartbreak to Inez and especially to George, who could rarely even bring himself to talk about his son. He had come all this way from Florida, and here was something that had turned out worse in ways he couldn't have thought possible.

Gerard would get himself together for a time but would never truly get on his feet. And during those moments of victory, his father preached at him.

"You owe God," he'd tell Gerard. "You owe it to him to go around and tell your generation the evil of dealing in drugs and how he rescued you."

Inez, who had adored and indulged Gerard, retreated into herself and seemed to take the sorrows out on those around her. She had a coat that Pat used to beg her to let her wear.

"A little coat that I loved," Pat said.

Pat had come up from the country with few clothes of her own, and when it got cold she wanted to wear one of Inez's coats, that one in particular. Pat was always talking about that coat.

"Uncle George knew I liked it," Pat said. "Everybody knew I liked it."

One day, after she had moved out, she saw her Uncle George.

"Pat, I got some bad news for you."

"What is it?"

"Your aunt threw that coat you so loved in the garbage can today," he said. "I begged her not to, but she did it anyway."

Pat went to their house and looked in the trash can for it.

"By the time I went there, it was gone," Pat said.

It all came back to Pat, the things the family used to say about Inez, that they could never make sense of "how when she was a little baby, how stubborn she was and how their grandmother would whip them and she refused to bow."

Pat would eventually make peace with her aunt. She would grow up, get married, have a family of her own, and join a church, which was what all of them had been raised to do. Inez never joined a church in New York. It reminded her too much of the hard life she'd had in Eustis and of a little girl's imaginings of how different life might have been if her mother had lived, the mother who died bringing Inez into the world.

Pat managed to convince Inez to go with her on occasion.

And every time, Pat remembered, "she would break down crying, and she'd have to leave the church."

LOS ANGELES, MAY 1962
ROBERT JOSEPH PERSHING FOSTER

THE SONG HIT the *Billboard* charts in May 1962. It stayed there for seven weeks and peaked at Number 20.

The song was by a famous migrant from Albany, Georgia, Robert's most high-maintenance patient, Ray Charles. It was about Robert or, rather, an idealized version of him in a smoke- and drug-filled world of airless recording studios, martini nightclubs, cross-country road tours, and shimmying, wig- and rouge-wearing backup-singer love triangles that was the life of Ray Charles in the sixties and which Robert entered unavoidably and not unhappily as his personal physician during the peak of both men's careers. The song was called "Hide Nor Hair," and the chorus went like this:

Well, I called my Dr. Foster and when the girl answered the phone,
I got a funny feeling, the way she said Dr. Foster had gone.
She said, "He left with a lady patient, about 24 hours ago."
I added two and two, and here's what I got: I got I'll never see that girl no
more.

I ain't seen hide nor hair of my baby, since she went away.
If Dr. Foster has got her, then I know I'm through,
Because he's got medicine and money, too.
I ain't seen hide nor hair of my baby, since that day.

Robert knew Ray was working on a song about him, or about a doctor at least. Ray asked Robert's permission to use his name before recording it. Coming as it did just months after Robert had put his hand back together and delivered his son, it was Ray's way of thanking a man he had come to depend on. Robert, always craving approval and enamored of show business, gave him the go-ahead.

Robert wasn't looking to be the subject of a song and really didn't need it. Years later, he didn't talk about it much and, the times he did, it was rather like a footnote. But when it first hit the airwaves back in 1962, his practice took off like never before. He could see the effects of the Migration in his waiting room—former sharecroppers from east Texas, schoolteachers from Baton Rouge, gamblers from Arkansas, Creoles from New Orleans. He ended up with more patients than he could handle, more than was really fair to him or to the patients, seeing as how he liked to spend so much time with each one, get to know them and their lives and desires, and seeing how much they took to that kind of attention. He had more business than he ever could have imagined back when he was dreaming of getting out of Louisiana, trying to convince himself as much as everybody else that he really could make it in California.

It reached the point where the hallway outside his office began to look like some of the train stations during the Migration. Patients started lining up hours before he got there, a reunion of Texans and Louisianans and migrants from Arkansas, spilling out of the reception room and into the outer corridor, patients sitting cross-legged on the floor, heads tilted back against the wall, all waiting to hear their names called. They knew he might still be at the racetrack or just in from Vegas. He'd step over the dangling legs and watch out for their feet as he waded through the crowd to get to his office door.

Some would end up waiting all day to see him, and somehow he made each one feel as if he or she were the only patient in the world. He would stay until ten or eleven at night or until he had seen the very last patient.

It got so crowded, like a Saturday-night rent party, that some people just couldn't take the waiting anymore, no matter how good he was. Reatha Gray Simon, his mentor Dr. Beck's granddaughter, had a brief falling-out with him over the fact that she practically had to block out a whole day to see him.

"I knew he was sometimes in surgery," she said, "but sometimes he was at the track. The waiting room was like the neighborhood barbershop."

That was just how he wanted it. Gambling and medicine were basically his life. He could lose himself in both and had a hard time walling off his professional and personal lives. He doted on his patients and sometimes went gambling with them. He didn't look down his speculum at the cooks and mailmen he treated and made sure to invite them to the parties he gave.

"Some wouldn't come for whatever reason," he said. The house was practically a mansion, and Robert threw out the red carpet, literally. "Most of them probably didn't feel comfortable. But I was gracious as I could be if they came. I'd bend over backwards to make them come."

THE PRODIGALS

[My father], along with
thousands of other Negroes,
came North after 1919
and I was part of that generation
which had never seen the landscape
of what Negroes sometimes call the Old Country.
        JAMES BALDWIN, *Notes of a Native Son*

'Sides, they can't run us all out.
That land's got more of our blood in it than theirs.
Not all us s'posed to leave. Some of us got to stay,
so y'all have a place to come back to.
        —A SHARECROPPER WHO STAYED IN
            NORTH CAROLINA, FROM MARITA
            GOLDEN, *Long Distance Life*

SOMEWHERE NEAR CARTERSVILLE, GEORGIA, SUMMER 1956

THE ROAD SIGNS were warning that the 1956 Pontiac with the shark-tooth grille and chrome racing stripes on the hood was drawing closer to the hill town of Rome, Georgia. My mother was driving, only it was clear from everything about her that she wouldn't become my mother for a while. She would have been wearing a poodle skirt with a cinched waist, a scarf folded Marilyn Monroe–style atop her head and knotted breezily at the neck, pressed curls peeking out from the sides. Dark, movie star sunglasses dwarfed her face and shielded her eyes, the eyes scanning for the one thing she needed, could not put off, had to do before pulling into her old hometown of Rome.

The car was brand-new, blue, the color of the flag, as my mother would remember it, with whitewall tires and white side panel trim. But it was dusty from the drive, its windshield spotted and speckled, and not looking anywhere close to the four thousand dollars she'd paid for it. Her sister Theresa, who had followed her up north, was with her, and they couldn't roll into town like that. No migrant could, none would dare let on that their new life was anything less than perfect; they had to prove that their decision to go north was the superior and right thing to do, that they were living the dream and everything was out of a Technicolor movie set.

Besides, the people back home would be disappointed if they didn't put on a show, and so they did. So she would have to find a car wash before she could get so close to town that some neighbor might see her in a dusty old automobile and conclude that things weren't nearly as swell up north as they had been claiming. If she did not find a car wash, it would be all over North Rome before she turned onto Gibbon Street to greet her mother and nieces, who, at that very moment, were praying she was running late because they weren't finished waxing the floors and shining the windows with old pages of the *Rome News Tribune,* hadn't smoothed out the chenille blankets with the cotton-ball fringe in the guest bedroom, the corn bread hadn't risen yet, the African violets needed watering, and what if she pulled up just now?

My mother delayed her arrival and the moment she would see her own beloved mother to stop in Cartersville to get the Pontiac washed and polished. That was the most important thing, after all. She had driven to Rome before, but it was in a Chevrolet, a used one at that. She had not long before started a new job teaching school, bought herself a row house in an all-white block in Northwest Washington, and now had this new car. But it wouldn't mean as much unless the people back home could see the manifestation of all this for themselves.

"We wanted to arrive in the daytime so people would come out looking at us," my mother remembered of the trip she made with her sister. "We tooted the horn, and Mother came out. I don't know why we went to Rome. To show off the car, I guess."

The car, with its precious Washington, D.C., license plates, would cause a commotion, like a UFO from another planet, which is just what she wanted, and all the little children would look at that shiny, chrome-plated car and inspect the tags and ask, "What is a 'District of Columbia'?"

———

At holidays and in summer, the migrants came home. They would leave a trail of Cadillac dust on Highway 61 in the Delta or along Route 1 through the Carolinas and Georgia. They had prepared all year for this moment of glory, and there were times when in some church parking lots in Grenada or Greenville, there were more Illinois license plates than those from Mississippi.

They had gone off to a new world but were still tied to the other. Over time, the language of geographic origin began to change; the ancestral home no longer the distant Africa of unknown forebears but the more immediate South of uncles and grandparents, where the culture they carried inside them was pure and familiar.

The homesick migrants loaded up their sleepy children in the dark hours of the morning for the long drive to the mother country when there was a death in the family or a loved one needing tending or just to show off how well they were making out up north. When they saw the cold airs of the New World seeping into their northern-bred children, they sent them south for the summer so the children would know where they came from. The migrants warned their children to be on their best behavior, especially when it came to the white people they might encounter.

But the children did not have the internalized deference of their southern cousins. They got into scrapes with the other children and couldn't remember all the rules. One migrant's son, Emmett Till, on a visit from Chicago to Mississippi in 1955, was killed for breaking protocol in some way that will probably never be known for sure, except that everyone agreed it involved something he had said to a white woman, which only served to remind those who left of the rightness of their decision and those who stayed how foolhardy it could be to forget for a moment where you were when you crossed into the very different country of the South.

———

Ida Mae did not go back often, not because she was afraid but because she had a family to tend to in Chicago. She went back for illnesses and funerals—when her mother, Miss Theenie, took ill and died, and years later, when her baby sister, Talma, got sick and died. Her husband,

George, went back only once—for the funeral of the brother who had raised him, Willie. And even then he did not stay the night; he left for Chicago right away.

Robert Foster did not go back often either. His goal was to get as many of his loved ones from Monroe to move out to California, and he went back only when he had to. Alice had no interest in going, and he did not insist on Alice or the girls visiting Monroe. They would grow up knowing little of their father's small-town Louisiana roots. When he returned home, he put on a show, as would have been expected of him, and made sure it was clear that he was now more California than Louisiana.

It would be a long time before George Starling would feel safe returning to Eustis, Florida, seeing how he had left. Southern sheriffs and planters were known to have long memories and even to go after migrants who had fled north. Some white southerners tried to convince the workers who had fled that conditions had improved. Some extradited people for whatever reason they saw fit.

"Even in the North, refugees were not always safe," wrote Arna Bontemps and Jack Conroy in the 1945 book *Anyplace but Here*. "One hard-working migrant was astonished when a detective from Atlanta approached him and informed him that he was wanted back home for 'spitting on the sidewalk.'"

So George was not inclined to linger in the vicinity of Eustis, Florida. His job on the railroad took him south, but on a line that usually veered west toward Birmingham. The times he worked a train that happened to take him through Florida, he did not leave the station or request permission to go home. The few relatives he trusted drove thirty or forty miles from Eustis or Alachua to meet him at the Wildwood station, bearing gossip, good wishes, and hams. George, in his porter's cap and uniform, leaned out of the coach door to see them and left weighed down with homemade cakes or fresh fish they had caught for him to take back up north.

"Where they stop the train and fuel up, they had to stop there a good little while," George's Uncle Andrew "Jack" Johnson said. "We'd go there and meet him. And most of the time we carry him something. Give him his handout, such as we had."

It was a measure of their pride and devotion that the uncle and his wife drove close to two hours in thunderstorms and waited for however long it took the train to get there for the few minutes they'd get to see him. "He'd have time enough to speak and pass a few words," the uncle remembered, "while the train was fueling up."

———

One time, George was hauling luggage at the train stop at Wildwood, when up stepped the most feared man in all of Lake County and one of the most notorious sheriffs in the South, Willis V. McCall. The sheriff was just one more reason that George went no closer to his hometown of Eustis than the depot at Wildwood.

McCall was the lawman who had shot two handcuffed prisoners, killing one, as he transported them from one jail to another for an upcoming trial in the Groveland rape case back in 1949. The trial and the subsequent shootings attracted nationwide attention partly because one of the men McCall thought he had killed had actually survived to tell what happened to him. The NAACP field secretary Harry T. Moore and his wife had died from a bomb placed under Moore's bed after Moore had accused McCall of police brutality in the case.

Over the years, McCall would be accused, implicated, or indicted in dozens of cases of prisoners dying under suspicious circumstances while in his custody. He patrolled the colored section in his ten-gallon hat, interrogating and pistol-whipping colored men for any suspicion and putting colored fruit pickers in jail if he caught them not working on a Saturday.

The colored people of Eustis and the rest of Lake County lived in fear of his patrol car crawling through their gravel streets.

"Here come the Big Hat Man," the people would say when they saw him approaching.

People scurried from the street. They cleared the benches on McDonald Avenue and fled behind the storefronts when they saw him coming.

"That bench would be cleared in two seconds," George said.

The sheriff had free rein and used to come into Big George's corner store and drink his sodas without paying.

"Well, see you, George," McCall would tell Big George, slurping on a soda to which he had helped himself.

The day Lil George saw Sheriff McCall, George was loading baggage on a train heading north. The sheriff was there to get an escaped prisoner from one of the railcars. The sheriff saw George on the station platform and recognized him from George's father's convenience store.

"Hey, don't I know you?"

"I guess you do."

"What's your name?"

"My name is George Starling, Jr."

"Oh, you George's boy, heh?"

"I'm George's son."

That was the only time in all the years that Willis McCall was sheriff that George actually spoke with him. George felt safe because he was about to jump up on the train, and so he spoke his mind as he never would have in Eustis.

"I was biggity then," George said. "And he got a little red in the face, and he kind of grinned a little bit."

McCall regained his composure.

"Well, when you coming home?"

"I ain't," George told him. "I live in New York. I ain't coming back to Eustis."

George turned away and hopped up on the train. "I ain't, not long as you still living," he said under his breath.

———

Emmett Till was perhaps the most memorialized black northerner ever to go south, if only because he never made it back alive and because of the brutal reasons that he didn't. His mother had sent her only child south for the summer in 1955 to spend time with his great-uncle in Mississippi. She never saw him alive again. He was bludgeoned and shot to death a month after his fourteenth birthday. Three days later, two fishermen found his body in the Tallahatchie River. Against the advice of those around her, his mother, Mamie Till, decided to hold the funeral with an open casket, so people could see what Mississippi had done to him.

Mourners and the curious clogged Fortieth and State Streets to line up and see his swollen, disfigured body inside the old barrel-vaulted Roberts Temple Church of God. Many of the people paying their respects had come from Mississippi like Emmett Till's family, had lived and escaped the violence, and here it was being brought back to Chicago in the form of a fourteen-year-old boy. It could just as easily have been one of their children lying there lifeless. How many of them had sent their children south to be with their cousins and grandparents, giving them the same warnings Mamie Till had given her son—that they mind themselves around white people?

Ida Mae went to Roberts Temple Church of God that day in early September and stood in line with the thousands of others waiting to see him. She felt she had to. It took hours to reach the casket. She was unprepared for what confronted her when she leaned over the glass-covered coffin. The undertakers had done what they could, but an eye was out of its socket and the face so disfigured that it did not resemble a human being's. She had to look away.

George said he didn't want to go, and he didn't. He had lived it and seen enough.

DISILLUSIONMENT

Let's not fool ourselves,
we are far from the Promised Land,
both north and south.
—DR. MARTIN LUTHER KING, JR.

It was a hoax if you ask me....
They're packed tight
into the buildings,
and can't do anything,
not even dream of going North,
the way I do
when it gets rough.
—A COLORED MAN WHO NEVER
LEFT ALABAMA, QUOTED IN
The New York Times IN 1967

CHICAGO, 1951
IDA MAE BRANDON GLADNEY

———

BY MIDCENTURY, the receiving cities of the Great Migration strained under the weight of millions of black southerners trying to situate themselves as tens of thousands more alighted from Pontiacs and railroad platforms each week. In the spring of 1951, a colored bus driver and former army captain named Harvey Clark, and his wife, Johnetta, faced an impossible living situation.

It was a dilemma confronting Ida Mae and her family and just about every colored household up from the South. There was not enough housing to contain them, and the white neighborhoods bordering the black belt were barricading themselves further, not flinching at the use of violence to keep the walls in place.

Ida Mae and her family moved from flat to flat within those walls. Once they lived in an apartment over a funeral home, where little Eleanor played among the caskets and rode with the undertaker to pick up bodies. As it was, Chicago was trying to discourage the migration of any more colored people from the South. In 1950, city aldermen and housing officials proposed restricting 13,000 new public housing units to people who had lived in Chicago for two years. The rule would presumably affect colored migrants and foreign immigrants alike. But it was the colored people who were having the most trouble finding housing and most likely to seek out such an alternative. And it was they who were seen as needing to be controlled, as they had only to catch a train rather than cross an ocean to get there. Nothing had worked before at keeping the migrants out once the Migration began, and this new plan wouldn't either. But it was a sign of the hostility facing people like Harvey Clark and Ida Mae, as white home owners stepped up pressure on the city to protect their neighborhoods.

"They don't want the Negro who has just moved out of rural Dixie as their neighbor," a city official told the *Chicago Defender* in a story that described what it called a "2-Year City Ban on Migrants."

With close to half a million colored people overflowing the black belt by 1950, racial walls that had been "successfully defended for a generation," in the words of the historian Allan Spear, were facing imminent collapse, but not without a fight. Chicago found itself in the midst of "chronic urban guerilla warfare" that rivaled the city's violent spasms at the start of the Migration, "when one racially motivated bombing or arson occurred every twenty days," according to the historian Arnold Hirsch.

———

Harvey Clark was from Mississippi like Ida Mae and brought his family to Chicago in 1949 after serving in World War II. Now that they were in the big city, the couple and their two children were crammed into half of a two-room apartment. A family of five lived in the other half. Harvey Clark was paying fifty-six dollars a month for the privilege, up to fifty percent more than tenants in white neighborhoods paid for the same amount of space. One-room tenement life did not fit them at all. The husband and wife were college-educated, well-mannered, and looked like movie stars. The father had saved up for a piano for his eight-year-old daughter with the ringlets down her back but had no place to put it. He had high aspirations for their six-year-old son, who was bright and whose dimples could have landed him in cereal commercials.

The Clarks felt they had to get out. By May of 1951, they finally found the perfect apartment. It had five rooms, was clean and modern, was closer to the bus terminal, and cost only sixty dollars a month. That came to four dollars a month more for five times more space. It was just a block over the Chicago line, at 6139 West Nineteenth Street, in the working-class suburb of Cicero. The Clarks couldn't believe their good fortune.

Cicero was an all-white town on the southwest border of Chicago. It was known as the place Al Capone went to elude Chicago authorities back during Prohibition. The town was filled with first- and second-generation immigrants—Czechs, Slavs, Poles, Italians. Some had fled fascism and Stalinism, not unlike blacks fleeing oppression in the South, and were still getting established in the New World. They lived in frame cottages and worked the factories and slaughterhouses. They were miles from the black belt, isolated from it, and bent on keeping their town as it was.

That the Clarks turned there at all was an indication of how closed the options were for colored families looking for clean, spacious housing they could afford. The Clarks set the move-in date for the third week of June. The moving truck arrived at 2:30 in the afternoon. White protesters met them as the couple tried to unload the truck.

"Get out of Cicero," the protesters told them, *"and don't come back."*

As the Clarks started to enter the building, the police stopped them at the door. The police took sides with the protesters and would not let the Clarks nor their furniture in.

"You should know better," the chief of police told them. "Get going. Get out of here fast. There will be no moving in that building."

The Clarks, along with their rental agent, Charles Edwards, fled the scene.

"Don't come back in town," the chief reportedly told Edwards, "or you'll get a bullet through you."

The Clarks did not let that deter them but sued and won the right to occupy the apartment. They tried to move in again on July 11, 1951. This time, a hundred Cicero housewives and grandmothers in swing coats and Mamie Eisenhower hats showed up to heckle them. The couple managed to get their furniture in, but as the day wore on, the crowds grew larger and more agitated. A man from a white supremacy group called the White Circle League handed out flyers that said, KEEP CICERO WHITE. The Clarks fled.

A mob stormed the apartment and threw the family's furniture out of a third-floor window as the crowds cheered below. The neighbors burned the couple's marriage license and the children's baby pictures. They overturned the refrigerator and tore the stove and plumbing fixtures out of the wall. They tore up the carpet. They shattered the mirrors. They bashed in the toilet bowl. They ripped out the radiators. They smashed the piano Clark had worked overtime to buy for his daughter. And when they were done, they set the whole pile of the family's belongings, now strewn on the ground below, on fire.

In an hour, the mob "destroyed what had taken nine years to acquire," wrote the historian Stephen Grant Meyer of what happened that night.

The next day, a full-out riot was under way. The mob grew to four thousand by early evening as teenagers got out of school, husbands returned home from work, and all of them joined the housewives who had kept a daylong vigil in protest of the Clarks' arrival. They chanted, "Go, go, go, go." They hurled rocks and bricks. They looted. Then they firebombed the whole building. The bombing gutted the twenty-unit building and forced even the white tenants out. The rioters overturned police cars and threw stones at the firefighters who were trying to put out the blaze.

Illinois Governor Adlai Stevenson had to call in the National Guard, the first time the Guard had been summoned for a racial incident since the 1919 riots in the early years of the Migration. It took four hours for more than six hundred guardsmen, police officers, and sheriff's deputies to beat back the mob that night and three more days for the rioting over the Clarks to subside. A total of 118 men were arrested in the riot. A Cook County grand jury failed to indict any of the rioters.

Town officials did not blame the mob for the riot but rather the people who, in their view, should never have rented the apartment to the Clarks in the first place. To make an example of such people, indictments were handed down against the rental agent, the owner of the apartment building, and others who had helped the Clarks on charges of inciting a riot. The indictments were later dropped. In spite of everything, the Clarks still felt they had a right to live in a city with good, affordable housing stock. But the racial hostility made it all but impossible to return.

Walter White, the longtime leader of the NAACP, kept close watch of the case. He had been challenging Jim Crow since the 1920s and compared the hatred he saw in the Cicero mob to the lynch mobs he had seen in the South. "It was appalling to see and listen to those who were but recently the targets of hate and deprivations," he said, "who, beneficiaries of American opportunity, were as virulent as any Mississippian in their willingness to deny a place to live to a member of a race which had preceded them to America by many generations."

It was the middle of the Cold War, and the famous columnist and broadcaster of the day Walter Winchell weighed in on what he called the "bigoted idiots out there," who "did as much for Stalin as though they had enlisted in the Red Army."

That fall, Governor Stevenson, who would go on to become the Democratic nominee for president the following year, told a newly convened state commission on human rights that housing segregation was putting pressure on the whole system. "This is the root of the Cicero affair," the governor said, "the grim reality underlying the tension and violence that accompany the efforts of minority groups to break through the iron curtain."

The Cicero riot attracted worldwide attention. It was front-page news in Southeast Asia, made it into the *Pakistan Observer,* and was remarked upon in West Africa. "A resident of Accra wrote to the mayor of Cicero," according to Hirsch, "protesting the mob's 'savagery' and asking for an 'apology to the civilized world.' "

It was U.S. Attorney Otto Kerner whose job it was to prosecute the federal case against the Cicero officials accused of denying the Clarks their civil rights. Kerner's name would later become linked to one of the most cited reports on race relations in this country. President Lyndon Johnson chose him to head a federal investigation into the racial disturbances of the 1960s. The commission's findings, released in February 1968 as the *Report of the National Advisory Commission on Civil Disorders,* would come to be known as the Kerner Report. Its recommendations would be revisited for decades as a measure of the country's progress toward equality, its stark pronouncement invoked many times over: *"Our nation is moving toward two societies,"* the report said, *"one black, one white—separate and unequal."*

Well into the twentieth century, Cicero would remain synonymous with intolerance and corruption. It would come to be seen in the same light as other symbolic places, like Ocoee, Florida, or Forsyth County, Georgia, where many blacks dared not think of living and thought twice before even driving through, well into the 1990s. By then Cicero was racked by a series of scandals involving a mayor who would ultimately serve prison time on federal corruption charges. Even white immigrant families were leaving Cicero, ceding it to Mexican immigrants. In 2000, the U.S. Census found that, of Cicero's population of 85,616, just one percent of the residents were black, nearly half a century after the riots that kept the Clarks from moving in.

——————

It was an article of faith among many people in Chicago and other big cities that the arrival of colored people in an all-white neighborhood automatically lowered property values. That economic fear was helping propel the violent defense of white neighborhoods.

The fears were not unfounded, but often not for the reasons white residents were led to believe, sociologists, economists, and historians have found. And the misunderstanding of the larger forces at work and the scapegoating of colored migrants, those with the least power of all, made the violence all the more tragic.

Contrary to conventional wisdom, the decline in property values and neighborhood prestige was a by-product of the fear and tension itself, sociologists found. The decline often began, they noted, in barely perceptible ways, before the first colored buyer moved in.

The instability of a white neighborhood under pressure from the very possibility of integration put the neighborhood into a kind of real estate purgatory. It set off a downward cycle of anticipation, in which worried whites no longer bought homes in white neighborhoods that might one day attract colored residents even if none lived there at the time. Rents and purchase prices were dropped "in a futile attempt to attract white residents," as Hirsch put it. With prices falling and the neighborhood's future uncertain, lenders refused to grant mortgages or made them more difficult to obtain. Panicked whites sold at low prices to salvage what equity they had left, giving the homeowners who remained little incentive to invest any further to keep up or improve their properties.

Thus many white neighborhoods began declining before colored residents even arrived, Hirsch noted. There emerged a perfect storm of nervous owners, falling prices, vacancies unfillable with white tenants or buyers, and a market of colored buyers who may not have been able to afford the neighborhood at first but now could with prices within their reach. The arrival of colored home buyers was often the final verdict on a neighborhood's falling property value rather than the cause of it. Many colored people, already facing wage disparities, either could not have afforded a neighborhood on the rise or would not have been granted mortgages except by lenders and sellers with their backs against the wall. It was the falling home values that made it possible for colored people to move in at all.

The downward spiral created a vacuum that speculators could exploit for their own gain. They could scoop up properties in potentially unstable white neighborhoods and extract higher prices from colored people who were anxious to get in and were accustomed to being overcharged in the black belt.

"The panic peddler and the 'respectable' broker earned the greatest profits," Hirsch wrote, "from the greatest degree of white desperation."

It seemed as if little had changed from the hostilities of the early years of the Migration, when colored tenants on Vincennes Avenue got the following notice: *"We are going to blow these flats to hell and if you don't want to go with them you had better move at once. Only one warning."* The letter writers carried out their threat. Three bombs exploded over the following two weeks.

Thirty years later, things were no better and may actually have been worse, as the black belt strained to hold the migrants still pouring in even as the borders with white neighborhoods were being more vigorously defended.

By the late 1950s, Ida Mae and George, now both working blue-collar jobs and their children now adults and with blue-collar jobs of their own, were dreaming of finding a place where they could pool their incomes and live together under one roof. But it would be some time before they were in a position to act or could find a safe and affordable place to go.

At the same time, an urban turf war had risen up around them. Bombings, shootings, riots, or threats greeted the arrival of nearly every new colored family in white-defended territory. The biggest standoffs came between the groups with the most in common, save race: the working-class white immigrants and the working-class black migrants, both with similar backgrounds and wanting the same thing—good jobs and a decent home for their families—but one group not wanting to be anywhere near the other and literally willing to fight to the death to keep the other out.

It was a chilling parallel to the war playing out at the very same time in the South, from the arrest of Rosa Parks in 1955 for refusing to give up a bus seat in Alabama to white troops blocking nine colored students in 1957 on their first day of school in Little Rock, Arkansas, after the Supreme Court said they had the right to enroll.

After World War II, Chicago, Detroit, Cleveland, and other northern and western cities would witness a fitful migration of whites out of their urban strongholds. The far-out precincts and the inner-ring suburbs became sanctuaries for battle-weary whites seeking, with government incentives, to replicate the havens they once had in the cities.

One such suburb was Dearborn, Michigan, just outside Detroit. By the mid-1950s, Dearborn was swelling with white refugees from the city. The suburb's mayor, Orville Hubbard, told the *Montgomery Advertiser* in Alabama that the whites had been "crowded out of Detroit by the colored people." He was more than happy to welcome these new white residents and said, to the delight of southern editorialists, "These people are so anti-colored, much more than you in Alabama."

Having already fled the cities, the newcomers were not going to let colored people into their new safehold. "Negroes can't get in here," Mayor Hubbard told the southerners. "Every time we hear of a Negro moving in, we respond quicker than you do to a fire."

———

Decades later, the message would still hang in the air, the calculus pretty much the same. By the end of the twentieth century, blacks would make up more than eighty percent of the population of Detroit. Just across the Ford Expressway, the black population of the suburb of Dearborn, the 2000 census found, was one percent.

NEW YORK, 1963
GEORGE SWANSON STARLING

———

EVERY NIGHT, the violence came into George Starling's living room. He had been watching the nightly news, the grainy black-and-white images of colored teenagers standing up to southern sheriffs, and he could see himself as a young man again, pressing against the barbed wall of the caste system in Florida. Sheriff's deputies were pounding the young people with fire hoses and beating them with batons. This was the South he left. He wondered if it would ever change.

He was on the subway one morning heading to work at Pennsylvania Station in the midst of this southern assault. He got settled in his seat and opened the newspaper. "I looked at the front page," he said, "and there's all these black people down on the ground, and dogs jumping all over them and the cops standing over them with billies and beating on them down in Alabama on a march."

Something welled up in George. Everything raced before him: the cheating foremen in the groves, his running for his life, the hangings and burnings, the little southern dog that would rather die than be black, the bomb going off on Christmas Day under the bed of a good man trying to bring justice to Florida. And then there was New York. Wide open and stifling at the same time. Yes, he was alive, but it was a slow death in a hard city. He was a baggage handler for all intents and purposes and would be no more than that no matter how much potential he had.

The city was pressing down on him and swallowing up his children. It never failed to remind him that he was seen as alien, the Yankee bartender taking the trouble to break the glass George had drunk from rather than use it again. There was no place else to run. And now the heat was turning up in the South again. Hosing and police dogs and people watching it as if it were a made-for-TV movie and the blacks just having to take it like they had for generations.

"I had the paper in front of my face," he said. *"And I got so mad. I dropped the paper down. And when I dropped the paper, I'm looking right in a white man's face just sitting across from me. I had never seen the man before, didn't know him from Adam, but he was white. And the hatred just surged up in me after looking at this thing in the paper. I just wanted to hurt somebody white. And I had to just really restrain myself to keep from just getting up. And that*

was the thing that went on during the whole campaign," as he called the
civil rights movement.

George got hold of himself. He pulled himself back from the edge.
This thing was driving him crazy, and there was nothing he could do
about it. The white man probably never had a clue. George would go
about his job on the train, and no one would know the difference. But
the despair did not leave him. He still had loved ones in the South. "I
was worried about all my family and friends," he said. "I had a lot of
people there. My father and mother were living. My brother and all the
kids that I went to school with and my wife's people. There were a lot of
people that I was concerned with."

He saw the fear firsthand on the faces of colored passengers heading
north and in his tense interactions with white southerners when he
worked the rails going south. As bad as it was, and as bad as it had been
all those decades before, some of the most boldfaced terrors of the civil
rights movement were yet to come—the bombing deaths of four little
girls just before a Sunday church service in Birmingham, the assassina-
tions of civil rights workers, black and white, Andrew Goodman, James
Chaney, and Michael Schwerner and Medgar Evers, the confrontation
on a bridge in Selma, Alabama. Those would not come until Jim Crow's
fitful last hours.

George kept close contact with the people back home and, like many
migrants in the North, sent money to support the protests because the
migrants knew more than most anyone what the people back home
were up against.

One day in 1962, in the middle of the civil rights movement, he heard
something that set him off again. By civil rights standards it was a rela-
tively small thing, and that is what drew him to it. For some reason
nothing seemed as fate-tempting and blasphemous as someone setting
fire to three defenseless colored churches, as in Georgia in September
1962. They were razed to the ground by white supremacists bent on
keeping colored people from something as basic as signing up to vote.
George was raised in the church and felt it hallowed and sanctified and
the only safe place even the old slaveholders had dared not enter. It represented a breach of the most private, holy space.

He read in the *New York Amsterdam News* that there was a drive on to
raise money to rebuild the churches. He started a collection himself. He
went to the underpaid cooks and baggage men and redcaps and porters

working the rails with him. He got fifty cents here and a dollar there from people like Walter Watkins from Washington, D.C., Ralph Covington from Brooklyn, Van Truett from the Bronx, G. T. Craig from Baltimore, J. E. Aaron of Brooklyn, and thirty-eight other co-workers. It took him four weeks to raise forty-one dollars. In January 1963, he walked over to the office of the *Amsterdam News* and handed a check in that amount to a rebuilding fund the paper was sponsoring.

With George, it was never the money when it came to these things but the sense of indignation over the injustice of it all and about doing something, anything, and getting other people as roused up about it as he was, just like he did back in the orange groves in Florida all those years ago. He had been in Harlem and working for the railroad for eighteen years now and knew he and his co-workers could raise more than a few dollars to help fight bigotry in the region they left.

The *Amsterdam News* soon closed the fund, figuring it had raised all it was going to get. The churches in Georgia had already begun rebuilding with donations that had come in from all over the country. But George hadn't stopped collecting money. He kept a ledger of all the men who contributed and what they contributed, each fifty-cent and dollar increment from Percy Brown of Mount Vernon, Yace Brown of Queens, Adolph Thomas of Philadelphia. In March, George showed up again at the newspaper office with a check for forty-four dollars more.

"I wanted to help in the only way I know," he told the *Amsterdam News*.

LOS ANGELES, AUGUST 1961
ROBERT JOSEPH PERSHING FOSTER

ROBERT WAS IN REGULAR CONTACT with the folks back home, and in one of his phone calls to Monroe, his big brother Madison mentioned that he was due for some upcoming surgery, what seemed on the face of it to be fairly routine, the problem being his gallbladder. But Robert, a surgeon of many years now, knew that nothing involving surgery was routine and urged his brother to come out to California, where he could get the best of medical care. Robert would make all the arrangements, and Madison wouldn't have to submit to the small-town, probably proficient, but still segregated medicine back in Louisiana.

"Come," Robert told him. "I don't want those white doctors in Monroe operating on you. You come out here so I'll know what kind of care you're getting."

Madison had heard about the state-of-the-art facilities in Los Angeles. He knew his brother would see to it that he got the very best—that was just the way Robert was and he couldn't help himself. So, although the trip out west would be taxing, he decided to leave his wife, Harriet, and son, Madison James, in Monroe and follow his little brother's advice and come to L.A.

"He had confidence in me," Robert said.

Robert set about planning the best medical care for his brother. He handpicked the surgeon—board-certified, it went without saying—who was one of his most trusted friends. On the day of the operation, Robert was there in his scrubs in the operating room, serving as second assistant and watching every move.

"And when he picked the knife up to make the incision," Robert remembered, "I closed my eyes and flinched. I felt it. I couldn't assist with that attitude. So the surgeon said, 'Bob, you let Palmer Reed move up, and you step back so I can sponge.' And I settled down."

Robert stayed for the duration of the surgery. "I saw everything, and it was a flawless operation. It was beautiful. There was no mistake made. None."

He felt proud and vindicated that he had insisted that his big brother come out to California and that things had gone so well. To Robert, it was just one more way to prove to the brother who had stayed in the South that he had made the right decision to migrate and that things really were better in California.

Robert was in a great mood and started joking with his brother that maybe he should recuperate at Robert's house or with their sister, Gold, who by now Robert had lured to California, too.

"You wasting money in a private room," Robert said. "Come to my house or go live with Gold."

"Okay," Madison said. "I'll be ready to go. I just don't feel good right now."

Three or four days after surgery, Madison was still saying he didn't feel good. He started sending out for antacids to relieve his abdominal pressure. But he wasn't complaining.

"And he didn't have any symptoms that would make us want to do anything special," Robert later said. "We know there's a certain amount of discomfort you gonna have. He was taking soft foods, and he was up. He was ambulated the next day after surgery. Temperature was flat. He was doing fine."

After several more days, a nurse woke Robert up one morning.

"Dr. Foster, this is Miss Smart. I'm calling you about Dr. Madison Foster."

"Yes."

"He went to the bathroom, Dr. Foster."

Robert heard the gravity in her voice, the succinctness of her message, and knew what it meant, could read her shorthand. Madison must have strained himself and, in the straining, dislodged some plaque that could be anywhere in his body, in his heart, his lungs, his brain. There was no telling where it could be. Robert got straight to the point.

"Is he alive?"

The nurse told him, yes, and that they had called in several doctors to attend to him.

"Fine," Robert said, suspecting that it wasn't.

At once he began calling in the specialists he knew, and then he rushed to the hospital. Madison's hospital room was full of doctors. They were surrounding his bedside, all working on him.

"And I'll never forget the look in his eyes," Robert said, his head down now. "And he's looking at me. And that look in his eye was saying, *'Is this it?'* Little Bubba, he called me. *'Little Bub, is this it?'* He was so worried. And I'm crying and talking."

Robert tried to comfort him.

"Don't worry, Bubba," Robert said. "It's alright. It's gonna be alright."

Madison was a physician himself and knew that it wasn't.

"He knew I was only reassuring him," Robert would later say, "because why would I be crying?"

Robert got on the phone with Madison's wife, Harriet, who was still awaiting word back in Monroe about how the gallbladder surgery had gone. "I gave her an hour-to-hour report," he said. "And that went on all day."

Instead of saving his brother in California, Robert would end up sending Madison back home in a casket, the people in Monroe clucking over Robert's so-called Promised Land and what a shame it all was. Harriet would hold it against him for years. Madison had died of a blood clot; that had been the source of his discomfort, and nothing, it seemed, could have prevented it. Robert would have been the first to blame the doctors if it had happened in the South, but this had been in California, and he had chosen the surgeons and seen the operation with his own eyes. Robert would blame himself for as long as he lived, torture himself with *"What would have happened if . . . ,"* and would never truly get over it.

REVOLUTIONS

I can conceive of no Negro native to this country
who has not, by the age of puberty, been irreparably scarred
by the conditions of his life. . . .
The wonder is not that so many are ruined
but that so many survive.
　　　　　　　—JAMES BALDWIN, *Notes of a Native Son*

CHICAGO, 1966
IDA MAE BRANDON GLADNEY

ONE DAY IN 1966, something hopeful called to Ida Mae, who was now fifty-three and a grandmother. She scuttled past the dime stores and beauty shops on Sixty-third Street with Eleanor's little children, Karen and Kevin, in tow. They were rushing in the direction of a quavering voice on a loudspeaker. Up ahead, she could see a crowd of onlookers, the faithful and the curious, packed in the street and on the sidewalks near Halsted and sober-faced police officers circling the crowd on horseback.

She arrived late and out of breath. Years later, all she would remember was the voice saying something about "little white children and little colored children," or so she thought, and all the people, hordes of them, straining to hear but tense from the police scrutiny and the vaguely dangerous nature of the moment.

Dr. Martin Luther King, Jr., was there in person and speaking before them. It was one of his rare appearances in Ida Mae's neighborhood during his first major attempt to bring the civil rights movement to the

North. Ida Mae almost missed it. She arrived too late to get anywhere near the podium. Neither she nor Karen or Kevin could see over the crowd that had gathered long before them.

"They had him way up on something high," she said decades later. "And you could hear his voice talking through those horns."

Ida Mae wanted to move closer to see him. That was what she had come for, after all. "I never did get close enough," she said. "I didn't want to push through the crowd. Everybody was so touchy. And I had kids, you see, and I just couldn't pull them up in there. I never did get to see him good."

Ida Mae was taken in by the sheer presence of the man, who by then had already won the Nobel Peace Prize, led the March on Washington, witnessed the signing of the 1964 Civil Rights Act, and overseen his epic battles against Jim Crow in places like Selma and Montgomery.

But Chicago was a turning point for King. His movement was aging, its actions drawing greater skepticism and its successes leaving him with fewer obvious dragons to slay. It was a campaign looking for a cause. The inroads into southern segregation gave King a greater awareness of the unresolved tensions in the North in the wake of the Great Migration.

"Negroes have continued to flee from behind the Cotton Curtain," King told a crowd at Buckingham Fountain near the Loop, testing out a new theme in virgin territory. "But now they find that after years of in-difference and exploitation, Chicago has not turned out to be the New Jerusalem."

Yet the very thing that made black life hard in the North, the very na-ture of northern hostility—unwritten, mercurial, opaque, and emi-nently deniable—made it hard for King to nail down an obvious right-versus-wrong cause to protest.

Blacks in the North could already vote and sit at a lunch counter or anywhere they wanted on an elevated train. Yet they were hemmed in and isolated into two overcrowded sections of the city—the South Side and the West Side—restricted in the jobs they could hold and the mort-gages they could get, their children attending segregated and inferior schools, not by edict as in the South but by circumstance in the North, with the results pretty much the same. The unequal living conditions produced the expected unequal results: blacks working long hours for overpriced flats, their children left unsupervised and open to gangs, the resulting rise in crime and drugs, with few people able to get out and the problems so complex as to make it impossible to identify a single cause or solution.

King was running headlong into what the sociologist Gunnar Myrdal called the Northern Paradox. In the North, Myrdal wrote, "almost everybody is against discrimination in general, but, at the same time, almost everybody practices discrimination in his own personal affairs"— that is, by not allowing blacks into unions or clubhouses, certain jobs, and white neighborhoods, indeed, avoiding social interaction overall.

"It is the culmination of all these personal discriminations," he continued, "which creates the color bar in the North, and, for the Negro, causes unusually severe unemployment, crowded housing conditions, crime and vice. About this social process, the ordinary white Northerner keeps sublimely ignorant and unconcerned."

Thus any civil rights campaign in the North would not be an attack on outrageous laws that, with enough grit and fortitude, could be overturned with the stroke of a pen. Instead, King would be fighting the ill-defined fear and antipathy that made northern whites flee at the sight of a black neighbor, turn away blacks at realty offices, or not hire them if they chose. The "enemy" was a feeling, a general unease that led to the flight of white people and businesses and sucked the resources out of the ghettos the migrants were quarantined into. No laws could make frightened white northerners care about blacks enough to permit them full access to the system they dominated.

"So long as this city is dominated by whites, whether because of their numbers without force or by their force if they were in the minority," the *Chicago Tribune* once wrote, "there will be limitations placed on the black people."

Still, despite the odds, King was compelled to go north—was called to it, he said—as had a good portion of his people in the still-unfolding Migration. He had made the journey himself when he went to Boston University for graduate school and while there met his wife, Coretta, another southerner. King's campaign in the North was "in one sense simply reacting to a major shift in the epicenter of black America," the historian James R. Ralph wrote. "It was following the great demographic flow of black Americans from the rural South to the urban North."

King actually moved into an apartment in the most hardscrabble section of town, the West Side neighborhood of North Lawndale, where the poorest and most recent arrivals from the South had shakily established themselves. He had a chesslike series of encounters with Mayor Richard J. Daley, the mayor-boss of Chicago, who managed to outwit the civil rights leader at nearly every turn. For one thing, Daley knew not to make the same mistakes as his southern counterparts. He met with King, appearing cooperative rather than ignoring him or having him thrown into jail. He vowed to protect the marchers with a heavy police presence that sometimes outnumbered the marchers. It worked so well that the protesters rarely had the chance to contrast their peaceable courage against foaming-at-the-mouth supremacists because Daley's police force didn't let any white mob get near them, which kept the protests off the news and kept the movement from gaining traction, just as Daley had hoped.

That is until, after months of buildup, King went to march against housing segregation in a neighborhood called Marquette Park on the city's southwest side. This was a working-class neighborhood of Poles, Lithuanians, Germans, and Italians who had not long since gotten their starter bungalows and were standing their ground against the very thought of colored people moving in.

It was August 5, 1966. A fist-shaking crowd of some four thousand residents had gathered in advance. Upon his arrival, they cursed King with epithets from a knoll overlooking the march. Many people in the crowd waved Confederate flags. Some wore Nazi-like helmets. One placard read KING WOULD LOOK GOOD WITH A KNIFE IN HIS BACK.

The march had barely begun when a heckler hurled a rock as big as a fist at King, striking him in the head, just above the right ear. He fell to his knees, and, as he tried to get up, the crowd pelted the demonstrators with bottles, eggs, firecrackers, and more rocks. Some in the crowd turned and smashed rocks into cars and buses that passed with colored people in them. Some twelve hundred police officers and two hundred plainclothesmen had gathered in anticipation of trouble, but this was one of the rare occasions that they were outnumbered by white residents primed for confrontation.

As the eight hundred King supporters tried to carry on the march, they passed men, women, and children on their front stoops, who called the marchers "cannibals," "savages," and worse. A column of three hundred jeering white teenagers sat in the middle of the street to block the marchers' path. The police dispersed the youths with nightsticks waving, and the march was able to resume. But the teenagers repositioned themselves half a block down and sat in the street again. It took a second charge from the police to break up the young hecklers.

When the march wound down, the mob chased the buses carrying King's people away. Rising in agitation that lasted for hours, the mob smashed an effigy of King, overturned a car on Marquette Road, stoned other cars, and fought police trying to clear the place out, requiring re-inforcements to beat the mob back with clubs and shots fired into the air. In the end, some thirty people were injured and forty were arrested.

Some of King's aides had warned him not to go to Chicago. He said he had to. "I have to do this," he said as he tried to steady himself after the stoning, "to expose myself—to bring this hate into the open."

He had marched in the deepest corners of Alabama but was unpre-pared for what he was in for in Chicago. "I have seen many demonstra-tions in the South," he said that violent day in the Promised Land. "But I have never seen anything so hostile and so hateful as I've seen here today."

Ida Mae watched it on the news that night and worried for the man she so badly had wanted to see. She expected this in Mississippi, not in the North. "No," she would say decades afterward, "some places I just trusted more than others."

NEW YORK, PENNSYLVANIA STATION, MID-1960S
GEORGE SWANSON STARLING

————

THE WORLD WAS CHANGING, and George, without trying, was on the front lines. In the South, the trains had been segregated for as long as most people had been alive. Now he was in the uncomfortable position of enforcing new laws that were just now filtering into everyday prac-tice.

There he was, scanning the crowds on the railroad platform as the southbound Silver Comet stretched down the track, belching and ready to board. The train would pull out of the station at 12:45 en route to Birmingham with some twenty-eight stops in between. Passengers packed the railway platform, suitcases, hatboxes, overnighters, trunks, briefcases, and Gimbel's shopping bags at their feet.

George went about his job of getting their luggage and helping them to their seats, but this time, he looked the passengers over in a way he never did before. He looked to see if they were in prim Sunday clothes or loud juke-joint get-ups, if the people seeing them off were self-

contained New Yorkers bidding people good-bye or excitable southerners still new to the spectacle. He checked to see if they haughtily took to
their reserved seats in the integrated railcar as if they owned it or if they
were wide-eyed and tentative about sitting in the same section as the
white passengers.

George was paying close attention because this was the mid-1960s.
The trains in the North had always been integrated, but blacks had to
move to separate cars before being permitted into the South. During the
run between New York and Alabama, it had been George's job to move
the colored passengers from their seats in the white section and into the
Jim Crow car before crossing from Washington into the segregated state
of Virginia.

But after the sit-ins and marches in the South, things were beginning
to change. President Lyndon B. Johnson signed the Civil Rights Act on
July 2, 1964, 101 years after Abraham Lincoln signed the Emancipation
Proclamation granting rights that would have to be spelled out again
long after Lincoln was gone. Now blacks were entitled to the same privileges as any other citizens. They were not to be segregated in any sphere
in life. But it would take time, up to a decade or more, for the message
to sink in to those who chose not to recognize the new law.

In addition, it was not as if a copy of the Civil Rights Act went out to
every black household. Some didn't know what their new rights were
exactly and had lived under the old order for so long that they were tentative about testing out the new one. In public conveyances, it fell to
workers like George Starling, if they were so inclined—which it so happened he was—to alert their fellow migrants to rights they weren't certain they could assert. On the train, it meant negotiating the tricky
business of reorienting the black passengers when the train passed into
or out of what had been Jim Crow territory.

For as long as most anyone alive could remember, this was the way
things had worked on the railroad: a black passenger boarding a southbound train at, say, Pennsylvania Station in New York would be assigned a seat anywhere on the train and could sit there without a second
thought until the train reached the border city of Washington, D.C.
From the time of Reconstruction in the 1870s, Washington had been the
dividing line between the free North and the segregated South. Black
passengers getting off in Washington had nothing to worry about. But
for those continuing south, the crews who ran the train, the porters who
helped passengers on and off, and the black passengers themselves knew

to gather their things and move to the Jim Crow car up front to make sure the races were separated when the train crossed into the state of Virginia.

The civil rights legislation of the mid-1960s changed all that, or was intended to. But custom had a way of lingering well after the ink was dry. So in the transition to integration, black passengers were not automatically granted the right to keep their seats no matter what their ticket or President Johnson said.

George was on the front lines in these early days of integration, when some conductors, many of them southern, held close the old traditions and ordered porters like George to move the colored passengers into the Jim Crow car, no matter the law. Some conductors, like many other southerners, resented the new laws that had been forced upon them. Others could always say that white southerners boarding the train below Washington were still not comfortable riding in the same coach as black people and might kick up a fuss.

As the train drew closer to Washington, the conductor gave George a passenger manifest identifying the passengers he wanted moved to the old Jim Crow car, meaning all the black passengers traveling below Washington.

George knew it wasn't right and began discreetly approaching colored passengers as the train pulled out of Baltimore en route to Washington. He tried to alert them to what was about to happen and let them know they had a right to stay where they were. But it was a perilous act on his part. The passengers might get scared and turn him in. He might be accused of inciting the passengers and disrupting the orderly relocation of passengers who didn't mind moving. It was especially dangerous because he was not heading north on the train but south into what might be considered enemy territory. Either way, he could be fired for what he was doing.

He knew he couldn't be seen openly advising black passengers to defy the conductor's orders. So from the moment he boarded the train in New York and began waiting on the black passengers in his charge, he paid close attention to them, scrutinized them to see which ones might be more receptive.

Then, as the train rumbled toward Union Station in Washington, and when he had made certain that the conductor wasn't around, he began approaching colored passengers, one by one. He leaned over the seat and began speaking in whispers.

"Look," he told them, "what I want to say to you is confidential, between you and me. If you don't think you can keep it confidential, let me know now, and I won't say any more. But it's to your benefit."

"Okay, okay."

Then he would explain the situation.

"Well, now, going below Washington," he would tell them, "they want us to move y'all up front in the Jim Crow car. But you have paid for a seat to wherever you're going. You paid an extra fee to reserve this seat, and you're entitled to keep this seat to your point of destination. But they not gonna tell you that. They gonna tell you, you got to move up front."

He waited for their response, checked for a show of interest and curiosity instead of fear and distrust. Then he would know whether to proceed. If he felt safe, he would go on.

"What you do," he continued, "is tell them that you don't care to move. Just tell them that."

Then he told them what to expect and gave them a little script. "They're gonna give you an argument," he said. "But just tell 'em, 'Look, I have a reserved seat here from New York to Jacksonville. Washington isn't my destination, and I'm not moving anywhere. Now, if you want me to move, you get the cops and come and move me. I'm not voluntarily moving anywhere.' "

He reassured them that they were within their rights. "They're not gon' bother you," he told them. "Because they know if you got nerve enough to tell 'em that you're not gonna move and if they force you to move, that they have a suit on their hands."

But it occurred to him that he needed to protect himself. He couldn't give any appearance of undermining the conductor's orders or inspiring the black passengers to do something that would otherwise never occur to them. So he admonished them further. "And don't go telling them, 'Well, the attendant told me I didn't have to move,' " George said. "Or you'll get me killed. Just tell 'em you're not gonna move. They not gonna move you."

Some of them got scared at that kind of talk. So George gave them an out. "If you feel more comfortable, and you think you should go up to that Jim Crow car when you have paid to ride like everybody else, then you go," he said. "I'll move you."

He forewarned them that if they decided to take the chance, they should know that he would have to feign indifference, pretend to have no knowledge of the matter if the conductor got involved. "He's gonna be telling me to take you up front, and you gonna be tellin' him that you're not going, and I'm gonna just be standing there. I'm gonna be saying, 'Naw, I ain't got nothin' to do with it.' "

By the time the train got halfway to Washington, he had a good idea of who he had in the railcar with him and which of them might be safe to approach.

"You could tell just by who brings them to the station," he said, "how they depart, the conversations."

But sometimes he would misjudge a passenger and come close to getting caught. Some passengers would loud-talk him.

"What? What the hell you talkin' 'bout?" they'd ask, not comprehending his plan.

George would speak in an even quieter whisper to get their voices down, which only meant they couldn't hear him and made them ask more questions, even louder than before.

"What? I don't have to move? How come I don't have to move?"

George would just shake his head and step away. "You know to leave them alone," he said.

What gave George the greatest sense of defeat were the people who went up to the Jim Crow car anyway. "They move anyway to avoid trouble," he said. "Quite a few would move up because the other attendants—they wouldn't tell the people. They wouldn't go to 'em like I would. Some of them would even support the conductor in telling them, 'You better move. You gotta move.' "

George didn't see it that way, and after all he had been through in the South, and even in the North, he felt it his duty to let the people know. It was the same George who tried to rouse the fruit pickers some twenty years before, to get them to stand up for what was due them.

In this case, on the train, George was fortunate. "None of them ever exposed me," he said.

And what's more, of the cases he saw, the people who resisted got to stay in their rightful seats. "Every incident that came up," George said, "they left them alone."

CHICAGO, SPRING 1967
IDA MAE BRANDON GLADNEY

―――――

IT HAD BEEN CLOSE TO THIRTY YEARS since Ida Mae and her family had come up north. The children were grown now. And by the late 1950s, the first generation born in the North had arrived. Eleanor, who had come north in Ida Mae's belly, had gotten married right out of high school and had two kids. James and his wife, Mary Ann, soon followed with four kids of their own. Ida Mae held the babies close and prayed for the first members of the family born free in the Promised Land.

There were different branches now, and they were getting by, but still renting and not settled in a place of their own. From flat to flat, in and around the straining borders of the South Side, Ida Mae and her family had moved more in Chicago than they had when they were sharecroppers in Mississippi, as they had never moved in Mississippi like some of the people they knew because they had always stayed with their one planter, Mr. Edd.

They had lived at Twenty-first and State, Thirty-third and State, Forty-fifth and St. Lawrence, and were now in the 700 block of West Sixty-sixth Place. They had been all over the South Side.

They felt they had been in Chicago long enough without owning something. George had been at Campbell Soup for years. Ida Mae was working as a nurse's aide at Walther Memorial Hospital. Velma was teaching, James was driving a bus for the Chicago Transit Authority. Eleanor was a ticket agent for the elevated train. So together, they had enough to put something down on some property.

Not unlike many immigrant families, they wanted to stay together and wanted a place big enough for all of them. Their search led them to a beige brick three-flat in a long-contested but, they believed, newly opened-up neighborhood called South Shore on the southern tip of the black belt. It was a few blocks west of Lake Michigan. The street was lined with oak trees along the sidewalk and brick bungalows and multiflats with little patches of yard in front.

They went to see the place at night.

An Italian car salesman and his family lived there. It had room enough for James and his family on the first floor, Ida Mae and her husband on the second, Eleanor and her kids on the third, or if necessary, a tenant to help with the house payments. Ida Mae and her family didn't have enough furniture to fill the flat. They wanted the place and every-thing in it: the plastic-covered upholstery, the marble-topped coffee table, the lamps, the dining room table, the breakfront and buffet, and the baby blue draperies over the front windows.

The Italian car salesman said he liked them and wanted them to have it. The family paid thirty thousand dollars and moved in without inci-dent. There was the little matter of a bullet hole in one of the windows in the front room, but Ida Mae didn't let it bother her as it appeared the shot had been fired sometime before they moved in. Thirty years after they arrived in the New World with little more than their kids and the clothes on their backs, Ida Mae and her husband were finally home-owners in Chicago.

"It was beautiful," Ida Mae said years later. "Trees everywhere, all up and down the block."

———

Weeks passed. Ida Mae went to work one morning and came back that evening on the streetcar over on Exchange. She walked down Colfax in the neighborhood of brick apartment buildings, barbershop storefronts, and frame bungalows along a route that she was just beginning to learn.

It was then that she noticed something missing across the street from her three-flat. A house had vanished. The people across from her had moved it, or so it appeared. There was now a small crater in the earth where, just that morning, a house used to be.

It was a wonderment to Ida Mae and to James and Eleanor and the grandkids. Why would their nice white neighbors move their house clear off the street? Where did they go? What did this mean?

They would never see them again to get the answers. They would never fully know for sure what had happened or why. It would become part of their family lore, one of the things they would tell over and over again, shaking their heads and hunching their shoulders as they looked out their second-floor window at the sociology unfolding beneath them.

As it was, too much was happening anyway. Within weeks of the dis-appearing house, moving vans clogged Colfax Street. More people were vanishing, but those people left their houses behind. They took their sofas and upright pianos and were gone.

"Lord, they move quick," Ida Mae said years later. "And then blacks started moving in. Oh, Lord."

The whites left so fast Ida Mae didn't get a chance to know any of them or their kids or what they did for a living or if they liked watching

The Ed Sullivan Show like she did Sunday nights. They didn't stick around long enough to explain. But some of the whites who left the South Side in a panic would talk about it years later and, to tell the truth, never got over the loss of their old neighborhoods.

"It happened slowly, and then all of a sudden, *boom,*" said a white homemaker who fled Ida Mae's neighborhood around that time and was quoted by the writer Louis Rosen, who had been a teenager when his parents fled South Shore, in the book *South Side*. "Everyone was gone. Everything changed. Before you know it, this one, that one. And then you heard, 'So-and-so's moving.' People didn't want to be the last."

A white father told Rosen, "I fought the good fight. I couldn't stay there with my three kids—my oldest was only fourteen at the time. I made a judgment. I did the best I could."

"It was like sitting around with a big group," said a white husband. " 'Okay, guys, in the next year, we're all going.' "

"It was who found a house first," the wife chimed in.

"Exactly. And we all went," the husband said.

To the colored people left behind, none of it made any sense. "It was like having a tooth pulled for no reason," said a black resident who moved his family in, only to watch the white neighbors empty out.

———

By the end of the year, the 7500 block of Colfax and much of the rest of South Shore went from all white to nearly totally black, which in itself might have been a neutral development, except that many houses changed hands so rapidly it was unclear whether the new people could afford the mortgages, and the rest were abandoned to renters with no investment or incentive to keep the places up. The turnover was sudden and complete and so destabilizing that it even extended to the stores on Seventy-fifth Street, to the neighborhood schools and to the street-sweeping and police patrols that could have kept up the quality of life. It was as if the city lost interest when the white people left.

The ice cream parlor closed. The five-and-dime shut down. The Walgreens on the corner became a liquor store. Karen and Kevin enrolled in Bradwell Elementary School and remember being, along with two other kids, the only black children in the entire school in 1968. By the time they graduated four years later, the racial composition had completely reversed: only four white children were left. South Shore would become as solidly black as the North Shore was solidly white. Ida

Mae's neighborhood never had a chance to catch up with all the up-heaval and was never the same again.

South Shore was one of the last white strongholds on the South Side, the completion of a cycle that had begun when the migrants first arrived and started looking for a way out of the tenements. There were fifty-eight bombings of houses that blacks moved into or were about to move into between 1917 and 1921 alone, bombings having become one of the preferred methods of intimidation in the North. In neighborhood after neighborhood, with the arrival of black residents the response during the Migration years was swift and predictable.

It happened to ordinary people like Ida Mae and to celebrities like Mahalia Jackson, the leading gospel singer of her day. When she began looking for a house in a well-to-do section of the South Side, people held meetings up and down the block. A Catholic priest rallied his parishioners and told them not to sell to her.

"You'd have thought the atomic bomb was coming instead of me," the singer said.

She got calls in the middle of the night, warning her, "You move into that house, and we'll blow it up with dynamite. You're going to need more than your gospel songs and prayers to save you."

She bought the house. It was a sprawling red brick ranch and the house of her dreams, coming as she had from the back country of Louisiana. A doctor had broken ranks and sold it to her. As soon as she moved in, the neighbors shot rifle bullets through her windows. The police were posted outside her house for close to a year.

"One by one," she said, "they sold their houses and moved away. As fast as a house came on the market a colored family would buy it."

Even Hyde Park, an island of sophistication just north of Ida Mae's working-class neighborhood of South Shore, succumbed to the same fears and raw emotion that overtook the rest of the city's South Side.

"Shall we sacrifice our property for a third of its value and run like rats from a burning ship," said a handbill circulated among white residents trying to keep blacks on the other side of State Street, "or shall we put up a united front to keep Hyde Park desirable for ourselves?"

Oddly enough, Hyde Park was one of the very few places where the alarmist rhetoric did not completely take. It was home to the venerable University of Chicago, which had its own interest in maintaining stability, and the neighborhood was blessed with some of the finest residential architecture in the city, giving many whites compelling and overriding reasons to stay. The neighborhood was one of the most expensive on the

South Side, so blacks who moved there had to have the means just to get in. Thus Hyde Park actually became a rare island of integration despite the initial hostilities.

Still, it was surrounded by all-black neighborhoods in a deeply divided city. Entire communities like the suburb of Cicero remained completely off-limits to blacks, and whites would avoid so much as driving through whole sections of the south and west sides for the remainder of the century.

By the time the Migration reached its conclusion, sociologists would have a name for that kind of hard-core racial division. They would call it hypersegregation, a kind of separation of the races that was so total and complete that blacks and whites rarely intersected outside of work. The top ten cities that would earn that designation after the 1980 census (the last census after the close of the Great Migration, which statistically ended in the 1970s) were, in order of severity of racial isolation from most segregated to least: (1) Chicago, (2) Detroit, (3) Cleveland, (4) Milwaukee, (5) Newark, (6) Gary, Indiana, (7) Philadelphia, (8) Los Angeles, (9) Baltimore, and (10) St. Louis—all of them receiving stations of the Great Migration.

NEW YORK, LATE SUMMER 1967
GEORGE SWANSON STARLING

———

THERE CAME A TIME in the lives of many migrants' children when the parents sent them south for the summer to protect them from the uncaring streets of the Promised Land or to learn the culture of their family of origin or of the Old Country itself. It was a ritual practiced more or less by most families to ensure that their children knew where they came from.

George and Inez Starling sent their daughter, Sonya, down to Eustis when she was thirteen. What happened there was the last thing they expected: she got pregnant.

"It almost killed my wife," George said.

It was devastating after all they had been through and was the beginning of the most trying season of their lives. They had been married for twenty-eight years. Theirs had not been a happy union, but at least they had a family and had made out okay in New York, almost in spite of themselves, because they were hard workers and deep down good and decent people.

They had the highest hopes for their children, raised in a world free of the hardships they had endured in Florida. And now, it was as if the South and the backbiting country town they had left had reached back and punished them for having had the nerve to leave.

George had made a winless bargain. He had taken a job that kept him away from the very people he was working so hard to take care of, and he could not undo the damage already done. His absence only created a bigger gulf between him and Inez and left the children without a father most of the time and a mother with demons of her own to raise them practically by herself.

When they learned of Sonya's pregnancy, George would not admit his pain. He reacted with resignation and had little sympathy for the despair Inez felt, just as, all those years before, she had had little sympathy for his earnestness in organizing the pickers in the citrus groves.

The wounds they both carried had hardened and calcified, and the crisis over Sonya—*What would become of her? What kind of future would she have? How would they manage to raise the baby?*—only widened the chasm. Each blamed the other and themselves.

When he finally spoke, George's words cut deep. He said Sonya was no different from Inez. "It wasn't on account of your purity," he told her with the barbed edge that seemed to characterize more and more of their interactions, "that it didn't happen to us. You can't deny it 'cause you were doing it with me."

Sonya gave birth to a baby boy she named Bryan. It was 1968. She was fourteen.

George, fatalistic now after all that they had been through, said all he could do was laugh. The sins of the father were visiting the children. He thought back to when he was in the tenth grade and a girl in his class turned up pregnant.

"She named me the father," he said.

His first reaction was how did she know that he was the father, that just about anybody could have been the father. His second reaction was that there went his future. For the rest of his life, he would be picking fruit during the citrus season and digging up palmetto roots the rest of the time, pretty much the only work around.

"Let me finish the eleventh grade," he remembered telling the grown folks. "I'd just like to finish out the eleventh grade. I don't mind doing the right thing."

The baby was born dead. "I was so relieved," George said. "I never tried to find out if it was mine."

Now his daughter had come to him with the same news the girl he dallied with in high school had broken to her family all those years ago.

"Now you know," he thought to himself. *"Now you know how that mother felt when her daughter said she was pregnant by you."*

And so when the crisis over Sonya came up, George could only laugh through his tears at how much of what he had sown he appeared to be reaping. "I never did tell my wife," George said. "I didn't try to tell my wife why I was laughing. It was retribution."

It was retribution on several fronts. At around the same time that Sonya got pregnant, so did another woman. It was a woman George had been going out with behind Inez's back. As their marriage strained under the weight of unspoken resentments, he gave in to temptation. It only made unpleasant matters even worse and life nearly unbearable for Inez, the discovery of two pregnancies she never would have imagined or wished for.

The sadness and irony seemed to be turning in on itself, and it all seemed to point back to the rash and fateful day that George tried to get back at his father by marrying Inez in the first place. It appeared in the end he was only getting back at himself.

The other woman gave birth to a son. The boy was named Kenny. He was born a few months after Sonya's baby was born.

Kenny would grow up as an outside son, knowing his father, George, from afar and valuing him more than perhaps anyone else on earth because he was in some ways more like his father than anyone else and loved what little he knew of him.

LOS ANGELES, 1967
ROBERT JOSEPH PERSHING FOSTER

RUFUS CLEMENT AND HIS SON-IN-LAW, Robert Foster, were at opposite ends of the Great Migration. They represented the two roads that stood before the majority of black people at the start of the century. One man had stayed in the South. One had left it behind. Both had worked long and hard and had all the material comforts most any American could dream of. Yet both men wanted to prove to the other and to everyone else that his was the wiser choice, his life the more meaningful one.

President Clement was the tight-buttoned scion of the southern black bourgeoisie. Robert was a brilliant but tortured free spirit who had run from the very strictures Clement stood for. Clement was a distinguished accommodationist in the Jim Crow South—a beneficiary of it, in fact. He was not unlike the colored university president in Ralph Ellison's *Invisible Man,* whose allegiance was, above all, to the institution he ran, which had become an extension of himself. He was a pragmatist who had learned the fine art of extracting whatever he needed from guilt-ridden northerners or poorly credentialed but powerful segregationists who wouldn't want him living next to them but might grant him a concession or donate to his cause, the colored graduate school Atlanta University. He was so vigilant as to his place in the colored hierarchy that he kept a card file near his desk, *Time* magazine reported, on every black person in the United States that he considered "worthy of a high position in Government and education" in case he got a query from Washington.

Without trying, Rufus Clement had become an unwitting rival of Robert, not only for the affections of Robert's wife and children but in both men's unspoken effort to prove that where each man had ended up was the better place for colored people.

Robert had made out well as a noted surgeon in Los Angeles. But it did not rate with his father-in-law, Rufus Clement, who had staked his claim in the South and prospered. President Clement had avoided the messy confrontations of the civil rights era, saying at one point that he had been disturbed, as any right-thinking southerner might be, by the sit-ins but recognized that "this is the way in which they have tried to dramatize the way in which the American Negro has to live in his own country." He reassured white southerners that "we don't want to sit beside you, we just want to sit when we eat, like other people sit. We don't want to intermarry with your people. We simply want to get a drink of water where there is a drinking fountain available."

His patient and deferential ambitions paid off in 1953, when, against the longest of odds, he was elected to the Atlanta Board of Education— a first for a colored person there, while Robert, by contrast, was doing physicals and collecting urine samples for Golden State Insurance in what then seemed an unpromising start in California.

———

The Clements hovered over Robert and pulled at his wife and daughters from afar. And as they did, Robert retreated further into the world of his patients, his bookies, and the B-list musicians he liked to hang around with. He was drinking more and coming in late. He had fallen hard for Vegas and now had discovered horse racing. He joined the club room at Santa Anita, since now he could well afford it, and liked to catch the trifectas at Hollywood Park racetrack down in Inglewood.

He would go to Vegas whenever the spirit hit him and could play long and well. "I don't need to eat and rarely need to go to the bathroom," Robert would say. "I can go thirty-six hours." He liked the Sands Hotel and the Las Vegas Hilton. He went so often and bet so much that the hotels started comping him rooms and meals. Some trips, he brought back tens of thousands of dollars. Some trips, he lost that much. But he was hooked.

While he was out betting heavy and looking for something that did not exist and that nobody could give him, Alice set about establishing herself as a proper surgeon's wife. She joined the Links and the auxiliary of doctors' wives and hosted teas and bridge parties for the same kind of social set she had grown accustomed to back in Atlanta. The girls took piano and voice lessons and came out at their cotillions in white princess gowns. They were living parallel lives, and Alice and the girls tried not to notice that Robert, whose long hours helped finance their ball gowns and socials, was trying to fill some hole that could not be filled and was hardly ever around.

At one point, Alice had had enough. She packed up the girls and moved back to Atlanta with the Clements, who surely had not approved of how their daughter and granddaughters were faring with Robert. Somehow Alice and Robert made up, and she came back to Los Angeles. But nothing really had changed. They had both come into their own and seemed less suited in some ways than before. Perhaps they had always been ill suited for each other but were just beginning to realize it, now that they had a life and a family and reputations to protect.

They reached a kind of understanding and came together on the shining occasions when their mutual love of hosting and socializing happened to intersect at the grand parties they threw and the costumes they wore.

It was a ritual, and they had an understanding. Robert dressed Alice. Robert bought the clothes. Robert chose the clothes. Dressing Alice was his personal project. He studied her as a surveyor would study an isthmus, knew her assets and liabilities as far as tailoring went, and accompanied her not so much as an advocate for her tastes but as a guardian of his own reputation.

When Alice started moving up in the Links and had more cotillions to go to, he was happy for her and wanted her to look good. But it was a defensive kind of happiness. He wanted Alice to outdress the other women. "I didn't want those women to say my wife had anything less than the best," Robert said.

In the early days, he would prep her before a big formal. *"You got to go out there first, baby,"* he would tell her. *"You represent me."*

Every entrance was a production. They would approach the doorway of a ballroom. Robert would adjust himself and pause to let his wife go before him. "I'd walk two paces to the right and the rear and just watch her make that entrance," he said. "And she could walk."

Before every big occasion, the ritual was the same: the two heading to the store's back room, the salesclerk bringing in dresses that Robert knew were all wrong for Alice, and Robert saying, "Pick what you like." Alice would try on a dress. Robert inspected her and directed her movements.

"Walk," he told her. And she would begin.

"Come to me." She moved toward him.

"Sit." She would find an ottoman and position herself.

"Stand." She lifted herself up.

"Turn." And she would do so.

"If the dress didn't talk to me, it wasn't her dress," he said. "The salespeople go crazy. 'Who is this man? Who *is* he?'"

Over time, he began to sort the big moments of his life by whatever Alice was wearing. It seemed as if he remembered the gown if he remembered nothing else. Those gowns got people talking, and it was exactly what he wanted to hear: *Foster, you dress your women well.* "I couldn't be betting a hundred dollars on a horse and skimping on my wife," he told me many years later. "I know I'm bragging, and I'm enjoying it."

———

Sometimes the Clements would come out to visit them in Los Angeles, and Robert would put on his most charming performance to prove how well he had made out in the Promised Land. He invited the colored men of importance in the city to meet with his father-in-law and alerted the *Los Angeles Sentinel* so that the visit could be captured for posterity, as the Clements would have expected. The two men would never be close, but Robert knew how to put on a show when he had to.

By 1966, President Clement had risen to such a level of esteem at Atlanta University that a building was named in his honor. Clement Hall, an august red brick classroom building on the campus promenade, had its formal dedication on October 16, 1966. Alice and Robert's youngest daughter, Joy, in bangs and a white headband, cut the ribbon with her grandfather right behind her. Alice stood watching in a pillbox hat and tailored dark suit and corsage. Bunny was there in a tweed peacoat and gloves, with her Jackie-Kennedy-in-the-White-House bob and beautifully chiseled sixties cover-girl face, in a show of support for her grandfather. Robert did not attend.

———

The man who had managed to oust W. E. B. Du Bois from Atlanta University by lobbying the university's board of trustees all those years ago was in New York in early November 1967 for the regular meeting of that same board of trustees.

On the afternoon of Tuesday, November 7, during a break in the board's proceedings, Clement collapsed in his suite at the Roosevelt Hotel. He died of an apparent heart attack. He was sixty-seven years old.

He and his wife, Pearl, had planned to embark on a round-the-world tour after the board meeting. Instead, plans for interment were made. Pearl would have to move out of the president's mansion at Atlanta University, which had been her home and decorated to her liking for most of her adult life. She would have to move in with her next of kin, her beloved only daughter, Alice, in Los Angeles. Robert would have a wing with a bedroom and sitting area built for his mother-in-law and would try to make the best of it.

News reports of Rufus Clement's death appeared in the *Atlanta Daily*

World, the *New York Amsterdam News,* the *Los Angeles Sentinel,* and else-where. The *New York Amsterdam News* wrote that, "in addition to his widow, he is survived by a daughter, Mrs. Robert Foster of Los Angeles." Robert himself went unmentioned.

CHICAGO, FEBRUARY 1968
IDA MAE BRANDON GLADNEY

A POLICE WAGON pulled up to a West Side hospital over at Division and Kedzie, amid a rabble of placard-waving protesters on strike against the hospital, Walther Memorial. The strikers marched at the entrance in the biting cold. They were picketing for higher wages for the orderlies and nurse's aides who did the kinds of things nobody notices until they go undone.

Inside the police wagon, bundled up with coats and purses, looking wide-eyed at the people protesting in circles along the sidewalk, were Ida Mae and her co-worker and friend Doris McMurray. For several weeks in February 1968, that was how Ida Mae went to work each day.

Ida Mae respected the strikers, knew them by name, had worked right beside them, and got along with most of them, but she wasn't going to stand out there and strike with them. She had been working since she was big enough to get behind a plow. She had had all kinds of backbreaking, mind-numbing, sometimes dangerous and usually thankless jobs and had finally come into a position as a hospital aide. She had gotten the job in 1949, after more than a decade of scuffling from domestic to steel worker to press operator. She had finally come into a job she liked and that suited her temperament. She had come a long way from the cotton fields in Mississippi for the chance to work indoors with people rather than outdoors with crops and to get paid for the job and feel some dignity doing it. She had never stood up to a boss or refused to work or tried to petition for more money, even though she surely could have used it and more than likely deserved it. She had faith that whatever she needed would eventually come to her. The concept of not working a job one had agreed to do was alien to Ida Mae.

So when her union local announced it was going on strike at the beginning of 1968, Ida Mae and her friend Doris never considered that they would stop going to work. Decades earlier, colored migrants, unaccustomed to unions and not understanding labor politics, had been brought in by northern industrialists specifically to break up strikes. White union members resented the migrants and beat them for breaching the picket lines they had unwittingly been brought in to cross.

Ida Mae was not schooled in the protocols of union organizing, but she knew she couldn't afford to lose her job and couldn't see how not working was going to help her keep it. She was under more pressure than ever. She and George had just bought their first house, the three-flat in South Shore, and had new and different bills coming at them than ever before—from the mortgage to the utilities to property taxes and hazard insurance.

"My pastor was just begging me," Ida Mae remembered. "Please don't cross that picket line."

Her children were worried for her. "They didn't want me to go," Ida Mae said. "But I wasn't studyin' them."

George was his usual contained self. If he was scared for her, he didn't let on. The idea of not going to work was as foreign to him as it was to Ida Mae. "I don't reckon he ever knowed no different," Ida Mae said.

She made no apology for doing what she felt was living up to her responsibilities. Even the union boss teased her and said he knew why Ida Mae couldn't strike.

"She can't stay off," he said. "She got to pay for that three-flat building. She got to pay that house note."

"You right," Ida Mae said.

When Ida Mae and Doris told management they were going to keep working, the hospital arranged for a driver to pick them up at a designated location and escort them into the building.

One day, the strikers beat up the hospital driver after he had dropped the women off, and, for the first time, Ida Mae realized the seriousness of this thing. Then the hospital came up with another way to get Ida Mae and Doris to work: it arranged for a police wagon to pick up the two women at a designated bus stop.

"It was just like we were going to jail," Ida Mae said.

They would climb out of the police wagon at the entrance to the hospital, and the police would walk them past the pickets into the building.

"Scabs!" some of the picketers, shivering on the cold sidewalk, would yell at Ida Mae and Doris.

"You a scab," Ida Mae would shoot back, not knowing the labor union meaning of the word but hurling it anyway because, to her, everybody should have been working.

Ida Mae couldn't let a heckler go unanswered, and it frightened Doris.

"Shut up, Ida," Doris whispered. *"Ida, hush."*

The two of them were working on the sixth floor in surgery and on their breaks could look out the window and see the pickets below. After so many hours outside, the strikers had to find ways to protect themselves from the freezing wind. They would scurry to their cars and sit for a while, and they would use buckets instead of the toilet in the building because the hospital wouldn't let them in.

The strikers never threw anything but names at Ida Mae and Doris, and when the two of them looked back on it years later, they marveled that they had never gotten hurt.

"I wouldn't do that now," Doris said.

Ida Mae turned to Doris. "Well, I didn't really understand," Ida Mae said. "We all supposed to be working."

CHICAGO, NEW YORK, LOS ANGELES, AND MEMPHIS, APRIL 1968

THE EVENING WAS unusually cool for Memphis in April. It was shortly before six o'clock, and Martin Luther King, Jr., was heading to dinner before attending a rally for striking sanitation workers. He was standing on the second-floor balcony of the Lorraine Motel on Mulberry Street just outside his room, room 306. A half dozen of his aides were with him, gathering themselves to leave. Someone reminded King of how chilly it was getting. He agreed and went to get his topcoat.

At the precise moment that he turned back to his room, a minute past six on April 4, 1968, a single .30-caliber bullet was fired into the balcony. The rifle shot, thought to have come from a flophouse across the street through the bare branches of the mimosa trees, struck him in the neck

and severed his spinal cord. King was pronounced dead at St. Joseph's
Hospital at 7:05 P.M., Central Time. Within hours, the poor, colored sections of more than a hundred cities went up in flames.

———

That night, George Starling was rounding the corner at 131st Street and
St. Nicholas Avenue in Harlem. He was returning home from a night
out with the guys and saw the fires rising up ahead. He was trying to get
to 132nd and Lenox, not yet knowing what had happened to set the people off. The whole thing was a blur, and he was looking for a way to get
around the mayhem.

"It was in the direction of St. Nicholas Avenue," he said. "It could
have been on Broadway, St. Nicholas, or Amsterdam. It was up on that
hill. They were burning everything up there. The sky was lit up like it
was the end of time."

He made his way home, and it was "only when I got into the house
and turned on the radio that I heard the news that Martin Luther King
had been shot in Memphis."

———

The evening of the assassination, Ida Mae would cup her face in disbelief at the news playing out in a scratchy, continuous, uncomprehensible
loop on the AM radio dial and the family's black-and-white television
set. She would pray for the soul of the man she so admired and had once
almost seen during his Chicago campaign two years before as he had
tried to free the people who had fled to the North.

On the other side of town, over on the West Side, police sirens wailed
and rocks crashed through the plate-glass windows of grocers and
liquor stores. Whole blocks went up in smoke in Chicago and on the
streets of Newark, Detroit, Boston, Kansas City, Baltimore, Washington, D.C., and elsewhere. The receiving stations of the Great Migration
would burn all through the night after Martin Luther King, Jr., was assassinated. And when it was over, some neighborhoods, the old places
the migrants had packed into when the Migration began, would look
like Berlin after an air strike during the Second World War.

The dispossessed children of the Great Migration but, more notably,
the lifelong black northerners broken by the big cities let out a fury that
made a mockery of the free harbor the North was reputed to be. A presidential commission examining the disturbances found that more black
northerners had been involved in the rioting than the people of the

Great Migration, as had mistakenly been assumed. "About 74 percent of the rioters were brought up in the North," wrote the authors of what would become known as the Kerner Report. "The typical rioter was a teenager or young adult, a lifelong resident of the city in which he rioted." What the frustrated northerners "appeared to be seeking was fuller participation in the social order and the material benefits enjoyed by the majority of American citizens," the commission found.

The discontent of the young people unsettled the migrant parents who had fled the violence of the South. They could do little to dissuade their children from whatever role they might play in the outburst. It was too late to try to get them jobs at now-closed factories or the education they missed if they gave up on school, or, maybe most of all, the grounding and strength they themselves had acquired after having endured so much. The parents had come from the Old Country, had been happy to have made it out alive and make a few dollars an hour. *What did they know of the frustration of the young people who had grown up in the mirage of equality but a whole different reality, in a densely packed world of drugs and gangs and disorder, with promises that seemed to have turned to dust?*

Ida Mae saw the destruction on the news and, as usual, tried not to worry about things she could not control. George Starling managed to negotiate his way through the burning streets of Harlem. They had long since left the South where Dr. King had been killed. And yet they were pulled into the aftermath. In the North, the migrants grieved for the man who had worked miracles in the land of their birth and thus for them from afar.

It was Thursday, a workday, and across the country, Robert Foster, workaholic that he was, would have been in his office attending his usual overflow of patients at what would have been late afternoon on the West Coast.

His office on Jefferson and his house in West Adams were comfortably situated far from Watts, where the fires had burned three years before. Ever conscious of appearances and propriety, he would be nearly as incensed at the violence as he was stunned at the assassination. To him, spite never settled anything. It only gave your detractors more ammunition and, as it had back when the colored people in Monroe had urinated in the colored section of the Paramount Theater, only ended up hurting the people themselves.

To Robert, the whole world had just about gone mad. A few years before King's death, Robert had been beside himself when he learned that Bunny, a student at Spelman College in Atlanta caught up in the zeitgeist of the movement, was talking about maybe picketing, too, as only a bourgeois daughter of the upper class would. It would not be trying to register poor people to vote in the backwoods of Mississippi—that was out of the question—but by, say, protesting Rich's department store in downtown Atlanta with a white-gloved delegation of other colored college girls.

On this, Rufus Clement and Robert agreed: Bunny simply could not be seen being arrested with the riffraff, all because Rich wouldn't let colored girls try on hats. Of course, Robert understood the indignity, had lived it after all, which is why he had raised her in Los Angeles and taken her to Beverly Hills for whatever she and Alice and the other girls might ever think they wanted.

It wasn't that he was against the civil rights movement. He was all for standing up for one's rights. It was just that, to his way of thinking, the way to change things was to be better than anybody at whatever you did, wear them down with your brilliance, and enjoy the heck out of doing it. So he had no patience for these sit-in displays, at least for his daughters anyway, much less actual violence. The day King died was a dark day all around.

———

It was around midnight that George encountered the destruction in Harlem. It wasn't all the people out in the streets that got his attention. It wasn't unusual for a lot of people to be out on the streets of Harlem if it were the least bit warm. What caught his eye were the flames.

That Thursday evening in April, George had been hanging out with the guys over on Prospect Avenue. He was talking baseball and downing boilermakers—a shot of Smirnoff's with orange juice and a chaser of beer. He was trying to escape the disappointments of an underutilized mind and a sand trap of a marriage he was too loyal and upright to leave.

The men were so distracted by the vodka and the joshing over the Yankees and the Mets and the Dodgers, who had years before left Brooklyn for Los Angeles, and over the baseball season that was to begin the very next week, that they failed to register the assassination of one of the most influential figures in American history.

It was only when George finally made it into his car and back into Harlem that he realized that something terrible had happened.

"The sky lit up," he remembered. "When I turned into 131st Street, as soon as I looked, I saw: 'The whole sky is on fire.' "

George Starling knew what it meant to stare an enemy down in a life-and-death sort of way and had respect for Dr. King. But by the time King was assassinated, George was unable to marshal much emotion. He had grown up with that kind of violence against people fighting the system and half expected it. No, what had really shaken him was the assassination five years earlier of John F. Kennedy, the president so many blacks had placed their hopes in, Kennedy having come from the North and from what they saw as a more enlightened generation than previous presidents.

George was in Florida in November 1963. "I used to go down every October or November. I had just passed through Ocala, on the way to Gainesville, and it was in the afternoon," George remembered.

"And I turned the radio on, and I heard them say, *'And the President of the United States has been assassinated. He was shot, and he did not survive.'* Or something like that. And I said, 'Now, what kind of joke is that?' And then it came back on. You know they wouldn't have risked repeating it over and over. And when I realized that Kennedy had really been killed, assassinated, that thing hit me. When I knew anything, I had run off the road. I don't know what I was doing. And it just so happened that the shoulder was grassy. It wasn't that much traffic. It was in the midafternoon, and I just brought the car to a stop, and I just sat there, and I cried like a baby."

For some reason it was different with King than with Kennedy. Perhaps the losses were piling up and George couldn't muster the same shock and pain anymore. "I didn't cry," he said. "I was just astonished. I was just numb. I couldn't believe it. Then I thought about his speech. He predicted his own death whether he knew it or not. He told it. *I've been to the top of the mountain, and I've looked over, and I've seen the Promised Land. I may not make it there with you, but you will get to the Promised Land.'* "

James Earl Ray, a forty-year-old drifter and prison escapee, would be convicted of the murder. Ray left a trail of evidence that he had been stalking King for months, but, until his own death in 1998, left questions as to what role he had actually played in the assassination.

Ray was not from the South, as the migrants who left it might have expected. He was from Alton, Illinois.

Precisely a week after King's death, and two years after King's brokered and dispiriting effort to end housing segregation in Chicago, President Lyndon Johnson signed the Fair Housing Act of 1968, banning discrimination on the basis of race, color, religion, or national origin in the renting or selling of property. King's bruising fight for the people in the North would not be won until King had died.

THE FULLNESS OF
THE MIGRATION

And so the root
Becomes a trunk
And then a tree
And seeds of trees
And springtime sap
And summer shade
And autumn leaves
And shape of poems
And dreams
And more than tree.
—Langston Hughes

THE NORTH AND WEST, 1970

THIS WAS THE YEAR that demographers called the turning point in the exodus of black Americans out of the South. It was the year that the revolutions of the 1960s began to bear fruit and black children were entering white schools in the South without death threats or the need for the National Guard. The people from the South continued to go north in great waves because nobody told them the Migration was over, but fewer were leaving than in previous decades and nearly as many blacks in the North and West, particularly the children of the original people of the Great Migration, began to contemplate or act upon a desire to return south, now that things appeared to be changing.

Ida Mae, the sharecropper's wife from Chickasaw County, Missis-

sippi, was not among them. She was like the majority of the original migrants, people who were not really migrants at all but who had left for
good and didn't look back. She was fifty-seven years old now, a grandmother, and had been in Chicago for more than half her life. The elevated train, the three feet of snow falling in April when it had no
business falling, the all-white neighborhood that had turned black in an
eye blink—it was all part of her now.

Her life revolved around family, church, and work, really no different than the order of things would have been in Mississippi, except that
the city that brought freedom also brought unforeseen hazards and
heartbreak.

She had gotten used to the concrete and congestion, the press of
buildings in place of the expanse of field. She had learned to quicken her
step as she walked to or from work, but she still smiled at people on the
bus or reached out to help young mothers balancing babies and strollers.
She was even getting to know the gangbangers who had begun to position themselves on the street corners to establish their turf and organize
their drug inventory. She spoke to them and they spoke back to her, calling her "Grandma" and watching out for her, to the dismay of her own
children, whose objections she largely ignored because the gangbangers
and their little lookouts were God's children too, to her way of thinking.

She was in the city but not fully wise to it, nor seeking to be.

One day, coming home from work, she stepped off the curb at the
green light for pedestrians to cross Eighty-seventh Street at the Dan
Ryan Expressway. The right turn on red had just been made legal. A
man in a late-model sedan pulled out in front of the bus just as she was
trying to cross. She fell onto the hood and then tumbled to the concrete.

"That was a good fall," she said. She was sore but not much else.

The man who hit her was worried for her and drove her to Jackson
Park Hospital, where she was declared fine, save for a few bruises to her
legs, arms, and ego. They called her husband to tell him what had happened.

"Oh, he fussed," she said, which looked to be the only way he knew to
show he cared.

"You should have watched where you were going!" he told her when
she got home. The idea of losing Ida Mae seemed to incite as much
anger as worry in him.

There was already a sense of lingering sadness in the house. Their
beloved Velma, the little girl Ida Mae hadn't wanted at first but whom
she had held close and cherished and who had ridden next to her, along

with little James, on the train ride north, was gone now. There had been a car accident a few years before. The details of the crash somehow didn't matter so much in the eternity between getting the call and making it to the hospital. Ida Mae saw her firstborn trying to hold on to life and then slip away. Ida Mae almost fell apart. Decades later, it would be the one thing she rarely talked about, as if not talking about it made it less real. And even though she knew full well that it was, she couldn't bear to let the thought of it slip into her subconscious. She acted as if it had never happened, and if it came up, her voice went uncharacteristically flat, and she quickly found something else to talk about. *"The police,"* she would say, *"they was riding last night. . . ."*

___

Ida Mae and her husband had settled into whatever they were going to be in the North. They were blue-collar, churchgoing, taxpaying home owners with now two, instead of three, grown children. Ida Mae now had six little grandchildren, all of whom had been born within the bonds of holy matrimony, even though Eleanor's didn't manage to last, which perfectly reflected the demographics of the times. Ida Mae's husband was a deacon in the church whose pastime was cheering the White Sox on television with their grandson Kevin and instructing him on the strategies of the game. Ida Mae and her husband were never going to go to college or rise much beyond where they were, but they had come a long way from where they had started, and that was an accomplishment in itself.

Many years later, people would forget about the quiet successes of everyday people like Ida Mae. In the debates to come over welfare and pathology, America would overlook people like her in its fixation with the underclass, just as a teacher can get distracted by the two or three problem children at the expense of the quiet, obedient ones. Few experts trained their sights on the unseen masses of migrants like her, who worked from the moment they arrived, didn't end up on welfare, stayed married because that's what God-fearing people of their generation did whether they were happy or not, and managed not to get strung out on drugs or whiskey or a cast of nameless, no-count men.

___

There were two sets of similar people arriving in Chicago and other industrial cities of the North at around the same time in the early decades of the twentieth century—blacks pouring in from the South and immi-

grants arriving from eastern and southern Europe in a slowing but continuous stream from across the Atlantic, a pilgrimage that had begun in
the latter part of the nineteenth century. On the face of it, they were so-
ciologically alike, mostly landless rural people, put upon by the landed
upper classes or harsh autocratic regimes, seeking freedom and auton-
omy in the northern factory cities of the United States.

But as they made their way into the economies of Chicago, Detroit,
Cleveland, Milwaukee, and other receiving cities, their fortunes di-
verged. Both groups found themselves ridiculed for their folk ways and
accents and suffered backward assumptions about their abilities and intelligence. But with the stroke of a pen, many eastern and southern Europeans and their children could wipe away their ethnicities—and those
limiting assumptions—by adopting Anglo-Saxon surnames and melt-
ing into the world of the more privileged native-born whites. In this
way, generations of immigrant children could take their places without
the burdens of an outsider ethnicity in a less enlightened era. Doris von
Kappelhoff could become Doris Day, and Issur Danielovitch, the son of
immigrants from Belarus, could become Kirk Douglas, meaning that
his son could live life and pursue stardom as Michael Douglas instead of
as Michael Danielovitch.

A name change would have had no effect in masking the ethnicity of
black migrants like Ida Mae, George, and Robert. It would have been
superfluous, given that their surnames, often inherited from the masters
of their forebears, were already Anglo-Saxon. They did not have the option of choosing for themselves a more favored identity. They could not
easily assimilate whether they sought to or not. They could send their
children to northern schools that were superior to anything back south,
acquire a northern accent, save up for suits to replace the overalls and
croker sack dresses of the field, but they would never be mistaken for an
English or Welsh arriviste the way a Czech or Hungarian immigrant
could if so inclined. Black migrants did not have the same shot at craft
unions or foreman jobs or country clubs or exclusive cul-de-sac lace-
curtain neighborhoods that other immigrants could enter if they were of
a mind to do so.

A daughter of white ethnics could instantly escape the perceived disadvantages of her origins by marrying a man of northern or western European descent and taking his surname. She and whatever children she
bore could thus assume the identity of a more privileged caste. With the
exception of extraordinarily light-skinned blacks passing into the white
world for these very same privileges, the daughter of the average black

migrants would gain no such advantage by intermarrying. She would still be seen as black and be subject to the scrutiny of the outside world, no matter whom she married or whose name she took.

Even without trying to pass oneself off as anything other than what he or she was, an ethnic immigrant would not likely be distinguishable from any other white person boarding a train, lining up for a foreman's job, or waiting for a loan officer at a bank—public situations that opened black migrants to immediate rejection but that white ethnic immigrants were protected from by virtue of their skin color.

Ultimately, according to the Harvard immigration scholar Stanley Lieberson, a major difference between the acceptance and thus life outcomes of black migrants from the South and their white immigrant counterparts was this: white immigrants and their descendants could escape the disadvantages of their station if they chose to, while that option did not hold for the vast majority of black migrants and their children. The ethnicity of the descendants of white immigrants "was more a matter of choice, because, with some effort, it could be changed," Lieberson wrote, and, out in public, might not easily be determined at all.

———

The hierarchy in the North "called for blacks to remain in their station," Lieberson wrote, while immigrants were rewarded for "their ability to leave their old world traits" and become American as quickly as possible. Society urged them to leave Poland and Latvia behind and enter the mainstream white world. Not so with their black counterparts like Ida Mae, Robert, and George.

"Although many blacks sought initially to reach an assimilated position in the same way as did the new European immigrants," Lieberson noted, "the former's efforts were apt to be interpreted as getting out of their place or were likely to be viewed with mockery." Ambitious black migrants found that they were not able to get ahead just by following the course taken by immigrants and had to find other routes to survival and hoped-for success.

Contrary to common assumptions about childbearing and welfare, many black migrants compensated for the disadvantages they faced by cutting back in every way they could, most notably by having fewer children than the eastern and southern Europeans arriving at the same time. Ida Mae, for example, bore no more children after the one she carried in her belly from Mississippi at the age of twenty-five, despite the many fertile years she spent in the North. She and her husband could not afford another mouth to feed.

It turned out that, during the first three decades of the Great Migration, fertility rates for black women migrants from the South were actually among the lowest of all newer arrivals to the North, according to Lieberson's compilation of census data. In 1940, for the fifteen-to-thirty-four age group, Ida Mae's at the time, there were 916 children per thousand black women, as against 951 for Austrians, 1,030 for Russians, 1,031 for Poles, 1,176 for Hungarians, and 1,388 for Italians. Czech women were virtually tied with black women at 923 children per thousand women. The disparities only widened with age. Among those in the forty-five-to-fifty-four age group, central and eastern European immigrant women had borne, in some cases, twice as many children per thousand as black migrant women in the North in 1940, with the Russians having borne 3,111, the Hungarians 3,305, the Austrians 3,683, the Czechs 4,045, the Poles 4,192, and the Italians 4,638 compared to 2,219 children having been born to black women by the same point in their lives in the North.

Clyde Vernon Kiser, a political scientist at Columbia University, studying the black migration from south Georgia to the Northeast in the 1930s, also found fertility to be "significantly reduced by migration" among black couples who went to both New York and Boston.

"The differences in most cases are of a massive nature," Lieberson reported.

Blacks, though native born, were arriving as the poorest people from the poorest section of the country with the least access to the worst education. Over the decades of the Migration, they came with every disadvantage and found themselves competing not only with newcomers like themselves but with second- and third-generation European immigrants already established in apprenticeships and factory jobs that were closed off to black migrants, the immigrants and their children permitted into the very trade unions that prohibited black citizens from joining.

Because they were largely excluded from well-paying positions in even unskilled occupations and were concentrated in servant work and other undesirable jobs, blacks were the lowest paid of all the recent arrivals. In 1950, blacks in the North and West made a median annual income of $1,628, compared to Italian immigrants, who made $2,295, Czechs, who made $2,339, Poles, who made $2,419, and Russians, who made $2,717.

"There is just no avoiding the fact that blacks were more severely discriminated against in the labor market and elsewhere," Lieberson wrote. They "had to work more hours to earn less money than anyone else," the historian Gilbert Osofsky wrote.

The people of the Great Migration had farther to climb because they started off at the lowest rung wherever they went. They incited greater fear and resentment in part because there was no ocean between them and the North as there was with many other immigrant groups. There was no way to stem the flow of blacks from the South, as the authorities could and did by blocking immigration from China and Japan, for instance. Thus, blacks confronted hostilities more severe than most any other group (except perhaps Mexicans, who could also cross over by land), as it could not be known how many thousands more might come and pose a further threat to the preexisting world of the North.

The presence of so many black migrants elevated the status of other immigrants in the North and West. Black southerners stepped into a hierarchy that assigned them a station beneath everyone else, no matter that their families had been in the country for centuries. Their arrival unwittingly diverted anti-immigrant antagonisms their way, as they were an even less favored outsider group than the immigrants they encountered in the North and helped make formerly ridiculed groups more acceptable by comparison.

Ida Mae was so isolated, living as she was in the all-black neighborhood of South Shore, that she had little contact with other immigrant groups except perhaps at work. She tried to make the best of it since she had no control over who had gotten to Chicago before she did or how they lived or what they thought of her. Her world was small, purposely so, built around her family and the people she knew from back home in Mississippi, and that was the way she and her husband preferred it.

NEW YORK, 1970
GEORGE SWANSON STARLING

———

THIS IS WHAT GEORGE STARLING'S LIFE had become at its midpoint. He had made it up north, alright, as he had dreamed so long ago. But he had an unhappy wife who could not be made happy and two teenage children who were good at heart but had been swallowed up by the worst aspects of the North and South while he and his wife were out working long hours to give the kids a life they themselves had never had. He had a two-year-old by another woman that he had to support and a decent-paying but dead-end job as essentially a servant to railroad passengers needing help with their luggage, directions to their seats, another pillow, their shoes shined.

He turned fifty-two in 1970. He had been in the North for a quarter of a century. He would never be the chemist or accountant he had seen for himself in his mind, would never work a white-collar job or any kind of job that would make use of his intellect. And, by an accident of birth, he had managed to suffer the terror and injustice of Jim Crow but just missed the revolution that opened up the best in education and unheard-of career opportunities for black people with the passage of the civil rights laws of the 1960s. The revolution had come too late for him. He was in his midforties when the Civil Rights Act was signed and close to fifty when its effects were truly felt.

He did not begrudge the younger generation their opportunities. He only wished that more of them, his own children, in particular, recognized their good fortune, the price that had been paid for it, and made the most of it. He was proud to have lived to see the change take place.

He wasn't judging anyone and accepted the fact that history had come too late for him to make much use of all the things that were now opening up. But he couldn't understand why some of the young people couldn't see it. Maybe you had to live through the worst of times to recognize the best of times when they came to you. Maybe that was just the way it was with people.

He did not dwell on this long or let it get him down. He stood as straight-backed now as he had when the South told him he didn't have a right to. He started going to church and found solace in that. He started singing in the choir. He had a way of sitting back and shaking his head at absurdities—whether segregationists training their terriers to mock black people in the South or black people with no hope or home training shooting each other over a nickel bag in the North.

The young people were letting their hair grow out and wearing Afros that his generation would never have been seen out in public with. They were living together—shacking up, they called it—in a flouting kind of way that even now, tortured as his marriage was, he couldn't bring himself to do. They were taking things farther than he ever would have had the nerve to contemplate, preaching black power, calling the white man a devil, walking arm in arm down the street with white women, all of those things that would have gotten him killed when he was their age.

The young people picked up on something strong and unnameable in him. They never bothered him as he climbed the stairs out of his basement apartment with his creaky and now-arthritic knees, heading to work at Pennsylvania Station or returning late at night from a forty-eight-hour run.

He knew more than most people of his generation precisely what he had missed out on, and what his life could have been. He had had a taste of college, knew he could do the work, and was convinced he could have succeeded.

How complicated had the ending of his college career been. Looking back on it, the course of his life had turned on that moment. He would not have been working in the citrus groves or had the standoff with the grove owners that had forced him to flee to the North if he had stayed in school. That moment would gnaw at him for as long as he lived. What if his father hadn't gotten it into his head that George had had enough schooling, if his father had helped out with the tuition George needed, if his father hadn't had a new family to support and chosen that obligation over college for his son? Then there was segregation. What if colored students had been allowed to attend the state schools near Eustis in George's day, as they could after the civil rights movement, where it would have been easier for George to make a go of it, work and go part-time if he had to?

Then there was George himself. At midlife, George had to search his soul and live with the regrets of his own missteps. If only he hadn't rushed to get back at his father by marrying a woman from the other side of the tracks, giving his father further reason to withhold his support and leaving George with a wife to take care of besides, perhaps he would have gotten the education that would have allowed him to fulfill his potential. As it was, he had only to look at Inez to be reminded of what could have been.

"It was spite," George would say of the decisions he made at that moment in his life.

He took every chance he got to warn young people not to make his mistakes, not knowing if they heard him but feeling he had to get it out.

"That's why I preach today, *Do not do spite,*" he said. "Spite does not pay. It goes around and misses the object that you aim and comes back and zaps you. And you're the one who pays for it."

LOS ANGELES, 1970
ROBERT JOSEPH PERSHING FOSTER

———

ON CHRISTMAS DAY 1970, Robert P. Foster turned fifty-two years old. He had been in Los Angeles for seventeen years. But, for some reason, he was unable to fill up on what he had acquired any more than he could carry fog in his satchel.

He had a practice that minted money. With all those migrants from Texas and Louisiana, he had patients spilling out of his office and into the hall, sitting like refugees on the floor all day, waiting for him to check their blood pressure.

By then he found it hard to walk down a hospital ward without orderlies and scrub nurses hailing him from closing elevator doors, *"Hey, Doc! Remember me?"* from some long-ago operation, and his feigning recollection so as not to disappoint them.

He was comfortably situated. There was the well-born wife, the three beautiful daughters, and the 3,600-square-foot house west of Crenshaw—if only by a block—with the white Cadillac in the driveway. He was famous even. Ray Charles's song about him, "Hide Nor Hair," spent seven weeks on the *Billboard* charts back in 1962. But he woke up that morning with the feeling that nothing mattered but the events that were about to unfold that day.

Until this moment, he had lived his life with the perpetual sense of watching a reception through a keyhole, of arriving too late and without the proper documentation. There he would be at the front gate, all dressed and superior to the people inside but afraid of being denied admittance. He craved acceptance from those most determined to withhold it from him and met slights and rejections at nearly every turn. The small-minded people in that Jim Crow town. Rufus and Pearl Clement scrutinizing his every move since the day he married Alice. The colonel from Mississippi who wouldn't let him operate on white women. The motel clerks in Phoenix who denied him a room. The colored people who happened to have gotten to L.A. first and wouldn't lend a newcomer a hand. That hotel in Vegas.

After all this time, he still couldn't shake these things. Rufus Clement had been dead for years. The run-in with the motel clerks in Phoenix—that was seventeen years ago. The colonel farther back than that. All the good and extraordinary things that had happened to him seemed never to make up for the rejection he had endured, and he set out to prove that he was better than what they took him for, even though the people who haunted him would never see it, no matter what he did.

Because of the fifty-one previous years of his life, he had a number of complexes. He had a Napoleon complex, a southern complex, a baby-of-the-family complex. He had both a superiority complex and an inferiority complex, and, because he was born on Christmas Day, a Christmas baby complex.

He had never had much of a birthday party, a fate known to just about anyone who enters the world on Christmas. His mother had tried to give him a birthday party once when he was a young boy in Monroe. She invited all the children in New Town. Only four came.

That would not happen this time. He finally had all the pieces in place to celebrate his having arrived. In a few hours, he would give a gala in honor of himself. It would make up for all the parties he'd never had, all the slights he had ever suffered. It would prove to everyone that he had put Monroe and the South behind him and made it in L.A. He had worked it all out in his head.

He would have guests from back east and up the coast and from all over the country. Monroe, too, of course. The best hams and the finest heavy bond paper for the invitations. Anything that anyone had ever thought of for a party, he would have. It would cost in the thousands, like the major motion picture wrap parties over in Beverly Hills, and he wanted the guests to see every dime of it. He had rehearsed the whole thing in his mind.

That morning he woke up early, just like when he was a teenager back in Monroe racing to lose himself in the celluloid illusion of California sophisticates from the colored balcony of the Paramount. Now he was in California, finally a sophisticate himself, and the urine-scented steps of the Paramount were from another lifetime.

But as he rewound a tape that had yet to be recorded, a thunderstorm gathered in his stomach. He could hear the sounds of a party forming on the first floor. Footsteps on linoleum, the help skittering between the refrigerator and the sink and around the avocado green Formica island back to the refrigerator again. The low screech of high chairs being positioned at the bar, the setting down of serving pieces and highball glasses, the opening and closing of the heavy front door with the arrival of roses and ice. He had done all he could, and now it was up to the

workers, who, sweet though they might be, could not possibly understand how crucial it was that there be only cashews and almonds and,
for God's sake, no peanuts in the nut bowls.

The sound of urgent disorder rose up the staircase and into his room.
Rather than being pleased that all was going more or less according to
plan, he was sickened at the prospect that, for all his preparation, things
might be less than perfect.

He could hear the assembling of a party. The storm grew worse in his
stomach.

———

For most of 1970, Robert had devoted himself to the second job of planning his own arrival party. He had told his wife, Alice, and daughter Joy
and his mother-in-law, Pearl, as soon as the thought had occurred to
him. He told Bunny and Robin in Chicago to be in Los Angeles that
Christmas and sent them checks for their gowns with instructions to
start shopping immediately. He told his nephew, Madison, a graduate
student at the University of Michigan, that he expected him in from
Ann Arbor. He told Madison's mother, Harriet, that he wanted her in
from Monroe.

He alerted the members of his wedding party, the former groomsmen in black tails and white kid gloves and the bridesmaids with tiaras
planted over their Bette Davis curls, so they could mark Friday, December 25, 1970, on their calendars. Leo, the maître d' at L'Escoffier, a
French restaurant at the Beverly Hilton, would oversee the whole affair.
The date fell within weeks of Alice's fiftieth birthday, as well as Bunny's
and Gold's birthdays. But the party would be essentially for him.

Robert began devising the guest list as if it were a state dinner. He
began thinking menu and decor. A tent over the patio. Belgian lace for
the tablecloths. Open bar with unpronounceable top-shelf spirits. He
slept with the thought of it. He carried it in his head to work. During
breaks in the day, he would think aloud to a nurse about this or that
entrée or particular band, not necessarily because he wanted a second
opinion—he would not have turned to them for that—but because he
assumed everyone was as captivated as he was.

In fact, some were. At the office one day, a patient overheard him
buzzing about the party. The patient joined in and offered to help. He said
he did a little printing work and could make Doc Foster some nice invitations for the party. Robert was horrified at the notion and thought it should
be obvious that no ordinary printer would do for a party of this caliber.

"Thank you very much," Robert said, "but they're already taken care of."

In truth, he had not begun looking. But he was grateful for the reminder and would track down an engraver immediately. "It had to be the best person in the city," he would say years later. "And I knew the best couldn't be a patient of mine."

He dispatched his mother-in-law to get on it right away. Her southern socialite airs would come in handy about now. It would give her something to occupy her mind and less time to scrutinize him. She spent an entire month choosing between white and ecru and the proper weight for the card stock. They found the invitations at the old Bullock's Wilshire in Beverly Hills, off Rodeo Drive. They had them engraved on Crane's paper, white with red lettering and a red border along the edge. "Etiquettely," he said, "it was perfect."

The invitations read:

> *Doctor and Mrs. Robert P. Foster*
> *At Home*
> *Friday, the twenty-fifth of December*
> *At nine o'clock in the evening*
> *1680 Victoria Avenue*
> *Regrets Only*　　　　*Cocktails—Dancing*

Two hundred invitations went out, and as Robert was at the peak of his practice and popularity, 194 accepted. "We counted all but six R.S.V.P.'s," he said, "and the six that declined were all out of town."

That raised the stakes for everything else, beginning with the costumes for the principals. He was the star and would have to look it. He went to the Beverly Hills couturiers, the tailors to Sammy Davis, Jr., who, from across a blackjack table some people said he favored, and found a suit to his liking. Crushed velvet had just hit the scene, very Fifth Dimension, Age of Aquarius, and all that. So that's what he would wear. Black crushed velvet suit. Black crushed velvet bow tie. Black velvet Bally slippers with a gold medallion above the instep. The suit had a red lining to match the red silk handkerchief in his breast pocket, and the shirt cuff fell precisely one inch below the jacket sleeve, just as it should.

Finding something for Alice would take more time. He was the show-off, just waiting for somebody to say, *Bob Foster, you too much*. They went all over Beverly Hills, to the back rooms of the designer floors of the finest department stores, Robert watching, advising, critiquing, and, for one reason or another, dismissing and rejecting as Alice tried on hanger after hanger of dresses.

One night after work, rather than heading straight home or to the track, Robert drove north and west from his medical office toward Beverly Hills. He went directly to the French Room at Bullock's Wilshire, which he had been known to keep open in search of the right attire. They had been there already, but he wanted to check again.

This time, he saw an organza gown loaded with beadwork. It was gaudy like New Orleans, and the skirt looked as if somebody had thrown rubies on the sidewalk. Robert told the salesclerk to wrap it up immediately. He carried it home and ran up the steps to show Alice. It was late, and he woke her up.

"Try it on, baby," he said.

She got up, and he positioned himself three feet to the right and rear in a corner of the yellow-trimmed bedroom to watch her move in it.

Walk.

Turn.

Come to me.

"It became alive when she walked," he said.

———

In Ann Arbor, his nephew, Madison, awaited word on the big party between sociology colloquia and trying to take over the administration building at the University of Michigan. He was a three-piece-suited militant who knew how to use a fish fork. Robert had given him a year's notice about the party. All year long, if the phone rang and it was Robert, he knew what it was about. *I'm having Mrs. Williams roast the nuts for the party. Hampton Hawes has agreed to do the jazz set. I'm flying the Smithfield hams in from Virginia.*

From the moment they accepted, he and the 194 other people on the guest list (and the guests they were bringing with them) were on a low-grade state of alert whether they liked it or not. Anyone deemed close enough to be invited also knew that Robert would expect them to look and act the part he assigned them. He wanted them to have a good time, of course, but he would also be sure to make note of the cut of their jackets and where a dress hem fell in relation to the ankle or knee. He

would be judging them all. It was just how he was, and he couldn't
help it.

Madison felt the heat as much as anyone. He was the only child
of Robert's deceased oldest brother. Theirs was the closest that either
had to a father-son relationship. They were the only Foster men left
after all the deaths in the family. Big Madison, when he was alive,
had made a point of not leaving the South, not running away and
chasing a dream as Robert and millions of others had done, but staying
and making the most of the angst and subtle shifts in sentiment of
southern whites watching their meal ticket disappear on north- and
westbound trains. Little Madison had thus been raised in the South,
with the pride and insecurities that came with it, and, despite his father's
decision to stay, looked up to his Uncle Robert, who had made good out
west.

A visit from Robert was a cause of great anxiety. Robert once visited
Michigan in the midsixties. Madison did his best to impress him. He
took him to the fanciest place he could afford. It took some time for the
guests to figure out what they wanted from the menu. But they ordered
and had a fine time. On the ride back, Robert gave his assessment of the
evening.

"That was B+," he said.

Madison sank into his seat and waited to hear what he had missed.

"You shouldn't have let your guests struggle with the menu," Robert
told him.

Madison never really got over it. Almost forty years later, and he was
still second-guessing the evening. "I didn't preorder the food," he would
say long afterward. "It was a painful lesson. I learned it."

He was southern and did everything he could to prove himself. He
tried to pull Robert's daughters back to their Louisiana roots, but they
looked upon him as their country cousin from back in Monroe, a place
they cared little about, growing up as they did in California.

Madison was a graduate student when Robert's oldest daughter,
Bunny, got her master's at the University of Iowa. He didn't have the
money for a new suit. He flew in anyway. At the commencement,
Robert pulled him aside.

"Your suit pants are shiny," Robert said. "You shouldn't go out like
that."

Madison would not let that happen again.

He had a year's notice on the party and made use of it. He went to a

tailor and had two suits cut for the occasion, hoping that one of them
might meet Robert's exacting standards.

———

December 25, 1970. A Friday. The florists draped pine leaf garlands
down the railing of the front staircase. To the branches they fastened red
plastic birds with glitter on the wing tips so that every four feet there
was a little bird in flight.

The caterers moved the dining room table in front of the gold
draperies. They covered it with $250 worth of white Belgian lace and set
sterling candelabras on each end, as the Clements would have done. The
Smithfield hams arrived from Virginia. The shrimp gumbo was set out
with instructions that it never hit empty.

The barkeep lined the liquor bottles behind the highball glasses at the
bar. "I told the bartender to give everybody two shots whether they
wanted it or not," Robert said.

All day, the heavy front door opened and closed with the arrival of
supplies, and the telephone rang on and off, people just landing at LAX,
people needing directions. Dusk fell, and the time drew near. Robert
began to feel sick. The thunderstorm grew worse in his stomach. He felt
weak and exhausted. His knees gave way. He fell back, collapsed. He
had to be helped upstairs, lie down, gather himself. He lay there staring
at the yellow walls in the master bedroom, fretting and unable to face
the possibility of imperfection.

He closed his eyes. He tried to rest. Soon, outside his window, he
could hear the rumble of car engines rounding St. Charles Place and
turning up South Victoria. The screeching came to a stop. The creak of
the passenger door of a Cadillac opening and the thud of its closing. The
engine shutting down and the valet taking the keys. The first guests had
arrived and were walking down the red-carpeted sidewalk he conceived
of months ago.

Round the corner and down the stairs, he could hear muffled conversation, a party being born. He reminded himself why he had spent the
better part of a year and really all of his life planning for this moment.
He got up, steadied himself. He checked himself in the mirror, practiced
his smile, and straightened his crushed-velvet tie.

"Let's get on with it," he said to himself, liking what he saw. "It's on."

———

He is wearing mutton-chop sideburns, flecked gray, and an Afro shaped like a mushroom cap. Hip as you got in those days. He greets his guests with a cigarette between his fingers and his legs purposely slew-footed, as if he were posing for Esquire. *It will make better pictures for the photographer he has hired to trail him and the guests all night.*

Soon the set piece begins to take shape. There's Joe Luellen, who hit town back in the thirties and played in The Great White Hope. *And three men standing together in velvet suits that forewarn the fashion crimes of the seventies.*

On a foot-high stand above the crowd, Sweets Edison is on trumpet under the green-striped tent over the patio. Hampton Hawes is playing piano with his head reared back. Everybody has a glass of something in one hand and a cigarette in the other like jewelry.

There's his mother-in-law near the hot pink tulip-upholstered love seat, in a four-hundred-dollar gown and a solid gold bracelet he bought her and which he complained she never gave him credit for. And she's greeting and upstaging as if she paid for the whole shebang. ("I ignored it, I ignored it," he would say years later, betraying that he most certainly had not.)

There are two or three wet bars, help everywhere, dressed in maid's uniforms and monkey suits, people checking coats, people parking cars, people pouring martinis, people picking up dishes before they have a chance to clink the top of an end table.

There's Bunny sticking her tongue out at the camera. And Ray Charles under the tent over the patio by the band. And Robert's bookie. And a judge. A postmaster. And a dentist. Robert's sister, Gold, in pink chiffon on a barstool, holding a pack of Marlboros. Keisha Brown, a gospel rock singer, sweating on stage in blood-red velvet. Madison, in a three-piece suit that thankfully met Robert's approval, doing the funky chicken with a woman in white bell-bottoms. Alice in her cat-eye glasses, posing for pictures, calm and dignified in that heavy beaded dress by the staircase.

The following Thursday, December 31, 1970, a breathless review ran on page C2 of the *Los Angeles Sentinel,* declaring it "certainly 'The Party of the Year,' without a doubt" (phrasing that unwittingly introduced the very doubt it sought to dispel). The column ran without pictures and began like this:

> *One of the Angel City's most fabulous parties to date was given by the Robert Fosters on Christmas Day, at their home on Victoria Avenue. The prominent physician and his wife, who is president of the L.A.*

Chapter of the Links, had their large back yard area tinted [sic] for the
occasion, and the View Park decorators had a field day. . . .

    For her party, Alice wore a Malcolm Star original that fairly
sparkled with jewels. . . . Mrs. Rufus E. Clement, formerly of Atlanta,
and Louisville, Ky., now makes her home in L.A. with her daughter
and son-in-law, and assisted in receiving the 400 guests.

    Who was there? Well, we could easily say the Who's Who of L.A. So-
ciety. . . . And believe it or not, at times there were as many as 200 beau-
tiful people, milling, sipping, and just having a marvelous time on
Christmas Day at the Robert Fosters. . . . This was certainly "The Party
of the Year,"without a doubt.

Robert had a photo album made of the night's festivities. It was made of
brown leather, and etched onto the front was "Robert's Birthday" in
gold italics. Over the succeeding decades, he would pull out the party
album before he would his wedding pictures or his medical degree. The
brown leather got worn in spots from the viewing. Usually, he would
not bother to mention the *Sentinel* story nor the party itself so much as
what went into it.

    "For some reason, it drops," he told me years later when I asked him
about the particulars. "It's not any less valuable or delicious. But for
some reason, it didn't seem as important as when I was putting it together."

    Some of the guests he never saw again. Some died. Some lost touch. It
was a wrap, and everyone was marvelous.

    He took comfort in any sign of the night's immortality. One day he
passed the stationery department at Bullock's. The invitations to his
party were mounted and on display. "I went in once and told the lady,
'That's mine,' " he said. "She looked at me like I was a fool. I just
smiled."

    Talking about it kept the party going, and so it never really ended in
his mind. He did not wait for reviews, he solicited them. He called
Jimmy Marshall, one of his oldest friends from back in Monroe, right
after the party.

    "Jimmy, did I wig 'em?" he asked.

    "Yeah, you hit it," Jimmy said.

    What are they saying, what are they thinking? Robert asked Jimmy.
Everyone was bowled over, of course. Jimmy didn't want to say it, but
the Monroe people thought he had gone too far. The black maid in the

black-and-white dress and white bow in the foyer was over the top even for Robert.

"We've been maids long enough," Jimmy told Robert. "People didn't go for that."

Robert didn't take it too well. "Either he answered or cussed," Jimmy said decades later, "which I didn't care, in either case."

As long as the two had known each other, Robert's fixations never made sense to Jimmy. "He always sought approval," Jimmy said. "And I never understood it because he had it all."

PART FIVE

AFTERMATH

*The migrants were gradually absorbed
into the economic, social, and political life of the city.
They have influenced and modified it.
The city has, in turn, changed them.*
— St. Clair Drake and Horace H. Cayton,
Black Metropolis

IN THE PLACES
THEY LEFT

The only thing
we are proud of
in connection with
the South
is that we left it.
—JEFFERSON L.
EDMONDS,
THE PUBLISHER
OF *The Liberator,*
ONE OF THE FIRST
COLORED NEWSPAPERS
IN LOS ANGELES

CHICKASAW COUNTY, MISSISSIPPI, 1970
IDA MAE BRANDON GLADNEY

———

THE RAW WOOD CABINS and gravel roads that broke the clearings in
the bottomlands of Chickasaw County did not change much in the
thirty years after Ida Mae and millions of other black people left the
South in a migration that was now slowing down as Mississippi began
fitfully opening up. Mr. Edd, whose land Ida Mae and her husband had
sharecropped, died of a heart attack back in 1945, a few years after Ida
Mae went north. Willie Jim, who came with Mr. Edd looking for Joe
Lee that night all those years ago over the missing turkeys, was still

alive. He ran a thousand-acre plantation with up to two hundred hoe hands and forty sharecropper families well into the 1960s.

The land was still devoted to cotton, but big combines and mechanical harvesters now did most of the work. The people who had not gone north now worked in factories, textile mills, and hardware plants, factories that made poly foam and felt for the manufacture of furniture, and factories that made trailers, sewer pipes, corrugated boxes, shipping crates.

The county and the rest of Mississippi and the old Confederacy had come out on the other side of a second civil war, the war over civil rights for the servant caste of the South. Chickasaw County had not been in the middle of it, had not been a focus of Martin Luther King or the freedom riders. It was too sparsely populated and too out of the way. But it was no less resistant to change, especially when it came to black people voting (where "intemperate individuals of both races created incidents best forgotten," the Chickasaw County Historical and Genealogical Society wrote dismissively of the era), and when it came to the integration of the schools, which had been segregated for longer than most anyone had been alive.

It was in 1954 that the Supreme Court ruled on *Brown v. Board of Education of Topeka,* declaring segregated schools inherently unequal and therefore unconstitutional. In a subsequent ruling in 1955, the Court ordered school boards to eliminate segregation "with all deliberate speed."

Much of the South translated that phrase loosely to mean whenever they got around to it, which meant a time frame closer to a decade than a semester. One county in Virginia—Prince Edward County—closed its entire school system for five years, from 1959 to 1964, rather than integrate.

The state funneled money to private academies for white students. But black students were left on their own. They went to live with relatives elsewhere, studied in church basements, or forwent school altogether. County supervisors relented only after losing their case in the U.S. Supreme Court, choosing finally to reopen the schools rather than face imprisonment.

It would take more than fifteen years before most of the South conceded to the *Brown* ruling and then only under additional court orders.

"This was passionately opposed," wrote the Chickasaw Historical Society, "not only by most of the whites—but by some of the blacks as well." That sentiment, if true, would have been explained away by the blacks who left as an indication that the blacks who stayed may have been more conciliatory than many of the people in the Great Migration.

It wasn't until the 1970–71 school year that integration finally came to Chickasaw County, and then only after a 1969 court order, *Alexander v. Holmes,* that gave county and municipal schools in Mississippi until February 1970 to desegregate. But even that deadline would be extended for years for particularly recalcitrant counties.

All the marching and court rulings did little to change some southerners' hearts. A 1968 survey found that eighty-three percent of whites said they preferred a system with no integration. And they acted on those preferences. By 1970, 158 new white private schools had opened up in Mississippi. By 1971, a quarter of the white students were in private schools, the white families paying tuition many could scarcely afford. Mothers went back to work to help cover tuition, "spent all their savings and forfeited luxuries and necessities in life," some splitting their children up and enduring the "expense and inconvenience of transporting the children long distances to and from school," according to the Mississippi-born scholar Mark Lowry, to avoid having their children sit in the same classroom with black children.

In the meantime, in the middle of the turmoil over what would become of the children of Mississippi, dozens of school districts forwent federal funding rather than integrate their schools. During the worst of things, at least one school superintendent, Lowry wrote, committed suicide.

EUSTIS, FLORIDA, 1970
GEORGE SWANSON STARLING

LAKE COUNTY, FLORIDA, began to join the rest of the free world in the late 1960s and early 1970s, six decades into the Great Migration, when black children and white children, for the first time in county history, began sitting in the same buildings to learn their cursive and multiplication tables.

Change did not come without incident. The first sign of trouble was a fight at the newly integrated high school between a white boy and a black boy. It fell to the black assistant principal, who had been demoted from principal of the colored high school to an assistant at the reconstituted school, to intervene. It was unclear who started what, but the black assistant principal ruled in favor of the white student to the outcries of reverse favoritism from the black parents.

"The black people could not understand why he should discipline this black kid that had an altercation with the white kid, and they been dogging us all our lives," George Starling, who had been keeping close contact, said years later. The assistant principal was his stepbrother in that small world of Eustis, Florida.

The black parents felt the white student had started the fight by provoking the black student and that the assistant principal should have ruled accordingly. But in the tinderbox of what was still very much an experiment in caste integration, he had little choice.

"We're crying out against prejudice and mistreatment," George said. "If you want it eliminated, you have to do unto others as you want them to do unto you."

When the next big fight broke out, Willis McCall rode up with his police dog to go after the black student. This time, the black parents rose up and protested. A church load of them, emboldened by the civil rights gains and the counterbalancing effect of all the people they knew up north, rode over to the county seat of Tavares, got a Reverend Jones to speak for them, and protested to the Lake County School Board.

"The people let Willis McCall know that they weren't scared of him or his dog," Viola Dunham, a long-time resident with three boys in school at the time, remembered. "We let him know he does not run the school system. We let them know we didn't want Willis McCall raising our children. And we did not back down that time."

———

Since the 1940s, Willis McCall had cast a long shadow over Lake County. His handling of the Groveland case, in which a white woman accused four black men of raping her back in 1949, had made national headlines and put Lake County on the map as a symbol of racial injustice. McCall had shot two shackled defendants while transporting them the night before their second trial. One of the men, Walter Irvin, actually survived the shooting and lived to tell how McCall had taken the backwoods, stopped in a remote location, told them to get out, and shot them.

After being hospitalized for his wounds, Irvin was retried, reconvicted, and once again sentenced to death. A few years later, a new governor, LeRoy Collins, reviewed his case and, in 1955, commuted Irvin's death sentence to life imprisonment. It was a stunning decision at that time in the Jim Crow South and one handed down against the vehement opposition of Sheriff McCall and other white Floridians.

The governor, a segregationist but otherwise a moderate by southern standards, was disturbed by the many shortcomings in the case. "My conscience told me it was a bad case, badly handled, badly tried and now, on this bad performance, I was asked to take a man's life," Collins later said. "My conscience would not let me do it."

His death sentence commuted, Walter Irvin would be imprisoned for eighteen years for a crime he maintained his whole life he had not committed. DNA testing was not yet in use to prove or disprove his claim. In 1969, he was paroled on the condition that he never set foot in Lake County again. But the following year, he was granted permission to visit his family there for a single day. Soon after he got there, "he dropped dead while sitting on a front porch." He was forty-two years old. Officials like McCall said he had a heart attack. But after all that had preceded Irvin's death, some black people in town believed it was no accident.

———

Into the early 1970s, Willis McCall was still the sheriff of Lake County. He was still wearing his ten-gallon hats. The Groveland case had made him something of a celebrity among Florida segregationists. He would become the center of case after case of alleged abuse and misconduct against black people in the county. He would be investigated forty-nine times and survive every one of them.

As the world began to change around him, he stood his ground in defense of the old order of things. When President John F. Kennedy was assassinated in November 1963, "the only public building in the United States that refused to lower its flag to half-staff was McCall's jail in Tavares," the Lake County seat, according to the author Ben Green.

COLORED ONLY and WHITE ONLY signs were coming down all over the South during the 1960s. But Sheriff McCall did not take down the COLORED WAITING ROOM sign in his office until September 1971, and then only under threat of a federal court order. He may have been the last elected official in the country to remove his Jim Crow sign, Green said.

McCall was reelected seven times, that is, until 1972, when Florida Governor Reubin Askew stepped in and suspended him after yet another violent assault on someone in his custody. This time, McCall was indicted for second-degree murder for allegedly kicking a black prisoner to death. The prisoner was in jail for a twenty-six-dollar traffic ticket. McCall was acquitted.

But he lost the election that November. Blacks were now able to vote, and they turned out in force to defeat him the first chance they got.

"We sent cars out and taxicabs," Viola Dunham, a longtime resident and a sister-in-law of George Starling, remembered. "We started getting these people out to vote."

Then, too, a new generation of whites had entered the Florida electorate, the younger people who may have identified with the young freedom riders in Mississippi and Alabama even if they would not have participated themselves, and the snowbirds, the white northerners who were buying up vacation homes or retiring to central Florida with the boom that came with the arrival of Disney World and who couldn't relate to the heavy-handedness of a small-town southern sheriff. And now it seemed that even the most steadfast traditionalists had finally tired of the controversies and felt it was time for him to go.

The defeated sheriff retreated to his ranch on Willis V. McCall Road in Eustis, where he tended his citrus grove, welcomed his partisans, and held forth on his decades of lordship over Lake County. He could take comfort in the fact that, for better or for worse, Lake County would not soon forget him, and he took pride in his role of protecting southern tradition.

The times might have changed, but he never would or sought to. Displayed in his home was the COLORED WAITING ROOM sign that once hung in his office and that he was forced to take down under threat of a court order. Nobody in the world was going to tell him what he could do or what he could hang in his own home on Willis V. McCall Road.

MONROE, LOUISIANA, EARLY 1970S
ROBERT JOSEPH PERSHING FOSTER

—————

THE FOSTERS HAD ALWAYS had a complicated relationship with their hometown of Monroe—or rather, with the few other ambitious and educated black people maneuvering among themselves for the few spoils allowed them in a segregated world. The rivalries would pass from one generation to the next until it no longer mattered because most of the Foster descendants had died or, like Robert, migrated away. As prominent as the Fosters had been, there would be no direct descendants living there by the 1970s, and the rivalries would play out from afar.

In the time since Robert drove away from Monroe for good, Robert's father had died, his brother Madison had visited Los Angeles for surgery and died from complications there, his brother Leland had moved to the Midwest, his sister, Gold, had followed Robert to L.A. in the 1960s, and his nephew, Madison James, was in graduate school at the University of Michigan and not likely to move back.

But even before Robert migrated west, the Fosters had begun to languish like deposed monarchs on the outskirts of influence in town. By the 1950s, Professor Foster had been edged out of his principalship and a new colored high school had gone up to replace the old one the Fosters had run for decades.

There was a time when hardly any black child in Monroe could get through high school without getting past a Foster. Now a whole new generation was growing up not knowing who they were. Not only had many of the Fosters left, but the Migration had drained away many of the people who remembered them. It was the price they paid for migrating.

Some old-timers expected that the new high school would be named after Professor Foster for all his years of service. He had taught, overseen, or influenced the education of most every black person in Monroe from the 1920s to the 1940s. But there were not enough partisans to push the case.

The new high school would take the name of a family that had stayed in Monroe, had not run north or west or forsaken Monroe for the so-called Promised Land. The Carrolls had been in Ouachita Parish since Reconstruction, and, like others who stayed, moved into greater prominence as possible competitors migrated away. When the new school went up, it was named after one of the Carrolls—Henry Carroll, who had become the first black member of the Monroe Board of Education—rather than the retired and nearly forgotten Professor Foster. Robert's father had to watch from the sidelines as the new school he had always dreamed of rose up in the name of a rival.

"Papa was hurting, dying inside," Robert said. "But he never let you know it."

The next year, the Foster name was affixed to something the Fosters would not, in principle, have been against but would not have otherwise chosen for themselves, given their preoccupation with high-minded achievement. The Fosters lost out with the high school, but as a consolation prize, a public housing project was named after Professor Foster, the Foster Heights Homes on Swayze Street, a few blocks from the new high school. It was as if all that Professor Foster had endured and devoted his life to had been boiled down to an assemblage of low-rise apartments of pink brick and struggling lawn. Every shooting or drug bust or robbery that might happen there and make it to the evening news ("Last night, in a drug raid at the Foster Heights Homes . . .") would resurrect the Foster name in a way that was counter to everything the family stood for.

Robert didn't want to go back to see the housing project with his surname on it, but he did and found it neatly spread out, rather like a roadside motel. He would have to go back to bury his father and big brother and sister-in-law Harriet.

Each visit was a time of melancholy. Finally, no immediate family was left. There were still no sidewalks in New Town, and the streets were still unpaved, just as they were when he was a boy. It only confirmed that he could not have lived out his life in this place.

By the early 1970s, integration was beginning to filter into everyday life in Monroe. So, after visiting the graves of his mother and father and his big brother Madison, Robert decided to walk into a diner that used to be only for white people. It was a place he could only have dreamed of entering as a young man. He sat down without incident, ordered and ate, and nobody commented on it one way or the other. It was nothing special and, in fact, underwhelming after all those years of being denied entrance and dreaming of being inside. How could it be that people were fighting to the death over something that was, in the end, so very ordinary? He had crossed into territory forbidden him growing up, and now the circle was complete. It was much like returning to a building that had seemed so imposing when you were a child but was, in fact, small and forgettable when seen through the eyes of an adult.

Before leaving Monroe, he passed the big new colored high school on Renwick Street and could not help but think of his father walking to his old schoolhouse in the dark of morning to open up Monroe Colored High with its used books from the white school and secondhand desks. The new Carroll High School was something Professor Foster could only have dreamt of in those early days, and, for as long as he lived, Robert would remain convinced that it should rightly have carried his name.

———

Robert returned to L.A. and again tried to put Monroe behind him. He would never fully be able to. And so he worked harder at everything he did. He gave all of himself to whatever was his fancy at the moment.

Each December 23, he put aside his patients and gambling to devote himself to commemorating his marriage to Alice. He made the reservations and all the arrangements. Every year, the plan was exactly the same.

Robert and Alice would go to Scandia on Sunset Boulevard. The maître d' would make a show of the appetizer and subsequent courses. There would be a gift immediately following the entrée—a diamond ring or a fur coat. There would be some grand gesture at the end and a toast to however many years it had been.

But things did not always go according to plan—not in any huge, irreversible way, but in the little ways that could easily rattle Robert, who was easily rattled anyway.

One anniversary, the maître d' happened to seat them at a table in a darkened corner in the back.

"I couldn't stand it," Robert said.

He fumed and sulked. He could barely enjoy the anniversary he was supposed to be celebrating. When he could stand it no longer, he summoned the maître d'.

"Please move me to another table," Robert said. "It's too dark."

(*I tipped him, and that will work wonders. You have to be careful not to overdo it. Then you show your ignorance.*)

Another year, the maître d' sat them at a booth. It was in the right place in the room. But something was wrong. The booth sank in where Robert was sitting.

"When I sat down in the booth, my wife was taller than I," he said. "I didn't like that."

He told Alice to switch places with him, "so that I wouldn't be shorter than she was." Alice, having already settled on her side of the booth, had to collect her purse. The two got up and circled each other to take the other's seat.

Only then could the evening commence.

"Leo, what are we going to eat tonight?"

There came the courses, and he would watch with pride and amazement as Alice negotiated whatever elaborate or towering concoction was put before her.

Then came the part Robert liked the most, the part he put the most ritual and planning into.

The morning of the dinner, he had called the florist.

"I want red roses and baby's breath," he had told the florist. "I want to be able to see over the table."

The florist fretted over what that meant for the arrangement, precisely what the dimensions should be.

"Alright, get me the width and the length of the table," Robert said. Someone called the restaurant and got the measurements for the particular table Robert had reserved for this particular anniversary, and the roses and ferns could then be cut and arranged.

"Each year I added one red rose to that bouquet," he said.

It was their thirty-third anniversary. "We're in the center of the dining room," Robert remembered. The maître d' came out with "thirty-three long-stemmed roses with white baby's breath and fern and ribbon," he remembered. "Each anniversary, one more ribbon."

LOSSES

It occurred to me that no matter where I lived,
geography could not save me.
— JACQUELINE JOAN JOHNSON,
WHO MIGRATED FROM CHARLESTON,
SOUTH CAROLINA, TO NEW YORK IN 1971

LOS ANGELES, DECEMBER 1974
ROBERT JOSEPH PERSHING FOSTER

———

WITHIN FOUR YEARS of Robert's big party of a lifetime, Alice, who had married him to the unspoken disappointment of her upper-crust parents, had followed him to Austria and Los Angeles and Vegas, allowed herself to be his mannequin and muse, given legitimacy to his aspirations and become his ticket to high society, which he both coveted and resented, Alice with her cat-eye glasses and teacher's solemnity, had fallen gravely ill and died.

Again, like his brother Madison, here was another family member passing away, and his medical certifications and surgical expertise could do nothing to stop it. She died of cancer, as had Robert's mother, on December 8, 1974, at the age of fifty-four. Her passing and burial rites were both headlined in the *Chicago Defender* and the *Atlanta Daily World,* the black newspaper that had charted her every coming and going for most of her life.

The *Defender,* taking interest from half a continent away, described her as "one of Los Angeles' most prominent civic and social figures," "wife of noted surgeon, Dr. Robert Pershing Foster," and "a tireless worker in numerous civic and philanthropic organizations."

She was interred far from the tinseled veneer of Los Angeles in Louisville, Kentucky, at her father's burial site, reclaimed in death as a Clement, not a Foster. They had been married thirty-three years, not one of them in Monroe. On that, they had both agreed.

As quiet and self-contained as she was, the house felt empty and unbearably silent after she was gone. The girls were all off on their own, two now married and living back east, the youngest away at college. Robert, along with Alice's mother, Pearl, returned disheartened from the interment and took up their positions in their respective corners of the echoing mansion. As big as it was, it was feeling too small for two people so different from each other, who had put up an appearance of cordiality only to appease the one thing they had in common—sweet and devoted Alice. Neither had liked how the other seemed to control her, and now the reason they endured each other was gone and not coming back.

Each missed her more than they could have possibly anticipated. Even Robert—who had directed her choice of clothing, dissected her every attribute and deficit, stayed out late tending his patients and his vices, and taken for granted that she would be there whenever he needed her—felt her absence perhaps more than her presence now that he no longer had it.

With each passing day, Pearl grew angrier and more resentful. Of all the people in her life and all the people she had known and loved, here she was left with the one she least wanted to be around. How was it that the two of them had survived? It would never have occurred to her when she moved to Los Angeles, a widow from Atlanta, into the new wing Robert had built for her that her daughter would precede both of them in death and that so full a house would come down to just these two.

Now Robert was asking her to contribute a little in rent each month, which she took as an insult, given how the Clements had helped them in the early years of their marriage and how she had just now lost her only child. Robert thought it was only fair, given that he had vowed to take care of her daughter, not her, but still had done so, even building a wing for her, from the time Rufus Clement had died seven years before. He knew that Pearl had the money to share the household expenses from Clement's pension and estate. And, besides, Robert said, "I had given

her anything she wanted." They could come to no agreement, and matters only grew worse.

The gambler and the socialite were marooned in a house that was big,
but not big enough to escape each other. They were the oddest of couples and each was all that the other had. Day after day, he went to his office, hoping to avoid her on the way out. Day after day, she was stuck in
the house where every lamp and figurine reminded her of the daughter
she had lost.

She had never wanted to be part of the Great Migration or come out
to California. She had lived her whole life in the South and was in Los
Angeles only because her daughter's husband had been so insistent on
fleeing the South and had taken Alice and the girls with him. Now, with
Alice gone, she was alone in a city she had never wanted to be in. She
had little to fill the hours. Robert and Pearl ground through their days
in slow motion and tried to pretend the other wasn't there.

It wasn't long until she realized she couldn't take it anymore. She
could no longer hold in the resentment. One day, she broke the silence.

"Why did you have to be the one to live, and not my daughter?" she
finally said.

She had gotten it out, and there was nothing left to say after that. The
tension had likely been building up from the moment they'd met. Her
time in the house couldn't last much longer. She packed her belongings
and moved back to Kentucky, where her late husband and daughter
were buried. And Robert was alone in the house and with himself for
the first time in his life.

CHICAGO, FEBRUARY 1975
IDA MAE BRANDON GLADNEY

———

IDA MAE'S SISTER IRENE, the one who had urged Ida Mae to come
north in the first place, saying, *"I just wouldn't stay down there if I was
you,"* and whom they moved in with upon arrival, was having eye
surgery. She hoped Ida Mae would come up to Milwaukee to help her

while she recovered. Ida Mae wanted to go but wasn't sure she would be able to.

There was so much going on in Ida Mae's household with everybody either coming or going to work and trying to take care of the grandkids, who were teenagers now, and get to church on time and pay the light bill and the house note. Ida Mae couldn't drive and didn't have a way to get there. And it was the darkest days of winter.

George and Ida Mae were not the youthful innocents fleeing the hard soil of the South for Chicago as they had been all those years ago. They were in their sixties now—George was sixty-eight and Ida Mae was sixty-two. They had lived in Chicago for longer than they had been in Mississippi and were still working, which they had been doing in one form or the other from the time they could pick up a hoe or reach over a wash pot.

They had reached the point in life where everyone around them seemed to be succumbing to something—high blood pressure, diabetes, which they called sugar, cancer, stroke, hysterectomies, heart attacks, or some combination of them all.

Ida Mae had had to go back to Mississippi some years before to see about her ailing mother. Miss Theenie had collapsed from a stroke and, isolated in the country as she was, had lain out in her yard, unable to move, for more than a day until someone happened to pass by on that lonely gravel road and see her. Miss Theenie did not live too much longer after that. Ida Mae went down to the funeral in the spring of 1959 and grieved mightily over it, but she had a family of her own to tend to.

Ida Mae herself had finally gotten over her fear of hospitals and had the hysterectomy her doctor said she needed. George had an enlarged heart and had already suffered two heart attacks. Each time, the family managed to get him to go to the hospital. But, stubborn as he was and disbelieving and suspicious of northern medicine, he wouldn't submit to any surgery or medication upon release—the nitroglycerin or beta-blockers that would have been standard at the time. To him that was just some kind of northern trickery and against his faith in God.

"He didn't have no medicine 'cause if he had it, he wouldn't take it," Ida Mae said. "He would never believe nothin' was wrong with him. He didn't believe in no doctors."

Whatever he was feeling, he just said it was indigestion. Once when he went to the hospital, the triage nurse was asking him about his symptoms.

"Don't ask so many questions," he told her. "Just do something for me and ask questions later."

Now her beloved big sister Irene was needing her, and Ida Mae was trying to figure out how to get to her. George told her she should stay home, tend to the family, and go to church. But it turned out that a friend named Evelyn happened to be heading to Milwaukee at around the same time, and Ida Mae's daughter Eleanor told her she should make up her own mind and go see about her sister. Eleanor agreed to go with her.

They helped Irene as best they could. When they arrived back in Chicago and pulled up to the house, they knew something was wrong. It was a Sunday, midday, and George's Chevrolet was still parked out front when he should have been at church.

Ida Mae and Eleanor walked into the vestibule. James came right out. He told them George had had another heart attack while Ida Mae was away. It was the third one her husband had had. It struck him that morning. This time he didn't come back from the hospital.

James broke the news to Ida Mae and Eleanor that George had passed away. "They had to pick both of us up off the floor of the vestibule," Ida Mae said.

She thought back to the start of the weekend. How she had chosen to see about her sister instead of staying home. How, the night before she left, the cat had slapped her in the face.

"I should have known then," Ida Mae said.

She remembered George's warning her over and over, "Now you work and make your own money," he used to say, " 'cause one day I ain't gon' be here."

She thought about his last heart attack. "The doctor said he'd never pull out of another one," she remembered.

Even Irene said she knew something was about to happen, although it wasn't clear exactly how. "Ida Mae, I started to tell you to go back home," Irene said after she learned that George had died.

James said he had found him.

"His arm was as hard as this seat."

"No, I found him," his wife, Mary Ann, said.

"No, you didn't," James said. "You fell out in the hallway."

———

"I should have been there," Ida Mae said in one of her rare displays of regret. For forty-five years, she had been the dutiful wife of a hardworking and stoic man, cooking and cleaning after him and obeying him—most of the time—like the pastor had said to do. And here, when he needed her, in his last moments on this, earth, she wasn't there.

She tried to remind herself why she had gone. "Eleanor said I was always doing what he said to do," she remembered. "She said I should go on up and see about my sister. I ain't saying he'd a lived. George went to a funeral that Saturday. Something told me, 'Ida Mae, you better stay here.' . . . You think about these things."

She mulled this over in the days after his death. Then Ida Mae dried her tears and consoled herself with something her husband used to say.

"He always said the Lord wasn't gon' let him suffer," Ida Mae said. He had suffered enough in his life. He had been a good provider, and he had kept his faith that God, who had delivered them from Mississippi, would look after him in the end.

He was right. He was the one who used to open up the church. He had set out his suit, shirt, shoes, and tie well in advance so he would be ready that Sunday. "He died in his sleep," Eleanor said, "with his hand over his heart like somebody had placed it there."

NEW YORK, 1978
GEORGE SWANSON STARLING

———

ALL THE SORROWS caught up with Inez. There would be scientific and medical explanations for what befell her. But those who knew her could see the storm whirling inside her, which she had tried to suppress, a thousand little heartaches since coming into the world just as her mother left it and being hooked now into a marriage born of adolescent love but mostly of spite.

Her churlishness had managed to alienate so many people, perhaps without intending to, but people didn't tend to stay around long enough to figure out the motivation. The one thing she categorically loved most in this life, her firstborn, Gerard, had broken her heart with his addictions. The drugs had turned him into a stranger and stolen her son from her.

She would never fully get over it. And as Gerard sank further and, by some miracle, came out of it, only to sink back again, she and George moved further apart. George practically had a second family, distant though he was, now that he had a son by another woman. But he stayed in the marriage out of a distorted sense of honor and duty rather than truly wanting to be there, and Inez had to live with that, too. The New World had been a land of milk and honey, of a hard-won measure of freedom and working-class achievements—the Harlem brownstone, the insurance policies and certificates of deposit, the upstairs tenants who brought in extra income, the furniture, cars, and appliances, the steady if monotonous jobs that impressed the folks back home—but they had come at a steep price.

Inez suffered under the weight of her disappointments and the mirage of what, from Florida, looked like a well-lived life in the North. By early 1978, the heartaches caught up with her. She was diagnosed with breast cancer and succumbed later that year.

Even as her body failed her and she had little time left on this earth, she and George circled each other, could not break through the hurts and recriminations that had built up over the decades since he had grabbed her by the hand and ushered her into the magistrate's office back in Florida to get back at his father. Her passing lent a finality to that error in judgment. They had lived with it but had not been happy, and the marriage ended more sorrowfully than either of them could have ever imagined that spring day back in Florida in 1939.

LOS ANGELES, 1978
ROBERT JOSEPH PERSHING FOSTER

WHEN ALICE DIED, so did the highbrow social theater she and Robert had shared in Los Angeles. Robert would no longer keep open the private salons of the finest department stores to find some heavily beaded gown for Alice. The invitations to this or that black-tie function evaporated. The phone didn't ring as much. With Pearl gone back to Kentucky, he had the whole house to himself.

Even the office didn't feel the same. What was he raking in all this money for if he couldn't spend it on someone he could show off and brag about? He was going on sixty now, and it was time he started thinking about letting his private practice go and taking a more predictable position at a hospital somewhere. He wouldn't have to worry about managing an office or patients needing him in the middle of the night. He could spend more time out in Vegas or at the track, doing what he wanted to do, what he came out to California for in the first place.

He decided to take a staff position at the Veterans Hospital in Brentwood. It would allow him to focus on medicine and his patients, not on rent, utilities, and payroll. It seemed a perfect fit. He was a veteran after all.

His life would now revolve around carpools to the hospital, treating the same kind of people he treated when he was in the army in Austria—rather like going back in time. And then there were the trips to Vegas whenever he could get away.

It was nothing for him to catch a plane to Vegas after work, gamble all night, fly back the next morning, and make it to his office just in time for his first patient.

"It was a sickness," said Limuary Jordan, who knew him in Monroe and in Los Angeles and had little patience for him. "I know for a fact that here's a man who could make five hundred or six hundred dollars a day in his office back in the seventies and still had to go and gamble in Vegas, go play his blackjack."

He would arrive at the Las Vegas Hilton and, unlike his first trip back in the fifties, would be ushered to one of the best rooms in the house. "The room was comp," Robert said.

"The meals were comp." He was betting so much money, the casino at the Hilton could be assured it would get the cost of them back, and more.

Robert would head to the casino and start playing blackjack or the roulette wheel. Mostly blackjack. Of course, there were no clocks or windows. None of the gamblers knew whether it was day or night. It didn't matter to Robert because he could play for almost twenty-four hours straight anyway.

"I don't know when to get up," Robert said.

There were times, lots of times, when he lost, in a matter of minutes, more than some people made in three or four years on a fairly decent job. And when he lost, he just kept playing, feeling it in his bones that the next hand, the next game, would be the one to turn things around.

He could rise out of the hole and get back in it for hours or days. He could get away with losing great sums of money because the casino knew he was good for it.

During one particularly rough stretch, he had a run of good luck and then sudden, heart-stoppingly bad luck. He was betting heavy and winning at first. He got cocky enough to tell the man in the casino cage that he was going to give him ten percent of whatever he won. He got to ten thousand, eleven thousand, twelve thousand, thirteen thousand dollars, and started attracting the attention of other gamblers around him.

Then nothing seemed to go his way.

He usually took someone with him—a nurse, a patient, another gambling buddy—to keep track of his winnings so he could concentrate on his game. When he hit it big, whoever was with him could count on getting a few thousand dollars from him to take back to Los Angeles. When he was losing, they sat helpless and watching. His nurse from the office was with him this time. As Robert's fortunes rose and fell by the hundreds with each bet, she started to notice something and tried to bring it to his attention.

"You know," the nurse began, "seems like every time you get to thirteen thousand dollars, you start losing."

That would not have been enough to stop him. It was not one of his better trips. But it was Vegas, and there was always another day. He was always playing to the crowd, knew all the casino workers, and loved it. Whatever he lost, he figured he would make it up tomorrow.

One time, Jimmy Gay, the man who had introduced Robert to Vegas and had been a boyhood friend of Limuary's in the small world of southerners in the L.A.-Vegas circuit, ran into Robert after a big win.

Robert had forty or fifty thousand dollars in front of him, and Jimmy wanted to intercede to keep him from losing it.

"Bob, let me go put it up for you," Jimmy said.

"No, I can handle my money," Robert shot back. "I'm a grown man. I don't need nobody to handle my money."

A couple hours later, Robert came back, wanting to borrow two thousand dollars.

"He done lost that fifty thousand and wanted two thousand to get it back," Limuary remembered. "Bob squandered a fortune."

But he seemed only to remember the times when he hit it big. It was what he lived for. Like the time when a friend who went with him had to keep up with the kind of money you only heard of in bank robberies.

"We brought back fifty-three thousand dollars," Robert said of one trip in the 1970s.

"He came back with a paper sack full of money," Limuary remembered, "and everybody knew his business on the job, and he'd pay all the people he owed."

But it was never really about the money for Robert. He had plenty coming in to begin with. It was hard really to know what it was about, except that he was weak for it and that deep inside him was a southerner with still a lot to prove. Gambling drew him, and he couldn't stay away. When he couldn't make it to Vegas, he bet on the horses at Santa Anita or played blackjack in a bare gymnasium of a space over by the Hollywood Park racetrack, anywhere he could escape into the nerve-jangling uncertainty and the rare seconds of elation that lasted only long enough to reel him back in.

He was handling sums of money that people back in Monroe could not fathom. "He won and lost several fortunes of a lifetime," Jimmy Marshall, his fellow migrant and friend, said.

In the midnineties, Robert, never a good driver to begin with, had a car accident, rammed into a median strip over on Crenshaw. He tore up his Cadillac. Someone came to help him out of the car.

"Are you hurt?" the man asked.

"No, I'm alright," Robert said.

"Did you get your bottle?" the man asked, figuring, why else would someone ram into a median strip?

"No, I don't drink," Robert told the man. Not anymore, anyway.

He would not be able to drive anymore. He shouldn't have been driving in the first place, his friends would say. But that wasn't going to stop him from getting to wherever he needed to gamble, even in a city of expressways and little in the way of public transportation.

He figured what he would do. *I'll take a taxi to the racetrack,* he thought to himself.

One day, he summoned a cab to his house on Victoria. He got in and directed the driver to Hollywood Park racetrack. Then it hit him. Why go to Hollywood Park when he knew where he really wanted to go?

"How much would it be to take me to Vegas?" he asked.

The cab driver told him the fare. He told the driver to head to Vegas. That time, he won big, which he would have needed to in order to get home, and flew back to Los Angeles with a sack full of money— triumph and self-esteem in a sack, to his mind.

More North and West
Than South

*I could come back down to New Orleans
for wonderful visits with my people,
but I couldn't stay.
Chicago and the North, where
I was used to Negroes being more free,
was where I belonged.*
—MAHALIA JACKSON, *Movin' On Up*

CHICAGO, 1978
IDA MAE BRANDON GLADNEY

IDA MAE SETTLED INTO HER ROLE as the sweet-natured but no-nonsense matriarch of the family now that her husband was gone. She had managed to re-create the village of extended family that existed on the plantations down south, her grown children and grandchildren surrounding her in the three-flat they had been in now for more than a decade.

The neighborhood had changed around them, had become all black and significantly poorer and more crime-ridden than it had been when they arrived. She and her family looked inward and lived their lives in the compound they created—her son, James, and his wife, Mary Ann, and their young children living on the first floor; Ida Mae living with Eleanor and her two children on the second floor; and a tenant named Betty, who was almost like a daughter to her, on the third floor.

There was always a commotion now that Kevin and Karen were out of high school and just starting their lives and Eleanor was divorced but with a full social schedule of house parties and lady friends from back in high school and new boyfriends, the phone always ringing for Eleanor.

Someone was always coming or going, wanting to know if the mail had arrived, if a job had come through, if a sweetheart had called yet, if a friend had said what time the party was, all of them expecting Ida Mae to keep up with this information since she was retired and home most of the time, and bending down and giving her a peck on the cheek as they got their coat and headed for the door again.

If they were all home at the same time, Kevin might be watching the White Sox in his room, Eleanor catching the news in hers, and Ida Mae watching a game show in the living room while keeping an eye on the drug busts and prostitutes on the street, which was usually better than any show on television anyway. There was a time back in Mississippi when nobody had a television—it hadn't been invented yet—and now everyone had one and retreated into his or her separate world.

Holidays brought everyone together, especially Thanksgiving. It's not clear whether anybody gave it any thought, but turkeys had been one of the reasons they were in Chicago in the first place. Maybe they would have come to Chicago anyway, it was just meant to be. In any case, in the fall of 1977, Ida Mae's family was chosen out of all the families on the South Side to represent the typical Chicago family at Thanksgiving. Someone at Jewel, the Chicago supermarket chain, knew someone who knew Ida Mae's family, knew James and Mary Ann, knew they were good solid people and that Ida Mae was beloved by all who came in contact with her.

Jewel brought a camera crew to their three-flat in South Shore. The dining room table was draped with white lace and candles, filled with platters of green beans and cranberry sauce and sweet potato pie and a roasted turkey at the head of the table. James with a mustachioed grin and his mother's narrow face, Mary Ann in auburn curls and a white silk blouse, and three of their four children sat smiling and happy as if in dinnertime conversation around the dining room table. A photographer captured the moment.

The picture ran as a full-page ad for Jewel Food Stores in the *Chicago Metro News* on Saturday, November 26, 1977. The headline read "Platters Full of Plenty Thanks." Near the center of the picture was Ida Mae with a platter full of salad, standing at the head of the table in a polyester dress, her white hair in a French twist, her big goggle glasses taking up most of her face. Her eyes looked directly into the camera and she smiled as if unburdened and free despite the turmoil outside her front windows. For now, she was taking up a whole page in an ad out of Norman Rockwell in a city that had resisted people like her coming north, and, for one brief holiday weekend, had made it to the big time in Chicago.

NEW YORK, 1978
GEORGE SWANSON STARLING

———

INEZ WAS GONE, but the churchwomen bearing homemade pound cakes held little interest for George Starling. Inez was the only woman he would ever consider as a wife, however unhappy they had been. Now that she was gone, he was left to watch helplessly as the children he was not around enough to raise got themselves into fixes. He would try to impart wisdom from what he had learned from his own mistakes to children and grandchildren who did not appear anxious to hear it. He was getting to be looked upon as just an old man from the South. What did he know of the frustrations of being young and black and wanting to be somebody and all the temptations and obstacles they faced and what it took to survive?

He had been the one to set the course of their lives by migrating to New York before they were born. The parts of the city that black migrants could afford—Harlem, Bedford-Stuyvesant, the Bronx—had been hard and forbidding places to raise children, especially for some of the trusting and untutored people from the small-town South. The migrants had been so relieved to have escaped Jim Crow that many underestimated or dared not think about the dangers in the big cities they were running to—the gangs, the guns, the drugs, the prostitution. They could not have fully anticipated the effects of all these things on children left unsupervised, parents off at work, no village of extended family to watch over them as might have been the case back in the South. Many migrants did not recognize the signs of trouble when they surfaced and so could not inoculate their children against them or intercede effectively when the outside world seeped into their lives.

George's two children would come to resent the overcrowding and the vice and concrete, the people on top of one another and the perils all around. Both Gerard and Sonya would succumb to them in one form or another then run from the toxic influences that caught root in the city. They would move to Florida, the Old Country, by the 1980s, Sonya to Eustis, of all places, which she found smaller and, after the death of Jim Crow, more welcoming, and Gerard to Miami, where he made unheard-of sums of money dealing drugs during the cocaine boom, falling deeper into the drug world he was initiated into as a boy in New York.

Gerard blamed New York for the road he had taken, and he hated the city for it, unable to own up to the choices he himself had made.

"If I hadn't been born and raised in New York," he once told his cousin Pat, "I never would have been on drugs. I wouldn't have lived the life that I lived. I hate New York."

Both of George's children went in the opposite direction from the one George had taken, went back to the place he had left and made decisions he couldn't understand. It was as if their return was a rebuke to his attempt to spare them the pain he had endured and to give them chances at decent schools and work options other than fruit picking, choices he himself had never had growing up.

George would rarely talk about his children, so great was his disappointment.

The one constant in his life was the job on the railroad that took him along the path of the Great Migration he had made himself back during the war. Down and back, South and North, New York to Florida and New York again. He was sixty years old and had been working the rails for thirty-five years. How many times had he plied this route, passed through Wildwood, Jacksonville, Savannah, Raleigh, Richmond, and Washington and on up to New York, again and again? How many thousands of migrants had he helped up the train steps carrying their luggage? How much history had he seen unfolding in the faces of the people boarding those trains?

He was nearing retirement and was doing precisely the same thing now that he was when he was twenty-five. He had not moved up or been promoted in all those years. He had tried to propose to his superiors improvements in service since he was in a position to see up close exactly what the passengers needed. But nothing ever came of it. He learned to accept his lot, and it got to the point where he just stopped applying for positions, like conductor or ticket taker, that it was clear he wasn't going to get. Toward the end of his career, he got to be in charge of the luggage in the club cars. But it was really not much different than before.

As he had done when he first started, he would walk from one end of the train to the other all night long. He could rarely sit and never sleep during a twenty-four-hour run. All through the night, he had to take people's luggage at every stop and put it away and reposition it and pull out the luggage for passengers disembarking. He walked back and forth, up and down.

Sometimes he would take Inez's niece Pat with him on those night runs. He would get her settled in her seat and go to work.

"There never was a time that I saw him sleep," she remembered. "He never complained. It wasn't a gravy job, and it was beneath his dignity. He never got a chance to use his mind. When he first started, it was an honor to be a porter on that train at that time. But in reality, it wasn't nothin' but hard labor."

The Great Migration had played out before his very eyes. Now it was coming to a close from a demographic, macroeconomic point of view. On the ground, it was maturing, the migrants and their families situated in the North, no longer nervous and starry-eyed, missing their stop or getting off too early or by accident in Newark. Now he was watching and helping the grown children and grandchildren of the Migration make their way back to the Old Country. The ways of the North had settled into most of them. Many of his passengers were born and raised in the North and were making their first visits to the South, rather than returning to a place they had known.

He could tell the original migrants. They were requiring more help getting up the steps, beginning to need canes, many still speaking in their southern accents. They were the ones sitting up straighter, more alert, their memories awakened, when they passed the fields of tobacco and cotton, the small church-steepled towns along the way and the groves of orange trees that George knew so well, because, mean and ornery as it may have been, the South was still the Old Country, the land where their fathers and mothers were buried, and these original migrants were heading home to it, at least for now.

LOS ANGELES, 1978
ROBERT JOSEPH PERSHING FOSTER

———

ROBERT, a widower nearing sixty now, had landed what would seem the perfect position. He was doing precisely what had been denied him back in Louisiana. He was on staff at a hospital. And not just any hospital. He was physician to the staff of the West Los Angeles Veterans Administration Medical Center in Brentwood. It took up twenty-two acres between UCLA and the Brentwood Country Club. Its curving drives were named after the great generals of history—MacArthur, Patton, Pershing, the name he had gone by for the first half of his life. It was bigger and better than St. Francis, the small-town hospital that had rejected doctors who looked like him during the days of Jim Crow and had given him one more reason to leave the South. It would be vindication for all that he had endured back home.

He would make less than when he was in private practice, when he was limited only by the hours in the day and the energy he could muster. But he no longer had to concern himself with patient billing and office leases and could concentrate on what he loved most—doting on his patients, the employees at the VA hospital. Immediately, he set about getting to know everyone.

Some of the staff took to him right away, especially the few black ones who had migrated from the South like he had. Before long, he was carpooling with some of them to get to work. They quickly learned that his other love was gambling, and they could tell when he had just gotten back from Vegas. They would drive up to his mansion early in the morning and toot the horn. Robert would scramble down the walkway, silk suit pressed and necktie in place, limping in his stocking feet with his dress shoes in his hand.

He brought his crushed velvet, jitterbug demeanor to the gray, humorless bureaucracy of a government hospital. He put his feet up on his desk as he always had and asked about his patients' complaints and worries before pulling out his stethoscope. He had built an entire practice on understanding his patients' personal troubles so that he could get to the bottom of their medical ailments, as he saw one as being connected to the other.

Migrants from the South treasured his bedside manner and had made up the majority of the patients in his private practice. But Robert was now in a world more like the one he worked in as an army doctor in Austria during the Korean War. Most of the patients, meaning the hospital staff members, were bureaucrats or military and not of his background. Some had come from the South in the parallel migration of whites seeking their own fortune in the wide-open world of California during the years of the Great Migration.

The whole enterprise was an adjustment for Robert. He was used to being in charge and the center of attention, running his office as he pleased. Now he had to be at work by eight in the morning. Bureaucrats wouldn't put up with what his adoring working-class patients would accept. They wouldn't put up with him coming in on a morning flight from Vegas, rushing in late with his silk suits and sacks full of money. He couldn't charm his way into everyone's good graces by offering to pick up everybody's lunch tab with his winnings.

"That didn't work when you working for another man," said Limuary Jordan's wife, Adeline, one of Robert's sometime critics. "You got to follow his orders. You just don't come and walk over them like that."

His breezy airs did not sit well with some of the bureaucrats and their assistants. His being one of the few blacks in authority could have put him under perhaps even greater scrutiny. The bureaucrats began complaining about him, and soon he clashed with one hospital worker in particular. It may never be known precisely what happened. The military would not disclose details of the dispute, and Robert took the Hippocratic oath so literally that he rarely spoke of the specifics of any one patient. There were no legal charges against him, and he received workers' compensation for the distress he suffered. But trouble flared, his colleagues said, after a white woman patient at the hospital complained about an examination. Robert had managed to survive decades in the Jim Crow South without crossing a white woman and had actually won the gratitude of one from Kentucky when he interceded in her delivery and helped her avoid a cesarean section.

Now, decades later, after he had built a name for himself and had taken a job he did not need, he was running into the very thing he had come to California to escape. There were whispers within the hospital of professional incompetency, perhaps the one thing he had never been accused of in his life.

Robert refused to give up his position. But it would be only a Pyrrhic victory. The hospital, he reported, moved him from the offices that he and the white doctors who preceded him had worked out of. It transferred him to an older building "in a cramped examining room next to a loud lavatory reeking with urine and feces," he wrote in the mid-1990s in a letter of complaint to the Labor Department.

It was as if he had been hurled back fifty years to the Paramount Theater back in Monroe. It was nearing the eve of the twenty-first century, and it seemed as if Jim Crow would not die. His every move was scrutinized and the stress of the isolation weighed on him more heavily than anything in his life. He had made it to the paradise he had so believed in all those decades ago that he had bragged about it before even seeing it. Now, it had betrayed him in ways he could not have imagined.

He told his friends and family of his plight and the plight of co-workers who had also migrated from the South and were now helpless as they witnessed what was happening to him. He was so incensed that he complained to the Labor Department about the "personal isolation, professional and personal slights, rumors, [and] professional slander" he was enduring. He described "a continuous racist and stressful environment," language that he rarely used in all his descriptions of life in the South.

He had given his life over to his patients to the detriment of his own family, a decision that would weaken his ties to his daughters and grieve him later in life when his choices could not be undone. He had sat at the bedside of patients who loved him for his devotion. And now a new one had turned on him and threatened the reputation that had taken him a lifetime to build.

Things only got worse. In seeking workers' compensation, Robert was required to be evaluated by a psychiatrist with ties to the VA hospital. The psychiatrist seemed to dismiss what Robert told him and directed Robert to prove to him the difference in the size of Robert's old office and the smaller one to which he had been demoted.

The psychiatrist "proceeded to command me to step forward," Robert wrote, "pick up a commercial tape from his desk and stoop down in a servile manner to measure his office for square footage." Something about a surgeon being commanded by anyone to stoop to the floor and take measurements brought back memories of the sirring and ma'aming back in the South and made him feel lower than at any time since perhaps his migration through the desert.

"I am humiliated and ensnared in an evaluation process which is untenable," Robert wrote.

He had never wanted to make a federal case out of the times in his life he had been ill-treated because of the caste into which he had been born and the era in which he lived. But here he was making a plea to the government as he fought for his good name. The stress forced him to seek treatment from a cardiologist and from vascular and orthopedic surgeons and a psychiatrist. They told him he needed to quit to protect his health, but Robert did not want to go out that way, not after all he had been through, proving himself at every turn, starting with the decision to migrate in the first place.

The only good thing about the situation was that Rufus Clement had not lived to see it. Surely he would have told him that this was proof of what Clement had believed all along, that Robert would have been better off casting his lot in the South. Better, too, that big Madison hadn't lived to see it either. Surely, he would have shed a tear for his little brother who so loved medicine and worked so hard at pleasing everyone.

———

The dispute dragged on for years as Robert sought relief through workers' compensation for the toll the situation had taken on his health. One day in the middle of this episode in his life, he was walking down the red-carpeted aisle toward the club room at Santa Anita when it felt as if he were being stabbed in the chest. He was suffering a heart attack. He would require bypass surgery and would see his life slow down considerably.

He would soon take his own physicians' advice and retire from the VA hospital. It was not how he wanted to end his career. The memory of what he felt was a forced ouster in his adopted home would stay with him for the rest of his life. He had seen roadblocks to black progress even in his beloved California. "And it's harder and heavier the higher the paycheck," he said.

As for Robert's reputation, the one he fought so hard to maintain during his dispute with the hospital, it remained as it had always been. Patients from the VA hospital continued to see him, dropping by the house on Victoria to seek his advice. And many years later, the State Medical Board in Sacramento showed the record of Dr. Robert P. Foster to be free of any sanctions during the forty-four years he was licensed to practice medicine in the state of California.

But he would never see California the same. He would have many moments of joy from the old patients who consulted him and brought their children for him to examine and allay their worries long after he had retired. But he would never get over what befell him.

"He was dying on the inside," his friend and patient Malissa Briley said.

REDEMPTION

*For our light
and momentary troubles
are achieving for us
an eternal glory
that far outweighs them all.*
—2 CORINTHIANS 4:17

I

CHICAGO, SUMMER 1996

IDA MAE GLADNEY IS EIGHTY-THREE YEARS OLD when I first meet her. She is a churchgoing pensioner with time on her hands. She spends most of her days alone while everyone else is out working. She does word puzzles and crosswords, whole paperback books of them, to keep her mind sharp. She collects the funeral programs of the people she knew and loved in Mississippi and Chicago, who are, one by one, passing away, getting extras for other mourners the way young people collect business cards and email addresses. It is the currency of the old. In the meantime, she manages to keep up with the job pursuits and love lives of her grandchildren and great-grandchildren.

She has little interest in soap operas and doesn't need to watch police dramas on television. She has one right outside her window. Hers is a bow-front window, curved like a movie screen. She can monitor the street day or night from her box seat, which is actually a baby blue, plastic-covered easy chair by the front window, on the second floor of her three-flat. Things are happening that she never saw growing up in Mississippi, and she isn't always certain of exactly what it is she is looking at. She is watching the street from her window the afternoon I meet her.

A man is selling drugs out of a trash can. She can see, plain as day, where he puts them and how he gets them out of the trash for the white customers in their SUVs with suburban license plates. Another hides his stash in his mouth. And when customers come up, he pulls a piece of his inventory from his tongue to sell to them. The police are on to it, too. "The police put flashlights down their mouth," she says. "Sometimes the police make them stoop over."

A man is climbing out of an old Pontiac he sleeps in. He and the car have been outside her house for weeks. A teenage mother has just popped her son for something Ida Mae can't make out because a car passes by just when the mother yells something at the boy. Usually it's "M—f—" or "G—d—," Ida Mae says, and it hurts her to see people do that to their children.

The other night, she says, she was setting out the trash and saw a woman on her knees in the alley doing something to a man who was up against the garage. "I was looking for her head, and I never did see it," Ida Mae says. She didn't know exactly what the woman was doing but she knew they shouldn't have been doing it and knew better than to say anything and thought it best to go back inside. "I just can't get it out of my mind," she says.

When the police aren't around, the people are out in the street like characters in a cable television drama and the drug dealers are up and down the block but mostly at the corner where there was once an ice cream parlor, back when she first moved here.

These are the lost grandchildren of the Migration who have grown hard in the big city and did not absorb the lessons of the past or the good to be found in the steadying rituals and folk wisdom of the South. Ida Mae and James and Eleanor can't understand how they do the things they do, how they would rather trawl the streets than go to work every day and be able to hold their heads high.

Something about too many people packed together and nothing to guide them makes the children worse than they used to be, to her mind. At the moment, the city is in a crisis because two grade-schoolers, one of them only seven, have been accused of killing another child. Nobody knows for sure what happened and she certainly couldn't say, but she knows one thing for sure: "They curse like sailors, they throw rocks, they do everything they big enough to do. They ain't got no home training, and they mama can't do nothing 'cause she on drugs. That seven-year-old, they say he was the ringleader. He know more than he telling. But they shouldn't put them in the penitentiary. They too young. They not gone ever forget it."

She keeps going. "I know kids 'cause I been one," she says. "I used to tease this girl that her mama was dead. I think about that a lot sometimes. She held that against me the rest of her life. She used to cry when I said it. I didn't know what it was to lose a mother. I had lost my father. I thought everyone should die. I was nine or ten years old. I was bad. Now they double worse. What go in the wash come out in the rain. *Watch what I say, now.* You got to start working on those little ones early. I ain't got much education, but I sho' know folks. I ain't scared of these kids but I stay out of their way."

———

The craziness has Ida Mae hemmed in on all sides. When she leaves to go to church, if she goes to buy groceries, if she takes a walk to get some exercise, the drug dealers and lookout boys greet her as she leaves and welcome her when she gets back. When she hears sirens or gunshots, she runs to the window to see what has happened now. She is an eyewitness to a war playing out on the streets below her. Staying on top of everything is how she makes peace with the craziness she cannot escape.

She would never dream of going outside at night by herself. But it is not because she is afraid of the gangbangers and the drug dealers. She speaks to them and prays for them, and in turn they look out for her. They call her "Grandma" and tell her not to come out on certain days.

"You better stay in the house," they tell her. "Because we don't know what time we gon' start shootin'."

———

On a July afternoon, she is telling her story about the ride up north and making her way in Chicago in those early days. We are in the middle of a conversation when something crashes outside the window. It rattles me, and I look toward the window to see what it might be. Ida Mae does not flinch. She has learned the difference between danger and mischief, between a gunshot and a rock through a window. Whatever it was, it's as if it didn't happen.

"Did you hear that?" I ask her. "Sounds like some glass broke."

"Honey, they does that. They throw bottles at each other."

"You didn't even look up."

"I hear too much of it," she says. "I'd be lookin' all day." She lets out a big laugh.

Every day, there is something or other. On an otherwise quiet afternoon, we look out the window and see two police officers leading a black man in a white windbreaker and baseball cap, hands cuffed, down the sidewalk in front of the apartment building next door.

"That's the janitor," she tells me. "He works there. Wonder what did he do?"

He lopes along, head up, scanning the street like a politician on a tour of his district. He looks both ways before stepping off the curb to cross the street to the patrol car. He nods his respects to the teenage girls walking past.

Ida Mae doesn't know what he has done, but figures she'll find out in due course.

"People talk," she says. "You don't have to ask."

She has an idea of what it was. There was a raid in the building a few weeks before. The police took seventeen or eighteen people out in handcuffs.

"Did it at night," she says. "They carried them all out tied together. I got tired of counting. You know that still ain't stop them? They still up in there. I don't know what'll stop 'em. I guess the Lord knows."

She watches and makes note of what's going on around her. Every month, there's a neighborhood crime watch meeting, and she is sure to attend. Trouble is, she believes some of the police are not much better than the criminals. "The detectives are the ones doing the dirt," she says. Somehow, some of the dealers are onto the police or get forewarning of their arrival. "They have a phone," she says. "They know when the police coming."

Still, she manages to stay out of everybody's way. She may be stuck in her own home, but she has too much faith or stubbornness to let fear take over.

"I ain't gone live nowhere scared," she says. "I ain't calling the police. Long as they don't bother me. If I know what's going on, they do, too."

And she refuses to put bars on the windows. "My husband say, he never be behind no bars," she says. "And neither am I."

2

HARLEM, 1996

———

IT REQUIRES descending down a narrow set of stairs into an airless vestibule in the basement of a three-story brownstone to get to where the owner lives. He has taken the dankest, darkest space for himself and given over the rest of the building, the rooms with light and space, to whatever tenants he has.

George Starling never cared about creature comforts and finery but about getting a square deal, which he on occasion achieved, and the right to exercise the free will he was not permitted in the South. His life is scattered in boxes all over his room, file folders stuffed with pictures of him and Inez as teenagers in Florida, mimeographed copies of his lawyerly letters to the railroad or union leaders about this or that provision or instance of inequity, and the funeral programs of loved ones who have passed away.

He is seventy-eight now, a grandfather and great-grandfather, a deacon in the church. He sits upright and stoic. He enunciates each syllable in this early conversation and speaks in the deliberate and formal manner of the professor he once wanted to be. But the longer he talks, the more comfortable he gets and the more he sounds like the southerner he is inside.

He feels it his responsibility to share what he knows and takes it upon himself to explain whatever he says in the greatest detail. He talks for forty-five patient and exacting minutes about what it takes to pick string beans and describes the difference between the walking buds, the junior buds, the uncle buds, and seedling trees he used to pick back in Florida.

A car pulls up. It's his pastor, Reverend Henry Harrison, dropping by to see Deacon Starling. The pastor, hearing the topic of the South and the Migration, begins telling the story of how his father escaped from a labor camp in South Carolina by swimming through a swamp, and, eventually, in 1930, finding his way to New York.

Both men start to lament the changes all around them, the sadder effects of the big city of the North on the people of the South. George waxes on about the days when "people would come down to 135th

Street with their house chairs, and they would baptize people in the Harlem River.

"We used to have a boat ride off 125th Street in the Dyckman section," he says.

"Spread the blankets out. Midsummer, people didn't have air-conditioning. People would stay up there all night and play card games.

"Things were so much different," he says. "Drugs wasn't heard of where I came from. When I came to New York, I didn't know what a reefer was."

"We got to being Americanized," Reverend Harrison is saying. "It got to where we don't help each other."

———

George has children and grandchildren and even a great-grandchild now, but there is an aloneness to the character of his life. He seems content in the solitude of his room with its dust-covered floor, barely made bed, and no sign of a woman's touch. He seems on a mission to sort through the paperwork of his life, find some meaning in all the railroad pamphlets and official letters he wrote on behalf of workers' rights that were politely dismissed or not acted upon.

His face turns ashen and he looks away when the subject turns to his children and grandchildren. His son by Inez had squandered the very opportunities George had left the South for, and he had limited contact with the now-grown son he had outside his marriage.

Then there was the daughter, Sonya. She was sweet but unsettled, too, back and forth between Florida and New York. George had been having heart trouble and had just come out of triple bypass surgery when he got word that Sonya had died in a car accident down in Eustis.

He flew down to Florida for the funeral. The people who had stayed in the South gathered around to console him.

"We would be in a room with a crowd of people," his niece Pat said, "and he would get up and leave the room. He'd come back and just carry on the conversation. You knew he had been crying."

He buried his daughter next to his wife.

3

LOS ANGELES, SPRING 1996

THIS IS THE 1970S set piece known as Dr. Robert Foster's living room. It is a room that is little changed, you learn, from the time when his wife, Alice, was alive. You are encased in cream and raspberry upholstery, sea foam carpet, and harvest gold draperies cascading down from ten-foot ceilings, more space than one person could possibly need and, by that measure alone, the very picture of success in California.

The host has momentarily disappeared down a hall and into the avocado green and harvest gold kitchen. He emerges, taking care with his steps, with a tray of lemon pound cake with vanilla ice cream, which you would really prefer not to take, since you have only just eaten; but it is clear from the formality with which he presents it and then watches as you pick up the fork that there is no choice but to accept this gesture of hospitality.

In a bookcase, there are volumes of Tolstoy, Freud, Goethe, and Herodotus. On his face is a smile of satisfaction at the interest being taken in a life he loves to talk about.

You learn the basics of what he wishes you to know about his growing up in Monroe, marrying the daughter of a university president, leaving the South for California, about the three daughters and now the grandchildren, the gambling and the current state of his health and how he views the world as a southern émigré in California. Those things will be fleshed out in due time over the course of several months.

You learn that right now he has heart problems, has already had bypass surgery. "The chest pain is growing more frequent," he says. "But I'm not going to have another operation. If anything happened to me tomorrow, I wouldn't have any regrets. I have lived. I've done it all. The world don't owe me nothin'."

He is retired from the practice of medicine and spends most of his time at the blackjack tables or on the phone dispensing free medical advice to former patients and old friends or ordering around a gardener who indulges his every whim as to precisely where the begonias should be. Years before, Robert woke up the morning of his oldest daughter's wedding, and, instead of taking his time dressing in his tuxedo, he got out and had the front yard dug up to plant flowers to match Bunny's wedding bouquet.

Now, on this late spring afternoon, he was fretting over the backyard. "Now turn it a little more," he was telling the gardener one day about a particular pot of geraniums. "Not to the left! To the right! To the right!"

———

He has come all this way and is living in a 3,600-square-foot monument to his success in California. But the most enduring accomplishments you cannot see: the cooks and teachers and postal workers all over southern California who would do just about anything for him because he had saved their lives or brought them into the world or repaired some broken piece of themselves. And the three daughters whom he spared from having to go to segregated schools in the South and who grew up free with their cotillions in California.

The daughters lead upper-middle-class lives, had married well if not long, and have children who can only be said to be brilliant. Bunny is now working as an artists' agent in Chicago. Robin is a city manager who is living outside Washington with her second husband and her son, who is being courted by the Ivies. The youngest daughter, Joy, is a physician—a radiologist—married to a day trader, and has two precocious young children in Long Beach, about thirty miles south of Robert.

Alice never got to see the fruits of her labor, and, at weddings and holidays, it falls to Robert to be mother and father, neither of which he is naturally suited for. But he rises to the occasion when called upon to do so. When Joy brought home a young man she appeared to be serious about, Robert stepped forward as a father protecting his youngest.

He asked the young man, Lee Ballard, to go out for a drive to the dry cleaners with him. He made it sound like a request, which, of course, it was not. Lee climbed into Robert's white Cadillac, and Robert began driving, erratic as usual. Then Robert began his inquiries.

"How do you like California?" he asked Lee once they were on their way. "And how do you plan to take care of my daughter?"

The drive lasted two hours. The beau survived the drive and ended up marrying Robert's youngest daughter. The marriage would last longer than those of the other girls.

———

The telephone rings. It's the third or fourth time in the space of a couple of hours. The phone usually starts ringing around three or four o'clock, after people get home from seeing their new doctors. Robert excuses himself to take the call in the kitchen. It's another friend and former patient calling about an ailment and how best to treat it and to check to see if his new doctor is prescribing the right medication. Robert indulges the man, addresses his worries, gives him advice.

"Demerol is the name of it," Robert is telling the person on the other end of the line. "Now, put something in your stomach."

The person has more questions for Robert about what he's been prescribed.

"Percodan? Any of those things nauseate the heck out of you," Robert tells him. "Take as little medicine as you can—"

The person interrupts, and Robert listens.

"Take your aspirin," Robert tells him.

The person cuts in again, still expressing concern. Robert reassures him.

"Sounds like you going to be alright, Phil. God bless you."

EUSTIS, FLORIDA, JULY 1996

GEORGE SWANSON STARLING

SOME FIFTY-ONE YEARS have passed since the standoff in the central Florida citrus groves that almost got George Starling killed. He has lived out his life in New York. The grove owners he stood up to are long dead, as is the high sheriff, old Willis McCall, who lorded over Lake County with a Smith and Wesson and a ten-gallon hat.

George has felt it safe to come back to visit and is now sitting at a diner out by Ocala with his old friend Reuben Blye, who was one of George's picking foremen back in the forties. They both had lived up north. Reuben, at age eighty-nine, is now living back in Florida with his sixth wife, having survived the treachery of the South and the temptations of the North and is at this moment reliving those days with George, who is back in town for a high school reunion.

"Do you know a Florida man got more sense than a born New Yorker, George?" Reuben asks, not really looking for George to answer. "You know that?"

"I had never given it a thought that way."

"One that's been around like us, George. We know our way around better than some of them up there."

"Well, you had to have a lot of sense to learn how to survive down here during those times to stay out of trouble, you know."

"George, you done run that railroad so long up and down from coast to coast on the train," Reuben says. "And look how we travel. Look at Rube, done travel, done made thirty-seven states. I already had it in my head. You don't get me every day."

As torn as George was about his time in Florida, he had never truly left it in his mind. Ever since his father had died, he had kept a little piece of property in Eustis, vacant land with live oaks and scrub brush near the house where his father had run the little convenience store. He never knew exactly what he would do with it and had no plans to live there ever again. He just liked the idea of having control over something in a place that had controlled his every step for so long.

"When I left, I swore that I would never come back under no circumstances anymore," he said. "When I left, I was just that bitter. I didn't intend to come back at all."

Ten years passed before he felt it safe to return. The deaths and illnesses lured him back and he began to see how the South seemed to be changing, in small ways and big ways, right before his eyes. "I never thought I would live to see the day," he said of some of the strides being made. "If anybody told me that there would be a black mayor in Birmingham, I would have told them they were crazy. Now they have black mayors all over the place down south. How many black mayors we got up north?"

He had once seen a black man and a white woman walking down the street in downtown Tavares, the county seat and the domain of old Willis McCall. George was having a hard time getting used to seeing what could have gotten him killed in his day.

"I never thought I'd see the day when a black man would walk down the street holding hands with a white woman," he said. "It amazes me when I see the intermingling. When I was a boy down here, when you went through the white neighborhood you had to be practically running. Now black people are living in there. They all mixed up with the whites right there in Eustis."

We are riding through Eustis and out to the orange groves near Sanford and the train station in Wildwood where the relatives would come to greet George when his train passed through. He and Reuben are returning to the places where they picked oranges and okra, the places they could and couldn't go and where the black people lived. Reuben does most of the directing because he has been living back in Florida for several years now. George sits up and starts pointing when he sees something he recognizes.

"They used to baptize us down here," George says as we wind past Lake Eustis. "To the left are the water oak trees."

We drive farther out. The land is wild scrub brush broken by stands of domed trees, the citrus that ruled their lives growing up.

"Over to the right, over here was woods," George says, "just like you see to the right, but they cleared that up."

"Here go the seedling groves," Reuben says.

"Is that Lake Ale there?"

"That Lake Ale. Those seedling groves right in here had all them pecan trees."

"Was this the Natural?" George asks of the legendary grove that has withstood the worst winters and hardest of freezes.

"The Natural's out there by Emaraldi Island."

"I told you Reuben would know where everything is," George says, turning in my direction.

"If you dropped an orange in the Natural Grove, five minutes and it would just be hittin' the ground. You could get up in one of those trees and look all over this south Florida."

"This is Ole Jones' place."

"I picked in that grove where I had a thirty-six-foot ladder spliced with a twenty-six-foot ladder, and it just reached the bottom limb."

"That's right. All us here, Charlie, Mud, me, we used to hunt coons and possum 'long here."

We drive further and further out.

"This here is Ole Cannon Grove."

"This is not the way it looked before the last big freeze," George says. "This is new. They reset, they put new trees there."

"All this here was froze out."

"Nineteen eighty-nine, it snowed in Florida. Had two and three inches of snow."

"Have you ever seen a forest that would burn out with a fire?" George asks me. "Well, that's just the way those trees look. Them trees looked just like somebody went through there with a flame-thrower."

George comes back to Eustis every two years for the biennial reunion of Curtwright Colored High School. He always comes down on the train he once worked. It's owned by Amtrak now and, as a pensioner with thirty-five years of service, he gets to ride for free. He can finally sit like the passengers he served and look out the window to see what they saw, reliving with each trip the migration he made all those years ago.

When George returns to Eustis, he is looked upon with a distant kind of respect. He was one of them once, but he chose a different path, knows things they couldn't know, survived in a place where they're not sure they could make it. He's been gone so long that whatever he knows about Eustis is either frozen in the 1940s or distorted through the sec-ondhand recounting in long-distance phone calls and letters and rumor. He's fuzzy on some of the names of the people who live there now.

Whole generations have been born since he left, and he searches out his connections to them, the ways he might know them—through a grandparent, great-aunt, or second cousin of theirs whom he grew up with but who may not be around anymore. He stays with Viola, the widow of his deceased stepbrother, and spends much of his time visiting with the few people who were around when he was here, reliving those days, and catching up on the things he has missed. When people hear that he's in town, they head over to Viola's bungalow and remove their hats before they walk in to see a prodigal son of Eustis.

It is Sunday on the July weekend of the high school reunion, and George puts on his burgundy polyester suit, burgundy tie, burgundy socks, and white straw hat to worship at the church he grew up in as a boy and where the doomed Harry T. Moore recruited him in the early drive for equal rights. Seventy parishioners take their places in the dark wood pews affixed to orange carpet.

Pastor William Hawkins beseeches the congregation to take up a spe-cial plate for the black churches that have recently been burned throughout the South. It is as if it is 1963 again.

"We ought to do something to assist them," he says. "And this is one of the reasons we better secure our own church."

People pull out money to give to the other churches and pray that they won't be next. The choir motions for George to come forward and sing the solo for the collection.

"What you give, what more He gives to you," he sings.

Then the pastor turns to George. "We are always glad to see our member from New York," Reverend Hawkins says, motioning to George to come to the pulpit to speak.

George stands before the congregation of mostly new faces, the descendants of those he knew, and looks around at a church that was as much a part of him as the South itself.

"Needless to say, I am grateful to be in your midst," he says. "I look over and see my father and my mother and my daughter. And it always makes me a little full. So if I become emotional, I hope you will understand."

He then sings a hymn, *"Without God I could do nothing . . . without him, I would fail. . . ."*

The congregation claps after he finishes, and he takes his glasses off and wipes the tears with his handkerchief before walking back to his seat at the side of the church. He takes his place and sits upright in a pew next to the pulpit with a silver cane beside him and tears escaping from his eyes.

LOS ANGELES, NOVEMBER 23, 1996
ROBERT JOSEPH PERSHING FOSTER

THE REGULARLY SCHEDULED BIMONTHLY MEETING of the Monroe, Louisiana, Club of Los Angeles, California, is not so much called to order as roused to life when ten of the sixteen surviving and currently active members trickle into the bungalow of Leo and Era Davis on Ninety-third Street east of Crenshaw. They gather in the Davises' den with the circular metal staircase and prepare to catch up with one another and with news from back home in Monroe.

It is surely one of the smallest Louisiana clubs in the city, not to mention its being overshadowed by all the Texas Clubs around town. "We're a dying breed," says Limuary Jordan, a club member who left Louisiana in his DeSoto more than half a century before. "It's a fact. Everybody in the club is over sixty. And without any new Monroe people . . . there are Monroe people here, but they don't affiliate with us. They don't belong to no club. So we are of a particular time."

"A lot of them don't have anything to do with the South," his wife, Adeline, says. "A lot of them, when they left, they were gone."

The few members who are still active approach the club with a sense of formality and ritual. Robert Foster had to secure approval before-hand to invite a guest, who brings the attendance at today's meeting to eleven. As the graying expatriates from Monroe begin to take their seats, I explain my presence as his guest and tell them about my work on the Great Migration. They listen without emotion or much in the way of comment, not seeing exactly what the Migration has to do with them, even though they had all been right in the middle of it. At the appointed hour, John Collins, whom they just call Collins, stands up like a proper reverend and prays stiffly in his black suit and gray vest and fedora.

"Lord, we thank you for this food we are about to receive, and we thank you for another day," he begins. "We pray for the lady visitor and the book she's trying to put together. Give her knowledge and wisdom and watch over her. In Jesus' name. Amen."

Spread out before the assembled are oxtails, collard greens, corn bread, sweet potatoes, potato salad, red beans and rice, and pound cake on an orange tablecloth in the wood-paneled dining room.

It is a time of unaccustomed quiet in the city after so much upheaval. The Rodney King beating, police acquittals, and ensuing riots were only a few years back, the business districts of South Central still in recovery. The people have been divided and whipsawed by the O. J. Simpson trial, the saga of a once-loved black football player acquitted of killing his white wife and her friend, the people by now just wishing the whole thing would go away but unable to escape it, billboards and headlines in every direction.

That very day, Robert passed a newspaper box with a poster about the O.J. trial. "I'm so sick of O.J.," he said, "I don't know what to do. They have choked us with this."

No one in the Monroe Club wants to talk about it. Instead, as if on cue, the never-ending loop of how people are faring back home and in Los Angeles and what they have been through in both places picks up where it left off from the last meeting as if it were fresh and new and has never come up before.

"If you look at it," Howard Beckwith begins, "we in the same instance as in the South. They throwing them in jail just like the South. The jails filled with colored people. The South has made a desperate change. Things you couldn't do in the South, you can do now. You can walk down the street with a white woman. The mayor is black."

"Who's that?" someone asks.

"You know Dr. Pierce what run the drugstore," Beckwith says. "One of his sons."

"No, it's not," someone breaks in, one-upping Beckwith and trying to prove who has the better connections to a place they still feel tied to even if nobody else cares about the distinctions. "It's one of Dr. Pierce's *cousin's* sons. The cousin of Dr. Pierce, one of his sons."

"That's Eliza Davis's son," a woman whispers to me by way of explanation. *"She was my classmate,"* she wants me to know.

Somehow the line of conversation reminds Collins about being black in the South and the talk turns to a kind of testifying rather than an interaction, each member reciting an experience independent from the others and at times seemingly unrelated. Here it is, fifty years after most of them left, and they can't stop talking about the South. They are exiles with ties to two worlds, still obsessed with the Old Country, and have never let it go.

Collins tells them about the time a white man slapped a ladle of water out of his hand as he was taking a drink. A woman describes being home from college and a policeman coming up and asking why she wasn't picking cotton or in the kitchen. Someone else mentions the movable sign on the trolley car and how "you had to sit and look at that sign that said 'Colored.' " Everyone nods in recognition.

Marshall brings up the segregated lines and the swiveling ticket agent at the Paramount Theater again. "The woman in the ticket counter swiveled to the white side to sell tickets and then swiveled to the colored," he says. "We walked up all those flights of stairs."

"That's all over the South," Beckwith says. "You didn't know nothing different."

Robert breaks in, momentarily distracted by the meal. "Era, what did you do with the oxtail? It's out of sight."

"Cake and ice cream? Cake and ice cream?" Mrs. Davis asks with a sugar voice, cake held up high.

Marshall then remembers an incident at Woolworth's, a seemingly small thing that let him know he was not meant to stay in the South.

"A white girl waited on me and gave me a token for my change," Marshall begins. "I went to tell on the woman, that she had taken my money and given me a token back that was worthless. All I got was the satisfaction of telling the man and of telling my mother when I got home."

He recounted what his mother told him: "You're going to have to leave this place, you keep that up."

Which is why Marshall ended up in California.

Then Robert joins in. "I had taken my bath in the tin tub," he begins. "I was clean."

"Was that the Saturday-night bath?" Beckwith's wife, Isabel, asks.

Everyone laughs in recognition. Like most black people in the South, none of them had had indoor plumbing back then, and Saturday was the one night in the week when they could manage the time-consuming ritual of boiling water from the well and filling a tin tub so everyone in a given family could take a bath.

They knew just what Robert meant. They let him finish his story.

"A white man called me over," Robert goes on. " 'Hey, boy, I'll pay you if you can tell me where I can find a clean colored girl.' "

He pauses for effect.

"I told him, 'I'll get you one if you get me your mother.' "

"Foster, did you really say that?"

"So help me God."

"You lucky to be alive."

And, Perhaps,
to Bloom

Most of them care nothing whatever about race.
They want only their proper place in the sun
and the right to be left alone,
like any other citizen of the republic.
　　—James Baldwin, *Notes of a Native Son*

CHICAGO, 1997
IDA MAE BRANDON GLADNEY

IDA MAE SETS HONEY on the window screen in her yellow-tiled kitchen to feed the bees. She gives away tiny seeds of four-o'-clocks and morning glories. They are a wonder to her, waking up as they do at the same time every day, more reliable than the best-intentioned people.

In her kitchen, she cooks no differently than if she were in Mississippi, folding the eggs and sugar, butter and nutmeg into softened sweet potatoes to make sweet potato pie, boiling her collards and mustard greens with ham hocks until they are rich and satiny and then making the corn bread to go with them. She has no use for recipes. It's all in her memory from what Miss Theenie taught her and her sisters-in-law back in Mississippi. She sifts cornmeal, white flour, a little baking powder, and a palmful of salt into a tin pan. She stirs in six eggs, sprinkles in a little sugar, and spreads a pool of vegetable oil in the baking pan before pouring in the batter.

Not too long ago, Eleanor went down south with a friend and came back reporting that the people were using self-rising meal for their corn bread in Mississippi now. Ida Mae didn't know what to make of it. She would have to rethink what she was doing. It was a revolutionary break from how they did things when she was there. For generations, they had used plain old cornmeal, back to slavery days, when that was all that they had. Everything in the recipes in their heads called for it. For years, they'd had self-rising meal in the North, but Ida Mae never tried it because that's not what they used down south when she was coming up. It wouldn't be authentic. But Ida Mae thought she might as well try it if that was the way they were doing things now. So she and Eleanor went out and bought some self-rising meal, and Ida Mae tried it. But the corn bread rose up like a pound cake. She wasn't sure if it was this newfangled meal or how she used it, but she never did try it again.

On this day, she puts the corn bread, made the way it was when she was coming up, into the oven and waits for it to bake. The corn bread grows plump and golden, and Ida Mae pulls it out when it is ready.

"Now you put you some butter and some buttermilk on it," she says, "and it make you want to hurt yourself."

At this stage of her life, the kitchen, where she whips up from memory the staples of the South, and the living room, where she monitors the streets of the North, are the center of her everyday world. Lately the invitations she gets are not to the weddings and baby showers of the young but to the funerals and wakes of her dwindling generation. It seems as though every week someone is admitted to the hospital or being eulogized. As she's the healthiest one in her circle of friends and the oldest member of her extended family, everyone expects to see her in their moments of grief.

———

She has just heard that another sister-in-law, Dessie, has died, and Ida Mae is getting ready to go to her funeral. The news hurls her back to the Pearson plantation in Mississippi, she and Dessie stopping to pick blackberries and Dessie teaching her how to make blackberry cobbler and tomato pie. She remembers being a young bride in a strange world, of all her husband's people on the plantation, all the brothers and their wives, the sisters and their kids, and how they took to her and brought her into their family.

"All them dead now," she says of her husband's generation of brothers and sisters.

The descendants want her to speak at the funeral since she is the oldest one left. Ida Mae doesn't like to dwell on the past or get mired in sadness. She doesn't want to do it.

"It's nothing I can say," she says. "Nothing I can say can bring her back."

She's beginning to dread funerals altogether but will go to this one and do what is expected of her. She will console the living, but it's getting harder and harder.

"I don't like going to funerals anymore," she says. "If it's sad, it just tears me to pieces."

———

One day she gets word that her beloved nephew Robert, whom they call Saint and who helped her and her family get out of Mississippi sixty years ago, has suffered a stroke. What is worse, his wife, Catherine, had a stroke just before he did. He had gone to the hospital every day to check on his wife before being stricken himself and each time was heartbroken over her blank stares and unmovable limbs. Now the two of them are separated for the first time in their marriage, she in the hospital, he in rehab. Ida Mae has to visit them both.

Today she is going to see Saint at a rehabilitation center at Ninety-fifth and Cicero. Saint had helped Ida Mae and her husband sell the things they didn't have time to dispense with or that, had they tried, would have attracted unwanted attention as they plotted their escape. He ended up following them up to Chicago with his wife and family in 1943, and they stayed with Ida Mae and George, as was the tradition among people migrating from the South, until they could get on their feet.

"I decided to come up because I had people up here," he is saying, sitting in his wheelchair. "People were coming up. I got in the crowd."

Saint and Ida Mae start reminiscing about the people they know from back home, how they are faring, who's a deacon now, who's moved into a nursing home, who's moved in with their grown kids out in the suburbs.

"It's a shame we all here and don't see each other," Robert says.

Then it hits him that he can't see his wife either. He starts to look down, and his eyes get moist. It's been the saddest of years, his wife taking sick and now him in a wheelchair from a stroke just like she had. His eyes well up.

Ida Mae looks at him, sorrowful and sad, too. This is her nephew by marriage. She is not much older than he is. She has known him for some

sixty-five years. She owes him in part for her safe passage out of the
South. His wife, Catherine, is one of the sweetest people she has ever
known. And they call the man before her Saint for a reason. He wants
to be with his wife, but he can't. The whole thing is breaking Ida Mae's
heart too. But then she catches herself, stiffens her back, and makes up
her mind to have none of that pity.

"Now, we not going to do that," she says staring at the floor, not able
to look Saint in the face. "God don't make no mistakes. Either you gon'
get better or you not. He's gon' see about you and do what he want.
Now, you be thankful you did all you could. You didn't miss a day."

She's older than all of them but fit and modern in her mint green
pantsuit and black pumps and copper mesh hat with her white curls
peeking from beneath it, while the younger nephew is bound for the
moment to a wheelchair.

She changes the subject, tries to lighten the heaviness in the air. "The
kids fuss at me," she tells him about how she eats everything put before
her. "They say, 'She don't let no food pass her mouth.' I say, 'Be a time
you won't have to worry about me eatin'.' They say, 'There she go
again.' "

"I told my kids, I'm doing pretty good to be seventy-seven years old,"
Saint says.

Ida Mae looks at him and smiles.

"That ain't old," she tells him.

On a late winter afternoon, Ida Mae is going through some old funeral
programs like other people go through family photo albums. She starts
to thinking about all the funerals she has been to, and one stands out in
her mind. It was of a nephew of her husband. The nephew had been
gay, and his companion, who was white, was distraught beyond words.

As she is recounting the story, Betty, the tenant from upstairs, happens to be there for a visit. Ida Mae describes how the companion was so
torn up about her nephew's death that he nearly climbed into the casket.

"It was a white fella he was living with," she says. "And when they
closed the casket, that white boy *fell* out. He said, 'Don't close the casket!' He took care of him to the end. Wouldn't let him go.

"I guess he musta really loved him," she says.

"That's not love," Betty breaks in. "God didn't mean for no man to be
with no other man. They can't love. They don't know what love is."

"You don't think they can love each other?" Ida Mae asks her.

"Can't no man love another man. Only men and women can love each other."

Ida Mae just looks straight ahead toward the couch. She knows what she saw. There are husbands who don't show out like that for their wives and wives looking relieved and near-gleeful at their husbands' funerals.

Ida Mae shakes her head. "Well, I don't know what it is," she says. "But it sure is something there."

———

Ida Mae is the last of her sisters and brothers still alive. The last one to go was Irene, the sister who urged her to come up north in the first place and whom she and her family stayed with in Milwaukee for a time.

Irene died in 1996, and it fell to Ida Mae to manage her affairs. It meant periodic trips to Milwaukee that Ida Mae took on without a great show of sentiment as just part of her duty as a sister.

It is the middle of October 1997. We are driving north toward Milwaukee on Lake Shore Drive along the curves of Lake Michigan. It is a blue glass sea with white waves like the ocean.

It has been a year since Irene's death, and still Ida Mae has business she must attend to. I had offered to drive Ida Mae and Eleanor to Milwaukee, and we are on our way on a steel gray morning. A storm gathers as we head north on the Edens Expressway. The rain beats down in sheets. Cars are having to slow to a crawl, and you can barely see ahead of you. The trip is going to take much longer than expected. This will cut into the time she will have to take care of things.

"It's really coming down," I say. "Of all days. I hope it won't be like this all day long."

This sets off an automatic response in Ida Mae, and she reframes the moment for everyone.

"Now, we ain't got nothing to do with God's business," she says, sitting back in her seat.

She adjusts herself and straightens her scarf, contenting herself with whatever the day has in store.

NEW YORK, 1997
GEORGE SWANSON STARLING

———

THERE IS A STIRRING among the original migrants and their children. The question is whether they should go back south again. Some haven't been back since they left and see no reason to go back now. Some go back and forth all the time and have already picked out a plot of land. George is somewhere in the middle.

He has diabetes now, and his knees are failing him. People in his circle from back in Florida are dying off or moving away. He's now under some pressure to move back to Florida from people who see the reconstituted South as the next refuge. People who left decades before, and even more likely their children, can't help but consider the prospects of a changed South, whether they act on it or not.

"Two more years, and I'll be able to retire and I'm gone," some of the people who came north have been saying. They say they are weary of the confined spaces, the cost of living, the crime, just the stress of living among so many millions of people.

"I don't know why you staying up here," some of them have been telling George. *"Better get out from here while you can."*

It reminds George of how people talked during the Migration. "People saying the same thing they said before, just in the reverse," he says.

But there are fundamental differences, as he sees it, between those who went north and those who stayed in the South, the people and the place he would be returning to if he chose to do so, and he doesn't see that changing. "Those who didn't leave learned to accept it," he says.

He never did.

"I think about leaving the North," he says. "But I would be a stranger down there. I've lived in New York for fifty-two years. I've spent more time here than there. I'm a New Yorker now. Almost all the ones I grew up with are in nursing homes. If I went back, what would I do?"

———

There is an unspoken fear among some migrants to the North that, no matter how much better you could live in the South on those northern pensions, going home is somehow moving backward, a retreat, an admission of failure or at worst something that, like retirement itself, could signal the end of the full part of life and perhaps the end of life it-self.

It was making George think back to what had happened to his old friend Babe Blye.

Babe was George's best friend and upstairs tenant who had worked with him in the orange groves when they were young men. Babe had come to New York in 1932 with his brother Reuben, well before George, and had gone back and forth between New York and Florida until George came up. For years, the two of them had lived in George's brownstone together with their wives, like the Ricardos and the Mertzes on *I Love Lucy*.

Babe so loved New York that he didn't go back to Florida "unless somebody was sick or died," Reuben said.

For years he worked at a car-painting factory in New York, caught possum in the Connecticut woods for their barbecues, and ran poker parties with George that almost got them killed. When Babe got sick, he went to George and told him he was going home. He asked George, whom he always called Son, a favor before he left.

"Son," Babe said. "I ain't gon' live long, Son. I'm going back. But I want you to sing 'Peace in the Valley' at my funeral."

"Babe, I ain't got no guarantee I'm a outlive you."

"Oh, yeah, you gon' outlive me."

"Well, close as we've been, I don't know if I can sing that."

"Goddammit, I want you to sing 'Peace in the Valley' now," Babe said. "Goddammit, I want you to promise me 'fore I go. You gon' sing 'Peace in the Valley'?"

"Okay. Yeah, Babe, I'm a sing 'Peace in the Valley.' "

In his heart he knew he couldn't. They were too close, like brothers, Babe and his wife, Hallie Q., upstairs from George and Inez all those years.

Babe left New York and went back to Eustis to live out his final years. He didn't live terribly long after that, a couple of years, as George and Reuben recalled.

He knew he was sick when he left. "He didn't tell me everything," George said. "But he knew something was wrong. And all of a sudden, he got it on his mind he wanted to go back home."

Babe died in 1976. The funeral was at the St. James Methodist Church, where George and Sam and Mud had eaten all those oranges back when they were little boys.

George went back for the funeral but didn't think he could get

through a song about his friend and onetime crew foreman who had
protected him in the orange groves. He figured he wouldn't have to,
what with Babe being gone and no one there to make him do it.

Apparently Babe had told his wife, Hallie Q. She went up to George
at the funeral.

"George, you supposed to sing 'Peace in the Valley,' " she said.

"Q., I can't do it."

"You promised Babe."

Somehow George got through the song Babe loved so much. George
had to take his handkerchief and wipe his eyes at the end of it. The original Migration people were falling away.

LOS ANGELES, AUTUMN 1996

ROBERT JOSEPH PERSHING FOSTER

———

ROBERT'S FRIENDS and former classmates are getting up in years and
facing one ailment or another, which puts Robert in almost as much demand as he was when he had a full-time practice. A friend called to
complain about a cough and thought he might need to go to the hospital. Robert calmed him down and told him to give the antibiotics a
chance to work.

Today he has gotten word that an old classmate from Morehouse is in
the hospital, and Robert wants to go by and see him. We drive to a hospital in South Central. As we walk out of the elevator to get to the man's
room, someone runs toward us.

"Dr. Foster, Dr. Foster!" the man is exclaiming.

It's an orderly who recognizes Robert from years ago and comes over
to him out of breath.

"Don't you remember me from that appendectomy over on Hoover?"

"Why, of course, I do," Robert says, not remembering the man exactly
but not letting on.

The orderly gets Robert caught up on what he has been doing the
past few years, excitedly trying to impress him, and Robert wishes him
well.

"You take care, Dr. Foster."
"And you as well."

Back at the house, he boils water for tea. He seems calm and at peace, distant now from the multiple recountings of the hard trek he made to get to California. He has thought things through and seems to have figured out his thinking now.

"I wanted to prove to them that I was worthy of a room," he says of his rejection along his journey. "I was not sure that I was good enough to be admitted. What good had it done me to get all this education and work as a surgeon in the army?"

"Have you ever been back through that stretch?" I ask him.

"Never," he shoots back. "I drove back south, but I went through Oklahoma."

He pauses and considers the effect his migration had on how he lived out the rest of his life and how he raised his daughters. He had demanded more of them than might have been necessary. He became obsessed with appearances and spent a fortune on their clothes and breeding so that there would be no reason for them to be rejected as he had been.

"I gave my daughters ballet so they could know how to walk," he said, "and create the picture I wanted. I wanted them to have an excellent education. I didn't want them to suffer the pains of racism. I didn't want them to have to sit in the back of the bus, suffer the unwelcome attention of low-class whites. I didn't want them to be open to being molested."

Unlike other parents raised in the South, he had never drilled into his children the hardships he had endured or dwelled on the limits of what they could or could not do based on the color of their skin. It was a strategy that worked beautifully in producing young women of grace and refinement but left them knowing little about the rituals and folk wisdom and history of the South or, in the end, that part of their father.

He remade himself in California and still does not fully know what to make of the place.

"It seemed like a fairyland the way they painted the picture," he says, "and I bought it."

"What do you think now?" I ask him.

"It's not the oasis that I thought it was," he says, "but I've got over that, too."

He pauses and considers the options of a stifled life under the deadly combination of Jim Crow and "little-townism," as he calls it, if he had stayed in Monroe or even Atlanta.

"I don't think I could have done any better," he finally says.

———

Robert has a taste for collard greens and corn bread, and we go to his favorite soul food restaurant in Inglewood, over by Crenshaw and Manchester, run by some people from Mississippi. He orders up yams and collards and smothered chicken and remembers that it was here that he sat when the riots over the Rodney King verdict broke out in May 1992. He remembers telling the waitress to wrap everything up.

"Let me get out of here," he told her. He turned north on Crenshaw and raced to get back home.

On this day four years later, the streets of his beloved adopted city are quiet, and Robert is momentarily back in the South with the comfort food of his youth. When it's time to leave, I prepare to take him home, but he tells me he'd rather be dropped off somewhere else. He wants to go to Hollywood Park racetrack, which all too conveniently happens to be right around the corner from the restaurant. He assures me he will have a way to get home. On the short ride to the track, he talks about how it feels, just going into a casino, which, for him, is more than a casino, but freedom itself.

"I walk into a casino," he says, "and I act like I own it."

Walking in like that attracts just the kind of attention he craves.

"What kind of surgeon *are* you?" a man asked him once, having heard he was a doctor.

"A damn good one," Robert told the man with a smile.

We arrive at the track, and Robert gets out of the car in his windbreaker and pensioner's slacks. He looks up at the exterior of the track, which looms high above him like a coliseum. He is a regal man, small-boned and slight in stature, and he looks out of place given his bearing and pedigree. But he quickens his step the closer he gets to the entrance. I watch him to make sure he gets in alright until he disappears into the crowd. He does not look back but straight ahead, as if he owns the place.

THE WINTER OF
THEIR LIVES

*That the Negro American has survived at all is extraordinary
—a lesser people might simply have died out, as indeed others have.*
— DANIEL PATRICK MOYNIHAN, *The Negro Family*

NEW YORK, 1997
GEORGE SWANSON STARLING

———

THE HARLEM THAT GEORGE STARLING FLED to in 1945 no longer exists. The Savoy Ballroom closed its doors in 1958. Small's Paradise closed in 1986, its patrons now frail and the children of the Migration not dressing up and dancing the Lindy Hop late into the night. The Sunday stroll died off with the top hat. The black elites—the surgeons and celebrities who would have made their homes on Sugar Hill in previous generations—can now move wherever they want. Many of them live in Westchester or Connecticut now.

The magnificent brownstones are aging and subdivided. Urban pioneers have only recently begun to turn them around. The streets have been given over to teenagers with boom boxes, to crack dealers and crack addicts, prostitutes and soapbox preachers, wig shops and liquor stores, corner stores selling single cigarettes for a nickel apiece and homeless people pushing their worldly possessions in shopping carts down what is no longer Lenox Avenue but Malcolm X Boulevard.

George Starling has lived in Harlem for half a century and knows and loves it in spite of itself. Many of the people who came up from the

South have passed away. There are fewer and fewer old-timers left. Still he makes his way around with a sense of ownership and belonging. He has lived there for longer than most of the people around him have been alive.

It has gotten to the point that his mind is still sharp but he can't drive anymore on account of his eyesight, and his knees fairly creak as he negotiates the steps to the basement apartment of his brownstone on 132nd Street.

When he returns home in the evening from church or the grocery store, and if someone happens to stop to talk to him, someone who, say, maybe has not been seen on the block before, a voice might holler out from across the street in the dark. It is a neighbor watching out for him.

"You alright, Mr. G.? Everything alright, Mr. George?"

"Yeah, I'm alright."

"Okay. We just want to be sure."

———————

Back in 1950, on the occasion of Harlem's fiftieth anniversary as a black community, the *New York Age* asked residents why they had moved to Harlem and why they stayed.

An ice vendor was one of the people who responded. "I know everybody in my block," he said, "and I don't think I want to go anywhere else to live, until I go to heaven."

George Starling knows how the ice vendor felt. As hard as the going has been up in Harlem, he has been free to live out his life as he chooses, been free to live, period, something he had not been assured of in Florida in the 1940s. He has made his mistakes, plenty of them, but he alone has made them and has lived with the consequences of exercising his own free will, which could be said to be the very definition of freedom.

A neighbor passes and yells, "Hey, Mr. George!" He smiles and nods and lifts his hand in the neighbor's direction.

Despite all the changes, it is still a neighborhood with its own sense of order and kinship.

"The people around here know more what's going on over here than I do," he says of his brownstone.

Anyone coming up to his door might face an inquiry.

"He know you?" somebody might ask on George's behalf.

When he was still driving, the crack addicts and prostitutes—or, more precisely, the addicts who were prostituting themselves to get more cocaine—would approach him as he pulled up to the curb.

"You need some company tonight?"

"No, darling, I don't need no company tonight."

Sometimes they come to him with good news, knowing how upright he carries himself.

"I'm going to school now, Mr. G.," they'll say. "Can you give me two dollars for some cigarettes?"

He looks them over and sees that they are only telling him what they think he wants to hear. "They come up, and they look like they just came out a garbage can," he says, shaking his head.

School is something he takes seriously because he hadn't been able to complete his own education. He calls them on it.

"Yeah? How long you been in school?"

They might not have an answer, but he gives them a couple dollars anyway.

"I give it to you Tuesday," they assure him.

"You don't owe me," George tells them. " 'Cause I don't want to get mad with you when you don't pay me back."

Sometimes they come up to him to report their progress, as if he were everybody's grandfather, and they feel the need to prove themselves to him.

"I just dropped out of rehab, but I'm going right back," they'll say, even though George can see full well that they can't be in rehab if they are running up and down the street as they have been all these months.

————

From his front stoop George Starling watches a most desperate parade. On these streets, there were once people gliding down the boulevard as if on a Paris runway, the men in overcoats and fedoras, the women in mink-collared swing coats and butterfly hats, all rushing to work for the rich white people or the manufacturers of paint or hats or lampshades. Now there are the hooded and disheveled descendants of the least able of the migrants living out their lives on the streets.

"I'm sitting out front now," he is saying to me over the telephone, *"and I see them ducking down these drug holes. They come here so beautiful, and in a few weeks look like they climbed out of a garbage can. We're the ones that's killing ourselves. I don't see one white person in this block selling drugs. They got the nerve to be mad at the blue-eyed devil. You don't have to take those drugs and sell 'em. Nobody's making you sell drugs. We're the ones that's killing ourselves. They won't learn in this century and maybe not in the next one."*

He wishes he could take all of them aside and warn them of the path they are taking. And, to those willing to listen, he does. But he has seen so much, it has begun to affect how he looks at them.

One time, a few years back, his door bell rang at two in the morning. He got up to see who or what it was.

"What do you want? You know what time it is?"

There before him was an addict, probably trying to sell him another trinket out of the trash that he didn't need.

"You know it's two in the morning?" George asked the addict.

"Your lights burning," the addict said. "The lights on your car, Mr. G. I'm sorry, Mr. G., but your lights're on in your car."

George thanked him. He rushed out to turn off the lights and promised himself he wouldn't prejudge these people anymore.

"I just thank the Lord," he says, "that, by his grace, it's not me."

LOS ANGELES, WINTER 1997

ROBERT JOSEPH PERSHING FOSTER

———

BY THE CLOSE OF 1996, Robert's body began to fail him. Everything that happened to him he knew precisely what it was because he had diagnosed it in everyone else, divined it before they or their other doctors even knew they had it. It was a gift to those who turned to him for help, a curse when applied to oneself. He calculated the symptoms and risks of whatever he saw happening to him, second-guessed his doctors, naturally, and then surrendered to whatever they suggested, depending on if he agreed with them.

His biggest frustration was not the natural breakdown of his body but not being able to reach his doctors when he wanted. He had always coddled his patients, brought a southern courtliness to his practice. He checked on them when they didn't expect it, went over impending procedures four or five times to make sure they understood because he felt they would come out of the procedure better if they went into it in the right state of mind. Now, aging and ill in an anonymous city out west, he can go days or weeks without hearing from a doctor. Test results come not with the reassuring words or stroke on the shoulder from his physician but in a form letter from some laboratory out in Riverside.

He has already had a heart attack and bypass surgery. Now his kidneys have succumbed, and he has to endure dialysis several times a week. He is growing frailer but is still sound of mind. He has a live-in nurse now, a sweet woman of good humor named Barbara Lemmons, who is from the South like most everybody else in his life and who indulges his idiosyncrasies.

He has taken care of everyone else, outlived his brothers Madison and Leland and his sister, Gold, the only one he had managed to lure out to California and then only after her marriage broke up. He misses them terribly, but especially Gold, whom he had tried to protect as a young boy back in Monroe and couldn't. Even when he had grown up, his money and status couldn't protect her from herself. She had taken to drinking, a Foster weakness, as their nephew Madison would put it. "She liked the parties, liquor, men," Madison said, "and broke up many a marriage." Robert couldn't protect her from her Billie Holiday of a life. And now she was gone.

His mentor, Dr. Beck, who took him in when he first got to Los Angeles, and Dr. Beck's son, William, who was almost like a brother to him, have passed away, along with so many others, Alice first among them. He has four grandchildren whom Alice did not live to see—Bunny's son and Robin's son, who are practically grown up and far away besides, and Joy's two little ones, who are growing up in Long Beach but whom he sees mainly at birthdays and holidays.

His world has grown smaller, and he is losing control, bit by bit, over his physical self. He seems to savor all the more the little joys in life—a perfectly broiled porterhouse steak, geraniums planted just so in the backyard, a call from a beloved patient.

There is a long list of things he is not supposed to have anymore—fatback and ham hocks, watermelon and barbecue sauce, biscuits, corn bread, tomatoes, and sweet potatoes—just torture to a southerner. But Barbara and his friends manage to slip him some corn bread with the collards anyway because it makes him so happy, and what is the point of living if you can't have a bit of joy in your life?

Every morning she gets up at eight, opens the drapes, and turns on the sprinklers. She invariably finds him at the side of his bed on the telephone. He comes into the kitchen. She gives him grits, which are on the approved list, but with a little salt, which is not. No matter what the list says, he refuses to give up his bacon.

He loves fried catfish, which is not approved, and he could eat that every day. "I know it's not on the list," he says. "But I don't care. Let's cook it."

She puts a chopping board onto the Formica-top island by the Thermador oven near the avocado green Frigidaire. She positions a chair so that he can watch her dust the fish in cornmeal and fry it.

When it is time to get dressed, she pulls some things from the closet for him to wear even if he is not expecting to see anyone that day.

"Yeah, that's fine, but run the iron over those pants," he'll say.

He has nothing but time on his hands, and he frets over the garden with its camellias and hollyhocks that he can no longer manage to his liking. He gets Barbara out there planting the annuals and worries over the placement and composition. They'll be watching the news and he'll be thinking about where he is going to put the begonias. They'll be having their grits and bacon at breakfast, and all of a sudden Robert will blurt out an idea.

"How do you think the geraniums would look over there in that corner?" he asks her. "I'm going to need some impatiens." And the two of them tramp out to the backyard to position them just so.

———

Robert has just gotten out of the hospital again, and the phone is ringing like mad. One time, Barbara picked up the phone and heard a gravel voice that sounded familiar.

"This is Ray Charles," the man said. "Let's speak to the old man. I'm calling to see if he wants some steaks."

Barbara was holding the receiver to her ear and the cradle to her hip. She whispered to Robert, "Ray Charles is on the phone!"

Robert took the receiver, and Ray got straight to the point.

"You gon' be at home?" Ray asked him. "You want these steaks? I'll be over there with them."

Barbara was in a panic. Ray Charles was on his way. She had just cleaned the living room, but she hadn't gotten to the kitchen or vacuumed the orange carpet in the den where Robert spent most of his day, when it occurred to her, what was the point of rushing?

He can't see anyway, she said to herself. *He won't know what room he's in.*

She calmed herself down. When the doorbell rang and Ray Charles arrived, she sent him through the kitchen. "You just say step up or step down," she later recounted. "Why should I let him trample through the living room I just finished vacuuming? He wasn't dressed up, and he don't know the difference."

Ray Charles came bearing ten or twelve steaks that Robert was not supposed to have but that no one in the world could stop Ray Charles from giving him—all New York cut and porterhouse, no T-bone, just as Robert liked it.

Ray chided Robert for not letting him know what hospital he had been in.

"Now, I had to call all over town, every hospital, looking for you," Ray said. "Where in the hell did you go? Why did you go way out there? I'm a shoot you if you go off again and don't let me know where you are."

The cancer diagnosis came in a form letter. He turned to Barbara and said, "Look at this." He would never have allowed a patient of his to discover such news this way.

"All he would do is look at it," Barbara remembered.

Now that he needed her more than ever, she would not be with him much longer. She already had high blood pressure and an enlarged heart. Now a blood clot had formed in her chest. It broke apart and traveled to her leg. "My leg felt like jelly," she said. "It felt like it wasn't there."

Barbara would no longer be able to work for Robert. By the late spring, a succession of nursing aides would come and go, but nothing would be the same after Barbara left.

Without her to keep him company and indulge his whims as his body grew weaker, he was finding fewer reasons to keep going.

Earlier in the year, he had received the most wonderful news about one of his grandchildren. Robin's son, Daniel Moss, a brilliant boy who took after all of his ambitious forebears, had been in the enviable position of having turned down early admission to Harvard and an offer from Princeton. He had chosen Yale, where he would be a goalie on the soccer team. He had been spared the pain of Jim Crow and the second-class schooling in the South because his mother had been spared it when Robert had moved the family to California.

Robert was too ill to fully enjoy the news about his grandson but could not help but contemplate how over the moon his mother, Ottie, would be if she were alive. All those years of scraping to send her four children to segregated colleges and never seeing her youngest son become the surgeon she so dreamed of. The idea of her great-grandson turning down Harvard and Princeton would have been beyond her comprehension.

His daughters were preparing a trip back east for Daniel's high school graduation. It was around the time of Father's Day. Robert had hoped to go but was not well enough to make the trip. And that made him all the sadder. While everyone else was at Daniel's graduation, a triumphant moment for the family and for Robert as the patriarch, he felt more alone than perhaps ever before. He started refusing to go to dialysis, knowing full well the consequences.

I visited him and found him inconsolable. I asked him if he wanted to go for a drive and get some sunshine. He shook his head no. I told him I had brought him some mangos and angel food cake. He looked away. "I hate to see you like this," I told him. "What can I do to cheer you up?" He stared out the patio door at the begonias growing unattended and a lawn that was not as it should be or would have been if he had been well.

––––

It got to the point that the only way he would go to dialysis was if someone insisted upon it. He was up and ready when I arrived to take him one day. His dark pants hung like draperies from his disappearing frame, and he took slow, labored steps as if he were walking in mud. He walked toward the stairs leading up to the landing above the den where the current aide, Renee, and I were setting up the wheelchair. As he neared the stairs, the hem of his pants got caught under his shoe and he teetered forward, reaching for my arm but missing it as he stumbled in a half-second fall on the top step. We rushed toward him and grabbed him at the waist and arm to lift him to an upright sitting position on the edge of the stairs. He sat flustered and defeated, his eyes lowered and looking at the floor in disbelief at his lot.

The dialysis center was at San Vicente and Third Street. He sat sinking into the passenger's seat, pointing to direct me to the center, his finger wagging becoming more rapid and insistent when I took a turn he did not think right. He shook his head to show his disapproval and struggled to clear his throat to say no, make a right at this corner. His mind was sharp. He knew exactly where we were going and how best to get there.

––––

It was getting to be late June. "I'm getting weaker and weaker," he told me. "As soon as I put the walker on the landing to the den, it slid beneath me. I hit the landing hard. I called the nurse. She didn't hear me. I tried three times. I took a hammer and banged on the coffee table to get her to help me."

He turned his thoughts to more pleasant things, the visitors who had stopped by to see him that day. "I just know so many beautiful people," Robert said.

Just the other day, he had told some friends, "I would give anything for a piece of watermelon," which he conveniently did not say he was not supposed to have.

Sylvester Brooks, the president of the Monroe Club and a faithful admirer, came by and brought Robert the watermelon he so craved. He sat on a bar stool and told Robert what folks in the club were up to.

Robert's old friend from back home Beckwith, who helped him set up his first office and even built furniture for it, stopped by to check on him. Robert was happy to see him. But it was a painful visit and did not last long.

"As well as I know him," Robert said, "we had so little to say. He was not completely comfortable. But that doesn't matter. No, it doesn't matter."

———

Then a man from back in Monroe, a man named Charles Spillers, dropped by. He had caught the bus from Slauson and Normandie in the center of South Central to see his old physician from the VA hospital.

He had heard of Dr. Foster before he'd ever gone to see him at the VA. He remembered Ray Charles's song about him. *"Dr. Foster got medicine and money too,"* the man sang to himself. "I said, that must be some doctor, that Dr. Foster."

Robert had been concerned about this new patient before him.

"You losing too much weight," Robert had told him. "You're sick. You need help."

The man had been a deckhand on a dredge and done ground maintenance at the VA hospital. He had dug up old graves, the graves of people who had died of tuberculosis, and he had dug them without a mask. He had worked in fields that leaked uranium, where some of his co-workers had died within weeks of exposure.

He was from the Old Country of Louisiana, believed in root doctors, and was suspicious after all he had seen in the South and West. He had pulled for Robert back at the VA, and he worried about what would happen to him after his trouble at the hospital.

"I'm not sure his kidneys went out on their own," Spillers confided to me. "You have to watch a rattlesnake if you get in the bed with him."

Charles Spillers felt he owed a debt to Robert as his physician even though he was too religious and superstitious to do some of what Robert told him. It was more that he felt inspired by him and appreciated Robert's forewarnings, which Spillers promptly used as a cue to go see his root doctor.

"If it wasn't for him, I would have been gone," Spillers said.

He remembered the first time he went to see Robert in his office. "You're just fading away right before me," Robert had told him during the exam. "I'm going to admit you to the hospital."

Spillers trusted the doctor but not the hospital and did not go. "The Holy Spirit came and told me don't go to the hospital," he said.

The man went to a root doctor instead, a woman from back south who was now in L.A. She plied him with root tea and Epsom salts in water. She made a fire in the house, even though it was August, and covered him with quilts until he sweated out the virus she believed to be in him. The fever broke, and he began to eat again and put weight back on.

Robert didn't take it personally or prejudge the man. He had grown up in the South and knew and accepted its ways. And that endeared Robert to the man all the more. He felt he had Robert to thank for alerting him to the problem and for saving his life.

"He meant so much to so many people," Spillers said. "I owe him so much."

He had ridden the bus to see his doctor, who was now sick himself. He sat with him for a while and then prepared to leave. As he headed toward the door to catch the bus back home—not knowing how long the wait would be; this was, after all, L.A.—he turned to his old doctor and friend from the VA hospital with a mixture of worry and gratitude, and the sweet folk spirit of the ancestral South.

"*Dr. Foster,*" he said with heavy eyes, "*I'm lighting seven candles for you.*"

By the summer of 1997, Robert Foster was finding his world constricted and fewer reasons to wake up in the morning. The things he loved to do, he could no longer do. He couldn't make it to the racetrack. Vegas was out of the question. His mansion on Victoria had become a glorious prison. The things he loved to eat, he could no longer get. His beloved nurse was ailing herself and no longer there to sneak him a half strip of bacon or a spoonful of peach cobbler. Then there were the twice-weekly trips to dialysis, which made him dread the start of every new week.

In late July, he went into the hospital for repair of a vein damaged by dialysis. He returned home weaker than before. Then, a few days later, on Sunday morning, August 3, he did not respond when called for breakfast. His left arm was motionless. He had suffered a massive stroke. He fell into a coma.

Word spread rapidly through the dwindling corps of original migrants from Monroe who had come out to California all those decades before.

Reatha Beck Smith, the widow of his old mentor Dr. Beck, who put Robert up when he first arrived in Los Angeles and who helped him get on his feet and open his office, rushed to the hospital as soon as she heard the news. She herself was in her nineties now and had her family and old friends from Louisiana with her. She saw him there lying motionless, the central and unforgettable figure of so many parallel worlds, who had saved so many lives but could not save his own.

"We went to see him at the hospital," she remembered. *"He wouldn't open his eyes. We called out our names, each one. And we could feel him squeezing our hand, each one."*

He never came out of the coma. He took his last breath on Wednesday, August 6, 1997. He was seventy-eight years old.

The memorial was the following Monday at the church where he had walked his three daughters down the aisle at their weddings but where he was rarely seen after Alice died.

Along the front pews sat the fruits of his labors and the embodiments of whatever dreams he carried with him while driving through the desert decades before: his eldest daughter, Bunny, now an artist's agent in Chicago, trim and regal in a black sculpted suit and with an upright bearing being consoled by her son Woodie White; his middle daughter, Robin, now a city manager in San Jose, sitting with her husband, Alan Christianson, and son, Daniel Moss, the pride of the family, who, having turned down Harvard and Princeton, would start at Yale a few weeks from now. Robert had lived long enough to know that. Then came Robert's youngest daughter, Joy, a radiologist, seated with her husband, Lee, a day trader, and their two small children, Lia and Adam.

The pews were filled with people from back in Monroe, old classmates from Morehouse, the people he knew from the racetrack, the people he had worked with at the VA hospital, the people whose gallbladders and appendixes he had removed and whose babies he had delivered and the babies that he had brought into the world and who were now grown men and women with gray hair and children of their own.

All of them showed up, their faces glazed and empty, to pay their respects. The daughters had had Robert cremated, which caused some grumbling among those who had wished to see him once more or who were grieving that they had not made it by to see him in time or who knew that it had simply not been the way southerners put away their dead.

The service was a tightly scripted affair.

"We gather in the faith and hope of Jesus Christ," the minister, who had not known Robert, intoned. "We come to comfort and support each other in our common loss—Robert Joseph Parish Foster."

Nobody remarked on the mispronunciation of "Pershing" in his final hour. Few people in California likely knew the name anyway. He had dispensed with it on his way to California for that very reason.

His nephew, Madison, read a scripture assigned to him from Ecclesiastes: "For everything there is a time, a time to be born and a time to die . . . "

Robert's gambling buddy Romie Banks rose and addressed his friend and those assembled: "Robert, you have fought so many battles, been a champion for so many people. He was a perfectionist at everything he did except winning at the racetrack."

Robert's son-in-law Lee went to the altar. "He let you know which way the wind was blowing," the son-in-law said, "whether you liked it or not."

The Morehouse alumni stood when asked to make themselves known.

Easter Butler, who had met Robert at the racetrack, declared simply, "Dr. Foster was one of the greatest men I ever knew."

———

Afterward, the people assembled back at the house on Victoria. Now, the street, unlike the last few weeks of his life when he was in his weakest, loneliest state, was crowded, overcome by cars—Mercedes, Cadillacs, sport utility vehicles, German and Japanese cars.

The people gathered around the crushed-velvet armchairs and the orange shag rug and the Zenith television console in the den, the room where Robert had thrown so many parties and had lived out the last months of his life.

A copy of *Life* magazine with Coretta Scott King in mourning sat in the bookcase, along with *Roots* by Alex Haley, surgery and gynecology textbooks, a book entitled *Difficult Diagnosis,* and, sitting alone, the brown desk plate that read, ROBERT P. FOSTER, MD.

The mourners partook of the honeydew and cantaloupe, cheesecake, lemon cake, and ham spread out on the dining room table. The testimonials continued all afternoon.

Della Bea Robinson, Ray Charles's ex-wife, showed up to pay her respects because "Bob delivered my son," she said. "My husband named our son after him."

The moment made Della Bea think about what a perfectionist Robert had been, which was a good thing to have in a surgeon. "We were going to a concert," she remembered, "and Alice came down the steps and couldn't find the right gloves. She put on a pair of gloves she found. Bob saw her when she came out. 'Something is wrong. The gloves are off,' he said. He noticed everything."

Leah Peterson, who had worked at the VA hospital with him, remembered turning to him for advice. "I used to go up and talk to him," she said. "I told him what I wanted to do with my years. Bob started buying me books."

A realtor named Nick White said simply, "He delivered me."

———

Madison, his nephew, left the memorial repast early and brooded over a glass of ice water at a restaurant over in Santa Monica. He was feeling alone as the only Foster left from that era and isolated from what he saw as the bourgeois pretensions of the day's proceedings, which, to him, did not reflect his uncle's southern joie de vivre. "He didn't get as good as he gave," Madison said after the funeral, "and he gave the best."

Madison was the self-described country cousin and one of Robert's biggest champions, a living reminder of the South that Robert had put behind him. Madison thought about all the things Robert had been through in the South and out west, the rejections despite the triumphs and never feeling good enough. These things made him an exacting, infuriating, insecure perfectionist who left a mark on everyone he met. The people around him knew to smooth their tie, check their hem, reach a little higher, do a little more because Robert Foster demanded it of them. He made everybody crazy and better for the sky-high expectations he had of them for even the smallest of things.

"If you bought him a melon," Madison said, "you couldn't just buy a melon. You had to stop and think about that melon. That's how he was with everything."

Madison thought back to how Robert had tried to get all of Monroe to come to Los Angeles. "Bob would say, 'You want some Monroe? Plenty Monroe out here. You can have Monroe in California.'"

Then Madison remembered the trips he had made to Los Angeles, his feeling tentative and unsure, being from small-town Louisiana as he was but exhilarated to be out in California with his uncle.

"Come on, chief," Bob would say. "Let's go to Beverly Hills and have breakfast on the veranda. Put your chain out. Put that gold chain out. You ain't on no college campus now. Put your chain out. That's why I gave you that damn chain."

This was Robert's Promised Land. He walked around as if he had been born to it. "You didn't have a care in the world," Madison remembered. "All your problems were gone. Nothing could happen to you. You were with Uncle Bob. He lightened a room. He created another world for you. The man had a certain magic to him."

———

The story of Robert Joseph Pershing Foster of Monroe, Louisiana, and Los Angeles, California, did not end with his death. Years later, people were still trying to decipher the meaning of his life. Some people were too distraught to speak of him with anyone outside their circle. Others could not stop referring to him in the present tense.

For some of his patients, Robert was the only doctor they had ever been to. They remember him making hospital rounds at midnight, stepping in with free medical advice upon hearing that an acquaintance of somebody's co-worker was in the least bit of trouble.

Perhaps it could be said that gambling was his mistress, medicine his beloved. Another migrant named Malissa Briley did not fully grasp it until she had to go into surgery herself. She was in her midforties at the time, a social worker in L.A. who had gone to Spelman with Alice. She was anxious about going into the hospital.

Robert did the surgery, and the surgery went well. But later that night, her blood pressure shot out of control. She was on the verge of having a stroke, which could have killed her or left her paralyzed. The hospital tried to get her blood pressure down but had no success. At midnight, the hospital called Robert to report the turn of events. He rushed over right away. He tried to lower her blood pressure, but he couldn't get it down either.

The next morning, Briley awoke to see Robert in a chair by her bed. She was stunned to see him there. It was early winter, the quiet time of the morning, so early that the hospital hadn't brought the breakfast tray yet. He was in his street clothes and uncharacteristically wrinkled. He hadn't shaved, had bags under his eyes.

"What are you doing here this early?" she asked him.

He told her she had gone through a crisis the night before and that neither he nor the hospital could get her blood pressure down.

"What did you do?" she asked.

"Well, I got to the point I couldn't do nothing but pray," he said.

He had stayed by her hospital bed all night. He had sat upright in a chair in his street clothes. Any patient he lost, he took it personally and especially hard. He took it as a sign of his own failure. So he had fought back sleep watching over this patient and praying for her to live.

By morning, her blood pressure had returned to a safe range. He made sure her vital signs were stable, gave instructions to the nurse to call him immediately should there be any change. Then he left to see about the rest of his patients.

"He had stayed through the night," she said forty years later, still almost in disbelief. "I woke up, and there he was. That I'll never forget, as long as I live."

———————

Robert Foster did not want to return to Louisiana, in life or in death. Nor did he choose to be interred with the Clements in Kentucky. He paid down on a place for himself at a cemetery in Los Angeles.

His body was cremated and placed in an urn in a granite mausoleum with rows of bronze plaques lining the wall like identical file cabinets. His sits in a corner high on the wall with a vase of purple silk roses. IN LOVING MEMORY OF ROBERT P. FOSTER, M.D., 1918–1997, the plaque reads.

The mausoleum is high on a hill at Inglewood Park Cemetery. The urns face a picture window with a view of the cemetery's manicured gardens and, beyond that, Hollywood Park racetrack. It is the closest

Robert could get to the track he so loved. Every so often one can see, set-tled along a curb of the cemetery road, a crumpled copy of the *Daily Racing Form* blown over from the track, and, if listening closely, hear the clomping roar of a horse race in progress over at Hollywood Park. Beloved California.

•

CHICAGO, AUGUST 1997

IDA MAE BRANDON GLADNEY

———

THE TRANSFORMATION of the South Shore section of Chicago from an all-white neighborhood to a near totally black one was complete by the time the Great Migration ended in the mid-1970s. But there was a less visible change that made life more difficult still for people like Ida Mae.

Had a study, like the 1968 Kerner Report on the state of race in America, been conducted of Ida Mae's adopted neighborhood, it might have concluded that there were, in fact, two neighborhoods—one, hard-working and striving to be middle class, the other, transient, jobless, and underclass; one, owners of property, the other, tenants and squatters; one, churchgoing and law-abiding, the other, drug-dealing and criminal—both coexisting on the same streets, one at odds with the other.

Ida Mae lived in the former world but had to negotiate the latter. The transformation had been so rapid that the city had not had a chance to catch up with it. Politicians came and went, but the problems were big-ger than one local official could solve. The problems were social, eco-nomic, geographic, perhaps even moral. A succession of mayors had appeased or looked away from the troubles of South Shore, it was but one of some fifty identifiable neighborhoods in the city and not any-where close to the worst. In fact, it had had a storied past as the home of the South Shore Country Club, a columned and grand clubhouse with its own golf course and riding stables that in its heyday had drawn celebrities like Jean Harlow and Amelia Earhart. By the time the neigh-borhood turned black in the mid-1970s, its membership had dwindled, and it was taken over by the Chicago Park District.

Mayors Richard J. Daley, Michael Bilandic, and Jane Byrne all relied on the votes of solidly Democratic South Shore to be elected, but life grew no better for Ida Mae. Ida Mae and other black residents had the highest hopes that their concerns might be heard when Harold Washington was elected mayor in 1983, but his election was so fraught with racial tension and his tenure so embattled that they could not look to him for much more than historic symbolism, which had a certain value but did not make their streets safer. Then Washington died unexpectedly at the start of his second term.

Thus the stalwart property owners of South Shore learned to rely on themselves to monitor the crime and mayhem around them. They formed block clubs and neighborhood watch groups, and, on the second Thursday of every month, the most dedicated believers turn out for police beat meetings to report what they are seeing, hear what the police are doing, and make their voices heard. The meetings are part of a community policing plan known as the Chicago Alternative Policing Strategy, or CAPS.

These days, Ida Mae goes to the beat meetings with the regularity and sense of obligation with which some people go to church. She never misses one because there is always so much to report. She and James and their friend and tenant Betty put on their coats and gather themselves for each meeting regardless of whether the problems are solved, which they frequently are not.

The four of us are in the car heading to a beat meeting one November when we see teenagers on the corner north of their three-flat.

"They're out there again," James says.

I ask him what they're doing.

"Drugs," he says matter-of-factly. "They're selling drugs."

———

Night is falling as a handful of people gathers for the meeting of Police Beat 421 at the South Shore Presbyterian Church. The people descend the steps to the church basement, where a man sits at a table in the back with a stack of flyers and neighborhood crime lists, called hot sheets, laid out in neat piles.

The hot sheets are like a neighborhood report card and are the first things the people reach for. They rifle through them, scanning for their street and block number to see the details of whatever crimes have been reported, if the knifing or carjacking they saw was ever called in, what the police say they are doing about it, and whether there have been any arrests.

About twenty people, including Ida Mae, James, and Betty, are still going over their hot sheets as they take their seats in the gray metal folding chairs in a basement with yellow cinder-block walls and a red-painted concrete floor, when the meeting is called to order.

The moderator asks what new problems there are. James and several others reach for the index cards being distributed to write out the things they have witnessed. The residents often do not put their names on the cards for fear of reprisal. Ida Mae rarely speaks up because she is convinced the gangs send moles to the meetings, which are public after all, to see who is snitching.

In the meeting, the people learn that Beat 422 held a march against gangs and crime, but they are not certain if they can muster such a march.

"We're at the last stand here," the moderator says. "We don't have any other alternative. If we don't do something, they will take us over."

Everyone knew who she meant by "they."

Someone brings up a worrisome but low-end priority: prostitution is getting worse over at Seventy-ninth and Exchange.

"We know that, okay," the moderator says. "That's a hot spot," she admits and quickly moves on to the robberies, shootings, and drug dealing.

After the meeting adjourns, Ida Mae pulls a policeman over to report one of the more benign sightings, but a measure of the general unruliness around them. "They pull up a truck and take the stoves out," Ida Mae says of theft going on in the building next door.

The police officer stares straight ahead. It's barely worth his time. He walks away to another conversation.

"They don't know nothing," Ida Mae says.

She buttons her coat and walks over to her son. "We ain't done nothing here," she says.

"The important thing is to keep coming," James says.

It is mid-May, the start of the crazy season in South Shore. The weather will be warm soon, and the kids will be out of school, roaming the streets with nothing to do. This time, a gang officer, a big, bearded man in a blue Nike sweatshirt and jeans, is there to brief the beat meeting.

"You have two gangs operating in 421," the officer is telling residents. "The Black Stones and the Mickey Cobras."

The residents listen, but they know they have a gang problem. They start to rattle off street names they want the police to check.

The officer jumps in. "We been hitting that area hard," the officer says. "Every day we've been locking someone up new. We're hitting Colfax, Kingston, Phillips real hard. They know our cars. They got so many guys out there doing lookout, hypes who work for them. They whistle when we get close."

He tells the residents to report whatever they see. "I call the police enough, they should know my name," a middle-aged woman in a brown beret says. "We got some terrible kids over where we are. It be raining and sleeting and they coming and going. And the girls are worse than the boys."

"Amen," Ida Mae chimes in.

The next meeting begins with a sober announcement: "We had a shooting of one of our CAPS members at Seventy-eighth and Coles."

"Did they catch the offender?" a resident asks.

"No, not as of yet." The people look down at their hot sheets.

The beat meetings attract all kinds of visitors—city hall bureaucrats, politicians running for reelection, people heading rape crisis centers or collecting names for this or that petition. This time, the visitor is a legal advocate in a beard and corduroy pants who doesn't live in the neighborhood. He rises to speak and tries to get the group to join him in opposing a city ordinance that would clamp down on loitering.

"It will make open season on all black youth," the man says of what he believes will happen if the ordinance were to pass.

The residents want the ordinance anyway, anything to bring them relief.

A man in his sixties stands up as if to speak for them all.

"We live in this neighborhood," the man says. "We own houses and pay taxes. We're scared to go outside. Practically every evening there's a shooting. I don't care about their rights. Maybe you have to get the good ones to get the bad."

This being Chicago, famously local in its politics, the residents of South Shore have learned where to get their immediate needs met—a broken hydrant fixed, a pothole patched, a house condemned. The alderman is the closest politician to turn to. Most Chicagoans know their alderman by sight or even personally and will call upon him without hesitation if they think he can help.

When Ida Mae's alderman, William Beavers, shows up at her beat meeting, there is great anticipation because he is one of the most powerful black politicians in the city and everyone knows him. He has been the Seventh Ward alderman for fourteen years. He arrives in a brown double-breasted suit and has cameras and lights and a television crew with him, which only adds to the sense of the drama of his visit.

"The area is coming back," he announces to the residents. He then lists what he's doing for the ward: "We got a new field house. We're building a senior home at Seventy-fourth and Kingston. We have a new shopping center at Ninety-fifth and Stoney."

Then he gets to what matters to them most, the crime, says he's seen it himself, especially the prostitutes over on Exchange Street. "They're on Exchange all day and all night," he says. "They be waving, 'Hey, Alderman Beavers!' "

A woman raises her hand with a complaint that is right up his alley. "There's no curb across the street for us," she says.

"I put them on the other side," he says without apology. "I put them where the people vote."

He then leaves them with a hotline number to call to report crime: the number, he says, is 1-800-CRACK-44.

———

South Shore is in Police Beat 421, Ward Seven, State Representative District 25, and State Senate District 13. The officeholders of the latter two districts rarely figure into the daily concerns of most people in Chicago. The state legislators are just low enough on the political food chain to go unrecognized, focused as they are on approving budgets and legislation. They are just lofty enough, however, to be seen as of little help in an immediate crisis as when, say, a drug dealer sets up shop in front of your house. It could be argued that many people could not name their state legislators off the top of their heads. As for state senators, there are fifty-nine of them, they meet in Springfield, and they are not usually household names, as would be the mayor or even one's alderman.

So when, in 1996, a young constitutional lawyer and community activist from Hyde Park ran for the Illinois State Senate seat in District 13, Ida Mae, voting her usual straight Democratic ticket, would become among the first people ever to have voted for the man. She would not have to give it much thought. He did not have Chicago roots and the name was unusual—Barack Obama. But he was running unopposed, having edged out the woman who had asked him to run in her place before changing her mind. His wife, Michelle, had grown up in South Shore, in the more stable section of bungalows further to the west. So

Ida Mae and an overwhelming majority of the Democratic stronghold of predominantly black South Shore voted him into office as their state senator.

———

On August 14, 1997, exactly one month before Alderman Beavers shows up with cameras and lights at Ida Mae's beat meeting, Barack Obama makes an appearance. He is introduced as the state senator for the district, which not everyone in the room could be expected to know, as he has only been in office since January. He is tall, slight of build, formal in speech and attire, looks like a college student, and he arrives without lights, cameras, or entourage.

He stands before them and gives a minilecture to these bus drivers, secretaries, nurse's aides, and pensioners about what state legislators do. He says that while the state legislature is not responsible for the police department, it passes laws that the police have to enforce. He describes the role of the legislature in education policy and in health care. And he invites those assembled to call his office anytime.

"Sometimes a call from the senator's office," he says like the professor he once was, "may be helpful in facilitating some issues that you have concerns about. Sometimes a call from my office will be answered much more quickly so we can move through some of the bureaucracy a little bit faster."

Ida Mae and the rest of the people listen politely and with appreciation. But, as this is just another meeting, they sit in anticipation of the reason they are here tonight: the discussion with police about the latest shootings, stabbings, and drug deals, the immediate dangers they will face just getting back home.

The thirty-six-year-old freshman state senator finishes his presentation to Beat 421. The people clap with gratitude as they always do and then turn back to their hot sheets.

That night, as he bounded up the steps and out of the church basement, nobody in the room could have imagined that they had just seen the man who, a decade from now, would become the first black president of the United States.

NEW YORK, SPRING 1998

———

THE TROUBLE BEGAN with a mysterious dark spot on the back of George Starling's foot. One of his grandsons had been the first to notice it. George was a diabetic and knew not to take chances with such things. He made an appointment to see his doctor right away.

The doctor admitted him to the hospital for tests. There was fear the foot might need to be amputated. "All these tests," Pat, the niece who used to live with him and Inez, said.

Pat came in from Washington, where she was now living, and her brother came in from New Jersey to see about their uncle. There was relief when it turned out that the foot would not need to be amputated. But George was now requiring dialysis. The knees that had always given him trouble could not be relied upon now to hold him up, and he was having a harder time keeping his balance.

Pat and her brother helped George get up when they were there. But after they and his other visitors left, George slipped and fell in the hospital. In time, he appeared to be recovering and was looking to go home.

"Well, they not gonna keep me no longer," he told Pat.

"Okay, now," Pat said. "I'll be up there to see about you."

But he was instead transferred to a nursing home for rehabilitation. While there, he lost his balance and fell again. This time he hit his head.

———

By now, Gerard, his firstborn, had been alerted in Florida as to his father's condition. The two had long been at odds. Gerard's lifestyle was counter to everything George had worked for. Gerard had been a drug hustler operating out of Miami and Gainesville. He had had money, homes, cars, women. Wherever he showed up, he gave everybody a hundred dollars just because he could. But in recent years, he had been down on his luck. He had diabetes, like his father, and was on dialysis and insulin.

Hearing that his father was in the hospital, he made plans to come up to New York. "We were all waiting on Gerard with great anticipation," Pat remembered.

It was while Gerard was trying to figure out what day to come to New York that George fell and hit his head. He suffered a cerebral hemorrhage and slipped into a coma. By the time Gerard made it to New

York, George was unconscious and hooked up to machines to sustain him on the chance he might come out of the coma.

Pat took Gerard to the hospital to see his father. "The moment he walked in and saw him, he broke down crying," Pat said.

Gerard had to leave the room. He said he couldn't stand to see his father that way. They didn't stay much longer.

Gerard had not realized how grave his father's condition was. He decided to head back to Florida, seeing as how there was nothing he could do to change things.

"Do you want to go and see him one more time before you get ready to go?" Pat asked him.

No, he said, he couldn't bear it.

Gerard drove back to Florida weak and in despair. He had missed several rounds of dialysis and had used cocaine in the interim, Pat discovered. When he got back to Gainesville, he still did not go to dialysis.

"He had already given up," Pat said.

Within days of seeing his father, Gerard suffered a massive seizure and died. He was fifty-one years old. His father was not conscious enough to know that he had lost his firstborn son. George, barely alive himself, was now the last one left of the nuclear family that had begun with him and Inez some sixty years before in Eustis.

There was no one in the hospital room when I went to see George Starling. The monitors attached to him beeped and flashed the minutest change in his vital signs. The robust onetime porter who could regale people for hours with his stories of the South and of the Great Migration was silent and motionless. He looked to be asleep, whatever wisdom or stories left now locked up inside of him. As much living as he had done, his seemed a life of missed chances and incompletion. Here was someone who had been born too early and in the wrong place to reach his true potential, had left to make a better way for himself, but had seemed to carry the sorrows of the South with him, without complaint.

I reached for his hand and squeezed it lightly and told him I had come from Chicago to see him. His face showed no reaction. His hand managed to press back into mine.

George Swanson Starling never came out of the coma. He died on September 3, 1998, a Thursday. Because he had migrated out of the South, lived most of his life in the North but remained connected to both, two funeral services were required. One was in New York, at the

Baptist House of Prayer on 126th Street in Harlem, on September 17; the other in Florida, at Gethsemane Baptist Church in Eustis, two days later.

———

In the North, in Harlem, where he had found refuge from the South, the people turned out to see him one last time. The Deacon Board, the Pastor's Aide Club, the 132nd Street Block Association, the neighbors who had looked out for him from across the street all packed into the church. The choir sang for him and shook the floor from the choir box as the fans whirred and oscillated around them.

One by one, people came forward to say they would miss his opening the church doors Sunday mornings, miss the sight of him reading the dictionary, and would remember him as "a gentleman of the first order."

A man, tentative in his steps and taking in the measure of the sanctuary, had arrived an hour early. He had a shaved head and full beard. He sat alone in the third pew as the church began to fill. His eyes were red. He stared at the silver casket, then leaned onto the pew in front of him and buried his face in his arms. When Pat arrived, she went over and sat beside him. It was Kenny, George's younger son, whose conception had broken Inez's heart. And that heartbreak kept him from feeling part of the family or ever truly knowing his father.

Before George took ill, Kenny went to George and let him know how he was doing. Kenny was married, had kids, was living in the Bronx. He told him he had converted to Islam, had changed his name to Amjad Mujaahid, which means, he said, "One who is noble, a warrior in the cause of God."

"Daddy," Kenny told George, "that name is in memory of you."

"That's real nice, son," Kenny remembers George saying. "I'm still calling you Kenny."

Now the man he wished he'd had more time to get to know was dead. The service was a blur of song and testimonials. He took off his glasses and used a handkerchief to wipe his eyes, as his father had done whenever he sang.

———

It was hurricane season at the time of George Starling's death. Hurricane Bonnie and Hurricane Danielle had gathered east of the Leeward Islands that August. By mid-September, when George Starling was transported back to the state of Florida for the last time, a new hurricane had formed and was nearing the Florida coast. The National Weather Service had named it Hurricane Georges.

Back in Eustis, the southern funeral commenced at Gethsemane Baptist Church. But Viola Dunham, the sister-in-law he used to stay with whenever he visited, could not bring herself to go. "It's killing me," she said. "I want to remember him sitting in my kitchen eating breakfast and running his mouth."

A cousin named Lila Mae went and spoke for the people who had stayed in the South, remembering him as the hometown boy who made good in the North with his railroad job and dignified bearing.

"As he journeyed to New York and became a porter," she began, "nothing was finer than to see this good-looking cousin come into Wildwood station and to bring him some sausage. All of his splendor and grace. It was something to see. Little George never forgot where he came from."

Reuben Blye, who'd known George most of his life, sat staring out into the sanctuary in a gray suit and tie in a front pew. Sam Gaskin, who had stood up with him against the grove owners back in the forties, was there, too. A processional of eight or ten cars led by a white hearse passed through town near the corner where George had stood and waited for the open-bed truck to take pickers to the citrus groves some sixty years before.

The cortege turned off a main thoroughfare and crept down a dirt path to a clearing of wild grass scattered with the headstones of nearly all the black people who had ever lived and died in Eustis. The cars crossed a pebbled, pitted clearing and came to a stop at a green tent pitched before two juniper bushes in the middle of Mount Olive Cemetery. A dozen people took their places before the casket. The pastor stood and said his last words: *"From dust thou art . . ."*

That evening, the sun fell behind the horizon and made what looked like streaks of fire across the sky after George Starling was returned for the last time to the Florida earth he had fled.

The Emancipation of Ida Mae

My presence will go with you. And I will give you rest.
—Exodus 33:14

CHICAGO, OCTOBER 15, 1998
IDA MAE BRANDON GLADNEY

————

IDA MAE WAS GOING BACK to visit Mississippi. It was early autumn, the same time of year she had left sixty-one years before. It would be her first time on Mississippi soil since her sister Talma had died in Tupelo in 1983. Ida Mae had gone down when she got word that her youngest sister had taken ill. She sat at the side of her sister's bed for her last hours on this earth.

Ida Mae remembered she had been watching Talma, and Talma had been trying to speak.

"Don't you see all them people in white singing?" Talma had said, delirious. "They just singing away."

Ida Mae looked in the direction Talma was facing and tried to see the people in white but couldn't. Days later, at Talma's funeral, the choir sang in all white.

"She saw them before," Ida Mae said, convinced of it.

————

Ida Mae and I are driving along Route 8, heading east toward Vardaman in the direction of Chickasaw County. We pass a cotton gin and bales of cotton bound in the field and covered with tarp. The bales are packed high and tight and look like cubes of Styrofoam the size of a school bus from a distance.

We cross a gravel road with cotton on either side of it. "That cotton's loaded," Ida Mae said, her eyes growing big. "Let's go pick some."

"You sure that's alright?" I ask. "That's somebody's cotton. What if they see us?"

"They not gon' mind what little bit we pick," she says, pushing open the passenger door.

She jumps out and heads into the field. She hasn't picked cotton in sixty years. It's as if she can't wait to pick it now that she doesn't have to. It's the first time in her life that she can pick cotton of her own free will.

I follow her out, and she starts pulling at the bolls, and I pull at them too. No cars or trucks pass by, and we are surrounded by cotton.

We carry a bouquet of cotton buds back to the car and head to her sister-in-law Jessie Gladney's house. Along the route, there are no street-lights, traffic lights, or stop signs. There are no street signs to identify what road you are on. The directions to the house call for looking for a cotton gin, passing and keeping count of five or six bridges that are merely dirt mounds over dry creek beds, making a right at a Baptist church, and looking for the sister-in-law's off-white double-wide on the right-hand side of the road, assuming we're on the correct one.

Jessie is Ida Mae's sister-in-law twice over, in the small, insular circles of rural Mississippi. She was married to Ida Mae's husband's brother Ardee, and she is the sister of the man Ida Mae's sister Talma married. Jessie moved up to Chicago in 1946 but recently returned to Mississippi, where her brother Aubrey lives. She went back south with her husband, but he was ill and not particular about moving back to Mississippi and did not live long after they had arrived. That left Jessie widowed and alone in the isolated double-wide with her sweet nature and bad knees.

Ida Mae and Jessie greet and hug each other like sisters, and Ida Mae rests herself in Jessie's recliner with a throw over it and starts talking about the cotton she and I picked by the side of the road.

"Ooh, it was so much cotton," she says. "Cotton everywhere."

"The highest I ever picked was one hundred eighty-seven pounds," Jessie says.

"I just couldn't do it," Ida Mae says. "I'd pick and cry. I ain't never liked the field."

The two of them catch up on the latest with the kids and nieces and nephews, and then Ida Mae starts talking about life back up in the North.

"You see everything up there, Jessie," she says. "Seem like they choose this block to do all they dirt. They sell drugs there. They open their mouths and put it down their throat. That's where they keep it. One lady died from swallowing it. It must have got hung up in her lung. I missed her and asked about her. She used to sit under the tree out there. She was in her fifties, and she died from it."

Ida Mae pauses and looks away. "I reckon people who've passed on wouldn't want to come back if they could. They couldn't take what's going on now days."

Jessie mostly listens. She's having trouble with her legs, and her husband's death is still weighing on her heart.

Which reminds Ida Mae of her husband. "I waited on George forty-seven years," she says. "And I mean I waited on him. When he come home from work, and when he wanted his breakfast, lunch, and dinner, I give it to him. I served him. They expect too much. When he passed, I wasn't thinking about no other husband. I laugh and talk with them, but that's as far as it go."

———

The next day we are riding through the curving hills of Chickasaw County, rising and sinking along the red dirt road. We are retracing the corners Ida Mae and her family lived and sharecropped and looking for anyone she might know who is still around. We drive through pine woods draped in kudzu and through tumbling fields down a gravel road that kicks up dirt as we pass.

Every now and then, the hills are broken by a cabin with a chicken-wire fence around it and a pickup truck at the side. The land is quiet, at peace, as if the bloodshed of the twentieth century never happened. There appears a black man riding high up on a tractor as it inches down a gravel road in a cloud of gravel dust, and he tips his hat as he passes us, a courtly gesture from another century that one would never see in Chicago.

Ida Mae's brother-in-law Aubrey, who was married to her late sister Talma, is leading her from place to place. He knows the land because he returned to Mississippi decades ago after trying Chicago and not liking it.

Aubrey tries to find Miss Theenie's house, the one where the men came courting Ida Mae on the front porch. They spot a weathered shack leaning on its side. They stop to inspect it and conclude that it might have been Miss Theenie's but they couldn't say for sure. Falling-down shacks look pretty much the same.

"Been so long," Ida Mae says.

In the car, Ida Mae looks out at all the cotton, the cotton that ruled her days and that she's free from now.

Aubrey points to a machine off in the distance.

"That machine can pick fifteen to twenty bales of cotton in a day," Aubrey says proudly of the advancements made since Ida Mae left.

"Sho' 'nough?" Ida Mae says blankly. She looks out with vague interest at the blur of field. Then she turns the conversation to the old friends she wants to see and how different things look to her now.

She is getting a little disoriented, one hill indistinguishable from another, nothing but trees or cabins as guideposts and the terrain seeming wilder than before. "I don't remember so many crooks and turns," she says of the land and the gravel road we are on.

She is having trouble with the heat after being in Chicago so long. "It's a different kind of hot down here," she says. And she's feeling a little sick, as people do when they drink the water they are warned about when they visit developing countries. Later in the day she will put some nutmeg in the palm of her hand and lick it to settle her stomach, and not draw the least attention to herself among the people in Mississippi, which is, after all, where she learned it.

———

In and around the settlements of Chickasaw County, Ida Mae visits with a succession of people who knew her. They greet her like a loved one they just discovered happens to be alive after all. She visits Isolena Harris, Marcelle Barr, Doretta Boston, a lady named Azaline.

Aubrey has taken charge and takes great pride in being the one to ask bewildered home folks, "You know who this is?"

The people inspect Ida Mae's face. She was a young mother in her twenties the last time some of them saw her. Now she's a great-grandmother. They look hard and see the pointed nose of her sister Talma or the nut butter coloring of Miss Theenie. Some catch on right away and startle themselves in the recognition.

"You know I know Miss Ida Mae! I declare! How you doing!" one lady says, after figuring it out, grabbing Ida Mae, and smothering her in hugs.

She stops by to see an old classmate named Castoria.

"You know who this is?" Aubrey asks again.

Castoria says she can't place her, doesn't know her.

"Yes, you do," Aubrey insists. "This is Ida Mae."

Castoria's face brightens. The two of them embrace each other and let out gap-toothed smiles.

"Girl, I ought to whoop you good!" Castoria says. "Lord have mercy on me. When have I seen Ida Mae?"

"It's been years and years and years," Ida Mae says. "I went to school with you. Just a few of us living now."

"Lord have mercy on my soul!" Castoria says, still staring at Ida Mae.

———

Aubrey takes her to the church cemetery where many of the black people of Chickasaw County are buried. She finds her mother, Miss Theenie, and some cousins and aunts, but not the father she loved so dearly.

One of the headstones appears to be testimony to the hard times the people faced under Jim Crow.

It reads simply: THY TRIAL'S ENDED.

Aubrey scans the headstones of all the people they once knew.

"Ida Mae, you gonna be buried down here?" Aubrey asks her.

"No, I'm gonna be in Chicago," she tells him.

———

We pull up to a frame house with a pickup truck and farm implements in the yard. It's where David McIntosh lives. He was the suitor who rode on horseback to court Ida Mae had when she was a young girl and who lost out to the man who married Ida Mae and carried her off to Chicago.

Had things turned out differently, had she not married George, this might be where Ida Mae would be living: on a Chickasaw County farm with chickens and pole beans in walking distance from where she grew up. She would never have lived in Chicago, might never have seen it. She wouldn't have been able to vote all those years or work in a big city hospital, to ride the elevated train and taste Polish sausage and be surrounded by family and friends most everywhere she went because most everyone she knew moved north like she did. Her children—James, Eleanor, Velma—not to mention the grandchildren, might not have existed or would surely have been different from what they were if they had. It's almost incomprehensible now.

David comes out of the house in his baseball cap. He has not seen her in half a lifetime. He recognizes her instantly. He breaks into a smile.

"How you, Ida Mae?"

"I'm blessed," she says, smiling back.

He is a compact man in soiled denim and bifocals, not much taller than Ida Mae. He stayed in Mississippi and lived his life close to the land, the opposite of how Ida Mae ended up. He studies her face across the decades and reaches out and grabs her hand.

Just then, David's wife, in white braids, comes out to see who is visiting, and Ida Mae and David keep it to a warm hug and a few words.

Ida Mae climbs into the car, still looking back at David, and he still looking at her.

"Bless his heart," Ida Mae says, as the car backs out of his dirt yard. "I knew him the minute I saw him."

That turned out to be the last time they would see each other. He died the next year, and she would not mourn so much as contemplate the meaning of what might have been and what their lives had turned out to be.

CHICAGO, MARCH 5, 1999
IDA MAE BRANDON GLADNEY

IDA MAE'S LIVING ROOM had a pink glow to it. The new venetian blinds she dreamed of had finally arrived. Their pink slats cast a rose-colored light in the room. It was just how she liked to see the world, and she was happier for it. She was all dressed up, her hair in cotton white Shirley Temple curls, pink lipstick on, smiling and free. It was her eighty-sixth birthday.

A thick snow was falling outside and coated the trees. Betty, who lived upstairs, waited with her for the guests to arrive.

The news was on. There was a report about a white man who had gotten the death penalty for dragging a black man to death in Jasper, Texas. But this was Ida Mae's birthday, and no one wanted to think about black men being dragged to death. They had lived it, and it hadn't gone away, and there was nothing they could do about it. Plus, that was Texas, not Mississippi. They were from Mississippi.

Outside, a man was parking his truck in front of the empty lot next to Ida Mae's house. She heard the screeching of the brakes and turned toward the window to see what was going on.

"He needs to move that truck," Ida Mae said. "That rusted-back truck is blocking my view."

Eleanor's daughter Karen arrived with a new boyfriend named Mike. He had a square jaw and specks of gray in his hair, looked to be late forties to midfifties. When Mike came in, Ida Mae noticed him right away. "I don't know who that is," she said, "but he sho' ain't bad on the eyes."

Their old friend Wilks Battle walked in and took a seat next to Ida Mae. He had just come from the hospital. His mother had been diagnosed with liver cancer. The doctor said there was no more they could do. He said it could be two months or two days, they just didn't know. He bent his head down, eyes cast to the carpet.

Ida Mae looked wide-eyed into his face with wonder and sympathy. All the people she had lost and buried, and still she listened as if this were the first she had heard of death and the first she had seen of grief.

"Well," she said in a low and gentle voice, "God don't make no mistakes."

"Yes, ma'am, I know," he said, looking away.

"No, God don't make no mistakes."

The meal was fish—"cat" and "buffalo" that Eleanor fried—coleslaw, and hush puppies. Mary Ann made the tuna macaroni salad and apple muffins. Karen brought a yellow layer cake with strawberries on top and the potato salad she was still refusing to divulge the recipe for no matter how much people begged.

The ten or so people gathered for Ida Mae's birthday that night stood in a circle around the dining room table as Mary Ann prayed, "Dear God, thank you for Grandmother . . ."

Ida Mae made sure to sit across the dining room table from Mike, her granddaughter notwithstanding, and proceeded to tell her story.

"I been in Chicago sixty-two years," she began. "I came here in 1937. Well, I came to Milwaukee first. I came when Eleanor was three month old and James was three year old. In them days on the train, everybody had shoe boxes full of food."

"The ways we got here . . . ," Mike said, shaking his head.

He had come up late, in 1969.

"I came up as a young man from Macomb, Mississippi," he said. "I guess it was coming to an end then. People stopped coming when things got better in the South."

A heavy snow fell outside. In a symbolic kind of way, snow was to Chicago what cotton was to Mississippi. It blanketed the land. It was inevitable. Both were so much a part of the landscape of either place that where you saw snow you by definition would not see cotton and vice versa. Coming to Chicago was a guarantee that you would not be picking cotton. The people sitting at the dining room table this late winter night had chosen snow over cotton.

It was a new century now. Ida Mae had never expected to see it. But here she was about to celebrate another birthday. She didn't know how many more she might live to see, and she didn't worry about it. It was March 2002. She was in a new chair by the window now. It was a gold velveteen recliner that could swivel and pivot, and she could watch the world play out beneath her from whatever angle she chose. She had replaced the baby blue carpet and the baby blue plastic-covered furniture she inherited from the nice Italian people when she bought the three-flat some thirty-five years ago. She had hung new draperies and kept the new blinds at half-mast to frame her view of the mayhem below. It was better than a movie.

"The police," she'd say, "they riding tonight. When it's a shooting, they ride for a good week. They been riding hard lately."

That meant the street might be quiet for a change. She lived with the daughter she had carried in her belly to the New World, the daughter who was now a grandmother herself, and with the daughter's son, whose quick mind and good nature couldn't protect him from the will of the streets. Just about every evening, James, the son who had balked at the shoes she had tried to put on him for the migration north and who was now a grandfather, his hair flecked with gray, would come up from the first floor to watch *Wheel of Fortune* with her on the Magnavox.

She had outlived her proud and stoic husband; her two oldest daughters; the suitor she might have married who would have kept her in the South; the hot-headed Willie Jim, who raised his chains up to her that night in Mississippi; old Mr. Edd, who was a decent boss man but still made life harder than it had to be down south; Miss Julie McClenna, blind and sweet though she was; and even the more tortured souls like Robert Foster and George Starling, whom she never knew but who, along with several million others, were on the train out of the South with her in spirit if not in fact.

Ida Mae Gladney, Robert Foster, and George Starling each left different parts of the South during different decades for different reasons and with different outcomes. The three of them would find some measure of happiness, not because their children had been perfect, their own lives without heartache, or because the North had been particularly welcoming. In fact, not a single one of those things had turned out to be true.

There had been sickness, disappointment, premature and unexpected losses, and, among their children, more divorces than enduring marriages, but at least the children had tried. The three who had come out of the South were left widowed but solvent, and each found some measure of satisfaction because whatever had happened to them, however things had unfolded, it had been of their own choosing, and they could take comfort in that. They believed with all that was in them that they were better off for having made the Migration, that they may have made many mistakes in their lives, but leaving the South had not been one of them.

———

Ida Mae outlasted them all. Here she was, well into a new millennium no one ever thought she would live to see, eighty-nine going on ninety, and dancing some old version of the black bottom that the old people wouldn't let her dance eight decades before. She was snapping her fingers to B. B. King, who had come north from Mississippi like her, from a place called Itta Bena. She was singing along with the words: *"To know you is to love you, is to see you being free as the wind . . . "*

Mississippi was deep inside her, but she gave no thought to ever living there again. Home was wherever she planted herself, and that happened to be Chicago. She had been there for sixty-six years, longer than some people get to live.

There were several dozen people in Chicago, Milwaukee, Beloit, and Toledo, descended from the original sharecroppers who had left the clay hills of northeastern Mississippi back in the 1930s and 1940s, including, among the descendants, Ida Mae's two surviving children, six grandchildren, seven great-grandchildren, and assorted nieces and nephews. Of those descendants, there were bus drivers, secretaries, teachers, administrators, a bank teller, a lawyer, a customer service representative, government workers.

Ida Mae was the only original migrant left in the family. She was held in high esteem in her white suit and with her cottony white hair combed into a French twist at annual reunion dinners at, say, a Holiday Inn on the outskirts of one of the arrival cities. She had a niece and a brother- and sister-in-law back in Mississippi. And that was pretty much all that was left back home.

She was a Chicagoan now but had seen and heard so much, so many wondrous, sad, and unspeakable things in her life, that there still wasn't time enough to tell all that she had witnessed.

"The half ain't been told," she said.

She put the disappointments in a lockbox in the back of her mind and lived in the moment, which is all anybody has for sure. She had learned long ago, when things were so much harder in the Old Country she left behind, that, after all she had been through, every day to her was a bless- ing and every breath she took a gift.

EPILOGUE

Because we have tasted
the bitter swill
of civil war and segregation,
and emerged from that dark chapter
stronger and more united,
we cannot help but believe
that the old hatreds shall someday pass;
that the lines of tribe shall soon dissolve;
that, as the world grows smaller,
our common humanity
shall reveal itself. . . .

—BARACK OBAMA,
PRESIDENTIAL INAUGURAL ADDRESS,
JANUARY 20, 2009

By the time the Great Migration was over, few Americans had not been touched by it. The descendants of those who left the South were raised in a world their ancestors could not have comprehended. Those who stayed had relatives up north or out west that they could boast about and options they had not had before if they, too, wanted to leave. In parts of old Abbeville County, South Carolina, for instance, "there is not one family that does not have close relatives in Philadelphia," wrote the scholar Allen B. Ballard. "It's always Philadelphia." Their world—the former Confederacy—was made better in part because of the pressures put upon it by those who made the sacrifice to leave it. The blacks who arrived from Africa and the Caribbean entered a country where people of African descent could breathe freer for all that had come before them.

They lived next to and did business with the great mass of people who had migrated from the South. So, too, did other immigrants and native whites who employed the migrants and their children, rented to them, sold goods to them, fled from them, or befriended them. And people the world over were enriched by the music the migrants carried north with them and, through translation, became—from Louis Armstrong to Miles Davis to Aretha Franklin to the Rolling Stones to Tupac Shakur, and many others—essentially the soundtrack of the twentieth century.

With all that grew out of this mass movement of people, did the Great Migration achieve the aim of those who willed it? Were the people who left the South—and their families—better off for having done so? Was the loss of what they left behind worth what confronted them in the anonymous cities they fled to?

Throughout the Migration, social scientists all but concluded that the answer to those questions was no, that the Migration had led to the troubles of the urban North and West, most scholars blaming the dysfunction of the inner cities on the migrants themselves. The migrants were cast as poor illiterates who imported out-of-wedlock births, joblessness, and welfare dependency wherever they went.

"Masses of ignorant, uncouth, and impoverished migrants flooded the city," the sociologist E. Franklin Frazier wrote of the migration to Chicago, "and changed the whole structure of the Negro community."

The presence of the migrants "in such large numbers crushed and stagnated the progress of Negro life," the economist Sadie Mossell wrote early in the migration to Philadelphia.

Newly available census records suggest the opposite to be true. According to a growing body of research, the migrants were, it turns out, better educated than those they left behind in the South and, on the whole, had nearly as many years of schooling as those they encountered in the North. Compared to the northern blacks already there, the migrants were more likely to be married and remain married, more likely to raise their children in two-parent households, and more likely to be employed. The migrants, as a group, managed to earn higher incomes than northern-born blacks even though they were relegated to the lowest-paying positions. They were less likely to be on welfare than the blacks they encountered in the North, partly because they had come so far, had experienced such hard times, and were willing to work longer hours or second jobs in positions that few northern blacks, or hardly anyone else for that matter, wanted, as was the case with Ida Mae

Gladney, George Swanson Starling, Robert Foster, and millions of others like them.

"The Southerners had their eye out for something," an old settler, Arthur Fauset, was quoted as saying in a book on the migration to Philadelphia. "These shrewd South Carolinians came here as if they knew there was something they could get and they went after it."

It could not have been imagined in the early decades of the Great Migration that some of those unwashed masses yearning to breathe free would end up leading the very cities that had rejected them upon arrival.

The first black mayors in each of the major receiving cities of the North and West were not longtime northern native blacks or those having arrived from the Caribbean but participants or sons of the Great Migration. Carl Stokes, whose parents migrated from Georgia to Ohio during World War I, would be elected, in 1967, mayor of Cleveland, the first black to hold that office in any major American city. Tom Bradley, the son of sharecroppers, whose family fled central Texas for California when he was six years old, would become, in 1973, the first black mayor of Los Angeles. Coleman Young, whose parents brought him north from Tuscaloosa, Alabama, would become, in 1974, mayor of Detroit. Harold Washington, whose father migrated from Kentucky to Illinois, would, in 1983, be elected, contentiously so, mayor of Chicago. Wilson Goode, the son of sharecroppers from North Carolina, would become, in 1984, the mayor of Philadelphia. David Dinkins, the son of a barber who migrated from Newport News, Virginia, to Trenton, New Jersey, would, in 1990, become mayor of New York. And Willie Brown, a onetime farmhand who left the cotton fields of east Texas for northern California, would become mayor of San Francisco in 1996, after having served as the Speaker of the California Assembly, the first black to do so. Many of these men would serve multiple, if often difficult, terms in office, but each had exceeded anything their origins would have foretold.

Over time, the Migration would transform American music as we know it. The three most influential figures in jazz were all children of the Great Migration. Miles Davis was born in Alton, Illinois, after his family migrated from Arkansas. Thelonious Monk migrated with his family from North Carolina when he was five. John Coltrane left High Point, North Carolina, for Philadelphia in 1943, when he was sixteen. Coltrane had never owned a saxophone before his mother bought him a used one once he got north. "He would just sit there all the time and practice and smoke cigarettes," a friend said. The neighbors complained, and a minister decided to give Coltrane the key to a Philadelphia church where he could play his sax whenever he wanted, which was often enough that his friends thought it bordered on the maniacal.

Such may be the sheer force of determination of any emigrant leaving one repressive place for something he or she hopes will be better. But for many of the migrants from the South, the stakes were especially high—there was no place left to go, no other refuge or other suns to search for, in their own country if they failed. Things had to work out, whatever it took, and that determination showed up in the statistics.

"Upon their arrival in northern cities, the recent southern migrants actually enjoyed greater family stability than their northern-born neighbors," the sociologists Stewart Tolnay and Kyle Crowder wrote in 1999.

"Compared with northern-born blacks," Tolnay wrote in 2003 as a result of his continuing research, "southern migrants had higher rates of participation in the labor force, lower levels of unemployment, higher incomes, lower levels of poverty and welfare dependency."

Something deep inside helped push them past the improbability of survival in a strange land and even past many people already there. "Whether one considers poverty status, earnings, or total income," the census analysts Larry H. Long and Lynne R. Heltman wrote, "independent studies are in unanimous agreement with the present finding that southern-born blacks are more economically successful in the North than northern born blacks."

In cases where things went awry, it turned out that the longer the migrants were exposed to the northern cities, the more vulnerable some became to the troubles of the preexisting world they had entered. If anything, the scholars found, the migrants who stumbled were brought down by the conditions of the northern cities, not the other way around.

"Instead of thinking of southern migrants as the 'culprits' in changes that have occurred in the urban black family during this century," Tolnay and Crowder wrote, "it may be more accurate to think of them as the 'victims' of their new residential milieu."

————

Just to leave, the migrants had to draw upon their inner reserves, transcend the limits of caste and geography and the station to which they had been assigned. The beneficiaries, despite the casualties, were many. The migrants would seem to be the prime beneficiaries of their actions. But they were the ones who had to face the unsettled in-betweenness of their emigrant status. Their individual actions, added together, benefited their children, their grandchildren, and even those they left behind in the South as much as if not more than themselves.

The Migration helped other people of color—the later arrivals from Asia, South and Central America, and the Middle East—whose worlds opened up further as the country liberalized its views of diversity. The Migration exposed white Americans outside the South to black culture and created an opportunity—much of it missed—to bridge the races in the New World. The Migration changed American culture as we know it. The migrants brought the blues and birthed whole genres of music— jazz, rock, rhythm and blues, hip-hop. The Migration would influence the language, food, dance, and dress we take for granted. The Migration "led to higher earnings, an influential black electorate and a black middle class," wrote the preeminent sociologist Reynolds Farley.

Regardless of their formal education, those who persevered in the New World, on the whole, enjoyed greater economic success than they would have otherwise. "Black migrants who left the South and did not return had higher incomes than those who never left or those who returned," the census analysts Larry H. Long and Kristin A. Hansen wrote. And, as the Migration spread the issue of race relations across the United States, forcing the entire country to face its centuries-old demons, it also helped inspire and pressure other racial regimes such as that of South Africa and, thus, was a gift to other parts of the world.

In their own lives, whatever individual success each migrant found was in part a function of how he or she adapted to the New World and made peace, or not, with the Old. Each of the three people in this book represented some aspect of the emigrant psyche, of the patterns of adjustment facing anyone who has ever left one place for another, desperate to make a go of it.

Robert Foster found financial success and walked taller in a land more suited to him. But he turned his back on the South and the culture he sprang from. He rarely went back. He plunged himself fully into an alien world that only partly accepted him and went so far as to change his name and assume a different persona to fit in. It left him a rootless soul, cut off from the good things about the place he had left. He put distance between himself and his own children, hiding his southern, perhaps truest, self. He sought to overcome his emigrant insecurities by trying to prove himself at the casinos, proving instead how much one could lose in so short a time. In later life, he hungered for any news or reminder of home, like many an exile. He became as obsessed with outward appearances as the city he fled to and nursed ancient wounds until the day he died. But he would have had it no other way.

George Starling succeeded merely by not being lynched. Just living was an achievement. He managed to reach a level of material solvency he might never have known in the South, assuming he had survived. He paid a price. He enjoyed the fruits of the North and the South but grieved over how he had to leave and what might have been. He was as northern as he was southern, biregional, one might say, not fully one or the other. His ultimate success was psychological freedom from the bonds of his origins. Leaving the South and working the railroads gave him a view of the world he might otherwise never have had. He became a master observer of people and events. And in the end, the thing he wanted most of all, the education denied him early in life, came to him perhaps without his realizing it. He got an education, not the formal one of his dreams, but one he could not have imagined, a fuller one, perhaps, for having left the limited world of his birth.

Ida Mae Gladney had the humblest trappings but was the richest of them all. She had lived the hardest life, been given the least education, seen the worst the South could hurl at her people, and did not let it break her. She lived longer in the North than in the South but never forsook her origins, never changed the person she was deep inside, never changed her accent, speaking as thick a Mississippi drawl in her nineties as the day she caught the train out of Okolona sixty-odd years before. She was surrounded by the clipped speech of the North, the crime on the streets, the flight of the white people from her neighborhood, but it was as if she were immune to it all. She took the best of what she saw in the North and the South and interwove them in the way she saw fit. She followed every jump shot of the Chicago Bulls and knew how to make sweet potato pie like the best of them in the Delta. She lived in the moment, surrendered to whatever the day presented, and remained her true, original self. Her success was spiritual, perhaps the hardest of all to achieve. And because of that, she was the happiest and lived the longest of them all.

———

From the moment the first migrants set foot in the North during World War I, scholars began weighing in on the motivations of people like Ida Mae, George, and Robert—whether it was the pull of the North or the push of the South, whether they were driven by economics or by injustice and persecution, whether changes in cotton production started the Migration or merely hastened what was already under way, and whether the Migration would end, as some wrongly anticipated, with World War I.

Scholars widely disagreed over the role of lynchings in sparking a particular wave of migration. Some scholars saw no connection between lynching and an exodus of blacks from a given community, suggesting that the people might have been too afraid to leave or had simply accepted violence as a part of life in the South. Others found evidence that blacks did, in fact, leave as might be expected after those public executions. Given the enormity of the Migration, it is quite possible that both observations could have been true, that blacks might have found it more daunting or were not in a position to leave in the immediate aftermath of a lynching but that such violence might have planted the seeds of a departure that may have taken months to actually pull off, as in the case of Ida Mae Gladney.

In any case, the turmoil in the South could be felt in the North. "Black school principals in Philadelphia," wrote the scholar Allen B. Ballard, could tell that "something had happened in a particular section of the South by the concentration of refugees from a certain place."

At the same time, the exodus forced change in the South, albeit a slow and fitful one, almost from the start: the number of lynchings in the South declined in each successive decade of the Great Migration as the number of black departures went up. Though the violence would continue into the 1960s and there were many factors that figured into that form of vigilantism, it took less than a decade of migration to begin making a difference. "Since 1924"—some eight years into the Great Migration—"lynchings have been on a marked decline," *The Montgomery Advertiser* of Alabama observed in 1959, four decades after the Migration began. "Lynchings have reached a vanishing point in recent years."

For decades, it was argued that the Great Migration was triggered by changes in cotton farming: the boll weevil infestation of the 1920s and the early mechanical cotton harvester unveiled in the 1940s. But whatever cotton's role in the Migration, it could, at best, account for only the subset of migrants who were picking cotton in the first place. Changes in cotton farming could not account for the Great Migration as a whole or for the motivations of the people who came from Virginia, Kentucky, Tennessee, North Carolina, western Texas, and Florida, for instance, where cotton was not the main industry, or for those in the cotton states who happened to be doing work other than picking cotton. Nor could it account for those who were in the industry but left for other reasons.

The timing of the Great Migration alone raises questions as to whether changes in cotton harvesting caused the Migration or whether it was the Migration that in fact set off changes in cotton production. The mechanical cotton picker did not exist when the exodus began. The Migration had been under way for some thirty years before the first viable prototypes were actually in use in the fields.

The Migration had siphoned off half a million black workers by 1920 alone. Not all of them were cotton pickers, but there was enough fretting over the loss of labor that the South began searching for a mechanical replacement for the workers the plantations were losing. The exodus of black southerners accelerated the drive toward finding a machine that could do what the pickers did. In the race toward an alternative, inventors registered nearly five hundred patents between 1901 and 1931, the early decades of the Migration, for some version of a hoped-for machine to pick cotton. That amounted to more than all the patents that had been issued in the entire second half of the nineteenth century, when the South did not have to worry about blacks leaving en masse.

Still, many planters were slow to accept the idea of such a machine or the implications of the growing black exodus. Nor did they welcome the sizable investment the new machines would require. Into the mid-1940s, the machines were plagued by imprecision, pulling up the stalks and all, and were seen as producing an inferior grade of cotton than what came from human hands. Thus, many planters did not then consider the machines a viable alternative.

It took World War II and the even bigger outflow of blacks to awaken them to what some agricultural engineers working on a mechanical harvester already knew: "Much of this labor is not returning to the farm," Harris P. Smith, the chief of agricultural engineering at Texas A&M University, wrote in 1946. "Therefore, the cotton farmer is forced to mechanize." As for the connection between the Migration and the machine, Smith concluded that "instead of the machines displacing labor, they were used to replace the labor that had left the farm."

It was not until the 1950s—close to two generations after the Great Migration began—that cotton harvesters were in wide enough use to do what human hands had done for centuries. But by then, some four million black people had already left.

In interviews with more than twelve hundred migrants across the country about their decisions to migrate, none mentioned the boll weevil or the economics of cotton. This in itself does not mean these things were not unseen forces in their lives, only that they were not thinking of them as they made their decision, or in hindsight. It appeared that when it came to a life-altering change of such gravity, it was not one thing; it was many things, some weighing more heavily in one migrant's heart than another but all very likely figuring into the calculus of departure.

———

All told, perhaps the most significant measure of the Great Migration was the act of leaving itself, regardless of the individual outcome. Despite the private disappointments and triumphs of any individual migrant, the Migration, in some ways, was its own point. The achievement was in making the decision to be free and acting on that decision, wherever that journey led them.

"If all of their dream does not come true," the *Chicago Defender* wrote at the start of the Great Migration, "enough will come to pass to justify their actions."

Many black parents who left the South got the one thing they wanted just by leaving. Their children would have a chance to grow up free of Jim Crow and to be their fuller selves. It cannot be known what course the lives of people like Toni Morrison, James Baldwin, Diana Ross, Aretha Franklin, Michelle Obama, Jesse Owens, Joe Louis, Jackie Robinson, Serena and Venus Williams, Bill Cosby, Condoleezza Rice, Nat King Cole, Oprah Winfrey, Berry Gordy (who founded Motown and signed children of the Migration to sing for it), the astronaut Mae Jemison, the artist Romare Bearden, the performers Jimi Hendrix, Michael Jackson, Prince, Sean "P. Diddy" Combs, Whitney Houston, Mary J. Blige, Queen Latifah, the director Spike Lee, the playwright August Wilson, and countless others might have taken had their parents or grandparents not participated in the Great Migration and raised them in the North or West. All of them grew up to become among the best in their fields, changed them, really, and were among the first generation of blacks in this country to grow up free and unfettered because of the actions of their forebears. Millions of other children of the Migration grew up to lead productive, though anonymous, lives in quiet, everyday ways that few people will ever hear about.

Most of these children would attend better schools than those in the South and, as a whole, outperform their southern white counterparts and nearly match the scores of northern-born blacks within a few years of arrival. Studies conducted in the early 1930s found that, after four years in the North, the children of black migrants to New York were scoring nearly as well as northern-born blacks who were "almost exactly at the norm for white children," wrote Otto Klineberg, a leading psychologist of the era at Columbia University.

"The evidence for an environmental effect is unmistakable," he reported. He found that the longer the southern-born children were in the North, the higher they scored. The results "suggest that the New York environment is capable of raising the intellectual level of the Negro children to a point equal to that of the Whites." Klineberg's studies of the children of the Great Migration would later become the scientific foundation of the 1954 Supreme Court decision in the school desegregation case, *Brown v. the Board of Education,* a turning point in the drive toward equal rights in this country.

In the end, it could be said that the common denominator for leaving was the desire to be free, like the Declaration of Independence said, free to try out for most any job they pleased, play checkers with whomever they chose, sit where they wished on the streetcar, watch their children walk across a stage for the degree most of them didn't have the chance to get. They left to pursue some version of happiness, whether they achieved it or not. It was a seemingly simple thing that the majority of Americans could take for granted but that the migrants and their forebears never had a right to in the world they had fled.

———

A central argument of this book has been that the Great Migration was an unrecognized immigration within this country. The participants bore the marks of immigrant behavior. They plotted a course to places in the North and West that had some connection to their homes of origin. They created colonies of the villages they came from, imported the food and folkways of the Old Country, and built their lives around the people and churches they knew from back home. They took work the people already there considered beneath them. They doubled up and took in roomers to make ends meet. They tried to instill in their children the values of the Old Country while pressing them to succeed by the standards of the New World they were in.

As with immigrant parents, a generational divide arose between the migrants and their children. The migrants couldn't understand their impatient, northern-bred sons and daughters—why the children who had been spared the heartache of a racial caste system were not more grateful to have been delivered from the South. The children couldn't relate to the stories of southern persecution when they were facing gangs and drive-by shootings, or, in the more elite circles, the embarrassment of southern parents with accents and peasant food when the children were trying to fit into the middle-class enclaves of the North.

And though this immigration theory may be structurally sound, with sociologists even calling them immigrants in the early years of the Migration, nearly every black migrant I interviewed vehemently resisted the immigrant label. They did not see themselves as immigrants under any circumstances, their behavior notwithstanding. The idea conjured up the deepest pains of centuries of rejection by their own country. They had been forced to become immigrants in their own land just to secure their freedom. But they were not immigrants and had never been actual immigrants. The South may have acted like a different country and been proud of it, but it was a part of the United States, and anyone born there was born an American.

The black people who left were citizens, and many of their forebears had been in this land before the country was founded. They were among the first nonnative people to set foot in the New World, brought by the Europeans to build it from wilderness and doing so without pay and by force from the time of the first arrivals in 1619 to their emancipation 246 years later. For twelve generations, their ancestors had worked the land and helped build the country. Into the twentieth century, their fourth century in America, they still had had to step aside and fall further down the economic ladder with each new wave of immigrants from all over the world, after generations as burden bearers.

It is one of those circular facts of history that, in the three great receiving cities to which southern blacks fled—the cities that drew Ida Mae, George, and Robert—blacks had been among the first nonnatives to set foot on the soil and to establish settlements centuries before. Black *mestizos* were among the forty-four Mexican settlers arriving in 1781 at the pueblo that would become Los Angeles. Jean Baptiste Point DuSable, a fur trader born of an African slave woman in Haiti, built, in 1779, the first permanent settlement in what is now known as Chicago. Jan Rodrigues, a sailor of African descent working for and later abandoned by Dutch merchants on an untamed island in the New World, created the first trading post on what is now known as Manhattan, in 1613.

And so when blacks who had migrated north and west showed resentment at being considered immigrants, it was perhaps because they knew in their bones that their ancestors had been here before there was a United States of America and that it took their leaving the South to achieve the citizenship they deserved by their ancestry and labors alone. That freedom and those rights had not come automatically, as they should have, but centuries late and of the migrants' own accord.

———

With the benefit of hindsight, the century between Reconstruction and the end of the Great Migration perhaps may be seen as a necessary stage of upheaval. It was a transition from an era when one race owned another; to an era when the dominant class gave up ownership but kept control over the people it once had owned, at all costs, using violence even; to the eventual acceptance of the servant caste into the mainstream.

The Great Migration was the final break from an abusive union with the South. It was a step in freeing not just the people who fled, but the country whose mountains they crossed. Their exodus left a still imperfect but far different landscape than before the Migration began.

It was, if nothing else, an affirmation of the power of an individual decision, however powerless the individual might appear on the surface. "In the simple process of walking away one by one," wrote the scholar Lawrence R. Rodgers, "millions of African-American southerners have altered the course of their own, and all of America's, history."

Over the decades, perhaps the wrong questions have been asked about the Great Migration. Perhaps it is not a question of whether the migrants brought good or ill to the cities they fled to or were pushed or pulled to their destinations, but a question of how they summoned the courage to leave in the first place or how they found the will to press beyond the forces against them and the faith in a country that had rejected them for so long. By their actions, they did not dream the American Dream, they willed it into being by a definition of their own choosing. They did not ask to be accepted but declared themselves the Americans that perhaps few others recognized but that they had always been deep within their hearts.

NOTES ON METHODOLOGY

I began this work because of what I saw as incomplete perceptions, outside of scholarly circles, of what the Great Migration was and how and why it happened, particularly through the eyes of those who experienced it. Because it was so unwieldy and lasted for so long, the movement did not appear to rise to the level of public consciousness that, by any measure, it seemed to deserve.

The first question, in my view, had to do with its time frame: what was it, and when precisely did it occur? The Great Migration is often described as a jobs-driven, World War I movement, despite decades of demographic evidence and real-world indicators that it not only continued well into the 1960s but gathered steam with each decade, not ending until the social, political, and economic reasons for the Migration began truly to be addressed in the South in the dragged-out, belated response to the Civil Rights Act of 1964.

The second question had to do with *where* it occurred. The migration from Mississippi to Chicago has been the subject of the most research through the years and has dominated discussion of the phenomenon, in part because of the sheer size of the black influx there and because of the great scholarly interest taken in it by a cadre of social scientists working in Chicago at the start of the Migration. However, from my years as a

national correspondent at *The New York Times* and my early experiences
growing up in a world surrounded by people who had come to the mid-
Atlantic region during the latter half of the migration from all over the
southeastern seaboard, I knew it to be a farther-reaching national resettlement than had been described by most studies of it.

Third, as most studies of the Migration focused on the important
questions of demographics, politics, economics, and sociology, I wanted
to convey the intimate stories of people who had dared to make the
crossing. I wanted to capture the enormity of the phenomenon by tracking unrelated people who had followed the multiple streams of the
Great Migration over the course of the decades it unfolded. I wanted to
reach as many as I could of this dwindling generation in the spirit of the
oral history projects with the last surviving slaves back in the 1930s.

Therefore, in the mid-1990s, I set out on a search for people who had
migrated from the South to the North and West during the Great Migration. That search led me to Mississippi Clubs, Masonic lodges, class
reunions, and union meetings of retired postal workers, bus drivers,
transit workers, and other retirees on the South Side of Chicago; to
quilting clubs, Baptist churches, and senior centers in Manhattan and
Brooklyn; to Louisiana Clubs, Texas Clubs, Sunday Masses, Creole lun-
cheons, and Juneteenth Day celebrations (commemorating the day the
last slaves in Texas learned they were free, two years after Emancipation) in Los Angeles; to senior centers, libraries, and community meetings in Oakland; and to funerals and family reunions in Milwaukee. In
these and dozens of other places frequented by seniors in these cities, I
collected names and stories, interviewing more than twelve hundred
people who shared with me preliminary versions of their experiences. I
conducted follow-up interviews with three dozen of the most promising
former migrants and settled on three complementary subjects through
whose lives I hoped to re-create the broad sweep of the movement.

The book is essentially three projects in one. The first was a collection
of oral histories from around the country. The second was the distillation of those oral histories into a narrative of three protagonists, each of
whom led a sufficiently full life to merit a book in his or her own right
and was thus researched and reported as such. The third was an examination of newspaper accounts and scholarly and literary works of the era
and more recent analyses of the Migration to recount the motivations,
circumstances, and perceptions of the Migration as it was in progress
and to put the subjects' actions into historical context.

As might be expected, the participants in the Migration had keener memories of their formative years and of the high and low points of their lives—the basis of this book—than of the more mundane and less relevant aspects of their retirement years. Some subjects recalled certain moments of their lives with greater detail than did other subjects recounting the same point in their own trajectory, which is reflected in the text. Furthermore, in their wisdom and commitment to an accurate rendering of events, they frequently declined to speculate or press beyond what they recollected. Where possible, I confirmed or clarified their accounts through interviews with the dwindling circle of surviving witnesses, cohorts, and family members; through newspaper accounts in the South and North dating back to 1900; and through census, military, railroad, school, state, and municipal records.

The primary subjects and many of the secondary informants were interviewed for dozens, if not hundreds, of hours, most of the interviews tape-recorded and transcribed. I returned to their counties of origin to interview the surviving people who knew them and to retrace their lives in the South. I then reenacted all or part of each subject's migration route, devoting most of my time to the migration of Robert Foster, which meant driving from Monroe, Louisiana, to Houston and Laredo, Texas, to Lordsburg, New Mexico, Phoenix, San Diego, Los Angeles, and on to Oakland, as Dr. Foster described in bitter detail, with my parents as generational tour guides for most of the journey. My father took notes and my mother offered commentary as I tried to re-create the experience of one person driving the entire distance through the desert night.

"You know he must have been ready to cry right about in here," my mother said as the car I had rented, a new Buick as was his when he made the crossing, hurtled into hairpin curves in total darkness with hundreds of miles yet to go. As it turned out, I was not able to reenact to the letter one of the most painful aspects of the drive. I was nearly ready to fall asleep at the wheel by the time we reached Yuma, Arizona. My parents insisted that we stop. We got a hotel room with, of course, no trouble at all, the one thing he had been so desperate for all those decades ago but that was denied him over and over again that long night in 1953.

———

The seeds of this project were sown within me years ago, growing up with parents who had migrated from the South and who sent me to an affluent white grade school that they themselves could never have dreamed of attending. There, classmates told of ancestors coming from Ireland or Scandinavia with little in their pockets and making something of themselves in the New World. Over time, I came to realize that the same could be said of my family and of millions of other black Americans who had journeyed north during the Great Migration.

I gravitated to the children of recent immigrants from Argentina, Nepal, Ecuador, El Salvador, with whom I had so much in common as the children of newcomers: the accents and folkways of overprotective parents suspicious of the libertine mores of the New World and our childish embarrassment at their nervous hovering; the exotic, out-of-step delicacies from the Old Country that our mothers lovingly prepared for our lunchboxes; the visits to my parents' fellow "immigrant" friends—all just happening to be from the South and exchanging the latest about the people from back home; the gentle attempts at instilling Old World values from their homelands, my father going so far as to nudge me away from city boys and toward potential suitors whose parents he knew from back home in Petersburg, Virginia, who were, to him, upstanding boys by definition and who would make a fine match in his view, which all but guaranteed that I'd have little interest in them.

Thus I grew up the daughter of immigrants, "a southerner once removed," as the Mississippi-born poet Natasha Trethewey once called me. My parents bore the subtle hallmarks of the immigrant psyche, except they were Americans who had taken part in an internal migration whose reach and nuances are still little understood.

———

The research into the world of the Great Migration required wading through dozens of scholarly works of the era, which were a revealing commentary on the attitudes and conditions the migrants lived under before and after their departures. Some of the works were benignly patronizing. Many betrayed such unquestioning bigotry as to be nearly unreadable. All were useful in some way or another. Yet, throughout my research, I was at times struck by the wisdom and compassion of otherwise detached social scientists, many of them white, privileged, and exhibiting unavoidable prejudices of the day but still often rendering prescient and even-handed conclusions. At the start of its 672-page report on the 1919 Chicago Riots, the sober, white-led Chicago Commission on Race Relations, presaging the sentiments of a yet-to-be-born African-American president, whose rise would have been beyond imagination at the time, admonished in 1922:

It is important for our white citizens always to remember that the Negroes alone of all our immigrants came to America against their will by the special compelling invitation of the whites; that the institution of slavery was introduced, expanded and maintained by the United States by the white people and for their own benefit; and they likewise created the conditions that followed emancipation.

Our Negro problem, therefore, is not of the Negro's making. No group in our population is less responsible for its existence. But every group is responsible for its continuance. . . . Both races need to understand that their rights and duties are mutual and equal and their interests in the common good are identical. . . . There is no help or healing in appraising past responsibilities or in present apportioning of praise or blame. The past is of value only as it aids in understanding the present; and an understanding of the facts of the problem—a magnanimous understanding by both races—is the first step toward its solution.

AFTERWORD

Ida Mae Gladney died peacefully in her sleep after a brief onset of leukemia in September 2004. Her family was so distraught that her children and grandchildren kept her room precisely as it was for years. The door remained closed in memoriam to her, and no one had the heart or strength to touch it.

ACKNOWLEDGMENTS

This book is the culmination of many years of research and distillation and could not have come to be without the faith and encouragement of critical people and institutions at crucial moments in its gestation.

I wish first to express gratitude for my parents—my mother and my late father, who gave me my earliest understanding of the Great Migration through their lives and experiences and through what they passed on to me, and who were the inspiration for what I did not know was possible when I first began pursuing the idea.

Thank you to the people who helped to create the groundwork necessary for my intuitions to become a reality: Denise Stinson, who believed in the book from the start, and Michael Winston, for his wise counsel.

I wish to thank my editors at Random House—Ann Godoff, who acquired it, Jonathan Karp, who cheered it on, and, most of all, Kate Medina, who embraced it, championed it, and brought it into the world. I also benefited from the support and insights of Lindsey Schwoeri, Millicent Bennett, Jonathan Jao, Amelia Zalcman, Sally Marvin, Carol Schneider, London King, Ashley Gratz-Collier, and Steve Messina and his team, among many others at Random House. Thank you ever so much.

During the course of the research, I was fortunate to have been able to rely on support from a fellowship from the John Simon Guggenheim Foundation; an Edith Kreeger Wolf endowed lectureship at Northwestern University; a semester as Ferris Professor of Journalism at Princeton University; and various lectures and seminars I delivered at such places as Brown University, the Nieman Foundation at Harvard University, the narrative journalism conference in Aarhus, Denmark, the University of Nevada at Reno, the University of Mississippi at Oxford, and, for three years, as the James M. Cox Professor of Journalism at Emory University. I am grateful to Boston University, where I now am on faculty, for its role in promoting narrative nonfiction such as this book and for the support of David Campbell, Thomas Fiedler, Louis Ureneck, Mitchell Zuckoff, Robert Manoff, Richard Lehr, Robert Zelnik, Caryl Rivers, Safoura Rafeizadeh, and James Brann.

I was on leave from *The New York Times* for much of the time I was researching the book with the good wishes of three executive editors, Bill Keller, Joseph Lelyveld, and Howell Raines, who showed patience and understanding as I pursued this calling, as well as the good cheer of Soma Golden Behr.

This has been a personal journey that, due to the nature of the work and the loss of the primary subjects, transformed me out of necessity from journalist to unintended historian. I am grateful for the insights of historians who have made rigorous examination of the American past, particularly of the Jim Crow era, their life's work. In particular, I wish to thank Leon Litwack, who shared with me his wisdom and made sure I left Berkeley with the books I needed from his favorite used book store, the old Cody's near campus.

Beyond these, I thank God for the will and fortitude to make it through this journey. But also for their encouragement at critical moments, I am grateful to Alex Reid, Jonathan Schwartz, Rick Jones, Gwendolyn Whitt, Fannye Jolly, Michael Elliston, D. J. Page, D. M. Page, Laleh Khadivi, Pat Harris, Marcia Lythcott, Debora Ott, and, for their belief in me over the years, Frances Ball, Gladys Pemberton, Beatrice Judge, Lawrence Kaggwa, Ronald Richardson, and the Taylor family of Richmond and Petersburg, Virginia. Thank you to Eva Harvey, Robert K. Watts, and Joseph Beck for sharing their memories of the Jim Crow South; and my sincerest gratitude to those who assisted in the research: Christine Savage in the final throes of production, Christine Li, Emily Truax, Sarah Stanton, and, especially, Kathryn Wilson for her hard work in the early years of the project.

I am deeply grateful for the time and contributions of the more than twelve hundred people who shared their stories in preliminary interviews in the first year and a half of the research and whose experiences, while not explicitly cited in the text, helped shape its direction. They were my initial teachers in the world of Jim Crow and the unseen chorus that validated the final narrative. For going out of their way to help identify people who had migrated from the South as they had done, I am grateful for the kindness shown me by Wilks Battle, Bennie Lee Ford, Aline Heisser-Ovid, and, especially, Almeta Washington.

I wish to thank the subjects' families for allowing me into their lives and entrusting me with their loved ones on trips both long and short that we made to the places they worked and lived and, for two of them, back to the Old Country. In particular, I want to thank Eleanor Smiley, James and Mary Ann Gladney, Karen Smiley, Kevin Smiley, Madison James Foster II, Bunny Fisher, Joy Foster, and Patricia George for their warmth and encouragement, and Amjad "Kenny" Mujaahid for his inspiring letters of support.

Finally, I reserve the greatest measure of gratitude for Ida Mae Gladney, George Swanson Starling, and Robert Pershing Foster, the people who gave so much of themselves to a book they would never see. They believed in me and in this project perhaps more than anyone else, perhaps, at times, even more than I did. Their unfailing faith in this work carried me through when I doubted what was possible. Meeting and sharing with them their final years on this earth has been one of the great joys and honors of my life, and I have been inspired and made better for having known them.

ISABEL WILKERSON
June 2010

SELECTED INTERVIEWS AND SOURCES

CALIFORNIA
Dr. Robert P. Foster
Cathryn Covington Baker
Lee Ballard
Romie Banks

Mrs. J. M. Beard
Howard and Isabelle Beckwith
Pat Botchekan
Malissa Briley
Sylvester Brooks

Claire Collins
John Collins
Joseph Cooper
Ivorye Covington
Leo DeJohn
John Dunlap
Dallas Evans
Sherman Ferguson
Bennie Lee Ford
Joy Foster
Warren Hollingsworth
Jessie Holmes
Charles Honore
Marilyn Hudson
Robert Johnson
Carrie Jones
Limuary and Adeline Jordan
Barbara Lemmons
Marguerite Lewis
Nellie Lutcher
Carl Kendall
James Marshall
Leola McMearn
Cleo Pierre
John Rachal, Sr.
Vera Roberts
Della B. Robinson
De Willow Sherman
Reatha Gray Simon
Reatha Beck Smith
Ida Bryant Spigener
Barbara Starks
Ruby Thomas
Melba Thompson
Almeta Washington
Inette Weasel
Betty S. White

FLORIDA
Reuben Blye

Viola Dunham
Watson Dunham
Cleave Frink
Patricia George
Reverend William Hawkins
Andrew "Jack" Johnson
Carla Mitchell
Virginia Sallet

GEORGIA
Joseph Beck
Sharon Seay
James C. Washington

ILLINOIS
Ida Mae Brandon Gladney
Laura Addison
Ruby Barnes
Wilks Battle
Bessie Baugard
Homer Betts
Erma Bien-Aimee
Marie Billingsley
Barbara Bowman
Isiah Bracy
Albert Brooks
George Brown
Joe L. Brown
Herbert Bruce
Albert Sidney Burchett
Tony Burroughs
Florine Burton
Betty Caldwell
Orlando Campbell
Joseph Chapman
James Clark
Elwood Crowder
Austin Cunningham
Grady Davis
Henrietta Dawson

John Harold Earl
Arthur Ellis
Lisa Ely
Mildred Elzie
Eddie Ervin
Robert David Fields
Bunny Fisher
Myrtis Francis
Lasalle Frelix
Phlenoid Gaiter
James and Mary Ann Gladney
Walter Goudy
Ruth Hamilton
Aaron Henderson
Leon "Jack" Hillman
James Hobbs
Spurgeon Holland
Karyne Islam
Urelle Jackson, Sr.
Isabel Joseph Johnson
Willie Johnson
Lola Jones
Spencer Leak
Emma Leonard
Clinton Lewis
Hollis Lewis
Carl Little
Ruth McClendon
Doris McMurray
Charles Mingo
Irene Nelson
Clara Piper
Raymar Pitchfork
Robena Porter
Robert Pulliam
Edna Robertson
William G. Samuels
James Seahorn
Eleanor Smiley
Karen Smiley

Kevin Smiley
Coy F. Smith
Ruby W. McGowan Mays Smith
Laura Starks
Howard Stephenson
Roma Stewart
Bennie Therrell
Riley Tubbs
John Valson
Mamie Westley
Mary Louise Wiley
Delores Woodtor

LOUISIANA
Joella Burton
Madison James Foster II
Faroker Johnson
Clara Poe
B. D. Robinson
Rosalie Taylor
Florence Todd
Clyde Walker

MISSISSIPPI
Marcelle Barr
Doretta Boston
Gilbert Elie
Aubrey Enochs
Gloria Enochs
Jessie Gladney
Isolena Harris
David McIntosh

NEW YORK
George Swanson Starling
Dees Abraham
Nathaniel M. Baker
Maxie Broughton
Bennie Brown
Gary Byrd

Franklin Caldwell
John Carter
Christine Chambers
Virginia DeBreaux Hall
Petite Bell Hammond
Reverend Henry V. Harrison
James Hobbs
Clarence Jerrell
Julia Johnson
Gardenia Joyner
Aurilla Moore
Ulysses Morris
Amjad "Kenny" Mujaahid
Onie Bell Carter Norwood
Donald Payne
Delphine Smith Peterman

Henry Roberts
Ruth Rudder
Jerry Ward
Robert K. Watts
Monifa White
Manier E. Webber
Eva Mae Williams

TENNESSEE
Richard Jarvis Enochs

WISCONSIN
Jerome Hervey
Freddie Knox
Manley Thomas

PARTIAL LIST OF ORGANIZATIONS THAT
OFFERED SUPPORT AND ACCESS TO MIGRANTS

CALIFORNIA
Betty Hill Recreation Center,
  Senior Line Dancing
East Texas Club of Los Angeles
Estelle Van Meter Senior Center
Grambling Alumni Association,
  Los Angeles
Independent Square Senior Center
Jefferson Council
Jim Gilliam Senior Center
Lake Charles, Louisiana, Club
LA–LA (Louisiana to Los
  Angeles), Inc.
Monroe, Louisiana, Club
Mount Carmel Senior Center
People Coordinated Services
St. Andrew's Senior Group
St. Bernadette Senior Center
Slauson Senior Recreation Center
Theresa Lindsay Senior Center

Vineyard Recreation Senior
  Center
Watts Senior Center
Xavier College Alumni Club of
  Los Angeles

FLORIDA
Gethsemane Baptist Church,
  Eustis
NAACP, South Brevard Chapter

GEORGIA
National Funeral Directors and
  Morticians Association

ILLINOIS
Ada S. Niles Senior Center
African-American Police League
Afro-American Genealogical and
  Historical Society of Chicago

AFSCME, Chicago District Council

Atlas Senior Center, Chicago Area Agency on Aging

Bethel Terrace Senior Center

Brookhaven, Mississippi, Club

Carter Funeral Home

Chicago Housing Authority Senior Housing

Chicago Pensioners Club

Chicago Urban League

Chicago Usher Board

Cotton Plant, Arkansas, Club

DuSable High School

Fourth District, Beat 414, South Chicago

Greater St. John's AME Church

Greenville, Mississippi, Club

Greenwood, Mississippi, Club

Grenada, Mississippi, Club

Happy Action Seniors, St. Joachim Church

Historic Pullman Foundation

Latney Funeral Home

Leak and Sons Funeral Home

Local 241/Chicago Transit Authority Bus Drivers Union

Metro Seniors in Action

National Alliance of Postal and Federal Employees, Chicago Branch, Retirees' Division

Neptune Seniors

Newton, Mississippi, Club

Old Friends of Chicago

Pastors of Englewood, Seventh District

Police Beat 713, Boulevard Arts Center

Prince Hall Masonic Lodge of the State of Illinois

Senior Advisory Committee, Third District

Senior Advisory Committee, Fourth District

Senior Steppers' Set at Mr. G's

Tabernacle Baptist Church

Third District, Beat 312, Grand Crossing

Third District, Beat 322, Grand Crossing

Third District, Beat 323, Grand Crossing

UBA A. Philip Randolph Center

Vicksburg, Mississippi, Club

Willa Rawls Manor

WBEZ-FM

WGCI-AM

WVON-AM

NEW YORK

African American Quilting Club, Brooklyn

Baptist House of Prayer, Harlem

Bridge Street Baptist Church, Brooklyn

Central Harlem Senior Center

First Baptist Church, Brooklyn

Lagree Baptist Church, Harlem

Metropolitan A.M.E. Church, Harlem

New York City Department of Aging

Wilson Major Morris Senior Center, Harlem

WLIB-AM

NOTES

vii **I was leaving the South:** Richard Wright, *Black Boy* (New York: HarperCollins, 1993, a reissue of Wright's autobiography, originally published in 1945 by Harper and Brothers). This passage is from a last-minute insertion in a restructuring of the book, which originally had been titled *American Hunger.* For its release in 1945, the title was changed to *Black Boy* and the second half of the book, describing Wright's adjustment in the North, was deleted at the behest of the Book-of-the-Month Club. Wright chose to insert this passage as a compromise ending to the revised autobiography. Because this passage was not part of the original manuscript, it is not included in the text of the modern-day version. The passage instead appears in the footnotes of the 1993 reprint, p. 496.

PART I: IN THE LAND OF THE FOREFATHERS

1 **Our mattresses were made:** Mahalia Jackson with Evan McLeod Wylie, *Movin' On Up* (New York: Hawthorn Books, 1966), pp. 22, 25.

LEAVING

3 **The land is first:** David L. Cohn, *God Shakes Creation* (New York: Harper and Brothers, 1935), pp. 32, 33.

3 **They fly from the land:** W. H. Stillwell, "Exode," *Chicago Inter-Ocean,* March 12, 1881. The stanza reads: "They fly from the land that bore them, as the Hebrews fled the Nile; from the heavy burthens [*sic*] o'er them; from unpaid tasks before them; from a serfdom base and vile."

5 **A man named Roscoe Colton:** Jonathan Rosen, "Flight Patterns," *The New York Times Magazine,* April 22, 2007, pp. 58–63.

THE GREAT MIGRATION, 1915–1970

8 **In our homes:** "The Negro Problem," *Independent* 54: 2221. The colored Alabama woman interviewed for this 1902 article requested that her name not be used, fearing retribution for expressing a desire to leave. The fear of being identified was common among southern black letter writers to the *Chicago Defender* inquiring about opportunities in the North and others discussing or considering migration. Often they explicitly pleaded that their identities not be revealed.

8 **"They left as though":** Emmett J. Scott, *Negro Migration During the War* (New York: Oxford University Press, 1920), p. 44.

9 **Over the course:** Estimates vary for the number of blacks who left the South during the Great Migration. Some have put the number at well over six million. The historian Jeffrey S. Adler writes that "the total for the three-decade period after 1940 exceeded 4.3 million" alone. David R. Colburn and Jeffrey S. Adler, eds., *African-American Mayors: Race, Politics, and the American City* (Urbana: University of Illinois Press, 2001), p. 4. Definitions vary as to which states make up the South, with the border states of Maryland, Delaware, and the District of Columbia often included. This book uses a definition based on the states that made up the Confederacy and the definitions and perceptions of the migrants who left the South. The migrants' decision to escape to those border regions and those states' participation in the Civil War on the Union side suggest that politically, psychologically, and demographically they were not southern but rather part of the North to which the migrants fled. Those states had net inflows of blacks in a dramatic departure from the states the migrants perceived of as the South. The estimate, just over five and a half million, used in this book is a conservative one and derives from data compiled from Public Use Microdata Sample (PUMS) Tapes of U.S. Census figures for out-migration of African Americans from the former Confederate states of Alabama, Arkansas, Florida, Georgia, Louisiana, Mississippi, North Carolina, South Carolina, Tennessee, and Virginia, along with Kentucky and Oklahoma, to the former Union states that attracted the bulk of the migrants, namely, New York, New Jersey, Connecticut, Massachusetts, Pennsylvania, Michigan, Indiana, Ohio, Illinois, Iowa, Wisconsin, Minnesota, Kansas, California, Nevada, Oregon, and the District of Columbia, along with the border states of Delaware, Maryland, and Missouri and the state of Washington, which was not admitted to the Union until after the Civil War. The number is considered to be an underestimate. "One estimate places the net under-enumeration of Negro males [alone] at about 20 per cent," wrote the sociologists Karl E. Taeuber and Alma F. Taeuber in "The Changing Character of Negro Migration," *The American Journal of Sociology* 70, no. 4 (January 1965), p. 433.

9 **"receiving station":** Carl Sandburg, *The Chicago Race Riots, July 1919* (New York: Harcourt, Brace and Howe, 1919), p. 60.

10 **Over time:** See Nicholas Mirkowich, "Recent Trends in Population Distribution in

NOTES557

California," *Geographical Review* 31, no. 2 (April 1941), pp. 300–307, for a general discussion of Gold Rush and Dust Bowl migrations.

10 **for far longer:** Blacks were enslaved in this country for 244 years, from 1619 to 1863. As of 2010, they have been free for 147 years.

10 **"The story of":** Neil R. McMillen, "The Migration and Black Protest in Jim Crow Mississippi," in *Black Exodus: The Great Migration from the American South,* ed. Alferdteen Harrison (Jackson: University Press of Mississippi, 1991), p. 81.

10 **By then nearly half:** U.S. Bureau of the Census, *Historical Statistics of the United States, Colonial Times to 1970, Part 1* (Washington, D.C.: U.S. Government Printing Office, 1975), table A, pp. 177–194; 1970 State Form 2 IPUS sample. From James N. Gregory, *The Southern Diaspora: How the Great Migrations of Black and White Southerners Transformed America* (Chapel Hill: University of North Carolina Press, 2005). See also Reynolds Farley and Walter Allen, *The Color Line and the Quality of Life in America* (Washington, D.C.: Russell Sage Foundation, 1987), pp. 112–13. Cited by Dernoral Davis in "Portrait of Twentieth-Century African-Americans," in *Black Exodus,* ed. Harrison, p. 12. See also John D. Reid, "Black Urbanization of the South," *Python* 35, no. 3 (1974), p. 259, for reference to the South's being 53 percent black in 1970, the end of the Migration.

10 **"Oftentimes, just to go":** John Dollard, *Caste and Class in a Southern Town* (New Haven, Conn.: Yale University Press, 1937), p. 302.

11 **In Chicago alone:** U.S. Census Bureau, Census 2000 Redistricting Data (Public Law 94-171) Summary File, Table PL1. In 2000, the black population was 1,084,221 in the city of Chicago and 1,033,809 in the state of Mississippi.

11 **"folk movement":** McMillen, "The Migration and Black Protest in Jim Crow Mississippi," p. 81.

11 **Farragut:** Union naval officer David G. Farragut, who rose to admiral, led the capture of the South's largest city during the Battle of New Orleans in April 1862.

12 **ten thousand:** Allan H. Spear, *Black Chicago: The Making of a Negro Ghetto, 1890–1920* (Chicago: University of Chicago Press, 1967), p. 209.

12 **"I went to the station":** Scott, *Negro Migration During the War,* p. 41.

12 **into the words of:** Lawrence R. Rodgers, *Canaan Bound: The African-American Great Migration Novel* (Urbana: University of Illinois Press, 1997), pp. x, xiii. The author notes that, among scholars, "the Great Migration, for many years, remained primarily an academic sideshow displaying only limited signs of penetrating the realm of national popular discourse and culture." However, in the arts, the Great Migration and the resulting issues of "movement and identity have, over the entire history of published black literature, occupied the center of African American consciousness." On p. 3, he adds, "As one of the most widely shared experiences of black America, migration, whether through force or volition, has remained a central subject of black literature and folklore." Blyden Jackson, professor of literature emeritus at the University of North Carolina at Chapel Hill, wrote that "no event, large or small, . . . has had an impact equal in mass or gavity upon the consciousness of black writers." Blyden Jackson, "Introduction," in *Black Exodus,* p. xv.

13 **"Less has been written":** Gregory, *The Southern Diaspora,* p. 5.

13 **the language changes:** Writers navigating the language of intolerance often struggle with how to convey old attitudes and norms with the authenticity the work demands but with the grace and sensitivity required to reach current and future generations. On issues of race and ethnicity, the debate often centers on how best to describe black Americans when the names for the group change with the political fashions of the times and with the origins and intentions of the speaker regarding whatever term is at issue. Based on my many interviews with people from the era, the term "colored" was the most common word they used among themselves. This is not to say that prominent blacks of the day did not use the term "Negro," many arguing that its capitalization bestowed greater status on a group hungry for recognition. But ordinary blacks seemed to wince at how the word could be so easily corrupted by the ruling class, coming out "nigra" instead of the more formal-sounding "Negro," and thus they tended to use the term somewhat derisively in everyday conversation. As for the N-word itself, I have chosen to use it only where required for context, which turned out to be rarer than might be assumed. I chose to use great care out of an acknowledgment of the violence and loss of life that often accompanied its utterance. On the whole, I found that people who had most felt the sting of the word and the violence that undergirded it were less likely to use the word in casual speech than people who had never had to step off a sidewalk because of the color of their skin.

14 **"Compared with northern-born":** Stewart E. Tolnay, "The African American 'Great Migration' and Beyond," *Annual Review of Sociology* 29 (2003): 219.

PART II: BEGINNINGS

17 **This was the culture:** Richard Wright, *Black Boy* (New York: HarperCollins, 1993), p. 303.

IDA MAE BRANDON GLADNEY

19 **From the open door:** Unless otherwise indicated, all references to Ida Mae Gladney are based on continual interviews and conversations with her from May 1996 to August 2004.

31 **Calhoun City, Mississippi:** Interview with Jarvis Enoch, Ida Mae's nephew and a professor at Tennessee State University, in September 1998 in Nashville, about his experiences growing up in Calhoun City, Mississippi, in the 1940s and 1950s.

33 **"hardware of reality":** Carrie Mae Weems, *Constructing History: A Requiem to Mark the Moment,* a film directed and narrated by Weems (Atlanta: Savannah College of Art and Design with the National Black Arts Festival, 2008).

THE STIRRINGS OF DISCONTENT

36 **Everybody seems to be:** *Macon Telegraph,* Editorial, September 15, 1916, p. 4.

36 **One of the earliest:** "Race Labor Leaving," *Chicago Defender,* February 5, 1916, p. 1. Though this is what scholars have cited as the earliest known reference to a group of colored people leaving the South during World War I, it can logically be assumed that other parties left before them in the early stages of the war without telling any-

one of their intentions. The full headline was "Race Labor Leaving. Much Concern over Possible Shortage of Labor—Exodus Steady—Treatment Doesn't Warrant Staying." The paragraph read: "Selma, Ala., Feb. 4—The white people of the extreme South are becoming alarmed over the steady moving of race families out of the mineral belt. Hundreds of families have left during the past few months and the stream is continuing. Every effort is being made to have them stay, but the discrimination and the race prejudice continues as strong as ever. Not many years ago there was a dearth of labor in this part of the country and the steerage passengers from Europe were sought. They cannot do the work of the race men, as they do not understand. Local editorials in white papers are pleading with the business men to hold the race men if possible."

37 **"treatment doesn't warrant staying":** Ibid.

37 **the long and violent hangover:** Some historians have termed the period between Reconstruction and the early twentieth century the Nadir. See Rayford Logan, *The Negro in American Life and Thought, The Nadir: 1887–1901* (New York: Dial Press, 1954).

37 **"I find a worse state":** Robert Preston Brooks, *The Agrarian Revolution in Georgia, 1865–1912,* doctoral dissertation (Madison: University of Wisconsin, 1914; reprinted New York: AMS Press, 1971), pp. 413–14.

37 **"They will almost":** "Laborers Wanted," *Southern Cultivator,* March 1867, a letter from a writer identified by the initials G.A.N. of Warrenton, Georgia, dated February 2, 1867, APS Online, p. 69.

38 **The fight over:** Harvey Fireside, *Separate and Unequal: Homer Plessy and the Supreme Court Decision That Legalized Racism* (New York: Carroll & Graf, 2004).

38 **Fourteenth Amendment:** The Fourteenth Amendment to the Constitution, of 1868, enacted to establish the rights of freed slaves after the Civil War, reads as follows: "All persons born or naturalized in the United States, and subject to the jurisdiction thereof, are citizens of the United States and of the State wherein they reside. No State shall make or enforce any law which shall abridge the privileges or immunities of citizens of the United States; nor shall any State deprive any person of life, liberty, or property, without due process of law; nor deny to any person within its jurisdiction the equal protection of the laws."

38 **Fifteenth Amendment:** The Fifteenth Amendment to the Constitution, of 1880, granting freed slaves the right to vote, reads: "The right of citizens of the United States to vote shall not be denied or abridged by the United States or by any State on account of race, color, or previous condition of servitude."

39 **"If it is necessary":** Ray Stannard Baker, *Following the Color Line* (New York: Doubleday and Page, 1908), p. 245 for Hoke Smith quotation, p. 246 for Vardaman remark on lynching.

39 **"The only effect":** *Jackson* (Mississippi) *Weekly Clarion-Ledger,* July 30, 1903, quoted in *The Oratory of Southern Demagogues,* ed. Calvin McLeod Logue and Howard Dorgan (Baton Rouge: Louisiana State University Press, 1981), p. 73.

39 **Fifteen thousand:** "Summary Punishment Administered by Mob," *Hobart* (Oklahoma) *Republican,* May 16, 1916, p. 1.

39 **"My son can't learn":** "Waco Horror Stirs to Action," *Savannah Tribune,* July 8, 1916, page 4. "Supreme Penalty for Murder Paid by Negro Ghoul," *Monroe News-Star,* March 5, 1935, p. 1—an example of newspaper headlines of the Migration era in the town where Pershing Foster grew up.

39 **someone was hanged:** Arthur F. Raper, *The Tragedy of Lynching* (Chapel Hill: University of North Carolina Press, 1933), p. 36.

39 **"insult to a white person":** Ibid.

39 **stealing seventy-five cents:** Baker, *Following the Color Line,* p. 176.

39 **"perhaps most":** Herbert Shapiro, *White Violence and Black Response: From Reconstruction to Montgomery* (Amherst: University of Massachusetts Press, 1988), p. 32.

40 **Soon Klansmen:** *Documented History of the Incident Which Occurred at Rosewood, Florida, in January 1923,* an investigation submitted to the Florida Board of Regents, December 22, 1993, p. 2. This seventy-nine-page report, commissioned by the State of Florida and conducted by a team of historians from the University of Florida, the State University of Florida, and Florida A&M University, provides a detailed account of the mob attack on the colored town of Rosewood and of the political and racial climate leading to the massacre, including the rebirth and rise to prominence of the Klan.

40 **"was much less":** Wilbur J. Cash, *The Mind of the South* (Garden City, N.Y.: Doubleday, 1941), pp. 124–25.

40 **White citizens, caught up:** The years and locations of the major riots of this era were: Wilmington, North Carolina (1898); Atlanta (1906); Springfield, Illinois (1908); East St. Louis, Illinois (1917); and Charleston; Nashville; Omaha; Elaine, Arkansas; Longview, Texas; Chicago; and Washington, D.C., among other places, in 1919, the year following the end of World War I.

40 **"I hope and trust":** Frederick Douglass, "The Lessons of the Hour," an address to the Metropolitan A.M.E. Church, Washington, D.C., delivered January 9, 1894 (Baltimore: Press of Thomas & Evans, 1894), p. 23.

40 **It was during that time:** See Gilbert Thomas Stephenson, "The Separation of the Races in Public Conveyances," *The American Political Science Review* 3, no. 2 (May 1909): 181 on the origins of the term "Jim Crow" and the first Jim Crow laws in Massachusetts, 1841. See also Ronald L. F. Davis, "Creating Jim Crow," http://www.jimcrowhistory.org/history/creating2.htm, as well as David Hinckley, "Natural Rhythm: Daddy Rice and the Original Jim Crow," New York *Daily News,* May 27, 2004. Mississippi, in 1865, required separate seating for all colored people except those "traveling with their mistresses, in the capacity of nurses." Florida, in 1865, made no such allowances and punished people of either race with standing in a "pillory for one hour" or a whipping "not exceeding thirty nine stripes." Texas, in 1866, simply required every railroad company to "attach to each passenger train run by said company one car for the special accommodation of Freedmen."

41 **Streetcars:** C. Vann Woodward, *The Strange Career of Jim Crow* (New York: Oxford University Press, 1966), pp. 97–102.

41 **"The measure of":** Howard Thurman, *The Luminous Darkness: A Personal Interpretation of the Anatomy of Segregation and a Ground of Hope* (New York: Harper and

Row, 1965), pp. 70–71. Thurman, a prominent theologian in the mid–twentieth century and a migrant himself, was born in Daytona Beach, Florida, in 1899. He was the dean of Rankin Chapel at Howard University and later the dean of Marsh Chapel at Boston University, where he became a mentor of Martin Luther King, Jr., while King was a seminary student at the university.

42 **"his fate":** David L. Cohn, *God Shakes Creation* (New York: Harper and Brothers, 1935), p. 156.

42 **"a premature":** Philip S. Foner, ed., *The Life and Writings of Frederick Douglass,* vol. 4, specifically from "The Negro Exodus from the Gulf States, an Address Before Convention of the American Social Science Association, Saratoga Springs, New York, September 12, 1879" (New York: International Publishers, 1955), p. 336.

42 **"The Negroes just quietly":** U.S. Department of Labor, Division of Negro Economics, *Negro Migration in 1916–17* (Washington, D.C.: U.S. Government Printing Office, 1919), p. 95.

43 **"You tell us":** Ibid., p. 31.

43 **"stabbed the next day":** Ibid., p. 95.

43 **"The sentiment":** *Proceedings of the Constitutional Convention of Alabama,* 1901, 4, p. 4441.

43 **"It is too much":** U.S. Department of Labor, *Negro Migration in 1916–17,* p. 13.

44 ***These were the facts:*** See Baker, *Following the Color Line,* pp. 29–36, for description of segregated elevators, waiting rooms, libraries, parks, and saloons and streetcar protocols. See Bertram Wilbur Doyle, *The Etiquette of Race Relations in the South: A Study in Social Control* (Port Washington, N.Y.: Kennikat Press, 1937), p. 147 (rules on amusement parks, theaters, and playhouses); p. 148 (rules on boarding and exiting streetcars); pp. 149–150 (rules on waiting rooms at depots and the protocol of colored people being served at ticket windows); p. 151 (different hours at colored and white schools, segregated ambulances); p. 152 (segregated hearses and cemeteries). See William H. Chafe, Raymond Gavins, and Robert Korstad, eds., *Remembering Jim Crow* (New York: New Press, 2001), p. 110, on separate windows for car license plates in Indianola, Mississippi.

44 **In 1958, a new:** Cal Brumley, "Segregation Costs: Dixie Firms Find Them More a Burden as Racial Tension Grows," *The Wall Street Journal,* December 17, 1957, p. 1.

44 **separate tellers:** See *Chicago Defender,* March 21, 1931, p. 3, on separate teller for colored people at an Atlanta bank.

44 **Colored people had:** Stetson Kennedy, *Jim Crow Guide to the U.S.A.* (Westport, Conn.: Greenwood Press, 1959), p. 227.

44 **the conventional rules:** Charles S. Johnson, *Patterns of Negro Segregation* (New York: Harper and Brothers, 1943), pp. 124–26. Johnson devoted an entire section to racial etiquette on the highway. "When driving their own cars," he wrote, "they were expected to maintain their role as Negros and in all cases to give whites the right-of-way." He later added, "If there is any doubt about whose turn it is to make a move in traffic, the turn is assumed to be the white person's."

44 **If he reached:** Hortense Powdermaker, *After Freedom: A Cultural Study of the Deep*

South (New York: Viking Press, 1939), p. 49. See also Kennedy, *Jim Crow Guide to the U.S.A.,* pp. 221–23.

45 **In everyday interactions:** Hugh Stephen Whitaker, "A Case Study in Southern Justice: The Emmett Till Case," unpublished dissertation for the Graduate School of Florida State University, August 1963. See p. 11 for description of taboos between blacks and whites in the South through the 1960s.

45 **The consequences:** James C. Cobb, *The Most Southern Place on Earth: The Mississippi Delta and the Roots of Regional Identity* (New York: Oxford University Press, 1992), p. 213.

45 **It was against the law:** Woodward, *The Strange Career of Jim Crow,* pp. 117–18, on Arkansas law on segregated racetrack betting and Birmingham ban on integrated playing of checkers.

45 **At saloons in Atlanta:** Baker, *Following the Color Line,* p. 36.

45 **There were white parking spaces:** "Confusion with Jim Crow Bible," *The Raleigh Evening Times,* March 29, 1906, p. 1. The story describes an incident during the trial of a black schoolteacher accused of disposing of a mule on which there was a mortgage. A defense witness, who was colored but looked white, took the stand and was being sworn in when the judge told the sheriff the man had been given the wrong Bible. "That one over this is the one for the use of the white people," Judge Amistead Jones said. "Not that I am a stickler about such matters, but if there are to be different Bibles kept for the races, then you must not get them mixed that way. Have a different place for them, and keep them there. Then such mistakes as this will not be made." Also practiced in Atlanta, and thus likely elsewhere in the South, as described by Baker in *Following the Color Line,* p. 36.

George Swanson Starling

47 **His world is the basement:** Unless otherwise indicated, all references to George Starling are based on numerous interviews and conversations with him from June 1995 to June 1998.

50 **"the caste barrier":** John Dollard, *Caste and Class in a Southern Town* (New Haven, Conn.: Yale University Press, 1937), p. 65.

50 **"The question of":** J. W. Johnson, *Along This Way* (New York: Viking Press, 1933), p. 56.

53 **In some parts:** Nell Irvin Painter, *Exodusters: Black Migration to Kansas after Reconstruction* (New York: Knopf, 1977), p. 83; original citation: Henry Adams, *Senate Report 693,* 2, p. 104.

54 **only a quarter:** Hortense Powdermaker, *After Freedom: A Cultural History of the Deep South* (New York: Viking Press, 1939), p. 86.

54 **"The Negro farm hand":** "The Negro Exodus," *Montgomery Advertiser,* a letter from J. Q. Johnson, pastor of St. Paul A.M.E. Church in Columbia, Tennessee, April 27, 1917, p. 4.

54 **"One reason for preferring":** Powdermaker, *After Freedom,* p. 86.

58 **"in a hurrying time":** Theodore Dwight Weld, *American Slavery as It Is: Testimony of a Thousand Witnesses* (New York: The American Anti-Slavery Society, 1839), p. 38.

58 **Florida went farther:** See Julia Floyd Smith, *Slavery and Plantation Growth in Ante-bellum Florida, 1821–1860* (Gainesville: University Press of Florida, 1973), p. 102, on punishment for slaves; p. 121 on law requiring free blacks to register or face arbitrary reenslavement.

59 **Florida, in the early winter:** The southern states did not all secede at the same time. There were two waves of secession following the November 1860 election of Abraham Lincoln and a Republican majority in Congress, portending abolition of a state's right to, among other things, maintain or expand slavery. The first wave of secession included seven slave states, beginning with South Carolina on December 20, 1860, followed by Mississippi on January 9, 1861; Florida on January 10, 1861; Alabama on January 11, 1861; Georgia on January 19, 1861; Louisiana on January 26, 1861; and Texas on February 1, 1861. The second wave of secession came after the outbreak of war at Fort Sumter, South Carolina, in April 1861. In the second wave were the marginally more moderate, previously fence-sitting slave states of Virginia, April 17, 1861; Arkansas, May 6, 1861; Tennessee, May 7, 1861; and North Carolina, May 20, 1861. The Confederacy also claimed portions of modern-day Oklahoma, New Mexico, and Arizona, as well as the support of Missouri and Kentucky, slave-holding border states that did not formally secede.

59 **"the great truth":** "The Southern Confederacy. Slavery the Basis of the New Government, An Official Manifesto. Speech of Vice-President Stephens," *The Philadelphia Inquirer,* March 28, 1861, p. 1. Stephens delivered this extemporaneous speech in Savannah, Georgia, on March 21, 1861, after the first Confederate states had seceded from the Union and drafted the Confederate Constitution. That document was largely based on the U.S. Constitution, setting forth three branches of government with duties nearly identical to those in the Union. The Confederate Constitution states in Part 4, Section 9: "No bill of attainder, ex-post facto law, or law denying or impairing the right of property in negro slaves shall be passed." The constitution was adopted by what was known as the Congress of the Confederate States (at the time, South Carolina, Mississippi, Florida, Alabama, Georgia, Louisiana, and Texas) at a joint meeting in Montgomery, Alabama, on March 11, 1861, precisely one week after Lincoln took the oath of office on March 4, 1861.

59 **"if any negro":** Gilbert Thomas Stephenson, "The Separation of the Races in Public Conveyances," *The American Political Science Review* 3, no. 2 (1909): 181.

59 **"anything that was black":** *Documented History of the Incident Which Occurred at Rosewood, Florida, in January 1923* (submitted to the Florida Board of Regents, December 22, 1993), p. 19.

59 **single worst act:** James R. McGovern, *Anatomy of a Lynching: The Killing of Claude Neal* (Baton Rouge: Louisiana State University Press, 1982), pp. 52–66.

60 **It was the early morning:** "Group Kills Negro; Disappoints Crowd," Associated Press, October 28, 1934; appeared in *The New York Times,* October 28, 1934.

60 **The crowd grew so large:** See *The Lynching of Claude Neal* (New York: National Association for the Advancement of Colored People, 1934), p. 2, for an account of the lynching. Also McGovern, *Anatomy of a Lynching,* pp. 79–90, for details of mob behavior, the lynching, and the rioting by whites after Neal's death.

61 **Soon afterward:** "Lynch Victim's Innocence Apparent as Father of Girl Is Sentenced," *Pittsburgh Courier,* June 15, 1935, p. A4. The Neal lynching cast a lingering cloud over race relations in Jackson County, Florida, decades after the killing. James R. McGovern, a historian examining the case in the early 1980s, found people who had clear memories of the lynching and its aftermath but were reluctant to speak about it out of fear of reprisal. This was especially true of black residents, one of whom, in finally relenting to give an interview, said, "Well, if I am going down, it will be for a good cause." McGovern, *Anatomy of a Lynching,* p. xi.

62 **"never had a negro":** Ben Green, *Before His Time: The Untold Story of Harry T. Moore, America's First Civil Rights Martyr* (New York: Free Press, 1999), p. 244.

62 **"he might be accused":** McGovern, *Anatomy of a Lynching,* p. 6.

ROBERT JOSEPH PERSHING FOSTER

72 **The paneled door:** Unless otherwise indicated, all references to Robert Pershing Foster are based on numerous interviews and visits with him from April 1996 to July 1997.

77 **1,139 pupils:** See "Louisiana States," *Chicago Defender,* October 10, 1931, p. 19, regarding the number of students at Monroe Colored High.

80 **the church broke into an uproar:** "Two Murdered in Baptist Church Riot: Four Others Wounded During Free for All Fight," *Chicago Defender,* September 17, 1932, p. 1.

80 **"the doors of the church":** "Eight Wounded, One Killed in Church Fight," *Atlanta Daily World,* September 8, 1932, p. 2.

85 **In Louisiana in the 1930s:** D. T. Blose and H. F. Alves, *Biennial Survey of Education in the U.S., Statistics of State School Systems, 1937–38,* U.S. Office of Education Bulletin, 1940, no. 2, p. 137. Cited in Charles S. Johnson, *Patterns of Negro Segregation* (New York: Harper and Brothers, 1943), p. 16.

85 **The disparity in pay:** Thomas M. Shapiro, *The Hidden Cost of Being African-American: How Wealth Perpetuates Inequality* (New York: Oxford University Press, 2004), p. 47.

85 **lopsided division of resources:** W. D. Weatherford and Charles S. Johnson, *Race Relations: Adjustment of Whites and Negroes in the United States* (Boston: D. C. Heath, 1934), pp. 358–59, on disparity of investment in white schools and colored schools in the South.

86 **"The money allocated":** Robert A. Margo, *Race and Schooling in the South, 1880–1950: An Economic History* (Chicago: University of Chicago Press, 1990), p. 44, citing Carleton Washburne, *Louisiana Looks at Its Schools* (Baton Rouge: Louisiana Educational Survey Commission, 1942), p. 111.

86 **"If these Negroes become":** see Ray Stannard Baker, *Following the Color Line* (New York: Doubleday, Page, 1908), p. 295, for quote lamenting the effect of education for black southerners.

88 **Sherman, Texas:** Arthur F. Raper, *The Tragedy of Lynching* (Chapel Hill: University of North Carolina Press, 1933; reprinted Mineola, New York: Dover Publications, 2003), pp. 319–55.

89 **And I'd whisper:** Mahalia Jackson with Evan McLeod Wylie, *Movin' On Up* (New York: Hawthorne Books, 1966), p. 36.

90 **Gilbert and Percy Elie:** Interview with Gilbert Elie, who migrated from Grenada, Mississippi, to Akron, Ohio. Conducted in Grenada, Mississippi, May 29, 1996.

92 **Hundreds of miles away:** Interview with Virginia Hall, a migrant from North Carolina, in Brooklyn, New York, February 22, 1998.

A BURDENSOME LABOR

97 **"one of the most backbreaking":** Donald Holley, *The Second Great Emancipation: The Mechanical Cotton Picker, Black Migration and How They Shaped the Modern South* (Fayetteville: University of Arkansas Press, 2000), p. xii.

97 **It took some seventy:** See ibid., p. 9, for a description of the basic mechanics of picking and the number of bolls per pound of seed cotton.

98 **"begin to dream":** Rupert B. Vance, *Human Factors in Cotton Culture* (Chapel Hill: University of North Carolina Press, 1929), p. 135, quoting the author Henry K. Webster from "Slaves of Cotton," *American Magazine,* July 1906, p. 19.

98 *"The first horn":* Ulrich B. Phillips, in Vance, *Human Factors in Cotton Culture,* p. 47.

99 **Sometime in the 1930s:** Interviews with Lasalle Frelix, a migrant from Brookhaven, Mississippi, in Chicago, 1996.

102 **A bale of cotton:** William C. Holley and Lloyd E. Arnold, *Changes in Technology and Labor Requirements in Crop Production: Cotton,* National Research Project Report no. A-7 (Philadelphia: Works Progress Administration, September 1937), pp. 19–54. Also Ronald E. Seavoy, *The American Peasantry: Southern Agricultural Labor and Its Legacy: A Study in Political Economy, 1850–1995* (Westport, Conn.: Greenwood Press, 1998), pp. 37–47, cited in Holley, *The Second Great Emancipation,* p. 56.

109 **The other brother:** Interviews with Reuben Blye in Eustis, Florida, July 1997 and July 1998.

113 **In North Carolina:** Gilbert Thomas Stephenson, "The Separation of the Races in Public Conveyances," *The American Political Science Review* 3, no. 2 (May 1909): 200–201.

120 **standing in the way:** David Levering Lewis, *W. E. B. Du Bois: The Fight for Equality and the American Century, 1919–1963* (New York: Henry Holt, 2000), pp. 491–92.

120 **"The result of this action":** Ibid., p. 495; Arnold Rampersad, *The Art and Imagination of W. E. B. Du Bois* (Cambridge: Harvard University Press, 1976), p. 22; W. E. B. Du Bois, *The Autobiography of W. E. B. Du Bois: A Soliloquy on Viewing My Life from the Last Decade of Its First Century* (New York: International Publishers, 1968), p. 323.

120 **"There was no earthly":** Lewis, *W. E. B. Du Bois,* pp. 493–95.

121 **His northern friends thought:** Ibid., p. 495, citing Shirley Graham Du Bois, *His Day Is Marching On: A Memoir of W. E. B. Du Bois* (Philadelphia: J. B. Lippincott, 1971), p. 71.

123 **In the winter of 1919:** Richard Panek, "The Loneliness of the Long-Distance Cosmologist," *The New York Times,* July 25, 1999, available at www.nytimes.com.

123 **It would confirm:** Alexander S. Sharov and Igor D. Novikov, *Edwin Hubble, the*

Discoverer of the Big Bang Universe, trans. Vitaly Kisin (Cambridge, England: Cambridge University Press, 1993), pp. 9, 10, 29–35.

THE AWAKENING

124 **You sleep over a volcano:** Glenda Elizabeth Gilmore, *Gender and Jim Crow: Women and the Politics of White Supremacy in North Carolina, 1896–1920* (Chapel Hill: University of North Carolina Press, 1996), pp. 132–33. Gilmore recounts a debate on a summer night in 1901 in Charlotte, North Carolina, between two well-educated young women, Addie Sagers and Laura Arnold, on the topic "Is the South the Best Home for the Negro?" Sagers argued against going north, where, she said, the only jobs open to blacks were "bell boy, waiter, cook or house maid," and where northern unions excluded blacks from their ranks. Arnold, her debate opponent, railed against the violence, segregation, and disenfranchisement of blacks in the South. She agreed that "the unknown was frightening," but added, "if the Puritans could cross the oceans in small boats, surely North Carolina's African-Americans could board northbound trains." Gilmore notes that Arnold's "received more points than any other speech that night." Two weeks later, Arnold "took her own advice and moved to Washington, D.C."

124 **I am in the darkness:** Emmett J. Scott, "Additional Letters of Negro Migrants, 1916–1918," *The Journal of Negro History* 4, no. 4 (October 1919): 412–45, quote on p. 440. This letter, dated May 13, 1917, was one of several hundred letters from anxious black southerners, written primarily to the *Chicago Defender* and collected and published by Emmett Scott in two series of articles at the end of World War I.

130 **a fight broke out:** Alfred McClung Lee and Norman D. Humphrey, *Race Riot* (New York: Dryden Press, 1943), p. 26.

131 **The Detroit riots:** Ibid., p. 28.

135 **A colored teacher:** William H. Chafe, Raymond Gavins, and Robert Korstad, eds., *Remembering Jim Crow: African Americans Tell About Life in the Segregated South* (New York: New Press, in association with Lyndhurst Books of the Center for Documentary Studies of Duke University), p. 201.

140 **Enlisting widespread interest:** "Alice Clarissa Clement to Wed Robert Foster: She Is a Spelman 1941 Graduate," *Chicago Defender,* June 21, 1941, p. 18.

140 **The *Atlanta Daily World*:** "Miss Clement Is Wed to Robert P. Foster Tuesday," *Atlanta Daily World,* December 25, 1941, p. 3.

143 **"because they were taking":** Baker, *Following the Color Line*, p. 250.

145 **In the spring of 1919:** "Army Uniform Cost Soldier His Life," *Chicago Defender,* April 5, 1919, p. 1.

147 **Pitocin:** The use of pitocin, a synthetic form of the hormone oxytocin, has grown more controversial in the decades since the Korean War, as more women seek natural childbirth with as few artificial inducements as possible. The emphasis on natural childbirth was not the prevailing view during the time of Pershing Foster's army service and was in fact considered the slower, more natural, and perhaps more progressive alternative to the cesareans preferred and commonly performed by many doctors of the era.

150 **fifty million dollars a year:** *Citrus Growing in Florida,* Bulletin no. 2, New Series, State of Florida, Department of Agriculture, October 1941, p. 5.

152 **It was an illegal form:** Terrell H. Shofner, "The Legacy of Racial Slavery: Free Enterprise and Forced Labor in Florida in the 1940s," *The Journal of Southern History* 47, no. 3 (August 1981): 414–16. The case against the Sugar Plantation Company in the Everglades was ultimately unsuccessful in the southern court system, which was sympathetic to the planters and hostile to the federal government, and may have in fact emboldened some planters to continue forcing colored people to work against their will. But it offered evidence and made public the extent of the alleged abuses. The company managed to evade prosecution when a Florida judge quashed the indictment.

152 **Willis Virgil McCall:** John Hill, "A Southern Sheriff's Law and Disorder," *The St. Petersburg Times,* November 28, 1999. See also Greg Lamm, "Willis V. McCall: Blood, Hatred, Fear: The Reign of a Traditional Southern Sheriff," *Leesburg* (Fla.) *Commercial,* May 20, 1987, p. A1.

153 **In February:** Shofner, "The Legacy of Racial Slavery," pp. 421–422.

153 **McCall struck:** "Terrorism Being Used to Frustrate Justice," *The Atlanta Daily World,* June 30, 1945, p. 1.

153 **"leaving all their possessions":** "Harlem Pair Tells of McCall's Acts," *New York Amsterdam News,* November 24, 1951, p. 1.

154 **"returns to the grower":** "Lake County Growers Shown Management Theories in Grove Tour," *The Sunday Orlando Sentinel Star,* December 21, 1941, p. 22.

154 **four dollars and forty cents:** Ibid., pp. 30–36.

154 **2.6 million citrus trees:** "Citrus Shipments Up 15% over Last Week; Tangerines in Van," *The Sunday Orlando Sentinel Star,* November 30, 1941, p. 10. See also "Growing Conditions," *The Sunday Orlando Sentinel Star,* December 28, 1941, p. 19. For ranking of citrus industry by county, see *Fruit and Vegetable Crops of Florida: A Compendium of Information on the Fruits and Vegetables Grown in Florida* (Tallahassee: Florida State Department of Agriculture, August 15, 1945).

157 **"the killing of a Negro":** Wilbur J. Cash, *The Mind of the South* (Garden City, N.Y.: Doubleday, 1941), p. 129.

161 **Later, in 1879:** Nell Irvin Painter, *Exodusters: Black Migration to Kansas After Reconstruction* (New York: Knopf, 1977), pp. 109–10, 184–85.

161 **Immigration plunged:** Florette Henri, *Black Migration: Movement North, 1900–1920* (Garden City, N.Y.:Anchor Press/Doubleday, 1975), p. 52. Original data on immigration of 1,218,480 in 1914 plunging to 110,618 in 1918 from the U.S. Census.

161 **So the North:** David L. Cohn, *God Shakes Creation* (New York: Harper and Brothers, 1935), p. 335.

161 **The recruiters would stride:** James R. Grossman, *Land of Hope* (Chicago: University of Chicago Press, 1989), p. 70.

162 **"As the North":** "Why the Negroes Go North," *Literary Digest* 77, no. 7 (May 19, 1923): 14, quoting *The Times-Picayune* (New Orleans). Appears in Grossman, *Land of Hope,* p. 43.

162 **"Where shall we get":** *Montgomery Advertiser,* quoted in "Negro Moving

North," *Literary Digest* 53, no. 15 (October 7, 1916): 877; from Grossman, *Land of Hope,* p. 40.

162 **"Black labor":** *Columbia State,* quoted in Emmett J. Scott, *Negro Migration During the War* (New York: Oxford University Press, 1920), p. 156, and Grossman, *Land of Hope,* p. 40.

162 **"It is the life":** *Report of the Industrial Commission on Agriculture and Agricultural Labor,* vol. 10 (Washington, D.C.: U.S. Government Printing Office, 1901), pp. 382–83, 518; cited in Gilbert Osofsky, *Harlem: The Making of a Ghetto* (New York: Harper and Row, 1963), p. 27.

162 **"With all our crimes":** Cohn, *God Shakes Creation,* p. 205.

162 **"We must have":** *The Macon Telegraph,* September 15, 1916, p. 4.

162 **"Why hunt for the cause":** *Montgomery Advertiser,* a letter in response to "Exodus of the Negroes to Be Probed," September 1916.

162 **"If you thought":** George Brown Tindall, *Emergence of the New South, 1913–1945* (Baton Rouge: Louisiana State University Press, 1967), p. 149; cited in Henri, *Black Migration,* p. 75.

162 **"Conditions recently":** U.S. Department of Labor, Division of Negro Economics, *Negro Migration in 1916–1917* (Washington, D.C.: U.S. Government Printing Office, 1919), p. 63.

163 **Macon, Georgia, required:** St. Clair Drake and Horace R. Cayton, *Black Metropolis: A Study of Negro Life in a Northern City* (Chicago: University of Chicago Press, 1945), p. 59.

163 **"Every Negro":** U.S. Department of Labor, *Negro Migration in 1916–1917,* p. 12.

163 **The chief of police:** Grossman, *Land of Hope,* p. 44.

163 **In Brookhaven, Mississippi:** Scott, *Negro Migration During the War,* p. 77.

163 **In Albany, Georgia:** U.S. Department of Labor, *Negro Migration in 1916–17,* p. 110.

163 **In Summit, Mississippi:** Grossman, *Land of Hope,* p. 48, from Junius B. Wood, *The Negro in Chicago* (Chicago: Chicago Daily News, 1916), p. 9; Scott, *Negro Migration,* p. 73; *Chicago Defender,* August 26, 1916; Emmett J. Scott, "Additional Letters of Negro Migrants of 1916–1918," *Journal of Negro History,* October 1919, p. 451; William F. Holmes, "Labor Agents and the Georgia Exodus," *South Atlantic Quarterly* 79 (1980), pp. 445–46, on dispersal of Georgia migrants at train station.

163 **"served to intensify":** Willis D. Weatherford and Charles S. Johnson, *Race Relations: Adjustment of Whites and Negroes in the United States* (Boston: D. C. Heath, 1934), p. 339.

163 **some migrants:** Scott, *Negro Migration During the War,* p. 77.

163 **one man disguising himself:** Interviews with Ruby Lee Welch Mays Smith, Chicago, January–October 1996.

163 **one delegation:** David L. Cohn, *Where I Was Born and Raised* (South Bend, Ind.: University of Notre Dame Press, 1967), pp. 340–45. Managers at King and Anderson plantation went to Chicago to convince sharecroppers to come back in the 1940s; cited in Nicholas Lemann, *The Promised Land* (New York: Knopf, 1991), pp. 47–48.

164 **In the 1920s:** Chicago Commission on Race Relations, *The Negro in Chicago: A Study*

of Race Relations and a Race Riot (Chicago: University of Chicago Press, 1922), p. 104.

164 **"Owing to the scarcity":** U.S. Department of Labor, *Negro Migration in 1916–17,* p. 96.

164 **Men hopped freight trains:** Grossman, *Land of Hope,* p. 40.

164 **"One section gang":** Arna Bontemps and Jack Conroy, *Anyplace but Here* (Columbia: University of Missouri Press, 1945), p. 164.

164 **the weeds grew up:** Grossman, *Land of Hope,* p. 40.

BREAKING AWAY

165 **I was leaving:** Richard Wright, *Black Boy* (New York: HarperCollins, 1993), p. 493.

167 **Of the few who got:** Hortense Powdermaker, *After Freedom: A Cultural Study of the Deep South* (New York: Viking Press, 1930), pp. 86–87.

167 **"How a man treats":** Ibid., p. 86.

168 **Like one planter:** Based on a letter sent to me by Ruth McClendon of Waukegan, Illinois. She heard me speaking about the Great Migration on WBEZ-FM, the public radio station in Chicago. The letter, dated August 17, 1995, was three pages, handwritten on yellow legal paper. In it, she shared the story of her grandparents leaving Alabama for Illinois during World War I.

172 **Pershing was working:** Ozeil Fryer Woolcock, "Social Swirl," *Atlanta Daily World,* March 8, 1953, p. 3, and March 15, 1953, p. 18. Both stories are useful in that they confirm the general timing of Robert Foster's departure. They note that he went to see his wife and daughters in Atlanta in early to mid-March before his migration trip to California. On Friday, March 13, 1953, the latter story notes, he was feted with "a small impromptu party by his wife, Alice Clement Foster, who invited a few former college mates in for an evening of dancing and chatting. The residence was most colorful with the St. Patrick motif, assisting Mrs. Foster was her mother, Mrs. Rufus E. Clement." The story said that Robert was to leave Atlanta that Tuesday, which would have been March 17. Robert would head back to Monroe one last time before his migration, as he would have to pass through Louisiana en route to California. There, he had at least two weeks to spend time with his own family and friends and to prepare for the long journey ahead. When he later recounted the time leading up to his departure, he went on at length about his final weeks in Monroe and the pre-Easter send-off given him by his close friends and family in his hometown, marking the beginning of his journey out of the South. He never mentioned the visit to Atlanta or the party given him by his in-laws, which suggests it did not figure into his definition of his migration journey or the moment of his emotional break from the South. It also reflected how he viewed the more formal, socially correct world of the Clements compared to the humbler circles of his origins, which seemed to have greater meaning to him.

177 **I pick up my life:** Langston Hughes, *One-Way Ticket* (New York: Knopf, 1949), p. 61.

178 **"Migratory currents flow":** E. G. Ravenstein, "The Laws of Migration," *Journal of the Royal Statistical Society,* no. 2 (June 1889): 284.

178 **"They are like":** Ibid., p. 280.

178 **Some participants:** Joe William Trotter, Jr., *Black Milwaukee: The Making of an Industrial Proletariat, 1915–1945* (Urbana: University of Illinois Press, 1985). Trotter recounts the especially convoluted migration of a man, identified as J.H., who was "born in Canton, Mississippi. At 16, he went to Memphis, Tennessee. From Memphis he went to Sapulpa, Oklahoma. From Sapulpa he went to the army and to France. After the war [World War I] he settled in Kansas City. From Kansas City [he migrated to] Chicago and then Milwaukee at the age of 40. He has lived in Milwaukee for six years." The account was originally published by the Milwaukee Urban League in its 1942–1943 Annual Report.

179 **"go no further":** Ravenstein, "Laws of Migration," p. 250.

179 **"The more enterprising":** Ibid., p. 279.

PART III: EXODUS

181 **There is no mistaking:** *The Cleveland Advocate,* April 28, 1917.

181 **We look up at:** Richard Wright, *12 Million Black Voices* (New York: Viking Press, 1941), p. 92.

THE APPOINTED TIME OF THEIR COMING

186 **A toddler named Huey Newton:** Dennis Hevesi, "Huey Newton Symbolized the Rising Black Anger of a Generation," *The New York Times,* August 23, 1989, p. 37.

186 **Another boy from Monroe:** Bill Russell, *Second Wind: The Memoirs of an Opinionated Man* (New York: Fireside, 1979), pp. 24–27.

190 **It carried so many:** Hollis R. Lynch, *The Black Urban Condition: A Documentary History, 1866–1971* (New York: Crowell, 1973), pp. 425–32. The black population of Chicago rose from 30,150 in 1900 to 44,103 in 1910, the last census before the Migration statistically began, and rose to 1,102,620 in 1970. In Detroit, the black population rose from 4,111 in 1900 to 5,741 in 1910 and 660,428 in 1970.

190 **the Illinois Central:** John F. Stover, *History of the Illinois Central Railroad* (New York: Macmillan, 1975), p. 15 on its founding, p. 89 on Lincoln's role.

200 **Later, it was the first stop:** Ray Stannard Baker, *Following the Color Line* (New York: Doubleday, Page, 1908), p. 113.

200 **"How a colored man":** Robert Russa Moton, *What the Negro Thinks* (Garden City, N.Y.: Doubleday, Doran, 1929), p. 82. See also Bertram Wilbur Doyle, *The Etiquette of Race Relations in the South: A Study in Social Control* (Port Washington, N.Y.: Kennikat Press, 1937), p. 156. Doyle was a professor of sociology at Fisk University.

201 **a family from Beaumont:** Interview with Pat Botshekan in Los Angeles, March 18, 1996.

CROSSING OVER

205 **Do you remember:** Charles H. Nichols, ed., *Arna Bontemps–Langston Hughes Letters, 1925–1967* (New York: Dodd, Mead, 1980), p. 24.

217 **In South Carolina:** Graham Russell Hodges, *Studies in African History and Culture* (New York: Garland, 2000), p. 155.

217 **Some of my people:** Chicago Commission on Race Relations, *The Negro in Chicago: A Study of Race Relations and a Race Riot* (Chicago: University of Chicago Press, 1922), pp. 97–98.

217 **The earliest departures:** Emmett J. Scott, *Negro Migration During the War* (New York: Oxford University Press, 1920), p. 13.

217 **Instead of the weakening stream:** E. G. Ravenstein, "The Laws of Migration," *Journal of the Royal Statistical Society* 52, no. 2 (1889), p. 278. "The most striking feature of the northern migration was its individualism," Emmett J. Scott wrote in 1920, as if the Migration were over.

218 **"A large error":** Florette Henri, *Black Migration: Movement North, 1900–1920* (Garden City, N.Y.: Anchor/Doubleday, 1975), p. 72.

218 **Robert Fields:** Interview with Robert Fields in Chicago, 1995.

219 **Eddie Earvin:** Interview with Eddie Earvin in Chicago, May 1995, after having been given his name at a reunion at DuSable High School.

PART IV: THE KINDER MISTRESS

223 **The lazy, laughing South:** Langston Hughes, "The South," *The Crisis,* June 1922.

CHICAGO

225 **Timidly, we get:** Richard Wright, *12 Million Black Voices* (New York: Viking Press, 1941), pp. 99–100.

NEW YORK

227 **A blue haze:** Arna Bontemps, "The Two Harlems," *American Scholar,* Spring 1945, p. 167.

LOS ANGELES

230 **Maybe we can start again:** John Steinbeck, *The Grapes of Wrath* (New York: Viking Press, 1939; updated edition New York: Penguin Books, 1997), p. 89.

232 **They went to court:** "Covenant Suit Arguments on August 22," *Los Angeles Sentinel,* July 31, 1947, p. 3, gives an overview of the case as it is about to go before the court.

233 **a small contingent:** Lawrence Brooks de Graaf, "Recognition, Racism and Reflections on the Writing of Western Black History," *Pacific Historical Review* 44, no. 1 (February 1975): 23.

233 **strongly discouraged:** Lawrence Brooks de Graaf, "Negro Migration to Los Angeles, 1930–1950," dissertation submitted to the University of California, Los Angeles, May 1962, p. 14.

233 **By 1900:** Ibid., p. 16.

233 **"Even the seeming":** Octavia B. Vivian, *The Story of the Negro in Los Angeles County* (Washington, D.C.: Federal Writers' Project, Works Progress Administration, 1936), p. 31.

234 **"In certain plants":** Ibid., p. 33.

THE THINGS THEY LEFT BEHIND

238 **There were no Chinaberry:** Clifton Taulbert, *The Last Train North* (Tulsa, Okla.: Council Oaks Books, 1992), pp. 43–44.

240 **had toiled:** It is not known precisely why there was a two-and-a-half-year delay in getting word to the slaves in Texas. One theory was that a messenger bearing the news of freedom was murdered on his way to Texas. Another was that slave masters deliberately withheld the news to keep their unpaid labor for as long as they could. Another was that there simply weren't enough Union troops in Texas to enforce the Proclamation, which was dated January 1, 1863. The announcement read by the Union troops in the form of General Order no. 3 was as follows: *"The people of Texas are informed that in accordance with a Proclamation from the Executive of the United States, all slaves are free. This involves an absolute equality of rights and rights of property between former masters and slaves, and the connection heretofore existing between them becomes that between employer and free laborer"* (available at www.juneteenth.com). Also see "An Obscure Texas Celebration Makes Its Way Across the U.S.," *The New York Times,* June 18, 2004.

241 **"If I were half":** Abraham Epstein, *The Negro Migrant in Pittsburgh* (New York: Arno Press, 1969 reissue of 1918 original), p. 27.

241 **Epstein found:** Ibid., p. 24.

TRANSPLANTED IN ALIEN SOIL

242 **Should I have come:** Richard Wright, *Black Boy* (New York: HarperCollins, 1993), pp. 306–7.

243 **A map:** Arna Bontemps and Jack Conroy, *Anyplace but Here* (Columbia: University of Missouri Press, 1945), p. 164.

243 **Beloit, Wisconsin:** Morton Rubin, "Migration Patterns from a Rural Northeastern Mississippi Community," *Social Forces* 39, no. 1, Oct. 1, 1960–May 1961, pp. 59–66. See also Paul Geib, "From Mississippi to Milwaukee: A Case Study of the Southern Black Migration to Milwaukee, 1940–1970, *The Journal of Negro History* 83, no. 4 (Autumn 1998): 229–48.

244 **Gary:** The Jackson Family of singers, including Michael and Janet, probably the most famous natives of Gary, Indiana, had roots in the South like most other black people born in Gary in the past century. The singing group's father, Joseph, was born in Fountain Hill, Arkansas, in 1929 and went to Chicago, just west of Gary, when he was eighteen. The group's mother, the former Katherine Scruse, was born in Barbour County, Alabama, and brought to East Chicago, Indiana, by her parents when she was four. Joseph and Katherine met in the Chicago area and married in November 1949. Their nine surviving children were born in Gary.

244 **But, as in the rest:** Joe William Trotter, Jr., *Black Milwaukee: The Making of an Industrial Proletariat, 1915–1945* (Chicago: University of Chicago Press, 1985), p. 42.

244 **"They are superior":** Ibid., p. 55.

245 **"only did the dirty work":** Ibid., p. 47.

245 **even those jobs:** Ibid., p. 152.

245 **"never did":** Ibid., p. 167.

247 **The first blacks in Harlem:** James Riker, *Revised History of Harlem (City of New York): Its Origin and Early Annals* (New York: New Harlem Publishing, 1904), p. 189; cited in Gilbert Osofsky, *Harlem: The Making of a Ghetto: Negro New York, 1890–1930* (New York: Harper and Row, 1963), p. 83.

248 **The trouble began:** Iver Bernstein, *The New York City Draft Riots: Their Significance for American Society and Politics in the Age of the Civil War* (New York: Oxford University Press, 1990); cited in Leslie M. Harris, *In the Shadow of Slavery: African Americans in New York City, 1826–1863* (Chicago: University of Chicago Press, 2003).

249 **By 1930:** Osofsky, *Harlem*, p. 130 on population, p. 139 on sleeping in shifts, p. 129 for Adam Clayton Powell quote.

249 **"a growing menace":** *Harlem Magazine,* February 1914, p. 21; cited in Osofsky, *Harlem,* p. 107.

249 **Panicked property owners:** Osofsky, *Harlem,* pp. 105–7.

249 **White leaders tried:** *The New York Age,* August 29 and November 14, 1912; January 9, 1913.

249 **White leaders warned:** Osofsky, *Harlem,* p. 108.

250 **"rent to colored":** Ibid., p. 110.

250 **NOTICE:** New York Urban League, "Twenty-four Hundred Negro Families in Harlem: An Interpretation of the Living Conditions of Small Wage Earners," typescript, Schomburg Collection, 1927, p. 7; cited in Osofsky, *Harlem,* p. 110.

251 **"The basic collapse":** Osofsky, *Harlem,* p. 109.

251 **"servants of the rich":** Jervis Anderson, *This Was Harlem, 1900–1950* (New York: Farrar, Straus and Giroux, Noonday Press, 1981), pp. 321–22.

252 **It had a marble:** Ibid., pp. 308–9.

253 **Golden State Mutual Life Insurance Company:** John N. Ingham and Lynne B. Feldman, *African-American Business Leaders: A Biographical Dictionary* (Westport, Conn.: Greenwood Press, 1994), pp. 58–65. William Nickerson, one of the founders of Golden State Mutual Life Insurance, left Houston, Texas, for Los Angeles in 1921 and attributed his migration to the fact that "things were happening in the state, one of which was the riot [Longview, Texas, in 1919 and perhaps Tulsa in 1921]. So becoming disgusted," he said, "I decided to take my wife and eight children and move to California." Four years later, he would become one of the founders of the largest black-owned insurance company in the state.

258 **"I didn't think":** Jim Pinson, "City School Board Seat Won by Negro," *The Atlanta Constitution,* May 15, 1953, p. 1.

258 **"For the first time":** "Negro Is Victor in Atlanta Vote; Defeats White School Board Member, 22,259 to 13,936—Mayor Renominated," *The New York Times,* May 15, 1953; "Atlanta Negro Is Elected to Board of Education," *New York Herald Tribune,* May 15, 1953, p. 1.

DIVISIONS

260 **I walked to the elevator:** Richard Wright, *Black Boy* (New York: HarperCollins, 1993), p. 303.

260 **"With few exceptions":** Sadie Tanner Mossell, "The Standard of Living Among One

Hundred Negro Migrant Families in Philadelphia," *Annals of the American Academy of Political and Social Science* 98 (November 1921): 216.

261 **"The inarticulate and resigned masses":** E. Franklin Frazier, *The Negro Family in Chicago, 1939* (Chicago: University of Chicago Press, 1932), pp. 80, 84.

261 **"a tangle of pathology":** Daniel Patrick Moynihan, *The Negro Family: The Case for National Action* (Washington, D.C.: Office of Policy Planning and Research, United States Department of Labor, 1965), p. 23.

261 **"the differential in payments":** Daniel Patrick Moynihan, "The Crisis in Welfare," *The Public Interest,* Winter 1968, pp. 3–29.

261 **"It is the higher":** Karl E. Taeuber and Alma F. Taeuber, "The Changing Character of Negro Migration," *The American Journal of Sociology* 70, no. 4 (January 1965): 429–41.

261 **"As the distance":** Everett S. Lee, "A Theory of Migration," *Demography* 3, no. 1 (1966): 57.

261 **"Migrants who overcome":** Ibid., pp. 55–56.

262 **"The move to northern":** J. Trent Alexander, "The Great Migration in Comparative Perspective: Interpreting the Urban Origins of Southern Black Migrants to Depression-Era Pittsburgh," *Social Science History,* Fall 1998, pp. 358–60. Alexander's analysis of census data found that, in 1940, only thirty-seven percent of black migrants to northern cities were from rural areas. Two-thirds were from towns with populations of 2,500 or more (p. 365).

262 **"Most Negro migrants":** Taeuber and Taeuber, "The Changing Character of Negro Migration," pp. 430–32.

262 **"averaged nearly two more years":** Stewart E. Tolnay, "Educational Selection in the Migration of Southern Blacks, 1880–1990," *Social Forces,* December 1998, pp. 492–97.

262 **A 1965 study:** Frank T. Cherry, "Southern In-Migrant Negroes in North Lawndale, Chicago, 1949–1959: A Study of Internal Migration and Adjustment," unpublished dissertation, University of Chicago, Department of Sociology, September 1965, p. 71.

262 **"There is no support":** Ibid., p. 98.

262 **"were *not* of lower":** Taeuber and Taeuber, "The Changing Character of Negro Migration," pp. 429–41.

262 **the 1965 census study:** Ibid., p. 439.

263 **"resemble in educational levels":** Ibid., pp. 436–39.

264 **"Black men who have been":** Larry H. Long and Lynne R. Heltman, "Migration and Income Differences Between Black and White Men in the North," *The American Journal of Sociology* 80, no. 6 (May 1975): 1396–97.

264 **"more successfully avoided poverty":** Larry H. Long and Kristin A. Hansen, "Selectivity of Black Return Migration to the South," *Rural Sociology* 42, no. 3 (Fall 1977): 318. Based on a paper presented at the annual meeting of the Southern Sociological Society, Atlanta, March 30–April 2, 1977.

264 **"not willing to risk":** Wen Lang Li and Sheron L. Randolph, "Return Migration and Status Attainment Among Southern Blacks," *Rural Sociology* 47, no. 2 (Summer 1982): 395.

264 **It made them "especially goal oriented":** Larry H. Long and Lynne R. Heltman, "Migration and Income Differences between Black and White Men in the North," *The American Journal of Sociology* 90, no. 6 (May 1975): 1406.

265 **In San Francisco, for instance:** Charles S. Johnson, Herman H. Long, and Grace Jones, *The Negro Worker in San Francisco* (San Francisco: YWCA, the Race Relations Program of the American Missionary Association, and the Julius Rosenwald Fund, May 1944), pp. 15–23.

265 **"more family-stable":** Thomas C. Wilson, "Explaining Black Southern Migrant Advantage in Family Stability: The Role of Selective Migration," *Social Forces* 80, no. 2 (December 2001): 555–71.

265 **"Colored pupils sometimes occupy":** W. A. Daniel, "Schools," in *Negro Problems in the Cities,* ed. T. J. Woofter (College Park, Md.: McGrath Publishing, 1928), p. 183.

265 **"is literally forced":** Ibid.

265 **James Cleveland Owens:** William J. Baker, *Jesse Owens: An American Life* (New York: Free Press, 1986), p. 16.

266 **The boy's first day:** Ibid., p. 19.

266 **It made headlines:** Larry Schwartz, "Owens Pierced a Myth," http://espn.go.com /sportscentury/features/00016393.html.

266 **"I wasn't invited":** Susan Robinson, "A Day in Black History: Jesse Owens," www.gibbsmagazine.com/Jessie%20Owens.htm.

267 **"My son's victories":** Donald McRae, *Heroes Without a Country: America's Betrayal of Joe Louis and Jesse Owens* (New York: Ecco, 2002), p. 168.

268 **"a narrow tongue":** St. Clair Drake and Horace Cayton, *Black Metropolis: A Study of Negro Life in a Northern City* (Chicago: University of Chicago Press, 1945), p. 12.

269 **There were temptations:** Ibid., p. 438. See Frazier, *The Negro Family in Chicago*, p. 103, on the mulatto woman running the biggest poker games on the South Side.

269 **This was the landing place:** Drake and Cayton, *Black Metropolis,* pp. 610–11.

269 **"rude cabin":** A. T. Andreas, *History of Chicago: From the Earliest Period to the Present Time* (Chicago: A. T. Andreas, 1884), pp. 70, 71.

269 **"A few goats":** Edith Abbott, *The Tenements of Chicago, 1908–1935* (Chicago: University of Chicago Press, 1936), pp. 121–23.

269 **"Families lived without light":** Ibid., p. 126.

270 **"Negro migrants confronted":** Ibid., p. 117.

270 **"attics and cellars":** Abraham Epstein, *The Negro Migrant in Pittsburgh* (New York: Arno Press, 1969), p. 13. Originally published by the University of Pittsburgh in 1918.

270 **New arrivals often paid:** Chicago Commission on Race Relations, *The Negro in Chicago: A Study of Race Relations and a Race Riot* (Chicago: University of Chicago Press, 1922), p. 93.

270 **"The rents in the South Side":** Abbott, *The Tenements of Chicago,* p. 125.

270 **Dwellings that went:** Thomas Jackson Woofter, *Negro Problems in Cities* (New York: Harper and Row, 1928), p. 127.

270 **"Lodgers were not disposed":** Epstein, *The Negro Migrant in Pittsburgh,* p. 8.

272 **Whites saw the migrants:** Chicago Commission on Race Relations, *The Negro in Chicago,* p. 3.

272 **"A colored boy swam":** Carl Sandburg, *The Chicago Race Riots* (New York: Harcourt, Brace and Howe, 1919), p. 3.

272 **"on a white man's complaint":** Chicago Commission on Race Relations, *The Negro in Chicago,* p. 4.

272 **Blacks stabbed a white peddler:** Ibid., p. 10.

272 **Two white men:** Ibid., p. 11.

273 **White gangs stormed:** Ibid., pp. 1–6.

273 **Initially, they came:** James N. Gregory, *The Southern Diaspora: How the Great Migrations of Black and White Southerners Transformed America* (Chapel Hill: University of North Carolina Press, 2005), p. 16.

274 **"By the conversation":** Alfred McClung Lee and Norman D. Humphrey, *Race Riot* (New York: Dryden Press, 1943), p. 81.

274 **"the immigration":** U.S. Department of Labor, Division of Negro Economics, *Negro Migration in 1916–17* (Washington, D.C.: Government Printing Office, 1919), p. 131.

274 **"stabbed, clubbed and hanged":** Oscar Leonard, "The East St. Louis Pogrom," *Survey,* July 14, 1917, p. 331; cited in Herbert Shapiro, *White Violence and Black Response: From Reconstruction to Montgomery* (Amherst: University of Massachusetts Press, 1988), p. 116.

274 **The police:** Chicago Commission on Race Relations, *The Negro in Chicago,* pp. 71–78.

275 **With a sense of urgency:** Ibid., pp. 640–51.

277 **"where they drank":** Arna Bontemps, "The Two Harlems," *The American Scholar,* Spring 1945, p. 168.

277 **There'll be brown skin mammas:** Frank Byrd, "Rent Parties," in *A Renaissance in Harlem: Lost Essays of the WPA,* ed. Lionel C. Bascom (New York: Amistad Press, 1999), pp. 59–67.

To Bend in Strange Winds

285 **I was a Southerner:** Zora Neale Hurston, "Backstage and the Railroad," *Dust Tracks on a Road* (Philadelphia: J. B. Lippincott, 1942), p. 98.

288 **"They have been our best":** E. Franklin Frazier, *The Negro Family in Chicago* (Chicago: University of Chicago Press, 1932), pp. 108–9.

288 **Businessmen jumped:** James R. Grossman, *Land of Hope: Chicago, Black Southerners, and the Great Migration* (Chicago: University of Chicago Press, 1989), p. 155.

288 **"I got a sharecropper":** Josh Sides, *L.A. City Limits: African American Los Angeles from the Great Depression to the Present* (Berkeley: University of California Press, 2003), p. 50.

288 **they ran notices:** Grossman, *Land of Hope,* pp. 156–57, on the effects of the Migration on churches in the North.

289 **"They tried to insulate":** Ibid., p. 139.

289 **"The same class of Negroes":** Frazier, *The Negro Family in Chicago,* p. 112.

289 **A colored newspaper:** Chicago Commission on Race Relations, *The Negro in Chicago: A Study of Race Relations and a Race Riot* (Chicago: University of Chicago Press, 1922), p. 304.

289 **A survey of new migrants:** Charles S. Johnson, Herman H. Long, and Grace Jones, *The Negro Worker in San Francisco* (San Francisco: YWCA, the Race Relations Program of the American Missionary Association, and the Julius Rosenwald Fund, May 1944), p. 19 on how migrants and nonmigrants viewed one another.

290 **"like German Jews":** Grossman, *Land of Hope,* p. 144.

290 **"Those who have long been":** "Our Part in the Migration," *Chicago Defender,* March 17, 1917, p. 9.

290 **"Well, their English":** Douglas Henry Daniels, *Pioneer Urbanites: A Social and Cultural History of San Francisco* (Philadelphia: Temple University Press, 1980), p. 171.

290 **"Eleanor":** Ibid., p. 175.

291 **"It is our duty":** *Chicago Defender,* March 17, 1917, and January 18, 1918, cited in Grossman, *Land of Hope,* pp. 144–45.

291 **Don't hang out the windows:** "A Few Do's and Don'ts," *Chicago Defender,* July 13, 1918, p. 16.

291 **Don't use vile language:** "Some Don'ts," *Chicago Defender,* May 17, 1919, p. 20.

291 **1. Do not loaf:** Grossman, *Land of Hope,* pp. 146–47.

The Other Side of Jordan

302 **We cannot escape:** James Baldwin, *Notes of a Native Son* (Boston: Beacon Press, 1955), p. 20.

303 **"If you succeed":** *Congressional Record,* 75, Session 3, pp. 893, 873.

310 **James Arthur Gay was perhaps:** Ed Koch, "Pioneering Civic Leader, Hotel Executive Gay Dies at 83," *Las Vegas Sun,* September 13, 1999, http://www.lasvegassun.com/news/1999/sep/13/pioneering-civic-leader-hotel-executive-gay-dies-a/.

315 **"What do you suppose":** Scott Nearing, *Black America* (New York: Schocken Books, 1929), p. 78; original reference: H. G. Duncan, *The Changing Race Relationship in the Border and Northern States* (Philadelphia, 1922), p. 77.

315 **Campbell Soup plant:** "Business & Finance: Soup," *Time,* September 2, 1929, www.time.com/time/magazine/article/0,9171,7737779,00.html.

315 **"the great clocks of the sky":** Robert Redfield, *Tepoztlán, A Mexican Village: A Study of Folk Life* (Chicago: University of Chicago Press, 1930), p. 83. Redfield describes the daily rhythms of life in his ethnography of a village in the Yucatán. His description could apply to rural people the world over who spend their days working the land. "In Tepoztlán," he writes, "as in other simple societies, the pulse of life is measured more directly than it is with us by the great clocks of the sky."

315 **The plant turned out:** Al Chase, "Chicago to Have One of the World's Largest Soup Factories," *Chicago Daily Tribune,* November 20, 1927, p. C1.

316 **"making conditions so unpleasant":** Abraham Epstein, *The Negro Migrant in Pittsburgh* (New York: Arno Press, 1969), p. 32.

316 **"friction in the washrooms":** Chicago Commision on Race Relations, *The Negro in*

Chicago: A Study of Race Relations and a Race Riot (Chicago: University of Chicago Press, 1922), p. 395.

317 **"I find a great resentment":** Ibid., pp. 394–95, on resistance to black workers at a millinery and on white women threatening to quit a laundry that introduced a black woman among them.

317 **"Their presence and availability":** Charles S. Johnson, *A Preface to Racial Understanding* (New York: Friendship Press, 1936), pp. 38–39.

318 **By 1940:** St. Clair Drake and Horace R. Cayton, *Black Metropolis: A Study of Negro Life in a Northern City* (Chicago: University of Chicago Press, 1945), p. 227, Figure 16 from the 1940 Census.

320 **"where no restaurant":** Ben Green, *Before His Time: The Untold Story of Harry T. Moore, America's First Civil Rights Martyr* (New York: Free Press, 1999), p. 5.

320 **These were the dark:** Paul Ortiz, *Emancipation Betrayed: The Hidden History of Black Organizing and White Violence in Florida from Reconstruction to the Bloody Election of 1920* (Berkeley: University of California Press, 2005), p. 61.

320 **"It is safe to predict":** Green, *Before His Time,* p. 43, citing a quote in the *Tampa Morning Tribune.*

320 **"We are in the hands":** "Florida Topics," *New York Freeman,* June 25, 1887.

321 **Florida school boards:** Charles Johnson, *Patterns of Negro Segregation* (New York: Harper and Brothers, 1943), p. 16.

323 **the authorities fired:** Green, *Before His Time,* p. 85.

324 **The three young men:** Ibid., p. 91.

324 **The trial had been so tense:** Ibid., pp. 103–6, for a detailed account of the car chase after the Groveland trial.

330 **Both men were from:** Ray Charles and David Ritz, *Brother Ray: Ray Charles' Own Story* (New York: Da Capo Press, 1978), p. 165.

331 **"even at a financial loss":** Josh Sides, *L.A. City Limits: African American Los Angeles from the Great Depression to the Present* (Berkeley: University of California Press, 2003), pp. 101–6.

COMPLICATIONS

332 **"What on earth was it":** Ralph Ellison, *Invisible Man* (New York: Vintage, 1995), p. 294 (reissue; originally published by Random House, New York, 1952).

333 **"positions in either":** Kimberley L. Phillips, *AlabamaNorth: African-American Migrants, Community and Working-Class Activism in Cleveland, 1915–1945* (Urbana: University of Illinois Press, 1999), pp. 241–42.

333 **Entire companies and classes:** Charles S. Johnson, *To Stem This Tide: A Survey of Racial Tension Areas in the United States* (Boston: Pilgrim Press, 1943), pp. 11–12.

333 **Those on the lowest rung:** Brenda Clegg Gray, *Black Female Domestics During the Depression in New York City, 1930–1940* (New York: Garland Publishing, 1993), pp. 57, 58.

333 **One was by:** Vivian Morris, "Slave Market" and "Domestic Price Wars," in *A Renaissance in Harlem: Lost Essays of the WPA,* ed. Lionel C. Bascom (New York: Amistad Press, 1999), pp. 146–57.

333 **In Chicago:** St. Clair Drake and Horace H. Cayton, *Black Metropolis: A Study of Negro Life in a Northern City* (Chicago: University of Chicago Press, 1945, reprinted 1993), pp. 245–46.

334 **"Someone would invariably":** Gray, *Black Female Domestics*, p. 51.

334 **One colored woman:** Keith Collins, *Black Los Angeles: The Maturing of the Ghetto, 1940–1950* (Saratoga, Calif.: Century Twenty One Publishing, 1980), pp. 53–54, cited in Kevin Leonard, *Years of Hope, Days of Fear: The Impact of World War II on Race Relations in Los Angeles*, pp. 40, 41.

334 **turning back the hands:** Morris, "Slave Market," p. 150.

334 **One housewife:** Gray, *Black Female Domestics*, p. 61.

334 **In many cases:** Ibid., p. 67.

339 **Boy Willie:** August Wilson, *The Piano Lesson* (New York: Penguin Books, 1990), p. 20.

340 **The bartender:** "Restaurant Keeper Who Breaks Dishes He Uses in Serving Negroes, Will Have to Get New Supply if This Plan Works," *The Pittsburgh Courier*, February 14, 1931, p. A7, a story about black resistance to the practice of restaurants breaking the dishes used by blacks.

346 **For several days:** Michael Lydon, *Ray Charles: Man and Music* (New York: Riverhead Books, 1998), p. 197. Ray Charles and David Ritz, *Brother Ray* (New York: Dial Press, 1978), p. 201.

346 **After the dealer's:** Charles and Ritz, *Brother Ray*, p. 201.

346 **It was around that time:** Lydon, *Ray Charles*, p. 197.

346 **They chose not to call:** Charles and Ritz, *Brother Ray*, p. 202; Lydon, *Ray Charles*, p. 198. These accounts differ in the timing and nature of Ray's arrival at the hospital. His biographer's account is more consistent with the sense of obligation and protocol with which Robert Foster was known to have treated his patients. Foster, honoring the patient-doctor privilege, did not speak in detail about individual patients.

347 **"Naturally, I refused":** Charles and Ritz, *Brother Ray*, p. 202.

347 **"Everyone I met":** Ibid.

347 **The tour was a dream:** Lydon, *Ray Charles*, p. 198.

348 **"one of the dearest":** Charles and Ritz, *Brother Ray*, p. 202.

349 **"Do you feel greater freedom":** Chicago Commission on Race Relations, *The Negro in Chicago: A Study of Race Relations and a Race Riot* (Chicago: University of Chicago Press, 1922), pp. 98–101.

THE RIVER KEEPS RUNNING

351 **"Why do they come?":** Ray Stannard Baker, *Following the Color Line* (New York: Doubleday, Page, 1908), p. 133.

351 **"Every train, every bus":** Interview with Manley Thomas, who migrated from Jackson, Tennessee, to Milwaukee in September 1950. Interview conducted June 26, 1998, in Milwaukee.

351 **Arrington High:** Dan Burley, "Mississippi Escapee Yearns to Return," *Chicago Defender*, February 24, 1958, p. A4.

354 **Henry Brown:** Henry Box Brown, *Narrative of the Life of Henry Box Brown* (Man-

chester, England: Lee and Glynn, 1851; reprint, Chapel Hill: University of North Carolina Press, 2008), p. 84.

355 **Brown was in agony:** From the account by William Still from *The Underground Rail Road* on the arrival of Henry Box Brown at the Pennsylvania Anti-Slavery Society offices. Cited in Appendix B of the 2008 reprint of *Narrative of the Life of Henry Box Brown,* pp. 160–63.

355 **They locked the door:** Henry Box Brown, *Narrative of Henry Box Brown, Who Escaped from Slavery Enclosed in a Box 3 Feet Long and 2 Wide. Written from a Statement Made by Himself. With Remarks upon the Remedy for Slavery by Charles Stearns* (Boston: Brown and Stearns, 1849); cited in Alan Govenar, *African American Frontiers: Slave Narratives and Oral Histories* (Santa Barbara, Calif.: ABC-CLIO, 2000), pp. 9–16.

356 **many funeral directors:** Interviews with black funeral directors in Chicago and at an annual National Funeral Directors Association meeting in Norfolk, Virginia, yielded polite changes of subject when directors were asked about the issue of funeral home involvement in these escapes out of the South.

356 **"That underground":** Burley, "Mississippi Escapee Yearns to Return."

THE PRODIGALS

364 **[My father], along with:** James Baldwin, *Notes of a Native Son* (Boston: Beacon Press, 1955), p. 72.

364 **'Sides, they can't run us:** Marita Golden, *Long Distance Life* (New York: Doubleday, 1989), p. 39.

367 **"Even in the North":** Arna Bontemps and Jack Conroy, *Anyplace but Here* (Columbia: University of Missouri Press, 1945), p. 170.

DISILLUSIONMENT

371 **Let's not fool ourselves:** Speech by Martin Luther King, Jr., May 17, 1956, MLK speech file, MLK Library, cited in James R. Ralph, Jr., *Northern Protest: Martin Luther King Jr., Chicago and the Civil Rights Movement* (Cambridge, Mass.: Harvard University Press, 1993), p. 30.

371 **It was a hoax:** Robert Coles, "When the Southern Negro Moves North," *The New York Times Magazine,* September 17, 1967, pp. 25–27.

372 **"They don't want":** L. Alex Wilson, "Plan 2-Year Ban on Migrants," *Chicago Defender,* July 1, 1950, p. 22.

372 **"successfully defended":** Allan H. Spear, *Black Chicago: The Making of a Negro Ghetto, 1890–1920* (Chicago: University of Chicago Press, 1967), p. 223.

372 **"chronic urban guerilla warfare":** Arnold R. Hirsch, *Making of the Second Ghetto: Race and Housing in Chicago, 1940–1960* (Chicago: University of Chicago Press, 1983), p. 41.

373 **The moving truck arrived:** "Justice Department Probes Case of Negro Kept Out of Home," *Atlanta Daily World,* July 11, 1951, p. 1.

373 **The Clarks did not let:** "Truman May Act in Cicero Case," *Chicago Defender,* September 29, 1951, p. 1.

374 **A mob stormed the apartment:** Stephen Grant Meyer, *As Long as They Don't Move Next Door: Segregation and Racial Conflict in American Neighborhoods* (Lanham, Md.: Rowman and Littlefield, 2000), pp. 118–19. Details of the mob's destruction of the Clarks' apartment and belongings from *Chicago Defender,* August 11, 1951, p. 7; *Chicago Defender,* July 21, 1951, p. 5; *Atlanta Daily World,* July 13, 1951, p. 1; "Ugly Nights in Cicero," *Time,* July 23, 1953.

374 **The next day:** "Chicago Called Guard for 1919 Riots," *Chicago Defender,* July 21, 1951, p. 5, for reference to National Guard in racial incidents. "Truman May Act in Cicero Case," *Chicago Defender,* September 29, 1951, p. 1, on arrests of 118 people in the Cicero rioting and the grand jury's decision not to indict.

375 **"It was appalling":** Walter White, "Probe of Cicero Outbreaks Reveals Rioters Not Red but Yellow," *Chicago Defender,* July 28, 1951, p. 7.

375 **"bigoted idiots":** "Support Is Growing for Cicero Riot Victims," *Atlanta Daily World,* p. 1.

375 **"This is the root":** "Illinois Gov. Blames Housing Shortage for Riot in Cicero," *Atlanta Daily World,* October 21, 1951, p. 1.

375 **"A resident of Accra":** Hirsch, *Making of the Second Ghetto,* p. 53.

375 ***"Our nation is moving":*** *Report of the National Advisory Commission on Civil Disorders* (New York: E. P. Dutton, 1968), p. 1. The 609-page report, issued by a commission chaired by Otto Kerner, then governor of Illinois, and at the behest of President Lyndon B. Johnson, examined the causes of a national outbreak of violence in twenty-three cities in the mid-1960s. The commission stated: "This is our basic conclusion: Our nation is moving toward two societies, one black, one white—separate and unequal."

377 **"The panic peddler":** Hirsch, *Making of the Second Ghetto,* pp. 31–35.

377 ***We are going to blow:*** "Bomb Explosion Wrecks Flat Building; Lives Imperiled When Angry Whites Hurl Dynamite: Police Failed to Protect Homes," *Chicago Defender,* September 28, 1918, p. 1.

378 **"crowded out of Detroit":** Meyer, *As Long as They Don't Move Next Door,* p. 122.

380 **He read in:** See "RR Employes Give to Church Fund," *New York Amsterdam News,* January 5, 1963, p. 24, for George Starling raising money to help rebuild churches in Georgia.

381 **In March, George:** See "Airline Workers Still Helping Razed Church," *New York Amsterdam News,* March 16, 1963, p. 5, for George Starling handing over the second check to help rebuild churches in Georgia.

REVOLUTIONS

385 **I can conceive:** James Baldwin, *Notes of a Native Son* (Boston: Beacon Press, 1955), p. 59.

386 **"Negroes have continued":** James R. Ralph, Jr., *Northern Protest: Martin Luther King Jr., Chicago and the Civil Rights Movement* (Cambridge, Mass.: Harvard University Press, 1993), p. 35.

387 **"almost everybody is against":** Gunnar Myrdal, *An American Dilemma: The Negro Problem and Modern Democracy,* vol. 2 (New York: Harper and Brothers, 1944), p. 1010.

387 **"So long as this city"**: "White and Black in Chicago," *Chicago Tribune,* August 3, 1919, p. F6. The editorial also said, "We admit frankly that if political equality had meant the election of Negro mayors, judges, and a majority of the city council, the whites would not have tolerated it. We do not believe that the whites of Chicago would be any different from the whites of the south in this respect. . . . Legally a Negro has a right to service anywhere the public generally is served. He does not get it. Wisely, he does not ask for it. There has been an illegal, nonlegal or extra legal adjustment founded upon common sense which has worked in the past, and it will work in the future."

387 **"in one sense"**: Ralph, *Northern Protest,* p. 34.

388 **It was August 5, 1966:** Gene Roberts, "Rock Hits Dr. King as Whites Attack March in Chicago," *The New York Times,* August 6, 1966, p. 1.

388 **The march had barely begun:** Ibid. on where the rock hit King. Ralph, *Northern Protest,* on the size of the rock.

388 **As the eight hundred:** Roberts, "Rock Hits Dr. King as Whites Attack March in Chicago."

389 **Some of King's aides:** See Ralph, *Northern Protest,* p. 33, for attempts by top advisers to dissuade King from going north. The advisers argued that their work in the South was far from complete, that the North would be unreceptive, and that such efforts would hurt northern support for their cause. "King thought otherwise, and rejected this counsel just as he would subsequent warnings," according to Ralph.

389 **"I have to do this"**: "Dr. King Is Felled by Rock: 30 Injured as He Leads Protesters; Many Arrested in Race Clash," *Chicago Tribune,* August 6, 1966, p. 1.

389 **"I have seen many demonstrations"**: Ibid.

396 **"It happened slowly"**: Louis Rosen, *The South Side: The Racial Transformation of an American Neighborhood* (Chicago: Ivan R. Dee, 1998), p. 118.

396 **"I fought the good fight"**: Ibid., p. 147.

396 **"It was like sitting around"**: Ibid., p. 120.

396 **"It was like having"**: Ibid., p. 26.

397 **Mahalia Jackson:** Mahalia Jackson and Evan McLeod Wylie, *Movin' On Up* (New York: Hawthorne Books, 1966), p. 119.

397 **"Shall we sacrifice"**: Arna Bontemps and Jack Conroy, *Anyplace but Here* (Columbia: University of Missouri Press, 1945), p. 176.

398 **The top ten cities:** Isabel Wilkerson, "Study Finds Segregation in Cities Worse than Scientists Imagined," *The New York Times,* August 5, 1989, an article on the findings of a five-year study of 22,000 census tracts conducted by University of Chicago sociologists Douglas S. Massey and Nancy A. Denton.

401 **kept a card file:** "The Extracurricular Clout of Powerful College Presidents," *Time,* February 11, 1966, p. 64.

405 **"in addition to his widow"**: "Dr. Rufus Clement of AU Dies Here," *New York Amsterdam News,* November 11, 1967, p. 45.

407 **The evening was unusually cool:** Earl Caldwell, "Martin Luther King Is Slain in Memphis; White Is Suspected; Johnson Urges Calm: Guard Called Out; Curfew

Ordered in Memphis, but Fires and Looting Erupt," *The New York Times,* April 5, 1968, p. 1.

409 **"About 74 percent":** *Report of the National Advisory Commission on Civil Disorders* (New York: Bantam Books, 1968), p. 6.

The Fullness of the Migration

413 **And so the root:** Langston Hughes, "For Russell and Rowena Jelliffe," *Cleveland Call and Post,* April 6, 1963, p. B1.

415 **There were two sets:** Stanley Lieberson, *A Piece of the Pie: Blacks and White Immigrants Since 1880* (Berkeley and Los Angeles: University of California Press, 1980), pp. 32–33.

416 **white immigrants:** Ibid., p. 34.

417 **"called for blacks":** Ibid., p. 35.

418 **fertility rates for black women:** Ibid., pp. 193–97. See also Clyde Vernon Kiser, *Sea Island to City* (New York: AMS Press, 1967), pp. 204, 205. This study from the 1930s found that the Migration "significantly reduced" fertility rates. In New York, "twenty-four out of forty wives married 1–10 years had borne no children. Five of the fourteen married 10–20 years were childless, as were the two wives married 20–30 years."

418 **blacks were the lowest paid:** Lieberson, *A Piece of the Pie,* pp. 292–93; Gilbert Osofsky, *Harlem: The Making of a Ghetto* (New York: Harper and Row, 1968), p. 16.

418 **"There is just no avoiding":** Ibid., p. 369.

Part V: Aftermath

433 **The migrants were gradually absorbed:** St. Clair Drake and Horace H. Cayton, *Black Metropolis: A Study of Negro Life in a Northern City* (Chicago: University of Chicago Press, 1945, reprinted 1993), p. 75.

In the Places They Left

435 **The only thing:** Lonnie G. Bunch III, "The Greatest State for the Negro: Jefferson L. Edmonds, Black Propagandist of the California Dream," in *Seeking El Dorado: African Americans in California,* ed. Lawrence B. de Graaf, Kevin Mulroy, and Quintard Taylor (Los Angeles: Autry Museum of Western Heritage in association with University of Washington Press, Seattle, 2001), p. 132. Jefferson Lewis Edmonds was a farmer, teacher, and state legislator in Mississippi during Reconstruction. He left Mississippi for Los Angeles in 1886, shortly after an incident in which whites, fearing that a group of colored residents were about to walk into the Carrollton County courthouse, opened fire on the unarmed people, killing twenty of them. Edmonds became editor of *The Liberator,* a colored newspaper in Los Angeles.

435 **Mr. Edd, whose land:** Chickasaw County Historical and Genealogical Society, *Chickasaw County History,* vol. 2 (Dallas: Curtis Media, 1997), p. 430 on Willie Jim Linn and p. 497 on Edd Monroe Pearson.

436 **The people who had not gone:** Ibid., p. 10.

436 **"intemperate individuals":** Ibid.

437 **"spent all their savings":** Mark Lowry II, "Schools in Transition," *Annals of the Asso-ciation of American Geographers* 63, no. 2 (June 1973): pp. 173, 178.

437 **In the meantime:** Ibid., p. 176.

439 **"My conscience told me":** Ben Green, *Before His Time: The Untold Story of Harry T. Moore, America's First Civil Rights Martyr* (New York: Free Press, 1999), pp. 206–7.

439 **"he dropped dead":** Ibid., p. 207.

439 **"the only public building":** Ibid., pp. 206–8.

439 **But Sheriff McCall did not:** Ibid., p. 207.

440 **McCall was reelected:** Ibid., p. 208. See also Ramsey Campbell, "Lake's Willis McCall Is Dead," *Orlando Sentinel,* April 29, 1994, p. A1.

441 **The new high school:** *Contributors of Ouachita Parish: A History of Blacks to Com-memorate the Bicentennial of the United States of America* (The Black Bicentennial Committee of Ouachita Parish, 1976), p. 10.

LOSSES

445 **It occurred to me:** Jacqueline Joan Johnson, *Rememory: What There Is for Us,* cited in Malaika Adero, *Up South* (New York: New Press, 1993), p. 108.

445 **"one of Los Angeles' ":** "Rites Held for L.A. Socialite Mrs. Alice Clement Foster, 54," *Chicago Defender,* December 17, 1974, p. 4.

MORE NORTH AND WEST THAN SOUTH

455 **I could come back:** Mahalia Jackson with Evan McLeod Wiley, *Movin' On Up* (New York: Hawthorne Books, 1966), p. 117.

456 **"Platters Full of Plenty Thanks":** An advertisement appearing in *Chicago Metro News,* November 26, 1977, p. 18.

462 **"personal isolation":** Based on an undated, registered letter written by Robert Fos-ter to Edward Bounds, director of the U.S. Labor Department in San Francisco, as part of a workers' compensation claim filed as a result of a dispute with the West Los Angeles Veterans Administration Medical Center in Brentwood.

AND, PERHAPS, TO BLOOM

481 **Most of them care nothing:** James Baldwin, *Notes of a Native Son* (Boston: Beacon Press, 1955), p. 21.

THE WINTER OF THEIR LIVES

491 **That the Negro American:** Daniel Patrick Moynihan, *The Negro Family: The Case for National Action* (Washington, D.C.: United States Department of Labor, Office of Policy Planning and Research, 1965), p. 23.

492 **"I know everybody":** "Why Do You Live in Harlem? Camera Quiz," *New York Age,* April 29, 1950.

EPILOGUE

527 **"there is not one family"**: Allen B. Ballard, *One More Day's Journey* (New York: McGraw-Hill, 1984), p. 13.

528 **"Masses of ignorant"**: E. Franklin Frazier, *The Negro Family in the United States* (New York: Dryden Press, 1948), p. 285. Originally published by the University of Chicago Press, 1939.

528 **"in such large numbers"**: Sadie Tanner Mossell, "The Standard of Living Among One Hundred Negro Migrant Families in Philadelphia," *Annals of the American Academy of Political and Social Science* 98 (November 1921): 216.

528 **better educated:** Stewart E. Tolnay, "Educational Selection in the Migration of Southern Blacks, 1880–1990," *Social Forces* (December 1998): 489–508. "The educational differences between southern migrants and native northerners were considerably smaller than the corresponding difference between migrants and their relatives and neighbors remaining in the South," Tolnay writes. Because a disproportionate number of educated blacks migrated out of the South, the number of years of schooling for migrants on the whole was higher than might otherwise have been expected and not far from the educational levels of blacks already in the North, a difference of one and a half years by 1950. The quality of their southern education, however, was generally considered inferior.

529 **"The Southerners had their eye"**: Allen B. Ballard, *One More Day's Journey* (New York: McGraw Hill, 1984), p. 191.

529 **John Coltrane:** Lewis Porter, *John Coltrane: His Life and His Music* (Ann Arbor: University of Michigan Press, 1998), p. 33.

530 **"Upon their arrival"**: Stewart E. Tolnay and Kyle D. Crowder, "Regional Origin and Family Stability in Northern Cities: The Role of Context," *American Sociological Review* 64 (1999): 109.

530 **"Compared with northern-born blacks"**: Stewart E. Tolnay, "The African American 'Great Migration' and Beyond," *Annual Review of Sociology* 29 (2003): 219. See also Larry H. Long and Lynne R. Heltman, "Migration and Income Differences Between Black and White Men in the North," *The American Journal of Sociology* 80, no. 6 (May 1975): 1395–1407.

530 **Something deep inside:** Long and Heltman, "Migration and Income Differences Between Black and White Men in the North," p. 1395.

530 **"Instead of thinking"**: Tolnay and Crowder, "Regional Origin and Family Stability in Northern Cities," p. 109.

531 **"led to higher earnings"**: Reynolds Farley, "After the Starting Line: Blacks and Women in an Uphill Race," *Demography* 25, no. 4 (November 1988): 477.

531 **"Black migrants who left"**: Larry H. Long and Kristin A. Hansen, "Selectivity of Black Return Migration to the South," *Rural Sociology* 42, no. 3 (Fall 1977): 325. Based on a paper presented at the annual meeting of the Southern Sociological Society, Atlanta, March 30–April 2, 1977.

533 **"Black school principals"**: Allen B. Ballard, *One More Day's Journey,* p. 186.

533 **"Since 1924"**: "4,733 Mob Action Victims Since '82, Tuskegee Reports," *Montgomery Advertiser,* April 26, 1959.

534 **The mechanical cotton picker:** Donald Holley, *The Second Great Emancipation: The Mechanical Cotton Picker, Black Migration, and How They Shaped the Modern South* (Fayetteville: University of Arkansas, 2000), pp. 38–40.

534 **Still, many planters:** Ibid., p. 101.

534 **"Much of this labor":** Harris P. Smith, "Late Developments in Mechanical Cotton Harvesting," *Agricultural Engineering,* July 1946, p. 321. Smith, the chief of the division of agricultural engineering at the Texas Agricultural Experiment Station, presented this paper at a meeting of the American Society of Agricultural Engineers at Fort Worth, Texas, in April 1946. See also Gilbert C. Fite, "Recent Changes in the Mechanization of Cotton Production in the United States," *Agricultural History* 24 (January 1950): 28, and Oscar Johnston, "Will the Machine Ruin the South?" *Saturday Evening Post* 219 (May 31, 1947): 37.

535 **"If all of their dream":** "Our Part in the Exodus," *Chicago Defender,* March 17, 1917, p. 9.

535 **Toni Morrison:** Toni Morrison's parents migrated from Alabama to Lorraine, Ohio. Diana Ross's mother migrated from Bessemer, Alabama, to Detroit, her father from Bluefield, West Virginia. Aretha Franklin's father migrated from Mississippi to Detroit. Jesse Owens's parents migrated from Oakville, Alabama, to Cleveland when he was nine. Joe Louis's mother migrated with him from Lafayette, Alabama, to Detroit. Jackie Robinson's family migrated from Cairo, Georgia, to Pasadena, California. Bill Cosby's father migrated from Schuyler, Virginia, to Philadelphia, where Cosby was born. Nat King Cole, as a young boy, migrated with his family from Montgomery, Alabama, to Chicago. Condoleezza Rice's family migrated from Birmingham, Alabama, to Denver, Colorado, when she was twelve. Thelonious Monk's parents brought him from Rocky Mount, North Carolina, to Harlem when he was five. Berry Gordy's parents migrated from rural Georgia to Detroit, where Gordy was born. Oprah Winfrey's mother migrated from Kosciusko, Mississippi, to Milwaukee, where Winfrey went to live as a young girl. Mae Jemison's parents migrated from Decatur, Alabama, to Chicago when she was three years old. Romare Bearden's parents carried him from Charlotte, North Carolina, to New York City. Jimi Hendrix's maternal grandparents migrated from Virginia to Seattle. Michael Jackson's mother was taken as a toddler from Barbour County, Alabama, by her parents to East Chicago, Indiana; his father migrated as a young man from Fountain Hill, Arkansas, to Chicago, just west of Gary, Indiana, where all the Jackson children were born. Prince's father migrated from Louisiana to Minneapolis. Sean "P. Diddy" Combs's grandmother migrated from Hollyhill, South Carolina, to Harlem. Whitney Houston's grandparents migrated from Georgia to Newark, New Jersey. The family of Mary J. Blige migrated from Savannah, Georgia, to Yonkers, New York. Queen Latifah's grandfather migrated from Birmingham, Alabama, to Newark. Spike Lee's family migrated from Atlanta to Brooklyn. August Wilson's mother migrated from North Carolina to Pittsburgh, following her own mother, who, as the playwright told it, had walked most of the way.

536 **"almost exactly at the norm":** Otto Klineberg, *Negro Intelligence and Selective Migration* (New York: Columbia University Press, 1935), pp. 43–45. The IQ tests were of

ten-year-old girls in Harlem, divided on the basis of how long they had lived in New York. Those in New York for less than a year scored 81.8, those in New York one to two years scored 85.8, those in New York for three to four years scored 94.1, and those born in New York scored 98.5. Other studies—of boys or with the use of other measurements—found what Klineberg described as an "unmistakable trend" of improved intellectual performance the longer the children were in the North.

536 **Klineberg's studies:** "Otto Klineberg, Who Helped Win '54 Desegregation Case, Dies at 92," *The New York Times,* March 10, 1992.

537 **Jean Baptiste Point DuSable:** Bessie Louise Pierce, *A History of Chicago,* vol. 1 (New York: Knopf, 1937), pp. 12, 13. Pierce describes Point DuSable as having been the son of a man from "one of France's foremost families" and says "that his mother was a Negro slave." Christopher R. Reed, "In the Shadow of Fort Dearborn: Honoring DuSable at the Chicago World's Fair of 1933–1934," *Journal of Black Studies* 21, no. 4 (June 1991): 412.

537 **Jan Rodrigues:** Leslie M. Harris, *In the Shadow of Slavery: African Americans in New York City, 1626–1863* (Chicago: University of Chicago Press, 2003), pp. 12–13.

538 **"In the simple process":** Lawrence R. Rodgers, *Canaan Bound: The African American Great Migration Novel* (Urbana: University of Illinois Press, 1997), p. 186.

NOTES ON METHODOLOGY

543 **It is important:** Chicago Commission on Race Relations, *The Negro in Chicago: A Study of Race Relations and a Race Riot* (Chicago: University of Chicago Press, 1922), pp. xxiii, xxiv.

INDEX

trials, 50, 152, 567n
 Groveland case and, 324, 325, 368, 438
trolleys, see streetcars
Trotter, Joe William, Jr., 570n
Truett, Van, 381
tuberculosis, 231
Tulsa, Ala., 131, 573n
turkeys, 101, 105–6, 125, 148, 165, 435, 456
Tuskegee, Ala., 197
Twain, Mark, 190–91
12 Million Black Voices (Wright), 181, 225
typhus, 103

Underground Railroad, 161, 190, 287, 354
Union, 556n
Union Army, 191, 240, 572n
Union Pacific, 190
unions, see labor unions
upward mobility, 21, 121, 300–301
Urban League, 291
urine, 77, 114, 409, 462
urine samples, 254, 256, 258, 259, 402
uterine inertia, 147

vagrancy, 152–53
Valentino, Rudolph, 218
Van Vleet, Miss., 20–35
 beauty of, 22–23
Vardaman, James K., 39
violence:
 black, 39, 130–34
 white, 39, 40, 45, 59–62, 130–33, 218, 320, 379
 see also bombing; lynchings; riots
Virginia, 161
 migration from, 178, 243, 251, 529, 533–34
 school desegregation in, 436
 secession of, 563n
 segregation in, 113, 390, 391
Virgin Mary, 33–34

voice tests, 333
voting, 44, 302–5, 320, 520
 in Chickasaw County, 436
 to defeat McCall, 440
voting rights, 38, 559n
 of black men, 38, 59

Waco, Tex., 39
waiting rooms, 44, 439–40
Wall Street, 98
Wall Street Journal, 44
Walter, James, 104
Walters African Methodist Episcopal Church, 288
Walther Memorial Hospital, 337–38, 394
 strike at, 405–7
Warmsley, Johnny, 235
Warren County, Ga., 37
washing, 101
Washington, Booker T., 42, 201
Washington, D.C., 90, 130, 197, 200, 355, 390, 472
 Charleston Ball in, 240
 Cleveland Park in, 335
 license plates from, 365–66
 migration to, 11–12, 124, 171, 178, 185, 200, 240
 native blacks in, 263
 riots in, 131, 408
 trains to, 294
Washington, Denzel, 10
Washington, Harold, 507, 529
Washington, Jesse, 39
Washington, Jimmy, 141
water boys, 98–99
watermelons, 64–65, 409
Watkins, Eleanor, 290
Watkins, Walter, 381
Weatherford, Willis T., 163
Weems, Carrie Mae, 33
welfare, 261, 415, 417, 528
Wen Lang Li, 264
West, 203, 260–67, 413–19
West Africa, 375

Permissions Acknowledgments

Grateful acknowledgment is made to the following for permission to reprint previously published material:

BEACON PRESS: Excerpts from *Notes of a Native Son* by James Baldwin, copyright © 1955 and copyright © renewed 1983 by James Baldwin. Reprinted by permission of Beacon Press, Boston.

DUTTON SIGNET, A DIVISION OF PENGUIN GROUP (USA) INC.: Excerpt from Act 1, Scene i, from *The Piano Lesson* by August Wilson, copyright © 1988, 1990 by August Wilson. Reprinted by permission of Dutton Signet, a division of Penguin Group (USA) Inc.

JOHN HAWKINS & ASSOCIATES, INC., AND THE ESTATE OF RICHARD WRIGHT: Excerpts from *12 Million Black Voices* by Richard Wright, copyright © 1940 by Richard Wright. Reprinted by permission of John Hawkins & Associates, Inc., and the Estate of Richard Wright.

HARPERCOLLINS PUBLISHERS: Excerpt from *Dust Tracks on a Road* by Zora Neale Hurston, copyright © 1942 by Zora Neale Hurston, copyright renewed 1970 by John C. Hurston. Excerpts from *Black Boy* by Richard Wright, copyright © 1937, 1942, 1944, 1945 by Richard Wright, copyright renewed 1973 by Ellen Wright. Reprinted by permission of HarperCollins Publishers.

ALFRED A. KNOPF, A DIVISION OF RANDOM HOUSE, INC., AND HAROLD OBER ASSOCIATES INCORPORATED: Excerpt from "For Russell and Rowena Jelliffe," excerpt from "One-Way Ticket," and an excerpt from "The South" from *The Collected Poems of Langston Hughes*, copyright © 1994 by the Estate of Langston Hughes. Reprinted by permission of Alfred A. Knopf, a division of Random House, Inc. Additional rights by permission of Harold Ober Associates Incorporated.

THE PHI BETA KAPPA SOCIETY: Excerpt from "The Two Harlems" by Arna Bontemps, *American Scholar*, Volume 14, No. 2, Spring 1945, p. 167, copyright © 1945 by The Phi Beta Kappa Society. Reprinted by permission of The Phi Beta Kappa Society.

ABOUT THE AUTHOR

ISABEL WILKERSON won the 1994 Pulitzer Prize for Feature Writing for her reporting as Chicago bureau chief of *The New York Times*. The award made her the first black woman in the history of American journalism to win a Pulitzer Prize and the first African American to win for individual reporting. She won the George Polk Award for her coverage of the Midwest and a John Simon Guggenheim Fellowship for her research into the Great Migration. She has lectured on narrative writing at the Nieman Foundation at Harvard University and has served as Ferris Professor of Journalism at Princeton University and as the James M. Cox Jr. Professor of Journalism at Emory University. She is currently Professor of Journalism and Director of Narrative Nonfiction at Boston University. During the Great Migration, her parents journeyed from Georgia and southern Virginia to Washington, D.C., where she was born and reared. This is her first book.

ABOUT THE TYPE

This book was set in Granjon, a modern recutting of a typeface produced under the direction of George W. Jones, who based Granjon's design upon the letter forms of Claude Garamond (1480–1561). The name was given to the typeface as a tribute to the typographic designer Robert Granjon.